KU-495-783

Crime and Delinquency

A Reader

Crime and Delinquency

A Reader

edited by

Carl A. Bersani

The Macmillan Company
Collier-Macmillan Limited, London

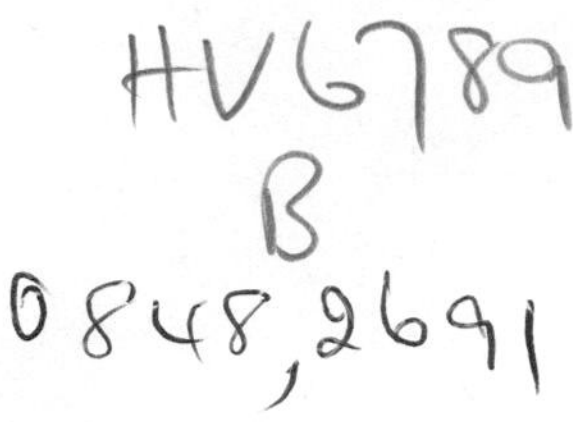

Second Printing, 1971

Library of Congress catalog card number: 70-95184

THE MACMILLAN COMPANY
COLLIER-MACMILLAN CANADA, LTD., Toronto, Ontario

Printed in the United States of America

For my Father

and Mother

Preface

This book of readings is designed to offer the student an integrated collection of the more important theoretical, empirical, and descriptive literature in criminology and in delinquency. Undergraduate students pursuing their first course in criminology or in delinquency, as well as graduate students who do not have an extensive background, are the intended audience. Those conducting programs of in-service correctional training, social welfare, and police science may also find the bulk of the material useful.

The development of this book is the result of the editor's experimentations in the use of most of these materials in courses in criminology and in delinquency. Additional content for these courses was provided through classroom discussions and through the use of library materials to emphasize other aspects of the field. The articles in this collection were also selected to supplement standard textbooks by emphasizing coverage not only of major foci but also directions in which the field is moving (e.g., interactionist perspective, labeling processes, collective violence, dissensus, change and legal norms, and structural variation and behavioral outcomes).

Hopefully, sufficient integration of materials is offered through placing the articles of each section within an innovative framework. This book is distinguished from other readers by the inclusion of articles in each section which provide general materials relevant to both crime and delinquency courses, followed by specific materials relevant to each. An attempt has been made for the most part to achieve a balance of materials in both crime and delinquency.

In addition, both the introductory remarks and the introductory article to each section, rather than being merely reviews of the readings, deal with the nature and the relevance of the sections, and thereby tie the readings together. The coherence of each section and between sections is also aided by the conceptual framework provided through the introductory remarks.

In striving for an integrated format it was my intent to stimulate reflection and discussion and to provide a framework from which students can examine the materials without the need for direction and clarification by the instructor. With few exceptions, the articles have been chosen by the standard that each could speak for itself. I have deliberately avoided the inclusion of highly specialized or technical articles requiring a degree of sophistication generally held neither by majors nor nonmajors pursuing their initial work in criminology or in delinquency.

Other sociological works related to the organizational theme could, of course, have been included, but space limitation did not so permit. Purely psychological works have been excluded, for to do otherwise would have been at the cost of adequately presenting the sociological perspective.

The addition of this book to the field was made possible only through the generosity of the authors and publishers in allowing materials to be reprinted. Although the final decision for inclusions and omissions is my own, the manuscript has benefited from the valuable suggestions and criticisms offered by David Matza, Harry Silverstein, John Stratton, and Robert Terry. To Charles E. Smith, Sociology Editor of The Macmillan Company, thanks are extended for making this project easier than it would have been otherwise.

Appreciation is extended to my colleagues within my department for their aid and the climate of encouragement they provided. I am especially indebted to John H. Lindquist for guidance in the mechanics of doing this type of book, and to Samuel C. Newman for the use of his abundant materials. To Diane M. Mingl, my secretary, and to Julia F. Siegenthaler, departmental secretary, much thanks for numerous tasks well done.

My special thanks to my wife, Carol, for her assistance with this work, and to her and our daughter, Lisa, for their patience and loving support.

C.A.B.

Contents

Crime and Delinquency

A Reader

Introduction

Crime and Victims in a Free Society

President's Commission on Law Enforcement and Administration of Justice

There is much crime in America, more than ever is reported, far more than ever is solved, far too much for the health of the Nation. Every American knows that. Every American is, in a sense, a victim of crime. Violence and theft have not only injured, often irreparably, hundreds of thousands of citizens, but have directly affected everyone. Some people have been impelled to uproot themselves and find new homes. Some have been made afraid to use public streets and parks. Some have come to doubt the worth of a society in which so many people behave so badly. Some have become distrustful of the Government's ability, or even desire, to protect them. Some have lapsed into the attitude that criminal behavior is normal human behavior and consequently have become indifferent to it, or have adopted it as a good way to get ahead in life. Some have become suspicious of those they conceive to be responsible for crime: adolescents or Negroes or drug addicts or college students or demonstrators; policemen who fail to solve crimes; judges who pass lenient sentences or write decisions restricting the activities of the police; parole boards that release prisoners who resume their criminal activities.

The most understandable mood into which many Americans have been plunged by crime is one of frustration and bewilderment. For "crime" is not a single simple phenomenon that can be examined, analyzed and described in one piece. It occurs in every part of the country and in every stratum of society. Its practitioners and its victims are people of all ages, incomes and backgrounds. Its trends are difficult to ascertain. Its causes are legion. Its cures are speculative and controversial. An examination of any single kind of crime, let alone of "crime in America," raises a myriad of issues of the utmost complexity.

Consider the crime of robbery, which, since it involves both stealing and violence or the threat of it, is an especially hurtful and frightening one. In 1965 in America there were 118,916 robberies known to the police: 326 robberies a day; a robbery for every 1,630 Americans. Robbery takes dozens of forms, but suppose it took

Reprinted from "The Challenge of Crime in a Free Society: Introduction, *The Challenge of Crime in a Free Society.*" Report by The President's Commission on Law Enforcement and Administration of Justice (Washington: Government Printing Office, 1967), ch. 1, pp. 1–51; ch. 12, pp. 273–274.

only four: forcible or violent purse-snatching by boys, muggings by drug addicts, store stickups by people with a sudden desperate need for money, and bank robberies by skillful professional criminals. The technical, organizational, legal, behavioral, economic and social problems that must be addressed if America is to deal with any degree of success with just those four kinds of events and those four kinds of persons are innumerable and refractory.

The underlying problems are ones that the criminal justice system can do little about. The unruliness of young people, widespread drug addiction, the existence of much poverty in a wealthy society, the pursuit of the dollar by any available means are phenomena the police, the courts, and the correctional apparatus, which must deal with crimes and criminals one by one, cannot confront directly. They are strands that can be disentangled from the fabric of American life only by the concerted action of all of society. They concern the Commission deeply, for unless society does take concerted action to change the general conditions and attitudes that are associated with crime, no improvement in law enforcement and administration of justice, the subjects this Commission was specifically asked to study, will be of much avail.

Of the everyday problems of the criminal justice system itself, certainly the most delicate and probably the most difficult concern the proper ways of dealing individually with individuals. Arrest and prosecution are likely to have quite different effects on delinquent boys and on hardened professional criminals. Sentencing occasional robbers and habitual robbers by the same standards is clearly inappropriate. Rehabilitating a drug addict is a procedure that has little in common with rehabilitating a holdup man. In short, there are no general prescriptions for dealing with "robbers." There are no general prescriptions for dealing with "robbery" either. Keeping streets and parks safe is not the same problem as keeping banks secure. Investigating a mugging and tracking down a band of prudent and well-organized bank robbers are two entirely distinct police procedures. The kind of police patrol that will deter boys from street robberies is not likely to deter men with guns from holding up store keepers.

Robbery is only one of 28 crimes on which the Federal Bureau of Investigation reports in its annual Uniform Crime Reports. In terms of frequency of occurrence, it ranks fifth among the UCR's "Index Crimes," the seven serious crimes that the FBI considers to be indicative of the general crime trends in the Nation. (The others are willful homicide, forcible rape, aggravated assault, burglary, theft of $50 or over, and motor vehicle theft.) The Index Crimes accounted for fewer than 1 million of the almost 5 million arrests that the UCR reports for 1965. Almost half of those arrests were for crimes that have no real victims (prostitution, gambling, narcotics use, vagrancy, juvenile curfew violations and the like) or for breaches of the public peace (drunkenness, disorderly conduct). Other crimes for which more than 50,000 people were arrested were such widely different kinds of behavior as vandalism, fraud, sex offenses other than rape or prostitution, driving while intoxicated, carrying weapons, and offenses against family or children. Each of the 28 categories of crime confronts the community and the criminal justice system, to a greater or a lesser degree, with unique social, legal, correctional, and law enforcement problems. Taken together they raise a multitude of questions about how the police, the courts, and corrections should be organized; how their personnel should be selected, trained and paid; what modern technology can do to help their work; what kinds of knowledge they need; what procedures they should use; what resources they should be given; what the relations between the community and the various parts of the criminal justice system should be.

• • •

Toward Understanding and Preventing Crime

A skid-row drunk lying in a gutter is crime. So is the killing of an unfaithful wife. A Cosa Nostra conspiracy to bribe public officials is crime. So is a strong-arm robbery by a 15-year-old boy. The embezzlement of a corporation's funds by an executive is crime. So is the possession of marihuana cigarettes by a student. These crimes can no more be lumped together for purposes of analysis than can measles and schizophrenia, or lung cancer and a broken ankle. As with disease, so with crime: if causes are to be understood, if risks are to be evaluated, and if preventive or remedial actions are to be taken, each kind must be looked at separately. Thinking of "crime" as a whole is futile.

In any case it is impossible to answer with precision questions about the volume or trends of crime as a whole, or even of any particular kind of crime. Techniques for measuring crime are, and probably always will be imperfect. Successful crime, after all, is secret crime. The best, in fact almost the only, source of statistical information about crime volumes is the Uniform Crime Reports of the FBI. The UCR is the product of a nationwide system of crime reporting that the FBI has painstakingly developed over the years. Under this system local police agencies report the offenses they know of to the FBI; the UCR is a compilation of these reports. This compilation can be no better than the underlying information that local agencies supply to the FBI. And because the FBI has induced local agencies to improve their reporting methods year by year, it is important to distinguish better reporting from more crime.

• • •

While it is impossible to offer absolute statistical proof that every year there are more crimes per American than there were the year before, both available statistics and the facts of social change in America suggest that there are.

Amounts and Kinds of Crime. Obviously the most serious crimes are the ones that consist of or employ physical aggression: willful homicide, rape, robbery, and serious assault. The injuries such crimes inflict are grievous and irreparable. There is no way to undo the damage done to a child whose father is murdered or to a woman who has been forcibly violated. And though medicine may heal the wounds of a victim of a mugging, and law enforcement may recover his stolen property, they cannot restore to him the feeling of personal security that has been violently wrested from him.

To be sure, the amount of pain that crime causes is a minute fraction of the amount Americans suffer accidentally every year. There were approximately 10,000 willful homicides in 1965 and more than 40,000 motor-accident fatalities. There were slightly more than 100 serious assaults for every 100,000 Americans, and more than 12,000 injuries due to accidents in the home for every 100,000 Americans. The risk of being attacked by a stranger on a street is far less than the total of violent crimes might lead one to believe. The UCR estimates that in fully two-thirds of the cases of willful homicide and aggravated assault, the criminals and the victims are known to each other; very often they are members of the same family. Studies of rape indicate that in perhaps half the cases the criminal and victim are acquainted. Robbery is the principal source of violence from strangers.

The most damaging of the effects of violent crime is fear, and that fear must not be belittled. Suddenly becoming the object of a stranger's violent hostility is as frightening as any class of experience. A citizen who hears rapid footsteps behind him as he walks down a dark and otherwise deserted street cannot be expected to calculate that the chance of those footsteps having a sinister meaning is only one in a hundred or in a thousand or, if he does make such a calculation, to be calmed by its results. Any chance at all is frightening. And, in fact, when Commission interviewers asked a sample of citizens what they would do in just such a situation, the majority replied, "Run as fast as I could or call for help." Commission studies in several cities indicate that just this kind of fear has impelled hundreds of thousands of Americans to move their homes or change their habits.

Controlling violent crime presents a number of distinct problems. To the extent that these crimes occur on private premises, as most murders and rapes and many assaults do, they are little susceptible to deterrence by police patrol. To the extent that they are the passionate culmination of quarrels between acquaintances or relatives—as again many murders and assaults are—there is little that can be done to increase the deterrent effect of the threat of punishment. More than nine-tenths of all murders are cleared by arrest, and a high proportion of those arrested are convicted. Yet people continue to commit murders at about the same rate year after year. Almost a third of all robberies are committed by juveniles and are, therefore, one aspect of the enormously complicated phenomenon of juvenile delinquency. Some robberies are committed by drug addicts, and a certain number of rapes are committed by sexually pathological men (or boys). Effective treatment for these diseases, in the community or in the criminal justice system, has not yet been found. Finally, more than one-half of all willful homicides and armed robberies, and almost one-fifth of all aggravated assaults, involve the use of firearms. As long as there is no effective gun-control legislation, violent crimes and the injuries they inflict will be harder to reduce than they might otherwise be.

Only 13 percent of the total number of Index Crimes in the UCR for 1965 were crimes of violence. The remaining 87 percent were thefts: thefts of $50 or over in money or goods, automobile thefts, and burglaries (thefts that involve breaking into or otherwise unlawfully entering private premises).[1] Of these three kinds of stealing,

[1] Editor's Note: The Uniform Crime Report for 1968 indicates crime nationally increased 17.5 percent (uncorrected for population growth) over 1967. Although crime continues to increase, the proportion of crimes of violence to crimes of theft continues to hold.

burglary was the most frequent; 1,173,201 burglaries were reported to the FBI in 1965, approximately one-half of them involving homes and one-half commercial establishments. Burglary is expensive; the FBI calculates that the worth of the property stolen by burglars in 1965 was some $284 million. Burglary is frightening; having one's home broken into and ransacked is an experience that unnerves almost anyone. Finally, burglars are seldom caught; only 25 percent of the burglaries known to the police in 1965 were solved, and many burglaries were not reported to the police.

Because burglary is so frequent, so costly, so upsetting and so difficult to control, it makes great demands on the criminal justice system. Preventing burglary demands imaginative methods of police patrol, and solving burglaries calls for great investigative patience and resourcefulness. Dealing with individual burglars appropriately is a difficult problem for prosecutors and judges; for while burglary is a serious crime that carries heavy penalties and many of its practitioners are habitual or professional criminals, many more are youthful or marginal offenders to whom criminal sanctions in their most drastic form might do more harm than good. Burglars are probably the most numerous class of serious offenders in the correctional system. It is a plausible assumption that the prevalence of the two crimes of burglary and robbery is a significant, if not a major, reason for America's alarm about crime, and that finding effective ways of protecting the community from those two crimes would do much to make "crime" as a whole less frightening and to bring it within manageable bounds.

Larceny—stealing that does not involve either force or illegal entry—is by far the most frequent kind of stealing in America. It is less frightening than burglary because to a large, perhaps even to a preponderant extent, it is a crime of opportunity, a matter of making off with whatever happens to be lying around loose: Christmas presents in an unlocked car, merchandise on a store counter, a bicycle in a front yard, and so forth. Insofar as this is so, it is a crime that might be sharply reduced by the adoption of precautionary measures by citizens themselves. The reverse side of this is that it is an extremely difficult crime for the police to deal with; there are seldom physical clues to go on, as there are more likely to be in cases of breaking and entering, and the likelihood of the victim identifying the criminal is far less than in the case of a face-to-face crime like robbery. Only 20 percent of reported major larcenies are solved, and the solution rate for minor ones is considerably lower.

A unique feature of the crime of automobile theft is that, although only a quarter of all automobile thefts—and there were 486,568 reported to the FBI in 1965—are solved, some 87 percent of all stolen automobiles are recovered and returned to their owners. The overwhelming majority of automobile thefts are for the purpose of securing temporary transportation, often for "joyriding."

More than 60 percent of those arrested for this crime in 1965 were under 18 years of age, and 88 percent were under 25. However, automobile theft for the purpose of stripping automobiles of their parts or for reselling automobiles in remote parts of the country is a lucrative and growing part of professional crime, a Commission study of professional criminals indicates. What is especially suggestive about these facts is that, while much automobile theft is committed by young joyriders, some of it is calculating, professional crime that poses a major law enforcement problem. The estimated value of the unrecovered stolen automobiles in 1965 is $60 million. In other words, coping with automobile theft, like coping with every kind of serious crime, is a matter of dealing with many kinds of people with many kinds of motives. No single response, by either the community or the criminal justice system, can be effective.

These three major crimes against property do not tell the whole story about stealing.[2] In fact, the whole story cannot be told. There is no knowing how much embezzlement, fraud, loan sharking, and other forms of thievery from individuals or commercial institutions there is, or how much price-rigging, tax evasion, bribery, graft, and other forms of thievery from the public at large there is. The Commission's studies indicate that the economic losses those crimes cause are far greater than those caused by the three index crimes against property. Many crimes in this category are never discovered; they get lost in the complications and convolutions of business procedures. Many others are never reported to law enforcement agencies. Most people pay little heed to crimes of this sort when they worry about "crime in America," because those crimes do not, as a rule, offer an immediate, recognizable threat to personal safety.

However, it is possible to argue that, in one sense, those crimes are the most threatening of all—not just because they are so expensive, but because of their corrosive effect on the moral standards by which American business is conducted. Businessmen who defraud consumers promote cynicism towards society and disrespect for law. The Mafia or Cosa Nostra or the Syndicate, as it has variously been called, is deeply involved in business crime, and protects its position there by bribery and graft and, all too often, assault and murder. White-collar crime and organized crime are subjects about which the criminal justice system, and the community as a whole, have little knowledge. Acquiring such knowledge in a systematic way is an extremely high-priority obligation of those entrusted with protecting society from crime.

"Crimes without victims," crimes whose essence is providing people with goods or services that, though illegal, are in demand, are peculiarly vexatious to the criminal justice system. Gambling, narcotics, and prostitution offenses, and their like, are not only numerous, but they present policemen, prosecutors, judges, and correctional officials with problems they are ill-equipped to solve. Since such crimes have no direct victims, or at any rate no victims with complaints, investigating them obliges policemen to employ practices like relying on informants who may turn out to be accomplices, or walking the streets hoping to be solicited by prostitutes. These practices may be legal, but they are surely distasteful and they can lead, in addition, to discriminatory enforcement or out-and-out corruption.

When offenders of this sort are arrested, corrections or punishment seldom has

[2]Editor's Note: The decision to systematically collect the above kinds of data that more likely reflect lower-class behavior does not relieve criminological theorists from explaining the vast amount of "white-collar" crime (usually undetected or unadjudicated) of the upper classes. See the appropriate articles in Sections I and II for a discussion of this form of crime.

much effect on them; they resume their activities as soon as they return to the street. Yet offenses of this sort cannot be ignored. Gambling is an activity that is controlled by organized criminals and is a major source of their wealth and power. The growing use of drugs, especially by young people, is a matter of profound concern to almost every parent in America and, of course, the distribution of narcotics is also an important part of the activities of organized crime. Often the statutes that deal with these offenses are obsolete or ambiguous. Treatment programs are still in an experimental stage. The connection between these offenses and social conditions is little understood. Finding ways of dealing with crimes without victims is not only a task for the criminal justice system but for legislators, doctors, sociologists, and social workers.

Finally, there are "petty offenses" and "breaches of the peace" like public drunkenness and public quarreling, which are the most numerous of all crimes. Most Americans have never actually seen a serious crime committed, but every American has seen a petty offense. Such offenses are undoubted public nuisances against which the public has every right to protect itself. Yet a curious thing about them is that usually the only person who suffers real damage from one of these crimes is the offender himself. Breaches of the peace are the most exasperating everyday problem of the criminal justice system.

Petty offenders, many of whom, like chronic alcoholics, are repeated and incurable lawbreakers, occupy much of the time of policemen, clog the lower courts and crowd city and county jails.

Crime and Social Conditions. Two striking facts that the UCR and every other examination of American crime disclose are that most crimes, wherever they are committed, are committed by boys and young men, and that most crimes, by whomever they are committed, are committed in cities. Three-quarters of the 1965 arrests for Index crimes, plus petty larceny and negligent manslaughter, were of people less than 25 years old. More 15-year-olds were arrested for those crimes than people of any other age, and 16-year-olds were a close second. Of 2,780,015 "offenses known to the police" in 1965—these were Index crimes—some 2 million occurred in cities, more than half a million occurred in the suburbs, and about 170,000 occurred in rural areas. The number of city crimes per hundred thousand residents was over 1,800, the suburban rate was almost 1,200, and the rural rate was 616.9. In short, crime is evidently associated with two powerful social trends: the increasing urbanization of America and the increasing numerousness, restlessness, and restiveness of American youth. The two trends are not separate and distinct, of course. They are entangled with each other in many ways, and both are entangled with another trend, increasing affluence, that also appears to be intimately associated with crime. An abundance of material goods provides an abundance of motives and opportunities for stealing, and stealing is the fastest growing kind of crime.

For as long as crime statistics of any kind have been compiled, they have shown that males between the ages of 15 and 24 are the most crime-prone group in the population. For the last 5 year, as the result of the "baby boom" that took place after the Second World War, the 15-24 age group has been the fastest growing group in the population.

The fact that young people make up a larger part of the population than they did 10 years ago accounts for some of the recent increase in crime. This group will continue to grow disproportionately for at least 15 years more. And so it is probable that crime will continue to increase during this period, unless there are drastic changes in general social and economic conditions and in the effectiveness of the criminal justice system. However, population changes cannot be shown to account for all of the increase that is reported in juvenile and youth crime, nor can the probability that police reporting is more complete every year account for the increase. Moreover, there have been marked improvements in police efficiency and correctional resourcefulness in many localities in recent years, which, all other things being equal, might have reduced crime. It may be that young people are not only more numerous than ever, but more crime prone; it is impossible to be sure.

...

The Extent of Unreported Crime. Although the police statistics indicate a lot of crime today, they do not begin to indicate the full amount. Crimes reported directly to prosecutors usually do not show up in the police statistics. Citizens often do not report crimes to the police. Some crimes reported to the police never get into the statistical system. Since better crime prevention and control programs depend upon a full and accurate knowledge about the amount and kinds of crime, the Commission initiated the first national survey ever made of crime victimization. The National Opinion Research Center of the University of Chicago surveyed 10,000 households, asking whether the person questioned, or any member of his or her household, had been a victim of crime during the past year, whether the crime had been reported and, if not, the reasons for not reporting.

More detailed surveys were undertaken in a number of high and medium crime rate precincts of Washington, Chicago, and Boston by the Bureau of Social Science Research of Washington, D.C., and the Survey Research Center of the University of Michigan. All of the surveys dealt primarily with households or individuals, although some data were obtained for certain kinds of businesses and other organizations.

These surveys show that the actual amount of crime in the United States today is several times that reported in the UCR.... The amount of personal injury crime reported to NORC is almost twice the UCR rate and the amount of property crime more than twice as much as the UCR rate for individuals. Forcible rapes were more than 3½ times the reported rate, burglaries three times, aggravated assaults and larcenies of $50 and over more than double, and robbery 50 percent greater than the reported rate. Only vehicle theft was lower and then by a small amount. (The single homicide reported is too small a number to be statistically useful.)

...

In the national survey of households those victims saying that they had not notified the police of their victimization were asked why. The reason most frequently given for all offenses was that the police could not do anything.... This reason was given by 68 percent of those not reporting malicious mischief, and by 60 or more percent of those not reporting burglaries, larcenies of $50 and over, and auto thefts. It is not clear whether these responses are accurate assessments of the victims' inability to help the police or merely rationalizations of their failure to report. The next most frequent reason was that the offense was a private matter or that the victim did not want to harm the offender. It was given by 50 percent or more of those who did not notify the police for aggravated and simple assaults, family crimes, and consumer frauds. Fear of reprisal, though least often cited, was strongest in the case of assaults and family crimes. The extent of failure to report to the police was highest for consumer fraud (90 percent) and lowest for auto theft (11 percent).

...

The picture portrayed by the official statistics in recent years, both in the total number of crimes and in the number of crimes per 100,000 Americans, is one of increasing crime. Crime always seems to be increasing, never going down. Up 5 percent this year, 10 the next, and the Commission's surveys have shown there is a great deal more crime than the official statistics show. The public can fairly wonder whether there is ever to be an end.

This official picture is also alarming because it seems so pervasive. Crimes of violence are up in both the biggest and smallest cities, in the suburbs as well as in the rural areas. The same is true for property crimes. Young people are being arrested in ever increasing numbers. Offense rates for most crimes are rising every year and in every section of the country. That there are some bright spots does not change this dismal outlook. Rates for some offenses are still below those of the early thirties and perhaps of earlier periods. Willful homicide rates have been below the 1960 level through most of the last few years. Robbery rates continue to decline in the rural areas and small towns, and arrest rates for many non-Index offenses have remained relatively stable.

...

Assessing the Amount and Trend of Crime. Because of the grave public concern about the crime problem in America today, the Commission has made a special effort to understand the amount and trend of crime and has reached the following conclusions:

1. The number of offenses—crimes of violence, crimes against property and most others as well—has been increasing. Naturally, population growth is one of the significant contributing factors in the total amount of crime.

2. Most forms of crime—especially crimes against property—are increasing faster than population growth. This means that the risk of victimization to the individual citizen for these crimes is increasing, although it is not possible to ascertain precisely the extent of the increase. All the economic and social factors discussed above support, and indeed lead to, this conclusion.

The Commission found it very difficult to make accurate measurements of crime trends by relying solely on official figures, since it is likely that each year police agencies are to some degree dipping deeper into the vast reservoir of unreported crime. People are probably reporting more to the police as a reflection of higher expectations and greater confidence, and the police in turn are reflecting this in their statistics. In this sense more efficient policing may be leading to higher rates of reported crime.

The diligence of the FBI in promoting more complete and accurate reporting through the development of professional police reporting procedures has clearly had an important effect on the completeness of reporting, but while this task of upgrading local reporting is under way, the FBI is faced with the problem, in computing national trends, of omitting for a time the places undergoing changes in reporting methods and estimating the amount of crime that occurred in those places in prior years.

3. Although the Commission concluded that there has been an increase in the volume and rate of crime in America, it has been unable to decide whether individual Americans today are more criminal than their counterparts 5, 10, or 25 years ago. To answer this question it would be necessary to make comparisons between persons of the same age, sex, race, place of residence, economic status and other factors at the different times: in other words, to decide whether the 15-year-old slum dweller or the 50-year-old businessman is inherently more criminal now than the 15-year-old slum dweller or the 50-year-old businessman in the past. Because of the many rapid and turbulent changes over these years in society as a whole and in the myriad conditions of life which affect crime, it was not possible for the Commission to make such a comparison. Nor do the data exist to make even simple comparisons of the incidence of crime among persons of the same age, sex, race, and place of residence at these different years.

4. There is a great deal of crime in America, some of it very serious, that is not reported to the police, or in some instances by the police. The national survey revealed that people are generally more likely to report serious crimes to the police, but the percent who indicated they did report to the police ranged from 10 percent for consumer fraud to 89 percent for auto theft. Estimates of the rate of victimization for Index offenses ranged from 2 per 100 persons in the national survey to 10 to 20 per 100 persons in the individual districts surveyed in 3 cities. The surveys produced rates of victimization that were from 2 to 10 times greater than the official rates for certain crimes.

5. What is needed to answer questions about the volume and trend of crime satisfactorily are a number of different crime indicators showing trends over a period of time to supplement the improved reporting by police agencies. The Commission experimented with the development of public surveys of victims of crime and feels this can become a useful supplementary yardstick. Further development of the procedure is needed to improve the reliability and accuracy of the findings. However, the Commission found these initial experiments produced useful results that justify more intensive efforts to gather such information on a regular basis. They should also be supplemented by new types of surveys and censuses which would provide better information about crime in areas where good information is lacking such as crimes by or against business and other organizations. The Commission also believes that an improved and greatly expanded procedure for the collection of arrest statistics would be of immense benefit in the assessment of the problem of juvenile delinquency.

6. Throughout its work the Commission has noted repeatedly the sharp differences in the amount and trends of reported crimes against property as compared with crimes against persons. It has noted that while property crimes are far more numerous than crimes against the person, and so dominate any reported trends, there is much public concern about crimes against persons. The more recent reports of the UCR have moved far toward separating the reporting of these two classes of crime altogether.

The Commission recommends:

The present Index of reported crime should be broken into two wholly separate parts, one for crimes of violence and the other for crimes against property.

The Commission also recommends, in principle, the development of additional indices to indicate the volume and trend of such other important crime problems as embezzlement, fraud, and other crimes against trust, crimes of vice that are associated with organized crime, and perhaps others. The Commission urges that consideration be given to practical methods for developing such indices.

The Commission also urges that the public media and others concerned with crime be careful to keep separate the various crime problems and not to deal with them as a unitary phenomenon. Whenever possible, crime should be reported relative to population as well as by the number of offenses, so as to provide a more accurate picture of risks of victimization in any particular locality.

7. The Commission believes that age, urbanization, and other shifts in the population already under way will likely operate over the next 5 to 10 years to increase the volume of offenses faster than population growth. Further dipping into the reservoirs of unreported crime will likely combine with this real increase in crime to produce even greater increases in reported crime rates. Many of the basic social forces that tend to increase the amount of real crime are already taking effect and are for the most part irreversible. If society is to be successful in its desire to reduce the amount of real crime, it must find new ways to create the kinds of conditions and inducements–social, environmental, and psychological–that will bring about a greater commitment to law-abiding conduct and respect for the law on the part of all Americans and a better understanding of the great stake that all men have in being able to trust in the honesty and integrity of their fellow citizens.

• • •

The Victims of Crime

Rather striking variations in the risk of victimization for different types of crime appear among different income levels in the population. The results shown in table 1 indicate that the highest rates of victimization occur in the lower income groups when all Index offenses except homicide are considered together. The risks of victimization from forcible rape, robbery, and burglary, are clearly concentrated in the

TABLE 1. Victimization by Income
(Rates per 100,000 population)

Offenses	*Income*			
	$0 to $2,999	*$3,000 to $5,999*	*$6,000 to $9,999*	*Above $10,000*
Total	2,369	2,331	1,820	2,237
Forcible rape	76	49	10	17
Robbery	172	121	48	34
Aggravated assault	229	316	144	252
Burglary	1,319	1,020	867	790
Larceny ($50 and over)	420	619	549	925
Motor vehicle theft	153	206	202	219
Number of respondents	(5,232)	(8,238)	(10,382)	(5,946)

SOURCE: NORC survey.

lowest income group and decrease steadily at higher income levels. The picture is somewhat more erratic for the offenses of aggravated assault, larceny of $50 and over, and vehicle theft. Victimization for larceny increases sharply in the highest income group.

National figures on rates of victimization also show sharp differences between whites and nonwhites (table 2). Nonwhites are victimized disproportionately by all Index crimes except larceny $50 and over.

TABLE 2. Victimization by Race
(Rates per 100,000 population)

Offenses	*White*	*Nonwhite*
Total	1,860	2,592
Forcible rape	22	82
Robbery	58	204
Aggravated assault	186	347
Burglary	822	1,306
Larceny ($50 and over)	608	367
Motor vehicle theft	164	286
Number of respondents	(27,484)	(4,902)

SOURCE: NORC survey.

The rates of victimization shown for Index offenses against men (table 3) are almost three times as great as those for women, but the higher rates of burglary, larceny and auto theft against men are in large measure an artifact of the survey procedure of assigning offenses against the household to the head of the household.

The victimization rate for women is highest in the 20 to 29 age group. In fact the victimization rates for women for all the Index offenses reported, with the exception of larceny, are greatest in this age group. The concentration of offenses against women in this age group is particularly noticeable for forcible rape and robbery and much less apparent in aggravated assault and the property crimes.

For men the highest Index total rate falls in the 30–39 age category, a result heavily influenced by the burglaries assigned to men as heads of households. Actually, all the Index property offenses against men show peak rates in the older age categories. This is probably due not only to their role as household heads but also to the fact that at older ages they are likely to possess more property to be stolen. Crimes against the person, such as aggravated assault and robbery, are committed relatively more often against men who are from 20 to 29 years of age.

Thus, the findings from the national survey show that the risk of victimization is highest among the lower income groups for all Index offenses except homicide, larceny, and vehicle theft; it weighs most heavily on the nonwhites for all Index offenses except larceny; it is borne by men more often than women, except, of course, for forcible rape; and the risk is greatest for the age category 20 to 29, except for larceny against women, and burglary, larceny, and vehicle theft against men.[3]

• • •

TABLE 3. Victimization by Age and Sex
(Rates per 100,000 population)

Offense	*Male*						
	10-19	*20-29*	*30-39*	*40-49*	*50-59*	*60 plus*	*All ages*
Total	951	5,924	6,231	5,150	4,231	3,465	3,091
Robbery	61	257	112	210	181	98	112
Aggravated assault	399	824	337	263	181	146	287
Burglary	123	2,782	3,649	2,365	2,297	2,343	1,583
Larceny ($50 and over)	337	1,546	1,628	1,839	967	683	841
Motor vehicle theft	31	515	505	473	605	195	268
	Female						
Total	334	2,424	1,514	1,908	1,132	1,052	1,059
Forcible rape	91	238	104	48	0	0	83
Robbery	0	238	157	96	60	81	77
Aggravated assault	91	333	52	286	119	40	118
Burglary	30	665	574	524	298	445	314
Larceny ($50 and over)	122	570	470	620	536	405	337
Motor vehicle theft	0	380	157	334	119	81	130

SOURCE: NORC survey.

Public Concern About Crime. The public sees crime as one of the most serious of all domestic problems. The Commission's NORC survey asked citizens to pick from a list of six major domestic problems the one they were paying the most attention to. As table 4 shows, crime was second to race relations as the most frequently mentioned problem, except in the case of nonwhites with annual incomes less than $6,000; they placed education second and crime third.

Crime is linked to other social problems by many people. In a 1964 Harris survey more people attributed increased crime in their neighborhood to "disturbed and restless teenagers" than to any other cause. A part of the crime problem that especially worries people is juvenile delinquency. A typical finding was reported by a Gallup poll in 1963. When persons were asked to name the top problems in their community from a list of 39 problems, "juvenile delinquency" was the second most

[3]Editor's Note: Unlike some countries which provide generous reimbursement to victims of crimes against person (e.g., Great Britain and New Zealand), in the United States, New York and California are the first states to develop a limited reimbursement plan, although other states are considering such a plan.

frequent selection–exceeded only by complaints about local real estate taxes. Also related to the problems of youth was a third frequently chosen problem–the need for more recreation areas.

TABLE 4. Most Important Domestic Problem by Race and Income

	Percent White		*Percent Nonwhite*	
Domestic Problem	*Under $6,000*	*Over $6,000*	*Under $6,000*	*Over $6,000*
Poverty	9	5	7	8
Inflation	15	17	4	4
Education	12	19	23	21
Crime	27	22	19	22
Race relations	29	34	32	38
Unemployment	8	3	15	7
Total	100	100	100	100
Number	(3,925)	(6,461)	(1,033)	(462)

SOURCE: NORC survey.

However, people are more inclined to think of crime in moral than in social terms. An August 1965 Gallup poll that asked people what they thought was responsible for the increase of crime found that most of the reasons people mentioned had to do directly with the moral character of the population rather than with changes in objective circumstances or with law enforcement. Over half of the answers fitted under the category "family, poor parental guidance." About 6 percent of the answers gave "breakdown of moral standards." A variety of other directly moral causes were given in addition, such as: "People expect too much," "people want something for nothing," and "communism." Relatively few (12 percent) of the responses cited objective conditions such as "unemployment," "poverty," "the automobile," or "the population explosion."

• • •

Personal Fear of Crime. Perhaps the most intense concern about crime is the fear of being attacked by a stranger when out alone. One-third of Americans feel unsafe about walking alone at night in their own neighborhoods, according to the NORC survey. As one would expect, the percentage of people feeling unsafe at night on the street is, according to an April 1965 Gallup survey, higher in large cities than in smaller ones and higher in cities than in rural areas.

Recently studies have been undertaken to develop an index of delinquency based on the seriousness of different offenses. They have shown that there is widespread public consensus on the relative seriousness of different types of crimes and these rankings furnish useful indicators of the types of crime that the public is most concerned about. Offenses involving physical assaults against the person are the most feared crimes and the greatest concern is expressed about those in which a weapon is used.

...

Fear of crime makes many people want to move from their homes. In the four police precincts surveyed for the Commission in Boston and Chicago, 20 percent of the citizens wanted to move because of the crime in their neighborhoods, and as many as 30 percent wanted to move out of the highest crime rate district in Boston.

Fear of crime shows variations by race and income. In the survey in Washington, the Bureau of Social Science Research put together an index of anxiety about crime. It found that Negro women had the highest average score, followed by Negro men, white women, and white men. Anxiety scores were lower at the higher income levels for both Negroes and whites.

Fear of crime is not always highest in the areas where official crime rates are highest or where rates of victimization based on the survey findings are highest. For example, the BSSR Washington study found that the average level of concern with crime in a predominately Negro police precinct that has one of the highest crime rates in the city, according to police data, was lower than it was in another Negro precinct that had a very low rate relative to the first.

...

Perhaps the most revealing findings on the impact of fear of crime on people's lives were the changes people reported in their regular habits of life. In the high-crime districts surveyed in Boston and Chicago, for example, five out of every eight respondents reported changes in their habits because of fear of crime, some as many as four or five major changes. Forty-three percent reported they stayed off the streets at night altogether. Another 21 percent said they always used cars or taxis at night. Thirty-five percent said they would not talk to strangers any more.

One of the most curious findings of the surveys was that fear of crime is less closely associated with having been a victim of crime than might be supposed. The national survey showed that victims tended to have somewhat more worry about burglary or robbery. This was true for both males and females as can be seen in table 5. However, females, whether they had been victimized or not, were more concerned about their safety than males. Furthermore, other data show that recent experience of being a victim of crime did not seem to increase behavior designed to protect the home. Almost identical proportions, 57 percent of victims and 58 percent of non-victims, took strong household security measures.

In its Washington study BSSR found similar results. An index of exposure to crime was developed based on having personally witnessed offenses or on whether one's self or one's friends had been victimized. Scores on this index, in general, were not associated with responses to a variety of questions on attitudes toward crime and toward law enforcement that respondents were asked. Nor did exposure to crime appear to determine the anxiety about crime manifested in the interviews. The one exception appeared in the case of the Negro male. Negro men showed a tendency to be influenced in their attitudes and behavior by their actual exposure to crime.

...

TABLE 5. Concern of Victims and Nonvictims About Burglary or Robbery
(In percentages)

Worry About Burglary or Robbery	*Victim*	*Nonvictim*
Males:		
Worried	69	59
Not worried	31	41
	100	100
Number of males	(1,456)	(3,930)
Females:		
Worried	84	77
Not worried	16	23
	100	100
Number of females	(2,399)	(6,189)

SOURCE: NORC survey.

Few domestic social problems more seriously threaten our welfare or exact a greater toll on our resources. But society has relied primarily on traditional answers and has looked almost exclusively to common sense and hunch for needed changes. The Nation spends more than $4 billion annually on the criminal justice system alone. Yet the expenditure for the kinds of descriptive, operational, and evaluative research that are the obvious prerequisites for a national program of crime control is negligible. Almost every industry makes a significant investment in research each year. Approximately 15 percent of the Defense Department's annual budget is allocated to research. While different fields call for different levels of research, it is worth noting that research commands only a small fraction of 1 percent of the total expenditure for crime control. There is probably no subject of comparable concern to which the Nation is devoting so many resources and so much effort with so little knowledge of what it is doing.

It is true, of course, that many kinds of knowledge about crime must await better understanding of social behavior. It is also true that research will never provide the final answers to many of the vexing questions about crime. Decisions as to the activities that should be made criminal, as to the limits there should be on search and seizure, or as to the proper scope of the right to counsel, cannot be made solely on the basis of research data. Those decisions involve weighing the importance of fairness and privacy and freedom–values that cannot be scientifically analyzed. But when research cannot, in itself, provide final answers, it can provide data crucial to making informed policy judgments.

There is virtually no subject connected with crime or criminal justice into which further research is unnecessary. The Commission was able to explore many of these subjects in connection with its work, and to develop the data that underlie the recommendations made in this report. Many of its projects sought to open up new areas of knowledge; many drew on the prior work of scholars, governmental agencies, and private organizations. Crime is a continuing and urgent reality with which we must deal as effectively as we can. We cannot await final answers. The alternatives are not whether to act or not, but whether to act wisely or unwisely.

•••

It would obviously be futile to attempt to catalog all the kinds of research that are needed. We do not even know all the questions that need to be asked. But we do know many of them and we also know that planning and organizing the search for knowledge is a matter of highest importance.

•••

[Editor's Note: For an insightful discussion concerning the controversy of "an ever increasing crime rate" see Fred P. Graham, "A Contemporary History of American Crime," in Violence in America: Historical and Comparative Perspectives, Vol. 2. A Report to the National Commission on the Causes and Prevention of Violence (Washington D.C.: Government Printing Office, June 1969), pp. 371–385.]

Section I

Interconnections: Normative Dissensus, Social Change and the Criminal Law

Introductory Remarks

In the study of human behavior, we encounter the obvious fact that those behaviors to be identified as criminal do not become so until the process of lawmaking defines them as such. It is difficult to maintain the position that the proscriptions and prescriptions of criminal laws are permanently fixed or that their contents duplicate the dictates of Divine Will as reflected in religious doctrines.

It is well known that criminal laws have been subject throughout history to marked shifts in emphasis and to pronounced changes; that is, as the years accumulate and new arrangements for social living emerge, criminal laws take on new forms and patterns.

If criminal laws lack permanency and invariability, what purpose can they serve? Whatever the defects of criminal laws, they are the means by which specialized institutions enact and enforce, among the many control rules in society, those which some view as crucial in the kinds of social relationships deemed necessary for proper order. Although the nature of criminal laws varies through history and in localities, one accepts the necessity of criminal laws if one desires a society that is ordered.

Nevertheless, if we are to understand the interrelationship of crime and society, it is upon this changeable quality, which is characteristic of legal norms, that we must focus our attention in our investigation. For this changing quality indicates that not only a response to processes occurs within society, but that the specific nature of the offender is not fixed forever.

Studies of various cultures do not reveal fixed, discernable steps in the emergence and development of all legal norms. Sociological analysis, however, does view legal norms as reflecting either underlying social values or the ever-changing conflicts of interest characterizing a particular society.

[1] For example, in the United States each of the 50 states, the Federal Government, the District of Columbia, Puerto Rico, and the military services have autonomous criminal codes. No two are identical in terms of offenses or penalties. The same variability between states occur in juvenile codes. However, in almost any jurisdiction many delinquent acts can be defined so broadly that, theoretically, any child could be referred to juvenile court (see Articles 7, 30 and 40).

This analysis applies particularly to a society such as ours. In American society there is much incorporated in the legal norms that reflects the shared norms and the actual behavior expressed by the vast majority of people. This category includes the prohibition of robbery, incest, murder, burglary, and many other behaviors. In these cases the legal norms are not substantially different from the expressed interests and concerns of the various subgroups within the nation.

Yet our recourse to legal norms in regulating behavior beyond that which is supported by shared norms has been frequently cited by numerous observers. Therefore, we have many types of behavior (e.g., truancy, vagrancy, loitering, premarital and extramarital sexual intercourse, abortions, gambling, drunkenness, homosexual behavior, narcotic and marijuana use) as part of juvenile or criminal codes that are viewed by many as self-indulgence rather than as clear-cut cases of social dangers.[2]

It is apparent that this society, noted for its heterogeneous population and normative dissensus,[3] *cannot reflect in all aspects of the legal norms the divergencies existing within the population. This being the case, it is conceivable that some groups are more susceptible to violation of laws.*

Such dilemmas call attention to the larger issue of how and why specific behaviors are defined as legal or illegal. Because existing legal norms reflect a preference by some men for this order, we must ask ourselves what men, whose rules, and why this order of things and not another? These are the generic questions to be answered.

This is far from a philosophical exercise. For if law precedes violation, and if laws are not invariable for all time, then what precedes the study of offenders is the study of why some laws come into being and others do not, why some men are offensive and others are not, why some laws change and others do not, and why some laws have an effect and others do not.

[2]It is interesting to note the paradox of juvenile "antisocial" behavior (e.g., truancy, incorrigibility, running away from home) treated as delinquency, and law violations by businessmen which threaten society and are punishable by political units mainly handled in civil courts or by regulatory agencies.

[3]Refers to disagreement as to behaviors that are allowable.

1. White-Collar Criminality

Edwin H. Sutherland

This paper[1] is concerned with crime in relation to business. The economists are well acquainted with business methods but not accustomed to consider them from the point of view of crime; many sociologists are well acquainted with crime but not accustomed to consider it as expressed in business. This paper is an attempt to integrate these two bodies of knowledge. More accurately stated, it is a comparison of crime in the upper or white-collar class, composed of respectable or at least respected business and professional men, and crime in the lower class, composed of persons of low socioeconomic status. This comparison is made for the purpose of developing the theories of criminal behavior, not for the purpose of muckraking or of reforming anything except criminology.

The criminal statistics show unequivocally that crime, *as popularly conceived and officially measured,* has a high incidence in the lower class and a low incidence in the upper class; less than two percent of the persons committed to prisons in a year belong to the upper class. These statistics refer to criminals handled by the police, the criminal and juvenile courts, and the prisons, and to such crimes as murder, assault, burglary, robbery, larcency, sex offenses, and drunkenness, but exclude traffic violations.

The criminologists have used the case histories and criminal statistics derived from these agencies of criminal justice as their principal data. From them, they have derived general theories of criminal behavior. These theories are that, since crime is concentrated in the lower class, it is caused by poverty or by personal and social characteristics believed to be associated statistically with poverty, including feeblemindedness, psychopathic deviations, slum neighborhoods, and "deteriorated" families. This statement, of course, does not do justice to the qualifications and variations in the conventional theories of criminal behavior, but it presents correctly their central tendency.

The thesis of this paper is that the conception and explanations of crime which have just been described are misleading and incorrect, that crime is in fact not closely correlated with poverty or with the psychopathic and sociopathic conditions associ-

Reprinted from *American Sociological Review,* 5:1 (February 1940), 1–12, by permission of The American Sociological Association.

[1]Thirty-fourth Annual Presidential Address delivered at Philadelphia, Pa., Dec. 27, 1939 in joint meeting with the American Economic Society (its Fifty-second) at which President Jacob Viner spoke on the relations of economic theory to the formulation of public policy.

ated with poverty, and that an adequate explanation of criminal behavior must proceed along quite different lines. The conventional explanations are invalid principally because they are derived from biased samples. The samples are biased in that they have not included vast areas of criminal behavior of persons not in the lower class. One of these neglected areas is the criminal behavior of business and professional men, which will be analyzed in this paper.

The "robber barons" of the last half of the nineteenth century were white-collar criminals, as practically everyone now agrees. Their attitudes are illustrated by these statements: Colonel Vanderbilt asked, "You don't suppose you can run a railroad in accordance with the statutes, do you?" A.B. Stickney, a railroad president, said to sixteen other railroad presidents in the home of J.P. Morgan in 1890, "I have the utmost respect for you gentlemen, individually, but as railroad presidents I wouldn't trust you with my watch out of my sight." Charles Francis Adams said, "The difficulty in railroad management ... lies in the covetousness, want of good faith, and low moral tone of railway managers, in the complete absence of any high standard of commercial honesty."

The present-day white-collar criminals, who are more suave and deceptive than the "robber barons," are represented by Krueger, Stavisky, Whitney, Mitchell, Foshay, Insull, the Van Sweringens, Musica-Coster, Fall, Sinclair, and many other merchant princes and captains of finance and industry, and by a host of lesser followers. Their criminality has been demonstrated again and again in the investigations of land offices, railways, insurance, munitions, banking, public utilities, stock exchanges, the oil industry, real estate, reorganization committees, receiverships, bankruptcies, and politics. Individual cases of such criminality are reported frequently, and in many periods more important crime news may be found on the financial pages of newspapers than on the front pages. White-collar criminality is found in every occupation, as can be discovered readily in casual conversation with a representative of an occupation by asking him, "What crooked practices are found in your occupation?"

White-collar criminality in business is expressed most frequently in the form of misrepresentation in financial statements of corporations, manipulation in the stock exchange, commercial bribery, bribery of public officials directly or indirectly in order to secure favorable contracts and legislation, misrepresentation in advertising and salesmanship, embezzlement and misapplication of funds, short weights and measures and misgrading of commodities, tax frauds, misapplication of funds in receiverships and bankruptcies. These are what Al Capone called "the legitimate rackets." These and many others are found in abundance in the business world.

In the medical profession, which is here used as an example because it is probably less criminalistic than some other professions, are found illegal sale of alcohol and narcotics, abortion, illegal services to underworld criminals, fraudulent reports and testimony in accident cases, extreme cases of unnecessary treatment, fake specialists, restriction of competition, and fee-splitting. Fee-splitting is a violation of a specific law in many states and a violation of the conditions of admission to the practice of medicine in all. The physician who participates in fee-splitting tends to send his patients to the surgeon who will give him the largest fee rather than to the surgeon who will do the best work. It has been reported that two thirds of the surgeons in New York City split fees, and that more than one half of the physicians in a central western city who answered a questionnaire on this point favored fee-splitting.

These varied types of white-collar crimes in business and the professions consist principally of violation of delegated or implied trust, and many of them can be reduced to two categories: misrepresentation of asset values and duplicity in the manipulation of power. The first is approximately the same as fraud or swindling; the second is similar to the double-cross. The latter is illustrated by the corporation director who, acting on inside information, purchases land which the corporation will need and sells it at a fantastic profit to his corporation. The principle of this duplicity is that the offender holds two antagonistic positions, one of which is a position of trust, which is violated, generally by misapplication of funds, in the interest of the other position. A football coach, permitted to referee a game in which his own team was playing, would illustrate this antagonism of positions. Such situations cannot be completely avoided in a complicated business structure, but many concerns make a practice of assuming such antagonistic functions and regularly violating the trust thus delegated to them. When compelled by law to make a separation of their functions, they make a nominal separation and continue by subterfuge to maintain the two positions.

An accurate statistical comparison of the crimes of the two classes is not available. The most extensive evidence regarding the nature and prevalence of white-collar criminality is found in the reports of the larger investigations to which reference was made. Because of its scattered character, that evidence is assumed rather than summarized here. A few statements will be presented, as illustrations rather than as proof of the prevalence of this criminality.

The Federal Trade Commission in 1920 reported that commercial bribery was a prevalent and common practice in many industries. In certain chain stores, the net shortage in weights was sufficient to pay 3.4 percent on the investment in those commodities. Of the cans of ether sold to the Army in 1923–1925, 70 percent were rejected because of impurities. In Indiana, during the summer of 1934, 40 percent of the ice cream samples tested in a routine manner by the Division of Public Health were in violation of law. The Comptroller of the Currency in 1908 reported that violations of law were found in 75 percent of the banks examined in a three months' period. Lie detector tests of all employees in several Chicago banks, supported in almost all cases by confessions, showed that 20 percent of them had stolen bank property. A public accountant estimated, in the period prior to the Securities and Exchange Commission, that 80 percent of the financial statements of corporations were misleading. James M. Beck said, "Diogenes would have been hard put to it to find an honest man in the Wall Street which I knew as a corporation lawyer" (in 1916).

White-collar criminality in politics, which is generally recognized as fairly prevalent, has been used by some as a rough gauge by which to measure white-collar criminality in business. James A. Farley said, "The standards of conduct are as high among officeholders and politicians as they are in commercial life," and Cermak, while mayor of Chicago, said, "There is less graft in politics than in business." John Flynn wrote, "The average politician is the merest amateur in the gentle art of graft, compared with his brother in the field of business." And Walter Lippmann wrote, "Poor as they are, the standards of public life are so much more social than those of business that financiers who enter politics regard themselves as philanthropists."

These statements obviously do not give a precise measurement of the relative criminality of the white-collar class, but they are adequate evidence that crime is not so highly concentrated in the lower class as the usual statistics indicate. Also, these statements obviously do not mean that every business and professional man is a criminal, just as the usual theories do not mean that every man in the lower class is a criminal. On the other hand, the preceding statements refer in many cases to the leading corporations in America and are not restricted to the disreputable business and professional men who are called quacks, ambulance chasers, bucket-shop operators, dead-beats, and fly-by-night swindlers.[2]

The financial cost of white-collar crime is probably several times as great as the financial cost of all the crimes which are customarily regarded as the "crime problem." An officer of a chain grocery store in one year embezzled $600,000, which was six times as much as the annual losses from five hundred burglaries and robberies of the stores in that chain. Public enemies numbered one to six secured $130,000 by burglary and robbery in 1938, while the sum stolen by Krueger is estimated at $250,000,000, or nearly two thousand times as much. *The New York Times* in 1931 reported four cases of embezzlement in the United States with a loss of more than a million dollars each and a combined loss of nine million dollars. Although a million-dollar burglar or robber is practically unheard of, these million-dollar embezzlers are small-fry among white-collar criminals. The estimated loss to investers in one investment trust from 1929 to 1935 was $580,000,000, due primarily to the fact that 75 percent of the values in the portfolio were in securities of affiliated companies, although it advertised the importance of diversification in investments and its expert services in selecting safe securities. In Chicago, the claim was made six years ago that householders had lost $54,000,000 in two years during the administration of a city sealer who granted immunity from inspection to stores which provided Christmas baskets for his constituents.

The financial loss from white-collar crime, great as it is, is less important than the damage to social relations. White-collar crimes violate trust and therefore create distrust, which lowers social morale and produces social disorganization on a large scale.

[2]Perhaps it should be repeated that "white-collar" (upper) and "lower" classes merely designate persons of high and low socioeconomic status. Income and amount of money involved in the crime are not the sole criteria. Many persons of "low" socioeconomic status are "white-collar" criminals in the sense that they are well-dressed, well-educated, and have high incomes, but "white-collar" as used in this paper means "respected," "socially accepted and approved," "looked up to." Some people in this class may not be well-dressed or well-educated, nor have high incomes, although the "upper" usually exceed the "lower" classes in these respects as well as in social status.

Other crimes produce relatively little effect on social institutions or social organization.

White-collar crime is real crime. It is not ordinarily called crime, and calling it by this name does not make it worse, just as refraining from calling it crime does not make it better than it otherwise would be. It is called crime here in order to bring it within the scope of criminology, which is justified because it is in violation of the criminal law. The crucial question in this analysis is the criterion of violation of the criminal law. Conviction in the criminal court, which is sometimes suggested as the criterion, is not adequate because a large proportion of those who commit crimes are not convicted in criminal courts. This criterion, therefore, needs to be supplemented. When it is supplemented, the criterion of the crimes of one class must be kept consistent in general terms with the criterion of the crimes of the other class. The definition should not be the spirit of the law for white-collar crimes and the letter of the law for other crimes, or in other respects be more liberal for one class than for the other. Since this discussion is concerned with the conventional theories of the criminologists, the criterion of white-collar crime must be justified in terms of the procedures of those criminologists in dealing with other crimes. The criterion of white-collar crimes, as here proposed, supplements convictions in the criminal courts in four respects, in each of which the extension is justified because the criminologists who present the conventional theories of criminal behavior make the same extension in principle.

First, other agencies than the criminal court must be included, for the criminal court is not the only agency which makes official decisions regarding violations of the criminal law. The juvenile court, dealing largely with offenses of the children of the poor, in many states is not under the criminal jurisdiction. The criminologists have made much use of case histories and statistics of juvenile delinquents in constructing their theories of criminal behavior. This justifies the inclusion of agencies other than the criminal court which deal with white-collar offenses. The most important of these agencies are the administrative boards, bureaus, or commissions, and much of their work, although certainly not all, consists of cases which are in violation of the criminal law. The Federal Trade Commission recently ordered several automobile companies to stop advertising their interest rate on installment purchases as 6 percent, since it was actually 11½ percent. Also it filed complaint against *Good Housekeeping,* one of the Hearst publications, charging that its seals led the public to believe that all products bearing those seals had been tested in their laboratories, which was contrary to fact. Each of these involves a charge of dishonesty, which might have been tried in a criminal court as fraud. A large proportion of the cases before these boards should be included in the data of the criminologists. Failure to do so is a principal reason for the bias in their samples and the errors in their generalizations.

Second, for both classes, behavior which would have a reasonable expectancy of conviction if tried in a criminal court or substitute agency should be defined as criminal. In this respect, convictability rather than actual conviction should be the criterion of criminality. The criminologists would not hesitate to accept as data a verified case history of a person who was a criminal but had never been convicted. Similarly, it is justifiable to include white-collar criminals who have not been convicted, provided reliable evidence is available. Evidence regarding such cases appears in many civil suits, such as stockholders' suits and patent-infringement suits. These cases might have been referred to the criminal court but they were referred to the civil court because the injured party was more interested in securing damages than in seeing punishment inflicted. This also happens in embezzlement cases, regarding which surety companies have much evidence. In a short consecutive series of embezzlements known to a surety company, 90 percent were not prosecuted because prosecution would interfere with restitution or salvage. The evidence in cases of embezzlement is generally conclusive, and would probably have been sufficient to justify conviction in all of the cases in this series.

Third, behavior should be defined as criminal if conviction is avoided merely because of pressure which is brought to bear on the court or substitute agency. Gangsters and racketeers have been relatively immune in many cities because of their pressure on prospective witnesses and public officials, and professional theives, such as pickpockets and confidence men who do not use strong-arm methods, are even more frequently immune. The conventional criminologists do not hesitate to include the life histories of such criminals as data, because they understand the generic relation of the pressures to the failure to convict. Similarly, white-collar criminals are relatively immune because of the class bias of the courts and the power of their class to influence the implementation and administration of the law. This class bias affects not merely present-day courts but to a much greater degree affected the earlier courts which established the precedents and rules of procedure of the present-day courts. Consequently, it is justifiable to interpret the actual or potential failures of conviction in the light of known facts regarding the pressures brought to bear on the agencies which deal with offenders.

Fourth, persons who are accessory to a crime should be included among white-collar criminals as they are among other criminals. When the Federal Bureau of Investigation deals with a case of kidnapping, it is not content with catching the offenders who carried away the victim; they may catch and the court may convict twenty-five other persons who assisted by secreting the victim, negotiating the ransom, or putting the ransom money into circulation. On the other hand, the prosecution of white-collar criminals frequently stops with one offender. Political graft almost always involves collusion between politicians and business men but prosecutions are generally limited to the politicians. Judge Manton was found guilty of accepting $664,000 in bribes, but the six or eight important commercial concerns that paid the bribes have not been prosecuted. Pendergast, the late boss of Kansas City, was convicted for failure to report as a part of his income $315,000 received in bribes from insurance companies but the insurance companies which paid the bribes have not been prosecuted. In an investigation of an embezzlement by the president of a bank, at least a dozen other violations of law which were related to this embezzlement and involved most of the other officers of the bank and the officers of the clearing house, were discovered but none of the others was prosecuted.

This analysis of the criterion of white-collar criminality results in the conclusion that a description of white-collar criminality in general terms will be also a description of the criminality of the lower class. The respects in which the crimes of the two classes differ are the incidentals rather than the essentials of criminality. They differ principally in the implementation of the criminal laws which apply to them. The crimes of the lower class are handled by policemen, prosecutors, and judges, with penal sanctions in the form of fines, imprisonment, and death. The crimes of the upper class either result in no official action at all, or result in suits for damages in civil courts, or are handled by inspectors, and by administrative boards or commissions, with penal sanctions in the form of warnings, orders to cease and desist, occasionally the loss of a license, and only in extreme cases by fines or prison sentences. Thus, the white-collar criminals are segregated administratively from other criminals, and largely as a consequence of this are not regarded as real criminals by themselves, the general public, or the criminologists.

This difference in the implementation of the criminal law is due principally to the difference in the social position of the two types of offenders. Judge Woodward, when imposing sentence upon the officials of the H. O. Stone and Company, bankrupt real estate firm in Chicago, who had been convicted in 1933 of the use of the mails to defraud, said to them, "You are men of affairs, of experience, of refinement and culture, of excellent reputation and standing in the business and social world." That statement might be used as a general characterization of white-collar criminals for they are oriented basically to legitimate and respectable careers. Because of their social status they have a loud voice in determining what goes into the statutes and how the criminal law as it affects themselves is implemented and administered. This may be illustrated from the Pure Food and Drug Law. Between 1879 and 1906, 140 pure food and drug bills were presented in Congress and all failed because of the importance of the persons who would be affected. It took a highly dramatic performance by Dr. Wiley in 1906 to induce Congress to enact the law. That law, however, did not create a new crime, just as the federal Lindbergh kidnapping law did not create a new crime; it merely provided a more efficient implementation of a principle which had been formulated previously in state laws. When an amendment to this law, which would bring within the scope of its agents fraudulent statements made over the radio or in the press, was presented to Congress, the publishers and advertisers organized support and sent a lobby to Washington which successfully fought the amendment principally under the slogans of "freedom of the press" and "dangers of bureaucracy." This proposed amendment, also, would not have created a new crime, for the state laws already prohibited fraudulent statements over the radio or in the press; it would have implemented the law so it could have been enforced. Finally, the Administration has not been able to enforce the law as it has desired because of the pressures by the offenders against the law, sometimes brought to bear through the head of the Department of Agriculture, sometimes through congressmen who threaten cuts in the appropriation, and sometimes by others. The statement of Daniel Drew, a pious old fraud, describes the criminal law with some accuracy, "Law is like a cobweb; it's made for flies and the smaller kinds of insects, so to speak, but lets the big bumblebees break through. When technicalities of the law stood in my way, I have always been able to brush them aside easy as anything."

The preceding analysis should be regarded neither as an assertion that all efforts to influence legislation and its administration are reprehensible nor as a particularistic interpretation of the criminal law. It means only that the upper class has greater influence in moulding the criminal law and its administration to its own interests than does the lower class. The privileged position of white-collar criminals before the law results to a slight extent from bribery and political pressures, principally from the respect in which they are held and without special effort on their part. The most powerful group in medieval society secured relative immunity by "benefit of clergy," and now our most powerful groups secure relative immunity by "benefit of business or profession."

In contrast with the power of the white-collar criminals is the weakness of their victims. Consumers, investors, and stockholders are unorganized, lack technical knowledge, and cannot protect themselves. Daniel Drew, after taking a large sum of money by sharp practice from Vanderbilt in the Erie deal, concluded that it was a mistake to take money from a powerful man on the same level as himself and declared that in the future he would confine his efforts to outsiders, scattered all over the country, who wouldn't be able to organize and fight back. White-collar criminality flourishes at points where powerful business and professional men come in contact with persons who are weak. In this respect, it is similar to stealing candy from a baby. Many of the crimes of the lower class, on the other hand, are committed against persons of wealth and power in the form of burglary and robbery. Because of this difference in the comparative power of the victims, the white-collar criminals enjoy relative immunity.

Embezzlement is an interesting exception to white-collar criminality in this respect. Embezzlement is usually theft from an employer by an employee, and the employee is less capable of manipulating social and legal forces in his own interest than is the employer. As might have been expected, the laws regarding embezzlement were formulated long before laws for the protection of investors and consumers.

The theory that criminal behavior in general is due either to poverty or to the psychopathic and sociopathic conditions associated with poverty can now be shown to be invalid for three reasons. First, the generalization is based on a biased sample which omits almost entirely the behavior of white-collar criminals. The criminologists have restricted their data, for reasons of convenience and ignorance rather than of principle, largely to cases dealt with in criminal courts and juvenile courts, and these agencies are used principally for criminals from the lower economic strata. Consequently, their data are grossly biased from the point of view of the economic status of criminals and their generalization that criminality is closely associated with poverty is not justified.

Second, the generalization that criminality is closely associated with poverty obviously does not apply to white-collar criminals. With a small number of exceptions, they are not in poverty, were not reared in slums or badly deteriorated families, and are not feebleminded or psychopathic. They were seldom problem children in their earlier years and did not appear in juvenile courts or child guidance clinics. The proposition, derived from the data used by the conventional criminologists, that "the criminal of today was the problem child of yesterday" is seldom true of white-collar criminals. The idea that the causes of criminality are to be found almost exclusively in childhood similarly is fallacious. Even if poverty is extended to include the economic stresses which afflict business in a period of depression, it is not closely correlated with white-collar criminality. Probably at no time within fifty years have white-collar crimes in the field of investments and of corporate management been so extensive as during the boom period of the twenties.

Third, the conventional theories do not even explain lower class criminality. The sociopathic and psychopathic factors which have been emphasized doubtless have something to do with crime causation, but these factors have not been related to a general process which is found both in white-collar criminality and lower class criminality and therefore they do not explain the criminality of either class. They may explain the manner or method of crime—why lower class criminals commit burglary or robbery rather than false pretenses.

In view of these defects in the conventional theories, an hypothesis that will explain both white-collar criminality and lower class criminality is needed. For reasons of economy, simplicity, and logic, the hypothesis should apply to both classes, for this will make possible the analysis of causal factors freed from the encumbrances of the administrative devices which have led criminologists astray. Shaw and McKay and others, working exclusively in the field of lower class crime, have found the conventional theories inadequate to account for variations within the data of lower class crime and from that point of view have been working toward an explanation of crime in terms of a more general social process. Such efforts will be greatly aided by the procedure which has been described.

The hypothesis which is here suggested as a substitute for the conventional theories is that white-collar criminality, just as other systematic criminality, is learned; that it is learned in direct or indirect association with those who already practice the behavior; and that those who learn this criminal behavior are segregated from frequent and intimate contacts with law-abiding behavior. Whether a person becomes a criminal or not is determined largely by the comparative frequency and intimacy of his contacts with the two types of behavior. This may be called the process of differential association. It is a genetic explanation both of white-collar criminality and lower class criminality. Those who become white-collar criminals generally start their careers in good neighborhoods and good homes, graduate from colleges with some idealism, and with little selection on their part, get into particular business situations in which criminality is practically a folkway and are inducted into that system of behavior just as into any other folkway. The lower class criminals generally start their careers in deteriorated neighborhoods and families, find delinquents at hand from whom they acquire the attitudes toward, and techniques of, crime through association with delinquents and in partial segregation from law-abiding people. The essentials of the process are the same for the two classes of criminals. This is not entirely a process of assimilation, for inventions are frequently made, perhaps more frequently in white-collar crime than in lower class crime. The inventive geniuses for the lower class criminals are generally professional criminals, while the inventive geniuses for many kinds of white-collar crime are generally lawyers.

A second general process is social disorganization in the community. Differential association culminates in crime because the community is not organized solidly against that behavior. The law is pressing in one direction, and other forces are pressing in the opposite direction. In business, the "rules of the game" conflict with the legal rules. A business man who wants to obey the law is driven by his competitors to adopt their methods. This is well illustrated by the persistence of commercial bribery in spite of the strenuous efforts of business organizations to eliminate it. Groups and individuals are individuated; they are more concerned with their specialized group or individual interests than with the larger welfare. Consequently, it is not possible for the community to present a solid front in opposition to crime. The Better Business Bureaus and Crime Commissions, composed of business and professional men, attack burglary, robbery, and cheap swindles, but overlook the crimes of their own members. The forces which impinge on the lower class are similarly in conflict. Social disorganization affects the two classes in similar ways.

I have presented a brief and general description of white-collar criminality on a framework of argument regarding theories of criminal behavior. That argument, stripped of the description, may be stated in the following propositions:

1. White-collar criminality is real criminality, being in all cases in violation of the criminal law.
2. White-collar criminality differs from lower class criminality principally in an implementation of the criminal law which segregates white-collar criminals administratively from other criminals.
3. The theories of the criminologists that crime is due to poverty or to psychopathic and sociopathic conditions statistically associated with poverty are invalid because, first, they are derived from samples which are grossly biased with respect to socioeconomic status; second, they do not apply to the white-collar criminals; and third, they do not even explain the criminality of the lower class, since the factors are not related to a general process characteristic of all criminality.
4. A theory of criminal behavior which will explain both white-collar criminality and lower class criminality is needed.
5. An hypothesis of this nature is suggested in terms of differential association and social disorganization.

2. The Study of Criminal Law and Social Norms

Richard Quinney

One of the basic assumptions in the study of criminal behaviour is that behaviour in violation of the criminal law also represents deviation from other norms. The criminologist in his research usually proceeds on the premise that the criminal law embodies important social norms and that these norms are held by most persons in society. While these assumptions are rarely questioned in most studies of criminal behaviour, a few criminologists have nevertheless recognised that the relationship between the criminal law and social norms is problematic. Some time ago, for example, Fuller (1942) observed that the criminal statute is the formal embodiment of someone's moral values and that, depending upon the particular law, all persons may not regard the law as valid according to their own values and group norms. Sellin (1938), touching upon similar matters even at an earlier time, noted that the criminal code is only one set of conduct norms, but one which is binding upon all who live within the boundaries of a political unit.

These and other writers, then, have questioned the degree of correspondence between criminal law and social norms. They have provided enough discussion to caution the criminologist in his research that care must be taken in inferring that legal violations are also deviations from other norms. The fact remains, however, that criminologists continue to ignore the problematic relation between legal and extra-legal norms. The result is that much of the behaviour that is studied as criminal behaviour is not actually deviant behaviour from the standpoint of the norms of the groups and subcultures that are being investigated. It is likely that some violations are nothing more than the breaking of a formal rule, a rule which has little or no support in any group.

This paper, then, will explore, on the one hand, the relation between criminal law and social norms and, on the other, the relation between crime and deviation. It is suggested that these relationships may be taken as objects of study in their own right. The strategy becomes one of exploring the relationships rather than taking them for granted. The degree of correspondence between criminal violation and normative deviation poses significant problems for study. Likewise, the relation be-

Reprinted from "Is Criminal Behaviour Deviant Behaviour?" in *The British Journal of Criminology,* 5 (April 1965), 132–142, by permission of the Institute for the Study and Treatment of Delinquency, London.

tween criminal law and social norms presents a number of important research problems.

Criminal Law and Social Norms

Criminal law may be regarded as an instrument of formal social control whereby an organised effort is made to regulate certain areas of behaviour (Davis, 1962, Chap. 2; Korn and McCorkle, 1959, Chap. 4; Parsons, 1962). As a particular type of formal social control, criminal law is characterised by (1) explicit rules of conduct created by political authority, (2) provisions for punishment, (3) designated officials to make, interpret and enforce the rules, and (4) uniform administration of the codes for all persons within a given territory.

Law has grown increasingly important as a means of social control as societies have grown in complexity. In preliterate and peasant societies where norms are relatively uniform, stable and consistent, intimate personal relationships exist to such an extent to control human interaction. The more modern societies, on the other hand, have become highly differentiated in terms of values and norms. Various social groupings have arisen with their own sets of values and norms. In these heterogeneous societies there are many values and norms which are agreed upon by most members, but there are many values and norms which are unique to the diverse groups. As Sellin (1938, p. 29) has noted: "The more complex a culture becomes, the more likely it is that the number of normative groups which affect a person will be large, and the greater the chance that the norms of these groups will fail to agree, no matter how much they may overlap as a result of a common acceptance of certain norms."

Criminal law, therefore, has emerged as a formal system of maintaining social order in differentiated societies. Other means of social control have proved inadequate in the uniform regulation of many areas of behaviour. Where correct conduct cannot be agreed upon, the criminal law serves to control the behaviour of all persons within a given political jurisdiction.

It is unlikely, then, that all criminal law incorporates the most cherished values and norms of all persons in a society. There are values and norms supported by some or possibly all persons which are not part of the law, and the law includes values and norms which are not important to some persons. It is going too far to argue, as have some (Michael and Adler, 1933, pp. 2–3), that "there is no surer way of ascertaining what kinds of behaviour are generally regarded as immoral or anti-social by the people of any community than by reference to their criminal code, for in theory, at least, the criminal code embodies social judgments with respect to behaviour, and perhaps, more often than not, fact conforms to theory," or that "most of the people in any community would probably agree that most of the behaviour which is proscribed by their criminal law is socially undesirable." Such thinking on the similarity between criminal law and other social norms ignores (1) social differentiation in modern society, (2) processes in the formulation of criminal law, and (3) the relation of social change to criminal law and social norms.

Social Differentiation. Some legal norms forbidding certain behaviours are supported by nearly all segments of a society, while others find little support. Many of our recent laws do not have the support of the majority of the people. There is little question that the traditional laws regarding such conventional crimes as murder, larceny, and robbery find support in public opinion. However, it is unlikely that laws which define such behaviours as restraint of trade, false advertising and misuse of trade marks as criminal are supported by most persons (Clinard, 1963, pp. 152–153; Sutherland, 1940). These latter laws are unrelated to the social norms of the vast majority of the population.

Due to the heterogeneity of modern society, with varied and often opposing subcultures, there cannot be complete agreement on all norms. "To a large number of persons who live in such a culture, certain life situations are governed by such conflicting norms that no matter what the response of the person in such a situation will be, it will violate the norms of some social group concerned" (Sellin, 1938, p. 60). Thus, many people in modern society, depending upon their particular attachments, do not regard the official, legal norms as legitimate. The criminal law may not overlap the social norms of some groups and thus may not be supported by some individuals. The result is that there is selective obedience to the law for most persons. Some laws are obeyed and others are not according to a person's own values and the norms of his groups (Clinard, 1963, pp. 172–174).

Formulation of Criminal Law. Another reason for the lack of agreement between criminal law and other social norms is due to the particular processes that operate in the formulation of the law. Cultural diversity creates special groups, and certain of these groups become organised to an extent that they are in a position to exert influence at strategic points in the formulation of criminal law (Williams, 1960, pp. 270–279; Key, 1958; Truman, 1951). The values and norms for some groups become a part of the criminal law, while other groups are not represented in the law which is binding upon all persons and groups.

The content of the criminal law, then, including the kind of conduct prohibited and the nature of sanctions attached, depends upon the norms of those groups in society which influence legislation, court decisions, and administrative rulings. In addition, these influential groups may not be in the majority in numbers or even represent the interests of the majority in the population. Indeed, as noted by Fuller (1942, p. 627), "Our parliamentary democracy is so constituted that much of our legislation is, in fact, the legislation of well-organized, articulate and powerful minorities." The social values and norms, then, "which receive the protection of the criminal law are ultimately those which are treasured by dominant interest groups" (Sellin, 1938, p. 21).

The ability of groups to influence the formulation of law is related to the power positions of the particular groups. A group that can get in a strategic power position can determine the content of criminal law. Furthermore, the criminal law changes as the values and norms of the dominant groups are modified and as the place of these groups is altered in the power structure itself. Therefore, what is defined as criminal behaviour in a society is related to the success of certain groups in influencing legislation, the values and norms of these groups, the compromises of these groups, and shifts in the power structure of the society. In addition the determination of what is criminal extends into the interpretation and enforcement of the law. The values and norms of groups in positions of power can enter at any point in establishing the criminality of any behaviour (Cuber, Harper and Kenkel, 1956, pp. 160–163).

Social Change. The degree of correspondence between criminal law and social norms is also affected by the changes in a society. For instance, many criminal laws lag behind the changing societal norms. The well-known "blue laws" are an example of criminal laws which were once related to the norms of several groups or segments of society but have since become dated and obsolete because of normative modifications and changes.

It is also the case that some laws precede the norms that will some day become established for a large portion of the society. In fact, law can serve as a device to induce social change (Rose, 1956). The recent civil rights legislation in the United States in reference to negro-white relations is forcing a change in social norms in some segments of the population. As has been noted by Segerstedt (1942a, 1942b), social codes—or imperatives—create social customs. Thus, in a number of ways, criminal law is related to social change. Social change and changes in the law are constant and interacting processes (Dror, 1959; Friedmann, 1959).

It can therefore be seen that the relationship between criminal law and social norms is a function of a number of factors, of which the most important appear to be social differentiation, processes in the formulation of criminal law, and social change. It is clear that the relationship between criminal law and social norms is a problematic one. Criminologists cannot take the relationship—in terms of complete correspondence—for granted. The nature of the relation of any criminal law to other social norms is far from certain.

Crime and Deviation

Much of what is called criminal behaviour may thus be viewed as behaviour that is oriented to norms other than those embodied in the criminal law. Such illegal behaviour is, of course, in a sense deviant behaviour in that there is deviation from a norm, the legal norm. However, in keeping with recent conceptualisation (Cohen, 1959, p. 462) deviant behaviour represents "behaviour which violates institutionalized expectations—that is, expectations which are shared and recognized as legitimate within a social system." Similarly (Clinard, 1963, p. 22), deviant behaviour consists of "only those situations in which behaviour is in a disapproved direction, and of sufficient degree to exceed the tolerance limit of the community." While behaviours in violation of many of a society's legal norms deviate from institutionalised expectations and exceed the tolerance limit of the community, it is also true that some crimes are not in violation of expectations (or social norms) and are not disapproved to such a degree as to exceed the tolerance limit of the community. Criminal behaviour and deviant behaviour can thus be treated as two separate orders of behaviour.

It follows that the formulation of hypotheses for research in criminology must take into consideration the deviant nature of the behaviour as well as its criminality. Behaviour that does not deviate from the group norm, but which is nevertheless illegal, will require an explanation different from behaviour which represents both normative deviation and criminal violation.

The problem of the correspondence between deviant behaviour and criminal behaviour becomes particularly crucial in the study of white collar crime–or occupational crime (Quinney, 1964). The question arises whether or not the behaviours which have been defined as criminal–many of them only recently–are also deviations from the normative structure of the occupation. If it can be established that the behaviours are regarded as deviant, as well as criminal, by the occupational members, the criminal violations can truly be studied as deviations from occupational norms, thus eliminating the cumbersome problem–usually not resolved–that criminal behaviour may not be normative deviation from the standpoint of the group being studied.

Methods must be developed to determine the correspondence between deviant and criminal behaviour. One procedure which appears to have promise involves the measurement of the attitudes of group members towards criminal cases. In a study of prescription violation by retail pharmacists, the author (Quinney, 1962, Chap. 9; Quinney, 1963) was able to determine the deviant nature of certain illegal behaviours by presenting the respondents with several cases of criminal violations. Through an analysis of forced choice responses, it was possible to establish whether or not the specific behaviours were regarded as criminal, deviant, or both.

The otherwise confusing problem that some criminal violations are not regarded as criminal by the group members becomes clear when it is found that these behaviours are not actually deviant. The eventual explanation of these behaviours cannot be based on a theory of deviant behaviour. On the other hand, behaviours that are deviant as well as criminal are subject to an explanation in terms of deviant behaviour. An understanding of the deviant nature of the criminal behaviour must precede any attempt to explain the behaviour.

The Study of Criminal Law and Social Norms in Criminology

To the criminologist, scientific interest in crime emerges when the important norms by which certain behaviours are defined as crime are themselves subjected to analysis rather than taken for granted. All too often the facile solution that the criminal behaviour under study is behaviour in deviation from social norms has been relied upon. Future studies must explore the relation between legal norms and extra-legal norms instead of resorting to the inference that the two are the same. An investigation which considers both the criminal law and social norms will provide valuable insights concerning the conditions under which behaviour becomes defined as crime. In addition, information regarding the process of law-making will be obtained. Such a study will be likely to produce knowledge regarding the structure of society itself.

The importance of criminal law to the study of criminal behaviour was forcefully noted some time ago by Michael and Adler (1933, p. 5) when they stated that criminal law is the formal cause of crime: "If crime is merely an instance of conduct which is proscribed by the criminal code it follows that the criminal law is the formal cause of crime." It is the criminal law that gives behaviour its quality of criminality. One might go on so far as to say, then, as did Michael and Adler (1933, p. 20), that "all of the problems of crime, practical and theoretical, have their roots in the criminal code."

The idea that criminal law should be given serious attention by criminologists has been suggested on several occasions. Vold (1958, p. 202) pointed out that in criminology there is "always a dual problem of explanation–that of accounting for the behaviour *as behaviour*, and equally important, accounting for the *definitions* by which specific behaviour comes to be considered as crime or noncrime." In a series of articles Jeffery (1956a, 1956b, 1959) has strongly stated that criminologists have over-emphasised the study of the behaviour of criminals to the neglect of the study of the way in which the behaviours become defined as crime. Moreover, he states (1959, p. 534): "Criminologists need a theory of crime, a theory which explains the origin and development of criminal law in terms of the institutional structure of society."

Likewise, Mannheim (1955, especially Chap. 12) has suggested a sociology of criminal law which examines the structure of society, the groups, values and attitudes in relation to the content of the criminal law; but actual research in the sociology of criminal law has been sparse. Some exceptions are Segerstedt's (1949) report on the attitudes towards the law and towards lawbreakers (also see Smigel, 1953), Hall's (1952) study of the relationship between social structure and the development of criminal law on theft, Rusche and Kirchheimer's (1961) recent observations on the use of legal procedures for political ends. In addition, there has been some research (Foote, 1956; Nagel, 1962; Newman, 1956) on the prosecution and adjudication of criminal cases.

The importance of the relation between criminal law and social norms has been acutely drawn to the attention of criminologists particularly through the study of white collar crime. As Aubert has noted (1952, p. 264): "The unexpected and somehow deviant nature of many recent laws defining white collar crimes has made it natural to ask for an explanation of the norms themselves and not only of their infringements. As soon as this happens new theoretical vistas are immediately opened." It is not altogether unlikely that the study of the process of law-making, the groups influencing legislation, and the social norms behind the criminal law may provide a level of analysis for the actual explanation of the behaviours that occur in violation of the law.

Administration of Criminal Justice

The relation between legal norms and other norms has consequences for violation and enforcement of the criminal law. In general, those laws which are in accord with the important extra-legal norms of most of the population are realised in actual behaviour (Davis, 1962, pp. 58-60; Dror, 1957-58). Enforcement becomes a problem when there is a lack of agreement on the norms embodied in the criminal law. Sutherland and Cressey (1960, p. 11) have summarised the problem of the correspondence between criminal law and the important norms as it relates to enforcement: "Laws have accumulated because the mores have been weak and inconsistent; and because the laws have not had the support of the mores they have been relatively ineffective as a means of control. When mores are adequate, laws are unnecessary; when the mores are inadequate, the laws are ineffective."

Finally, in reference to the relation between criminal law and social norms, it may be suggested that much criminal behaviour in modern, heterogeneous society represents a normal response to the accumulation of criminal laws. There is a tendency in modern societies to make laws as a first reaction to situations which are defined by some as difficult and unpleasant. The result is that today our criminal codes consist of many laws which contradict one another and many which are antiquated (Barnes and Teeters, 1959, pp. 70-75; Bloch and Geis, 1962, pp. 63-64). Each year there are thousands of new laws added to the statute books, creating many new crimes. It has been estimated (Jeffery, 1962, p. 300), for example, that since 1900 in the United States the number of offences for which a person can be arrested has doubled. Many of the laws no longer incorporate the social norms on which they were once based. Changes both in norms and scientific knowledge have made many laws obsolete. Such laws are likely to meet with resistance. Violation may occur where the usefulness of the proscribed action is doubtful. Violation of these laws may be the only possible solution to present-day problems and situations.

Several undesirable consequences result from such an unwieldy accumulation of criminal law. A genuine disrespect and disregard for the particular laws may be created and, what is more, even for law in general. This may be furthered when law enforcement agencies must often ignore the offence when the law is obsolete but still exists on the statute books. Enforcement and administrative procedures in general tend to break down. Furthermore, there may be an outright attempt by the public to outwit the law enforcement agencies in violation of these laws and others. Thus, as stated by Michael and Adler (1933, p. 353), "Laws which make certain types of behaviour criminal may be more undesirable in their consequences than the behaviour itself."

When criminal laws no longer receive social support, or the laws become obsolete because of scientific knowledge, the laws should be changed with old and inefficient ones repealed and, if necessary, new ones enacted. It may also be desirable to bring within the scope of the criminal law behaviours which deviate from the basic values of the society (Mannheim, 1946). Thus, as has been suggested by several writers (Beutel, 1957; Mannheim, 1946, especially Chap. 11; Michael and Adler, 1933), the study of criminal law by criminologists could provide the necessary knowledge for rational legislation. Further investigation of the relation between criminal behaviour and deviant behaviour could contribute to this purpose.

REFERENCES

AUBERT, V. (1952) "White Collar Crime and Social Structure," *American Journal of Sociology 58,* 263–271.

BARNES, H. E. and TEETERS, N. K. (1959) *New Horizons in Criminology.* Englewood Cliffs, N.J.: Prentice-Hall.

BEUTEL, F. (1957) *Some Potentialities of Experimental Jurisprudence as a New Branch of Social Science.* Lincoln: University of Nebraska Press.

BLOCH, H. A. and GEIS, G. (1962) *Man, Crime, and Society.* New York: Random House.

CLINARD, M. B. (1963) *Sociology of Deviant Behavior.* New York: Holt, Rinehart & Winston.

COHEN, A. K. (1959) "The Study of Social Disorganization and Deviant Behavior" in R. K. Merton, L. B. Broom and L. S. Cottrell, Jr. (eds.): *Sociology Today,* pp. 461–484. New York: Basic Books.

CUBER, J. F., HARPER, R. A. and KENKEL, W. F. (1956) *Problems in American Society: Values in Conflict.* New York: Henry Holt.

DAVIS, F. J. (1962) "Law as a Type of Social Control" in F. J. Davis, H. H. Foster, Jr., C. R. Jeffery and E. E. Davis (eds.): *Society and the Law,* Chap. 2. New York: The Free Press of Glencoe.

DROR, Y. (1957–58) "Values and the Law," *The Antioch Review 17,* 440–454.

DROR, Y. (1959) "Law and Social Change," *Tulane Law Review 35,* 787–802.

FOOTE, C. (1956) "Vagrancy-Type Law and Its Administration," *University of Pennsylvania Law Review 104,* 603–650.

FRIEDMANN, F. (1959) *Law in a Changing Society.* London: Stevens & Sons.

FULLER, R. C. (1942) "Morals and the Criminal Law," *Journal of Criminal Law, Criminology and Police Science 32,* 624–630.

HALL, J. (1952) *Theft, Law and Society.* 2nd edition. Indianapolis: Bobbs-Merrill.

JEFFERY, C. R. (1956a) "The Structure of American Criminological Thinking," *Journal of Criminal Law, Criminology and Police Science 46,* 658–672.

JEFFERY, C. R. (1956b) "Crime, Law and Social Structure," *Journal of Criminal Law, Criminology and Police Science 47,* 423–435.

JEFFERY, C. R. (1959) "An Integrated Theory of Crime and Criminal Behavior," *Journal of Criminal Law, Criminology and Police Science 49,* 533–552.

JEFFERY, C. R. (1962) "Criminal Justice and Social Change" in F. J. Davis, H. H. Foster, Jr., C. R. Jeffery and E. E. Davis (eds.): *Society and the Law,* Chap. 8. New York: The Free Press of Glencoe.

KEY, V. O., Jr. (1958) *Politics, Parties and Pressure Groups.* New York: Thomas Y. Crowell.

KIRCHHEIMER, O. (1961) *Political Justice: The Use of Legal Procedure for Political Ends.* Princeton: Princeton University Press.

KORN, R. R. and McCORKLE, L. W. (1959) *Criminology and Penology.* New York: Holt, Rinehart & Winston.

MANNHEIM, H. (1946) *Criminal Justice and Social Reconstruction.* New York: Oxford University Press.

MANNHEIM, H. (1955) *Group Problems in Crime and Punishment.* London: Routledge & Kegan Paul.

MICHAEL, J. and ADLER, M. J. (1933) *Crime, Law, and Social Science.* New York: Harcourt, Brace.

NAGEL, S. S. (1962) "Judicial Backgrounds and Criminal Cases," *Journal of Criminal Law, Criminology and Police Science 53,* 333–339.

NEWMAN, D. J. (1956) "Pleading Guilty for Consideration: A Study of Bargain Justice," *Journal of Criminal Law, Criminology and Police Science 46,* 780–790.

PARSONS, T. (1962) "The Law and Social Control" in W. M. Evan (ed.): *Law and Sociology,* pp. 56–72. New York: The Free Press of Glencoe.

QUINNEY, E. R. (1962) *Retail Pharmacy as a Marginal Occupation: A Study of Prescription Violation,* unpublished Ph. D. dissertation, University of Wisconsin.

QUINNEY, E. R. (1963) "Occupational Structure and Criminal Behavior Prescription Violation by Retail Pharmacists," *Social Problems 11,* 179–185.

QUINNEY, E. R. (1964) "The Study of White Collar Crime: Toward a Reorientation in Theory and Research," *Journal of Criminal Law, Criminology and Police Science 55,* 208–214.

ROSE, A. M. (1956) "The Use of Law to Induce Social Change," *Transactions of the Third World Congress of Sociology 6,* 52–63.

RUSCHE, G. and KIRCHHEIMER, O. (1939) *Punishment and Social Structure.* New York: Columbia University Press.

SEGERSTEDT, T. T. (1942a) "Customs and Codes" (Part I), *Theorica 8,* 3–22.

SEGERSTEDT, T. T. (1942b) "Customs and Codes" (Part II), *Theorica 8,* 126–153.

SEGERSTEDT, T. T. (1949) "A Research in the General Sense of Justice," *Theorica 15,* 323–338.

SELLIN, S. (1938) *Culture, Conflict and Crime.* New York: Social Science Research Council.

SMIGEL, E. O. (1953) "Public Attitudes Toward 'Chiseling' with Reference to Unemployment Compensation," *American Sociological Review 18,* 59–67.

SUTHERLAND, E. H. (1940) "White Collar Criminality," *American Sociological Review 5,* 1–12.

TRUMAN, D. (1951) *The Governmental Process.* New York: Alfred A. Knopf.

VOLD, G. B. (1958) *Theoretical Criminology.* New York: Oxford University Press.

WILLIAMS, R. M., Jr. (1960) *American Society.* New York: Alfred A. Knopf.

3. A Sociological Analysis of the Law of Vagrancy

William J. Chambliss

With the outstanding exception of Jerome Hall's analysis of theft[1] there has been a severe shortage of sociologically relevant analyses of the relationship between particular laws and the social setting in which these laws emerge, are interpreted, and take form. The paucity of such studies is somewhat surprising in view of widespread agreement that such studies are not only desirable but absolutely essential to the development of a mature sociology of law.[2] A fruitful method of establishing the direction and pattern of this mutual influence is to systematically analyze particular legal categories, to observe the changes which take place in the categories and to explain how these changes are themselves related to and stimulate changes in the society. This paper is an attempt to provide such an analysis of the law of vagrancy in Anglo-American Law.

Legal Innovation: The Emergence of the Law of Vagrancy in England

There is general agreement among legal scholars that the first full fledged vagrancy statute was passed in England in 1349. As is generally the case with legislative innovations, however, this statute was preceded by earlier laws which established a climate favorable to such change. The most significant forerunner to the 1349 vagrancy statute was in 1274 when it was provided:

> Because that abbies and houses of religion have been overcharged and sore grieved, by the resort of great men and other, so that their goods have not been sufficient for themselves, whereby they have been greatly hindered and impoverished, that they cannot maintain themselves, nor such charity as they have been accustomed to do;

Reprinted from *Social Problems,* 12:1 (Fall 1964), 67–77, by permission of The Society for the Study of Social Problems and the author.

For a more complete listing of most of the statutes dealt with in this report the reader is referred to Burn, *The History of the Poor Laws.* Citations of English statutes should be read as follows: 3 Ed. 1. c. 1. refers to the third act of Edward the first, chapter one, etc.

[1] Hall, J., *Theft, Law and Society,* Bobbs-Merrill, 1939. See also, Alfred R. Lindesmith, "Federal Law and Drug Addiction," *Social Problems,* Vol. 7, No. 1, 1959, p. 48.

[2] See, for example, Rose, A., "Some Suggestions for Research in the Sociology of Law," *Social Problems,* Vol. 9, No. 3, 1962, pp. 281–283, and Geis, G., "Sociology, Criminology, and Criminal Law," *Social Problems,* Vol. 7, No. 1, 1959, pp. 40–47.

it is provided, that none shall come to eat or lodge in any house of religion, or any other's foundation than of his own, at the costs of the house, unless he be required by the governor of the house before his coming hither.[3]

Unlike the vagrancy statutes this statute does not intend to curtail the movement of persons from one place to another, but is solely designed to provide the religious houses with some financial relief from the burden of providing food and shelter to travelers.

The philosophy that the religious houses were to give alms to the poor and to the sick and feeble was, however, to undergo drastic change in the next fifty years. The result of this changed attitude was the establishment of the first vagrancy statute in 1349 which made it a crime to give alms to any who were unemployed while being of sound mind and body. To wit:

Because that many valiant beggars, as long as they may live of begging, do refuse to labor, giving themselves to idleness and vice, and sometimes to theft and other abominations; it is ordained, that none, upon pain of imprisonment shall, under the colour of pity or alms, give anything to such which may labour, or presume to favour them towards their desires; so that thereby they may be compelled to labour for their necessary living.[4]

It was further provided by this statute that:

... every man and woman, of what condition he be, free or bond, able in body, and within the age of threescore years, not living in merchandize nor exercising any craft, not having of his own whereon to live, nor proper land whereon to occupy himself, and not serving any other if he in convenient service (his estate considered) be required to serve, shall be bounded to serve him which shall him require... And if any refuse, he shall on conviction by two true men,... be commited to gaol till he find surety to serve.

And if any workman or servant, of what estate or condition he be, retained in any man's service, do depart from the said service without reasonable cause or license, before the term agreed on, he shall have pain of imprisonment.[5]

There was also in this statute the stipulation that the workers should receive a standard wage. In 1351 this statute was strengthened by the stipulation:

An none shall go out of the town where he dwelled in winter, to serve the summer, if he may serve in the same town.[6]

By 34 Ed 3 (1360) the punishment for these acts became imprisonment for fifteen days and if they "do not justify themselves by the end of that time, to be sent to gaol till they do."

A change in official policy so drastic as this did not, of course, occur simply as a matter of whim. The vagrancy statutes emerged as a result of changes in other

[3] 3 Ed. 1. c. 1.
[4] 35 Ed. 1. c. 1.
[5] 23 Ed. 3.
[6] 25 Ed. 3 (1351).

parts of the social structure. The prime-mover for this legislative innovation was the Black Death which struck England about 1348. Among the many disastrous consequences this had upon the social structure was the fact that it decimated the labor force. It is estimated that by the time the pestilence had run its course at least fifty per cent of the population of England had died from the plague. This decimation of the labor force would necessitate rather drastic innovations in any society but its impact was heightened in England where, at this time, the economy was highly dependent upon a ready supply of cheap labor.

Even before the pestilence, however, the availability of an adequate supply of cheap labor was becoming a problem for the landowners. The crusades and various wars had made money necessary to the lords and, as a result, the lord frequently agreed to sell the serfs their freedom in order to obtain the needed funds. The serfs, for their part, were desirous of obtaining their freedom (by "fair means" or "foul") because the larger towns which were becoming more industrialized during this period could offer the serf greater personal freedom as well as a higher standard of living. This process is nicely summarized by Bradshaw:

> By the middle of the 14th century the outward uniformity of the manorial system had become in practice considerably varied ... for the peasant had begun to drift to the towns and it was unlikely that the old village life in its unpleasant aspects should not be resented. Moreover the constant wars against France and Scotland were fought mainly with mercenaries after Henry III's time and most villages contributed to the new armies. The bolder serfs either joined the armies or fled to the towns, and even in the villages the free men who held by villein tenure were as eager to commute their services as the serfs were to escape. Only the amount of 'free' labor available enabled the lord to work his demense in many places.[7]

And he says regarding the effect of the Black Death:

> ... in 1348 the Black Death reached England and the vast mortality that ensued destroyed that reserve of labour which alone had made the manorial system even nominally possible.[8]

The immediate result of these events was of course no surprise: Wages for the "free" man rose considerably and this increased, on the one hand, the landowners' problems and, on the other hand, the plight of the unfree tenant. For although wages increased for the personally free laborers, it of course did not necessarily add to the standard of living of the serf, if anything it made his position worse because the landowner would be hard pressed to pay for the personally free labor which he needed and would thus find it more and more difficult to maintain the standard of living for the serf which he had heretofore supplied. Thus the serf had no alternative but flight if he chose to better his position. Furthermore, flight generally meant both freedom and better conditions since the possibility of work in the new weaving industry was great and the chance of being caught small.[9]

[7]Bradshaw, F., *A Social History of England*, p. 54.
[8]*Ibid.*
[9]*Ibid.*, p. 57.

It was under these conditions that we find the first vagrancy statutes emerging. There is little question but that these statutes were designed for one express purpose: to force laborers (whether personally free or unfree) to accept employment at a low wage in order to insure the landowner an adequate supply of labor at a price he could afford to pay. Caleb Foote concurs with this interpretation when he notes:

> The anti-migratory policy behind vagrancy legislation began as an essential complement of the wage stabilization legislation which accompanied the breakup of feudalism and the depopulation caused by the Black Death. By the Statutes of Labourers in 1349-1351, every ablebodied person without other means of support was required to work for wages fixed at the level preceding the Black Death; it was unlawful to accept more, or to refuse an offer to work, or to flee from one county to another to avoid offers of work or to seek higher wages, or go give alms to able-bodied beggars who refused to work.[10]

In short, as Foote says in another place, this was an "attempt to make the vagrancy statutes a substitute for serfdom."[11] This same conclusion is equally apparent from the wording of the statute where it is stated:

> Because great part of the people, and especially of workmen and servants, late died in pestilence; many seeing the necessity of masters, and great scarcity of servants, will not serve without excessive wages, and some rather willing to beg in idleness than by labour to get their living: it is ordained, that every man and woman, of what condition he be, free or bond, able in body and within the age of three score years, not living in merchandise, (etc.) be required to serve. ...

The innovation in the law, then, was a direct result of the afore-mentioned changes which had occurred in the social setting. In this case these changes were located for the most part in the economic institution of the society. The vagrancy laws were designed to alleviate a condition defined by the lawmakers as undesirable. The solution was to attempt to force a reversal, as it were, of a social process which was well underway; that is, to curtail mobility of laborers in such a way that labor would not become a commodity for which landowners would have to compete.

Statutory Dormancy: A Legal Vestige. In time, of course, the curtailment of the geographical mobility of laborers was no longer requisite. One might well expect that when the function served by the statute was no longer an important one for the society, the statutes would be eliminated from the law. In fact, this has not occurred. The vagrancy statutes have remained in effect since 1349. Furthermore, as we shall see in some detail later, they were taken over by the colonies and have remained in effect in the United States as well.

The substance of the vagrancy statutes changed very little for some time after the first ones in 1349–1351 although there was a tendency to make punishments more harsh than originally. For example, in 1360 it was provided that violators of the

[10]Foote, C., "Vagrancy Type Law and Its Administration," *Univ. of Pennsylvania Law Review* (104), 1956, p. 615.

[11]*Ibid.*

statute should be imprisoned for fifteen days[12] and in 1388 the punishment was to put the offender in the stocks and to keep him there until "he find surety to return to his service."[13] That there was still, at this time, the intention of providing the landowner with labor is apparent from the fact that this statute provides:

> and he or she which use to labour at the plough and cart, or other labour and service of husbandry, till they be of the age of 12 years, from thenceforth shall abide at the same labour without being put to any mistery or handicraft: and any covenant of apprenticeship to the contrary shall be void.[14]

The next alteration in the statutes occurs in 1495 and is restricted to an increase in punishment. Here it is provided that vagrants shall be "set in stocks, there to remain by the space of three days and three nights, and there to have none other sustenance but bread and water; and after the said three days and nights, to be had out and set at large, and then to be commanded to avoid the town."[15]

The tendency to increase the severity of punishment during this period seems to be the result of a general tendency to make finer distinctions in the criminal law. During this period the vagrancy statutes appear to have been fairly inconsequential in either their effect as a control mechanism or as a generally enforced statute.[16] The processes of social change in the culture generally and the trend away from serfdom and into a "free" economy obviated the utility of these statutes. The result was not unexpected. The judiciary did not apply the law and the legislators did not take it upon themselves to change the law. In short, we have here a period of dormancy in which the statute is neither applied nor altered significantly.

A Shift in Focal Concern

Following the squelching of the Peasants' Revolt in 1381, the services of the serfs to the lord "...tended to become less and less exacted, although in certain forms they lingered on till the seventeenth century... By the sixteenth century few knew that there were any bondmen in England...and in 1575 Queen Elizabeth listened to the prayers of almost the last serfs in England...and granted them manumission."[17]

In view of this change we would expect corresponding changes in the vagrancy laws. Beginning with the lessening of punishment in the statute of 1503 we find these changes. However, instead of remaining dormant (or becoming more so) or being negated altogether, the vagrancy statutes experienced a shift in focal concern. With this shift the statutes served a new and equally important function for the social

[12] 34 Ed. 3 (1360).

[13] 12 R. 2 (1388).

[14] *Ibid.*

[15] 11 H. & C. 2 (1495).

[16] As evidenced for this note the expectation that "...the common gaols of every shire are likely to be greatly pestered with more numbers of prisoners than heretofore..." when the statutes were changed by the statute of 14 Ed. c. 5 (1571).

[17] Bradshaw, *op. cit.*, p. 61.

order of England. The first statute which indicates this change was in 1530. In this statute (22 H.8.c. 12 1530) it was stated:

If any person, being whole and mighty in body, and able to labour, be taken in begging, or be vagrant and can give no reckoning how he lawfully gets his living;...and all other idle persons going about, some of them using divers and subtle crafty and unlawful games and plays, and some of them feigning themselves to have knowledge of... craft sciences... shall be punished as provided.

What is most significant about this statute is the shift from an earlier concern with laborers to a concern with *criminal* activities. To be sure, the stipulation of persons "being whole and mighty in body and able to labour, be taken in begging, or be vagrant" sounds very much like the concerns of the earlier statutes. Some important differences are apparent however when the rest of the statute includes those who "...can give no reckoning how he lawfully getshis living"; "some of them using divers subtil and unlawful games and plays." This is the first statute which specifically focuses upon these kinds of criteria for adjudging someone a vagrant.

It is significant that in this statute the severity of punishment is increased so as to be greater not only than provided by the 1503 statute but the punishment is more severe than that which had been provided by *any* of the pre-1503 statutes as well. For someone who is merely idle and gives no reckoning of how he makes his living the offender shall be:

...had to the next market town, or other place where they [the constables] shall think most convenient, and there to be tied to the end of a cart naked, and to be beaten with whips throughout the same market town or other place, till his body be bloody by reason of such whipping.[18]

But, for those who use "divers and subtil crafty and unlawful games and plays," etc., the punishment is "...whipping at two days together in manner aforesaid."[19] For the second offense such persons are:

...scourged two days, and the third day to be put upon the pillory from nine of the clock till eleven before noon of the same day and to have one of his ears cut off.[20]

And if he offend the third time "... to have like punishment with whipping, standing on the pillory and to have his other ear cut off."

This statute (1) makes a distinction between types of offenders and applies the more severe punishment to those who are clearly engaged in "criminal" activities, (2) mentions a specific concern with categories of "unlawful" behavior, and (3) applies a type of punishment (cutting off the ear) which is generally reserved for offenders who are defined as likely to be a fairly serious criminal.

Only five years later we find for the first time that the punishment of death is

[18] 22 H. 8. c. 12 (1530).
[19] *Ibid.*
[20] *Ibid.*

applied to the crime of vagrancy. We also note a change in terminology in the statute:

> and if any ruffians...after having been once apprehended...shall wander, loiter, or idle use themselves and play the vagabonds...shall be eftfoons not only whipped again, but shall have the gristle of this right ear clean cut off. And if he shall again offend, he shall be committed to gaol till the next sessions; and being there convicted upon indictment, he shall have judgment to suffer pains and execution of death, as a felon, as an enemy of the commonwealth.[21]

It is significant that the statute now makes persons who repeat the crime of vagrancy a felon. During this period then, the focal concern of the vagrancy statutes becomes a concern for the control of felons and is no longer primarily concerned with the movement of laborers.

These statutory changes were a direct response to changes taking place in England's social structure during this period. We have already pointed out that feudalism was decaying rapidly. Concomitant with the breakup of feudalism was an increased emphasis upon commerce and industry. The commercial emphasis in England at the turn of the sixteenth century is of particular importance in the development of vagrancy laws. With commercialism came considerable traffic bearing valuable items. Where there were 169 important merchants in the middle of the fourteenth century there were 3,000 merchants engaged in foreign trade alone at the beginning of the sixteenth century.[22] England became highly dependent upon commerce for its economic support. Italians conducted a great deal of the commerce of England during this early period and were held in low repute by the populace. As a result, they were subject to attacks by citizens and, more important, were frequently robbed of their goods while transporting them. "The general insecurity of the times made any transportation hazardous. The special risks to which the alien merchant was subjected gave rise to the royal practice of issuing formally executed covenants of safe conduct through the realm."[23]

Such a situation not only called for the enforcement of existing laws but also called for the creation of new laws which would facilitate the control of persons preying upon merchants transporting goods. The vagrancy statutes were revived in order to fulfill just such a purpose. Persons who had committed no serious felony but who were suspected of being capable of doing so could be apprehended and incapacitated through the application of vagrancy laws once these laws were refocused so as to include "...any ruffians... [who] shall wander, loiter, or idle use themselves and play the vagabonds..."[24]

The new focal concern is continued in 1 Ed. 6. c. 3 (1547) and in fact is made more general so as to include:

[21] 27 H. 8. c. 25 (1535).
[22] Hall, *op. cit.*, p. 21.
[23] *Ibid.*, p. 23.
[24] 27 H. 8. c. 25 (1535).

> Whoever man or woman, being not lame, impotent, or so aged or diseased that he or she cannot work, not having whereon to live, shall be lurking in any house, or loitering or idle wandering by the highway side, or in streets, cities, towns, or villages, not applying themselves to some honest labour, and so continuing for three days; or running away from their work; every such person shall be taken for a vagabond. And...upon conviction of two witnesses...the same loiterer (shall) be marked with a hot iron in the breast with the letter V, and adjudged him to the person bringing him, to be his slave for two years...

Should the vagabond run away, upon conviction, he was to be branded by a hot iron with the letter S on the forehead and to be thenceforth declared a slave forever. And in 1571 there is modification of the punishment to be inflicted, whereby the offender is to be "branded on the chest with the letter V" (for vagabond). And, if he is convicted the second time, the brand is to be made on the forehead. It is worth noting here that this method of punishment, which first appeared in 1530 and is repeated here with somewhat more force, is also an indication of a change in the type of person to whom the law is intended to apply. For it is likely that nothing so permanent as branding would be applied to someone who was wandering but looking for work, or at worst merely idle not particularly dangerous *per se.* On the other hand, it could well be applied to someone who was likely to be engaged in other criminal activities in connection with being "vagrant."

By 1571 in the statute of 14 El. C. 5 the shift in focal concern is fully developed:

> All rogues, vagabonds, and sturdy beggars shall...be committed to the common gaol...he shall be grievously whipped, and burnt through the gristle of the right ear with a hot iron of the compass of an inch about;...And for the second offense, he shall be adjudged a felon, unless some person will take him for two years in to his service. And for the third offense, he shall be adjudged guilty of felony without benefit of clergy.

And there is included a long list of persons who fall within the statute: "proctors, procurators, idle persons going about using subtil, crafty and unlawful games or plays; and some of them feigning themselves to have knowledge of...absurd sciences... and all fencers, bearwards, common players in interludes, and minstrels...all juglers, pedlars, tinkers, petty chapmen...and all counterfeiters of licenses, passports and users of the same." The major significance of this statute is that it includes all the previously defined offenders and adds some more. Significantly, those added are more clearly criminal types, counterfeiters, for example. It is also significant that there is the following qualification of this statute: "Provided also, that this act shall not extend to cookers, or harvest folks, that travel for harvest work, corn or hay."

That the changes in this statute were seen as significant is indicated by the following statement which appears in the statute:

> And whereas by reason of this act, the common gaols of every shire are like to be greatly pestered with more number of prisoners than heretofore hath been, for that

the said vagabonds and other lewd persons before recited shall upon their apprehention be committed to the said gaols; it is enacted...[25]

And a provision is made for giving more money for maintaining the gaols. This seems to add credence to the notion that this statute was seen as being significantly more general than those previously.

It is also of importance to note that this is the first time the term *rogue* has been used to refer to persons included in the vagrancy statutes. It seems, *a priori,* that a "rogue" is a different social type than is a "vagrant" or a "vagabond"; the latter terms implying something more equivalent to the idea of a "tramp" whereas the former (rogue) seems to imply a more disorderly and potentially dangerous person.

The emphasis upon the criminalistic aspect of vagrants continues in Chapter 17 of the same statute:

Whereas divers *licentious* persons wander up and down in all parts of the realm, to countenance their *wicked behavior;* and do continually assemble themselves armed in the highways, and elsewhere in troops, *to the great terror* of her majesty's true subjects, *the impeachment of her laws,* and the disturbance of the peace and tranquility of the realm; and whereas many outrages are daily committed by these dissolute persons, and more are likely to ensue if speedy remedy be not provided. (Italics added)

With minor variations (*e.g.,* offering a reward for the capture of a vagrant) the statutes remain essentially of this nature until 1743. In 1743 there was once more an expansion of the types of persons included such that "all persons going about as patent gatherers, or gatherers of alms, under pretense of loss by fire or other casualty; or going about as collectors for prisons, gaols, or hospitals; all persons playing of betting at any unlawful games; and all persons who run away and leave their wives or children...all persons wandering abroad, and lodging in alehouses, barns, outhouses, or in the open air, not giving good account of themselves," were types of offenders added to those already included.

By 1743 the vagrancy statutes had apparently been sufficiently reconstructed by the shifts of concern so as to be once more a useful instrument in the creation of social solidarity. This function has apparently continued down to the present day in England and the changes from 1743 to the present have been all in the direction of clarifying or expanding the categories covered but little has been introduced to change either the meaning or the impact of this branch of the law.

We can summarize this shift in focal concern by quoting from Halsbury. He has noted that in the vagrancy statutes:

"... elaborate provision is made for the relief and incidental control of destitute wayfarers. These latter, however, form but a small portion of the offenders aimed at by what are known as the Vagrancy Laws, ... many offenders who are in no ordinary sense of the word vagrants, have been brought under the laws relating to vagrancy,

[25] 14 Ed. c. 5. (1571).

and the great number of the offenses coming within the operation of these laws have little or no relation to the subject of poor relief, but are more properly directed towards the prevention of crime, the preservation of good order, and the promotion of social economy."[26]

Before leaving this section it is perhaps pertinent to make a qualifying remark. We have emphasized throughout this section how the vagrancy statutes underwent a shift in focal concern as the social setting changed. The shift in focal concern is not meant to imply that the later focus of the statutes represents a completely new law. It will be recalled that even in the first vagrancy statute there was reference to those who "do refuse labor, giving themselves to idleness and vice and sometimes to theft and other abominations." Thus the possibility of criminal activities resulting from persons who refuse to labor was recognized even in the earliest statute. The fact remains, however, that the major emphasis in this statute and in the statutes which followed the first one was always upon the "refusal to labor" or "begging." The "criminalistic" aspect of such persons was relatively unimportant. Later, as we have shown, the criminalistic potential becomes of paramount importance. The thread runs back to the earliest statute but the reason for the statutes' existence as well as the focal concern of the statutes is quite different in 1743 than it was in 1349.

Vagrancy Laws in the United States

In general, the vagrancy laws of England, as they stood in the middle eighteenth century, were simply adopted by the states. There were some exceptions to this general trend. For example, Maryland restricted the application of vagrancy laws to "free" Negroes. In addition, for *all* states the vagrancy laws were even more explicitly concerned with the control of criminals and undesirables than had been the case in England. New York, for example, explicitly defines prostitutes as being a category of vagrants during this period. These exceptions do not, however, change the general picture significantly and it is quite appropriate to consider the U.S. vagrancy laws as following from England's of the middle eighteenth century with relatively minor changes. The control of criminals and undesirables was the *raison de etre* of the vagrancy laws in the U.S. This is as true today as it was in 1750. As Caleb Foote's analysis of the application of vagrancy statutes in the Philadelphia court shows, these laws are presently applied indiscriminately to persons considered a "nuisance." Foote suggests that " ...the chief significance of this branch of the criminal law lies in its quantitative impact and administrative usefulness." [27] Thus it appears that in America the trend begun in England in the sixteenth, seventeenth and eighteenth centuries has been carried to its logical extreme and the laws are now used principally as a mechanism for "clearing the streets" of the derelicts who inhabit the "skid roads" and "Bowerys" of our large urban areas.

[26]Earl of Halsbury, *The Laws of England,* Butterworth & Co., Bell Yard, Temple Bar, 1912, pp. 606–607.

[27]Foote, *op. cit.,* p. 613. Also see in this connection, Irwin Deutscher, "The Petty Offender," *Federal Probation,* XIX, June, 1955.

Since the 1800's there has been an abundant source of prospects to which the vagrancy laws have been applied. These have been primarily those persons deemed by the police and the courts to be either actively involved in criminal activities or at least peripherally involved. In this context, then, the statutes have changed very little. The functions served by the statutes in England of the late eighteenth century are still being served today in both England and the United States. The locale has changed somewhat and it appears that the present day application of vagrancy statutes is focused upon the arrest and confinement of the "down and outers" who inhabit certain sections of our larger cities but the impact has remained constant. The lack of change in the vagrancy statutes, then, can be seen as a reflection of the society's perception of a continuing need to control some of its "suspicious" or "undesirable" members.[28]

A word of caution is in order lest we leave the impression that this administrative purpose is the sole function of vagrancy laws in the U.S. today. Although it is our contention that this is generally true it is worth remembering that during certain periods of our recent history, and to some extent today, these laws have also been used to control the movement of workers. This was particularly the case during the depression years and California is of course infamous for its use of vagrancy laws to restrict the admission of migrants from other states.[29] The vagrancy statutes, because of their history, still contain germs within them which make such effects possible. Their main purpose, however, is clearly no longer the control of laborers but rather the control of the undesirable, the criminal and the "nuisance."

Discussion

The foregoing analysis of the vagrancy laws has demonstrated that these laws were a legislative innovation which reflected the socially perceived necessity of providing an abundance of cheap labor to landowners during a period when serfdom was breaking down and when the pool of available labor was depleted. With the eventual breakup of feudalism the need for such laws eventually disappeared and the increased dependence of the economy upon industry and commerce rendered the former use of the vagrancy statutes unnecessary. As a result, for a substantial period the vagrancy statutes were dormant, undergoing only minor changes and, presumably, being applied infrequently. Finally, the vagrancy laws were subjected to considerable alteration through a shift in the focal concern of the statutes. Whereas in their inception the laws focused upon the "idle" and "those refusing to labor" after the turn of the sixteenth century and emphasis came to be upon "rogues," "vagabonds," and others who were suspected of being engaged in criminal activities. During this period the focus was particularly upon "roadmen" who preyed upon citizens who transported goods from one place to another. The increased importance of commerce

[28]It is on this point that the vagrancy statutes have been subject to criticism. See for example, Lacey, Forrest W., "Vagrancy and Other Crimes of Personal Condition," *Harvard Law Review* (66), p. 1203.

[29]Edwards *vs* California. 314 S: 160 (1941).

to England during this period made it necessary that some protection be given persons engaged in this enterprise and the vagrancy statutes provided one source for such protection by re-focusing the acts to be included under these statutes.

Comparing the results of this analysis with the findings of Hall's study of theft we see a good deal of correspondence. Of major importance is the fact that both analyses demonstrate the truth of Hall's assertion that "the functioning of courts is significantly related to concomitant cultural needs, and this applies to the law of procedure as well as to substantive law."[30]

Our analysis of the vagrancy laws also indicates that when changed social conditions create a perceived need for legal changes that these alterations will be effected through the revision and refocusing of existing statutes. This process was demonstrated in Hall's analysis of theft as well as in our analysis of vagrancy. In the case of vagrancy, the laws were dormant when the focal concern of the laws was shifted so as to provide control over potential criminals. In the case of theft the laws were re-interpreted (interestingly, by the courts and not by the legislature) so as to include persons who were transporting goods for a merchant but who absconded with the contents of the packages transported.

It also seems probable that when the social conditions change and previously useful laws are no longer useful there will be long periods when these laws will remain dormant. It is less likely that they will be officially negated. During this period of dormancy it is the judiciary which has principal responsibility for *not* applying the statutes. It is possible that one finds statutes being negated only when the judiciary stubbornly applies laws which do not have substantial public support. An example of such laws in contemporary times would be the "Blue Laws." Most states still have laws prohibiting the sale of retail goods on Sunday yet these laws are rarely applied. The laws are very likely to remain but to be dormant unless a recalcitrant judge or a vocal minority of the population insist that the laws be applied. When this happens we can anticipate that the statutes will be negated.[31] Should there arise a perceived need to curtail retail selling under some special circumstances, then it is likely that these laws will undergo a shift in focal concern much like the shift which characterized the vagrancy laws. Lacking such application the laws will simply remain dormant except for rare instances where they will be negated.

This analysis of the vagrancy statutes (and Hall's analysis of theft as well) has demonstrated the importance of "vested interest" groups in the emergence and/or alteration of laws. The vagrancy laws emerged in order to provide the powerful landowners with a ready supply of cheap labor. When this was no longer seen as necessary and particularly when the landowners were no longer dependent upon cheap labor

[30] Hall, *op. cit.*, p. XII.

[31] Negation, in this instance, is most likely to come about by the repeal of the statute. More generally, however, negation may occur in several ways including the declaration of a statute as unconstitutional. This later mechanism has been used even for laws which have been "on the books" for long periods of time. Repeal is probably the most common, although not the only, procedure by which a law is negated.

nor were they a powerful interest group in the society the laws became dormant. Finally a new interest group emerged and was seen as being of great importance to the society and the laws were then altered so as to afford some protection to this group. These findings are thus in agreement with Weber's contention that "status groups" determine the content of the law.[32] The findings are inconsistent, on the other hand, with the perception of the law as simply a reflection of "public opinion" as is sometimes found in the literature.[33] We should be cautious in concluding, however, that either of these positions are necessarily correct. The careful analysis of other laws, and especially of laws which do not focus so specifically upon the "criminal," are necessary before this question can be finally answered.

In conclusion, it is hoped that future analyses of changes within the legal structure will be able to benefit from this study by virtue of (1) the data provided and (2) the utilization of a set of concepts (innovation, dormancy, concern and negation) which have proved useful in the analysis of the vagrancy law. Such analyses should provide us with more substantial grounds for rejecting or accepting as generally valid the description of some of the processes which appear to characterize changes in the legal system.

[32]M. Rheinstein, *Max Weber on Law in Economy and Society*, Harvard University Press, 1954.
[33]Friedman, N., *Law in a Changing Society*, Berkeley and Los Angeles: University of California Press, 1959.

4. An Illustrative Case: The Marihuana Tax Act

Howard S. Becker

It is generally assumed that the practice of smoking marihuana was imported into the United States from Mexico, by way of the southwestern states of Arizona, New Mexico, and Texas, all of which had sizable Spanish-speaking populations. People first began to notice marihuana use in the nineteen-twenties but, since it was a new phenomenon and one apparently confined to Mexican immigrants, did not express much concern about it. (The medical compound prepared from the marihuana

Reprinted with permission of the Macmillan Company from *Outsiders: Studies in the Sociology of Deviance*, pp. 135–46, by Howard S. Becker. Copyright by The Free Press, a Corporation, 1963.

plant had been known for some time, but was not often prescribed by U.S. physicians.) As late as 1930, only sixteen states had passed laws prohibiting the use of marihuana.

In 1937, however, the United States Congress passed the Marihuana Tax Act, designed to stamp out use of the drug. According to the theory outlined above, we should find in the history of this Act the story of an entrepreneur whose initiative and enterprise overcame public apathy and indifference and culminated in the passage of Federal legislation. Before turning to the history of the Act itself, we should perhaps look at the way similar substances had been treated in American law, in order to understand the context in which the attempt to suppress marihuana use proceeded.

The use of alcohol and opium in the United States had a long history, punctuated by attempts at suppression.[1] Three values provided legitimacy for attempts to prevent the use of intoxicants and narcotics. One legitimizing value, a component of what has been called the Protestant Ethic, holds that the individual should exercise complete responsibility for what he does and what happens to him; he should never do anything that might cause loss of self-control. Alcohol and the opiate drugs, in varying degrees and ways, cause people to lose control of themselves; their use, therefore, is evil. A person intoxicated with alcohol often loses control over his physical activity; the centers of judgment in the brain are also affected. Users of opiates are more likely to be anesthetized and thus less likely to commit rash acts. But they become dependent on the drug to prevent withdrawal symptoms and in this sense have lost control of their actions; insofar as it is difficult to obtain the drug, they must subordinate other interests to its pursuit.

Another American value legitimized attempts to suppress the use of alcohol and opiates: disapproval of action taken solely to achieve states of ecstasy. Perhaps because of our strong cultural emphases on pragmatism and utilitarianism, Americans usually feel uneasy and ambivalent about ecstatic experiences of any kind. But we do not condemn ecstatic experience when it is the by-product or reward of actions we consider proper in their own right, such as hard work or religious fervor. It is only when people pursue ecstasy for its own sake that we condemn their action as a search for "illicit pleasure," an expression that has real meaning to us.

The third value which provided a basis for attempts at suppression was humanitarianism. Reformers believed that people enslaved by the use of alcohol and opium would benefit from laws making it impossible for them to give in to their weaknesses. The families of drunkards and drug addicts would likewise benefit.

These values provided the basis for specific rules. The Eighteenth Amendment and

[1]See John Krout, *The Origins of Prohibition* (New York: Columbia University Press, 1928); Charles Terry and Mildred Pellens, *The Opium Problem* (New York: The Committee on Drug Addiction with the Bureau of Social Hygiene, Inc., 1928); and *Drug Addiction: Crime or Disease?* Interim and Final Reports of the Joint Committee of the American Bar Association and the American Medical Association on Narcotic Drugs (Bloomington, Indiana: Indiana University Press, 1961).

the Volstead Act forbade the importation of alcoholic beverages into the United States and their manufacture within the country. The Harrison Act in effect prohibited the use of opiate drugs for all but medical purposes.

In formulating these laws, care was taken not to interfere with what were regarded as the legitimate interests of other groups in the society. The Harrison Act, for instance, was so drawn as to allow medical personnel to continue using morphine and other opium derivatives for the relief of pain and such other medical purposes as seemed to them appropriate. Furthermore, the law was carefully drawn in order to avoid running afoul of the constitutional provision reserving police powers to the several states. In line with this restriction, the Act was presented as a revenue measure, taxing unlicensed purveyors of opiate drugs at an exorbitant rate while permitting licensed purveyors (primarily physicians, dentists, veterinarians, and pharmacists) to pay a nominal tax. Though it was justified constitutionally as a revenue measure, the Harrison Act was in fact a police measure and was so interpreted by those to whom its enforcement was entrusted. One consequence of the passage of the Act was the establishment, in the Treasury Department, of the Federal Bureau of Narcotics in 1930.

The same values that led to the banning of the use of alcohol and opiates could, of course, be applied to the case of marihuana and it seems logical that this should have been done. Yet what little I have been told, by people familiar with the period, about the use of marihuana in the late 'twenties and early 'thirties leads me to believe that there was relatively lax enforcement of the existing local laws. This, after all, was the era of Prohibition and the police had more pressing matters to attend to. Neither the public nor law enforcement officers, apparently, considered the use of marihuana a serious problem. When they noticed it at all, they probably dismissed it as not warranting major attempts at enforcement. One index of how feebly the laws were enforced is that the price of marihuana is said to have been very much lower prior to the passage of Federal legislation. This indicates that there was little danger in selling it and that enforcement was not seriously undertaken.

Even the Treasury Department, in its report on the year 1931, minimized the importance of the problem:

> A great deal of public interest has been aroused by newspaper articles appearing from time to time on the evils of the abuse of marihuana, or Indian hemp, and more attention has been focused on specific cases reported of the abuse of the drug than would otherwise have been the case. This publicity tends to magnify the extent of the evil and lends color to an inference that there is an alarming spread of the improper use of the drug, whereas the actual increase in such use may not have been inordinately large.[2]

The Treasury Department's Bureau of Narcotics furnished most of the enterprise that produced the Marihuana Tax Act. While it is, of course, difficult to know what the motives of Bureau officials were, we need assume no more than that they per-

[2]U.S. Treasury Department, *Traffic in Opium and Other Dangerous Drugs for the Year ended December 31, 1931* (Washington: Government Printing Office, 1932), p. 51.

ceived an area of wrongdoing that properly belonged in their jurisdiction and moved to put it there. The personal interest they satisfied in pressing for marihuana legislation was one common to many officials: the interest in successfully accomplishing the task one has been assigned and in acquiring the best tools with which to accomplish it. The Bureau's efforts took two forms: cooperating in the development of state legislation affecting the use of marihuana, and providing facts and figures for journalistic accounts of the problem. These are two important modes of action available to all entrepreneurs seeking the adoption of rules: they can enlist the support of other interested organizations and develop, through the use of the press and other communications media, a favorable public attitude toward the proposed rule. If the efforts are successful, the public becomes aware of a definite problem and the appropriate organizations act in concert to produce the desired rule.

The Federal Bureau of Narcotics cooperated actively with the National Conference of Commissioners on Uniform State Laws in developing uniform laws on narcotics, stressing among other matters the need to control marihuana use.[3] In 1932, the Conference approved a draft law. The Bureau commented:

> The present constitutional limitations would seem to require control measures directed against the intrastate traffic in Indian hemp to be adopted by the several State governments rather than by the Federal Government, and the policy has been to urge the State authorities generally to provide the necessary legislation, with supporting enforcement activity, to prohibit the traffic except for bona fide medical purposes. The proposed uniform State narcotic law...with optional text applying to the restriction of traffic in Indian hemp, has been recommended as an adequate law to accomplish the desired purposes.[4]

In its report for the year 1936, the Bureau urged its partners in this cooperative effort to exert themselves more strongly and hinted that Federal intervention might perhaps be necessary:

> In the absence of additional Federal legislation the Bureau of Narcotics can therefore carry on no war of its own against this traffic...the drug has come into wide and increasing abuse in many states, and the Bureau of Narcotics has therefore been endeavoring to impress upon the various States the urgent need for vigorous enforcement of local cannabis [marihuana] laws.[5]

The second prong of the Bureau's attack on the marihuana problem consisted of an effort to arouse the public to the danger confronting it by means of "an educational campaign describing the drug, its identification, and evil effects."[6] Apparently

[3] *Ibid.*, pp. 16–17.

[4] Bureau of Narcotics, U.S. Treasury Department, *Traffic in Opium and Other Dangerous Drugs for the Year ended December 31, 1932* (Washington: Government Printing Office, 1933), p. 13.

[5] Bureau of Narcotics, U.S. Treasury Department, *Traffic in Opium and Other Dangerous Drugs for the Year ended December 31, 1936* (Washington: Government Printing Office, 1937), p. 59.

[6] *Ibid.*

hoping that public interest might spur the States and cities to greater efforts, the Bureau said:

In the absence of Federal legislation on the subject, the States and cities should rightfully assume the responsibility of providing vigorous measures for the extinction of this lethal weed, and it is therefore hoped that all public-spirited citizens will earnestly enlist in the movement urged by the Treasury Department to adjure intensified enforcement of marihuana laws.[7]

The Bureau did not confine itself to exhortation in departmental reports. Its methods in pursuing desired legislation are described in a passage dealing with the campaign for a uniform state narcotic law:

Articles were prepared in the Federal Bureau of Narcotics, at the request of a number of organizations dealing with this general subject [uniform state laws] for publication by such organizations in magazines and newspapers. An intelligent and sympathetic public interest, helpful to the administration of the narcotic laws, has been aroused and maintained.[8]

As the campaign for Federal legislation against marihuana drew to a successful close, the Bureau's efforts to communicate its sense of the urgency of the problem to the public bore plentiful fruit. The number of articles about marihuana which appeared in popular magazines indicated by the number indexed in the *Reader's Guide,* reached a record high. Seventeen articles appeared in a two-year period, many more than in any similar period before or after [as shown in Table 1].

TABLE 1. Articles on Marihuana Indexed in The Reader's Guide to Periodical Literature

Time Period	*Number of Articles*
January, 1925–December, 1928	0
January, 1929–June, 1932	0
July, 1932–June, 1935	0
July, 1935–June, 1937	4
July, 1937–June, 1939	17
July, 1939–June, 1941	4
July, 1941–June, 1943	1
July, 1943–April, 1945	4
May, 1945–April, 1947	6
May, 1947–April, 1949	0
May, 1949–March, 1951	1

[7]Bureau of Narcotics, U.S. Treasury Department, *Traffic in Opium and Other Dangerous Drugs for the Year ended December 31, 1935* (Washington: Government Printing Office, 1936), p. 30.

[8]Bureau of Narcotics, U.S. Treasury Department, *Traffic in Opium and Other Dangerous Drugs for the Year ended December 31, 1933* (Washington: Government Printing Office, 1934), p. 61.

Of the seventeen, ten either explicitly acknowledged the help of the Bureau in furnishing facts and figures or gave implicit evidence of having received help by using facts and figures that had appeared earlier, either in Bureau publications or in testimony before the Congress on the Marihuana Tax Act. (We will consider the Congressional hearings on the bill in a moment.)

One clear indication of Bureau influence in the preparation of journalistic articles can be found in the recurrence of certain atrocity stories first reported by the Bureau. For instance, in an article published in the *American Magazine,* the Commissioner of Narcotics himself related the following incident:

> An entire family was murdered by a youthful [marihuana] addict in Florida. When officers arrived at the home they found the youth staggering about in a human slaughterhouse. With an ax he had killed his father, mother, two brothers, and and a sister. He seemed to be in a daze. ... He had no recollection of having committed the multiple crime. The officers knew him ordinarily as a sane, rather quiet young man; now he was pitifully crazed. They sought the reason. The boy said he had been in the habit of smoking something which youthful friends called "muggles," a childish name for marihuana.[9]

Five of the seventeen articles printed during the period repeated this story, and thus showed the influence of the Bureau.

The articles designed to arouse the public to the dangers of marihuana identified use of the drug as a violation of the value of self-control and the prohibition on search for "illicit pleasure," thus legitimizing the drive against marihuana in the eyes of the public. These, of course, were the same values that had been appealed to in the course of the quest for legislation prohibiting use of alcohol and opiates for illicit purposes.

The Federal Bureau of Narcotics, then, provided most of the enterprise which produced public awareness of the problem and coordinated action by other enforcement organizations. Armed with the results of their enterprise, representatives of the Treasury Department went to Congress with a draft on the Marihuana Tax Act and requested its passage. The hearings of the House Committee on Ways and Means, which considered the bill for five days during April and May of 1937, furnish a clear case of the operation of enterprise and of the way it must accommodate other interests.

The Assistant General Counsel of the Treasury Department introduced the bill to the Congressmen with these words: "The leading newspapers of the United States have recognized the seriousness of this problem and many of them have advocated Federal legislation to control the traffic in marihuana."[10] After explaining the

[9]H. J. Anslinger, with Courtney Ryley Cooper, "Marihuana: Assassin of Youth," *American Magazine,* CXXIV (July, 1937), 19, 150.

[10]*Taxation of Marihuana* (Hearings before the Committee on Ways and Means of the House of Representatives, 75th Congress, 1st Session, on H.R. 6385, April 27–30 and May 4, 1937), p. 7.

constitutional basis of the bill—like the Harrison Act, it was framed as a revenue measure—he reassured them about its possible effects on legitimate business:

> The form of the bill is such, however, as not to interfere materially with any industrial, medical, or scientific uses which the plant may have. Since hemp fiber and articles manufactured therefrom [twine and light cordage] are obtained from the harmless mature stalk of the plant, all such products have been completely eliminated from the purview of the bill by defining the term "marihuana" in the bill so as to exclude from its provisions the mature stalk and its compounds or manufacturers. There are also some dealings in marihuana seeds for planting purposes and for use in the manufacture of oil which is ultimately employed by the paint and varnish industry. As the seeds, unlike the mature stalk, contain the drug, the same complete exemption could not be applied in this instance.[11]

He further assured them that the medical profession rarely used the drug, so that its prohibition would work no hardship on them or on the pharmaceutical industry.

The committee members were ready to do what was necessary and, in fact, queried the Commissioner of Narcotics as to why this legislation had been proposed only now. He explained:

> Ten years ago we only heard about it throughout the Southwest. It is only in the last few years that it has become a national menace. ... We have been urging uniform State legislation on the several States, and it was only last month that the last State legislature adopted such legislation.[12]

The commissioner reported that many crimes were committed under the influence of marihuana, and gave examples, including the story of the Florida mass-murderer. He pointed out that the present low prices of the drug made it doubly dangerous, because it was available to anyone who had a dime to spare.

Manufacturers of hempseed oil voiced certain objections to the language of the bill, which was quickly changed to meet their specifications. But a more serious objection came from the birdseed industry, which at that time used some four million pounds of hempseed a year. Its representative apologized to the Congressmen for appearing at the last minute, stating that he and his colleagues had not realized until just then that the marihuana plant referred to in the bill was the same plant from which they got an important ingredient of their product. Government witnesses had insisted that the seeds of the plant required prohibition, as well as the flowering tops smokers usually used, because they contained a small amount of the active principle of the drug and might possibly be used for smoking. The birdseed manufacturers contended that inclusion of seed under the provisions of the bill would damage their business.

To justify his request for exemption, the manufacturers' representative pointed to the beneficial effect of hempseed on pigeons:

> [It] is a necessary ingredient in pigeon feed because it contains an oil substance that is a valuable ingredient of pigeon feed, and we have not been able to find any

[11] *Ibid.*, p. 8.

[12] *Ibid.*, p. 20.

seed that will take its place. If you substitute anything for the hemp, it has a tendency to change the character of the squabs produced.[13]

Congressman Robert L. Doughton of North Carolina inquired: "Does that seed have the same effect on pigeons as the drug has on human beings?" The manufacturers' representative said: "I have never noticed it. It has a tendency to bring back the feathers and improve the birds."[14]

Faced with serious opposition, the Government modified its stern insistence on the seed provision, noting that sterilization of the seeds might render them harmless: "It seems to us that the burden of proof is on the Government there, when we might injure a legitimate industry."[15]

Once these difficulties had been ironed out, the bill had easy sailing. Marihuana smokers, powerless, unorganized, and lacking publicly legitimate grounds for attack, sent no representatives to the hearings and their point of view found no place in the House and Senate the following July. The enterprise of the Bureau had produced a new rule, whose subsequent enforcement would help create a new class of outsiders–marihuana users.

I have given an extended illustration from the field of Federal legislation. But the basic parameters of this case should be equally applicable not only to legislation in general, but to the development of rules of a more informal kind. Wherever rules are created and applied, we should be alive to the possible presence of an enterprising individual or group. Their activities can properly be called *moral enterprise,* for what they are enterprising about is the creation of a new fragment of the moral constitution of society, its code of right and wrong.

Wherever rules are created and applied we should expect to find people attempting to enlist the support of coordinate groups and using the available media of communication to develop a favorable climate of opinion. Where they do not develop such support, we may expect to find their enterprise unsuccessful.[16]

And, wherever rules are created and applied, we expect that the processes of enforcement will be shaped by the complexity of the organization, resting on a basis of shared understandings in simpler groups and resulting from political maneuvering and bargaining in complex structures.

[13] *Ibid.*, pp. 73–74.

[14] *Ibid.*

[15] *Ibid.*, p. 85.

[16] Gouldner has described a relevant case in industry, where a new manager's attempt to enforce rules that had not been enforced for a long time (and thus, in effect, create new rules) had as its immediate consequence a disruptive wildcat strike; he had not built support through the manipulation of other groups in the factory and the development of a favorable climate of opinion. See Alvin W. Gouldner, *Wildcat Strike* (Yellow Springs, Ohio: Antioch Press, 1954).

5. Moral Passage: The Symbolic Process in Public Designations of Deviance

Joseph R. Gusfield

Recent perspectives on deviant behavior have focused attention away from the actor and his acts and placed it on the analysis of public reactions in labelling deviants as "outsiders."[1] This perspective forms the background for the present paper. In it I will analyze the implications which defining behavior as deviant has for the public designators. Several forms of deviance will be distinguished, each of which has a different kind of significance for the designators. The symbolic import of each type, I argue, leads to different public responses toward the deviant and helps account for the historical changes often found in treatment of such delinquents as alcoholics, drug addicts, and other "criminals," changes which involve a passage from one moral status to another.

Instrumental and Symbolic Functions of Law[2]

Agents of government are the only persons in modern societies who can legitimately claim to represent the total society. In support of their acts, limited and specific group interests are denied while a public and societal interest is claimed.[3] Acts of government "commit the group to action or to perform coordinated acts for

Reprinted from *Social Problems,* **15**:2 (Fall 1968), 175–188, by permission of The Society for the Study of Social Problems and the author.

[1]Howard S. Becker, *Outsiders: Studies in the Sociology of Deviance,* Glencoe: The Free Press 1963, Chap. 1. A similar view is presented in John Kitsuse, "Societal Reaction to Deviant Behavior," *Social Problems,* 9 (Winter, 1962), pp. 247–56; Kai Erikson, "Sociology of Deviance," in E. McDonagh and J. Simpson, editors, *Social Problems,* New York: Holt, Rinehart and Winston, Inc., 1965, pp. 457–464, p. 458.

[2]The material of this section is more fully discussed in my book *Symbolic Crusade: Status Politics and the American Temperance Movement,* Urbana: University of Illinois Press, 1963, esp. Chap. 7.

[3]See the analysis of power as infused with collective goals in Parsons' criticism of C. Wright Mills, *The Power Elite:* Talcott Parsons, "The Distribution of Power in American Society," *World Politics, 10* (October, 1957), p. 123, 144. [See his book, *Structure and Process,* Glencoe, Illinois: Free Press, 1960.]

general welfare."[4] This representational character of governmental officials and their acts makes it possible for them not only to influence the allocation of resources but also to define the public norms of morality and to designate which acts violate them. In a pluralistic society these defining and designating acts can become matters of political issue because they support or reject one or another of the competing and conflicting cultural groups in the society.

Let us begin with a distinction between *instrumental* and *symbolic* functions of legal and governmental acts. We readily perceive that acts of officials, legislative enactments, and court decisions often affect behavior in an instrumental manner through a direct influence on the actions of people. The Wagner Labor Relations Act and the Taft-Hartley Act have had considerable impact on the conditions of collective bargaining in the United States. Tariff legislation directly affects the prices of import commodities. The instrumental function of such laws lies in their enforcement; unenforced they have little effect.

Symbolic aspects of law and government do not depend on enforcement for their effect. They are symbolic in a sense close to that used in literary analysis. The symbolic act "invites consideration rather than overt reactions."[5] There is a dimension of meaning in symbolic behavior which is not given in its immediate and manifest significance but in what the action connotes for the audience that views it. The symbol "has acquired a meaning which is added to its immediate intrinsic significance."[6] The use of the wine and wafer in the Mass or the importance of the national flag cannot be appreciated without knowing their symbolic meaning for the users. In analyzing law as symbolic we are oriented less to behavioral consequences as a means to a fixed end; more to meaning as an act, a decision, a gesture important in itself.

An action of a governmental agent takes on symbolic import as it affects the designation of public norms. A courtroom decision or a legislative act is a gesture which often glorifies the values of one group and demeans those of another. In their representational character, governmental actions can be seen as ceremonial and ritual performances, designating the content of public morality. They are the statement of what is acceptable in the public interest. Law can thus be seen as symbolizing the public affirmation of social ideals and norms as well as a means of direct social control. This symbolic dimension is given in the statement, promulgation, or announcement of law unrelated to its function in influencing behavior through enforcement.

It has long been evident to students of government and law that these two func-

[4] Francis X. Sutton, "Representation and the Nature of Political Systems," *Comparative Studies in Society and History, 2* (October, 1959), pp. 1–10. In this paper Sutton shows that in some primitive societies, political officials function chiefly as representatives to other tribes rather than as law enforcers or policy-makers.

[5] Phillip Wheelwright, *The Burning Fountain,* Bloomington: Indiana University Press, 1964, p. 23.

[6] Talcott Parsons, *The Social System,* Glencoe: The Free Press, 1954, p. 286.

tions, instrumental and symbolic, may often be separated in more than an analytical sense. Many laws are honored as much in the breach as in performance.[7] Robin Williams has labelled such institutionalized yet illegal and deviant behavior the "patterned evasion of norms." Such evasion occurs when law proscribes behavior which nevertheless occurs in a recurrent socially organized manner and is seldom punished.[8] The kinds of crimes we are concerned with here quite clearly fall into this category. Gambling, prostitution, abortion, and public drunkenness are all common modes of behavior although laws exist designating them as prohibited. It is possible to see such systematic evasion as functioning to minimize conflicts between cultures by utilizing law to proclaim one set of norms as public morality and to use another set of norms in actually controlling that behavior.

While patterned evasion may perform such harmonizing functions, the passage of legislation, the acts of officials, and decisions of judges nevertheless have a significance as gestures of public affirmation. First, the act of public affirmation of a norm often persuades listeners that behavior and norm are consistent. The existence of law quiets and comforts those whose interests and sentiments are embodied in it.[9] Second, public affirmation of a moral norm directs the major institutions of the society to its support. Despite patterned practices of abortion in the United States, obtaining abortions does require access to a subterranean social structure and is much more difficult than obtaining an appendectomy. There are instrumental functions to law even where there is patterned evasion.

A third impact of public affirmation is the one that most interests us here. The fact of affirmation through acts of law and government expresses the public worth of one set of norms, of one sub-culture vis-à-vis those of others. It demonstrates which cultures have legitimacy and public domination, and which do not. Accordingly it enhances the social status of groups carrying the affirmed culture and degrades groups carrying that which is condemned as deviant. We have argued elsewhere that the significance of Prohibition in the United States lay less in its enforcement than in the fact that it occurred.[10] Analysis of the enforcement of Prohibition law indicates that it was often limited by the unwillingness of Dry forces

[7]Murray Edelman has shown this in his analysis of the discrepancy between legislative action and administrative agency operation. Murray Edelman, *The Symbolic Uses of Politics,* Urbana: University of Illinois Press, 1964.

[8]Robin Williams, *American Society,* New York: A. A. Knopf, 1960, pp. 372–96. Hyman Rodman's analysis of "lower-class value stretch" suggests yet another ambiguity in the concept of norm. He found that in Trinidad among lower-class respondents that *both* marriage and non-legal marital union are normatively accepted, although marriage is preferred. Hyman Rodman, "Illegitimacy in the Caribbean Social Structure," *American Sociological Review, 31* (October, 1966), pp. 673–683.

[9]Edelman, *op. cit.,* Chap. 2. The author refers to this as a process of political quiescence. While Edelman's symbolic analysis is close to mine, his emphasis is on the reassurance function of symbols in relation to presumed instrumental affects. My analysis stresses the conflict over symbols as a process of importance apart from instrumental effects.

[10]Gusfield, *op. cit.,* pp. 117–126.

to utilize all their political strength for fear of stirring intensive opposition. Great satisfaction was gained from the passage and maintenance of the legislation itself.[11]

Irrespective of its instrumental effects, public designation of morality is itself an issue generative of deep conflict. The designating gestures are dramatistic events, "since it invites one to consider the matter of motives in a perspective that, being developed in the analysis of drama, treats language and thought primarily as modes of action."[12] For this reason the designation of a way of behavior as violating public norms confers status and honor on those groups whose cultures are followed as the standard of conventionality, and derogates those whose cultures are considered deviant. My analysis of the American Temperance movement has shown how the issue of drinking and abstinence became a politically significant focus for the conflicts between Protestant and Catholic, rural and urban, native and immigrant, middle class and lower class in American society. The political conflict lay in the efforts of an abstinent Protestant middle class to control the public affirmation of morality in drinking. Victory or defeat were consequently symbolic of the status and power of the cultures opposing each other.[13] Legal affirmation or rejection is thus important in what it symbolizes as well or instead of what it controls. Even if the law was broken, it was clear whose law it was.

Deviant Nonconformity and Designator Reaction

In Durkheim's analysis of the indignant and hostile response to norm-violation, all proscribed actions are threats to the existence of the norm.[14] Once we separate the instrumental from the symbolic functions of legal and governmental designation of deviants, however, we can question this assumption. We can look at norm-violation from the standpoint of its effects on the symbolic rather than the instrumental character of the norm. Our analysis of patterned evasion of norms has suggested that a law weak in its instrumental functions may nevertheless perform significant symbolic functions. Unlike human limbs, norms do not necessarily atrophy through disuse. Standards of charity, mercy, and justice may be dishonored every day yet remain important statements of what is publicly approved as virtue. The sexual behavior of the human male and the human female need not be a copy of the socially sanctioned rules. Those rules remain as important affirmations of an acceptable

[11] Joseph Gusfield, "Prohibition: The Impact of Political Utopianism," in John Braeman, editor, *The 1920's Revisited,* Columbus: Ohio State University Press, forthcoming; Andrew Sinclair, *The Era of Excess,* New York: Harper Colophon Books, 1964, Chap. 10, pp. 13–14.

[12] Kenneth Burke, *A Grammar of Motives,* New York: Prentice-Hall, 1945, p. 393. Burke's writings have been the strongest influence on the mode of analysis presented here. Two other writers, whose works have been influential, themselves influenced by Burke, are Erving Goffman and Hugh D. Duncan.

[13] Gusfield, *Symbolic Crusade, op. cit.,* Chap. 5.

[14] Emile Durkheim, *The Division of Labor in Society,* trans. George Simpson, Glencoe: The Free Press, 1947, especially at pp. 96–103. For a similar view see Lewis Coser, "Some Functions of Deviant Behavior and Normative Flexibility," *American Journal of Sociology, 68* (September 1962), pp. 172–182.

code, even though they are regularly breached. Their roles as ideals are not threatened by daily behavior. In analyzing the violation of norms we will look at the implications of different forms of deviance on the symbolic character of the norm itself. *The point here is that the designators of deviant behavior react differently to different norm-sustaining implications of an act.* We can classify deviant behavior from this standpoint.

The Repentant Deviant. The reckless motorist often admits the legitimacy of traffic laws, even though he has broken them. The chronic alcoholic may well agree that both he and his society would be better if he could stay sober. In both cases the norm they have violated is itself unquestioned. Their deviation is a moral lapse, a fall from a grace to which they aspire. The homosexual who seeks a psychiatrist to rid himself of his habit has defined his actions similarly to those who have designated him as a deviant. There is a consensus between the designator and the deviant; his repentance confirms the norm.

Repentance and redemption seem to go hand-in-hand in court and church. Sykes and Matza have described techniques of neutralization which juvenile delinquents often use with enforcement agencies.

> The juvenile delinquent would appear to be at least partially committed to the dominant social order in that he frequently exhibits guilt or shame when he violates its proscriptions, accords approval to certain conforming figures and distinguishes between appropriate and inappropriate targets for his deviance.[15]

A show of repentance is also used, say Sykes and Matza, to soften the indignation of law enforcement agents. A recent study of police behavior lends support to this. Juveniles apprehended by the police received more lenient treatment, including dismissal, if they appeared contrite and remorseful about their violations than if they did not. This difference in the posture of the deviant accounted for much of the differential treatment favoring middle-class "youngsters" as against lower-class "delinquents."[16]

The Sick Deviant. Acts which represent an attack upon a norm are neutralized by repentance. The open admission of repentance confirms the sinner's belief in the sin. His threat to the norm is removed and his violation has left the norm intact. Acts which we can perceive as those of sick and diseased people are irrelevant to the norm; they neither attack nor defend it. The use of morphine by hospital patients in severe pain is not designated as deviant behavior. Sentiments of public hostility and the apparatus of enforcement agencies are not mobilized toward the morphine-user. His use is not perceived as a violation of the norm against drug use, but as an uncontrolled act, not likely to be recurrent.[17]

[15] Gresham Sykes and David Matza, "Techniques of Neutralization: A Theory of Delinquency," *American Sociological Review, 22* (December, 1957), pp. 664–670, at p. 666.

[16] Irving Pilliavin and Scott Briar, "Police Encounters with Juveniles," *American Journal of Sociology, 70* (September, 1964), pp. 206–214.

[17] This of course does not mean that the patient using morphine may not become an addict.

While designations of action resulting from sickness do not threaten the norm, significant consequences flow from such definitions. Talcott Parsons has pointed out that the designation of a person as ill changes the obligations which others have toward the person and his obligations toward them.[18] Parsons' description sensitizes us to the way in which the sick person is a different social object than the healthy one. He has now become an object of welfare, a person to be helped rather than punished. Hostile sentiments toward sick people are not legitimate. The sick person is not responsible for his acts. He is excused from the consequences which attend the healthy who act the same way.[19]

Deviance designations, as we shall show below, are not fixed. They may shift from one form to another over time. Defining a behavior pattern as one caused by illness makes a hostile response toward the actor illegitimate and inappropriate. "Illness" is a social designation, by no means given in the nature of medical fact. Even left-handedness is still seen as morally deviant in many countries. Hence the effort to define a practice as a consequence of illness is itself a matter of conflict and a political issue.

The Enemy Deviant. Writing about a Boston slum in the 1930's, William F. Whyte remarks:

> The policeman is subject to sharply conflicting pressures. On one side are the "good people" of Eastern City, who have written their moral judgments into law and demand through their newspapers that the law be enforced. On the other side are the people of Cornerville, who have different standards and have built up an organization whose perpetuation depends upon the freedom to violate the law.[20]

Whyte's is one of several studies that have pointed out the discrepancies between middle-class moralities embodied in law and lower-class moralities which differ sharply from them.[21] In Cornerville, gambling was seen as a "respectable" crime, just as antitrust behavior may be in other levels of the social structure. In American society, conflicts between social classes are often also cultural conflicts reflecting moral differences. Coincidence of ethnic and religious distinctions with class differences accentuates such conflicts between group values.

In these cases, the validity of the public designation is itself at issue. The publicly-defined deviant is neither repentant nor sick, but is instead an upholder of an oppo-

[18]Talcott Parsons and Renee Fox, "Illness, Therapy and the Modern Urban Family," *Journal of Social Issues, 8* (1952), pp. 25–54.

[19]A somewhat similar distinction as that presented here can be found in Vilhelm Aubert and Sheldon Messinger, "The Criminal and the Sick," in V. Aubert, *The Hidden Society,* New York: The Bedminister Press, 1965, pp. 25–54.

[20]William F. Whyte, *Street-Corner Society,* Chicago: University of Chicago Press, 2nd edition, 1955, p. 138.

[21]See William Westley's analysis of the differences between the morality shared by the lower class and the police in contrast to that of the courts over such matters as gambling, prostitution, and sexual perversion. The courts take a sterner view of gamblers and prostitutes than do the police, who take a sterner view of the sexual offender. William Westley, "Violence and the Police," *American Journal of Sociology, 59* (July, 1953), pp. 34–42.

site norm. He accepts his behavior as proper and derogates the public norm as illegitimate. He refuses to internalize the public norm into his self-definition. This is especially likely to occur in instances of "business crimes." The buyer sees his action as legitimate economic behavior and resists a definition of it as immoral and thus prohibitable. The issue of "off-track" betting illustrates one area in which clashes of culture have been salient.

The designation of culturally legitimate behavior as deviant depends upon the superior power and organization of the designators. The concept of convention in this area, as Thrasymachus defined Justice for Socrates, is the will of the stronger. If the deviant is the politically weaker group, then the designation is open to the changes and contingencies of political fortunes. It becomes an issue of political conflict, ranging group against group and culture against culture, in the effort to determine whose morals are to be designated as deserving of public affirmation.

It is when the deviant is also an enemy and his deviance is an aspect of group culture that the conventional norm is most explicitly and energetically attacked. When those once designated as deviant have achieved enough political power they may shift from disobedience to an effort to change the designation itself. This has certainly happened in the civil rights movement. Behavior viewed as deviant in the segregationist society has in many instances been moved into the realm of the problematic, now subject to political processes of conflict and compromise.

When the deviant and the designator perceive each other as enemies, and the designator's power is superior to that of the deviant, we have domination without a corresponding legitimacy. Anything which increases the power of the deviant to organize and attack the norm is thus a threat to the social dominance symbolized in the affirmation of the norm. Under such conditions the need of the designators to strengthen and enforce the norms is great. The struggle over the symbol of social power and status is focused on the question of the maintenance or change of the legal norm. The threat to the middle class in the increased political power of Cornerville is not that the Cornerville resident will gamble more; he already does gamble with great frequency. The threat is that the law will come to accept the morality of gambling and treat it as a legitimate business. If this happens, Boston is no longer a city dominated by middle-class Yankees but becomes one dominated by lower-class immigrants, as many think has actually happened in Boston. The maintenance of a norm which defines gambling as deviant behavior thus symbolizes the maintenance of Yankee social and political superiority. Its disappearance as a public commitment would symbolize the loss of that superiority.

The Cynical Deviant. The professional criminal commits acts whose designation as deviant is supported by wide social consensus. The burglar, the hired murderer, the arsonist, the kidnapper all prey on victims. While they may use repentance or illness as strategies to manage the impressions of enforcers, their basic orientation is self-seeking, to get around the rules. It is for this reason that their behavior is not a great threat to the norms although it calls for social management and repression. It does not threaten the legitimacy of the normative order.

Drinking as a Changing Form of Deviance

Analysis of efforts to define drinking as deviant in the United States will illustrate the process by which designations shift. The legal embodiment of attitudes toward drinking shows how cultural conflicts find their expression in the symbolic functions of law. In the 160 years since 1800, we see all our suggested types of non-conforming behavior and all the forms of reaction among the conventional segments of the society.

The movement to limit and control personal consumption of alcohol began in the early nineteenth century, although some scattered attempts were made earlier.[22] Colonial legislation was aimed mainly at controlling the inn through licensing systems. While drunkenness occurred, and drinking was frequent, the rigid nature of the Colonial society, in both North and South, kept drinking from becoming an important social issue.[23]

The Repentant Drinker. The definition of the drinker as an object of social shame begins in the early nineteenth century and reaches full development in the late 1820's and early 1830's. A wave of growth in Temperance organizations in this period was sparked by the conversion of drinking men to abstinence under the stimulus of evangelical revivalism.[24] Through drinking men joining together to take the pledge, a norm of abstinence and sobriety emerged as a definition of conventional respectability. They sought to control themselves and their neighbors.

The norm of abstinence and sobriety replaced the accepted patterns of heavy drinking countenanced in the late eighteenth and early nineteenth century. By the 1870's rural and small-town America had defined middle-class morals to include the Dry attitude. This definition had little need for legal embodiment. It could be enunciated in attacks on the drunkard which assumed that he shared the normative pattern of those who exhorted him to be better and to do better. He was a repentant deviant, someone to be brought back into the fold by moral persuasion and the techniques of religious revivalism.[25] His error was the sin of lapse from a shared standard of virtue. "The Holy Spirit will not visit, much less will He dwell within he who is under the polluting, debasing effects of intoxicating drink. The state of heart and mind which this occasions to him is loathsome and an abomination."[26]

Moral persuasion thus rests on the conviction of a consensus between the deviant and the designators. As long as the object of attack and conversion is isolated in individual terms, rather than perceived as a group, there is no sense of his deviant act as part of a shared culture. What is shared is the norm of conventionality; the ap-

[22]The best single account of Temperance activities before the Civil War is that of John Krout, *The Origins of Prohibition*, New York: A. A. Knopf, 1925.

[23]*Ibid.*, Chapters 1 and 2; also see Alice Earle, *Home Life in Colonial Days*, New York: Macmillan, 1937, pp. 148–149; 156–165.

[24]Gusfield, *Symbolic Crusade, op. cit.*, pp. 44–51.

[25]*Ibid.*, pp. 69-86.

[26]*Temperance Manual* (no publisher listed, 1836), p. 46.

peal to the drinker and the chronic alcoholic is to repent. When the Woman's Anti-Whiskey Crusade of 1873-1874 broke out in Ohio, church women placed their attention on the taverns. In many Ohio towns these respectable ladies set up vigils in front of the tavern and attempted to prevent men from entering just by the fear that they would be observed.[27] In keeping with the evangelical motif in the Temperance movement, the Washingtonians, founded in 1848, appealed to drinkers and chronic alcoholics with the emotional trappings and oratory of religious meetings, even though devoid of pastors.[28]

Moral persuasion, rather than legislation, has been one persistent theme in the designation of the drinker as deviant and the alcoholic as depraved. Even in the depictions of the miseries and poverty of the chronic alcoholic, there is a decided moral condemnation which has been the hallmark of the American Temperance movement. Moral persuasion was ineffective as a device to wipe out drinking and drunkenness. Heavy drinking persisted through the nineteenth century and the organized attempts to convert the drunkard experienced much backsliding.[29] Nevertheless, defections from the standard did not threaten the standard. The public definition of respectability matched the ideals of the sober and abstaining people who dominated those parts of the society where moral suasion was effective. In the late nineteenth century those areas in which temperance sentiment was strongest were also those in which legislation was most easily enforceable.[30]

The Enemy Drinker. The demand for laws to limit alcoholic consumption appears to arise from situations in which the drinkers possess power as a definitive social and political group and, in their customary habits and beliefs, deny the validity of abstinence norms. The persistence of areas in which Temperance norms were least controlling led to the emergence of attempts to embody control in legal measures. The drinker as enemy seems to be the greatest stimulus to efforts to designate his act as publicly defined deviance.

In its early phase the American Temperance movement was committed chiefly to moral persuasion. Efforts to achieve legislation governing the sale and use of alcohol do not appear until the 1840's. This legislative movement had a close relationship to the immigration of Irish Catholics and German Lutherans into the United States in this period. These non-evangelical and/or non-Protestant peoples made up a large

[27]See the typical account by Mother Stewart, one of the leaders in the 1873-74 Woman's War on Whiskey, in Eliza D. Steward, *Memories of the Crusade,* Columbus, Ohio: W. G. Hibbard, 2nd edition, 1889, pp. 139-143; also see *Standard Encyclopedia of the Alcohol Problem, 6* (Westerville, Ohio: American Issue Publishing Co., 1930), pp. 2902-2905.

[28]Krout, *op. cit.,* Chap. 9.

[29]See the table of consumption of alcoholic beverages, 1850-1957, in Mark Keller and Vera Effron, "Selected Statistics on Alcoholic Beverage," reprinted in Raymond McCarthy, editor, *Drinking and Intoxication,* Glencoe: The Free Press, 1959, p. 180.

[30]Joseph Rowntree and Arthur Sherwell, *State Prohibition and Local Option,* London: Hodden and Stoughton, 1900, using both systematic observation and analysis of Federal tax payments, concluded (p. 253) that "... local veto in America has only been found operative outside the larger towns and cities."

proportion of the urban poor in the 1840's and 1850's. They brought with them a far more accepting evaluation of drinking than had yet existed in the United States. The tavern and the beer parlor had a distinct place in the leisure of the Germans and the Irish. The prominence of this place was intensified by the stark character of the developing American slum.[31] These immigrant cultures did not contain a strong tradition of Temperance norms which might have made an effective appeal to a sense of sin. To be sure, excessive drunkenness was scorned, but neither abstinence nor constant sobriety were supported by the cultural codes.

Between these two groups—the native American, middle-class evangelical Protestant and the immigrant European Catholic or Lutheran occupying the urban lower class—there was little room for repentance. By the 1850's the issue of drinking reflected a general clash over cultural values. The Temperance movement found allies in its political efforts among the nativist movements.[32] The force and power of the anti-alcohol movements, however, were limited greatly by the political composition of the urban electorate, with its high proportion of immigrants. Thus the movement to develop legislation emerged in reaction to the appearance of cultural groups least responsive to the norms of abstinence and sobriety. The very effort to turn such informal norms into legal standards polarized the opposing forces and accentuated the symbolic import of the movement. Now that the issue had been joined, defeat or victory was a clear-cut statement of public dominance.

It is a paradox that the most successful move to eradicate alcohol emerged in a period when America was shifting from a heavy-drinking society, in which whiskey was the leading form of alcohol, to a moderate one, in which beer was replacing whiskey. Prohibition came as the culmination of the movement to reform the immigrant cultures and at the height of the immigrant influx into the United States.

Following the Civil War, moral persuasion and legislative goals were both parts of the movement against alcohol. By the 1880's an appeal was made to the urban, immigrant lower classes to repent and to imitate the habits of the American middle class as a route to economic and social mobility. Norms of abstinence were presented to the non-abstainer both as virtue and as expedience.[33] This effort failed. The new, and larger, immigration of 1890–1915 increased still further the threat of the urban lower class to the native American.

The symbolic effect of Prohibition legislation must be kept analytically separate from its instrumental, enforcement side. While the urban middle class did provide

[31] See the accounts of drinking habits among Irish and German immigrants in Oscar Handlin, *Boston's Immigrants,* Cambridge, Massachusetts: Harvard University Press, 1941, pp. 191–192, 201–209; Marcus Hansen, *The Immigrant in American History,* Cambridge, Massachusetts: Harvard University Press, 1940.

[32] Ray Billington, *The Protestant Crusade, 1800–1860,* New York: Macmillan, 1938, Chap. 15; Gusfield, *Symbolic Crusade, op. cit.,* pp. 55–57.

[33] William F. Whyte, *op. cit.,* p. 99. Whyte has shown this as a major attitude of social work and the settlement house toward slum-dwellers he studied in the 1930's. "The community was expected to adapt itself to the standards of the settlement house." The rationale for adaptation lay in its effects in promoting social mobility.

much of the organizational leadership to the Temperance and Prohibition movements, the political strength of the movement in its legislative drives was in the rural areas of the United States. Here, where the problems of drinking were most under control, where the norm was relatively intact, the appeal to a struggle against foreign invasion was the most potent. In these areas, passage of legislation was likely to make small difference in behavior. The continuing polarization of political forces into those of cultural opposition and cultural acceptance during the Prohibition campaigns (1906–1919), and during the drive for Repeal (1926–1933), greatly intensified the symbolic significance of victory and defeat.[34] Even if the Prohibition measures were limited in their enforceability in the metropolis there was no doubt about whose law was public and what way of life was being labelled as opprobrious.

After Repeal, as Dry power in American politics subsided, the designation of the drinker as deviant also receded. Public affirmation of the temperance norm had changed and with it the definition of the deviant had changed. Abstinence was itself less acceptable. In the 1950's the Temperance movement, faced with this change in public norms, even introduced a series of placards with the slogan, "It's Smart *Not* to Drink."

Despite this normative change in the public designation of drinking deviance, there has not been much change in American drinking patterns. Following the Prohibition period the consumption of alcohol has not returned to its pre-1915 high. Beer has continued to occupy a more important place as a source of alcohol consumption. "Hard drinkers" are not as common in America today as they were in the nineteenth century. While there has been some increase in moderate drinking, the percentage of adults who are abstainers has remained approximately the same (one-third) for the past 30 years. Similarly, Dry sentiment has remained stable, as measured by local opinion results.[35] In short, the argument over deviance designation has been largely one of normative dominance, not of instrumental social control. The process of deviance designation in drinking needs to be understood in terms of symbols of cultural dominance rather than in the activities of social control.

The Sick Drinker. For most of the nineteenth century, the chronic alcoholic as well as the less compulsive drinker was viewed as a sinner. It was not until after Repeal (1933) that chronic alcoholism became defined as illness in the United States. Earlier actions taken toward promotion of the welfare of drinkers and alcoholics through Temperance measures rested on the moral supremacy of abstinence and the demand for repentance. The user of alcohol could be an object of sympathy, but his social salvation depended on a willingness to embrace the norm of his exhorters. The designation of alcoholism as sickness has a different bearing on the question of normative superiority. It renders the behavior of the deviant indifferent to the status of norms enforcing abstinence.

[34] Although a well-organized Temperance movement existed among Catholics, it was weakened by the Protestant drive for Prohibition: See Joan Bland, *Hibernian Crusade*, Washington, D.C.: Catholic University Press, 1951.

[35] See my analysis of American drinking in the post-Repeal era. Gusfield, "Prohibition: The Impact of Political Utopianism," *op. cit.*

This realization appears to have made supporters of Temperance and Prohibition hostile to efforts to redefine the deviant character of alcoholism. They deeply opposed the reports of the Committee of Fifty in the late nineteenth century.[36] These volumes of reports by scholars and prominent men took a less moralistic and a more sociological and functional view of the saloon and drinking than did the Temperance movement.

The soundness of these fears is shown by what did happen to the Temperance movement with the rise of the view that alcoholism is illness. It led to new agencies concerned with drinking problems. These excluded Temperance people from the circle of those who now define what is deviant in drinking habits. The National Commission on Alcoholism was formed in 1941 and the Yale School of Alcoholic Studies formed in 1940. They were manned by medical personnel, social workers, and social scientists, people now alien to the spirit of the abstainer. Problems of drinking were removed from the church and placed in the hands of the universities and the medical clinics. The tendency to handle drinkers through protective and welfare agencies rather than through police or clergy has become more frequent.

"The bare statement that 'alcoholism is a disease' is most misleading since ... it conceals what is essential—that a step in public policy is being recommended, not a scientific discovery announced."[37] John Seeley's remark is an apt one. Replacement of the norm of sin and repentance by that of illness and therapy removes the onus of guilt and immorality from the act of drinking and the state of chronic alcoholism. It replaces the image of the sinner with that of a patient, a person to be helped rather than to be exhorted. No wonder that the Temperance movement has found the work of the Yale School, and often even the work of Alcoholics Anonymous, a threat to its own movement. It has been most limited in its cooperation with these organizations and has attempted to set up other organizations which might provide the face of Science in league with the tone of the movement.[38]

The redefinition of the alcoholic as sick thus brought into power both ideas and

[36]The Committee of Fifty, a group of prominent educators, scientists, and clergymen sponsored and directed several studies of drinking and the saloon. Their position as men unaffilated to temperance organizations was intended to introduce unbiased investigation, often critical of Temperance doctrine. For two of the leading volumes see John Shaw Billing's, *The Physiological Aspects of the Liquor Problem,* Boston and New York: Houghton Mifflin Co., 1903; Raymond Calkins, *Substitutes for the Saloon,* Boston and New York: Houghton Mifflin Co., 1903.

[37]John Seeley, "Alcoholism Is a Disease: Implications for Social Policy," in D. Pittman and C. Snyder, editors, *Society, Culture and Drinking Patterns,* New York: John Wiley and Sons, 1962, pp. 586–593, at p. 593. For a description of the variety of definitions of alcoholism and drunkenness, as deviant and non-deviant, see the papers by Edwin Lemert, "Alcohol, Values and Social Control" and by Archer Tongue, "What the State Does About Alcohol and Alcoholism," both in the same volume.

[38]The WCTU during the 1950's persistently avoided support to Alcoholics Anonymous. The Yale School of Alcohol Studies was attacked and derogated in Temperance literature. A counter-organization, with several prominent pro-Dry scientists, developed, held seminars, and issued statements in opposition to Yale School publications.

organizations antithetical to the Temperance movement. The norm protected by law and government was no longer the one held by the people who had supported Temperance and Prohibition. The hostility of Temperance people is readily understandable; their relative political unimportance is crucial to their present inability to make that hostility effective.

Movement of Moral Passage

In this paper we have called attention to the fact that deviance designations have histories; the public definition of behavior as deviant is itself changeable. It is open to reversals of political power, twists of public opinion, and the development of social movements and moral crusades. What is attacked as criminal today may be seen as sick next year and fought over as possibly legitimate by the next generation.

Movements to redefine behavior may eventuate in a moral passage, a transition of the behavior from one moral status to another. In analyzing movements toward the redefinition of alcohol use, we have dealt with moral crusades which were restrictive and others which were permissive toward drinking and toward "drunkards." (We might have also used the word "alcoholics," suggesting a less disapproving and more medical perspective.) In both cases, however, the movements sought to change the public designation. While we are familiar with the restrictive or enforcing movements, the permissive or legitimizing movement must also be seen as a prevalent way in which deviants throw off the onus of their actions and avoid the sanctions associated with immoral activities.

Even where the deviants are a small and politically powerless group they may nevertheless attempt to protect themselves by influence over the process of designation. The effort to define themselves as ill is one plausible means to this end. Drug addiction as well as drunkenness is partially undergoing a change toward such redefinition.[39] This occurs in league with powerful groups in society, such as social workers, medical professionals, or university professors. The moral passage achieved here reduces the sanctions imposed by criminal law and the public acceptance of the deviant designation.

The "lifting" of a deviant activity to the level of a political, public issue is thus a sign that its moral status is at stake, that legitimacy is a possibility. Today the moral acceptance of drinking, marijuana and LSD use, homosexuality, abortion, and other "vices" is being publicly discussed, and movements championing them have emerged. Such movements draw into them far more than the deviants themselves. Because they become symbols of general cultural attitudes they call out partisans for both repression and permission. The present debate over drug addiction laws in

[39] Many of the writings of sociologists interested in drug addiction have contained explicit demands for such redefinitions. See Becker, *op. cit.;* Alfred Lindesmith, *The Addict and the Law,* Bloomington: Indiana University Press, 1965, and David Ausubel, *Drug Addiction,* New York: Random House, 1958. The recent movement to redefine marijuana and LSD as legitimate is partially supported by such writings but is more saliently a movement of enemy deviants. The activities of Timothy Leary, Allen Ginsberg, and the "hipsters" is the most vocal expression of this movement.

the United States, for example, is carried out between defenders and opposers of the norm rather than between users and non-users of the drugs involved.

As the movement for redefinition of the addict as sick has grown, the movement to strengthen the definition of addiction as criminal has responded with increased legal severity. To classify drug users as sick and the victims or clients as suffering from "disease" would mean a change in the agencies responsible for reaction from police enforcement to medical authorities. Further, it might diminish the moral disapproval with which drug use, and the reputed euphoric effects connected with it, are viewed by supporters of present legislation. Commenting on the clinic plan to permit medical dispensing of narcotics to licensed addicts, U.S. Commissioner of Narcotics Anslinger wrote:

> This plan would elevate a most despicable trade to the avowed status of an honorable business, may, to the status of practice of a time-honored profession; and drug addicts would multiply unrestrained, to the irrevocable impairment of the moral fiber and physical welfare of the American people.[40]

In this paper we have seen that redefining moral crusades tends to generate strong counter-movements. The deviant as a cultural opponent is a more potent threat to the norm than is the repentant, or even the sick deviant. The threat to the legitimacy of the norm is a spur to the need for symbolic restatement in legal terms. In these instances of "crimes without victims" the legal norm is *not* the enunciator of a consensus with the community. On the contrary, it is when consensus is least attainable that the pressure to establish legal norms appears to be greatest.

[40] Harry Anslinger and William Tompkins, *The Traffic in Narcotics,* New York: Funk and Wagnalls Co., Inc. 1953, p. 186.

6. Limits of the Criminal Law as a Means of Social Regulation

The President's Commission on Law Enforcement and Administration of Justice

The substantive criminal law is of fundamental and pervasive importance to law enforcement and the administration of justice. In defining criminal conduct and authorizing punishment it constitutes the basic source of authority, directing and controlling the State's use of the criminal sanction. It has a profound effect upon the functioning of law enforcement. Sir Robert Peel, the father of the English police, saw this early in the last century. Before undertaking to reform the police system he insisted on the need to reform the criminal law itself. A leading British police historian has noted:

> Peel realized what the Criminal Law reformers had never done, that Police reform and Criminal Law reform were wholly interdependent; that a reformed Criminal Code required a reformed police to enable it to function beneficially; and that a reformed police could not function effectively until the criminal and other laws which they were to enforce had been made capable of being respected by the public and administered with simplicity and clarity. He postponed for some years his boldly announced plans for police, and concentrated his energies on reform of the law.[1]

• • •

These and other problems have been confronted by the American Law Institute's Model Penal Code. The code, the product of 10 years' work, is a thoughtful and comprehensive examination of the substantive criminal law. It was designed not as a ready-made statute for adoption by the States but as a plan for criminal law revision, a source of research material, and a guide to the development and modernization of the law. With the Code as a guide Illinois and New York have already revised their penal codes. At the present time 30 States, including California, Michigan, and Texas, are taking a new look at their criminal codes. In 1966 at the request of

Reprinted from "Substantive Law Reform and the Limits of Effective Law Enforcement," *Task Force Report: The Courts,* a Report by The President's Commission on Law Enforcement and Administration of Justice (Washington: Government Printing Office, 1967), ch. 8, pp. 97–107.

[1] Reith. The Police Idea–Its History and Evolution in England in the Eighteenth Century and after 236 (1938).

President Johnson, Congress created a commission to conduct a three-year study of the Federal Criminal Code.

...

The Limits of Effective Law Enforcement

The prohibitions of the criminal law are not limited to conduct that involves major injuries to persons, property and institutions. Not all cases involve assault, homicide, kidnapping, arson, burglary, robbery, theft, bribery, perjury, and the like. How and to what extent the criminal law, rather than other means of social control, is the appropriate vehicle for dealing with such conduct as gambling, public drunkenness, disorderly conduct, and vagrancy should receive closer examination.

In many instances legislatures have responded to difficult problems of social control by making the undesired conduct criminal. And many people are prepared to argue that if the legislature has not included a criminal penalty as a means of enforcement, it is not really serious about the matter.

> If we are deeply disturbed by something which we know to be happening, and feel that we ought to be doing something to prevent it, this feeling can be partly relieved by prohibiting it on paper. Even if we merely succeed in persuading some organization to issue a statement deploring whatever it is, we have done something: but of course, the supreme form of prohibition on paper is the act of Parliament.[2]

The criminal law is not the sole or even the primary method relied upon by society to motivate compliance with its rules. The community depends on a broad spectrum of sanctions to control conduct. Civil liability, administrative regulations, licensing, and noncriminal penalties carry the brunt of the regulatory job in many very important fields, with little additional force contributed by such infrequently used criminal provisions as may appear in the statute books. Internal moral compunctions and family, group, and community pressures are some of the obvious informal sanctions that often are more effective than the prohibitions of the criminal law. The overready assumption that the way to control behavior is by making it criminal may interfere with the operation of the criminal law and inhibit the development of solutions to underlying social problems. Too infrequently have the limits of the effectiveness of criminal law been critically examined and the costs that must be paid for its use appraised.

Dean Francis Allen has described the extent of overreliance upon the criminal law:

> No one scrutinizing American criminal justice can fail to be impressed by the tremendous range of demands that are placed upon the system. This can be demonstrated in various ways. First, we may note the sheer bulk of penal regulations and observe the accelerating rate at which these accretions to the criminal law have occurred. ...
>
> More interesting than the mere volume of modern criminal legislation is the re-

[2] Walker, *Morality and the Criminal Law*, 11 Howard Society Journal 209, 215 (1964).

markable range of human activities now subject to the threat of criminal sanctions. Many years ago, before the most striking modern developments had occurred, the late Professor Ernst Freund remarked: "Living under free institutions we submit to public regulation and control in ways that appear inconceivable to the spirit of oriental despotism."...

Moreover, we should not assume that this striking expansion of criminal liability has proceeded in a rational and orderly fashion or that, until recently, it has attracted any substantial amount of thoughtful and scholarly inquiry. The precise contrary is very nearly true. Thus, it is more than poetic metaphor to suggest that the system of criminal justice may be viewed as a weary Atlas upon whose shoulders we have heaped a crushing burden of responsibilities relating to public policy in its various aspects. This we have done thoughtlessly without inquiring whether the burden can be effectively borne.[3]

This chapter examines several types of conduct which has been declared criminal but for which criminal enforcement has proven either ineffective or unduly costly. It tries to identify some circumstances in which the criminal law proves ineffective and the nature and extent of the costs paid for its use, costs measured in terms of the sacrifice of other social values and in terms of law enforcement generally. For this purpose the instances selected are principally exemplitive. Often the problem lies in excessively broad definitions of the crime. Appropriate redefinition might leave as criminal most of the kinds of conduct now proscribed in some categories, although in other instances there would be a substantial contraction of the area of criminality.[4] This contraction of the formal proscription would in all cases tend to bring the written law in closer conformity with the law as it in fact operates.

In the final analysis each legislature must decide whether preserving a given criminal penalty is justified by the costs. The difficulty of this choice was aptly put by Michael and Adler over 30 years ago:

If the social consequences of the enforcement of a law are themselves undesirable, for one reason or another, it may be difficult to determine whether the behavior in question should be prohibited. The decision may rest in part upon the balance of the disadvantages involved or upon the availability of other than legal means of preventing the undesirable behavior. Empirical investigation may be needed to decide questions of this sort. In some cases it may be impossible to answer the question except by the hazard of guesses or opinions.[5]

But precisely because of the subtlety and elusiveness of the considerations involved and the common legislative tendency to ignore them in favor of the easy remedy of remitting difficult social problems to the police and to the courts, it may be useful to call attention to the undesirable consequences of indiscriminately dealing with undesirable conduct by making it criminal.

Drunkenness. Almost all jurisdictions treat public drunkenness as criminal either

[3]Allen, The Borderland of Criminal Justice, 3–4 (1964).

[4]Editor's Note: In recent years England has abolished or greatly restricted its criminal laws dealing with drug use, gambling, homosexual behavior, and prostitution.

[5]Michael & Adler, Crime, Law and Social Science 357 (1933).

by laws expressly so providing or by disorderly conduct statutes. Few would question the need to retain criminal provisions to protect the public against disorderly behavior, whether committed by sober or intoxicated persons. The problem is the stuporous drunk in the public streets or alleyways who constitutes a danger to himself and an ugly inconvenience to others. Since these problems are discussed in greater detail in chapter 9 of the Commission's General Report, only the principal ways in which the use of the criminal process has proven costly and ineffective are summarized here. They indicate that a major reconsideration of alternatives is imperative.

The costs are a substantial burden upon law enforcement resources, since approximately one-third of all reported arrests are for drunkenness. In addition there is a substantial amount of prosecutors' and magistrates' time expended dealing with the public drunk, and there is added strain upon courtrooms, jails, and correctional facilities. Should the right to counsel and other procedural protections be expanded to include drunkenness proceedings, the cost of employing the criminal process would be a financial and administrative burden of even greater proportions.

The return for these costs is disappointing. The public drunk is rarely the normal but undisciplined drinker who might be deterred from public intoxication by the prospect of a spell in the city jail. He is usually the alcoholic and the homeless for whom alcohol, poverty, and rootlessness have become a way of life. The data reveal that a large percentage of those swelling the arrest figures for public drunkenness are the compulsive repeaters, drunks who have been arrested and run through the process time and time again.

From every indication, therefore, deterrence is virtually inoperative. Rehabilitation also proves illusory because a correctional regimen for these persons is largely nonexistent. Some relief to the public and protection to the drunk are afforded, to be sure, by the temporary removal from the streets of some of the public drunks. This is about the only return the public receives for the costly labors of the criminal process.

The search for alternatives is imperative, for it would at least identify the problem for what it really is, a social problem of alcoholism and poverty, for which social services, not the penal-correctional process of the criminal law, are indicated.

Gambling. The laws of most States prohibiting gambling sweep within their ban various activities with significantly different social and law enforcement connotations. Many Americans engage in casual social gambling, the weekly poker game, the wager among friends on Saturday's football game, the church-sponsored evening of bingo. But the Report of the Organized Crime Task Force describes a very different kind of gambling activity. This is a highly organized illicit business, involving large and sometimes national organizations dealing in billions of dollars a year. Gambling is reported to be a prime source of funds for organized crime and is inevitably associated with political and police corruption. It is a substantial social evil preying particularly on the poor and the gullible.

Most States now countenance some legalized forms of gambling, commonly betting at race tracks, bingo, or limited forms of lotteries. The laws of some States attempt to distinguish between the casual player and the professional gambling promoter.

Because of the variety of gambling activity and the costs of the approach now commonly followed, more careful legislative definition of the evil sought to be prohibited is needed.

The substantial demand for gambling, like the demand for alcohol during prohibition, has survived the condemnations of the criminal law. The conduct proscribed by gambling laws is basically a commercial transaction between a willing seller and a willing buyer. People have been arrested, prosecuted, and convicted, but the prohibited conduct has flourished. The law may operate in some measure to diminish demand, but it is clear that criminal enforcement does not begin to control the problem. Illicit suppliers, protected against competition by the ban of the criminal law itself, enter the market to seek the profits made available by the persistence of the demand and the reduction of legitimate sources of supply. The risk of conviction appears to have a very limited effect.

The use of the criminal sanction serves to raise the stakes, for while the risk becomes greater, so do the prospects of reward. The process of filling the demand under these circumstances encourages the formation of large-scale, organized groups, often of national scope, with a multitude of persons each carrying out a phase of an integrated and continuous operation.

Once created these organized systems of crime tend to extend and diversify their operations much after the fashion of legitimate business. Racketeering organizations which found their market flooded by prohibition repeal moved into gambling and the illegal drug market. Organizations which purvey drugs and supply gambling find it profitable to extend their successful organization and mode of operation into loan sharking and labor racketeering. And in order to enhance their effectiveness as business operations, they are led to engage in collateral forms of crime of which murder and governmental corruption are the most notable examples. Hence in some measure crime is encouraged, and successful modes of criminality are produced, by the criminal law itself. As is made clear in the Report of the Task Force on Organized Crime, the ordinary processes of criminal law enforcement are particularly ineffective in dealing with crime conducted in these businesslike ways.

The difficulties of enforcement produced by the consensual character of the illegal conduct and the organized methods of operation have sometimes driven enforcement agencies to excesses in pursuit of evidence. Not only is this excessive enforcement activity undesirable in itself, but it has produced an adverse reaction by the public and the courts, often in the form of restrictions upon the use of evidence. No single phenomenon is more responsible for the whole pattern of judicial restraints upon methods of law enforcement than the unfortunate experience with enforcing laws against vice. Thurman Arnold's observation on this in 1935 has been further documented in the subsequent 30 years:

> Before...prohibition...the problem of search and seizures was a minor one. Thereafter, searches and seizures became the weapon of attack which could be used against prohibition enforcement. For every "dry" speech on the dangers of disobedience, there was a "wet" oration on the dangers of invading the privacy of the home. Reflected in the courts the figures are startling. In six States selected for the purpose

of study we find 19 search-and-seizure cases appealed in the 12 years preceding Prohibition and 347 in the 12 years following.

Because the creed of law enforcement has a habit of arising out of laws which are impossible of being enforced, it seems to be more of an influence in this country today than in any other.[6]

A considerable amount of police, prosecutorial, and judicial time, personnel, and resources is invested in enforcing laws against gambling. At a time when the volume of crime is steadily increasing and the burden on law enforcement agencies is becoming more onerous, this diversion of resources impairs the ability of law enforcement to deal effectively with more dangerous and threatening conduct.

This catalog of practical costs should not be understood as a recommendation for the elimination of the criminal penalty from all forms of gambling. The exploitation of the weaknesses of vulnerable people often results in economic loss and deprivation of major proportions, and as the Task Force Report on organized crime indicates, gambling is a major source of funds for criminal syndicates. The criminal law is necessary to deal with these evils, but its use should be carefully and objectively explored and measured against the costs to law enforcement.

Such reexamination may lead to abandoning the traditional approach which sweeps all forms of gambling within the scope of the prohibition and relies on the discretion of the police to exempt private gambling and charitable and religious fundraising enterprises. One of the objectives of reexamination might be to relieve the latter types from criminal penalties while seeking to bring the law to bear more effectively on the organized gambling promoter. This should be accomplished by legislative definition rather than by the haphazard and uneven application of police or prosecutorial discretion.

Narcotics and Dangerous Drugs. Although the conduct forbidden by narcotics and dangerous drugs laws has a more serious direct effect on those who engage in it, it shares many of the same characteristics as gambling. Those who use narcotics and dangerous drugs, like those who gamble, do so voluntarily. Similarly the profits available because of the illicit nature of the activity encourage persons to engage in the business of supplying drugs despite the legal risks involved. And these profits, coupled with the continued demand, have contributed to the growth of organized criminal groups. In addition there is a substantial investment of law enforcement resources seeking to suppress or deal with drug abuse. But it is evident that law enforcement alone cannot handle the problem.

Chapter 8 of the Commission's General Report considers these matters in some detail and suggests the need for careful study of the criminal laws controlling the possession, sale, and use of drugs. Change should include provision for severe penal sanctions against those who trade in drugs for profit, with appropriate provision of alternate treatment for those who have some psychic or physical dependence on drugs.

[6] Arnold, The Symbols of Government 164 (1935).

A new approach in Federal legislation was taken by the Drug Abuse Control Amendments of 1965, which restrict criminal penalties to persons who unlawfully sell and distribute nonnarcotic stimulant, depressant, and hallucinogenic drugs and provide no criminal penalty for those who use these drugs or possess them solely for personal use.

In 1966 Federal legislation was enacted which provides alternate civil commitment procedures for persons addicted to the use of narcotics. This legislation is a first step toward reducing the anomalous disparity between the criminal treatment of those dependent on narcotics and the approach taken with those dependent on other dangerous drugs.

...

Disorderly Conduct and Vagrancy. Disorderly conduct and vagrancy laws, found in virtually all jurisdictions, are another example of statutes that are used to achieve purposes other than controlling the proscribed conduct by punishing those who engage in it. Disorderly conduct laws grant the police authority to act in numerous minor situations where it is considered desirable for them to do so, but where the conduct has not otherwise been specifically defined as criminal. Vagrancy laws provide authority to hold a suspect for investigation and interrogation when the police could not legally arrest him for another offense.

Disorderly conduct statutes vary in their precise formulation, and the conduct is variously labeled, as, for example, riot, breach of the peace, unlawful assembly, disturbing the peace, or loitering. These laws tend to embrace an excessively broad range of conduct, some of it dangerous, some merely annoying, some harmless, some constitutionally protected. While these statutes protect important interests, they often are excessively general and do not adequately discriminate and identify the kinds of behavior legitimately to be prohibited. In California, for example, it is a misdemeanor to make noise in the area of a religious meeting which disturbs the solemnity of the meeting; willfully to disturb any assembly or meeting without authority of law; to commit a lawful act with another in a violent, boisterous, or tumultuous manner; maliciously and willfully to disturb the peace or quiet of any neighborhood by loud or unusual noise or offensive conduct; to commit any act willfully and wrongfully which seriously disturbs or endangers the public peace or health or which openly outrages public decency.

The generality and imprecision of most disorderly conduct statutes allow the police to exercise a broad discretionary authority in deciding which conduct to treat as criminal. More arrests are made for disorderly conduct than for any other crime except drunkenness. Of all arrests reported by the 1965 Uniform Crime Reports over 10 percent were for disorderly conduct, over 500,000 out of a total of nearly 5 million arrests. Studies of reported decisions and of the activities of lower courts reveal that a wide gamut of conduct is covered by these statutes.

These excessively broad laws are applied in excessively broad ways that lead to convictions for some conduct that properly is subject to criminal control and to convictions for some conduct that is harmless or should be protected. Some of these convictions are reversed, but not the overwhelming majority. There is little appellate review of the work of the often ill-trained magistrates who work with these vague laws. A New York study revealed that although over 70,000 disorderly conduct arraignments occurred in 1957 alone, there have been only approximately 150 reported opinions since the enactment of the statute in 1923.

As observed in the commentary to the Model Penal Code, "If the disorderly conduct statutes are troublesome because they require so little in the way of misbehavior, the vagrancy statutes offer the astounding spectacle of criminality with no misbehavior at all!" Vagrancy laws define criminality essentially in terms of a person's status or a set of circumstances reflecting a judgment that such persons are apt to commit antisocial acts. For some forms of the offense no conduct need be committed at all, although other forms rest on the commission of an act. As the offense developed through the common law, it came to include idle and disorderly persons and vagabonds; persons who refused to work or engaged in begging, threatened to desert their families, or returned from whence they were legally removed; and persons who wandered abroad without giving a good account of themselves.

The usual components of vagrancy in its modern statutory form include living in idleness without employment and having no visible means of support; roaming, wandering, or loitering; being a common prostitute, drunkard, or gambler; and sleeping outdoors or in a nonresidential building without permission.

These laws have an ancient lineage. In feudal days they served to protect the rights of the lord in his fugitive serfs. As feudal ties began to dissolve, they were used to control wandering bands of rootless workmen turned robbers. During the acute labor shortage following the Black Plague they served to hold laborers to their jobs. Subsequently they served the purpose of protecting against abuse of the poor laws by wandering indigents. Their current and widespread use, as documented in a number of recent studies, is to afford police justification, which otherwise would not be present under prevailing constitutional and statutory limitations, to arrest, search, question, and detain persons because of suspicion that they have committed or may commit a crime. They are also used by the police to clean the streets of undesirables, to harass persons believed to be engaged in crime, and to investigate uncleared offenses. An American Bar Foundation study found that although brief on-the-street or stationhouse detention without a formal arrest occurred fairly frequently in the absence of express legal authority, most investigations were carried out under the guise of a vagrance or a related minor statute arrest.

Persons held for investigation purposes were found to be frequently booked for "vagrancy and investigation." This practice was advocated in one police duty manual in cases in which there is some specific crime for which the person should be investigated, or there is some specific reason for general investigation. The American Bar Foundation study found that detectives obtained an arrest warrant of vagrancy when they were uncertain whether there were adequate grounds for arrest on a serious charge.

Precisely because disorderly conduct and vagrancy charges are so commonly relied upon by law enforcement authorities, as well as because penalties involved are generally minor, and defendants are usually from the lowest economic and social levels, they have proved largely resistant to scrutiny and change. Yet

this is a most important area of criminal administration, affecting the largest number of defendants, involving a great portion of police activity, and powerfully influencing the view of public justice held by millions of people.[7]

The Model Penal Code offers some constructive guidelines for redefining these offenses. It confines disorderly conduct to behavior that is itself disorderly and excludes that which "tends to provoke a breach of peace." Although inevitably imprecise the definition is much less vague and commodious than usual disorderly conduct laws. To constitute disorderly conduct the defined disturbances must be genuinely public.

The code also provides a model for defining the crime of vagrancy which eliminates all traces of the ancient offense except that thought justified by the legitimate needs of law enforcement, namely, situations in which a person "loiters or prowls in a place, at a time, or in a manner not usual for law-abiding individuals under circumstances that warrant alarm for the safety of persons or property in the vicinity." Although the concept of justifiable "alarm" for the safety of persons or property rather than justifiable "suspicion" of criminality is employed, the net effect appears to authorize arrest and search in circumstances short of probable cause.

It is evident that the real issue in vagrancy cases is not one of defining criminal conduct but of defining the circumstances in which police may intervene short of arrest to make inquiries and dispel suspicion. The police must have reasonable, though carefully limited, authority to make this type of inquiry. In attempting to meet this problem, New York has authorized a police officer to "stop any person abroad in a public place [who] he reasonably suspects is committing, has committed or is about to commit" a felony or serious misdemeanor and to demand his name, address, and an explanation of that person's action. A section of the American Law Institute Model Code of Pre-Arraignment Procedure offers a similar solution. Both offer a more direct response to the central problem of providing the police with a means other than a vagrancy arrest for dealing with persons encountered in suspicious circumstances.

Improvements in laws such as these are of great importance. The high price paid for extending to the police wide and largely uncontrollable power of traditional disorderly conduct and vagrancy laws should be recognized. Foremost among its disadvantages is that it constitutes an abandonment of the basic principle upon which the whole system of criminal justice in a democratic community rests, close control over exercise of the authority delegated to officials to employ force and coercion. This control is to be found in carefully defined laws and in judicial and administrative accountability. The looseness of the laws constitutes a charter of authority of the street whenever the police deem it desirable. The practical costs of this departure from principle are significant. One of its consequences is to communicate to the people who tend to be the object of these laws the idea that law enforcement is not

[7] Model Penal Code 2 (Tent. Draft No. 13, 1961).

a regularized, authoritative procedure, but largely a matter of arbitrary behavior by the authorities. The application of these laws often tends to discriminate against the poor and subcultural groups in the population. It is unjust to structure law enforcement in such a way that poverty itself becomes a crime. And it is costly for society when the law arouses the feelings associated with these laws in the ghetto, a sense of persecution and helplessness before official power and hostility to police and other authority that may tend to generate the very conditions of criminality society is seeking to extirpate.

Sexual Behavior. In virtually all States the criminal law is used to govern sexual relationships and activities between consenting adults. There are laws against sexual intercourse between unmarried people (fornication), between persons one or both of whom is married to another (adultery), and where the woman is paid for her services (prostitution). There are laws against deviant sexual activities such as those between males or between partners, even persons married to each other, where unnatural modes of intercourse are used (sodomy).

Basic social interests demand the use of the strongest sanctions to protect the individual against forcible sexual acts and those induced by fraud and overreaching, to protect the young from the sexual advances of more mature individuals, to protect the public against open and notorious solicitation and commercialized vice, and to protect the institutions of marriage and family. Protection of these interests warrant criminal sanctions for their violation. Thus in recent statutory revisions, notably the Illinois Criminal Code of 1961 and the Model Penal Code, they were the interests protected by criminal prohibitions. When these interests are not at stake, as in the case of most consensual misbehavior between adults, the situation is less clear.

Available information indicates that laws against fornication, adultery, and heterosexual deviancy are generally unenforced. In New York, where adultery was the only ground for divorce until recently, there were countless divorces based on documented instances of adultery but no adultery prosecutions. Certainly there is no greater enforcement of prohibitions against premarital sexual relations. In many if not most jurisdictions adultery and fornication laws have been repealed in practice, although in form they persist on the books. There is surely some truth in Thurman Arnold's comment that these laws "survive in order to satisfy moral objections to established modes of conduct. They are unenforced because we want to continue our conduct, and unrepealed because we want to preserve our morals."

But widespread and obvious winking at violations of the criminal law by those charged with their enforcement may well influence law enforcement generally. It tends to breed a cynicism and indifference to the criminal law which augments the tendency to disrespect those who make and enforce the law.

Homosexual practices are condemned as criminal in virtually all States, usually as a felony with substantial punishment. There are some attempts at enforcement, particularly in cases involving public conduct, solicitation, or corruption of the young. When the activity is private and consensual, however, the deterrent efficacy of law enforcement is limited; only the indiscreet have reasons for fear.

Homosexuality entails deviation from social mores and the flouting of community attitudes having greater apparent capacity to deter and shape conduct than that possessed by the criminal law. It is questionable whether there is significant additional deterrent force provided by the criminal sanction above that coming from other forms of social pressure not to engage in such acts. Moreover, the present penal system is no better suited than other social institutions to deal with the homosexual or to rehabilitate or reintegrate him. In addition, the presence of these laws creates opportunities for extortion, and opens the door for discriminatory enforcement.

Despite this nonenforcement and the costs the presence of these laws on the books can impose, there is understandable and deeply felt reluctance to repeal them. This stems from a fear that the affirmative act of repeal might be mistaken as an abandonment of social disapproval for the prohibited acts and an invitation to license. Opponents of repeal emphasize the symbolic effect of unenforced laws and the difficulty of removing what may be an inappropriate sanction without appearing to condone the forbidden act. The appropriateness and the scope of criminal sanctions with respect to these sexual activities deserves discussion and analysis by those concerned with the improvement of criminal administration.

Prostitution is an ancient and widespread social problem which has proven virtually immune to the threats of the criminal sanction. It is a consensual crime for which the market is persistent. Although it is prohibited in all States, the laws are widely violated. Enforcement tends to be associated with degradation of the image of the police, harassment, discriminatory treatment, and endemic official corruption.

The social interest in repressing prostitution is strong, primarily because of the elements of commercialism and exploitation that are involved in its more organized forms. Society is also concerned with controlling venereal disease and with reducing the affront involved in public acts of solicitation. These interests justify the maintenance and enforcement of laws directed against pandering, operating disorderly houses, public solicitation, and the commercial forms of meretricious behavior.

But a more careful definition of the offense would seem desirable to ensure that it is limited to situations where a person engages in sexual activity as a business or where public solicitation is involved.

Concluding Observations. This chapter has sought to examine the problem of overreliance upon the criminal law as a means of social regulation by identifying instances in which the use of the penalties and processes of the criminal law have proven particularly ineffective or costly or both. Certain generalizations emerge.

The absence of a complaining victim appears to mark many ineffective criminal laws. Any system of law enforcement must rely heavily upon the cooperation of those who are unwillingly victimized. When the conduct is consensual on both sides and particularly when it occurs in private, the normal techniques of law enforcement inevitably tend to be frustrated. The laws prohibiting certain consensual sexual relations, both heterosexual and homosexual, as well as the laws against abortion, drunkenness, gambling, and narcotics, display these characteristics in varying degrees.

Where the nature of the crime is such that there are added difficulties of detection and proof, a lack of strong enthusiasm for the criminal prosecution, plus a persistent demand to engage in the conduct, the potential effectiveness of the criminal process is further reduced.

The criminal prohibitions against some types of sexual behavior reflect an idealized moral code, not what a substantial percentage of the population, judged by their conduct, regard as beyond the margin of tolerability for the average fallible citizen. Consensual homosexuality, on the other hand, is repugnant to large segments of the community. But the general feeling that those who engage in such acts are psychologically disturbed rather than wicked, tends to sap enthusiasm for criminal prosecution. Prostitution is certainly not viewed as a tolerable form of behavior by the general community. Yet the existence of professionalized sex, not only in this country but historically in all cultures, availed of by otherwise reputable citizens in all walks of life, plus the mildness of the usual sanctions, are sure evidence that it is not regarded unequivocally as condemnable.

Abortion and gambling share these qualities in varying degrees. There are compelling reasons for liberalizing abortion laws to accommodate manifest health needs. Gambling attracts a legal response that is ambiguous on its face: Within the same jurisdiction some kinds of gambling are prohibited and some are permitted, on the basis of distinctions with scarcely any relevance to the moral quality of the participant's conduct. Narcotics use does commonly arouse sentiments of condemnation and fear. But the continued demand for drugs, generated by deep-rooted and complex social and psychological drives, and the sentiment that it should be treated as sickness serve to limit the efficiency of criminal law enforcement.

In several instances the criminal process is directed at objectives quite different from deterring the outlawed conduct through surveillance, prosecution, and correction of offenders. The role of law enforcement in the case of public drunkenness, for example, is to remove unsightly annoyances from the public streets, to protect the drunk against physical dangers, and to provide a respite for him from his self-destructive habits. In the case of family support laws its role is largely to ensure the performance of family obligations. With the insufficient fund check writer its role is often to collect debts in behalf of creditors. Obviously measuring effectiveness in traditional law enforcement terms is inappropriate in these cases. The issue is how well the use of the criminal process in these instances attains its special objectives. There is evidence to support the hypothesis of one observer that "when the criminal law is relied upon to perform social services, those services are not likely to be effectively rendered."[8]

No doubt the criminal process is filling a need in these situations. It would seem, however, that civil processes or institutions designed to handle particular social problems would be more effective than the criminal process in many cases. The increasing demands of due process in all criminal proceedings, the requirements of appointment of counsel, prohibition of interrogation in certain circumstances, high standards with respect to waiver of constitutional rights, and others, add to the

[8] Allen, The Borderland of Criminal Justice 5 (1964).

difficulty of enforcing the criminal law in many of the situations described in this chapter.

One substantial cost of overextended use of the criminal process is the risk of creating cynicism and indifference to the whole criminal law and its agencies of enforcement at a time when precisely the opposite is needed. This indifference tends to occur particularly where the criminal sanction is generally unenforced. As observed by Roscoe Pound many years ago,

> However impressive the state-declared ideal may be to the contemplative observer, the spectacle of statutory precepts with penal sanctions, which are not and perhaps are not intended to be put in force in practice, casts doubts upon the whole penal code and educates in disrespect for law more than the high pronouncement can educate for virtue.[9]

These attitudes also occur when the substantive criminal law is used as a device for circumventing constitutional restrictions upon police practices. The disorderly conduct and vagrancy laws are cases in point. The same consequence is also produced by inherent difficulties in enforcement which sometimes lead police to excesses degrading to themselves as well as to the public.

Another kind of cost is imposed when criminal enforcement itself produces social behavior which may be more undesirable than that prohibited by the law. We have seen how the bans on gambling tend to foster organized forms of criminality which, with alarming business efficiency and the use of systematic means of coercion, violence, and governmental corruption, continue to supply the persistent demand. In the case of the abortion laws the criminal prohibition forces thousands of women each year to incompetent abortionists, with the loss of a substantial number of lives as a consequence.

Still another variety of cost is the substantial impairment of the effectiveness of the police in performing the tasks, which only they can perform, of protecting the public against serious threats. This occurs when men and resources that could be employed in meeting problems of serious criminality are diverted into areas where the use of the criminal law is problematical. Every man-hour spent in running down bad check passers or in rounding up or processing drunks is a man-hour lost to other purposes. As a representative of the FBI stated to the Commission:

> The criminal code of any jurisdiction tends to make a crime of everything that people are against, without regard to enforceability, changing social concepts, etc. The result is that the criminal code becomes society's trash bin. The police have to rummage around in this material and are expected to prevent everything that is unlawful. They cannot do so because many of the things prohibited are simply beyond enforcement both because of human inability to enforce the law and because, as in the case of prohibition, society legislates one way and acts another way. If we would restrict our definition of criminal offenses in many areas, we would get the criminal codes back to the point where they prohibit specific, carefully defined, and serious conduct, and the police could then concentrate on enforcing the law in that context

[9] Pound, Criminal Justice in America 67 (1930).

and would not waste its officers by trying to enforce the unenforceable as is now done.

There is also the loss of morale and self-esteem among police who are obligated to engage in tasks which must seem to them demeaning or degrading or of little relevance to the mission of law enforcers. What must be counted as another indirect impairment of police effectiveness is the whole pattern of judicial restraints upon police surveillance, detection, and interrogation which have been provoked in substantial measure by excesses growing out of attempts to enforce laws which are particularly resistant to enforcement.

Also associated with overreliance upon the criminal law is the creation of undesirably wide areas of discretionary authority by law enforcement agencies. Excessive discretion is invited when the substantive law creates an implicit authorization for agencies to employ the process for purposes other than deterring the prohibited conduct and correcting the offender. This is the case in varying degrees with disorderly conduct and vagrancy laws, public drunkenness and family support laws, and laws relating to insufficient fund checks. Excessive discretion also occurs when the criminal prohibition is one that is generally not enforced or probably not intended to be enforced, for example, certain of the sex laws. Finally, it occurs where the legislature has deliberately defined the prohibited conduct to include conduct beyond the borders of the target social evil in order to ease prosecutorial burdens of proof. Of those crimes discussed, the ban on all forms of gambling, including such innocuous forms as church and charitable socials and the friendly poker game, is the clearest example. Some ameliorative discretion is of course inevitable as well as desirable in any system, but discretion becomes excessive and threatening when it is used as a substitute for law itself. Moreover, when exercised under a broad character of discretion, police authority tends to be viewed in many sections of the community, usually those in which crime is a serious problem, as an episodic and arbitrary exercise of naked power rather than as the impartial command of the law. And finally the delegated authority affords the opportunity for abuse and discrimination either through malice or untempered zeal. What Professor Wechsler wrote concerning prosecutorial discretion is equally applicable to all law enforcement agency discretion:

> A society that holds, as we do, to belief in law cannot regard with unconcern the fact that prosecuting agencies can exercise so large an influence on dispositions that involve the penal sanction, without reference to any norms but those that they may create for themselves. Whatever one would hold as to the need for discretion of this order in a proper system or the wisdom of attempting regulation of its exercise, it is quite clear that its existence cannot be accepted as a substitute for a sufficient law. Indeed, one of the major consequences of the state of penal law today is that administration has so largely come to dominate the field without effective guidance from the law. This is to say that to a large extent we have, in this important sense, abandoned law—and this within an area where our fundamental teaching calls most strongly for its vigorous supremacy.[10]

[10] Wechsler, *The Challenge of a Model Penal Code,* 65 Harv. L. Rev. 1097, 1102 (1952).

Undoubtedly a great deal of research is needed on the uses and limitations of the criminal law as a means of social regulation, on the circumstances in which it is more likely to be effective, and on the situations in which its use overbalances social disadvantages and consequences and those in which it does not. But enough is now known to warrant abandonment of the common legislative premise that the criminal law is a sure panacea for all social ailments. Only when the load of law enforcement has been lightened by stripping away those responsibilities for which it is not suited will we begin to make the criminal law a more effective instrument of social protection.

7. The Concepts of Tolerance and Contraculture as Applied to Delinquency*

Ruth Shonle Cavan

In defining juvenile delinquency, laws are of little use. Usually laws are specific only in relation to serious adult offenses such as murder, assault, robbery, burglary, and so forth. Children are delinquent if they are found guilty in court of breaking any of the federal, state, or local laws designed to control adult behavior. Delinquency statistics, however, indicate that these serious offenses account for only a

Reprinted from *The Sociological Quarterly,* 2 (1961), 243–258, by permission of the publisher and the author.

*Presidential Address, Midwest Sociological Society, April 28, 1961. In addition to the titles cited in the notes, the reader's attention is directed to the following general references:

Marshall Clinard, *Sociology of Deviant Behavior* (New York: Rinehart, 1957), Chap. 1; Richard A. Cloward, "Illegitimate Means, Anomie, and Deviant Behavior," *American Sociological Review,* 24:164–76 (1959); Albert K. Cohen, "The Study of Social Disorganization and Deviant Behavior," in Robert K. Merton, Leonard Broom, and Leonard S. Cottrell (eds.), *Sociology Today: Problems and Prospects* (New York: Basic Books, 1959) Chap. 21; Robert Dubin, "Deviant Behavior and Social Structure: Continuities in Social Theory," *American Sociological Review,* 24:147–76 (1959); Robert K. Merton, "Social Conformity, Deviation, and Opportunity Structures: A Comment on the Contributions of Dubin and Cloward," *American Sociological Review,* 24:177–89 (1959); Robert K. Merton, *Social Theory and Social Structure* (rev. ed., Glencoe, Ill.: Free Press, 1957); Talcott Parsons, *The Social System* (Glencoe, Ill.: Free Press, 1951).

small proportion of the delinquencies of children. Most of the behavior that gets a child into trouble with the police and courts comes under a much less definite part of the law on juvenile delinquency.[1] Examples are easy to find. The Illinois law defines as delinquent a child who is incorrigible or who is growing up in idleness, one who wanders about the streets in the nighttime without being on any lawful business, or one who is guilty of indecent or lascivious conduct. Laws in some other states are still more vague. New Mexico rests its definition on the word habitual. A delinquent child is one who, by habitually refusing to obey the reasonable and lawful commands of his parents or other persons of lawful authority, is deemed to be habitually uncontrolled, habitually disobedient, or habitually wayward; or who habitually is a truant from home or school; or who habitually so deports himself as to injure or endanger the morals, health, or welfare of himself or others. In these laws there is no definition of such words or phrases as incorrigible, habitual, indecent conduct, or in the nighttime. How much disobedience constitutes incorrigibility? How often may a child perform an act before it is considered habitual?

The federal Children's Bureau dodges all this by stating flatly that juvenile delinquency cases are those referred to courts for certain violations of laws or for conduct so seriously antisocial as to interfere with the rights of others or to menace the welfare of the delinquent himself or of the community.[2] This approach does not help much. Someone has to decide when the child has violated a law or when his conduct is antisocial. Parents, teachers, and police make the decisions. What guides them in deciding when a child's behavior justifies a court hearing? Is a court hearing the only measure of delinquency? Or are there gradations in delinquency? If so, where along the line of gradation does a child become so out of line that his behavior merits calling him a delinquent? If delinquent behavior has gradations, does good behavior also have gradations?

This paper is an attempt to assign misbehavior to a place in the total social structure, and to determine when misbehavior should be termed delinquency. The Children's Bureau definition is tentatively used: behavior that interferes with the rights of others, or menaces the welfare of the delinquent or the welfare of the community. I am concerned chiefly with the last, construed to mean the effective functioning of the social organization.

The Behavior Continuum

A word now about Figure 1. The figure represents the social structure, the framework of which consists of the institutions and less formal but fairly permanent organizations that, operating together, carry on the functions of the society. Area *D*

[1] Editor's Note: In many countries (e.g., England, Canada, Sweden) adjudication as a delinquent is reserved for serious offenses. Both Illinois and New York, unlike the remaining states, now call "delinquent" those youth who violate the criminal law and call "in need of supervision" those youth committing noncriminal misbehavior.

[2] *Juvenile Court Statistics, 1957,* Statistical Series No. 52 (Washington, D.C.: Children's Bureau, 1959), p. 4.

represents the central or dominant part of the social structure, where institutions are found that set the formal standards for behavior and exert the formal means of control. The base line represents the extent of deviations from the central social norms. According to this hypothetical formulation, behavior falls into a continuum from condemnable behavior (area *A*) through decreasing degrees of disapproved behavior to the central area *D* and then through increasing degrees of good behavior to near perfection in area *G*.

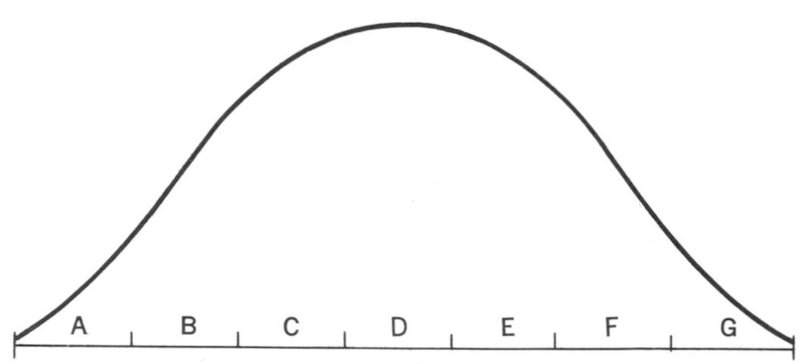

FIGURE 1. Hypothetical formulation of behavior continuum

A. Underconforming contraculture
B. Extreme under-conformity
C. Minor under conformity
D. Normal conformity
E. Minor over-conformity
F. Extreme over-conformity
G. Over conforming conformity

The area above the line represents the volume of behavior—or more concretely the number of people—that falls into the area controlled by the norms and into successive segments of deviation. There is sufficient evidence, that I will not quote, to support a bell-shaped curve.[3]

Even though we know that behavior falls into a continuum, nevertheless we tend to think in terms of dichotomies. We have the sinner and the saint, the devil and the angel, the alcoholic and the teetotaller, the criminal and the upright citizen, the juvenile delinquent and the model child. We tend to think in terms of black and white, whereas between these two rare extremes are many shades of gray. For instance, one might set up such a series as pitch black, charcoal gray, slate gray, tattletale gray, dingy white, off white, and lily white. In this series of seven, the modal term (area *D*) is not white but tattletale gray. (This term is borrowed from the advertisements of a few years ago in which the sheets flapping on the line were tattletale gray because the housewife had not used the right kind of laundry soap.) Observed behavior falls into similar gradations. The child may break into a store at

[3]Floyd H. Allport, "The J-Curve Hypothesis of Conforming Behavior," *Journal of Social Psychology*, 5:141–83 (1934); R. T. LaPiere, and P. R. Farnsworth, *Social Psychology* (McGraw-Hill: New York, 1936), p. 400.

night and steal (black); deliberately pick up valuables during store hours; occasionally pick up things as opportunity arises; pilfer small objects (tattletale gray); be meticulous about not taking things; remonstrate with others who steal; or report other children to teachers or police for even minor pilfering (lily white).

Social Norms and Modal Behavior

To avoid confusion, certain terms require clarification. The formal standards that dominate area *D* are social norms. They are related to but not identical with values. Values are ideals or ultimate goals, perhaps never attained. They are abstractions. Social norms are the specific formulations to implement the values in practical, attainable form. They constitute the expectations of society and often are stated in terms implying that exact conformity is expected. However, a third level may be identified, the working plans or modal behavior of the majority of people.

For adequate functioning of society a balance must be maintained between the rigid social norms and the more flexible modal behavior. Complete conformity to the social norms, always, by everyone, is rarely demanded. A concession is made to human nature itself–to the difficulty of always observing rules, or always suppressing impulses, or always standing at attention. Some of these concessions have been institutionalized in the familiar swing back and forth between consecration and carnival. After the religious rites at Christmas we have our modern New Year's Eve; and Mardi Gras precedes Lenten abstinence. Concessions are often made in areas of behavior not vital to the main social functions. Other concessions are made to certain groups, especially the young and the very old. The behavior in the central area *D* therefore is not strict conformity to social norms, but permits some deviations. *D* is an area of flexibility or tolerance, but only to the extent that the social organization itself is not threatened.

Normally, children are taught to accept the social norms and to confine their behavior to the area of tolerance. Most people find in this area a satisfactory way of life. Their behavior is reasonably well restrained and predictable. The society functions adequately.

Underconformity and Overconformity

In the illustration of the continuum given above, pilfering of small objects was given as the modal type of behavior falling within the area of tolerance although not rigidly conforming to the social norm of honesty. With this formulation, both more serious forms of stealing and meticulous avoidance of taking things are deviations from the social norms and the modal behavior. There is deviation in the nature of underconformity to the social norms, shown to the left on Figure 1, and deviation in the nature of overconformity to the social norms, shown to the right. Underconformity is an exaggeration of the tolerance allowed by the modal norms; for example, if the modal behavior permits a small amount of pilfering of candy and comic books in the corner store, the underconformer expands the tolerance to include stealing of more valuable objects. Overconformity is an exaggeration of the strict observance of formal social norms. Honesty may be exaggerated to the point where a person would not keep even a pencil that he found nor use an article belonging to someone else even in an emergency.

Either underconformity or overconformity that exceeds the limits of tolerance poses a threat to the operation of the social organization. Overconformity, as a threatening type of deviation, has often been omitted from the formulations of sociologists or has been only casually mentioned. It is true that overconformity usually does not constitute delinquency or crime in the same degree as underconformity. However, it should be included in any discussion providing a complete picture of the social structure, of which delinquency and crime are one kind of deviation and overconformity the opposite kind.

The issue with reference to overconformity has sometimes been obscured by the tendency to think of the social norms not as our workable expectations of behavior but as ideal or perfect standards. An example may be drawn from the introductory text by Lundberg, Schrag, and Larsen.[4] These authors establish the institutional expectations and the area of tolerance in the middle, with most people fitting their behavior into this area. They also show disapproved behavior to the left, as is done in Figure 1. However, to the right they show approved deviations, whereas Figure 1 and Table 1 define these deviations as disapproved and a threat to area *D.* According to Lundberg, *et al.*, approved deviations exceed the standard set by the group, and include at the extreme some 2 or 3 per cent of people who are given public recognition for their overconformity. According to this formulation, the ideal standards for behavior would be at the extreme right, would constitute virtual perfection, and practically, would be attained by almost no one. Everyone except the 2 or 3 per cent would be deviants.

Research studies of juvenile delinquents sometimes ignore the central area of modal behavior and compare delinquent children (area *A*) with near-perfect children (area *G*). Sheldon and Eleanor Glueck in their much discussed book, *Unraveling Juvenile Delinquency,* make such a comparison.[5] They matched each of 500 correctional-school boys with a boy of the same age, intelligence, and social background, whose behavior was exemplary. Not only were these control boys without any police, court, or correctional-school record, but 74 per cent were without any known delinquency of even a minor nature. The Gluecks had difficulty in finding 500 such overly good boys, and eventually had to include a few boys guilty of such misbehavior as smoking in their early years, hopping trucks, once or twice swiping much desired articles in five-and-ten-cent stores, crap shooting, sneaking into movies, occasional truancy, being stubborn to their mothers, and a very occasional occurrence of staying out late at night, using vile language, drinking, running away from home, and bunking out. Some of the deficiencies were very trivial and had occurred when the boy was seven or eight years old. The Gluecks then were comparing boys from

[4]George A. Lundberg, Clarence C. Schrag, and Otto N. Larsen, *Sociology,* rev. ed. (Harper: New York, 1958), p. 349.

[5]Sheldon and Eleanor Glueck, *Unraveling Juvenile Delinquency* (Cambridge, Mass.: Harvard University Press, 1950), pp. 23–39, Chap. 21.

TABLE 1. Characteristics of Stages of Continuity in Behavior

	A *Delinquent Contraculture*	*B* *Extreme Underconformity*	*C* *Minor Underconformity*	*D* *Normal Conformity*	*E* *Minor Overconformity*	*F* *Extreme Overconformity*	*G* *Overconforming Contraculture*
Public attitude	Condemnation; "hard core"	Disapproval	Toleration without approval	Tolerance with approval	Toleration without approval	Disapproval	Condemnation
Public reaction	Rejection; school expulsion; commitment to correctional school	Police warnings; school suspension; referral to social agency	Disciplinary action by school or parent	Indifference; acceptance; mild reproofs	Ignoring	Ostracizing	Rejection
Child's attitude toward public	Rejection of values of *D*	Wavering between acceptance and rejection of *D* values	Acceptance of values of *D*; feelings of guilt	Acceptance of values of *D*; no guilt feelings	No deviation in personal conduct	Criticism of *D* behavior in others	Rejection of *D* values
Child's self-concept	As delinquent, outlaw	Confused, marginal to *C* and *A*	As misbehaving nondelinquent	As a conforming nondelinquent	As a true conformer	Better than others	His way is the only right way
Examples	Armed robbery; burglary	Larceny of valuables	"Borrowing" and keeping; pilfering	Minor pilfering; unauthorized borrowing	Borrowing only with permission	Extreme care not to use other's possessions; criticism of others	Report even minor pilfering to teacher or police
	Rape; serious sex deviations	Promiscuity; minor sex deviations	Extensive normal sex relations	Minor normal sex relations; petting	Normal, only in marriage; no petting	Restrained, even in marriage	Celibacy as a philosophy
	Drug addiction	Occasional use of drugs	Smoking of marihuana	Smoking tobacco	No smoking; use coffee or tea	No stimulating drinks, even though mild	Opposition to use by others

area *A*—the most seriously underconforming—with boys from area *G*—the most seriously overconforming. This selection may account for the fact that, whereas the delinquents tended to be active, aggressive, impulsive, and rebellious, the control group tended to be neurotic, fearful of failure or defeat, and submissive to authority. The middle group of boys with normal conformity or *D*-type behavior, who live within the tolerance limits of the community, is completely ignored. In the Glueck study the control group is fully as deviant as the delinquent group, but in the opposite direction.

Actually, it seems very doubtful whether so much admiration is really accorded the overconforming group as some sociologists and researchers state or imply. The good behavior and achievements that are rewarded by society seem much more likely to be in area *D* or *E* than in area *F* or *G*. For example, consider the descriptive terms and epithets that are applied to youths whose behavior falls into the different areas. Boys in area *A* are often referred to as little savages, hoodlums, punks, bums, or gangsters—not very complimentary terms. But boys in area *G* also are not complimented; they are often referred to as sissies, goody-goods, teacher's pet, drips, brains, fraidy-cats, wet blankets, or squares. Adults and youth alike admire the boys in area *D*, who are essentially conforming but not rigidly so. The area *D* youth is "all boy," or the all-American boy; he can take care of himself; he is ambitious; he can hold his own with the best of them; he is a good sport. A little later, in college, he makes a "gentleman's *C*." He may occasionally borrow small things that he needs and forget to return them, truant off and on but not enough to damage his school record, cheat on tests in subjects that he doesn't like, mark up the walks and walls of a rival high school, do some property damage under the stress of excitement, outwork and outsmart his rivals, lie for his own advantage, and occasionally sass his parents and neglect his home chores. But he stays within the tolerance limits; he is developing, even in misbehavior, traits that will help him fit into the adult competitive *D* pattern of behavior; he is moving toward the social expectations for his future as an adult.

Areas C and E

Let us look at areas *C* and *E*, representing minor deviations from the social norms and the modal behavior of area *D*. Minor deviations only are involved, whether they are under- or overconforming. Parents, teachers, employers, and other adults keep a wary eye out for these deviations. They are not a serious threat to the social organization but might become so if they increased in frequency or seriousness. The general attitude is toleration without approval, as indicated in Table 1 after "public attitude." Efforts to rectify or prevent these deviations usually are handled by parents or school officials. More attention is given to the underconformers than the overconformers. However, overconformers are admonished not to interfere with other people's fun, and are urged to get into the swing of things, to enjoy themselves, and to let themselves go in normal fashion.

The youth who falls into one of these two areas is regarded as a member of the social institutions and groups that control area *D*. He is "one of ours," erring a little, but to be brought back into the groups, disciplined if need be, and forgiven.[6]

The youth in areas *C* and *E* accepts the standards of area *D*. He identifies himself with groups in area *D*, and would be lost without them. He feels guilty about not meeting the expectations of groups in area *D* and tends to rationalize his shortcomings. In the *C* area the boy agrees that stealing is wrong and insists he meant to return the property he took; he is contrite and filled with good intentions. He thinks of himself as nondelinquent.[7] The overly conscientious youth in area *E* also feels guilty because he is not measuring up to the expectations of area *D*. He also rationalizes: he doesn't join the boys on Saturday night because he doesn't want to worry his parents; he needs the time to study, and so on.

Areas B and F

Behavior in areas *B* and *F* is definitely disapproved according to the social norms and the modal behavior patterns of area *D*. *B*- and *F*-type behaviors are a threat to the smooth operation of the social organization. The chronic truant of area *B* interferes with the effective operation of the school; but the boy who always is perfectly prepared or who is always on hand after school to do the schoolroom chores is also a hindrance in a school that wishes to draw all boys into participation. He may of course be temporarily rewarded by appreciation from an overworked teacher who welcomes his help even though it is at the expense of the boy's participation with other boys in nonschool activities.

The underconformers in area *B* are made to feel that they are violators of the social norms; but they are not abandoned by representatives of area *D*.[8] Police warn or arrest but do not necessarily refer boys to the juvenile court. The school may suspend disorderly boys but does not expel them. Parents inflict severe penalties. These disapproved underconformers are made to feel that they are on the outer margin of area *C* and in danger of losing their membership in conforming groups. One more misstep and they are out.

Youth in overconforming area *F* are handled somewhat differently. The attitude toward them is one of impatience, sometimes of scorn. They too are made to feel that they are on the outer margin of acceptability. They are socially ostracized, ignored in invitations to parties, and excluded by youth from membership in many

[6]This analysis was drawn from Solomon Kobrin, "Problems in the Development of the Image of the Delinquent in Mass Society," paper presented at the annual meeting of the Illinois Academy of Criminology, Chicago, May 6, 1960.

[7]William W. Wattenberg, "Ten-Year-Old Boys in Trouble," *Child Development*, 28:43–46 (1957); Wattenberg and F. Quiroz, "Follow-up Study of Ten-Year-Old Boys with Police Records," *Journal of Consulting Psychology*, 17:309–13 (1953); Wattenberg, "Eleven-Year-Old Boys in Trouble," *Journal of Educational Psychology*, 44:409–17 (1953); Wattenberg, "Normal Rebellion–or Real Delinquency?" *Child Study*, 34:15–20 (Fall, 1957).

[8]Stanley Schachter, "Deviation, Rejection, and Communication," *Journal of Abnormal and Social Psychology*, 46:190–207 (April, 1951). In an experiment with small groups, the dissenter at first is the object of increased interaction in the effort to restore him to consensus; when this fails, he is rejected.

groups because they would hamper activities. If adults take any action it is in the nature of trying to stimulate them to normal youth activities, or in some cases referring them to psychiatric clinics for diagnosis and treatment of their extremely overconforming behavior.

Youth themselves in either area *B* or *F* feel themselves to be in a marginal position, neither in nor out of the normal social organization. They waver between accepting and adjusting to modal behavior and social norms of the *D* area, and abandoning these norms altogether. They are in contrast to youth in areas *C* and *E* with slightly deviating behavior who feel that they are wanted by groups in area *D*. The more seriously nonconforming youth in areas *B* and *F* feel alternately wanted and rejected by the conforming groups in area *D*. The youth is in an anomalous position and often feels isolated from all groups. He may become involved in a spiral type of interaction in which each move on the part of the representative of area *D* calls for a countermove on his part. If the youth perceives the approach to him as friendly he may respond with friendliness and a spiral will be set up that carries him back into conforming groups. But if he perceives the approach of conforming groups as hostile and rejective, he will respond in kind and the process of alienation will increase until he breaks off all contacts with the various conforming groups. Underconformers show their hostility by stealing, vandalism, and attacks of various sorts. Overconformers show hostility by vociferous criticism of conforming groups.

Areas *B* and *F* are the ones where reclamation of youth must occur if it is to take place at all. Much of what is done with nonconformers is punitive and tends to push a youth further along in the process of alienation from conforming groups. The reverse process might pull him back into conformity. He should be made to feel that he is not a threat to society or permanently outside the approved area of behavior, unworthy of association, even though he has seriously transgressed the codes or social norms.

Areas A and G

Areas *A* and *G* differ from the ones already considered in that they do not represent simply deviation from the central modal behavior and social norms, but rather detachment from social norms and opposition to them. In full development, areas *A* and *G* are *contracultures*, one of which is built up around disregard for the social norms, the other around overcompliance with the norms.

The term "contraculture" is new in sociology and calls for clarification. It is a replacement for the term subculture when applied to sharply deviating types of behavior. The term subculture refers to a body of beliefs and behavior that differs to some extent from the main culture but is not in conflict with it in destructive fashion. The term contraculture has been proposed by J. Milton Yinger to signify certain qualities of detached groups.[9] According to Yinger's analysis, the contraculture

[9] J. Milton Yinger, "Contraculture and Subculture," *American Sociological Review*, 25:625–35 (1960). Albert K. Cohen used the term "delinquent subculture" for essentially the same type of behavior as found in a contraculture.–*Delinquent Boy* (Glencoe, Ill.: Free Press, 1955).

has developed values and modes of behavior that are in conflict with the prevailing social norms (area *D*). The values and behavior of the contraculture are not only different from but are opposed to the social norms.

The logical end result is that people who accept the contraculture tend to organize into small contra-organizations with their own social norms, hierarchy of status positions, roles, and methods of control. A contracultural organization is not only a threat to the social norms but an active disintegrative element in the total social structure. Youth in areas *B* and *F* who are rejected by socially conforming groups may in turn reject these groups and pass into the appropriate contraculture. They are then no longer responsive to either the social norms or the efforts of members of area *D* to reclaim them.

Let us consider area *A*, extreme underconformity. Youth in this area are condemned not only in terms of their behavior but as persons. They are referred to as the "hard core" or "real" delinquents. They are physically exiled at least for a period of time. The school may expel them permanently, the judge may commit them to a correctional school or a prison. Occasionally such a youth may receive the death sentence.

The delinquent youth in the delinquent contraculture for his part rejects the conforming groups of society. He no longer measures his behavior against the expectations of area *D*. His standard of measurement is the small, more restricted, less demanding standard of the delinquent contraculture. Here he may be applauded for stealing, chronic truancy, or fighting. Toward groups in area *D* he is indifferent, hostile, or vengeful.

The effort to draw members of the delinquent contraculture back into area *D* is often doomed to failure. The street workers in New York City and other large cities, who have been successful in re-establishing approved social behavior in many street clubs or gangs, note that they cannot influence the hard-core delinquents who are thoroughly incorporated into a delinquent or youthful criminal gang. The street workers, who represent the values and norms of area *D*, are to the members of the contraculture outsiders and enemies who threaten the little structure of the contraculture.[10] If the street workers or other adults were able to influence individual members of the contraculture, the youth would again have to traverse the disorganizing experiences of area *B* before he could reach the relative security of area *C*. He would meet the scorn and rejection of his own gang-mates without having assurance that members of area *C* or *D* would accept him.

What of the overconforming contraculture? Criticism, ostracism, and rejection of youth in area *F* also drive many of them into withdrawal into small closed groups with their own social organization. Many enter already formed adult contracultures that have values and customs opposed to those of the central culture. As examples we have conscientious objection to war, refusal to salute the flag, rejection of medical care when ill or for ill children, refusal to have children vaccinated, refusal to send children to school for the number of years required by law, celibacy, and com-

[10] *Reaching the Fighting Gang* (New York: New York City Youth Board, 1960).

munity ownership of property. Each of these practices is an exaggeration of some value of social norm contained in the general culture. Each is socially disapproved according to the norms of area *D* or is illegal. They are attacks on the general social values and norms, and if they were to spread throughout the nation they would undermine the social structure seriously. Some overconforming contracultures are content to withdraw into isolation; some attack the general social norms through propaganda or legislation. Others, however, are more militant and occasionally some members physically attack members or symbols of the general culture. (Carrie Nation, smashing the windows of saloons, might be an example of a member of a militant overconforming contraculture.)

Further Applications to Juvenile Delinquency

This analysis of deviancy in the social organization clarifies several problems connected with juvenile delinquency. Three of these will be discussed.

1. The relation of public attitudes to social class.[11] Each social class or other large subcultural group has its own definition of what behavior falls into the area of tolerance, what is disapproved mildly or seriously, and what is condemned. Even when these groups share a basic culture and verbally accept the social norms, their concepts of approved and disapproved behavior may differ. The difference between middle- and lower-class definitions of behavior is especially pertinent, since most school officers and judges represent the middle class and most seriously misbehaving youth come from the lower class. Figure 2 is an attempt to indicate the difference between lower-class and middle-class judgments of what may and may not be tolerated.

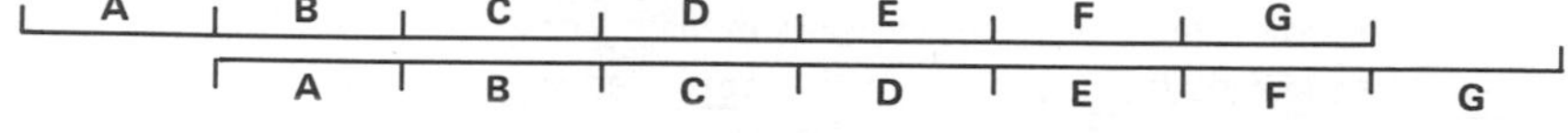

FIGURE 2. Discrepancies Between Lower-class and Middle-class Evaluations of Identical Behavior

The behavior that the lower-class would regard as falling in area *D*, to be accepted with tolerance, might be placed by the middle class in area *C* (barely tolerated behavior), or even in area *B*. Lower-class parents, other adults, and children might regard certain behavior as acceptable, whereas teachers and judges might regard it as unacceptable or reprehensible. An example is the case of the father whose son was in a correctional school for taking a car for joy riding. The father said, "Of course, he took a few cars, but he did not strip them; he just wanted to use them. He is not a bad boy." But in the eyes of the judge, the boy had stolen the cars. This shifting of the class judgments on behavior is especially interesting at the left-hand extreme. The middle class tends to regard certain acts as type *A*, condemned behavior, that the lower class would regard as either *B* or *A*. This gives a wide range of everyday lower-class behavior that receives middle-class condemnation.

[11] Marshall Clinard, "Areas for Research in Deviant Behavior," *Sociology and Social Research*, 42:415–19 (1958). Among areas for research, Clinard suggests differences among social classes.

At the overconforming end of the scale the situation is reversed. Behavior that the middle class regards as acceptable and approved (type *D*), the lower class might regard as overconforming type *E* behavior. The lower class would perhaps regard behavior that is either *F* or *G* by middle-class standards as all extremely overconforming.

These shifts can be illustrated briefly by sexual attitudes and behavior in the two social classes. The casual sex relations of boys and girls that are regarded as natural and normal in some lower-class groups are regarded as underconformity and delinquency by middle-class standards. On the other hand the petting that some middle-class groups regard as an acceptable substitute for intercourse, the lower class would regard as prudish overconformity. At the extreme left, however, the two classes would tend to agree in condemning serious sex deviations, forcible rape, incest, exploitation of little children, and prostitution. At the extreme right, also, there would tend to be agreement, since both classes would probably look with disfavor on universal advocacy of celibacy, for example, as practiced by the Shakers. The argument would not apply to religious organizations where celibacy affects only a small portion of the total religious subculture. Such differences in attitudes of the two social classes lead to misunderstandings. Mishandling of the deviants of one social class by authorities in the other class almost automatically follows from such differences in judgment of the same behavior.

2. The evaluation of the behavior continuum is important in the expectations of behavior for delinquent youth on probation or parole. Usually probation or parole entails laying upon the youth a number of stringent restrictions on behavior. The penalty for disobedience often is commitment or return to correctional school. Such conditions as the following are typical: obedience to parents; regular school attendance; return home at an early hour of the evening, sometimes with the hour specified; and avoidance of disreputable companions and places. At least some of these requirements are overconforming by lower-class standards and virtually impossible for the youth to follow if he is to remain in the lower-class community and not be isolated from his natural social groups. The result is disregard for the requirements and deception on the part of the youth. Probation and parole might more often be successful if the youth were required to meet reasonably conforming lower-class standards.

3. The third point that may be clarified by the behavior continuum is the often repeated statement that all boys are delinquent but only poor boys are pulled into court or committed to correctional schools. It is true, according to several studies, that much delinquent behavior is overlooked and that most middle-class boys and girls at some time have behaved in such a way that they might have been brought into juvenile court. A recent study by Short and Nye compares misbehavior of high-school students with that of correctional school students.[12] Some boys and girls in both groups had committed each of a long list of delinquencies. But it was apparent that the correctional school boys and girls far outstripped the high-school students in the seriousness of their acts and the frequency with which they had committed them. For example, half of high-school boys but almost 100 per cent of correctional-school boys had skipped school; a fourth of high-school boys but 85 per cent of correctional-school boys had skipped school more than once or twice. Or, take a more serious offense, the theft of something worth fifty dollars or more. Five per cent of high-school boys compared with 90 per cent of correctional-school boys

[12] James F. Short, Jr., and F. Ivan Nye, "Extent of Unrecorded Juvenile Delinquency, Tentative Conclusions," *Journal of Criminal Law, Criminology and Police Science,* 49:296–309 (1958).

had taken things of this value. Almost no high-school boys compared with almost half of the correctional-school boys had committed this offense more than once or twice. An examination of the entire set of data leads to the conclusion that the high-school students had confined their delinquencies to acts within the area of tolerance of the community, whereas the correctional-school boys were guilty of behavior of types *B* or *A*, highly disapproved and regarded as threatening to the social organization.

Conclusion

In conclusion, this paper has attempted to state a hypothesis whereby behavior may be placed in a continuum running from an underconforming contraculture through various degrees of disapproved behavior to normal conformity and then through stages of overconforming behavior to an overconforming contraculture. The reaction of the normally conforming segment of the population to deviations varies in severity according to the threat posed to the social norms by either under- or overconformity. Minor deviants usually are drawn back into conformity. Serious deviants often are treated so severely that they are alienated and withdraw into a contraculture.

Section II

Interconnections: Positions Within a Differentiated Society and Forms of Criminal and Delinquent Behavior

Introductory Remarks

Within the population of American society obviously many differences exist. There are social and biological differences–for example, social class, religion, ethnicity, race, age, sex; functional differences–for example, occupational, family, and associational roles; differences in residential patterns–for example, farm, rural, slum, suburb; and differences in proscriptions and prescriptions concerning how individuals should act.

It would be expected that these differences would promote variations in behavior, and available research documents this. For example, we find that differences in interests and in experiences are influenced by education; differences in style of living are influenced by income; and differences in participation and involvements are influenced by occupation, neighborhood, and race. When groups of people possessing many similar attributes cluster in a restrictive web of interaction, sociocultural[1] *distinctions (e.g., occupational, neighborhood, ethnic and peer groups) may be nurtured.*

Although American society possesses consensus regarding some values and norms, their meanings will receive different emphases because socialization to them primarily occurs within these varied sociocultural groupings. Values, norms, and social relations unique from other groups may also develop as one sociocultural grouping responds to problems of adjustment peculiar to itself.

Because of their distinctiveness in values, norms, and social relations, specific forms and patterns of crime and delinquency may readily emerge in a given sociocultural grouping. In other words, in a given sociocultural arrangement, specific forms of deviance are facilitated by existant pressures and tolerances, by the legitimate and illegitimate opportunities available, and by the perceptions and attitudes nurtured in that setting.[2]

For example, in middle-class neighborhoods with a stable opportunity system, organized criminal enterprises (prostitution, gambling, handling of stolen goods by "fences") could not easily exist; whereas, some slum areas are not organizationally equipped to prevent these activities. There are yet other areas in which criminal and

[1] Refer to both cultural orientations (e.g., values, goals, norms) and to established patterns of social interaction.

[2] The readings in this section deal with these points in detail.

conventional groups tolerate one another, and in many ways integrate their political, commercial, and social activities.[3]

Within other kinds of sociocultural arrangements persons of upper-level occupations and social classes similarly perpetuate forms of crimes[4] *unique to their setting. Of course these settings, having alternate means for deviance, would have an almost complete absence of traditional offenders such as burglars or robbers. Nor would there be predatory and conflict subcultural activities which do exist in other settings. The reading in this section by Gilbert Geis, "White Collar Crime: The Heavy Electrical Equipment Antitrust Cases of 1961," deals with price-fixing conspiracy. This reading illustrates how pressures, tolerances, and opportunities facilitate price-fixing, and indicates the processes of learning and patterns of association necessary in the commission of this deviance.*

There are yet other forms of criminal behavior not uniformly distributed throughout the American society. Notwithstanding student violence, the empirical evidence is abundant that violence (e.g., murder, forcible rape, aggravated assault, riots) varies a great deal with race, ethnicity, occupational level, social class and neighborhood.[5] *For example, in some communities mostly all incidences of murder can be attributed to blacks or to several neighborhoods. These types of violence rarely occur in the upper ends of the occupational and social class scales.*

Most youth during their adolescent years have from time to time engaged in various minor delinquent activities. However, the career type delinquents emerge from the lower social classes and specific neighborhoods. The career type is distinquishable from other youth by greater frequency and seriousness of offenses committed. Career type delinquents may begin with vandalism and minor theft and through progressive stages advance to serious larcencies, burglaries, robberies, and so on. Usually middle-class youth begin and end their delinquencies with vandalism and minor theft.[6]

Much of the literature in the past viewed both criminal and delinquent behavior as unitary terms. Because of the diversity of behaviors included within the terms crime *and* delinquency, *increased attention is being directed to sociocultural distinctions in the development of forms and patterns.*

[3]The reader may know personally of the existence of such an area.

[4]Examples are illegal rebates, bribes, tax evasion, monopolies, embezzlement, doctor-abortionist, fee-splitting, unfair labor practices, black-marketeering, misrepresentation in advertising, price-rigging, graft, etc.

[5]For most types of violence, this would apply equally to victims.

[6]Although middle-class youth do engage in vandalism and minor theft, it is usually not a frequent and patterned activity. The less visible "auto-sex-alcohol" behavioral complex within some middle-class youth groups is patterned and recurring.

8. Deviance and Social Differentiation

Marshall B. Clinard

Social Norms

A major interest of sociologists is the definition of the norms involved and the differences in society's tolerance of various types of norm violations. All deviations from social norms are by no means always disapproved. Inventions, for example, represent violations of norms which may be strongly approved. Other violations may be tolerated, and still others may be mildly disapproved.

Deviant behaviour consists of those violations of norms which are of a sufficient degree to exceed the general tolerance limit of society (Clinard, 1957). This means, of course, that the norms which constitute deviant behaviour are not necessarily the same in various cultures, nor are they the same in a given culture over a period of time. Homosexual behaviour, prostitution, or drunkenness do not constitute deviant behaviour in some societies today. Some Scandinavian countries, for example, have such different interpretations of sexual norms that many delinquent and criminal acts in American society would not be regarded as such there. Changed attitudes in the United States over the past fifty years toward tobacco smoking by juveniles and young adults are an indication of how deviant behaviour can be redefined in time. Formerly there was great preoccupation with smoking among younger groups, laws were passed forbidding it, and often they were strictly enforced. Smoking was thought to be related to a variety of other social problems.

In studying deviant behaviour the sociologist is interested in having the norms involved stated fairly explicitly. On this basis, certainly, one cannot assume that there is a "non-conformist personality type," for such would depend upon the assumption that all norms were violated regardless of their nature. For that reason most sociologists are also sceptical of loose terms like "socially maladjusted," "anti-social," "emotionally disturbed," "abnormal," "mentally ill," "sexually deviant," and even an omnibus category like "delinquency." For example, an operational definition of delinquent norms appears to be more useful than the inclusion of undefined areas of behaviour. The definition of excessive drinking and alco-

Reprinted from "Contributions of Sociology to Understanding Deviant Behaviour," *The British Journal of Criminology* (October 1962), pp. 110–129, by permission of the Institute for the Study and Treatment of Delinquency, London, and the author.

holism involves a deviation from the norms of drinking behaviour within a culture and dependence on alcohol in the life organisation of the individual. Such a definition includes the amount of alcohol consumed, the purpose and meaning of the drinking, the social handicap to the individual, and the degree of inability to refrain from excessive drinking. Even the norms involved in mental disorder need to be so stated that we can determine with some precision who is mentally ill and who is not, whom we are to treat and whom not to treat. Even here an operational definition may turn out to be more satisfactory than the usual vague, unprecise and value-laden definition of "mental health" (Redlich, 1957).

Sociological studies on a broad front of strongly disapproved norm violations have shown marked differences between the official visibility and the actual extent of norm violations. Social visibility varies according to the type of deviant behaviour, as well as the sex, age, or social class to which a person belongs. Some deviations, like kidnapping or murder, may become highly visible. Others, like homosexuality, pre-marital sexual relations, or drunkenness which is not public may be only slightly visible. White collar crime, *i.e.*, among higher status groups committed in connection with their occupations, has a very low social visibility. Sociological studies using broader samples have revealed extensive violations of many norms among groups which had been thought not to have many deviants. Such studies have also shown that only a small part of most deviant behaviour becomes officially recognised, and that it often may represent biased samples of delinquents, sex deviants, criminals, alcoholics or mental patients.

Sub-Cultures and Social Groups

The sociologist is particularly concerned with the effect of the culture, sub-cultures, and group relationships on deviant behaviour (see, for example, Mannheim, 1955). The term culture refers to normative standards of behaviour, and the sociologist is interested in how the conflicting norms and values of the general culture and sub-cultures are related to deviant behaviour. Society or social groups refer to the interaction and relationships among human beings, and the sociologist is interested in the effect of all types of such group relationships.

The family, while important, is only one of many groups which may be related to deviant behaviour either in terms of norms or social relationships. Among others are neighbourhoods, schools, gangs, cliques, occupations, and religious groups. Alcoholism, for example, represents far more than simply a product of anxieties or personality traits left over from early family interaction or other childhood experiences. Alcoholism implies changes in the nature of interpersonal relationships with others, in attitudes toward drinking, in social roles and in conception of self. This process may take as long as fifteen or twenty years. Some interesting sociological findings support the conclusion that the groups to which a person belongs are related to his excessive drinking, and that alcoholism may be largely a product of the difficulties arising from the excessive drinking itself (Clinard, 1957, pp. 306–307). Group drinking and cultural factors play an important part in determining who becomes an excessive drinker. In modern society there seem to be pronounced differences in excessive drinking according to the drinking habits of one's companions as shown by differences in the incidence of alcoholism by sex, social class, occupation, religious and ethnic affiliation. Jews and Italians, for example, have a low rate of alcoholism (Lolli, 1958; Snyder, 1958).

Large modern societies consist of a variety of sub-cultures and social groups, each often with its own set of norms and values not only as to what constitutes proper conduct but also even as to the goals of life itself. Sub-cultures, like cultures, tell a person what he must do, ought to do, should do, may do, and must not do (Williams, 1954, p. 23). Cohen (1955, p. 59) has suggested that sub-cultures emerge in a highly differentiated society when, in effective interaction with one another, a number of persons have similar problems. Sociological research has shown the existence of pronounced differences in normative structures of sub-cultures involving persons of different age groups, social classes, occupations, racial, religious and ethnic groups, neighbourhoods and regions. In addition, there are some even more limited sub-cultures such as those among teenage gangs, prostitutes, alcoholics, drug addicts, homosexuals, professional and organised criminals. Even institutions for the treatment of deviants, such as prisons, are actually sub-cultures with their own social systems (Clemmer, 1960; Cressey, 1961; Cloward *et al.,* 1960). In fact, so diverse are the norms of most large societies that there are probably only a few norms which are accepted as binding on all persons.

This means three things: (1) that within a modern society there may be almost as pronounced differences among various groups about the norms of accepted behaviour as there are between large cultures; (2) that to explain logically how members of certain deviant groups in a society come to act the way they do can be explained in the same way, for example, that an Eskimo learns culturally to become an Eskimo; and (3) that when we speak of the norms of a given family we are likely to be referring actually to the social class, occupational, or other sub-cultural group to which the family belongs.

Some, of course, will raise the question, and correctly so, that intimate contact with deviant sub-cultures does not affect all persons in the same manner. Sociological research has suggested that the explanation for this lies in the fact that, first, no deviant sub-culture exists as a closed system for all its members, for even in a high delinquency area they are exposed to other norms. Second, the self-conception of the individual may serve as an insulator against participation in deviant norms. Recent sociological studies of delinquency, for example, indicate that the conception of self as a "good boy" is one of the chief insulators in areas of high delinquency (Reckless *et al.,* 1957). Such a self-conception is not only acquired in the family, but also through the school and neighbourhood.

Another useful concept for explaining differential behaviour is whether group membership constitutes a reference group to the person. Membership in a group has little meaning for deviant behaviour unless the individual comes to identify with it. (For a discussion of differential response, see Clinard, 1959.)

Recognition of sub-cultures in a society seems to have further implications. Rather than seeing a society, neighbourhood, or family as "disorganised" we come to see that the issue is one of conflicting norms. The presence of gambling, the wide use of alcohol, patronage of pubs or taverns, or greater freedom in sexual relations do not necessarily mean that these conditions are naturally "bad" or "disorganised." The slum sex code may be as highly organised and normative regarding pre-marital relations in one direction as the middle-class sex code is in the other (Whyte, 1943[a], pp. 24-32).

Another criticism of the loose use of the term "disorganisation" is that actually modern society consists of competing systems of organised sub-cultures. Many sub-cultures of deviant behaviour such as delinquent gangs, homosexuality, organised crime, prostitution, and white collar crime including political corruption, may be highly organised. The norms and values of the slums are highly organised, as Whyte (1943[b]) has shown in his *Street Corner Society*. Finally, as several sociologists have suggested, it is possible that a variety of sub-cultures may contribute, through their diversity, to the unity or integration of a society rather than weaken it (Williams, 1957, pp. 1–8).

Class Structure

Modern societies are socially differentiated in many ways; probably no differentiation is greater than the variations in behaviour among the social classes based on occupation, income, residence and way of life. Studies of class structure have shown how value orientation, patterns of family life, and behaviour in general not only represent but serve actually to integrate class ways of life. So different are the social norms and other behaviour of, for example, various American social classes, that the differences in behaviour are probably actually greater than between the accepted conduct of members of the same social class but, say, from some other Western European or even Asiatic societies. Kinsey and others, for example, have shown the existence of great class differences in sex behaviour and even the nature of the sex relation itself. Studies by Green (1946, pp. 31–41), Davis (1955), and others have shown that even family-rearing patterns of the lower and middle classes are greatly different. The use of physical punishment is an acceptable form of disciplining children in lower-class families. The middle-class boy is more likely to be whipped if he fights; the lower-class boy if he does not, or if he loses. Studies have shown great differences in the norms, behaviour, and family structure of teen-age youth by social class (Hollingshead, 1949).

...

The rates for crime in general are higher in lower-class areas. Nearly all crimes of violence such as murder are committed by lower-class adults, and the nature of lower-class sub-culture and family life seems to offer an explanation of the origin of most murders (Bullock, 1955; Wolfgang, 1958).

Sociological studies have shown the existence of wide-scale violations of law by persons in the upper and middle classes, politicians, government officials, businessmen, labour union leaders, doctors and lawyers (Sutherland, 1949; Clinard, 1952). These findings indicate that general theories of the relation of crime to poverty, bad housing or low intelligence have little validity. Moreover, sociological research suggests that it is hard to see how psychiatric or psychoanalytic theory can explain most crime in the face of evidence of widespread violations of law among all classes and the existence generally of a low order of business, political and labour ethics in many societies.

Probably in no area has social class shown more pronounced differences than in mental disorder. Faris and Dunham (1939) showed this years ago in their Chicago study of the residences of public and private mental patients. More recently, Hollingshead, a sociologist, and Redlich, a psychiatrist (1958), have shown great differences in the relative incidence and nature of neuroses and psychoses by social class (see also Myers and Roberts, 1959). Schizophrenia was nine times more prevalent among those of the lowest social class. There were even class differences in the type of the neuroses.

The incidence of suicide is related to occupation and social class. This has been established by many studies including Sainsbury's (1955) study of London suicides.

• • •

Role Theory and Self-Conception

Deviant behaviour, like all human behaviour, develops out of a process of social interaction and communication with other persons. The study of social roles, organised systems of behaviour expectations and attitudes, and particularly the concepts of role playing and role taking are especially important theoretical tools in the study of deviant behaviour (Lement, 1951; Clinard, 1957; Bernard, 1957). In the course of the day the activities of a human being are the performance of a series of roles, the behaviour for which he has largely learned from the groups to which he belongs. The diversity of social roles, provided by the variety of sub-cultures and urbanism, is an important factor in the extent of certain types of social deviation in a society. Much of delinquent and criminal behaviour represents the acting out of roles. Moreover, because of the diversity of roles in modern urban society and their lack of co-ordination, the responses of persons to certain situations may often fail to conform to what is expected. A person's evaluation of his role and the evaluation of others may not always be the same. Such role conflicts become important in the analysis of mental disorder and the problems of older persons. Even minority discrimination is a problem of role conflict.

Self-conception is an important corollary in the sociological and social psychological analysis of roles. Self-conception is the image in our minds of the "self" (ourselves) that we try to enhance or defend. It is when individuals have their behaviour socially defined and identify with this definition that they take on behaviour patterns and attitudes characteristic of a definite deviant type. When deviant behaviour is consciously incorporated into the self-image this identification itself is a motive for further behaviour. Societal reaction may reinforce the deviant's self-image.

Whether of deviants or non-deviants, self-conception does not appear to be a static entity fixed as the result of family experience. It can be modified throughout life. The self-conception of a mentally ill person, alcoholic, or suicide is the product not only of the reactions of the father and mother, but of wife and husband, employer, neighbours, other relatives and friends. The self-conception of some types of deviants is the product of the sub-cultures to which they belong. The identification and label, for example, of "delinquent," "criminal," "neurotic," "psychotic," "alcoholic," or "drug addict" may later result in serious consequences on self-conception. Certainly minor deviations, such as certain acts of delinquency, may become intensified through this labelling process.

• • •

Urbanism

The rapid spread of urbanism, or the "mass society," has contributed a great deal to the increase in deviant behaviour in the contemporary world (Rose, 1954). By urbanism is meant a way of life accompanied by characteristics such as individualism, rapid cultural change, emphasis on materialism, culture conflict, and, above all, a decline in intimate communication and informal social control. These characteristics have generally accompanied urbanisation, which refers to population concentration, and which, in turn, is largely but not exclusively a product of industrialisation. Urbanism is not always associated with urbanisation, however, for rural areas are increasingly displaying these characteristics. Conversely, one may have enclaves within large cities which display little of the characteristics of urbanism, and cities themselves may vary in the degree to which they have urban characteristics.

The process is transforming social relations all over the world. Two out of three Americans and four out of five persons in Great Britain now live in urban areas, some of them of immense size. In the Russell Sage Foundation volume, *Industrial Society and Social Welfare,* it was recognised that industrial-urban society is the central stage for an increasing amount of the social problems of mankind and that "These massive changes in American society are the major determinants of the social problems which create the demand for social welfare services" (Wilensky and Lebeaux, 1958, p. 17).

• • •

Most of all, urban life has fractured much of the conventional family system and has, instead, brought new groupings mainly on the basis of age, occupation and the like. Urbanism has made possible the growth of teenage subcultures which are often at variance with family, school and adult norms. This conflict, as yet, has not been as great in the middle class but appears to be on the increase. To these effects of urbanism can be traced a great deal of the explanation for contemporary delinquency among youths. Much teenage delinquency in an urban society probably represents a definition of excitement and a means of gaining status among the peer group (Lowson, 1960; Bloch and Neiderhoffer, 1958).

The problem of an urban society such as ours can be illustrated by studies of the extent and effect of contemporary mobility on deviant behaviour. According to estimates based on contemporary trends, a worker in his lifetime today in America is likely to change his residence eight times and two or three of them would involve an entirely different community (Bogue, 1957). Such mobility, even within a community, often means a loss of relatives and neighbours. Children and adults are faced with new norms and social roles, as well as the reconciliation of old norms and roles with new ones. Personal reputation comes to mean less to the mobile person as the influence of personal social controls declines. Controls become more secondary, the urban family comes to be, as Reuben Hill has termed it, "the lonely family."

• • •

Studies of many kinds of deviant behaviour have shown the pronounced effects of urbanisation and urbanism. Rates for delinquency and most crimes, for example, vary directly with the degree of urbanisation of the community. With few exceptions the same is true for rates of alcoholism, suicide and many other forms of deviant behaviour.

REFERENCES

BERNARD, J. (1957). *Social Problems at Midcentury.* New York: Dryden Press.

BLOCH, H. A. and NIEDERHOFFER, A. (1958). *The Gang: A Study in Adolescent Behaviour.* New York: Philosophical Library.

BOGUE, D. (1957). "Residential Mobility and Migration of Workers." In W. Hober (Ed.). *Manpower in the United States.* New York: Dryden Press.

BULLOCK, H. A. (1955). "Urban Homicide in Theory and Fact." *Journal of Criminal Law, Criminology and Police Science 45,* 565–575.

CLEMMER, D. (1960). *The Prison Community.* Revised edition. New York: Rinehart & Co.

CLINARD, M. B. (1952). *The Black Market: A Study of White Collar Crime.* New York: Rinehart & Co.

CLINARD, M. B. (1957). *Sociology of Deviant Behaviour.* New York: Rinehart & Co.

CLINARD, M. B. (1959). "Criminological Research." In Merton *et al. Sociology Today.* New York: Basic Books.

CLOWARD, R. A. *et al.* (1960). *Theoretical Studies in Social Organisation of the Prison.* New York: Social Science Research Council, Pamphlet 15.

COHEN, A. K. (1955). *Delinquent Boys: The Culture of the Gang.* Glencoe, Ill.: Free Press.

CRESSEY, D. (Ed.) (1961). *The Prison: Studies in Institution Organisation and Change.* New York: Rinehart & Co.

DAVIS, K. (1955). "Mental Hygiene and the Social Structure." In A. Rose (ed.). *Mental Health and Mental Disorder.* New York: W. W. Norton & Co.

FARIS, R. A., and DUNHAM, H. W. (1939). *Mental Disorders in Urban Areas.* Chicago: Univ. of Chicago Press.

GREEN, A. W. (1946). "The Middle-Class Male Child and Neurosis." *Amer. Sociol. Review 11,* 31–41.

HOLLINGSHEAD, A. B. (1949). *Elmtown's Youth.* New York: J. Wiley & Co.

HOLLINGSHEAD, A. B., and REDLICH, F. (1958). *Social Class and Mental Illness.* New York: John Wiley & Sons.

LEMERT, E. H. (1951). *Social Pathology.* New York: McGraw-Hill Book Co.

LOLLI, G., *et al.* (1958). *Alcohol in Italian Culture.* Glencoe, Ill.: Free Press.

LOWSON, D. (1960). "Delinquency in Industrial Areas." *Brit. J. Criminol. 1,* 50–56.

MANNHEIM, H. (1955). *Group Problems in Crime and Punishment.* London: Routledge and Kegan Paul.

MYERS, J. K., and ROBERTS, B. H. (1959). *Family and Class Dynamics in Mental Illness.* New York: John Wiley & Sons.

RECKLESS, W., *et al.* (1957). "Self-component in Potential Delinquency and Non-Delinquency," *Amer. Social. Rev. 22,* 566–570.

REDLICH, F. (1957). "The Concept of Health in Psychiatry." In A. H. Leighton *et al.* (ed.). *Explorations in Social Psychiatry.* New York: Basic Books.

ROSE, A. (1954). "The Problem of the Mass Society." *In Theory and Methods in the Social Sciences.* Minneapolis: Univ. of Minnesota Press.

SAINSBURY, P. (1955). *Suicide in London.* London: Chapman & Hall.

SNYDER, C. R. (1958). *Alcohol and the Jews.* Glencoe, Ill.: Free Press.

SUTHERLAND, E. H. (1949). *White Collar Crime.* New York: Dryden Press.

WHYTE, W.F. (1943[a]). "A Slum Sex Code." *Amer. J. Sociol. 49,* 24–32.

WHYTE, W. F. (1943[b]). *Street Corner Society.* Chicago: Univ. of Chicago Press.

WILENSKY, H., and LEBEAUX, C. N. (1958). *Industrial Society and Social Welfare.* New York: Russell Sage Foundation.

WILLIAMS, R., Jr. (1954). *American Society.* New York: A. A. Knopf.

WILLIAMS, R., Jr. (1957). "Unity and Diversity in Modern America." *Social Forces 35,* 1–8.

WOLFGANG, M. E. (1958). *Patterns in Criminal Homicide.* Philadelphia: Pennsylvania Press.

9. Ecology of Crime and Delinquency

The President's Commission on Law Enforcement and Administration of Justice

One of the most striking facts about crime, especially in the big cities, is the consistent fashion in which the rates for different types of crime vary from one area to another.* It is remarkable that these rates in any one city stay as steady as they do, allowing for the changes in the population from year to year. It is also surprising that the pattern of relationships between high- and low-rate crime areas changes so slowly.

• • •

The first systematic and sustained effort to investigate the regularities in the variation of crime within a large city in the United States started in Chicago in 1921.[1] This analysis of the delinquency areas of Chicago by Clifford Shaw and his associates set off a wave of studies in other cities and a spirited debate about the interpretation of the findings, which is still being fed by new studies using different techniques, different measures, and competing theories. This development has been greatly aided by the growth and increasing sophistication of the field of human ecology which involves the study of the relationship of human individuals and groups to their physical, social, and cultural environment by geographers, demographers, and other social scientists.[2]

Reprinted from "Crime and the Inner City," *Task Force Report: Crime and Its Impact–An Assessment,* a Report by the President's Commission on Law Enforcement and Administration of Justice (Washington: Government Printing Office, 1967), ch. 4, pp. 60–76.

*Editor's Note: The criminal behaviors reported and adjudicated reflect the actions of authorities and the concerns of Americans. Although the data reviewed in this selection are the forms of criminal behavior most likely to occur in lower income groups, it does not overstate the criminal behavior of the lower income groups. It does, however, understate the particular forms of criminal behavior committed by upper income groups. These latter crimes are not systematically detected or recorded, not often criminally adjudicated, and not generally perceived by most Americans as "real" crime. This state of affairs is unlike some countries (particularly U.S.S.R.) where punishment for these forms of crimes is quite severe. See Articles 1, 2, 13, 14, 15, 36 and the Introductory Remarks to Sections I and II for further comments concerning crimes and delinquencies of the upper income groups.

[1]Clifford R. Shaw, "Delinquency Areas" (Chicago: The University of Chicago Press, 1929), p. ix.

[2]Amos H. Hawley, "Human Ecology" (New York: The Ronald Press, 1950).

Patterns of Crime Variation in City Areas

The National Commission on Law Observance and Enforcement published the second major ecological study of the Institute of Juvenile Research in Chicago in 1931.[3] This study was of particular significance since it demonstrated that the characteristic patterns for delinquency rates in Chicago could also be found in Philadelphia, Richmond, Cleveland, Birmingham, Denver, and Seattle. Three of their major findings about the distribution of delinquency rates have been repeatedly borne out in subsequent studies, subject only to local and usually accountable variations:[4]

"1. Juvenile delinquents are not distributed uniformly over the City of Chicago but tend to be concentrated in areas adjacent to the central business district and to heavy industrial areas.

"2. There are wide variations in the rates of delinquents between areas in Chicago ...

"3. The rates of delinquents tend to vary inversely with distance from the center of the City..."

These patterns in the distribution of delinquency rates have stood up remarkably well under tests in many cities throughout the country and have also been found in Mexico City and Honolulu.[5] ... The study in Honolulu found that the distribution of arrests for vice followed most closely the distribution for delinquency court cases while suicide cases were much more widely dispersed than the other two series.[6]

A much more intensive and detailed study of the distribution of different offenses known to the police and the residences of arrested persons has recently been completed in Seattle.[7] The offenses known to the police were analyzed for the 3-year period 1949–51, and a second series based on persons arrested by the police was drawn for the 2-year period 1950–51.

When the crime rates for the various census tracts of the city were correlated with each other, certain offenses could be grouped together because they showed very similar patterns of distribution in the city. The closest degree of correspondence (intercorrelations over 0.90) was found in the spatial distribution of drunkenness, disorderly conduct, vagrancy, lewdness, petty larcenies and robbery (highway and car). Another closely related clustering of offenses (intercorrelations over 0.87) was found for burglary of residence by day and night and check fraud.[8]

...

[3] Clifford R. Shaw and Henry D. McKay, "Social Factors in Juvenile Delinquency" Report on the Causes of Crime (Washington, D.C.: National Commission on Law Observance and Enforcement, 1931), pp. 2, 13.

[4] Id. at pp. 383–385.

[5] Andrew W. Lind, "Some Ecological Patterns of Community Disorganization in Honolulu," American Journal of Sociology, 36:206–220, September 1930. Norman S. Hayner, "Criminogenic Zones in Mexico City," American Sociological Review, 11:429–438, August 1946.

[6] Andrew W. Lind, id. at p. 212.

[7] Calvin F. Schmid, "Urban Crime Areas: Part I," American Sociological Review, 25:527–542, August 1960, and Calvin F. Schmid, "Urban Crime Areas: Part II," American Sociological Review, 25: 655–678, October 1960.

[8] Id. at pp. 529–534.

When the city is divided into six 1-mile zones radiating out from the city center, the usual pattern of high rates in the central zones and low rates on the outskirts is shown for most crimes.[9] As one might expect, this is most pronounced for the crime of embezzlement since the rates are based on place of occurrence of offense. The rate of embezzlement is 18.3 for zone I and 0.03 for zone VI. Bicycle theft is the only offense which runs counter to this pattern, showing a rate of 65.3 in zone I and 149.5 in zone VI. It should be noted, however, that the differences between the inner and outer zones for such offenses as peeping tom, obscene telephone calls, indecent liberties, and carnal knowledge are relatively small.[10]

Distribution of Juvenile Offenses. Most of the studies dealing with juvenile delinquents show spatial distributions in the city only according to the total delinquency rate or occasionally the rate of truancy. A recent study in Madison, Wis., however, divides the city into three relatively distinct areas and provides information on the types of acts by juveniles which resulted in a contact with the police.[11] A police contact in this study meant any interaction between a Madison police officer and a juvenile which resulted in a report being filed with the Crime Prevention Bureau of the police department.

The distribution of different types of acts by juveniles resulting in a police contact are shown distributed among the three districts of Madison in table 1 according to the place of residence of the offenders. The rates are for the period 1950–55 and are based on school estimates of the juvenile population age 6 to 18. They reflect the results of a sample of 1,876 juveniles whose records showed a total of 4,554 acts or police contacts, an average of 2.47 acts per person. The west district in table 1 is an area of high income, middle and upper class residents. The east district is composed of laboring and middle class residents of moderate income, and the central zone has residents of the working class and lower working class with generally low incomes.

Comparison of Area Offense Rates and Area Offender Rates. In describing the distribution of crime and delinquency rates by city areas, one can calculate the area rates on the basis of where the offense took place or where the offender resided. These procedures produce different pictures of the distribution of the crime problem. ... This type of comparison has been made possible by use of the data on offenses known to the police and on arrests by the police developed by Schmid and his associates in Seattle.

... the central segment and the remainder of the city differ considerably in the rate with which they contribute either criminal opportunities or criminals for different types of offenses. For example, 41 percent of the persons arrested for robbery resided in the central segment, while 63 percent of the robberies occurred there. This suggests that some robbers seek the greater opportunity and anonymity of the cen-

[9] Id. at p. 666.

[10] Id. at p. 666.

[11] Lyle W. Shannon, "Types and Patterns of Delinquency in a Middle-sized City," The Journal of Research in Crime and Delinquency, v. 1:53–66, January 1964.

tral segment when their area of residence is some place else. This may also be true of the crime of sodomy, since 64 percent of the offenses are reported in the central segment but only 37 percent of those arrested for this offense reside there....

TABLE 1. Delinquent Acts Resulting in Police-Juvenile Contacts by Zone of City: Madison, Wis. 1950–55[1]

Acts	*Average Acts per 1,000 Juveniles per Year*			
	Central	*West*	*East*	*Total City*
Incorrigible, runaway	34.10	13.55	29.97	26.65
Disorderly conduct	31.82	14.05	22.40	23.65
Contact–Suspicion, investigation, information	25.92	6.47	17.80	17.61
Theft	23.35	4.37	13.30	14.61
Traffic (operation)	16.45	11.45	12.37	13.73
Vagrancy	19.77	4.27	12.90	13.03
Liquor	9.17	1.65	7.77	6.49
Burglary	4.77	.67	4.17	3.36
Auto theft	4.15	1.77	2.85	3.06
Sex offenses	2.13	.20	1.23	1.27
Traffic (parking)	1.27	.87	.90	1.06
Truancy	1.12	.47	1.00	.91
Assault	.75	.00	.40	.42
Other delinquent acts	10.08	3.04	6.02	6.76
Total delinquent acts	185.05	63.13	133.08	132.65

[1] Sample of City of Madison juveniles from files of Crime Prevention Bureau, 1950–55.

SOURCE: Lyle W. Shannon, "Types and Patterns of Delinquency in a Middle-sized City," The Journal of Research in Crime and Delinquency, v. 1, January 1964, p. 60–62.

• • •

The degree to which the mobility of the offender varies for different offenses is addressed more directly in recent data reported to the Task Force from Seattle.[12] This information from the statistical bureau of the Seattle Police Department compares the census tract of occurrence of the offense with the tract of residence of the offender for 19,327 persons arrested in Seattle in 1965. In table 2 is shown for different offense categories whether the offender resided in the same tract in which he committed his offense, whether he resided elsewhere in the city, or whether he resided outside the city. In general, offenders are much more likely to move out of their neighborhood in connection with crimes against property than in crimes against persons. ...

These findings corroborate the general conclusions drawn from a study of resi-

[12] Albert J. Reiss, Jr., "Place of Residence of Arrested Persons Compared With Place Where the Offense Charged in Arrest Occurred For Part I and II Offenses," A report to the President's Commission on Law Enforcement and the Administration of Criminal Justice, (min:co) 1966.

dence of offender and place of occurrence of offense carried out in Indianapolis in 1931.[13] The data, based on all cases disposed of in the Marion County Criminal Court in 1930, made it possible to measure on a map the distance from the center of the residence census tract to the center of the offense census tract for the 481 cases shown by offense category in table 3. The mobility patterns for different of-

TABLE 2. Comparison of Place of Offense and Residence of Offender for Parts I and II Crimes, Seattle, 1965

Offense Charged on Arrest	*Residence of Arrested Offender (percent)*			
	Same Tract	*Elsewhere Seattle*	*Outside Seattle*	*Unknown*
Part I offenses:				
Forcible rape	15	69	16	0
Assault to rape, attempts	54	38	8	0
Robbery	29	53	12	5
Aggravated assault	35	47	14	4
Other assaults	42	45	10	3
Burglary, breaking or entering	26	59	12	2
Larceny, theft	13	68	14	6
Auto theft	13	68	17	2
Part II offenses:				
Arson	40	57	3	0
Forgery and counterfeiting	20	59	17	5
Fraud	19	47	28	6
Embezzlement	18	45	28	9
Stolen property buying, receiving, possessing	27	54	16	4
Vandalism	27	60	12	1
Weapons: carrying, possessing, etc.	15	65	14	5
Prostitution and commercialized vice	34	59	3	4
Other sex offenses	30	51	16	3
Narcotic drug law	41	43	11	4
Gambling	14	69	9	8
Offenses against family and children	67	33	0	0
Driving under the influence	13	64	20	4
Liquor laws	38	43	13	6
Drunkenness	33	48	6	12
Disorderly conduct	27	55	12	6
Vagrancy	26	61	4	9

SOURCE: Special Tabulation of 1965 Arrests: Seattle Police Department Cited in Reiss, supra, note 12, table 1, pp. 13–21.

[13] Clyde R. White, "The Relation of Felonies to Environmental Factors in Indianapolis," Social Forces, v. 10–498–509, May 1962.

fenses do not seem greatly different in Seattle 35 years later, though the data are not exactly comparable.

...

TABLE 3. Distance[1] Between Offender's Residence and Place of Offense for Specific Crimes in Indianapolis, 1930[1]

Crime	*Number of Cases*	*Mean Distance[2] (miles)*
Against person	37	.84
Rape	11	1.52
Assault and battery	16	.91
Manslaughter	9	.11
Against property	444	1.72
Auto banditry	9	3.43
Embezzlement	21	2.79
Robbery	20	2.14
Vehicle taking	76	1.77
Burglary	121	1.76
Grand larceny	117	1.53
Obtaining money falsely	38	1.47
Petty larceny	25	1.42

[1]Felonies disposed of by the Marion County Criminal Court during the calendar year 1930.

[2]The distance from the middle of the residence census tract to the middle of the offense census tract.

SOURCE: Clyde R. White, "The Relation of Felonies to Environmental Factors in Indianapolis," Social Forces, v. 10, May 1932, p. 507.

Trends in the Crime and Delinquency Rates of City Areas. As we have seen, the studies of different types of crime and delinquency rates have established that these rates follow a fairly consistent pattern in their distribution throughout the geographical areas of the city, and that this pattern shows a considerable amount of similarity among American cities. A further question concerns the stability of this pattern of crime rates from one time period to another. Do these rates show any trends? Do changes in the area rates alter the relative standing of these areas in the total crime distribution pattern of the city? Do the higher crime rate areas remain the higher crime rate areas?

...

The answer appears to be that the general pattern of distribution of crime and delinquency rates among the various areas of the city remains the same, even though some of these rates may change drastically in a few areas where major shifts in land use and population composition have occurred. This conclusion rests, however, on relatively few studies that have been carried out in the same fashion, for the same city, and at different time periods. ...

The most fully developed time series of the geographic distribution of crime and delinquency rates in a city are those assembled for Chicago.[14] Table 4 shows the rates for different series of delinquents who were referred to the Juvenile Court of Cook County over a 40-year period from 1900 to 1940. The rates are shown for the city of Chicago, which is divided into five 2-mile concentric zones with the focal point of the zones located in the center of the central business district. Though the *absolute* sizes of the rates differ, the same *relative* tendency for the rates to be highest in zone 1 (the central district zone) and lowest in zone 5 (the outermost part of the city) holds for all series, except for the reversal of rank in zones 4 and 5 in the first series, 1900–1906. During this 40-year period Chicago experienced enormous growth in population and industrial and economic power. It also was confronted with the task of assimilating wave after wave of new immigrants with very different cultural values and expectations. In the light of this ceaseless turmoil of change and new development, the relative stability of the relationships between the zonal rates is impressive.

TABLE 4. Rates of Delinquents Per 100 Males, 10–17 Years of Age, in Chicago by 2-Mile Concentric Zones, For Selected Time Periods 1900–40

Years	*Zone*				
	I	*II*	*III*	*IV*	*V*
1900–1906	16	9	6	4	6
1917–23	10	7	4	3	3
1927–33	10	7	5	3	2
1934–40	9	9	6	4	2

SOURCE: Henry D. McKay and Solomon Kobrin, "Nationality and Delinquency" (Chicago: Institute of Juvenile Research, Department of Mental Health, State of Illinois, 1966).

Though the comparison of rates by city zones is useful to demonstrate the stability of relationships between delinquency areas, it also obscures important changes in neighborhood rates of delinquency as the result of social and economic change. We need much more detailed study of the way in which the changing character of life in the city affects the rates of delinquency and crime in the many different geographical areas of the city. It will require more intensive study of the trends in rates in the same areas in relation to the various physical, demographic, economic, and cultural changes which may have occurred. Such studies should also take account of the effects of changes in the organization, policies, and practices of the criminal

[14] For the most current statement on these studies see Henry D. McKay and Solomon Kobrin, "Nationality and Delinquency" (Chicago: Institute of Juvenile Research, Department of Mental Health, State of Illinois, 1966).

justice system itself. From such studies we could obtain a much clearer idea than we now possess of the way delinquency rates reflect the existing structure of life within these areas and the way they are affected by changes both inside the area and in the city as a whole.

McKay has taken a beginning step in this direction by drawing trend lines of delinquency rates for 74 community areas of the city of Chicago.[15] These trend lines are based on five different series of delinquents appearing before the Juvenile Court of Cook County from 1927 to 1962. Selected for special study were the five community areas where the trend in rates showed the greatest increase and the five areas showing the greatest decrease in rates. The areas showing the greatest increase were areas where "a largely middle class white population was replaced by a Negro population coming partly from other city areas and partly from outside of the city." Four of the areas showing the greatest decrease in rates extend directly southward from the central business district and are areas which have formed the heart of the Negro community for more than 30 years. The fifth area of greatest decrease is on the outskirts of the city where there has been a rapid increase of population, but where the population is 93 percent white...The increase in area rates were attributed to the breakdown of institutional controls and the disruption of roles and opportunities to participate in local political and economic institutions due to the fact that a new racial group moved in and displaced the former residents. Conversely, it was suggested that the areas showing decreasing delinquency rates are areas where new institutional controls and more stable role relationships have had time to become established.

One cannot assume on the basis of these findings that order will gradually emerge from disorder by some "self healing" process. Much effort has been expended to develop more stable institutions and community relationships in these decreasing rate Negro areas, and the delinquency rates are still above the average for the city. These findings do indicate, however, the great importance of studying more closely what happens to the institutions in an area when a new group moves in. If it is true that the period of transition creates a chaotic situation which becomes resolved only when the new group develops its own network of institutionalized roles, then crime prevention programs might concentrate on how these roles, so essential for social control, might be developed more swiftly.

Sources of Irregularity in Crime Patterns. The presentation of the distribution of crime and delinquency rates by census tracts, community areas, or concentric mile or 2-mile zones sometimes gives the impression of disjointed and abrupt breaks in the delinquency patterns. This is to some extent an artifact of the manner of presentation, reflected by the necessity to use somewhat arbitrary boundaries for areas. The general assumption that has characterized these studies is that the distribution

[15] Henry D. McKay, "A Note on Trends in Rates of Delinquents in Certain Areas of Chicago," in Task Force Report on Juvenile Delinquency, President's Commission of Law Enforcement and Administration of Justice, Appendix F, (Washington, D.C.: Government Printing Office, 1967).

of offenses and offenders shows a fairly continuous decreasing density from the center of the city outward to the suburban areas. Even within census tracts offenses and offenders usually show up on spot maps more heavily concentrated toward the central district side of the tract rather than the side toward the periphery of the city.[16]

This assumption of a fairly continuous decline in rates outward from the city center, while apparently a generally valid description for most American cities, must allow for many exceptions. Cities are broken up by physical and social barriers which often create sharply juxtaposed contrasts in the economic and cultural characteristics of adjacent city areas. In the growth of a city the existence of physical barriers such as rivers, railroads, canals, viaducts, lakes, parks, elevated lines, and high-speed limited access highways turn and shape the flow of population so that great differences in the characteristics of adjoining areas and their population may result, which in turn find reflection in very different rates of delinquency. Such contrasts show up in nearly all of the studies. These natural or artificial barriers sometimes create the circumstances for the development of rather homogeneous settlements of racial and ethnic groups whose measures for social control may produce much lower delinquency rates than neighboring groups.[17]

• • •

The Relation of Crime to Other Social Indicators

...The studies in Chicago found a high degree of relationship between delinquency rates and the existence of other social problems in urban areas, such as school truancy (0.89), infant mortality (0.64), tuberculosis (0.93), and mental disorder (0.72).[18] In addition to showing that areas having high rates of crime also show high rates for other social or health problems, indicators were developed on the physical and economic status of these areas and the composition of the population. The concentration of delinquency in or adjacent to areas of heavy industry and commerce has already been noted. In addition, high crime rate areas tend to show the following characteristics: decreasing population (a correlation of 0.52 for one series of rates and 0.69 with another), a high percentage of families on relief (0.89), low monthly rents (-0.61), low rates of home ownership (-0.49), and a high percentage of foreign born or Negro heads of family (0.60).[19]

• • •

In general, there has been a considerable amount of agreement among the various studies as to the social and demographic characteristics of areas which are most closely associated with crime. In part, this agreement is attributable to the fact that correlations have been made with total rates of crime or delinquency based on the

[16] See spot-maps in Clifford R. Shaw and Henry D. McKay, "Juvenile Delinquency in Urban Areas," (Chicago: The University of Chicago Press, 1942).

[17] See discussion on cultural enclaves, infra.

[18] Shaw and McKay, "Juvenile Delinquency in Urban Areas," supra note 16, pp. 86-101.

[19] Id. at pp. 134-163.

offender's residence. When the crime rates are based on offenses known to police, rather than on arrests or court appearance, the factor of opportunity at the place of occurrence of the crime comes more into focus, and somewhat different area characteristics emerge as most important.

Important differences also can be seen when crimes against property are treated separately from crimes against the person. These differences can be illustrated from data collected in Atlanta, Ga.[20] Table 5 shows the number and rate of crimes against the person and crimes against property classified by the medium family income of the area in which the crime was committed. Victimization by crimes against the person is much more concentrated in the low income areas than crimes against property. The rate of crimes against the person is over eight times as great in the lowest income areas as compared to the highest, while for crimes against property it is less than twice as great. The high rates for the downtown area reflect the opportunity factor and are inflated by the high transient and low resident population of the area.

TABLE 5. Crimes by Income of Area in Which Committed[1]

1959 Median Family Income	*Number of Reported Crimes*			*Crimes per 1,000 Residents*		
	Against the person[2]	*Against property*[3]	*Total*	*Against the person*[2]	*Against property*[3]	*Total*
Under $3,000	470	2,112	2,582	5.8	26.2	32.1
$3,000 to $3,999	361	1,771	2,132	4.6	22.7	27.3
$4,000 to $4,999	196	1,689	1,885	2.5	21.6	24.1
$5,000 to $5,999	193	1,721	1,914	2.4	21.4	23.8
$6,000 to $6,999	92	1,609	1,701	1.3	22.2	23.4
$7,000 to $7,999	24	436	460	0.8	15.3	16.1
$8,000 to $8,999	21	509	530	0.8	18.7	19.4
$9,000 and over	45	918	963	0.7	13.7	14.4
Subtotal	1,402	10,765	12,167	2.7	21.0	23.7
Tracts F-19, 27, and 35[4]	86	1,182	1,268	22.8	313.0	335.8
Total	1,488	11,947	13,435	2.9	23.1	26.0

[1]Crimes reported, July 1, 1964–June 30, 1965, Atlanta Police Department.
[2]Murder, rape, aggravated assault, and robbery.
[3]Burglary, larceny from buildings, and auto theft (based on samples of reported cases).
[4]Downtown tracts with high rates due to characteristics other than median family income (less than $2,000)

SOURCE: Opportunity for Urban Excellence: Report of the Atlanta Commision on Crime and Juvenile Delinquency, February, 1966, p. 59.

[20] Atlanta Commission on Crime and Juvenile Delinquency, "Opportunity For Urban Excellence," February, 1966.

These results, however, present a relatively diffused picture of the distribution of crime when they are compared to the distribution of convicted offenders in crimes against the person and crimes against property classified by the same categories of median family income in their area of residence, as shown in table 6. The residences of the offenders show more concentration in the low income areas than do the crimes. Family income areas with medians under $4,000 account for 71 percent of the offenders against the person and only 51 percent of the crimes against the person. Similarly, the areas below $4,000 median family income account for over 58 percent of the persons convicted of crimes against property but only 36 percent of the crimes against property.

TABLE 6. Crimes by Income of Area in Which Offender Resided[1]

1959 Median Family Income of Area	*Number of Offenses*			*Offenders per 1,000 Residents*		
	Against the person[2]	*Against property*[3]	*Total*	*Against the person*[2]	*Against property*[3]	*Total*
Under $3,000	43	124	167	0.51	1.47	1.98
$3,000 to $3,999	31	91	122	.40	1.47	1.56
$4,000 to $4,999	9	74	83	.11	.94	1.06
$5,000 to $5,999	16	43	59	.20	.53	.73
$6,000 to $6,999	2	18	20	.03	.25	.28
$7,000 to $7,999	1	11	12	.04	.39	.42
$8,000 to $8,999	2	2	4	.07	.07	.15
$9,000 and over	0	6	6		.09	.09
Total	104	369	473	.20	.71	.91

[1]Crimes reported, July 1, 1964–June 30, 1965, Atlanta Police Department.
[2]Murder, rape, aggravated assault, and robbery.
[3]Burglary, larceny from buildings, and auto theft (based on sample of reported cases).

SOURCE: Opportunity for Urban Excellence: Report of the Atlanta Commission on Crimes and Juvenile Delinquency, February 1966, p. 61.

•••

Many of the variables which are highly associated with crime rates have also been shown to be highly associated with each other. In recent years a number of attempts have been made to coalesce these diverse indicators into simpler sets of variables which could be used to characterize more directly the basic features of the urban areas relevant to crime. The mathematical techniques of factor analysis make it possible to manipulate the statistical interrelationships between these various indicators to identify the ones which best hang together. These efforts have yielded anywhere from two to eight basic factors depending in part on the number and types of variables introduced.

One of the most recent studies of this type also re-analyzed two previous studies and showed that all three reached a remarkable degree of agreement despite the fact that they were done in different cities for different time periods, in Baltimore,

Detroit, and Indianapolis.[21] The results suggest that a basic socioeconomic factor is at work in the production of high delinquency rates based on residence of offenders that can be indicated best by such variables as overcrowded housing, the percentage of unrelated individuals, and mobility which is negatively represented by the "proportion of persons reporting that they did not move during the preceding year."...

To be most useful these techniques need to be applied to the distribution of different types of offenses in relation to area characteristics. An attempt to do this with 20 offenses, using the Seattle data, produced eight basic factors which brought together different groupings of offenses with such descriptive variables of the areas as low occupational status, low family status, low economic status, high or low mobility, and race.[22] An indication of the potential usefulness of this technique is evident in the clarity with which the "Skid Road" syndrome of characteristics emerged. This factor reflected "a social pattern characterized by large proportions of unmarried and unemployed males."[23] Significant relationships emerged for percentage of the population classified as male (0.782), percentage unemployed (0.647), and low proportion of the population married (-0.375). The crime pattern showed very close relationships for common drunkenness, vagrancy, drunkenness, lewdness, petty larceny, fighting, and robbery (highway and car).

This study goes on to develop profiles for individual census tracts based on the relative applicability of the eight basic factors to each tract.[24] Many of the profiles of the individual tracts on these factors were very similar and others very different. This opens up the possibility that a smaller set of typical crime pattern profiles can be developed for classifying the criminal potential of city areas in a more precise, distinctive, and useful way. ...

Studies to achieve this objective have recently been undertaken under the heading of "social area" analysis. The goal is to identify a set of census variables which will make it possible to classify the various social areas of the city into as distinctive types as possible. One can then use these groupings to study the distribution of social problems or to make other useful comparisons. The basic problem is to derive a set of variables that will yield the most distinctive and useful groupings for a variety of purposes. Tryon solved this by using a technique of cluster analysis on census data for San Francisco and the East Bay area.[25] Shevky and his associates developed a typology based on an analysis of previous ecological and social studies and tested it for the Los Angeles Area and the San Francisco Bay Region.[26] The

[21] Roland J. Chilton, "Continuity in Delinquency Area Research: A Comparison of Studies for Baltimore, Detroit, and Indianapolis," American Sociological Review, 29:71-83, February 1964.

[22] Schmid, supra, note 7, pp. 535-539.

[23] Id. at p. 538.

[24] Id. at pp. 539-541.

[25] Robert C. Tryon, "Identification of Social Areas by Cluster Analysis" (Berkeley and Los Angeles: University of California Press, 1955).

[26] Eshref Shevky and Wendell Bell, "Social Area Analysis" (Stanford: Stanford University Press, 1955). See also references to earlier explorative work by Shevky and his associates.

Shevky-Bell typology has been used most frequently in analyzing the distribution of crime and delinquency. This typology contains three dimensions. The first is called economic status and is based on measures of occupational status (total number of craftsmen, operatives, and laborers per 1,000 employed persons), and educational level (number of persons who have completed no more than grade school per 1,000 persons 25 years old and over).[27] The second is named family status and is based on the fertility ratio (number of children under 5 years per 1,000 females age 15 through 44), women in the labor force ratio (number of females in the labor force per 1,000 females 14 years old and over), and single family detached dwelling units ratio (number of single-family dwelling units per 1,000 dwelling units of all types). The third dimension is called ethnic status and is based on race and nativity (high proportion of non-native-born white persons in total population of tract).

Only a few studies have been made using these typologies, but the results, particularly in studies of delinquency, show promise. In Seattle it was found that the two typologies yielded very similar results in that the comparable dimensions showed high intercorrelations.[28] It was also discovered that for certain crime patterns, particularly the "Skid Road" variety, single indexes, such as percent male or percent male unemployed, frequently showed higher correlations than did the typologies.[29]

One of the most informative applications of the Shevky-Bell typology occurred in the study of crime and delinquency rates in Lexington, Ky.[30] The distribution of the crime rates showed little relationship to family status (-0.16) but a closer relationship to economic status (-0.52) and racial status (0.47) of the areas. The delinquency rates however, showed a relationship to all three (-0.35, -0.38, and -0.48 respectively).[31]

One of the interesting results involved the computation of the ratio of juvenile to adult arrest rates. It was found that the proportion of delinquency to adult crime *increases* as family status (-0.53) and racial status (-0.28) of areas *decrease*. However, the proportion of delinquency to adult crime *increases* with an *increase* in the economic status (0.40) of social areas. Putting these relationships together shows the proportion of delinquency to adult crime will be greatest when high economic status is combined with low family status, as can be seen from the following progression in the delinquency/crime ratio: low economic-low family status, 22.0; low economic-high family status, 28.1; high economic-high family status, 33.5; high

[27]In this presentation the alternative typological designations suggested by Bell have been used instead of the original designations, which were social rank for economic status, urbanization for family status, and segregation for ethnic status. See Wendell Bell, "The Utility of the Shevky Typology for the Design of Urban Sub-Area Field Studies," Journal of Social Psychology, 47:71–83, February 1953.

[28]Schmid, supra, note 7, p. 672.

[29]Id. at pp. 672–673.

[30]Richard Quinney, "Crime, Delinquency, and Social Areas," The Journal of Research in Crime and Delinquency, 1:49–154, July 1954.

[31] Id. at table 1, p. 151.

economic-low family status, 62.2.[32] One possible interpretation of this finding is that high economic status areas show fewer adult arrests, and a condition of low family status tends to be associated with more delinquency. Thus, the combined interactive effect of these two tendencies becomes evident in a sharp increase in the proportion of delinquency to adult crime for areas characterized as high economic-low family status areas.

Several significant relationships are obtained between the social areas variables and crime and delinquency rates for specific age, sex, race, and offense categories.[33] For example, nonwhite delinquency shows no relation to economic status (0.05) or racial status (0.03) of census tracts but is significantly related to low family status (-0.49). The nonwhite adult crime rate shows mildly negative relationships to all three factors in the social areas typology, but it is the only category that shows the crime rate increasing as the percent nonwhite in the area decreases. The association of the family status variable is primarily with youth delinquency, though it seems to be more closely related to male delinquency (-0.38) than female delinquency (-0.12). The young adult age group 18 to 24 contributes heavily to the crime totals, and here the high association with economic status (-0.58) and racial status (0.63) and the lack of association with family status (-0.03) are particularly striking. With respect to the offense categories, racial status shows especially high associations with juvenile (0.68) and adult (0.59) sex offenses, criminal homicide, and assault (0.67), but very little relationship with juvenile homicide and assault (0.18).

These studies using social area analysis have raised many issues that are unresolved, such as the relative value of the typologies versus single variables for different problems and the applicability of social area analysis to offense as compared to offender data. However, further exploration of the usefulness of these typologies in revealing the significant dimensions of social areas for the crime problem is clearly indicated.

The Relationships of Nationality and Race with Crime and Delinquency by City Areas

From the data presented thus far it appears that the application of ecological methods to the description and understanding of crime and delinquency has yielded only fragmentary insights and guidelines for action. However, a better realization of the potential and value of this type of analysis can be secured from the results relating nationality and race with crime and delinquency.

•••

The greatest contribution of data for public consideration of this problem was made through the series of studies in Chicago.[34] The use of ecological methods

[32] Id. at table 2, p. 152.

[33] The following results are drawn from Qinney, ibid., table 4, p. 153.

[34] See Shaw and McKay, "Juvenile Delinquency in Urban Areas," supra, note 16. Also see McKay and Kobrin, supra, note 14.

permitted them to go beyond the simple relationship between crime rates and nationality. It enabled them to demonstrate the operation of a relatively effective process of assimilation of these different nationality groups into the mainstream of American economic and social life. With this assimilation the high rates of crime and delinquency as well as a number of other social problems disappeared. It enabled them to focus public attention on the conditions of life, and on cultural and social change, rather than on inherent criminality as a function of national origin.

• • •

Marked changes were noted in the composition of the population inhabiting the high delinquency and crime rate areas near the central district over a period of many years. The Germans, Irish, English-Scotch, and Scandanavians in Chicago were gradually replaced by the Italians, Polish, and persons from Slavic countries. Despite the change in population the rates remained high relative to other areas in the city. Nor were those families left behind by each nationality group the most delinquent. They actually produced fewer delinquents than their proportion in the population of the area would lead one to expect.[35]

As the older immigrant group moved out, their children appeared proportionately less often in the Juvenile Court, and the court intake reflected instead the disproportionate appearance of the new arrivals. Nor did the children of the disappearing nationality groups raise the court intake in their new areas either for foreign-born or native-born children.[36]

Comparison of the rates for white and Negroes, native and foreign-born, and old and new immigrants, classified by the area rates for white delinquents, shows that all of these groups have rates that range from high to low. Each racial and nationality group shows a considerable range in rates. At the same time these different groups produce much the same rate when they live in the same areas.[37]

• • •

The Cultural Enclave. One of the most significant findings of the ecological studies has been the identification of enclaves of culturally different insulated groups who have maintained low rates of crime and delinquency despite exposure to poverty, discrimination, exploitation, and disadvantageous conditions. Perhaps the most striking capacity to do this has been observed in areas of Oriental settlement in large cities. In Seattle a school district comprised of 90 percent Japanese boys showed a low delinquency rate of 5.7 despite the fact that the rate for the rest of the area was 27.7.[38] This district was located in a very deteriorated section of town with "the highest concentration of homicides, houses of prostitution, unidentified suicides, and cheap lodging-houses in Seattle."[39] Of the 710 boys who were sent to

[35] Shaw and McKay at pp. 151–152.

[36] Id. at p. 152.

[37] Id. at pp. 152–153.

[38] Norman S. Hayner, "Delinquency Areas in the Puget Sound Region," American Journal of Sociology, 39:319, November 1933.

[39] Ibid.

the Parental School (a boy's reform school) from 1919 to 1930 from Seattle, only three were Japanese, and the cases of these three indicated that they had lost "vital contact with the racial colony."[40]

• • •

Explanations and Implications of the Distribution of Crime Rates

Studies of the patterns in the geographical distribution of crime and delinquency rates in cities have persistently tried to establish the chief characteristics of the areas in which the rates of both offenses and offenders are highest. They have tried many types of indicators with varying degrees of success. Considering that these studies have been undertaken in different cities containing very different populations, in different regions of the country with diverse cultural traditions, and in different time periods ranging back to the beginning of the century, the results have shown a considerable degree of consistency concerning the location of serious crime problems.

These studies have not assumed that the factors found to be associated with these delinquency rates are causative. Instead they are regarded simply as indicators of characteristics of urban areas with spatial variations similar to those shown by the crime rates. There is also the underlying assumption that both the crime rates and other related social problems are being produced by certain common structural features of a social, economic, physical, and demographic character in the high rate areas that are not present or do not interact in the same way in the low rate areas. The interaction of these distinctive structural features of the area are regarded as setting the conditions and resources for living. To the extent that these conditions are so disadvantageous that it becomes difficult for the family to assert and maintain its authority in training children, or the schools to teach effectively, or the employment system to recruit and sustain motivations toward successful conventional careers, higher rates of social problems, such as delinquency and crime, will occur.

• • •

Though these ecological studies of the distribution of crime and delinquency rates in cities have not been specifically addressed to a search for causes of crime, they have produced many useful insights about the conditions of life with which crime and delinquency are most often associated. In calling attention to the close relation between the social and economic conditions of life and the adequacy of local institutions in meeting the needs of residents of high delinquency areas, such studies have pointed to the need for much more detailed investigation of these connections. This more intensive analysis would be greatly facilitated if police districts and the reporting of crime data coincided with the area boundaries used in reporting census data. It would also be extremely helpful if other types of social and economic data reported by public and private institutions, such as education, health, and welfare agencies, used comparable census area boundaries. This failure to use comparable

[40] Ibid.

area units has been one of the major restraints on the full exploitation of ecological methods for the analysis of crime problems. Nevertheless, the ecological studies have provided the beginnings of a theoretical explanation of the distribution of crime rates which justifies a broad attack on the underlying social and economic conditions which produce such heavy concentrations of both offenses and offenders in some areas of the city rather than others.

10. Crime as an American Way of Life

Daniel Bell

Americans have had an extraordinary talent for compromise in politics and extremism in morality. The most shameless political deals (and "steals") have been rationalized as expedient and realistically necessary. Yet in no other country have there been such spectacular attempts to curb human appetities and brand them as illicit, and nowhere else such glaring failures. From the start America was at one and the same time a frontier community where "everything goes," and the fair country of the Blue Laws. At the turn of the century the cleavage developed between the Big City and the small-town conscience. Crime as a growing business was fed by the revenues from prostitution, liquor and gambling that a wide-open urban society encouraged and which a middle-class Protestant ethos tried to suppress with a ferocity unmatched in any other civilized country. Catholic cultures rarely have imposed such restrictions, and have rarely suffered such excesses. Even in prim and proper Anglican England, prostitution is a commonplace of Piccadilly night life, and gambling one of the largest and most popular industries. In America the enforcement of public morals has been a continuing feature of our history.

Some truth may lie in Svend Ranulf's generalization that moral indignation is a peculiar fact of middle-class psychology and represents a disguised form of repressed envy. The larger truth lies perhaps in the brawling nature of American development and the social character of crime. Crime, in many ways, is a Coney Island mirror, caricaturing the morals and manners of a society. The jungle quality of the American business community, particularly at the turn of the century, was reflected in the mode of "business" practiced by the coarse gangster elements, most of them from

From *Antioch Review*, **13**:2 (June 1953), 132–154, abridged and reprinted by permission of The Antioch Press.

new immigrant families, who were "getting ahead," just as Horatio Alger had urged. In the older, Protestant tradition the intense acquisitiveness, such as that of Daniel Drew, was rationalized by a compulsive moral fervor. But the formal obeisance of the ruthless businessman in the workaday world to the church-going pieties of the Sabbath was one that the gangster could not make. Moreover, for the young criminal, hunting in the asphalt jungle of the crowded city, it was not the businessman with his wily manipulation of numbers but the "man with the gun" who was the American hero. "No amount of commercial prosperity," once wrote Teddy Roosevelt, "can supply the lack of the heroic virtues." The American was "the hunter, cowboy, frontiersman, the soldier, the naval hero." And in the crowded slums, the gangster. He was a man with a gun, acquiring by personal merit what was denied to him by complex orderings of a stratified society. And the duel with the law was the morality play *par excellence:* the gangster, with whom rides our own illicit desires, and the prosecutor, representing final judgment and the force of the law.

Yet all this was acted out in a wider context. The desires satisfied in extra-legal fashion were more than a hunger for the "forbidden fruits" of conventional morality. They also involved, in the complex and ever shifting structure of group, class and ethnic stratification, which is the warp and woof of America's "open" society, such "normal" goals as independence through a business of one's own, and such "moral" aspirations as the desire for social advancement and social prestige. For crime, in the language of the sociologists, has a "functional" role in the society, and the urban rackets—the illicit activity organized for continuing profit rather than individual illegal acts—is one of the queer ladders of social mobility in American life. Indeed, it is not too much to say that the whole question of organized crime in America cannot be understood unless one appreciates (1) the distinctive role of organized gambling as a function of a mass consumption economy; (2) the specific role of various immigrant groups as they one after another became involved in marginal business and crime; and (3) the relation of crime to the changing character of the urban political machines.

As a society changes, so does, in lagging fashion, its type of crime. As American society became more "organized," as the American businessman became more "civilized" and less "buccaneering," so did the American racketeer. And just as there were important changes in the structure of business enterprise, so the "institutionalized" criminal enterprise was transformed too.

In the America of the last fifty years the main drift of society has been toward the rationalization of industry, the domestication of the crude self-made captain[1] of industry into the respectable man of manners, and the emergence of a mass-consumption economy. The most significant transformation in the field of "institutionalized" crime was the increasing relative importance of gambling as against other kinds of illegal activity. And, as a multi-billion-dollar business, gambling un-

[1]Editor's Note: Refers to so-called robber barons, who were noted for utilizing any means to acquire wealth and power.

derwent a transition parallel to the changes in American enterprise as a whole. This parallel was exemplified in many ways: in gambling's industrial organization (e.g., the growth of a complex technology such as the national racing wire service and the minimization of risks by such techniques as lay-off betting); in its respectability, as was evidenced in the opening of smart and popular gambling casinos in resort towns and in "satellite" adjuncts to metropolitan areas; in its functional role in a mass-consumption economy (for sheer volume of money changing hands, nothing has ever surpassed this feverish activity of fifty million American adults); in the social acceptance of the gamblers in the important status world of sport and entertainment, i.e., "cafe society."

In seeking to "legitimize" itself, gambling had quite often actually become a force against older and more vicious forms of illegal activity. In 1946, for example, when a Chicago mobster, Pat Manno, went down to Dallas, Texas, to take over gambling in the area for the Accardo-Guzik combine, he reassured the sheriff as to his intent as follows: "Something I'm against, that's dope peddlers, pickpockets, hired killers. That's one thing I can't stomach, and that's one thing the fellows up there—the group won't stand for, things like that. They discourage it, they even go to headquarters and ask them why they don't do something about it."

...

The criminal world of the last decade, its tone set by the captains of the gambling industry, is in startling contrast to the state of affairs in the two decades before. If a Kefauver report had been written then, the main "names" would have been Lepke and Gurrah, Dutch Schultz, Jack "Legs" Diamond, Lucky Luciano, and, reaching back a little further, Arnold Rothstein, the czar of the underworld. These men (with the exception of Luciano, who was involved in narcotics and prostitution) were in the main industrial racketeers. Rothstein, it is true, had a larger function: he was, as Frank Costello became later, the financier of the underworld—the pioneer big businessman of crime, who, understanding the logic of co-ordination, sought to *organize* crime as a source of regular income. His main interest in this direction was in industrial racketeering, and his entry was through labor disputes. At one time, employers in the garment trades hired Legs Diamond and his sluggers to break strikes, and the Communists, then in control of the cloakmakers union, hired one Little Orgie to protect the pickets and beat up the scabs; only later did both sides learn that Legs Diamond and Little Orgie were working for the same man, Rothstein.

...

But in the last decade and a half, industrial racketeering has not offered much in the way of opportunity. *Like American capitalism itself, crime shifted its emphasis from production to consumption.* The focus of crime became the direct exploitation of the citizen as consumer, largely through gambling. And while the protection of these huge revenues was inextricably linked to politics, the relation between gambling and "the mobs" became more complicated.

...

While Americans made gambling illegal, they did not in their hearts think of it as wicked—even the churches benefited from the bingo and lottery crazes. So they gambled—and gamblers flourished. Against this open canvas, the indignant tones of Senator Wiley and the shocked righteousness of Senator Tobey during the Kefauver investigation rang oddly. Yet it was probably this very tone of surprise that gave the activity of the Kefauver Committee its piquant quality. Here were some Senators who seemingly did not know the facts of life, as most Americans did. Here, in the person of Senator Tobey, was the old New England Puritan conscience poking around in industrial America, in a world it had made but never seen. Here was old-fashioned moral indignation, at a time when cynicism was rampant in public life.

Commendable as such moralistic fervor was, it did not make for intelligent discrimination of fact. Throughout the Kefauver hearings, for example, there ran the presumption that all gamblers were invariably gangsters. This was true of Chicago's Accardo-Guzik combine, which in the past had its fingers in many kinds of rackets. It was not nearly so true of many of the large gamblers in America, most of whom had the feeling that they were satisfying a basic American urge for sport and looked upon their calling with no greater sense of guilt than did many bootleggers. After all, Sherman Billingsley did start out as a speakeasy proprietor, as did the Kreindlers of the "21" Club; and today the Stork Club and the former Jack and Charlie's are the most fashionable night and dining spots in America (one prominent patron of the Stork Club: J. Edgar Hoover).

...

Apart from the gamblers, there were the mobsters. But what Senator Kefauver and company failed to understand was that the mobsters, like the gamblers, and like the entire gangdom generally, were seeking to become quasi-respectable and establish a place for themselves in American life. For the mobsters, by and large, had immigrant roots, and crime, as the pattern showed, was a route of social ascent and place in American life.

The mobsters were able, where they wished, to "muscle in" on the gambling business because the established gamblers were wholly vulnerable, not being able to call on the law for protection. The Senators, however, refusing to make any distinction between a gambler and a gangster, found it convenient to talk loosely of a nationwide conspiracy of "illegal" elements. Senator Kefauver asserted that a "nationwide crime syndicate does exist in the United States, despite the protestations of a strangely assorted company of criminals, self-serving politicians, plain blind fools, and others who may be honestly misguided, that there is no such combine." The Senate Committee report states the matter more dogmatically: "There is a nationwide crime syndicate known as the Mafia. ... Its leaders are usually found in control of the most lucrative rackets in their cities. There are indications of a centralized direction and control of these rackets. ... The Mafia is the cement that helps to bind the Costello-Adonis-Lansky syndicate of New York and the Accardo-Guzik-Fischetti syndicate of Chicago. ... These groups have kept in touch with Luciano since his deportation from the country."

Unfortunately for a good story—and the existence of the Mafia would be a whale of a story—neither the Senate Crime Committee in its testimony, nor Kefauver in his book, presented any real evidence that the Mafia exists as a functioning organization. One finds police officials asserting before the Kefauver committee their *belief* in the Mafia; the Narcotics Bureau *thinks* that a worldwide dope ring allegedly run by Luciano is part of the Mafia; but the only other "evidence" presented—aside from the incredulous responses both of Senator Kefauver and Rudolph Halley when nearly all the Italian gangsters asserted that they didn't know about the Mafia—is that certain crimes bear "the earmarks of the Mafia."

•••

The salient reason, perhaps, why the Kefauver Committee was taken in by its own myth of an omnipotent Mafia and a despotic Costello was its failure to assimilate and understand three of the more relevant sociological facts about institutionalized crime in its relation to the political life of large urban communities in America, namely: (1) the rise of the American Italian community, as part of the inevitable process of ethnic succession, to positions of importance in politics, a process that has been occurring independently but almost simultaneously in most cities with large Italian constituencies—New York, Chicago, Kansas City, Los Angeles; (2) the fact that there are individual Italians who play prominent, often leading roles today in gambling and in the mobs; and (3) the fact that Italian gamblers and mobsters often possessed "status" within the Italian community itself and a "pull" in city politics.[2] These three items are indeed related—but not so as to form a "plot."

The Italian community has achieved wealth and political influence much later and in a harder way than previous immigrant groups. Early Jewish wealth, that of the German Jews of the late nineteenth century, was made largely in banking and merchandising. To that extent, the dominant group in the Jewish community was outside of, and independent of, the urban political machines. Later Jewish wealth, among the East European immigrants, was built in the garment trades, though with some involvement with the Jewish gangster, who was typically an industrial racketeer (Arnold Rothstein, Lepke and Gurrah, etc.). Among Jewish lawyers, a small minority, such as the "Tammany lawyer" (like the protagonist of Sam Ornitz's *Haunch, Paunch and Jowl)* rose through politics and occasionally touched the fringes of crime. Most of the Jewish lawyers, by and large the communal leaders, climbed rapidly, however, in the opportunities that established and legitimate Jewish wealth provided. Irish immigrant wealth in the northern urban centers, concentrated largely in construction, trucking and the waterfront, has, to a substantial extent, been wealth

[2]Toward the end of his hearings, Senator Kefauver read a telegram from an indignant citizen of Italian descent, protesting against the impression the committee had created that organized crime in America was a distinctly Italian enterprise. The Senator took the occasion to state the obvious: that there are racketeers who are Italian does not mean that Italians are racketeers. However, it may be argued that to the extent the Kefauver Committee fell for the line about crime in America being organized and controlled by the Mafia, it did foster such a misunderstanding. Perhaps this is also the place to point out that insofar as the relation of ethnic groups and ethnic problems to illicit and quasi-legal activities is piously ignored, the field is left open to the kind of vicious sensationalism practiced by Mortimer and Lait.

accumulated in and through political alliance, e.g., favoritism in city contracts.[3] Control of the politics of the city thus has been crucial for the continuance of Irish political wealth. This alliance of Irish immigrant wealth and politics has been reciprocal; many noted Irish political figures lent their names as important window-dressing for business corporations (Al Smith, for example, who helped form the U.S. Trucking Corporation, whose executive head for many years was William J. McCormack, the alleged "Mr. Big" of the New York waterfront) while Irish businessmen have lent their wealth to further the careers of Irish politicians. Irish mobsters have rarely achieved status in the Irish community, but have served as integral arms of the politicians, as strong-arm men on election day.

The Italians found the more obvious big city paths from rags to riches pre-empted. In part this was due to the character of the early Italian immigration. Most of them were unskilled and from rural stock. Jacob Riis could remark in the '90's, "the Italian comes in at the bottom and stays there." These dispossessed agricultural laborers found jobs as ditch-diggers, on the railroads as section hands, along the docks, in the service occupations, as shoemakers, barbers, garment workers, and stayed there. Many were fleeced by the "padrone" system, a few achieved wealth from truck farming, wine growing, and marketing produce; but this "marginal wealth" was not the source of coherent and stable political power.

Significantly, although the number of Italians in the U.S. is about a third as high as the number of Irish, and of the 30,000,000 Catholic communicants in the United States, about half are of Irish descent and a sixth of Italian, there is not one Italian bishop among the hundred Catholic bishops in this country, or one Italian archbishop among the 21 archbishops. The Irish have a virtual monopoly. This is a factor related to the politics of the American church; but the condition also is possible because there is not significant or sufficient wealth among Italian Americans to force some parity.

The children of the immigrants, the second and third generation, became wise in the ways of the urban slums. Excluded from the political ladder—in the early '30's there were almost no Italians on the city payroll in top jobs, nor in books of the period can one find discussion of Italian political leaders—finding few open routes to wealth, some turned to illicit ways. In the children's court statistics of the 1930's, the largest group of delinquents were the Italian; nor were there any Italian communal or social agencies to cope with these problems. Yet it was, oddly enough, the quondam racketeer, seeking to become respectable, who provided one of the major supports for the drive to win a political voice for Italians in the power structure of the urban political machines.

• • •

[3] A fact which should occasion little shock if one recalls that in the nineteenth century American railroads virtually stole 190,000,000 acres of land by bribing Congressmen, and that more recently such scandals as the Teapot Dome oil grabs during the Harding administration, consummated, as the Supreme Court said, "by means of conspiracy, fraud and bribery," reached to the very doors of the White House.

Frank Costello made his money originally in bootlegging. After repeal, his big break came when Huey Long, desperate for ready cash to fight the old-line political machines, invited Costello to install slot machines in Louisiana. Costello did, and he flourished. Together with Dandy Phil Kastel, he also opened the Beverly Club, an elegant gambling establishment just outside New Orleans, at which have appeared some of the top entertainers in America. Subsequently, Costello invested his money in New York real estate (including 79 Wall Street, which he later sold), the Copacabana night club, and a leading brand of Scotch whiskey.

Costello's political opportunity came when a money-hungry Tammany, starved by lack of patronage from Roosevelt and La Guardia, turned to him for financial support. The Italian community in New York has for years nursed a grievance against the Irish and, to a lesser extent, the Jewish political groups for monopolizing political power. They complained about the lack of judicial jobs, the small number—usually one—of Italian Congressmen, the lack of representation on the state tickets. But the Italians lacked the means to make their ambitions a reality. Although they formed a large voting bloc, there was rarely sufficient wealth to finance political clubs. Italian immigrants, largely poor peasants from Southern Italy and Sicily, lacked the mercantile experience of the Jews, and the political experience gained in the seventy-five-year history of Irish immigration.

• • •

That the urban machines, largely Democratic, have financed their heavy campaign costs in this fashion rather than having to turn to the "moneyed interests," explains in some part why these machines were able, in part, to support the New and Fair Deals without suffering the pressures they might have been subjected to had their source of money supply been the business groups. Although he has never publicly revealed his political convictions, it is likely that Frank Costello was a fervent admirer of Franklin D. Roosevelt and his efforts to aid the common man. The basic measures of the New Deal, which most Americans today agree was necessary for the public good, would not have been possible without the support of the "corrupt" big-city machines.

There is little question that men of Italian origin appeared in most of the leading roles in the high drama of gambling and mobs, just as twenty years ago the children of East European Jews were the most prominent figures in organized crime, and before that individuals of Irish descent were similarly prominent. To some extent statistical accident and the tendency of newspapers to emphasize the few sensational figures gives a greater illusion about the domination of illicit activities by a single ethnic group than all the facts warrant. In many cities, particularly in the South and on the West Coast, the mob and gambling fraternity consisted of many other groups, and often, predominantly, native white Protestants. Yet it is clear that in the major northern urban centers there was a distinct ethnic sequence in the modes of obtaining illicit wealth, and that uniquely in the case of the recent Italian elements, the former bootleggers and gamblers provided considerable leverage for the growth of political influence as well. A substantial number of Italian judges sitting on the bench in New York today are indebted in one fashion or another to Costello; so too are many

Italian district leaders—as well as some Jewish and Irish politicians. And the motive in establishing Italian political prestige in New York was generous rather than scheming for personal advantage. For Costello it was largely a case of ethnic pride. As in earlier American eras, organized illegality became a stepladder of social ascent.

...

As happens with all "new" money in American society, the rough and ready contractors, the construction people, trucking entrepreneurs, as well as racketeers, polished up their manners and sought recognition and respectability in their own ethnic as well as in the general community. The "shanty" Irish became the "lace curtain" Irish, and then moved out for wider recognition.[4] Sometimes acceptance came first in established "American" society, and this was a certificate for later recognition by the ethnic community, a process well illustrated by the belated acceptance in established Negro society of such figures as Sugar Ray Robinson and Joe Louis, as well as leading popular entertainers.

Yet, after all, the foundation of many a distinguished older American fortune was laid by sharp practices and morally reprehensible methods. The pioneers of American capitalism were not graduated from Harvard's School of Business Administration. The early settlers and founding fathers, as well as those who "won the west" and built up cattle, mining and other fortunes, often did so by shady speculations and a not inconsiderable amount of violence. They ignored, circumvented or stretched the law when it stood in the way of America's destiny, and their own—or, were themselves the law when it served their purposes. This has not prevented them and their descendants from feeling proper moral outrage when under the changed circumstances of the crowded urban environments later comers pursued equally ruthless tactics.

...

Apart from these considerations, what of the larger context of crime and the American way of life? The passing of the Fair Deal signalizes, oddly, the passing of an older pattern of illicit activities. The gambling fever of the past decade and a half was part of the flush and exuberance of rising incomes, and was characteristic largely of new upper-middle class rich having a first fling at conspicuous consumption. This upper-middle class rich, a significant new stratum in American life (not rich in the nineteenth century sense of enormous wealth, but largely middle-sized businessmen and entrepreneurs of the service and luxury trades—the "tertiary economy" in Colin Clark's phrase—who by the tax laws have achieved sizable incomes often much

[4]The role of ethnic pride in corralling minority group votes is one of the oldest pieces of wisdom in American politics; but what is more remarkable is the persistence of this identification through second and third generation descendants, a fact which, as Samuel Lubell noted in his *Future of American Politics,* was one of the explanatory keys to political behavior in recent elections. Although the Irish bloc as a solid Democratic bloc is beginning to crack, particularly as middle-class status impels individuals to identify more strongly with the G.O.P., the nomination in Massachusetts of Jack Kennedy for the United States Senate created a tremendous solidarity among Irish voters and Kennedy was elected over Lodge although Eisenhower swept the state.

higher than the managers of the super-giant corporations) were the chief patrons of the munificent gambling casinos. During the war decade when travel was difficult, gambling and the lush resorts provided important outlets for this social class. Now they are settling down, learning about Europe and culture. The petty gambling, the betting and bingo which relieve the tedium of small town life, or the expectation among the urban slum dwellers of winning a sizable sum by a "lucky number" or a "lucky horse" goes on. To quote Bernard Baruch: "You can't stop people from gambling on horses. And why should you prohibit a man from backing his own judgment? It's another form of personal initiative." But the lush profits are passing from gambling, as the costs of coordination rise. And in the future it is likely that gambling, like prostitution, winning tacit acceptance as a necessary fact, will continue on a decentralized, small entrepreneur basis.

But passing, too, is a political pattern, the system of political "bosses" which in its reciprocal relation provided "protection" for and was fed revenue from crime. The collapse of the "boss" system was a product of the Roosevelt era. Twenty years ago Jim Farley's task was simple; he had to work only on some key state bosses. Now there is no longer such an animal. New Jersey Democracy was once ruled by Frank Hague; now there are five or six men each top dog, for the moment, in his part of the state or faction of the party. Within the urban centers, the old Irish-dominated political machines in New York, Boston, Newark, and Chicago have fallen apart. The decentralization of the metropolitan centers, the growth of suburbs and satellite towns, the break-up of the old ecological patterns of slum and transient belts, the rise of functional groups, the increasing middle-class character of American life, all contribute to this decline.

With the rationalization and absorption of some illicit activities into the structure of the economy, the passing of an older generation that had established a hegemony over crime, the general rise of minority groups to social position, and the break-up of the urban boss system, the pattern of crime we have discussed is passing as well. Crime, of course, remains as long as passion and the desire for gain remain. But big, organized city crime, as we have known it for the past seventy-five years, was based on more than these universal motives. It was based on certain characteristics of the American economy, American ethnic groups, and American politics. The changes in all these areas means that it too, in the form we have known it, is at an end.

11. The Subculture of Violence

Marvin E. Wolfgang and Franco Ferracuti

Like all human behavior, homicide and other violent assaultive crimes must be viewed in terms of the cultural context from which they spring. De Cahmpneuf, Guerry, Quetelet early in the nineteenth century, and Durkheim later, led the way toward emphasizing the necessity to examine the *physique sociale*, or social phenomena characterized by 'externality', if the scientist is to understand or interpret crime, suicide, prostitution, and other deviant behavior. Without promulgating a sociological fatalism, analysis of broad macroscopic correlates in this way may obscure the dynamic elements of the phenomenon and result in the empirical hiatus and fallacious association to which Selvin refers.[1] Yet, because of wide individual variations, the clinical, idiosyncratic approach does not necessarily aid in arriving at Weber's *Verstehen,* or meaningful adequate understanding of regularities, uniformities, or patterns of interaction. And it is this kind of understanding we seek when we examine either deviation from, or conformity to, a normative social system.

Sociological contributions have made almost commonplace, since Durkheim, the fact that deviant conduct is not evenly distributed throughout the social structure. There is much empirical evidence that class position, ethnicity, occupational status and other social variables are effective indicators for predicting rates of different kinds of deviance.

...

That there is a conflict of value systems, we agree. That is, there is a conflict between a prevailing culture value and some subcultural entity. But commission of homicide by actors from the subculture at variance with the prevailing culture cannot be adequately explained in terms of frustration due to failure to attain normative-goals of the latter, in terms of inability to succeed with normative-procedures (means) for attaining those goals, nor in terms of an individual psychological condition of anomie. Homicide is most prevalent, or the highest rates of homicide occur, among a relatively homogeneous subcultural group in any large urban community. Similar prevalent rates can be found in some rural areas. The value system of this group, we

Reprinted from *The Subculture of Violence–Towards an Integrated Theory in Criminology* by Marvin E. Wolfgang and Franco Ferracuti (London: Tavistock Publications Ltd., 1967), pp. 150–152, 153–161, 181–185, by permission of Tavistock Publications Ltd., London.

[1] Hanan C. Selvin, 'Durkheim's *Suicide* and Problems of Empirical Research', *American Journal of Sociology* (1958) 63:607–619.

are contending, constitutes a subculture of violence. From a psychological viewpoint, we might hypothesize that the greater the degree of integration of the individual into this subculture, the higher the probability that his behavior will be violent in a variety of situations. From the sociological side, there should be a direct relationship between rates of homicide and the extent to which the subculture of violence represents a cluster of values around the theme of violence.

Except for war, probably the most highly reportable, socially visible, and serious form of violence is expressed in criminal homicide. Data show that in the United States rates are highest among males, non-whites, and the young adult ages. Rates for most serious crimes, particularly against the person, are highest in these same groups. In a Philadelphia study of 588 criminal homicides,[2] for example, non-white males aged 20-24 had a rate of 92 per 100,000 compared with 3.4 for white males of the same ages. Females consistently had lower rates than males in their respective race groups (non-white females, 9.3; white females, 0.4, in the same study), although it should be noted, as we shall discuss later, that non-white females have higher rates than white males.

It is possible to multiply these specific findings in any variety of ways; and although a subcultural affinity to violence appears to be principally present in large urban communities and increasingly in the adolescent population, some typical evidence of this phenomenon can be found, for example, in rural areas and among other adult groups....

We suggest that, by identifying the groups with the highest rates of homicide, we should find in the most intense degree a subculture of violence; and, having focused on these groups, we should subsequently examine the value system of their subculture, the importance of human life in the scale of values, the kinds of expected reaction to certain types of stimulus, perceptual differences in the evaluation of stimuli, and the general personality structure of the subcultural actors. In the Philadelphia study it was pointed out that:

> ...the significance of a jostle, a slightly derogatory remark, or the appearance of a weapon in the hands of an adversary are stimuli differentially perceived and interpreted by Negroes and white, males and females. Social expectations of response in particular types of social interaction result in differential "definitions of the situations." A male is usually expected to defend the name and honor of his mother, the virtue of womanhood...and to accept no derogation about his race (even from a member of his own race), his age, or his masculinity. Quick resort to physical combat as a measure of daring, courage, or defense of status appears to be a cultural expression, especially for lower socioeconomic class males of both races. When such a culture norm response is elicited from an individual engaged in social interplay with others who harbor the same response mechanism, physical assaults, altercations, and violent domestic quarrels that result in homicide are likely to be common. The upper-middle and upper social class value system defines subcultural mores, and considers many of the social and personal stimuli that evoke a combative reaction

[2] Marvin E. Wolfgang, *Patterns in Criminal Homicide,* Philadelphia, Pennsylvania: University of Pennsylvania Press, 1958.

in the lower classes as "trivial." Thus, there exists a cultural antipathy between many folk rationalizations of the lower class, and of males of both races, on the one hand, and the middle-class legal norms under which they live, on the other.[3]

This kind of analysis, combined with other data about delinquency, the lower-class social structure, its value system, and its emphasis on aggression, suggest the thesis of a violent subculture, or, by pushing the normative aspects a little further, a *subculture of violence.* Among many juvenile gangs, as has repeatedly been pointed out, there are violent feuds, meetings, territorial fights, and the use of violence to prove 'heart', to maintain or to acquire 'rep'.[4]

Physical aggression is often seen as a demonstration of masculinity and toughness. We might argue that this emphasis on showing masculinity through aggression is not always supported by data. If homicide is any index at all of physical aggression, we must remember that in the Philadelphia data non-white females have rates often two to four times higher than the rates of white males. Violent behavior appears more dependent on cultural differences than on sex differences, traditionally considered of paramount importance in the expression of aggression. It could be argued, of course, that in a more matriarchal role than that of her white counterpart, the Negro female both enjoys and suffers more of the male role as head of the household, as parental authority and supervisor; that this imposed role makes her more aggressive, more male-like, more willing and more likely to respond violently. Because most of the victims of Negro female homicide offenders are Negro males, the Negro female may be striking out aggressively against the inadequate male protector whom she desperately wants but often cannot find or hold.[5]

It appears valid to suggest that there are, in a heterogeneous population, differences in ideas and attitudes toward the use of violence and that these differences can be observed through variables related to social class and possibly through psychological correlates. There is evidence that modes of control of expressions of aggression in children vary among the social classes.[6] Lower-class boys, for example, appear more

[3] Wolfgang, *Patterns in Criminal Homicide,* pp. 188–189.

[4] We have elsewhere, in Chapter II, referred to the many studies of delinquency that discuss these matters. For recent items, see especially Lewis Yablonsky, *The Violent Gang,* New York: Macmillan, 1962; also, Dorothy Hayes and Russell Hogrefe, 'Group Sanction and Restraints Related to Use of Violence in Teenagers', paper read at the 41st annual meeting of the American Orthopsychiatric Association, Chicago, Illinois, March 20, 1964.

[5] For an especially insightful comment that aided our thinking on this topic, see Otto Pollak, 'Our Social Values and Juvenile Delinquency', *The Quarterly of the Pennsylvania Association on Probation, Parole and Correction* (September, 1964) 21:12–22.

[6] Excellent summaries of the literature in current works are found in Paul Henry Mussen (ed.) *Handbook of Research Methods in Child Development,* New York: Wiley, 1960; in Martin L. Hoffman and Lois W. Hoffman, *Review of Child Development Research,* Vol. I, New York: Russell Sage Foundation, 1964; and in the rich bibliography noted in John J. Honigmann and Richard J. Preston, 'Recent Developments in Culture and Personality', Supplement to *The Annals of the American Academy of Political and Social Science* (July, 1964) 354:153–162.

All of the recent literature we have been able to examine from anthropology, psychology, and sociology buttressed the general position of our thesis regarding class, punishment, and aggression.

likely to be oriented toward direct expression of aggression than are middle-class boys. The type of punishment meted out by parents to misbehaving children is related to this class orientation toward aggression. Lower-class mothers report that they or their husbands are likely to strike their children or threaten to strike them, whereas middle-class mothers report that their type of punishment is psychological rather than physical; and boys who are punished physically express aggression more directly than those who are punished psychologically. As Martin Gold[7] has suggested, the middle-class child is more likely to turn his aggression inward; in the extreme and as an adult he will commit suicide. But the lower-class child is more accustomed to a parent-child relationship which during punishment is for the moment that of attacker and attacked. The target for aggression, then, is external; aggression is directed toward others.[8]

The existence of a subculture of violence is partly demonstrated by examination of the social groups and individuals who experience the highest rates of manifest violence. This examination need not be confined to the study of one national or ethnic group. On the contrary, the existence of a subculture of violence could perhaps receive even cross-cultural confirmation. Criminal homicide is the most acute and highly reportable example of this type of violence, but some circularity of thought is obvious in the effort to specify the dependent variable (homicide), and also to infer the independent variable (the existence of a subculture of violence). The highest rates of rape, aggravated assaults, persistency in arrests for assaults (recidivism) among these groups with high rates of homicide are, however, empirical addenda to the postulation of a subculture of violence. Residential propinquity of these same groups reinforces the socio-psychological impact which the integration of this subculture engenders. Sutherland's thesis of 'differential association', or a psychological reformulation of the same theory in terms of learning process, could effectively be employed to describe more fully this impact in its intensity, duration, repetition, and frequency. The more thoroughly integrated the individual is into this subculture, the more intensely he embraces its prescriptions of behavior, its conduct norms, and integrates them into his personality structure. The degree of integration may be measured partly and crudely by public records of contact with the law, so high arrest rates, particularly high rates of assault crimes and high rates of recidivism for assault crimes among groups that form the subculture of violence, may indicate allegiance to the values of violence.

We have said that overt physical violence often becomes a common subculturally expected response to certain stimuli. However, it is not merely rigid conformity to

[7] Martin Gold, 'Suicide, Homicide and the Socialization of Aggression', *American Journal of Sociology* (May, 1958) 63:651–661.

[8] *Ibid.*

the demands and expectations of other persons, as Henry and Short[9] seem to suggest, that results in the high probability of homicide. Excessive, compulsive, or apathetic conformity of middle-class individuals to the value system of their social group is a widely recognized cultural malady. Our concern is with the value elements of violence as an integral component of the subculture which experiences high rates of homicide. It is conformity to *this* set of values, and not rigid conformity *per se,* that gives important meaning to the subculture of violence.

If violence is a common subcultural response to certain stimuli, penalties should exist for deviation from *this* norm. The comparatively nonviolent individual may be ostracized,[10] but if social interaction must occur because of residential propinquity to others sharing in a subculture of violence, he is most likely to be treated with disdain or indifference. One who previously was considered a member of the ingroup, but who has rebelled or retreated from the subculture, is now an outgroup member, a possible threat, and one for the group to avoid. Alienation or avoidance takes him out of the normal reach of most homicide attacks, which are highly personal offenses occurring with greatest frequency among friends, relatives, and associates. If social interaction continues, however, the deviant from the subculture of violence who fails to respond to a potentially violent situation, may find himself a victim of an adversary who continues to conform to the violence values.

It is not far-fetched to suggest that a whole culture may accept a value set dependent upon violence, demand or encourage adherence to violence, and penalize deviation. During periods of war the whole nation accepts the principle of violence against the enemy. The nonviolent citizen drafted into military service may adopt values associated with violence as an intimately internalized re-enforcement for his newly acquired rationalization to kill. War involves selective killing of an outgroup enemy, and in this respect may be viewed as different from most forms of homicide. Criminal homicide may be either 'selective' or non-discriminate slaying, although the literature on homicide consistently reveals its intragroup nature. However, as in wartime combat between opposing individuals when an 'it-was-either-him-or-me' situation arises similar attitudes and reactions occur among participants in homicide. It may be rel-

[9] This is different from the 'strength of the relational system' discussed by Henry and Short in their provocative analysis (Andrew F. Henry and James F. Short, Jr., *Suicide and Homicide,* Glencoe, Ill.: The Free Press, 1954, pp. 16–18, 91–92, 124–125). Relative to the Henry and Short suggestion, see Wolfgang, *Patterns in Criminal Homicide,* pp. 278–279. The attempt of Gibbs and Martin to measure Durkheim's reference to 'degree of integration' is a competent analysis of the problem, but a subculture of violence integrated around a given value item or value system may require quite different indices of integration than those to which these authors refer (Jack P. Gibbs and Walter T. Martin, 'A Theory of Status Integration and Its Relationship to Suicide', *American Sociological Review* (April, 1958) 23:140–147.

[10] Robert J. Smith, 'The Japanese World Community: Norms, Sanctions, and Ostracism', *American Anthropologist* (1961) 63:522–533. Withdrawal from the group may be by the deviant's own design and desire, or by response to the reaction of the group. Cf. Robert A. Dentler and Kai T. Erikson, 'The Functions of Deviance in Groups', *Social Problems* (Fall 1959) 7:98–107.

evant to point out that in the Philadelphia study of criminal homicide, 65 per cent of the offenders and 47 per cent of the victims had previous arrest records. Homicide, it appears, is often a situation not unlike that of confrontations in wartime combat, in which two individuals committed to the value of violence came together, and in which chance, prowess, or possession of a particular weapon dictates the identity of the slayer and of the slain. The peaceful non-combatant in both sets of circumstances is penalized, because of the allelomimetic behavior of the group supporting violence, by his being ostracized as an outgroup member, and he is thereby segregated (imprisoned, in wartime, as a conscientious objector) from his original group. If he is not segregated, but continues to interact with his original group in the public street or on the front line that represents the culture of violence, he may fall victim to the shot or stab from one of the group who still embraces the value of violence.

An internal need for aggression and a readiness to use violence by the individual who belongs to a subculture of violence should find their psychological foundation in personality traits and in attitudes which can, through careful studies, be assessed in such a way as to lead to a differential psychology of these subjects. Psychological tests have been repeatedly employed to study the differential characteristics of criminals; and if a theoretical frame of reference involving a subculture of violence is used, it should be possible to sharpen the discriminatory power of these tests. The fact that a subject belongs to a specific subculture (in our case, a deviant one), defined by the ready use of violence, should, among other consequences, cause the subject to adopt a differential perception of his environment and its stimuli. Variations in the surrounding world, the continuous challenges and daily frustrations which are faced and solved by the adaptive mechanism of the individual, have a greater chance of being perceived and reacted upon, in a subculture of violence, as menacing, aggressive stimuli which call for immediate defense and counter-aggression. This hypothesis lends itself to objective study through appropriate psychological methodologies. The word of Stagner[11] on industrial conflict exemplifies a similar approach in a different field. This perceptual approach is of great importance in view of studies on the physiology of aggression, which seem to show the need of outside stimulation in order to elicit aggressive behavior.[12]...

Confronted with many descriptive and test statistics, with some validated hypotheses and some confirmed replications of propositions regarding aggressive crime in psychological and sociological studies, interpretative analysis leading to the building of a theory is a normal functional aspect of the scientific method.

But there are two common and inherent dangers of an interpretative analysis that yields a thesis in an early stage of formulation, such as our thesis of a subculture of violence. These are: (*a*) the danger of going beyond the confines of empirical data

[11] Ross Stagner, *Psychology of Industrial Conflict,* New York: Wiley, 1956.

[12] See, for example, John Paul Scott, *Aggression,* Chicago: University of Chicago Press, 1958, pp. 44-64.

which have been collected in response to some stated hypothesis; and (*b*) the danger of interpretation that produces generalizations emerging inductively from the data and that results in tautologous reasoning. Relative to the first type of danger, the social scientist incurs the risk of 'impressionistic', 'speculative' thinking, or of using previous peripheral research and trying to link it to his own data by theoretical ties that often result in knotted confusion typically calling for further research, the *caveat* of both 'good' and 'poor' analyses. Relative to the second danger, the limitations and problems of tautologies are too well known to be elaborated here. We hope that these two approaches to interpretation are herein combined in degrees that avoid compounding the fallacies of both, but that unite the benefits of each. We have made an effort to stay within the limits imposed by known empirical facts and not to become lost in speculative reasoning that combines accumulated, but unrelated, facts for which there is no empirically supportive link.

We have said that overt use of force or violence, either in interpersonal relationships or in group interaction, is generally viewed as a reflection of basic values that stand apart from the dominant, the central, or the parent culture. Our hypothesis is that this overt (and often illicit) expression of violence (of which homicide is only the most extreme) is part of a subcultural normative system, and that this system is reflected in the psychological traits of the subculture participants. In the light of our discussion of the caution to be exercised in interpretative analysis, in order to tighten the logic of this analysis, and to support the thesis of a subculture of violence, we offer the following corollary propositions:

1. *No subculture can be totally different from or totally in conflict with the society of which it is a part.* A subculture of violence is not entirely an expression of violence, for there must be interlocking value elements shared with the dominant culture. It should not be necessary to contend that violent aggression is the predominant mode of expression in order to show that the value system is set apart as subcultural. When violence occurs in the dominant culture, it is usually legitimized, but most often is vicarious and a part of phantasy. Moreover, subcultural variations, we have earlier suggested, may be viewed as quantitative and relative. The extent of difference from the larger culture and the degree of intensity, which violence as a subcultural theme may possess, are variables that could and should be measured by known socio-psychological techniques.[13] At present, we are required to rely almost entirely upon expressions of violence in conduct of various forms—parent-child relationships, parental discipline, domestic quarrels, street fights, delinquent conflict gangs, criminal records of assaultive behavior, criminal homicides, etc.—but the number of psychometrically oriented studies in criminology is steadily increasing in both quantity and sophistication, and from them a reliable differential psychology of homicides should emerge to match current sociological research.

[13] For the concept of subculture to have psychological validity, psychologically meaningful differences should, of course, be evident in subjects belonging to the subculture of violence. From a diagnostic point of view, a number of signs and indicators, of both psychometric and projective type, can be used. The differential perception of violent stimuli can be used as an indicator. Partial studies in this direction are those of Shelley and Toch (E. L. V. Shelley and H. Toch, 'The Perception of Violence As an Indicator of Adjustment in Institutionalized Offenders', *Journal of Criminal Law, Criminology and Police Science*, (1962) 53:463–469).

2. *To establish the existence of a subculture of violence does not require that the actors sharing in these basic value elements should express violence in all situations.* The normative system designates that in some types of social interaction a violent and physically aggressive response is either expected or required of all members sharing in that system of values. That the actors' behavior expectations occur in more than one situation is obvious. There is a variety of circumstances in which homicide occurs, and the history of past aggressive crimes in high proportions, both in the victims and in the offenders, attests to the multisituational character of the use of violence and to its interpersonal characteristics.[14] But, obviously, persons living in a subcultural milieu designated as a subculture of violence cannot and do not engage in violence continuously; otherwise normal social functioning would be virtually impossible. We are merely suggesting, for example, that ready access to weapons in this milieu may become essential for protection against others who respond in similarly violent ways in certain situations, and that the carrying of knives or other protective devices becomes a common symbol of willingness to participate in violence, to expect violence, and to be ready for its retaliation.[15]

3. *The potential resort or willingness to resort to violence in a variety of situations emphasizes the penetrating and diffusive character of this culture theme.* The number and kinds of situations in which an individual uses violence may be viewed as an index of the extent to which he has assimilated the values associated with violence. This index should also be reflected by quantitative differences in a variety of psychological dimensions, from differential perception of violent stimuli to different value expressions in questionnaire-type instruments. The range of violence from minor assault to fatal injury, or certainly the maximum of violence expected, is rarely made explicit for all situations to which an individual may be exposed. Overt violence may even occasionally be a chance result of events. But clearly this range and variability of behavioral expressions of aggression suggest the importance of psychological dimensions in measuring adherence to a subculture of violence.

4. *The subcultural ethos of violence may be shared by all ages in a subsociety, but this ethos is most prominent in a limited age group, ranging from late adolescence to middle age.* We are not suggesting that a particular ethnic, sex, or age group all share in common the use of potential threats of violence. We are contending merely that the known empirical distribution of conduct, which expresses the sharing of this violence theme, shows greatest localization, incidence, and frequency in limited subgroups and reflects differences in learning about violence as a problem-solving mechanism.

5. *The counter-norm is nonviolence.* Violation of expected and required violence is most likely to result in ostracism from the group. Alienation of some kind, depending on the range of violence expectations that are unmet, seems to be a form of punitive action most feasible to this subculture. The juvenile who fails to live up to the conflict gang's requirements is pushed outside the group. The adult male who

[14] The Philadelphia study (Wolfgang, *Patterns in Criminal Homicide*) showed that 65 per cent of the offenders and 47 per cent of the victims had a previous police record of arrests and that 75 per cent of these arrests were for aggravated assaults. Here, then, is a situation in homicide often not unlike that of combat in which two persons committed to the value of violence come together and in which chance often dictates the identity of the slayer and of the slain.

[15] A recent study (L. G. Schultz, 'Why the Negro Carries Weapons', *Journal of Criminal Law, Criminology and Police Science* (1962) 53:476–483) on weapon-carrying suggests that this habit is related, within the colored population, to lower-class status, rural origin from the South, and prior criminal record.

does not defend his honor or his female companion will be socially emasculated. The 'coward' is forced to move out of the territory, to find new friends and make new alliances. Membership is lost in the subsociety sharing the cluster of attitudes positively associated with violence. If forced withdrawal or voluntary retreat are not acceptable modes of response to engaging in the counter-norm, then execution, as is reputed to occur in organized crime, may be the extreme punitive measure.

6. *The development of favorable attitudes toward, and the use of, violence in a subculture usually involve learned behavior and a process of differential learning,*[16] *association,*[17] *or identification.*[18] Not all persons exposed—even equally exposed—to the presence of a subculture of violence absorb and share in the values in equal portions. Differential personality variables must be considered in an integrated social-psychological approach to an understanding of the subcultural aspects of violence. We have taken the position that aggression is a learned response, socially facilitated and integrated, as a habit, in more or less permanent form, among the personality characteristics of the aggressor. Aggression, from a psychological standpoint, has been defined by Buss as 'the delivery of noxious stimuli in an interpersonal context'.[19] Aggression seems to possess two major classes of reinforcers: the pain and injury inflicted upon the victim and its extrinsic rewards.[20] Both are present in a subculture of violence, and their mechanism of action is facilitated by the social support that the aggressor receives in his group. The relationship between aggression, anger, and hostility is complicated by the habit characteristics of the first, the drive state of the second, and the attitudinal interpretative nature of the third. Obviously, the immediacy and the short temporal sequence of anger with its autonomic components make it difficult to study a criminal population that is some distance removed from the anger-provoked event. Hostility, although amenable to easier assessment, does not give a clear indication or measure of physical attack because of its predominantly verbal aspects. However, it may dispose to or prepare for aggression.[21]

Aggression, in its physical manifest form, remains the most criminologically relevant aspect in a study of violent assaultive behavior. If violent aggression is a habit and possesses permanent or quasi-permanent personality trait characteristics, it should be amenable to psychological assessment through appropriate diagnostic techniques. Among the several alternative diagnostic methodologies, those based on a perceptual approach seem to be able, according to the existing literature,[22] to elicit signs and symptoms of behavioral aggression, demonstrating the existence of this 'habit' and/or trait in the personality of the subject being tested. Obviously, the same set of techniques being used to diagnose the trait of aggression can be used to assess the

[16] As previously mentioned, differential reactions to conditioning may be the cause of differential adherence to the subculture by equally exposed subjects.

[17] Alternative hypotheses make use of the concept of differential association (Edwin H. Sutherland and Donald E. Cressey, *Principles of Criminology,* Philadelphia: Lippincott, 1955).

[18] Differential identification has been presented as a more psychologically meaningful alternative to simple association (Daniel Glaser, 'Criminality Theories and Behavioral Images', *American Journal of Sociology* (1956) 5:433–444).

[19] A. H. Buss, *The Psychology of Aggression,* New York: Wiley, 1961, pp. 1–2.

[20] *Ibid.*, pp. 2–4.

[21] *Ibid.,* Chapter 1, *passim.*

[22] For an analysis of relevant literature on diagnostic psychological instruments, see Buss, *op. cit.,* Chapters VIII and IX. For discussion of a preventive psychiatric system, see Leon D. Hankoff, 'Prevention of Violence', paper read at the annual meeting of the Association for the Psychiatric Treatment of Offenders, New York, May 7, 1964.

presence of major psychopathology, which might, in a restricted number of cases, have caused 'aggressive behavior' outside, or in spite of, any cultural or subcultural allegiance.

7. *The use of violence in a subculture is not necessarily viewed as illicit conduct and the users therefore do not have to deal with feelings of guilt about their aggression.* Violence can become a part of the life style, the theme of solving difficult problems or problem situations. It should be stressed that the problems and situations to which we refer arise mostly within the subculture, for violence is used mostly between persons and groups who themselves rely upon the same supportive values and norms. A carrier and user of violence will not be burdened by conscious guilt, then, because generally he is not attacking the representatives of the nonviolent culture, and because the recipient of this violence may be described by similar class status, occupational, residential, age, and other attribute categories which characterize the subuniverse of the collectivity sharing in the subculture of violence. Even law-abiding members of the local subculture area may not view various illegal expressions of violence as menacing or immoral. Furthermore, when the attacked see their assaulters as agents of the same kind of aggression they themselves represent, violent retaliation is readily legitimized by a situationally specific rationale, as well as by the generally normative supports for violence.

Probably no single theory will ever explain the variety of observable violent behavior. However, the subculture-of-violence approach offers, we believe, the advantage of bringing together psychological and sociological constructs to aid in the explanation of the concentration of violence in specific socio-economic groups and ecological areas.

12. Differentiated Structures, Differential Opportunities, and Delinquent Subcultures

Richard A. Cloward and Lloyd E. Ohlin

We believe that each individual occupies a position in both legitimate and illegitimate opportunity structures. This is a new way of defining the situation. The theory of anomie views the individual primarily in terms of the legitimate opportunity structure. It poses questions regarding differentials in access to legitimate routes to success-goals; at the same time it assumes either that illegitimate avenues to success-goals are freely available or that differentials in their availability are of little significance. This tendency may be seen in the following statement by Merton:

> Several researchers have shown that specialized areas of vice and crime constitute a "normal" response to a situation where the cultural emphasis upon pecuniary success has been absorbed, but where there is little access to conventional and legitimate means for becoming successful. The occupational opportunities of people in these areas are largely confined to manual labor and the lesser white-collar jobs. Given the American stigmatization of manual labor *which has been found to hold rather uniformly for all social classes,* and the absence of realistic opportunities for advancement beyond this level, the result is a marked tendency toward deviant behavior. The status of unskilled labor and the consequent low income cannot readily compete *in terms of established standards of worth* with the promises of power and high income from organized vice, rackets and crime.... [Such a situation] leads toward the gradual attenuation of legitimate, but by and large ineffectual, strivings and the increasing use of illegitimate, but more or less effective, expedients.[1]

The cultural-transmission and differential-association tradition, on the other hand, assumes that access to illegitimate means is variable, but it does not recognize the

Reprinted with permission of The Macmillan Company from "Illegitimate Means and Delinquent Subcultures," and "Subcultural Differentiation," *Delinquency and Opportunity: A Theory of Delinquent Gangs* by Richard A. Cloward and Lloyd E. Ohlin. Copyright by The Free Press, a Corporation, 1960.

[1] R. K. Merton, *Social Theory and Social Structure,* Rev. and Enl. Ed. (Glencoe, Ill.: Free Press, 1957), pp. 145–46.

significance of comparable differentials in access to legitimate means. Sutherland's "ninth proposition" in the theory of differential association states:

> *Though criminal behavior is an expression of general needs and values, it is not explained by those general needs and values since non-criminal behavior is an expression of the same needs and values.* Thieves generally steal in order to secure money, but likewise honest laborers work in order to secure money. The attempts by many scholars to explain criminal behavior by general drives and values, such as the happiness principle, striving for social status, the money motive, or frustration, have been and must continue to be futile since they explain lawful behavior as completely as they explain criminal behavior.[2]

In this statement, Sutherland appears to assume that people have equal and free access to legitimate means regardless of their social position. At the very least, he does not treat access to legitimate means as variable. It is, of course, perfectly true that "striving for social status," "the money motive," and other socially approved drives do not fully account for either deviant or conforming behavior. But if goal-oriented behavior occurs under conditions in which there are socially structured obstacles to the satisfaction of these drives by legitimate means, the resulting pressures, we contend, might lead to deviance.

The concept of differential opportunity structures permits us to unite the theory of anomie, which recognizes the concept of differentials in access to legitimate means, and the "Chicago tradition," in which the concept of differentials in access to illegitimate means is implicit. We can now look at the individual, not simply in relation to one or the other system of means, but in relation to both legitimate and illegitimate systems. This approach permits us to ask, for example, how the relative availability of illegitimate opportunities affects the resolution of adjustment problems leading to deviant behavior. We believe that the way in which these problems are resolved may depend upon the kind of support for one or another type of illegitimate activity that is given at different points in the social structure. If, in a given social location, illegal or criminal means are not readily available, then we should not expect a criminal subculture to develop among adolescents. By the same logic, we should expect the manipulation of violence to become a primary avenue to higher status only in areas where the means of violence are not denied to the young. To give a third example, drug addiction and participation in subcultures organized around the consumption of drugs presuppose that persons can secure access to drugs and knowledge about how to use them. In some parts of the social structure, this would be very difficult; in others, very easy. In short, there are marked differences from one part of the social structure to another in the types of illegitimate adaptation that are available to persons in search of solutions to problems of adjustment

[2] E. H. Sutherland, *Principles of Criminology*, 4th ed. (Philadelphia: Lippincott, 1947), pp. 7–8.

arising from the restricted availability of legitimate means.[3] In this sense, then, we can think of individuals as being located in two opportunity structures–one legitimate. Given limited access to success-goals by legitimate means, the nature of the delinquent response that may result will vary according to the availability of various illegitimate means.[4]

...

Slum Organization and Subculture Differentiation

Before we turn to a discussion of the relationship between particular forms of slum organization and the differentiation of subcultural content, it might be useful to note a recent article by Cohen and Short pertaining to subcultural differentiation.[5]...

The point they make is that subcultural content varies depending on the age-level of the participants. Among younger delinquents, they suggest, a universal or generic form of subculture emerges which is *independent* of its specific social milieu. This subcultural form is characterized by a diffuse agglomeration of cultural traits, including an orientation toward the "kick," a "conflict" orientation, and an orientation toward the illegal acquisition of money or goods. These traits or orientations, some of which are more or less incompatible with others, can nevertheless coexist because the subculture is loosely organized and thus capable of considerable cultural versatility. As the participants mature, however, additional (unspecified) forces intervene which intensify the latent conflict between these orientations. Cliques within the subculture may then break away and form a more specialized subsubculture which tends to value one orientation more than others (*e.g.*, disciplined theft rather than indiscriminate violence and destruction). If a particular cultural orientation comes to be widely diffused through the group, the generic culture as a whole may tend to become specialized. In either case, Cohen and Short believe that the process of subcultural differentiation occurs at later stages in the age cycle.

We question the validity of this point of view, for it rests upon what we consider an unwarranted premise; namely, that the social milieu influences the content of

[3] For an example of restrictions on access to illegitimate roles, note the impact of racial definitions in the following case: "I was greeted by two prisoners who were to be my cell buddies. Ernest was a first offender, charged with being a 'hold-up' man. Bill, the other buddy, was an old offender, going through the machinery of becoming a habitual criminal, in and out of jail....The first thing they asked me was, 'What are you in for?' I said, 'Jack-rolling.' The hardened one (Bill) looked at me with a superior air and said, 'A hoodlum, eh? An ordinary sneak thief. Not willing to leave jack-rolling to the niggers, eh? That's all they're good for. Kid, jack-rolling's not a white man's job.' I could see that he was disgusted with me, and I was too scared to say anything" (C. R. Shaw, *The Jack-Roller,* (Chicago: University of Chicago Press, 1930), p. 101).

[4] For a discussion of the way in which the availability of illegitimate means influences the adaptations of inmates to prison life, see R. A. Cloward, "Social Control in the Prison," *Theoretical Studies of the Social Organization of the Prison,* Bulletin No. 15 (New York: Social Science Research Council, March 1960), pp. 20-48.

[5] A. K. Cohen and J. F. Short, Jr., "Research in Delinquent Subcultures," *Journal of Social Issues,* Vol. 14, No. 3 (Summer 1958), pp. 20–37.

subcultural solutions at some points in the age cycle but not at other points. We prefer to make a quite different assumption; namely, that *the social milieu affects the nature of the deviant response whatever the motivation and social position* (i.e., *age, sex, socioeconomic level*) *of the participants in the delinquent subculture.* We assume that the local cultural and social structure impinges upon and modifies deviant responses from the very outset. The delinquent subculture may or may not be fully specialized at first, but we should not expect it to manifest all three delinquent orientations to the same extent, even at an early stage of development. In other words, we should expect the content of delinquent subcultures to vary predictably with certain features of the milieu in which these cultures emerge. And we should further expect these predominant traits to become all the more articulated and specialized as the subcultures become stabilized and integrated with their respective environments. With these notions in mind, we turn now to a discussion of the three types of subculture and their relationship to features of slum social structure.

•••

We come now to the question of the specific social conditions that make for the emergence of distinctive delinquent subcultures. Throughout this analysis, we shall make extensive use of the concepts of social organization: ...namely, integration of different age-levels of offenders, and integration of carriers of conventional and deviant values. Delinquent responses vary from one neighborhood to another, we believe, according to the articulation of these structures in the neighborhood. Our object here is to show more precisely how various forms of neighborhood integration affect the development of subcultural content.

The Criminal Subculture

The criminal subculture, like the conflict and retreatist adaptations, requires a specialized environment if it is to flourish. Among the environmental supports of a criminal style of life are integration of offenders at various age-levels and close integration of the carriers of conventional and illegitimate values.

Integration of Age-Levels. Nowhere in the criminological literature is the concept of integration between different age-levels of offender made more explicit than in discussions of criminal learning. Most criminologists agree that criminal behavior presupposes patterned sets of relationships through which the requisite values and skills are communicated or transmitted from one age-level to another. What, then, are some of the specific components of systems organized for the socialization of potential criminals?

Criminal Role-Models. The lower class is not without its own distinctive and indigenous illegitimate success-models. Many accounts in the literature suggest that lower-class adults who have achieved success by illegitimate means not only are highly visible to young people in slum areas but often are willing to establish intimate relationships with these youth.

"Every boy has some ideal he looks up to and admires. His ideal may be Babe Ruth, Jack Dempsey, or Al Capone. When I was twelve, we moved into a neighborhood with a lot of gangsters. They were all swell dressers and had big cars and carried "gats." Us kids saw these swell guys and mingled with them in the cigar store on the corner. Jack Gurney was the one in the mob that I had a fancy to. He used to take my sis out and that way I saw him often. He was in the stick-up rackets before he was in the beer rackets, and he was a swell dresser and had lots of dough....I liked to be near him and felt stuck up over the other guys because he came to my home to see my sis."[6]

Just as the middle-class youth, as a consequence of intimate relationships with, say, a banker or a businessman, may aspire to *become* a banker or a businessman, so the lower-class youth may be associated with and aspire to become a "policy king": " 'I want to be a big shot....Have all the guys look up to me. Have a couple of Lincolns, lots of broads, and all the coppers licking my shoes.' "[7] The crucial point here is that success-goals are not equally available to persons in different positions in the social structure. To the extent that social-class lines act as barriers to interaction between persons in different social strata, conventional success-models may not be salient for lower-class youth. The successful criminal, on the other hand, may be an intimate, personal figure in the fabric of the lower-class area. Hence one of the forces leading to rational, disciplined, crime-oriented delinquency may be the availability of criminal success-models.

Age-grading of Criminal Learning and Performance. The process by which the young acquire the values and skills prerequisite for a stable criminal career has been described in many studies. The central mechanism in the learning process is integration of different age-levels of offender. In an extensive study of a criminal gang on the Lower East Side of New York City, Bloch and Niederhoffer found that

...the Pirates [a group of young adults] was actually the central organizing committee, the party headquarters for the youthful delinquents in the area. They held regular conferences with the delegates from outlying districts to outline strategy.... The younger Corner Boys [a gang of adolescents in the same vicinity] who ... were trying to join with the older Pirates ... were on a probationary status. If they showed signs of promise, a couple of them were allowed to accompany the Pirates on tours of exploration to look over the terrain around the next "job."[8]

At the pinnacle of this age-graded system stood an adult, Paulie.

Paulie had real prestige in the gang. His was the final say in all important decisions. Older than the other members [of the Pirates] by seven or eight years, he maintained a certain air of mystery....From talks with more garrulous members, it was learned that Paulie was the mastermind behind some of the gang's most impressive coups.[9]

[6] C. R. Shaw, "Juvenile Delinquency–A Group Tradition," *Bulletin of the State University of Iowa,* No. 23, N. S. No. 700, 1933, p. 8.

[7] *Ibid.*, p. 9.

[8] H. H. Bloch and Arthur Niederhoffer, *The Gang: A Study in Adolescent Behavior* (New York: Philosophical Library, 1958), pp. 198–99.

[9] *Ibid.*, p. 201.

The basis of Paulie's prestige in the gang is apparent in the following account of his relationship with the full-fledged adult criminal world:

> From his contacts, information was obtained as to the most inviting locations to burglarize. It was he who developed the strategy and outlined the major stages of each campaign of burglary or robbery.... Another vital duty which he performed was to get rid of the considerable loot, which might consist of jewelry, clothing, tools, or currency in large denominations. His contact with professional gangsters, fences, bookies, made him an ideal choice for this function.[10]

Learning alone, as we have said, does not ensure that the individual can or will perform the role for which he has been prepared. The social structure must also support the actual performance of the role. To say that the individual must have the opportunity to discharge a stable criminal role as well as to prepare for it does not mean that role-preparation necessarily takes place in one stage and role-performance in a succeeding stage. The apprentice may be afforded opportunities to play out a particular role at various points in the learning process.

> When we were shoplifting we always made a game of it. For example, we might gamble on who could steal the most caps in a day, or who could steal in the presence of a detective and then get away. This was the best part of the game. I would go into a store to steal a cap, by trying one on when the clerk was not watching, walk out of the store, leaving the old cap. With the new cap on my head I would go into another store, do the same thing as in the other store, getting a new hat and leaving the one I had taken from the other place. I might do this all day.... It was the fun I wanted, not the hat. I kept this up for months and *then began to sell the things to a man on the West Side. It was at this time that I began to steal for gain.*[11]

This quotation illustrates how delinquent role-preparation and role-performance may be integrated even at the "play-group" stage of illegitimate learning. The child has an opportunity to actually perform illegitimate roles because such activity finds support in his immediate neighborhood milieu. The rewards–monetary and other–of successful learning and performance are immediate and gratifying at each age level.

Integration of Values. Unless the carriers of criminal and conventional values are closely bound to one another, stable criminal roles cannot develop. The criminal, like the occupant of a conventional role, must establish relationships with other categories of persons, all of whom contribute in one way or another to the successful performance of criminal activity. As Tannenbaum says, "The development of the criminal career requires and finds in the immediate environment other supporting elements in addition to the active 'criminal gangs'; to develop the career requires the support of middlemen. These may be junk men, fences, lawyers, bondsmen, 'backers,' as they are called."[12] The intricate systems of relationship between these

[10] *Ibid.*

[11] C. R. Shaw, *op. cit.*, p. 3.

[12] Frank Tannenbaum, *Crime and the Community* (New York: Columbia University Press, 1938), p. 60.

legitimate and illegitimate persons constitute the type of environment in which the juvenile criminal subculture can come into being.[13]

An excellent example of the way in which the content of a delinquent subculture is affected by its location in a particular milieu is afforded by the "fence," a dealer in stolen goods who is found in some but not all lower-class neighborhoods. Relationships between such middlemen and criminals are not confined to adult offenders; numerous accounts of lower-class life suggest not only that relationships form between fences and youngsters but also that the fence is a crucial element in the structure of illegitimate opportunity. He often caters to and encourages delinquent activities among the young. He may even exert controls leading the young to orient their stealing in the most lucrative and least risky directions. The same point may be made of junk dealers in some areas, racketeers who permit minors to run errands, and other occupants of illegitimate or semilegitimate roles.

As the apprentice criminal passes from one status to another in the illegitimate opportunity system, we should expect him to develop an ever-widening set of relationships with members of the semilegitimate and legitimate world. For example, a delinquent who is rising in the structure might begin to come into contact with mature criminals, law-enforcement officials, politicians, bail bondsmen, "fixers," and the like. As his activities become integrated with the activities of these persons, his knowledge of the illegitimate world is deepened, new skills are acquired, and the opportunity to engage in new types of illegitimate activity is enhanced. Unless he can form these relationships, the possibility of a stable, protected criminal style of life is effectively precluded.

The type of environment that encourages a criminal orientation among delinquents is, then, characterized by close integration of the carriers of conventional and illegitimate values. The *content* of the delinquent subculture is a more or less direct response to the local milieu in which it emerges. And it is the "integrated" neighborhood, we suggest, that produces the criminal type of delinquent subculture.

Structural Integration and Social Control. Delinquent behavior generally exhibits a component of aggressiveness. Even youth in neighborhoods that are favorable learning environments for criminal careers are likely to engage in some "bopping" and other forms of violence. Hence one feature of delinquency that must be explained is its tendency toward aggressive behavior. However, aggressiveness is not the primary component of all delinquent behavior; it is much more characteristic of some delinquent groups than of others. Therefore, we must also concern ourselves with the conditions under which the aggressive component becomes ascendant.

The importance of assessing the relative dominance of the case of Murder, Inc. Abe Reles, a former member of the syndicate who turned state's evidence, made certain comments about Murder, Inc. which illustrate perfectly Max Weber's famous characterization of the norms governing role performance and interpersonal relation-

[13]In this connection, see R. A. Cloward, "Social Control in the Prison," *Theoretical Studies of the Social Organization of the Prison,* Bulletin No. 15 (New York: Social Science Research Council, March 1960), pp. 20–48, which illustrates similar forms of integration in a penal setting.

ships in bureaucratic organizations: *"Sine ira et studio"* ("without anger or passion").

The crime trust, Reles insists, never commits murder out of passion, excitement, jealousy, personal revenge, or any of the usual motives which prompt private, unorganized murder. It kills impersonally, and solely for business considerations. Even business rivalry, he adds, is not the usual motive, unless "somebody gets too balky or somebody steps right on top of you." No gangster may kill on his own initiative; every murder must be ordered by the leaders at the top, and it must serve the welfare of the organization....The crime trust insists that that murder must be a business matter, organized by the chiefs in conference and carried out in a disciplined way. "It's a real business all the way through," Reles explains. "It just happens to be that kind of business, but nobody is allowed to kill from personal grievance. There's got to be a good business reason, and top men of the combination must give their okay."[14]

The pressure for rational role performance in the adult criminal world is exerted downward, we suggest, through interconnected systems of age-graded statuses. At each point in this illegitimate hierarchy, instrumental rather than expressive behavior is emphasized. In their description of the Pirates, for example, Bloch and Niederhoffer observe that Paulie, the adult mastermind of the gang, avoided expressive behavior: "The younger Pirates might indulge in wild adolescent antics. Paulie remained aloof."[15] Paulie symbolized a mode of life in which reason, discipline, and foresight were uppermost. To the extent that younger members of the gang identified with him, they were constrained to adopt a similar posture. Rico, the leader of a gang described in a recent book by Harrison Salisbury, can be characterized in much the same way:

> This youngster was the most successful kid in the neighborhood. He was a dope pusher. Some weeks he made as much as $200. He used his influence in some surprising ways. He persuaded the gang members to stop bopping because he was afraid it would bring on police intervention and interfere with his drug sales. He flatly refused to sell dope to boys and kicked out of the gang any kid who started to use drugs. He sold only to adults. With his money he bought jackets for the gang, took care of hospital bills of members, paid for the rent on his mother's flat, paid most of the family expenses and sometimes spent sixty dollars to buy a coat as a present for one of his boys.[16]

The same analysis helps to explain a puzzling aspect of delinquent behavior; namely, the apparent disregard delinquents sometimes exhibit for stolen objects. Some theorists have concluded from this that the ends of stealing are not utilitarian, that delinquents do not steal because they need or want the objects in question or for any other rational reason. Cohen, for example, asserts that "were the participant in the delinquent subculture merely employing illicit means to the end of acquiring

[14] Joseph Freeman, "Murder Monopoly: The Inside Story of a Crime Trust," *The Nation,* Vol. 150, No. 21 (May 25, 1940), p. 648. This is but one of many sources in which the bureaucratization of crime is discussed.

[15] Bloch and Niederhoffer, *op. cit.,* p. 201.

[16] H. E. Salisbury, *The Shook-up Generation* (New York: Harper & Bros., 1958), p. 176.

economic goods, he would show more respect for the goods he has thus acquired."[17] Hence, Cohen concludes, the bulk of stealing among delinquents is "for the hell of it" rather than for economic gain. Whether stealing is expressive or instrumental may depend, however, on the social context in which it occurs. Where criminal opportunities exist, it may be argued that stealing is a way of expressing solidarity with the carriers of criminal values and, further, that it is a way of acquiring the various concrete skills necessary before the potential criminal can gain full acceptance in the group to which he aspires. That is, a certain amount of stealing may be motivated less by immediate need for the objects in question than by a need to acquire skill in the arts of theft. When practice in theft is the implicit purpose, the manner of disposing of stolen goods is unimportant. Similarly, the status accruing to the pickpocket who can negotiate a "left-front-breech" derives not so much from the immediate profit attaching to this maneuver as from the fact that it marks the individual as a master craftsman. In other words, where criminal learning environments and opportunity structures exist, stealing beyond immediate economic needs may constitute anticipatory socialization. But where these structures do not exist, such stealing may be simply an expressive act in defiance of conventional values.

Shaw pointed to a related aspect of the social control of delinquent behavior. Noting the prestige ordering of criminal activities, he commented on the way in which such definitions, once internalized, tend to regulate the behavior of delinquents:

> It is a matter of significance to note... that there is a general tendency among older delinquents and criminals to look with contempt upon the person who specializes in any form of petty stealing. The common thief is not distinguished for manual dexterity and accomplishment, like the pickpocket or mobsman, nor for courage, ingenuity and skill, like the burglar, but is characterized by low cunning and stealth—hence the term "sneak thief." ... It is possible that the stigma attaching to petty stealing among members of older delinquent groups is one factor which gives impetus to the young delinquent's desire to abandon such forms of petty delinquency as stealing junk, vegetables, breaking into freight cars ... and to become identified with older groups engaged in such crimes as larceny of automobiles and robbery with a gun, both of which are accredited "rackets" among older delinquents....[18]

To the extent that an area has an age-graded criminal structure in which juvenile delinquents can become enmeshed, we suggest that the norms governing adult criminal-role performance filter down, becoming significant principles in the life-organization of the young. The youngster who has come into contact with such an age-graded structure and who has won initial acceptance by older and more sophisticated delinquents will be less likely to engage in malicious, destructive behavior than indisciplined, instrumental, career-oriented behavior. In this way the adult

[17] A. K. Cohen, *Delinquent Boys: The Culture of the Gang* (Glencoe, Ill.: Free Press, 1955), p. 36.

[18] Shaw, *op. cit.*, p. 10.

criminal system exerts controls over the behavior of delinquents. Referring to urban areas characterized by integration of different age-levels of offender, Kobrin makes an observation that tends to bear out our theoretical scheme:

> ... delinquency tends to occur within a partial framework of social controls, insofar as delinquent activity in these areas represents a tolerated means for the acquisition of an approved role and status. Thus, while delinquent activity here possesses the usual characteristics of violence and destructiveness, there tend to develop effective limits of permissible activity in this direction. Delinquency is, in other words, encompassed and contained within a local social structure, and is marginally but palpably related to that structure.[19]

In summary, the criminal subculture is likely to arise in a neighborhood milieu characterized by close bonds between different age-levels of offender, and between criminal and conventional elements. As a consequence of these integrative relationships, a new opportunity structure emerges which provides alternative avenues to success-goals. Hence the pressures generated by restrictions on legitimate access to success-goals are drained off. Social controls over the conduct of the young are effectively exercised, limiting expressive behavior and constraining the discontented to adopt instrumental, if criminalistic, styles of life.

The Conflict Subculture

Because youngsters caught up in the conflict subculture often endanger their own lives and the lives of others and cause considerable property damage, the conflict form of delinquency is a source of great public concern. Its prevalence, therefore, is probably exaggerated. There is no evidence to suggest that the conflict subculture is more widespread than the other subcultures, but the nature of its activities makes it more visible and thus attracts public attention. As a consequence, many people erroneously equate "delinquency" and "conflict behavior." But whatever its prevalence, the conflict subculture is of both theoretical and social importance, and calls for explanation.

We have questioned the common belief that slum areas, because they are slums, are necessarily disorganized. We have pointed to forms of integration which give some slum areas unity and cohesion. Areas in which these integrative structures are found, we suggested, tend to be characterized by criminal rather than conflict or retreatist subcultures. But not all slums are integrated. Some lower-class urban neighborhoods lack unity and cohesiveness. Because the prerequisites for the emergence of stable systems of social relations are not present, a state of social disorganization prevails.

The many forces making for instability in the social organization of some slum areas include high rates of vertical and geographic mobility; massive housing projects in which "site tenants" are not accorded priority in occupancy, so that tradi-

[19] Solomon Kobrin, "The Conflict of Values in Delinquency Areas," *American Sociological Review*, Vol. 16 (Oct. 1951), p. 657.

tional residents are dispersed and "strangers" re-assembled; and changing land use, as in the case of residential areas that are encroached upon by the expansion of adjacent commercial or industrial areas. Forces of this kind keep a community off balance, for tentative efforts to develop social organization are quickly checked. Transiency and instability become the overriding features of social life.

Transiency and instability, in combination, produce powerful pressures for violent behavior among the young in these areas. First, an unorganized community cannot provide access to legitimate channels to success-goals, and thus discontent among the young with their life-chances is heightened. Secondly, access to stable criminal opportunity systems is also restricted, for disorganized neighborhoods do not develop integration of different age-levels of offender or integration of carriers of criminal and conventional values. The young, in short, are relatively deprived of *both* conventional and criminal opportunity. Finally, social controls are weak in such communities. These conditions, we believe, lead to the emergence of conflict subcultures.

Social Disorganization and Opportunity. Communities that are unable to develop conventional forms of social organization are also unable to provide legitimate modes of access to culturally valued success-goals. The disorganized slum is a world populated with failures, with the outcasts of the larger society. Here families orient themselves not toward the future but toward the present, not toward social advancement but toward survival. The adult community, being disorganized, cannot provide the resources and opportunities that are required if the young are to move upward in the social order.

Just as the unintegrated slum cannot mobilize legitimate resources for the young, neither can it provide them with access to stable criminal careers, for illegitimate learning and opportunity structures do not develop. The disorganized slum, populated in part by failures in the conventional world, also contains the outcasts of the criminal world. This is not to say that crime is nonexistent in such areas, but what crime there is tends to be individualistic, unorganized, petty, poorly paid, and unprotected. This is the haunt of the small-time thief, the drifter, the pimp, the jackroller, the unsophisticated "con" man, the pickpocket who is all thumbs, and others who cannot graduate beyond "heisting" candy stores or "busting" gas stations. Since they are unorganized and without financial resources, criminals in these areas cannot purchase immunity from prosecution; they have neither the money nor the political contacts to "put in the fix." Hence they are harassed by the police, and many of them spend the better part of their lives in prison. The organized criminal world is generally able to protect itself against such harassment, prosecution, and imprisonment. But professional crime and organized rackets, like any business enterprise, can thrive only in a stable, predictable, and integrated environment. In this sense, then, the unintegrated area does not constitute a promising launching site for lucrative and protected criminal careers. Because such areas fail to develop criminal learning environments and opportunity structures, stable criminal subcultures cannot emerge.

Social Disorganization and Social Control. As we have noted, social controls originate in both the conventional and the illegitimate sectors of the stable slum area. But this is apparently not the case in the disorganized slum. The basic disorganization of the conventional institutional structure makes it impossible for controls to originate there. At the same time, Kobrin asserts, "Because adult crime in this type of area is itself unorganized, its value system remains implicit and hence incapable of generating norms which function effectively on a groupwide basis." Hence "juvenile violators readily escape not merely the controls of conventional persons in the community but those of adult violators as well." Under such conditions,

> ... [the] delinquencies of juveniles tend to acquire a wild, untrammelled character. Delinquents in this kind of situation more frequently exhibit the personality traits of the social type sometimes referred to as the hoodlum. Both individually and in groups, violent physical combat is engaged in for its own sake, almost as a form of recreation. Here groups of delinquents may be seen as excluded, isolated conflict groups dedicated to an unending battle against all forms of constraint. The escape from controls originating in any social structure, other than that provided by unstable groupings of the delinquents themselves, is here complete.[20]

Unlike Kobrin, we do not attribute conflict behavior in unorganized urban areas to the absence of controls alone. The young in such areas are also exposed to acute frustrations, arising from conditions in which access to success-goals is blocked by the absence of any institutionalized channels, legitimate or illegitimate. They are deprived not only of conventional opportunity but also of criminal routes to the "big money." In other words, precisely when frustrations are maximized, social controls are weakened. Social controls and channels to success-goals are generally related: where opportunities exist, patterns of control will be found; where opportunities are absent, patterns of social control are likely to be absent too. The association of these two features of social organization is a logical implication of our theory.

Social Disorganization and Violence. Those adolescents in disorganized urban areas who are oriented toward achieving higher position but are cut off from institutionalized channels, criminal as well as legitimate, must rely upon their own resources for solving this problem of adjustment. Under these conditions, tendencies toward aberrant behavior become intensified and magnified. These adolescents seize upon the manipulation of violence as a route to status not only because it provides a way of expressing pent-up angers and frustrations but also because they are not cut off from access to violent means by vicissitudes of birth. In the world of violence, such attributes as race, socioeconomic position, age, and the like are irrelevant; personal worth is judged on the basis of qualities that are available to all who would cultivate them. The principal prerequisites for success are "guts" and the capacity to endure pain. One doesn't need "connections," "pull," or elaborate technical skills in order to achieve "rep." The essence of the warrior adjustment is an expressed feeling-state: "heart." The acquisition of status is not simply a consequence of skill in the use of violence or of physical strength but depends, rather, on one's

[20] *Ibid.*, p. 658.

willingness to risk injury or death in the search for "rep." A physically immature boy may find a place among the warrior elite if, when provoked, he will run such risks, thus demonstrating "heart."

As long as conventional and criminal opportunity structures remain closed, violence continues unchecked. The bulk of aggressive behavior appears to be channeled into gang warfare; success in street combat assures the group that its "turf" will not be invaded, that its girls will not be molested, that its members will otherwise be treated deferentially by young and old in the local community. *If new opportunity structures are opened, however, violence tends to be relinquished.* Indeed, the success of certain efforts to discourage violent, aggressive behavior among warrior gangs has resulted precisely from the fact that some powerful group has responded deferentially to these gangs. (The group is powerful because it can provide, or at least hold out the promise of providing, channels to higher position, such as jobs, education, and the like.) The most dramatic illustration of this process may be seen in programs conducted by social group workers who attach themselves to street gangs....

...

In summary, severe limitations on both conventional and criminal opportunity intensify frustrations and position discontent. Discontent is heightened further under conditions in which social control is relaxed, for the area lacking integration between age-levels of offender and between carriers of conventional and criminal values cannot generate pressures to contain frustrations among the young. These are the circumstances, we suggest, in which adolescents turn to violence in search of status. Violence comes to be ascendant, in short, under conditions of relative detachment from all institutionalized systems of opportunity and social control.

The Retreatist Subculture

The consumption of drugs—one of the most serious forms of retreatist behavior—has become a severe problem among adolescents and young adults, particularly in lower-class urban areas. By and large, drug use in these areas has been attributed to rapid geographic mobility, inadequate social controls, and other manifestations of social disorganization. In this section, we shall suggest a hypothesis that may open up new avenues of inquiry in regard to the growing problem of drug use among the young.

Pressures Leading to Retreatist Subcultures. Retreatism is often conceived as an isolated adaptation, characterized by a breakdown in relationships with other persons. Indeed, this is frequently true, as in the case of psychotics. The drug-user, however, must become affiliated with others, if only to secure access to a steady supply of drugs. Just as stable criminal activity cannot be explained by reference to motivation alone. neither can stable drug use be fully explained in this way. Opportunity to use drugs must also be present. But such opportunities are restricted. As Becker notes, the illegal distribution of drugs is limited to "sources which are not available to the ordinary person. In order for a person to begin marihuana use, he must begin participation in some group through which these sources of supply become available to him."[21]

Because of these restrictions on the availability of drugs, new users must become affiliated with old users. They must learn the lore of drug use, the skills required in making appropriate "connections," the controls which govern the purchase of drugs (*e.g.*, drugs will not generally be made available to anyone until he is "defined as a person who can safely be trusted to buy drugs without endangering anyone else"), and the like. As this process of socialization proceeds, the individual "is considered more trustworthy, [and] the necessary knowledge and introductions to dealers [then become] available to him." According to Becker, the "processes by which people are emancipated from the larger set of controls *and become responsive to those of the subculture*" are "important factors in the genesis of deviant behavior."[22] The drug-user, in other words, must be understood not only in terms of his personality and the social structure, which create a readiness to engage in drug use, but also in terms of the new patterns of associations and values to which he is exposed as he seeks access to drugs. The more the individual is caught in this web of associations, the more likely that he will persist in drug use, for he has become incorporated in a subculture that exerts control over his behavior.

Despite these pressures toward subcultural formation, it is probably also true that the resulting ties among addicts are not so solidary as those among participants in criminal and conflict subcultures. Addiction is in many ways an individualistic adaptation, for the "kick" is essentially a private experience. The compelling need for the drug is also a divisive force, for it leads to intense competition among addicts for money. Forces of this kind thus limit the relative cohesion which can develop among users.

"Double Failure" and Drug Use. We turn now to a discussion of the social conditions which give rise to retreatist reactions such as drug use among adolescents. According to Merton,

> Retreatism arises from continued failure to near the goal by legitimate measures and from an inability to use the illegitimate route because of internalized prohibitions, this process occurring while the supreme value of the success-goal has not yet been renounced. The conflict is resolved by abandoning both precipitating elements, the goals and the norms. The escape is complete, the conflict is eliminated and the individual is associalized.[23]

[21] H. S. Becker, "Marihuana Use and Social Control," *Social Problems*, Vol. 3, No. 1 (July 1955), pp. 36–37.

[22] *Ibid.*, p. 35. Emphasis added.

[23] R. K. Merton, *Social Theory and Social Structure*, Rev. and Enl. Ed. (Glencoe, Ill.: Free Press, 1957), pp. 153–54. For discussions of drug use among juveniles, see D. L. Gerard and Conon Kornetsky, "Adolescent Opiate Addiction–A Study of Control and Addict Subjects," *Psychiatric Quarterly*, Vol. 29 (April 1955), pp. 457–86; Isidor Chein *et al.*, *Studies of Narcotics Use Among Juveniles* (New York University, Research Center for Human Relations, mimeographed, Jan. 1956); Harold Finestone, "Cats, Kicks, and Color," *Social Problems*, Vol. 5, No. 1 (July 1957), pp. 3–13; and D. M. Wilmer, Eva Rosenfeld, R. S. Lee, D. L. Gerard, and Isidor Chein, "Heroin Use and Street Gangs," *Criminal Law, Criminology and Police Science*, Vol. 48, No. 4 (Nov.-Dec. 1957), pp. 399–409.

Thus he identifies two principal factors in the emergence of retreatist adaptations: (1) continued failure to reach culturally approved goals by legitimate means, and (2) inability to employ illegitimate alternatives because of internalized prohibitions. We take it that "internalized prohibitions" have to do with the individual's attitudes toward norms. Retreatists, according to Merton, do not call into question the legitimacy of existing institutional arrangements—a process which might then be followed by the use of illegitimate alternatives. Rather, they call into question their own adequacy, locating blame for their dilemma in personal deficiencies. One way of resolving the intense anxiety and guilt which ensue is to withdraw, to retreat, to abandon the struggle.

This definition of the processes giving rise to retreatist behavior is useful in connection with some types of retreatism, but it does not, we believe, fit the facts of drug use among lower-class adolescents. It is true that some youthful addicts appear to experience strong constraints on the use of illegitimate means; the great majority of drug-users, however, had a history of delinquency before becoming addicted. In these cases, unfavorable attitudes toward conventional norms are evident. Hence we conclude that internalized prohibitions, or favorable attitudes toward conventional norms, may not be a necessary condition for the emergence of retreatist behavior.

If internalized prohibitions are not a necessary component of the process by which retreatism is generated, then how are we to account for such behavior? We have noted that there are differentials in access both to illegitimate and to legitimate means; not all of those who seek to attain success-goals by prohibited routes are permitted to proceed. There are probably many lower-class adolescents oriented toward success in the criminal world who fail; similarly, many who would like to acquire proficiency in the use of violence also fail. We might ask, therefore, what the response would be among those faced with failure in the use of *both* legitimate and illegitimate means. We suggest that persons who experience this "double failure" are likely to move into a retreatist pattern of behavior. That is, retreatist behavior may arise as a consequence of limitations on the use of illegitimate means, whether the limitations are internalized prohibitions or socially structured barriers. For our purpose, the two types of restriction are functional equivalents. Thus we may amend Merton's statement as follows:

> Retreatism arises from continued failure to near the goal by legitimate measures and from an inability to use the illegitimate route because of internalized prohibitions *or socially structured barriers,* this process occurring while the supreme value of the success-goal has not yet been renounced.

This hypothesis permits us to define two general classes of retreatist: those who are subject to internalized prohibitions on the use of illegitimate means, and those who seek success-goals by prohibited routes but do not succeed. If we now introduce a distinction between illegitimate opportunity structures based on the manipulative use of violence and those based on essentially criminal means, such as fraud, theft, and extortion, we can identify four classes of retreatist.

Types I and II both arise in the manner described by Merton—that is, as a consequence of internalized restrictions on the use of illegitimate means. The two types differ only with respect to the content of the internalized restraints. In type II, it is the use of criminal means that is precluded; in type I, it is the use of violence. Resort to illegitimate means, violent or criminal, apparently evokes extreme guilt and anxiety among persons in these categories; such persons are therefore effectively cut off from criminal or violent routes to higher status. For persons of types III and IV, access to illegitimate routes is limited by socially structured barriers. They are not restrained by internal prohibitions; they would employ illegitimate means if these were available to them.

Retreatist Adaptations

Basis of Illegitimate Opportunity Structure	Restrictions on Use of Illegitimate Means: Internalized Prohibitions	Restrictions on Use of Illegitimate Means: Socially Structured Barriers
Violence	I	III
Criminal Means	II	IV

Generally speaking, it has been found that most drug addicts have a history of delinquent activity prior to becoming addicted. In Kobrin's research, conducted in Chicago, "Persons who become heroin users were found to have engaged in delinquency *in a group-supported and habitual form* either prior to their use of drugs or simultaneously with their developing interest in drugs."[24] And from a study of drug addicts in California, "A very significant tentative conclusion [was reached]: namely, that the use of drugs follows criminal activity and criminal association rather than the other way around, which is often thought to be the case."[25] In other words, adolescents who are engaged in group-supported delinquency of the criminal or conflict type may eventually turn to drug use. Indeed, entire gangs sometimes shift from either criminal or conflict to retreatist adaptations.

We view these shifts in adaptation as responses to restrictions on the use of illegitimate means. Such restrictions, as we have seen, are always operative; not all who

[24] Solomon Kobrin, *Drug Addiction Among Young Persons in Chicago* (Illinois Institute for Juvenile Research, Oct. 1953), p. 6. Harold Finestone, in a study of the relationship between addicts and criminal status, comments: "The impression gained from interviewing ... was that these addicts were petty thieves and petty 'operators' who, status-wise, were at the bottom of the criminal population of the underworld" ("Narcotics and Criminality," *Law and Contemporary Problems,* Vol. 22, No. 1 [Winter 1957], pp. 69–85).

[25] *Narcotics in California* (Board of Corrections, State of California, Feb. 18, 1959), p. 9.

would acquire success by violence or criminal means are permitted to do so. It is our contention that retreatist behavior emerges among some lower-class adolescents because they have failed to find a place for themselves in criminal or conflict subcultures. Consider the case of competition for membership in conflict gangs. To the extent that conflict activity—"bopping," street-fighting, "rumbling," and the like—is tolerated, it represents an alternative means by which adolescents in many relatively disorganized urban areas may acquire status. Those who excel in the manipulation of violence may acquire "rep" within the group to which they belong and respect from other adolescent groups in the vicinity and from the adult world. In areas which do not offer criminal opportunities, the use of violence may be the only available avenue to prestige. But prestige is, by definition, scarce—just as scarce among adolescents who seek to acquire it by violence as it is elsewhere in the society. Not only do juvenile gangs compete vigorously with one another, but within each gang there is a continual struggle for prestigeful positions. Thus some gangs will acquire "rep" and others will fail; some persons will become upwardly mobile in conflict groups and others will remain on the periphery.

If the adolescent "failure" then turns to drugs as a solution to his status dilemma, his relationships with his peers become all the more attenuated. Habitual drug use is not generally a valued activity among juvenile gangs. Ordinarily the drug-user, if he persists in such behavior, tends to become completely disassociated from the group. Once disassociated, he may develop an even greater reliance upon drugs as a solution to status deprivations. Thus adolescent drug-users may be "double failures" who are restrained from participating in other delinquent modes of adaptation because access to these illegitimate structures is limited.

Our hypothesis states that adolescents who are double failures are more vulnerable than others to retreatist behavior; it does not imply that *all* double failures will subsequently become retreatists. Some will respond to failure by adopting a law-abiding lower-class style of life—the "corner boy" adaptation. It may be that those who become retreatists are incapable of revising their aspirations downward to correspond to reality. Some of those who shift to a corner-boy adaptation may not have held high aspirations initially. It has frequently been observed that some adolescents affiliate with delinquent groups simply for protection in gang-ridden areas; they are motivated not by frustration so much as by the "instinct of self-preservation." In a less hostile environment, they might simply have made a corner-boy adjustment in the first place. But for those who continue to exhibit high aspirations under conditions of double failure, retreatism is the expected result.

Sequences of Adaptation. Access to success-goals by illegitimate means diminishes as the lower-class adolescent approaches adulthood. Illegitimate avenues to higher status that were available during early adolescence become more restricted in later adolescence. These new limitations intensify frustration and so create pressures toward withdrawal or retreatist reactions.

With regard to criminal means, late adolescence is a crucial turning point, for it is during this period that the selection of candidates for stable adult criminal roles takes place. It is probably true that more youngsters are exposed to criminal learning environments during adolescence than can possibly be absorbed by the adult criminal structure. Because of variations in personality characteristics, criminal proficiency, and capacity to make "the right connections," or simply because of luck, some persons will find this avenue to higher status open and some will find it closed off. In effect, the latter face a dead end. Some delinquents, therefore, must cope with abrupt discontinuity in role-preparation and role-performance which may lead to retreatist reponses.

In the case of conflict patterns, a similar process takes place. As adolescents near adulthood, excellence in the manipulation of violence no longer brings high status. Quite the contrary, it generally evokes extreme negative sanctions. What was defined as permissible or tolerable behavior during adolescence tends to be sharply proscribed in adulthood. New expectations are imposed, expectations of "growing up," of taking on adult responsibilities in the economic, familial, and community spheres. The effectiveness with which these definitions are imposed is attested by the tendency among fighting gangs to decide that conflict is, in the final analysis, simply "kid stuff": "As the group grows older, two things happen. Sports, hell raising, and gang fights become 'kid stuff' and are given up. In the normal course of events, the youthful preoccupations are replaced with the more individual concerns about work, future, a 'steady' girl, and the like." [26] In other words, powerful community expectations emerge which have the consequence of closing off access to previously useful means of overcoming status deprivations. Strains are experienced, and retreatist behavior may result.

As we have noted, adolescents who experience pressures leading to retreatist reactions are often restrained by their peers. Adolescent gangs usually devalue drug use (except on an experimental basis or for the sake of novelty) and impose negative sanctions upon those who become "hooked." The very existence of the gang discourages the potential user:

> The activities of the gang offer a measure of shared status, a measure of security and a sense of belonging. The boys do not have to face life alone—the group protects them. Escape into drugs is not necessary as yet.[27]

In the post-adolescent period, however, the cohesiveness of the peer group usually weakens. Those who have the requisite skills and opportunities begin to make the transition to adulthood, assuming conventional occupational and kinship roles. As the solidarity of the group declines, it can no longer satisfy the needs or control the behavior of those who continue to rely upon it. These members may try to reverse the trend toward disintegration and, failing this, turn to drugs:

> This group organized five years ago for self-protection against other fighting groups in the area. Recently, as the majority grew cool to bopping, a group of three boys

[26] D. M. Wilmer, *et al.*, "Heroin Use and Street Gangs," *Criminal Law, Criminology, and Police Science,* Vol. 48, No. 8 (Nov.-Dec. 1957), p. 409.

[27] *Ibid.*

broke off in open conflict with the president; *soon after, these three started using heroin and acting "down with the cats."* They continue making efforts to get the gang back to fights.... The three users are still out and it is unlikely that they will be readmitted.[28]

For some adolescents, the peer group is the primary avenue to status as well as the primary source of constraints on behavior. For these youngsters, the post-adolescent period, during which the group may disintegrate or shift its orientation, is one in which social controls are weakened precisely when tensions are heightened.

Whether the sequence of adaptations is from criminal to retreatist or from conflict to retreatist, we suggest that limitations on legitimate and illegitimate opportunity combine to produce intense pressures toward retreatist behavior. When both systems of means are simultaneously restricted, it is not strange that some persons become detached from the social structure, abandoning cultural goals and efforts to achieve them by any means.

[28] *Ibid.*, p. 405. Emphasis added.

13. White Collar Crime: The Heavy Electrical Equipment Antitrust Cases of 1961

Gilbert Geis

An inadvertent bit of humor by a defense attorney provided one of the major criminological motifs for "the most serious violations of the antitrust laws since the time of their passage at the turn of the century."[1] The defendants, including several vice-presidents of the General Electric Corporation and the Westinghouse Electric

[1] Judge J. Cullen Ganey in "Application of the State of California," *Federal Supplement*, 195 (Eastern District, Pennsylvania, 1961), p. 39.

Corporation–the two largest companies in the heavy electrical equipment industry–stood somberly in a federal courtroom in Philadelphia on February 6, 1961. They were aptly described by a newspaper reporter as "middle-class men in Ivy League suits–typical business men in appearance, men who would never be taken for lawbreakers."[2] Several were deacons or vestrymen of their churches. One was president of his local chamber of commerce, another a hospital board member, another chief fund raiser for the community chest, another a bank director, another a director of the taxpayer's association, another an organizer of the local little league.

The attorney for a General Electric executive attacked the government's demand for a jail sentence for his client, calling it "cold-blooded." The lawyer insisted that government prosecutors did not understand what it would do to his client, "this fine man," to be put "behind bars" with "common criminals who have been convicted of embezzlement and other serious crimes."[3]

The difficulty of defense counsel in considering antitrust violations "serious crimes," crimes at least equivalent to embezzling, indicates in part why the 1961 prosecutions provide such fascinating material for criminological study. Edwin H. Sutherland, who originated the term "white collar crime" to categorize offenders such as antitrust violators, had lamented that his pioneering work was handicapped by the absence of adequate case histories of corporate offenders. "No first hand research from this point of view has ever been reported,"[4] Sutherland noted and, lacking such data, he proceeded to employ rather prosaic stories of derelictions by rather unimportant persons in small enterprises upon which to build an interpretative and theoretical structure for white collar crime.

To explain corporate offenses and offenders, Sutherland had to rely primarily upon the criminal biographies of various large companies, as these were disclosed in the annals of trial courts and administrative agencies. In the absence of information about human offenders, the legal fiction of corporate humanity, a kind of economic anthropomorphism, found its way into criminological literature. Factual gaps were filled by shrewd guesses, definitional and semantic strategies, and a good deal of extrapolation. It was as if an attempt were being made to explain murder by reference only to the listed rap sheet offenses of a murderer and the life stories and identification data of several lesser offenders.[5]

Sutherland was writing, of course, before the antitrust violations in the heavy electrical equipment industry became part of the public record. Though much of the

[2] *New York Times,* Feb. 7, 1961.

[3] *New York Times,* Feb. 7, 1961.

[4] Edwin H. Sutherland, *White Collar Crime,* New York: Holt, Rinehart and Winston, Inc., 1949, p. 240. Note: "Private enterprise remains extraordinarily private....We know more about the motives, habits, and most intimate arcana of primitive peoples in New Guinea...than we do of the denizens of executive suites in Unilever House, Citroen, or General Electric (at least until a recent Congressional investigation)."–Roy Lewis and Rosemary Stewart, *The Managers,* New York: New American Library, 1961, pp. 111–112.

[5] For an elaboration of this point, see Gilbert Geis, "Toward a Delineation of White-Collar Offenses," *Sociological Inquiry,* 32 (Spring 1962), pp. 160–171.

data regarding them is tantalizingly incomplete, unresponsive to fine points of particular criminological concern, the antitrust offenses nonetheless represent extraordinary case studies of white collar crime, that designation which, according to Sutherland, applies to behavior by "a person of high socioeconomic status who violates the laws designed to regulate his occupational activities"[6] and "principally refers to business managers and executives."[7] In particular, the antitrust cases provide the researcher with a mass of raw data against which to test and to refine earlier hunches and hypotheses regarding white collar crime.

Facts of the Antitrust Violations

The most notable characteristic of the 1961 antitrust conspiracy was its willful and blatant nature. These were not complex acts only doubtfully in violation of a highly complicated statute. They were flagrant criminal offenses, patently in contradiction to the letter and the spirit of the Sherman Antitrust Act of 1890, which forbade price-fixing arrangements as restraints upon free trade.[8]

The details of the conspiracy must be drawn together from diverse secondhand sources because the grand jury hearings upon which the criminal indictments were based were not made public. The decision to keep the records closed was reached on the ground that the traditional secrecy of grand jury proceedings took precedence over public interest in obtaining information about the conspiracy and over the interest of different purchasers in acquiring background data upon which to base civil suits against the offending corporations for allegedly fraudulent sales.[9]

The federal government had initiated the grand jury probes in mid-1959, apparently after receiving complaints from officials of the Tennessee Valley Authority concerning identical bids they were getting from manufacturers of highly technical electrical equipment, even though the bids were submitted in sealed envelopes.[10] Four grand juries were ultimately convened and subpoenaed 196 persons, some of whom obviously revealed the intimate details of the price-fixing procedures. A package of twenty indictments was handed down, involving 45 individual defendants and 29

[6] Edwin H. Sutherland in Vernon C. Branham and Samuel B. Kutash, *Encyclopedia of Criminology*, New York: Philosophical Library, Inc., 1949, p. 511.

[7] Sutherland, *White Collar Crime*, p. 9, fn. 7.

[8] *United States Statutes*, 26 (1890), p. 209; *United States Code*, 15 (1958), pp. 1,2. See also William L. Letwin, "Congress and the Sherman Antitrust Law, 1887-1890," *University of Chicago Law Review*, 23 (Winter 1956), pp. 221–258, and Paul E. Hadlick, *Criminal Prosecutions under the Sherman Anti-Trust Act*, Washington, D.C.: Ransdell, 1939. The best interpretation of *American antitrust law is* A. D. Neale, *Antitrust Laws of the United States*, New York: Cambridge University Press, 1960.

[9] Note: "Release of the Grand Jury Minutes in the National Deposition Program of the Electrical Equipment Cases," *University of Pennsylvania Law Review*, 112 (June 1964), pp. 1130–1145.

[10] John Herling, *The Great Price Conspiracy*, Washington, D.C.: Robert B. Luce, 1962, pp.1-12; John G. Fuller, *The Gentleman Conspirators*, New York: Grove Press, Inc., 1962, pp. 7-11. See also Myron W. Watkins, "Electrical Equipment Antitrust Cases—Their Implications for Government and Business," *University of Chicago Law Review*, 29 (August 1961), pp. 97–110.

corporations. Almost all of the corporate defendants pleaded guilty; the company officials tended to enter pleas of nolo contendere (no contest) which, in this case, might reasonably be taken to indicate that they did not see much likelihood of escaping conviction.

The pleas negated the necessity for a public trial and for public knowledge of the precise machinations involved in the offenses. At the sentencing hearing, fines amounting to $1,924,500 were levied against the defendants, $1,787,000 falling upon the corporations and $137,000 upon different individuals. The major fines were set against General Electric ($437,500) and Westinghouse ($372,500). Much more eye-catching were the jail terms of thirty days imposed upon seven defendants, of whom four were vice-presidents, two were division managers, and one was a sales manager.

The defendants sentenced to jail were handled essentially the same as other offenders with similar dispositions. They were handcuffed in pairs in the back seat of an automobile on their way to the Montgomery County Jail in Norristown, Pennsylvania, fingerprinted on entry, and dressed in the standard blue denim uniforms. During their stay, they were described as "model prisoners," and several were transferred to the prison farm. The remainder, working an eight-hour day for 30 cents, earned recognition from the warden as "the most intelligent prisoners" he had had during the year on a project concerned with organizing prison records. None of the seven men had visitors during the Wednesday and Saturday periods reserved for visiting; all indicated a desire not to be seen by their families or friends.[11]

Good behavior earned the men a 5-day reduction in their sentence. Toward the end of the year, the remaining defendants, who had been placed on probation, were released from that status, despite the strong protests of government officials. The judge, the same man who had imposed the original sentences, explained his action by noting that he "didn't think that this was the type of offense that probation lent itself readily to or was designed for." Supervision was seen as meaningless for men with such past records and such little likelihood of recidivism, particularly since the probation office was already "clogged to the gunwales" with cases.[12]

The major economic consequences to the corporations arose from civil suits for treble damages filed against them as provided in the antitrust laws. The original fines were, of course, negligible: For General Electric, a half-million dollar loss was no more unsettling than a $3 parking fine would be to a man with an income of $175,000 a year. Throughout the early stages of negotiations over the damage suits, General Electric maintained that it would resist such actions on grounds which are noteworthy as an indication of the source and the content of the rationale that underlay the self-justification of individual participants in the price-fixing conspiracy:

> We believe that the purchasers of electrical apparatus have received fair value by any reasonable standard. The prices which they have paid during the past years

[11] United Press International, Feb. 16, 1961; *New York Times*, Feb. 25, 1961.

[12] Telephone interview with Judge Ganey, Philadelphia, Aug. 31, 1964; *New York Times*, Dec. 20, 1961.

were appropriate to value received and reasonable as compared with the general tends of prices in the economy, the price trends for similar equipment and the price trends for materials, salaries, and wages. The foresight of the electrical utilities and the design and manufacturing skills of companies such as General Electric have kept electricity one of today's greatest bargains.[13]

By 1962, General Electric was granting that settlements totaling between $45 and $50 million would have to be arranged to satisfy claimants.[14] Municipalities and other purchasers of heavy electrical equipment were taking the period of lowest prices, when they assumed the price-rigging was least effective, using these prices as "legitimate," and calculating higher payments as products of the price conspiracy.[15] The initial G.E. estimate soon proved as untenable as its original thesis regarding value received. A mid-1964 calculation showed that 90 percent of some 1800 claims had been settled for a total of $160 million,[16] but General Electric could derive some solace from the fact that most of these payments would be tax-deductible.[17]*

Techniques of the Conspiracy

The modus operandi for the antitrust violations shows clearly the awareness of the participants that their behavior was such that it had better be carried on as secretly as possible. Some comparison might be made between the antitrust offenses and other forms of fraud occurring in lower economic classes. It was one of Sutherland's most telling contentions that neither the method by which a crime is committed nor the manner in which it is handled by public agencies alters the essential criminal nature of the act and the criminal status of the perpetrator.[18] Selling faucet water on a street corner to a blind man who is led to believe that the product is specially prepared to relieve his ailment is seen as no different from selling a $50 million turbine to a city which is laboring under the misapprehension that it is purchasing the product at the best price possible from closed competitive bidding. The same may be said in regard to methods of treatment. Tuberculosis, for example, remains tuberculosis and its victim a tubercular whether the condition is treated in a sanitarium or whether it is ignored or even condoned by public authorities. So too with crime. As Miss Stein might have said: A crime is a crime is a crime.

Like most reasonably adept and optimistic criminals, the antitrust violators had hoped to escape apprehension. "I didn't expect to get caught and I went to great

[13] *New York Times,* Feb. 7, 1961.

[14] *New York Times,* July 27, 1962.

[15] *New York Times,* March 14, 1961.

[16] *New York Times,* Apr. 29, 1964. Regarding Westinghouse see *Wall Street Journal,* Sept. 3, 1964.

[17] *Wall Street Journal,* July 27, 1964.

*(Editor's Note: The ruling by the Internal Revenue Service classified most of these payments as ordinary and necessary business expenses and therefore could be deducted from taxable corporate income).

[18] Edwin H. Sutherland, "White-Collar Criminality," *American Sociological Review,* 5 (February 1940), pp. 1–12.

lengths to conceal my activities so that I wouldn't get caught," one of them said.[19] Another went into some detail concerning the techniques of concealment:

...it was considered discreet to not be too obvious and to minimize telephone calls, to use plain envelopes if mailing material to each other, not to be seen together on traveling, and so forth....not to leave wastepaper, of which there was a lot, strewn around a room when leaving.

The plans themselves, while there were some slight variations over time and in terms of different participants, were essentially similar. The offenders hid behind a camouflage of fictitious names and conspiratorial codes. The attendance roster for the meetings was known as the "Christmas card list" and the gatherings, interestingly enough, as "choir practice."[20] The offenders used public telephones for much of their communication, and they met either at trade association conventions, where their relationship would appear reasonable, or at sites selected for their anonymity. It is quite noteworthy, in this respect, that while some of the men filed false travel claims, so as to mislead their superiors regarding the city they had visited, they never asked for expense money to places more distant than those they had actually gone to—on the theory, apparently, that whatever else was occurring, it would not do to cheat the company.

At the meetings, negotiations centered about the establishment of a "reasonable" division of the market for the various products. Generally, participating companies were allocated essentially that part of the market which they had previously garnered. If Company A, for instance, had under competitive conditions secured 20 percent of the available business, then agreement might be reached that it would be given the opportunity to submit the lowest bid on 20 percent of the new contracts. A low price would be established, and the remainder of the companies would bid at approximately equivalent, though higher, levels. It sometimes happened, however, that because of things such as company reputation, or available servicing arrangements, the final contract was awarded to a firm which had not submitted the lowest bid. For this, among other reasons, debate among the conspirators was often acrimonious about the proper division of spoils, about alleged failures to observe previous agreements, and about other intramural matters. Sometimes, depending upon the contract, the conspirators would draw lots to determine who would submit the lowest bid; at other times the appropriate arrangement would be determined under a rotating system conspiratorially referred to as the "phase of the moon."

[19] Senate Committee on the Judiciary, Subcommittee on Antitrust and Monopoly, 87th Cong., 2d Sess., 1961, "Administered Prices," *Hearings, Pts.* 27 and 28. Unless otherwise indicated, subsequent data and quotations are taken from these documents. Space considerations do not permit citation to the precise pages.

[20] The quotation is from an excellent two-part article by Richard Austin Smith, "The Incredible Electrical Conspiracy," *Fortune,* 63 (April 1961), pp. 132–137, and 63 (May 1961), 161–164, which is reproduced in *Hearings,* Pt. 27, pp. 17094–17105 and 17172–17182.

Explanations of the Conspiracy

Attempts to understand the reasons for and the general significance of the price-fixing conspiracy have been numerous. They include re-examinations of the antitrust laws[21] as well as denunciations of the corporate ethos and the general pattern of American life and American values. For example, "This is the challenge of the grim outcome in Philadelphia. Can corporations outgrow the idea that employees must produce, whatever the moral cost, or lose their prerequisites? Is it possible to create a business ethic favoring honesty even at the expense of profit? Can our society get away from its pervasive attitude that a little cheating is harmless? The electrical cases raise those questions not only in the antitrust field, but in others, especially taxation. And they are questions not only for large corporations and not only for business but for all of us."[22]

A not inconsiderable number of the defendants took the line that their behavior, while technically criminal, has really served a worthwhile purpose by "stabilizing prices" (a much-favored phrase of the conspirators). This altruistic interpretation almost invariably was combined with an attempted distinction among illegal, criminal, and immoral acts, with the offender expressing the view that what he had done might have been designated by the statutes as criminal, but either he was unaware of such a designation or he thought it unreasonable that acts with admirable consequences should be considered criminal. The testimony of a Westinghouse executive during hearings by the Senate Subcommittee on Antitrust and Monopoly clearly illustrates this point of view:

Committee Attorney: Did you know that these meetings with competitors were illegal?

Witness: Illegal? Yes, but not criminal. I didn't find that out until I read the indictment....I assumed that criminal action meant damaging someone, and we did not do that....I thought that we were more or less working on a survival basis in order to try to make enough to keep our plant and our employees.

This theme was repeated in essentially similar language by a number of witnesses. "It is against the law," an official of the Ingersoll-Rand Corporation granted, but he added: "I do not know that it is against public welfare because I am not certain that the consumer was actually injured by this operation." A Carrier Corporation executive testified that he was "reasonably in doubt" that the price-fixing meetings violated the antitrust law. "Certainly, we were in a gray area. I think the degree of violation, if you can speak of it that way, is what was in doubt." Another offender said: "We were not meeting for the purpose of getting the most that traffic could bear. It was to get a value for our product." Some of these views are gathered together in a statement by a former sales manager of the I-T-E Circuit Breaker Company:

[21] See, for instance, Leland Hazard, "Are Big Businessmen Crooks?" *Atlantic,* 208 (November 1961), pp. 57–61.

[22] Anthony Lewis, *New York Times,* Feb. 12, 1961.

One faces a decision, I guess, at such times, about how far to go with company instructions, and since the spirit of such meetings only appeared to be correcting a horrible price level situation, that there was not an attempt to actually damage customers, charge excessive prices, there was no personal gain in it for me, the company did not seem actually to be defrauding, corporate statements can evidence the fact that there have been poor profits during all these years.... So I guess morally it did not seem quite so bad as might be inferred by the definition of the activity itself.

For the most part, personal explanations for the acts were sought in the structure of corporate pressures rather than in the avarice or lack of law-abiding character of the men involved. The defendants almost invariably testified that they came new to a job, found price-fixing an established way of life, and simply entered into it as they did into other aspects of their job. This explanatory scheme fit into a pattern that Senator Philip A. Hart of Michigan, during the subcommittee hearings, labeled *imbued fraud.*[23]

There was considerable agreement concerning the precise method in which the men initially became involved in price-fixing. "My first actual experience was back in the 1930's," a General Electric official said. "I was taken there by my boss...to sit down and price a job." An Ingersoll-Rand executive said: "[My superior] took me to a meeting to introduce me to some of our competitors, none of whom I had met before, and at that meeting pricing of condensers was discussed with the competitors." Essentially the same comment is repeated by witness after witness. "I found it this way when I was introduced to competitive discussion and just drifted into it," a Carrier Corporation man noted. A General Electric officer echoed this point: "Every direct supervisor that I had directed me to meet with competition.... It had become so common and gone on for so many years that I think we lost sight of the fact that it was illegal." Price-fixing, whether or not recognized as illegal by the offenders, was clearly an integral part of their jobs. "Meeting with competitors was just one of the many facets of responsibility that was delegated to me," one witness testified, while an Allis-Chalmers executive responded to the question: "Why did you go to the meetings?" with the observation: "I thought it was part of my duty to do so."

What might have happened to the men if, for reasons of conscience or perhaps through a fear of the possible consequences, they had objected to the "duty" to participate in price-fixing schemes? This point was raised only by the General Electric employees, perhaps because they alone had some actual evidence upon which to base their speculations. In 1946, General Electric had first issued a directive, number 20.5, which spelled out the company's policy against price-fixing, in terms stronger than those found in the antitrust laws. A considerable number of the executives believed, in the words of one, that the directive was only for "public

[23] Analysis of the relationship between occupational norms and legal violations could represent a fruitful line of inquiry. See Richard Quinney, "The Study of White Collar Crime: Toward a Reorientation in Theory and Research," *Journal of Criminal Law, Criminology and Police Science,* 55 (June 1964), pp. 208–214.

consumption," and not to be taken seriously. One man, however, refused to engage in price-fixing after he had initialed the document forbidding it. A witness explained to the Senate subcommittee what followed:

> [My superior] told me, "This fellow is a fine fellow, he is capable in every respect except he was not broad enough for his job, that he was so religious that he thought in spite of what his superiors said, he thought having signed that, that he should not do any of this and he is getting us in trouble with competition."

The man who succeeded the troublesome official, one of the defendants in the Philadelphia hearing, said that he had been told that he "would be expected to do otherwise" and that this "was why I was offered that promotion to Philadelphia because this man would not do it." At the same time, however, the General Electric witnesses specified clearly that it was not their jobs with the company that would be in jeopardy if they failed to price-fix, but rather the particular assignment they had. "If I didn't do it I felt that somebody else would," said one, with an obvious note of self-justification. "I would be removed and somebody else would do it."

Westinghouse and General Electric differed considerably in their reactions to the exposure of the offenses, with Westinghouse electing to retain in its employ persons involved in the conspiracy, and General Electric deciding to dismiss the employees who had been before the court. The reasoning of the companies throws light both on the case and on the relationship between antitrust offenses and the more traditionally viewed forms of criminal behavior.

Westinghouse put forward four justifications for its retention decision. First, it declared, the men involved had not sought personal aggrandizement: "While their actions cannot in any way be condoned, these men did not act for personal gain, but in the belief, misguided though it may have been, that they were furthering the company's interest." Second, "the punishment incurred by them already was harsh" and "no further penalties would serve any useful purpose." Third, "each of these individuals is in every sense a reputable citizen, a respected and valuable member of the community and of high moral character." Fourth, there was virtually no likelihood that the individuals would repeat their offense.[24]

General Electric's punitive line toward its employees was justified on the ground that the men had violated not only federal law but also a basic company policy, and that they therefore deserved severe punishment. The company's action met with something less than wholehearted acclaim; rather, it was often interpreted as an attempt to scapegoat particular individuals for what was essentially the responsibility of the corporate enterprise and its top executives. "I do not understand the holier-than-thou attitude in GE when your directions came from very high at the top," Senator Kefauver said during his committee's hearings, while Senator John A. Carroll of Colorado expressed his view through a leading question: "Do you think you were thrown to the wolves to ease the public relations situation...that has de-

[24] Sharon (Pa.) *Herald,* Feb. 6, 1961.

veloped since these indictments?" he asked a discharged General Electric employee. The witness thought that he had.

Perhaps most striking is the fact that though many offenders quite clearly stressed the likely consequences for them if they failed to conform to price-fixing expectations, not one hinted at the benefits he might expect, the personal and professional rewards, from participation in the criminal conspiracy. It remained for the sentencing judge and two top General Electric executives to deliver the harshest denunciations of the personal motives and qualities of the conspirators to be put forth during the case:

The statement of Judge J. Cullen Ganey, read prior to imposing sentence, received widespread attention. In it he sharply criticized the corporations as the major culprits, but he also pictured the defendants in a light other than that they chose to shed upon themselves in their subsequent discussions of the offenses:

> ...they were torn between conscience and an approved corporate policy, with the rewarding objective of promotion, comfortable security, and large salaries. They were the organization or company man, the conformist who goes along with his superiors and finds balm for his conscience in additional comforts and security of his place in the corporate set-up.[25]

The repeated emphasis on "comfort" and "security" constitutes the basic element of Judge Ganey's view of the motivations of the offenders. Stress on passive acquiescence occurs in remarks by two General Electric executives viewing the derelictions of their subordinates. Robert Paxton, the retired company president, called antitrust agreements "monkey business" and denounced in vitriolic terms one of his former superiors who, when Paxton first joined General Electric, had put him to work attempting to secure a bid on a contract that had already been prearranged by a price-fixing agreement. Ralph Cordiner, the president and board chairman of General Electric, thought that the antitrust offenses were motivated by drives for easily acquired power. Cordiner's statement is noteworthy for its dismissal of the explanations of the offenders as "rationalizations":

> One reason for the offenses was a desire to be "Mr. Transformer" or "Mr. Switchgear"*...and to have influence over a larger segment of the industry.... The second was that it was an indolent, lazy way to do business. When you get all through with the rationalizations, you have to come back to one or the other of these conclusions.

There were other explanations as well. One truculent offender, the 68-year-old president of a smaller company who had been spared a jail sentence only because of his age and the illness of his wife, categorically denied the illegality of his behavior. "We did not fix prices," he said. "I can't agree with you. I am telling you

[25] *New York Times*, Feb. 7, 1961.

*Earlier, a witness had quoted his superior as saying: "I have the industry under my thumb. They will do just about as I ask them." This man, the witness said, "was known as Mr. Switchgear in the industry."

that all we did was recover costs." Some persons blamed the system of decentralization in the larger companies, which they said placed a heavy burden to produce profit on each of the relatively autonomous divisions, particularly when bonuses—"incentive compensation"—were at stake, while others maintained that the "dog-eat-dog" business conditions in the heavy electrical equipment industry were responsible for the violations. Perhaps the simplest explanation came from a General Electric executive. "I think," he said, "the boys could resist everything but temptation."

Portrait of an Offender

The highest paid executive to be given a jail sentence was a General Electric vice-president, earning $135,000 a year—about $2600 every week. The details of his career and his participation in the conspiracy provide additional insight into the operations of white-collar crime and white-collar criminals.

The General Electric vice-president was one of a disporportionate number of Southerners involved in the antitrust violations. He had been born in Atlanta and was 46 years old at the time he was sentenced to jail. He had graduated with a degree in electrical engineering from Georgia Tech, and received an honorary doctorate degree from Sienna College in 1958, was married, and the father of three children. He had served in the Navy during the Second World War, rising to the rank of lieutenant commander, was a director of the Schenectady Boy's Club, on the board of trustees of Miss Hall's School, and, not without some irony, was a member of Governor Rockefeller's Temporary State Committee on Economic Expansion.[26]

Almost immediately after his sentencing, he issued a statement to the press, noting that he was to serve a jail term "for conduct which has been interpreted as being in conflict with the complex antitrust laws." He commented that "General Electric, Schenectady, and its people have undergone many ordeals together and we have not only survived them, but have come out stronger, more vigorous, more alive than ever. We shall again." Then he voiced his appreciation for "the letters and calls from people all over the country, the community, the shops, and the offices...expressing confidence and support."[27]

The vice-president was neither so sentimental about his company nor so certain about the complexity of the antitrust regulations when he appeared before the Kefauver committee five months later. "I don't get mad, Senator," he said at one point, referring to his behavior during a meeting with competitors, but he took another line when he attempted to explain why he was no longer associated with General Electric:

> ...when I got out of being a guest of the Government for 30 days, I had found out that we were not to be paid while we were there,* and I got, frankly, madder than hell....

[26] *New York Times,* Feb. 7, 1961.

[27] *Schenectady Union-Star,* Feb. 10, 1961.

* A matter of some $11,000 for the jail term.

Previously, he had been mentioned as a possible president of General Electric, described by the then president, as "an exceptionally eager and promising individual." Employed by the company shortly after graduation from college, he had risen dramatically through the managerial ranks, and passed that point, described by a higher executive, "where the man, if his work has been sufficiently promising, has an opportunity to step across the barrier out of his function into the field of general management." In 1946, he had his first contact with price-fixing, being introduced to competitors by his superior and told that he "should be the one to contact them as far as power transformers were concerned in the future."

The meetings that he attended ran a rather erratic course, with numerous squabbles between the participants. Continual efforts had to be made to keep knowledge of the meetings from "the manufacturing people, the engineers, and especially the lawyers," but this was achieved, the witness tried to convince the Kefauver committee, because commercial transactions remained unquestioned by managerial personnel so long as they showed a reasonable profit. The price-fixing meetings continued from 1946 until 1949. At that time, a federal investigation of licensing and cross-patent activities in the transformer industry sent the conspirators scurrying for shelter. "The iron curtain was completely down" for a year, and sales people at General Electric were forbidden to attend gatherings of the National Electrical Manufacturers' Association, where they had traditionally connived with competitors.

Meetings resumed, however, when the witness's superior, described by him as "a great communicator, a great philosopher, and, frankly, a great believer in stabilities of prices," decided that "the market was getting in chaotic condition" and that they "had better go out and see what could be done about it." He was told to keep knowledge of the meetings from Robert Paxton, "an Adam Smith advocate," then the plant works manager, because Paxton "don't understand these things."

Promoted to general manager in 1954, the witness was called to New York by the president of General Electric and told specifically, possibly in part because he had a reputation of being "a bad boy," to comply with the company policy and with the antitrust laws, and to see that his subordinates did so too. This instruction lasted as long as it took him to get from New York back to Massachusetts, where his superior there told him: "Now, keep on doing the way that you have been doing but just...be sensible about it and use your head on the subject." The price-fixing meetings therefore continued unabated, particularly as market conditions were aggravated by overproduction which had taken place during the Korean War. In the late 1950s foreign competition entered the picture, and lower bids from abroad often forced the American firms to give up on particular price-fixing attempts.

In 1957, the witness was promoted to vice-president, and again brought to New York for a lecture from the company president on the evils of price-fixing. This time, his "air cover gone"—he now had to report directly to top management—he decided to abandon altogether his involvement in price-fixing. He returned to his plant and issued stringent orders to his subordinates that they were no longer to attend meetings with competitors. Not surprisingly, since he himself had rarely obeyed such injunctions, neither did the sales persons in his division.

The witness was interrogated closely about his moral feelings regarding criminal behavior. He fumbled most of the questions, avoiding answering them directly, but ultimately came to the point of saying that the consequences visited upon him represented the major reason for a re-evaluation of his actions. He would not behave in the same manner again because of what "I have been through and what I have done to my family." He was also vexed with the treatment he had received from the newspapers: "They have never laid off a second. They have used some terms which I don't think are necessary–they don't use the term price fixing. It is always price rigging or trying to make it as sensational as possible."[28] The taint of a jail sentence, he said, had the effect of making people "start looking at the moral values a little bit." Senator Hart drew the following conclusions from the witness's comments:

Hart: This was what I was wondering about, whether absent the introduction of this element of fear, there would have been any re-examination of the moral implications.

Witness: I wonder, Senator. That is a pretty tough one to answer.

Hart: If I understand you correctly, you have already answered it....After the fear, there came the moral re-evaluation.

Nevertheless, the former General Electric vice-president viewed his situation rather philosophically. Regarding his resignation from the company, it was "the way the ball has bounced." He hoped that he would have "the opportunity to continue in American industry and do a job," and he wished some of the other men who had been dismissed a lot of good luck. "I want to leave the company with no bitterness and go out and see if I can't start a new venture along the right lines." Eight days later, he accepted a job as assistant to the president in charge of product research in a large corporation located outside Philadelphia.[29] Slightly more than a month after that, he was named president of the company, at a salary reported to be somewhat less than the $74,000 yearly received by his predecessor.[30]

A Summing Up

The antitrust violations in the heavy electrical industry permit a re-evaluation of many of the earlier speculations about white collar crime. The price-fixing behavior, flagrant in nature, was clearly in violation of the criminal provisions of the Sherman Act of 1890, which had been aimed at furthering "industrial liberty." Rather, the

[28] A contrary view is expressed in Note, "Increasing Community Control over Corporate Crime–A Problem in the Law of Sanctions," *Yale Law Journal,* 71 (December 1961), footnoted material pp. 287–289. It has been pointed out that Time Magazine (Feb. 17, 1961, pp. 64 ff.) reported the conspiracy in its "Business" section, whereas it normally presents crime news under a special heading of its own–Donald R. Taft and Ralph W. England, Jr., *Criminology,* 4th ed., New York: The Macmillan Company, 1964, p. 203.

[29] *New York Times,* May 12, 1961.

[30] *New York Times,* June 23, 1961.

price-fixing arrangements represented attempts at "corporate socialism," and in the words of Senator Kefauver to a subcommittee witness:

> It makes a complete mockery not only of how we have always lived and what we have believed in and have laws to protect, but what you were doing was to make a complete mockery of the carefully worded laws of the Government of the United States, ordinances of the cities, rules of the REA's [Rural Electrification Administration], with reference to sealed secret bids in order to get competition.

The facts of the antitrust conspiracy would seem clearly to resolve in the affirmative debate concerning the criminal nature and the relevance for criminological study of such forms of white collar crime,[31] though warnings regarding an indefinite and unwarranted extension of the designation "crime" to all acts abhorrent to academic criminologists must remain in force.[32] Many of Sutherland's ideas concerning the behavior of corporate offenders also receive substantiation. His stress on learning and associational patterns as important elements in the genesis of the violations receives strong support.[33] So too does his emphasis on national trade conventions as the sites of corporate criminal conspiracies.[34]

Others of Sutherland's views appear to require overhaul. His belief, for example, that "those who are responsible for the system of criminal justice are afraid to antagonize businessmen"[35] seems less than totally true in terms of the electrical industry prosecutions. Sutherland's thesis that "the customary pleas of the executives of the corporation...that they were ignorant of and not responsible for the action of the special department...is akin to the alibi of the ordinary criminal and need not be taken seriously"[36] also seems to be a rather injudicious blanket condemnation. The accuracy of the statement for the antitrust conspiracy must remain moot, but it would seem important that traditional safeguards concerning guilty knowledge as a basic ingredient in criminal responsibility be accorded great respect.[37] Nor,

[31] See Edwin H. Sutherland, "Is 'White Collar Crime' Crime?" *American Sociological Review,* 10 (April 1945), pp. 132-139. Note: "It may be hoped that the Philadelphia electric cases have helped to dispel this misapprehension... It should now be clear that a deliberate or conscious violation of the antitrust laws...is a serious offense against society which is as criminal as any other act that injures many in order to profit a few. Conspiracy to violate the antitrust laws is economic racketeering. Those who are apprehended in such acts are, and will be treated as criminals."–Lee Loevinger, "Recent Developments in Antitrust Enforcement," Antitrust Section, American Bar Association, 18 (1961), p. 102.

[32] Paul W. Tappan, "Who Is the Criminal?" *American Sociological Review,* 12 (February 1947), pp. 96-102.

[33] Sutherland, *White Collar Crime,* pp. 234-257.

[34] Sutherland, p. 70.

[35] Sutherland, p. 10.

[36] Sutherland, p. 54.

[37] For an excellent presentation, see Sanfor H. Kadish, "Some Observations on the Use of Criminal Sanctions in Enforcing Economic Regulations," *University of Chicago Law Review,* 30 (Spring 1963), pp. 423–449. See also Richard A. Whiting, "Antitrust and the Corporate Executive," *Virginia Law Review,* 47 (October 1961), pp. 929–987.

in terms of the antitrust data, does Sutherland appear altogether correct in his view that "the public agencies of communication, which continually define ordinary violations of the criminal code in a very critical manner, do not make similar definitions of white collar crime."[38]

Various analytical schemes and theoretical statements in criminology and related fields provide some insight into elements of the price-fixing conspiracy. Galbraith's caustic observation regarding the traditional academic view of corporate price-fixing arrangements represents a worthwhile point of departure:

> Restraints on competition and the free movement of prices, the principal source of uncertainty to business firms, have been principally deplored by university professors on lifelong appointments. Such security of tenure is deemed essential for fruitful and unremitting thought.[39]

It seems apparent, looking at the antitrust offenses in this light, that the attractiveness of a secure market arrangement represented a major ingredient drawing corporate officers to the price-fixing violations. The elimination of competition meant the avoidance of uncertainty, the formalization and predictability of outcome, the minimization of risks. It is, of course, this incentive which accounts for much of human activity, be it deviant or "normal," and this tendency that Weber found so pronounced in bureaucracies in their move from vital but erratic beginnings to more staid and more comfortable middle and old age.[40]

For the conspirators there had necessarily to be a conjunction of factors before they could participate in the violations. First, of course, they had to perceive that there would be gains accruing from their behavior. Such gains might be personal and professional, in terms of corporate advancement toward prestige and power, and they might be vocational, in terms of a more expedient and secure method of carrying out assigned tasks. The offenders also apparently had to be able to neutralize or rationalize their behavior in a manner in keeping with their image of themselves as law-abiding, decent, and respectable persons.[41] The ebb and flow of the price-fixing conspiracy also clearly indicates the relationship, often overlooked in explanations of criminal behavior, between extrinsic conditions and illegal acts. When the market behaved in a manner the executives thought satisfactory, or when enforcement agencies seemed particularly threatening, the conspiracy desisted. When market

[38] Sutherland, *White Collar Crime,* p. 247.

[39] John Kenneth Galbraith, *The Affluent Society,* Boston: Houghton Mifflin Company, 1958. p. 84. See also Richard Hofstadter, "Antitrust in America," *Commentary,* 38 (August 1964), pp. 47–53. An executive of one corporation is said to have remarked regarding the collusive antitrust arrangements: "It is the only way business can be run. It's free enterprise." Quoted by Mr. Justice Clark to Antitrust Section, American Bar Association, St. Louis, Aug. 8, 1961, p. 4.

[40] Max Weber, *The Theory of Social and Economic Organization,* translated by A. M. Henderson and Talcott Parsons, New York: Oxford University Press, 1947, pp. 367–373.

[41] See Donald R. Cressey, *Other People's Money,* New York: The Free Press of Glencoe, 1953; Gresham M. Sykes and David Matza, "Techniques of Neutralization: A Theory of Delinquency," *American Sociological Review,* 22 (December 1957), pp. 664–670.

conditions deteriorated, while corporate pressures for achieving attractive profit-and-loss statements remained constant, and enforcement activity abated, the price-fixing agreements flourished.

More than anything else, however, a plunge into the elaborate documentation of the antitrust cases of 1961, as well as an attempt to relate them to other segments of criminological work, points up the considerable need for more and better monographic field studies of law violators and of systems of criminal behavior, these to be followed by attempts to establish theoretical guidelines and to review and refine current interpretative viewpoints. There have probably been no more than a dozen, if that many, full-length studies of types of criminal (not delinquent) behavior in the past decade. The need for such work seems overriding, and the 1961 antitrust cases represent but one of a number of instances, whether in the field of white collar crime, organized crime, sex offenses, personal or property crimes, or similar areas of concern, where we are still faced with a less than adequate supply of basic and comparative material upon which to base valid and useful theoretical statements.

14. Automobile Theft: A "Favored-Group" Delinquency

William W. Wattenberg and James Balistrieri

The purpose of this paper is to explore certain implications of "white-collar criminality." That concept, based largely on evidence dealing with adults, challenges the adequacy of some generalizations concerning crime and its causation. The point of impact of the concept lies in its assumption that the form of antisocial or illegal conduct rather than its frequency varies from social class to class in our society. If this is so, then there is need to search for factors common to the causation of delinquency or similar misconduct at all social levels rather than to accept without reservation the vast mass of research linking juvenile misconduct with neighborhood situations which in turn reflect the economic status of the adult population.

In general, the ecological findings are that delinquency rates are highest in those sections of a city where, among other things, rentals are low and the occupations are typically unskilled or semiskilled labor. The relative poverty of the population is associated with high transiency rates, substandard housing, and a breakdown of

Reprinted from *American Journal of Sociology,* 57:6 (May 1952), 575–579, permission of The University of Chicago Press and the authors.

family and other controls. Often youth is also exposed to a conflict of cultures. This constellation of influences is assumed to give rise to a neighborhood subculture of which delinquency patterns are one aspect. This subculture transmits to youth a readiness to embark upon delinquent behavior.

Challenging all this is the contention that crime is culturally defined rather than culturally determined and that it is not the fact of criminality but the form of it which varies with socioeconomic level. Thus, we have burglars and embezzlers, holdup men and black-marketeers, prostitutes and fashionable mistresses. The antisocial conduct of the "lower classes" affronts the middle-class legal norms and so leads to prison terms and criminal records. The antisocial deeds of "respectable" folk are likely to draw much milder treatment. All this casts doubt on many research data by implying that we have not been measuring the extent of crime or of delinquency but only of the varieties we do not like. By such reasoning, no theory of delinquency or criminality can be adequate unless it explains the "white-collar" offenses as well as the more obvious forms of theft and violence. It is assumed that, if this were done, the present emphasis on relationship of socioeconomic variables to crime might have to be discarded.

For the field of juvenile delinquency, the existence of "white-collar" offenses is difficult to establish. We have fairly good figures on assaults, burglary, truancy, and similar offenses. However, the early manifestations of patterns which could develop into bribery, bucket-shop operations, and price-control evasions are not likely to draw police attention. Certainly, statistical evidence would be hard to get. Apparently the best we could do would be to assume that among juveniles there was much hidden misconduct analogous to adult "white-collar" crime.

An alternative would be to search for some class of offense which departed from the usual high correlation with socioeconomic or ecological variables. Then, by exploring the similarities and differences between the offenders thus identified and a run-of-the-mill group, we might find more clues as to causal factors common to antisocial character formation in privileged as well as underpriviledged groups. To be most helpful, in this respect the offense must be sufficiently common and widespread so that it is not peculiar to a single neighborhood. Also, to avoid argument as to antisocial quality, the offense should be clearly illegal and generally condemned. Otherwise, as in the case of the recent debate between Hartung and Burgess,[1] we would be bogged down in claims and counterclaims as to whether or not the offenders were real delinquents.

Evidence of the existence of such an offense was turned up in connection with another investigation.[2] In a study of the complete police records of 1,170 boys all

[1]Frank E. Hartung, "White-Collar Offenses in the Wholesale Meat Industry in Detroit," *American Journal of Sociology,* XLI, No. 1 (1950), 25–32. See "Comment" by Ernest W. Burgess, "Rejoinder," by Frank E. Hartung, and "Concluding Comment," by Ernest W. Burgess, on pp. 32–34 of the same issue.

[2]William W. Wattenberg and David Faigenbaum, "Completed Delinquent Careers" (Detroit: Crime Prevention Bureau, Detroit Police Department, 1949). (Mimeographed.)

of whom had passed their seventeenth birthdays it was found that during the period when they had been ten to sixteen years old automobile thefts were proportionately three times as frequent among white boys as among Negroes. (The general ratio of delinquencies was two to one; automobile theft approached seven to one; results were significant well beyond the 1 per cent level of confidence.) The same offense was proportionately heavier among boys of West European parentage. Again, results were statistically reliable. This is significant because the largest recent foreign immigration to Detroit's transitional areas was from Eastern Europe.

The police explanation of the small proportion of Negroes involved in automobile theft was one of danger and difficulty. Veteran police officials said that colored youngsters were almost sure to be challenged by parking-lot attendants and thus were barred from some opportunity to take cars. Also, it was widely believed that squad-car crews were prone to investigate credentials of Negro young people driving automobiles. However, these explanations, even if accurate, did not account for the nationality differentials among white boys. Therefore, it was decided to dig deeper.

All investigations made by Detroit police of boys aged ten to sixteen inclusive for 1948 were secured and analyzed. These reports included some fifty items of information obtained by interview with the boys and their parents on such matters as housing, neighborhood conditions, family relationships, peer-group activities, and recreation. In all, data were available for 3,870 boys, of whom 2,774 were white. These records were carefully sorted, and all records involving any form of automobile theft were segregated. There were 260 such records. As shown in Table 1, the previously discovered tendency for automobile theft to be a "white" offense was thoroughly verified.

TABLE 1. Relationship Between Automobile Theft and Race of All Boys Interviewed on Complaint by Detroit Police, 1948*

Race	Total	*Number*		*Per Cent*	
		Involved in Automobile Theft	*All Others*	*Involved in Automobile Theft*	*All Others*
White	2,774	230	2,544	88.5	70.5
Nonwhite	1,096	30	1,066	11.5	29.5
Total	3,870	260	3,610	100.0	100.0

* $\chi^2 = 38.29; n = 1; P < 0.01$.

In order to avoid various possible distorting influences, such as the correlations between race and such variables as housing, employment discriminations and the like, it was decided to confine the remainder of the study to comparisons among white boys only. The 230 involved in automobile theft were compared on every available recorded item of information with the 2,544 charged with other offenses.

In all cases the chi-square computation was employed to establish the degree of statistical reliability with which the null hypothesis could be rejected. A total of fifty tables was prepared and tested. Of these, nine proved significant at the 1 per cent level of confidence; five more, at the 5 per cent level. Thus, the number of tables showing statistical significance was more than five times chance expectation. For convenience, the statistically significant factors will be discussed below in terms of the clusters into which they fell.

Socioeconomic Level. The automobile-theft group again met the requirements of the category denoted by the title of this article. As compared with the other boys in trouble, they were reliably more likely to come from neighborhoods rated "above average" by the police and less likely to come from neighborhoods rated as "slums." This was borne out by the more objective evidence of the ratio between the number of rooms in the dwelling unit and the number of persons occupying the unit. The proportion of boys from dwellings with less than one room per person was significantly smaller than for all other boys contacted by the police. There were other tables of inconclusive reliability which supported this general picture. In these the tendency was for the automobile-theft group to come from racially homogeneous neighborhoods, to live in single-family homes, to come from homes not showing need of repairs, and to have only one parent employed.

On one socioeconomic item no relationship with automobile theft was found. When police were asked to classify the family income as either "adequate" or "inadequate," both the automobile-theft group and all other boys came from the same percentage of homes classed as having "adequate" income. However, fewer boys involved in automobile thefts had parents both of whom had to work to secure that level of income.

Age. As might be expected, automobile theft was largely confined to the older boys; it was relatively rare below the age of fourteen. Accordingly, a number of items in which chronological age was a factor were significantly related to the offense. These included reliable tendencies for the boys involved in automobile theft to be better developed physically, to have completed sex development, to be in the junior high school grades in school, to have records of previous offenses, to have laboring jobs, and to use some of their earnings to purchase their own clothing.

Peer-Group Relationships. This group also showed evidence of socializing well with other young people. The statistically reliable tables showed they were less likely to be classed by the investigating officers as social "lone wolves" and were more likely to be members of definite gangs with a reputation of either being rambunctious or engaging in organized theft. Although the statistical reliability was inconclusive, it seemed likely that they also got along well with their classmates in school.

Miscellaneous. There were three statistically reliable tables that do not fit into any of the three clusters described above. When police officers rated the attitude of the boys toward themselves, they were more likely to class it as "responsive." Also, in disposing of the cases, the police were more likely to be stern and either file an official complaint or otherwise refer the case to the juvenile court. This, of course, was an indication of the seriousness of the offense in the eyes of the police, even though they were not required to file delinquency petitions in such cases. The third significant table dealt with the degree of the parents' participation in their sons' recreation; for the automobile-theft group this was more likely to be ranked in the medium level of "occasional," as contrasted to "regular," on the one hand, or "seldom," on the other. Interestingly, this was the only item involving family relationships where statistical significance appeared.

More consequential for the purpose of this article were the similarities between the automobile-theft group and the less privileged other white boys involved in all other offenses. In the list below we give only those items not previously mentioned which failed of significance in the present series of comparisons but were found reliably linked to repeating among all boys interviewed by Detroit police in 1948.[3]

1. Number and sex of siblings
2. Boys' expressed attitude toward home
3. Boys' expressed attitude toward parents
4. Boys' feeling of being "picked on"
5. Boys' appearance
6. Estimated intelligence
7. Hobby and sports interests
8. Membership in organized youth groups
9. Church attendance
10. Attitude toward school
11. Attitude toward teachers
12. School grades
13. Chores around home
14. Method by which parents gave boys money
15. Comparability of boys' recreational equipment with playmates
16. Attitude toward adult neighbors
17. Distance of home from nearest recreational facility
18. Parents' attitude toward boys
19. Parents' attitude toward police
20. Marital status of parents
21. Degree of quarreling between parents
22. Family ownership of a car

In summary of the chi-square-tested comparisons, then, we get the following general picture of white juveniles involved in automobile theft: they were more likely to come from relatively favored neighborhoods, to be older, and to have good social relationships with their peers. On indexes of family relationships, school adjustment, and religious training they were like a cross-section of all other white boys interviewed on complaint by the Detroit police.

Discussion

To some extent the above findings buttress the implied contentions of the writers on "white-collar" criminality. That is to say, there is here shown to exist at least one

[3] William W. Wattenberg and James J. Ballistrieri, "New Offenders, 1948" (Detroit: Youth Bureau, Detroit Police Department, 1950). (Mimeographed.)

type of offense which is relatively less correlated with low socioeconomic level and neighborhood distintegration than the general run of juvenile offenses. This being the case, it is fair to argue that we need to look for formulations of causal influences beyond the customary "bad"-neighborhood factors. We have reason to assume that there may be other varieties of antisocial conduct which would not so swiftly be indicated by police or court statistics and which are sufficiently prevalent in good neighborhoods and among high socioeconomic folk to rule out their being dismissed as exceptions.

Interestingly, in the case of automobile theft, we are dealing with a group that is well socialized as far as primary-group relationships are concerned. These boys are not isolated, peculiar individuals. In the rubrics of the Hewitt and Jenkins[4] study of clinic cases they are neither the quarrelsome, "unsocialized aggressives" nor the pathetically neurotic "overinhibited" children. Rather, they are similar to the "socialized delinquents" in all respects save residence in deteriorated neighborhoods.

There may be a possible systematic explanation in the general picture of this last-mentioned "type." On the basis of a very elaborate statistical analysis, Hewitt and Jenkins described this group as characterized by good ability to relate to people and by a conscience partially formed in the sense that it did not include the prohibitions of the wider society. The value systems of such individuals were quite responsive to the immediately present code of interpersonal relations pertaining to their friends but only weakly responsive to the more abstract rules codified in statutes and ordinances. Thus, if a boy's friends got pleasure from riding in automobiles, he would oblige in carefree fashion by borrowing a car. Similarly, if an adult with a similar value system found he could get along well in business by violating price controls or by bribing public officials, he would be untroubled by compunctions. However, if his immediate associates would react hostilely to such crude or dangerous crimes as burglary or physical assault, he would shun such behavior. Of course, in a "bad" neighborhood where such out-and-out criminality was tolerated, that might enter into his conduct. Much would depend upon the limits prevalent among his associates.

The common element in all this is a rather general type of personality structure. If such is indeed the case, the causes of all varieties of antisocial conduct having this quality are to be found in how that personality structure is formed. Hewitt and Jenkins believe they could trace it to a lax kind of family in which children are not rejected but rather have weak affectional relationships with their parents, who exercise little supervision over them. It is easy to see that such a pattern might be relatively prevalent where parents are bedeviled by a struggle for existence and are bewildered by the culture conflict found in slums. However, with some variations, it also could be found in better neighborhoods where parents are forever "on the go" or even where children are reared by a succession of servants.

[4] L. E. Hewitt and R. L. Jenkins, *Fundamental Patterns of Maladjustment* (Springfield: State of Illinois, 1946).

Using methods very different from Hewitt and Jenkins, the studies conducted by the Committee on Human Development of the University of Chicago in "Prairie City" led to a description of a very similar type of personality. In their reports it is called "the adaptive person."[5] This "type" is described as having high "social intelligence" and as conforming easily to the expectations of whatever group in which it is found. Their case studies led them to believe that the family relationships were the important factor in its development. The relationships in the home were characterized as easygoing and the parents as having "broad and tolerant" moral views and as setting few restrictions on the social activities of the children.

Whether we accept the formulation of Hewitt and Jenkins or that of Havighurst and Taba, the principal point would be that a variety of permissive upbringing produces a personality "type" with little moral courage and a potentiality for engaging in antisocial behavior finding support among associates. Obviously, this is only a hypothesis, to be tested by carefully designed studies. In all probability, as our storehouse of scientifically verified knowledge grows, such a hypothesis would undoubtedly have to be modified. At best it would apply to only one of a number of patterns leading to delinquency and crime. It would hardly cover adequately all types of misconduct, delinquency, crime, and fraud.

It should be pointed out that even the admittedly incomplete hypothesis now being advanced hardly negates the theories built on statistics showing high correlations between delinquency rates and socioeconomic variables. Rather, it would offer an explanation of how some cases contributing to such correlations might arise. The tensions induced by relative poverty, culture conflict, and social pressures might interfere with the parents' supervision over their children or otherwise lead parents to be lax in a fashion which would produce in slum areas a relatively high proportion of young people prone to engage lightheartedly in the theft, violence, and immorality tolerated by the neighborhood's culture.

Summary

In this study 230 white boys charged with automobile theft were compared with 2,544 others in trouble with the Detroit police in 1948. They had good peer-group relationships, came from relatively more favored neighborhoods, but were otherwise similar to juvenile offenders in general. It was suggested that the common factor accounting for one general class of antisocial behavior regardless of socioeconomic factors was a personality structure which readily accepted the values of immediate associates but responded weakly to the enactments of larger social entities.

[5] Robert J. Havighurst and Hilda Taba, *Adolescent Character and Personality* (New York: John Wiley & Sons, 1949), chap. xiii.

15. Socio-Economic Class and Area as Correlates of Illegal Behavior Among Juveniles*

John P. Clark and Eugene P. Wenninger

Until recently almost all efforts to discover characteristics that differentiate juveniles who violate legal norms from those who do not have compared institutional and non-institutional populations. Though many researchers still employ a "delinquent" or "criminal" sample from institutions,[1] there is a growing awareness that the process through which boys and girls are selected to populate our "correctional" institutions may cause such comparison studies to distort seriously the true picture of illegal behavior in our society. Therefore, conclusions based upon such studies are subject to considerable criticism[2] if generalized beyond the type of population of the particular institution at the time of the study. Although the study of adjudicated offenders is important, less encumbered studies of the violation of legal norms hold more promise for those interested in the more general concept of deviant behavior.

Though it, too, has methodological limitations, the anonymous-questionnaire procedure has been utilized to obtain results reflecting the rates and patterns of illegal behavior among juveniles from different social classes, ages, sexes, and ethnic groups in the general population.[3] The results of these studies have offered sufficient

Reprinted from "Research Reports and Notes," *American Sociological Review,* **27**:6 (December 1962), 826–834, by permission of The American Sociological Association and the authors.

*The total project of which this paper is a part was sponsored by the Ford Foundation and the University of Illinois Graduate Research Board. Professor Daniel Glaser was very helpful throughout the project and in the preparation of this paper.

[1] An outstanding example of this type of research design is Sheldon and Eleanor Glueck, *Unraveling Juvenile Delinquency,* New York: The Commonwealth Fund, 1950.

[2] See Marshall B. Clinard, *Sociology of Deviant Behavior,* New York: Rinehart, 1958, p.124, for his assessment of the validity of the study by Sheldon and Eleanor Gluecks *Unraveling Juvenile Delinquency.*

[3] Most outstanding are those by Austin L. Porterfield, *Youth in Trouble,* Fort Worth, Texas: Leo Potishman Foundation, 1946; F. Ivan Nye and James F. Short, "Scaling Delinquent Behavior," *American Sociological Review,* 22 (June, 1957), pp. 325–331; and Robert A. Dentler and Lawrence J. Monroe, "Early Adolescent Theft," *American Sociological Review,* 26 (October, 1961), 733–743; Fred J. Murphy, Mary M. Shirley, and Helen L. Witmer, "The Incidence of Hidden Delinquency,"*American Journal of Orthopsychiatry,* 16 (October, 1946), pp.686–696.

evidence to indicate that the patterns of illegal behavior among juveniles may be dramatically different than was heretofore thought to be the case.

Some of the most provocative findings have been those that challenge the almost universally-accepted conclusion that the lower socio-economic classes have higher rates of illegal behavior than do the middle or upper classes. For example, neither the Nye-Short study[4] nor that of Dentler and Monroe[5] revealed any significant difference in the incidence of certain illegal or "deviant" behaviors among occupational-status levels–a finding quite at odds with most current explanations of delinquent behavior.

Although most of the more comprehensive studies in the social class tradition have been specifically concerned with a more-or-less well-defined portion of the lower class (i.e., "delinquent gangs,"[6] or "culture of the gang," or "delinquent subculture"[7]), some authors have tended to generalize their findings and theoretical formulations rather specifically to the total lower class population of juveniles.[8] These latter authors certainly do not profess that *all* lower class children are equally involved in illegal behavior, but by implication they suggest that the incidence of illegal conduct (whether brought to the attention of law enforcement agencies or not) is more pervasive in this class than others because of some unique but fundamental characteristics of the lower social strata. For example, Miller has compiled a a list of "focal concerns" toward which the lower class supposedly is oriented and because of which those in this class violate more legal norms with greater frequency than other classes.[9] Other authors point out that the lower classes are disadvantaged in their striving for legimate goals and that they resort to deviant means to attain them.[10] Again, the result of this behavior is higher rates of illegal behavior among the lower socio-economic classes.

Therefore, there *appears* to be a direct conflict between the theoretical formulations of Miller, Cohen, Merton, Cloward and Ohlin, and those findings reported by Nye and Short and Dentler and Monroe. This apparent discrepancy in the literature can be resolved, however, if one hypothesizes that the rates of illegal conduct among

[4] James F. Short, "Differential Association and Delinquency," *Social Problems,* 4 (January, 1957), pp. 233–239; F. Ivan Nye, *Family Relationships and Delinquent Behavior,* New York: John Wiley, 1958; James E. Short and F. Ivan Nye, "Reported Behavior as a Criterion of Deviant Behavior," *Social Problems,* 5 (Winter, 1957–1958), pp. 207–213; F. Ivan Nye, James F. Short, and Virgil J. Olson, "Socio-Economic Status and Delinquent Behavior," *American Journal of Sociology,* 63 (January, 1958), pp. 381–389.

[5] Dentler and Monroe, *op. cit.*

[6] Richard A. Cloward and Lloyd E. Ohlin, *Delinquency and Opportunity: A Theory of Delinquent Gangs,* New York: The Free Press of Glencoe, 1961.

[7] Albert K. Cohen, *Deliquent Boys: The Culture of the Gang,* Glencoe, Ill.: Free Press, 1955.

[8] Walter B. Miller, "Lower Class Culture as a Generating Milieu of Gang Delinquency," *Journal of Social Issues,* 14 (No. 3, 1958), pp. 5–19.

[9] *Ibid.* The matter of class differences in "focal concerns" or values will be explored in subsequent articles.

[10] Cohen, *op. cit.,* Cloward and Ohlin, *op. cit.,* and Robert K. Merton, *Social Theory and Social Structure,* Glencoe, Ill.: Free Press, 1957, pp. 146–149.

the social classes vary with the type of community[11] in which they are found. Were this so, it would be possible for studies which have included certain types of communities to reveal differential illegal behavior rates among social classes while studies which have involved other types of communities might fail to detect social class differences.

Whereas the findings and formulations of Merton, Cohen, Cloward and Ohlin, and Miller are oriented, in a sense, toward the "full-range" of social situations, those of Nye-Short and Dentler-Monroe are very specifically limited to the types of populations used in their respective studies. It is important to note that the communities in which these latter studies were conducted ranged only from rural to small city in size. As Nye points out, "They are thus urban but not metropolitan."[12] Yet, most studies of "delinquent gangs" and "delinquent subcultures" have been conducted in metropolitan centers where these phenomena are most apparent. Perhaps, it is only here that there is a sufficient concentration of those in the extreme socio-economic classes to afford an adequate test of the "social class hypothesis."

In addition to the matter of social class concentration and size, there is obviously more than one "kind" of lower class and each does not have rates or types of illegal behavior identical to that of the others. For example, most rural farm areas, in which occupations, incomes, and educational levels are indicative of lower class status, as measured by most social class indexes, consistently have been found to have low rates of misconduct–in fact lower than most urban middle class communities.

Therefore, to suggest the elimination of social class as a significant correlate to the quantity and quality of illegal behavior before it has been thoroughly examined in a variety of community situations, seems somewhat premature. Reiss and Rhodes concluded as a result of a study of class and juvenile court rates by school district that "it is clear, that there is no simple relationship between ascribed social status and delinquency."[13] In order to isolate the factor of social class, to eliminate possible effects of class bias in the rate of which juvenile misbehavior is referred to court, as well as to vary the social and physical environs in which it is located, we chose in this study to compare rates of admitted illegal behavior among diverse communities within the northern half of Illinois. Our hypotheses were:

1. Significant differences in the incidence of illegal behavior exist among communities differing in predominant social class composition, within a given metropolitan area.
2. Significant differences in the incidence of illegal behavior exist among similar social class strata located in different types of community.

[11] In this report "type of community" is used to refer in a general way to a geographic and social unit having certain distinctive demographic qualities, such as occupational structure, race, social class, and size. Designations such as "rural farm," or "Negro lower class urban," or "middle class suburbia," have long been utilized to describe such persistent physical-social characteristics.

[12] Nye, Short, and Olson, *op. cit.,* p. 383.

[13] Albert J. Reiss and Albert L. Rhodes, "The Distribution of Juvenile Delinquency in the Social Class Structure," *American Sociological Review,* 26 (October, 1961), pp. 720–732.

3. Differences in the incidence of illegal behavior among different social class populations within a given community are not significant.

The Study

The data used to test the above hypotheses were gathered in 1961 as part of a larger exploratory study of illegal behavior (particularly theft) among juveniles, and its relationship to socio-economic class, type of community, age, race, and various attitudinal variables, such as attitude toward law, feelings of alienation, concept of self, and feelings of being able to achieve desired goals. Subsequent reports will deal with other aspects of the study.

A total of 1154 public school students from the sixth through the twelfth grades in the school systems of four different types of communities were respondents to a self-administered, anonymous questionnaire given in groups of from 20 to 40 persons by the senior author. Considerable precaution was taken to insure reliability and validity of the responses. For example, assurances were given that the study was not being monitored by the school administration; questions were pretested to eliminate ambiguity; and the administration of the questionnaire was made as threat-free as possible.

The four communities represented in the study were chosen for the unique social class structure represented by each. The Duncan "Socio-Economic Index for All Occupations,"[14] was used to determine the occupational profile of each community by assigning index scores to the occupation of the respondents' fathers. The results are summarized in Table 1.

TABLE 1. Duncan Socio-Economic-Index Scores Based on Occupation of Father

	Type of Community			
Score	*Rural Farm* %	*Lower Urban* %	*Industrial City* %	*Upper Urban* %
(1) 0–23	75.9	40.4	36.4	5.7
(2) 24–47	9.9	15.5	19.3	4.8
(3) 48–71	4.7	12.5	22.9	43.9
(4) 72–96	1.5	4.2	10.0	34.6
(5) Unclassifiable*	8.0	27.4	11.4	11.0
Total	100 (N=274)	100 (N=265)	100 (N=280)	100 (N=335)

*This category included those respondents from homes with no father and those respondents who did not furnish adequate information for reliable classification. The 27.4 per cent figure in the lower urban community reflects a higher proportion of "father-less" homes rather than greater numbers of responses which were incomplete or vague in other ways.

[14] Albert J. Reiss, Jr., Otis Dudley Duncan, Paul K. Hatt, and Cecil C. North, *Occupations and Social Status*, New York: The Free Press of Glencoe, 1961, especially pp. 109–161 prepared by Otis D. Duncan.

The overwhelming majority of the respondents comprising the *rural farm* population live on farms, farming being by far the most common occupation of their fathers. Many of the fathers who were not listed as farmers were, in fact, "part-time" farmers. Therefore, though the Duncan Index would classify most of the residents in the lower class, most of these public school children live on farms in a prosperous section of the Midwest. The sixth, seventh, and eighth graders were drawn from schools located in very small villages. Grades 9-12 were drawn from the high school which was located in open-farm land.

The *lower urban* sample is primarily composed of children of those with occupations of near-equal ranking but certainly far different in nature from those of the rural farm community. The lower urban sample was drawn from a school system located in a very crowded and largely-Negro area of Chicago. The fathers (or male head of the family) of these youngsters are laborers in construction, waiters, janitors, clean-up men, etc. Even among those who place relatively high on the Duncan Scale are many who, in spite of their occupational title, reside, work, and socialize almost exclusively in the lower class community.

As Table 1 demonstrates, the occupational structure of the *industrial city* is somewhat more diffuse than the other communities, though consisting primarily of lower class occupations. This city of about 35,000 is largely autonomous, although a small portion of the population commutes daily to Chicago. However, about two-thirds of these students have fathers who work as blue-collar laborers in local industries and services. The median years of formal education of all males age 25 or over is 10.3.[15] The median annual family income is $7,255.[16] The population of this small city contains substantial numbers of Polish and Italian Americans and about fifteen per cent Negroes.

Those in the *upper urban* sample live in a very wealthy suburb of Chicago. Nearly three-fourths of the fathers in these families are high-level executives or professionals. The median level of education for all males age 25 or over is 16 plus.[17] The median annual family income is slightly over $20,000–80 per cent of the families make $10,000 or more annually.[18]

With two exceptions, representative sampling of the public school children was followed within each of these communities: (1) those who could not read at a fourth grade level were removed in all cases, which resulted in the loss of less than one-half per cent of the total sample, and (2) the sixth-grade sample in the industrial city community was drawn from a predominantly Negro, working class area and was, therefore, non-representative of the total community for that grade-level only. All the students from grades six through twelve were used in the rural farm community "sample."

[15] U. S. *Census of Population: 1960.* Final Report PC (1)–15C, p. 15–296.

[16] *Ibid.*, p. 15–335.

[17] *Ibid.*, p. 15–305.

[18] *Ibid.*, p. 15–344.

Measure of Illegal Behavior

An inventory of 36 offenses was initially assembled from delinquency scales, legal statutes, and the FBI Uniform Crime Reports. In addition to this, a detailed list of theft items, ranging from candy to automobiles, was constructed. The latter list was later combined into two composite items (minor theft, and major theft) and added to the first list, enlarging the number of items in this inventory to 38 items as shown in Table 2. No questions on sex offenses were included in this study, a restriction found necessary in order to gain entrance into one of the school systems.

All respondents were asked to indicate if they had committed each of these offenses (including the detailed list of theft items) *within the past year,* thus furnishing data amenable to age-level analysis.[19] If the respondents admitted commission of an offense, they so indicated by disclosing the number of times (either 1, 2, 3, or 4 or more) they had done so. The first four columns of Table 2 reveal the percentage of students who admitted having indulged in each specific behavior one or more times *during the past year.*

Specific offense items were arranged in an array from those admitted by the highest percentage of respondents to those admitted by the lowest percentage of respondents. Obviously the "nuisance" offenses appear near the top while the most serious and the more situationally specific fall nearer the end of the listing.[20] Several offenses are apparently committed very infrequently by school children from the sixth to twelfth grades regardless of their social environs.

Findings

In order to determine whether significant differences exist in the incidence of illegal behavior among the various types of communities, a two-step procedure was followed. First, each of the four communities was assigned a rank for each offense on the basis of the percentage of respondents admitting commission of that offense. These ranks were totaled across all offenses for each community. The resultant numerical total provided a very crude over-all measure of the relative degree to which the sample population from each community had been involved in illegal behavior during the past year. The results were (from most to least illegal behavior): industrial city, lower urban, upper urban, and rural farm. However, there was little over-all difference in the sum of ranks between upper urban and rural farm and even less difference between the industrial city and lower urban areas.

[19] Rates of illegal behavior were found to increase until age 14–15 and then to decrease.

[20] Ordinarily, not receiving 100 per cent admission to the first few offenses listed would have raised doubt as to the validity of those questionnaries on which these extremely common offenses were not admitted. In the Nye-Short study such questionnaires were discarded. However, since the respondents were asked in this study to admit their offenses during the past year only, it was thought that less than 100 per cent admission would be highly possible when one considers the entire age range. Undoubtedly some of the respondents who did not admit these minor offenses were falsifying their questionnaires.

TABLE 2. Percentage of Respondents Admitting Individual Offenses and Significance of Differences Between Selected Community Comparisons

Offense	*Community* (1) Indus-trial City N=280	(2) Lower Urban N=265	(3) Upper Urban N=335	(4) Rural Farm N=274	*Significance of Differences** (1-2)	(2-3)	(3-4)
1. Do things my parents told me not to do.	90	87	85	82	X	X	X
2. Minor theft (compilation of such items as the stealing of fruit, pencils, lipstick, candy, cigarettes, comic books, money less than $1, etc.)	79	78	80	73	X	X	X
3. Told a lie to my family, principal, or friends.	80	74	77	74	X	X	X
4. Used swear words or dirty words out loud in school, church, or on the street so other people could hear me.	63	58	54	51	X	X	X
5. Showed or gave someone a dirty picture, a dirty story, or something like that.	53	39	58	54	1	3	X
6. Been out at night just fooling around after I was supposed to be home.	49	50	51	35	X	X	3
7. Hung around other people who I knew had broken the law lots of times or who were known as "bad" people.	49	47	27	40	X	2	4
8. Threw rocks, cans, sticks, or other things at passing car, bicycle, or person.	41	37	33	36	X	X	X
9. Slipped into a theater or other place without paying.	35	40	39	22	X	X	3
10. Major theft (compilation of such items as the stealing of auto parts, autos, money over $1, bicyles, radios and parts, clothing, wallets, liquor, guns, etc.)	37	40	29	20	X	2	3
11. Gone into another person's house, a shed, or other building without their permission.	31	16	31	42	1	3	4
12. Gambled for money or something else with people other than my family.	30	22	35	26	X	3	3
13. Got some money or something from others by saying that I would pay them back even though I was pretty sure I wouldn't.	35	48	26	14	2	2	3
14. Told someone I was going to beat-up on them unless they did what I wanted them to do.	33	28	24	32	X	X	4
15. Drank beer, wine, or liquor without my parents' permission.	38	37	26	12	X	2	3
16. Have been kicked out of class or school for acting up.	27	28	31	22	X	X	3
17. Thrown nails, or glass, or cans in the street.	31	29	21	17	X	X	X
18. Used a slug or other things like this in candy, coke, or coin machines.	24	35	18	12	2	2	3
19. Skipped school without permission.	24	36	18	11	2	2	3
20. Helped make a lot of noise outside church, or school, or any other place in order to bother the people inside.	17	37	18	15	X	2	X

TABLE 2 *(Continued)*

Offense	*Community*				*Significance of Differences**		
	(1) Indus-trial City N=280	*(2) Lower Urban N=265*	*(3) Upper Urban N=335*	*(4) Rural Farm N=274*	*(1-2)*	*(2-3)*	*(3-4)*
21. Threw rocks, or sticks or any other thing in order to break a window, or street light, or thing like that.	24	26	22	16	X	X	3
22. Said I was going to tell something on someone unless they gave me money, candy, or something else I wanted.	23	28	17	19	X	2	X
23. Kept or used something that I knew had been stolen by someone else.	29	36	15	16	X	2	X
24. Tampered or fooled with another person's car, tractor, or bicycle while they weren't around.	26	13	19	24	1	3	X
25. Started a fist fight.	26	22	15	18	X	2	X
26. Messed up a restroom by writing on the wall, or leaving the water running to run onto the floor, or upsetting the waste can.	18	33	14	17	X	2	X
27. Hung around a pool hall, bar, or tavern.	21	18	10	23	X	2	4
28. Hung around the railroad tracks and trains.	16	13	23	16	X	3	3
29. Broken down or helped to break down a fence, gate, or door on another person's place.	15	14	8	8	X	2	X
30. Taken part in a "gang fight."	12	18	7	7	X	2	X
31. Ran away from home.	12	12	8	7	X	X	X
32. Asked for money, candy, a cigarette or other things from strangers.	12	12	6	7	X	2	X
33. Carried a razor, switch-blade, or gun to be used against other people.	8	16	3	4	2	2	X
34. "Beat up" on kids who hadn't done anything to me.	8	5	5	6	X	X	X
35. Broke or helped break up the furniture in a school, church, or other public building.	8	4	2	8	X	X	4
36. Attacked someone with the idea of killing them.	3	6	1	3	2	n	n
37. Smoked a reefer or used some sort of dope (narcotics).	3	4	1	3	X	n	n
38. Started a fire or helped set a fire in a building without the permission of the owner.	3	2	1	3	X	n	n

*Code: X = No significant difference.
1, 2, 3, or 4 = significant differences at .05 level or higher. The numbers indicate which of the communities in the comparison is higher in incidence of the offense.
n = too few offender cases to determine significant level.

In the second step the communities were arranged in the order given above and then the significance of the difference between adjacent pairs was determined by applying the Wilcoxon matched-pairs signed-ranks test. Only those comparisons which involve either industrial city or lower urban versus upper urban or rural farm result in any significant differences.[21] This finding is compatible with the above crude ranking procedure.

On the basis of these findings the first hypothesis is supported, while the second hypothesis received only partial support. Lower urban juveniles reported significantly more illegal behavior than did the juveniles of the upper urban community, and the two lower class communities of industrial city and lower urban appear to be quite similar in their high rates, but another lower class area composed largely of farmers has a much lower rate, similar to that of the upper urban area.

Much more contrast among the rates of juvenile misconduct in the four different communities, than is indicated by the above results, becomes apparent when one focuses on individual offenses. As the last column in Table 2 reveals, and as could be predicted from the above, there are few significant differences in the rates on each offense between the industrial city and lower urban communities. The few differences that do occur hardly fall into a pattern except that the lower urban youth seem to be oriented more toward violence (carrying weapons and attacking persons) than those in the industrial city.

However, 16 of a possible 35 relationships are significantly different in the upper urban-rural farm comparison, a fact that could not have been predicted from the above results. Apparently, variation in one direction on certain offenses tends to be neutralized by variation in the opposite direction on other offenses when the Wilcoxon test is used. There are greater actual differences in the nature of illegal behavior between these two communities than is noticeable when considered in more summary terms. (It might be pointed out here, parenthetically, that this type of finding lends support to the suggestion by Dentler and Monroe that the comparison of criterion groups on the basis of "omnibus scales" may have serious shortcomings.)[22]

Rural farm youngsters are more prone than those in the upper urban area to commit such offenses as trepassing, threatening to "beat up" on persons, hanging around taverns and being with "bad" associates—all relatively unsophisticated acts. Although some of the offenses committed more often by those who live in the upper urban

[21] Significance of differences were calculated between pairs of communities across *all 38* offenses by using the Wilcoxon Matched-Pairs Signed-Ranks test (described in Sidney Siegel, *Non-Parametric Statistics,* New York: McGraw-Hill Book Company, Inc., 1956, pp. 75–83). The results of this procedure were:

1–2 – P .35	1–3 – P .00006
2–3 – P .0034	1–4 – P .0006
3–4 – P .90	2–4 – P .016

[22] Dentler and Monroe, *op. cit.* p. 734.

community are also unsophisticated (throwing rocks at street lights, getting kicked out of school classes, and hanging around trains), others probably require some skill to perform successfully and probably depend on supportive peer-group relationships. For example, these data reveal that upper urban juveniles are more likely than their rural farm counterparts to be out at night after they are supposed to be at home, drink beer and liquors without parents' permission, engage in major theft, gamble, skip school, and slip into theaters without paying. In addition to their likely dependence upon peer-groups, perhaps these offenses are more easily kept from the attention of parents in the urban setting than in open-farm areas.

The greatest differences between rates of illegal conduct occur between the lower urban and upper urban communities, where 21 of a possible 35 comparisons reach statistical significance, the lower urban rates being higher in all except five of these. Although the upper urban youngsters are more likely to pass "dirty pictures," gamble, trespass, hang around trains, and tamper with other people's cars, their cousins in the lower class area are more likely to steal major items, drink, skip school, destroy property, fight, and carry weapons. The latter offenses are those normally thought to be "real delinquent acts" while the upper urban offenses (with the exception of vehicle tampering) are not generally considered to be such.

To summarize briefly, when the rates of juvenile misconduct are compared on individual offenses among communities, it appears that as one moves from rural farm to upper urban to industrial city and lower urban, the incidence of most offenses becomes greater, especially in the more serious offenses and in those offenses usually associated with social structures with considerable tolerance for illegal behavior.

While most emphasis is placed here on the differences, one obvious finding, evident in Table 2, is that in most of the nuisance offenses (minor theft, lying to parents, disobeying parents, swearing in public, throwing objects to break things or into the streets) there are no differences among the various communities. Differences appear to lie in the more serious offenses and those requiring a higher degree of sophistication and social organization.

The Reiss-Rhodes findings tend to refute theories of delinquent behavior which imply a high delinquency proneness of the lower class regardless of the "status area" in which it is found.[23] In view of this report, and since Nye-Short and Dentler-Monroe were unable to detect inter-class differences, inter-class comparisons were made within the four community types of this study. Following the technique employed by Nye and Short, only those students age 15 and younger were used in these comparisons in order to neutralize the possible effects of differential school drop-out rates by social classes in the older categories.

With the exception of the industrial city, no significant inter-class differences in illegal behavior rates were found within community types when either the Wilcoxon

[23] Reiss and Rhodes, *op. cit.*, p. 729. The concept of "status areas" is used here as it was used by Reiss and Rhodes to designate residential areas of a definite social class composition.

test was used for all offenses or when individual offense comparisons were made.[24] This finding supports hypothesis #3. It could account for the inability of Nye-Short and Dentler-Monroe to find differences among the socio-economic classes from several relatively similar communities in which their studies were conducted. It is also somewhat compatible with the Reiss and Rhodes findings. However, we did not find indications of higher rates of illegal conduct in the predominant socio-economic class within most areas, as the Reiss and Rhodes data suggested.[25] This may have been a function of the unique manner in which the socio-economic categories had to be combined for comparison purposes in this study. These findings, however, are logical in that boys and girls of the minority social classes within a "status area" would likely strive to adhere to the norms of the predominant social class as closely as possible whether these norms were legal or illegal.

Within the industrial city the second socio-economic category (index scores 24–47) was slightly significantly lower than either extreme category when the Wilcoxon test was used. Since the largest percentage of the sample of the industrial city falls in the lowest socio-economic category (0–23) and since this category evidences one of the highest rates of misconduct, the finding for this community is somewhat similar to the Reiss-Rhodes findings.

Conclusions

The findings of this study tend to resolve some of the apparent conflicts in the literature that have arisen from previous research concerning the relationship between the nature of illegal behavior and socio-economic class. However, some of the results contradict earlier reports.

Our findings are similar to those of Nye-Short and Dentler-Monroe in that we failed to detect any significant differences in illegal behavior rates among the social classes or rural and small urban areas. However, in keeping with the class-oriented theories, we did find significant differences, both in quantity and quality of illegal acts, among communities or "status areas," each consisting of one predominant socio-economic class. The lower class areas have higher illegal behavior rates, particularly in the more serious types of offenses. Differences among the socio-economic classes within these "status areas" were generally insignificant (which

[24] Because of small numbers in social classes within certain communities, categories were collapsed or ignored for comparison purposes as shown below. Refer to Table 1 for designation of categories. The Wilcoxon matched-pairs signed-ranks test was used.

Rural farm	category 1 versus 2, 3, 4	insignificant
Lower urban	category 1 versus 2, 3, 4	insignificant
	category 1 versus 5	insignificant
	categories 2, 3, 4 versus 5	insignificant
Industrial city	category 1 versus 2	significant
	category 2 versus 3, 4	significant
	category 1 versus 3, 4	insignificant
Upper urban	category 3 versus 4	insignificant

[25] Reiss and Rhodes, *op. cit.,* p. 729.

does not agree with the findings of Reiss and Rhodes), although when social class categories were compared across communities, significant differences were found. All this suggests some extremely interesting relationships.

1. The pattern of illegal behavior within small communities or within "status areas" of a large metropolitan center is determined by the predominant class of that area. Social class differentiation within these areas is apparently not related to the incidence of illegal behavior. This suggests that there are community-wide norms which are related to illegal behavior and to which juveniles adhere regardless of their social class origins. The answer to the obvious question of how large an urban area must be before socio-economic class becomes a significant variable in the incidence of illegal behavior is not provided by this study. It is quite likely that in addition to size, other considerations such as the ratio of social class representation, ethnic composition, and the prestige of the predominant social class relative to other "status areas" would influence the misconduct rates. The population of 20,000 of the particular upper urban community used in this study is apparently not of sufficient size or composition to provide for behavior autonomy among the social classes in the illegal behavior sense. There is some evidence, however, that an industrial city of roughly 40,000 such as the one included here is on the brink of social class differentiation in misconduct rates.

2. Though the juveniles in all communities admitted indulgence in several nuisance offenses at almost equal rates, serious offenses are much more likely to have been committed by lower class urban youngsters. Perhaps the failure of some researchers to find differences among the social classes in their misconduct rates can be attributed to the relatively less-serious offenses included in their questionnaires or scales. It would seem to follow that any "subculture" characterized by the more serious delinquencies, would be found only in large, urban, lower-class areas. However, the data of this study, at best, can only suggest this relationship.

3. Lastly, these data suggest that the present explanations that rely heavily on socio-economic class as an all-determining factor in the etiology of illegal behavior should be further specified to include data such as this study provides. For example, Cohen's thesis that a delinquent subculture emerges when lower class boys discover that they must satisfy their need for status by means other than those advocated in the middle class public schools should be amended to indicate that this phenomenon apparently occurs only in large metropolitan centers where the socio-economic classes are found in large relatively-homogeneous areas. In the same manner, Miller's theory of the relationship between the focal concerns of the lower class culture and delinquency may require closer scrutiny. If the relationship between focal concerns to illegal behavior that Miller has suggested exists, then those in the lower social class (as determined by father's occupation) who live in communities or "status areas" that are predominantly of some other social class, are apparently not participants in the "lower class culture;" or, because of their small numbers, they are being successfully culturally intimidated by the predominant class. Likewise, those who are thought to occupy middle class positions apparently take on lower class illegal behavior patterns when residing in areas that are predominantly lower class. This suggests either the great power of prevailing norms within a "status area" or a limitation of social class, as it is presently measured, as a significant variable in the determination of illegal behavior.

Research Questions

At least three general questions that demand further research emerge from this study:

1. What dimension (in size and other demographic characteristics) must an urban area attain before socio-economic class becomes a significant variable in the determination of illegal behavior patterns?

2. What are the specific differences between lower class populations and social structures located in rural or relatively small urban areas and those located in large, concentrated areas in metropolitan centers that would account for their differential rates, especially in the more serious offenses?

3. The findings of this study suggest that the criteria presently used to determine social class levels may not be the most conducive to the understanding of variation in the behavior of those who fall within these classes, at least for those within the juvenile ages. A substitute concept is that of "status area" as operationalized by Reiss and Rhodes. For example, the differentiating characteristics of a large, Negro, lower-class, urban "status area" could be established and would seem to have greater predictive and descriptive power than would the social class category as determined by present methods. Admittedly, this suggestion raises again the whole messy affair of "cultural area typologies" but area patterns of behaviors obviously exist and must be handled in some manner. Research effort toward systematically combining the traditional socio-economic class concept with that of cultural area might prove extremely fruitful by providing us with important language and concepts not presently available.

16. The Offense Patterns and Family Structures of Urban, Village and Rural Delinquency

*Theodore N. Ferdinand**

Benjamin Whorf's hypothesis that the ontology a group develops depends upon its language structure is illustrated nicely in the manner in which the data supplied by state and federal agencies have shaped the research efforts of sociologists seeking to unravel delinquency. Not only have these agencies supplied the ammunition with which many of the sociological battles concerning delinquency have been fought, but the manner in which they have unself-consciously grouped their information has

Reprinted from *The Journal of Criminal Law, Criminology and Police Science,* **55** (1964), 86–93, by permission of the publisher and the author.

*The author is deeply grateful to the Michigan Department of Social Welfare and Mr. Willis M. Oosterhof for making available to him the data upon which this study is based.

also determined to some degree the specific points over which the skirmishes have contended.

The fact, for example, that official agencies routinely report the sex, race, family structure, and offense of the delinquent but not the social characteristics of his community has inclined researchers to ask many questions about the contribution of the family to delinquency but relatively few about the way in which community organization induces delinquency. The question, for example, as to whether broken homes, *per se,* are causally related to delinquency today has largely been resolved thanks to the efforts of men like Monahan,[1] Nye,[2] and Toby.[3] The consensus among sociologists seems to be that broken homes, while often themselves the product of conditions that encourage delinquency, e.g., alienated and anomic marriage partners, also deprive the adolescents involved of the parental guidance that would help insulate them from other pressures toward delinquency.

A second issue that has consumed much energy is based upon the well-known fact that family disorganization is more prominent in the history of delinquent girls than delinquent boys. One explanation asserts that girls are more sensitive to rents in their social fabric than boys and, therefore, when exposed to the trauma that surrounds a broken home, they are more likely to respond in maladaptive, deviant ways.[4] Another interpretation suggests that families at a given level of cohesiveness provide their female adolescents considerably more guidance and supervision than their male teen-agers, and when the family is ruptured through divorce or death, the consequent collapse is much more significant for girls than boys.[5]

Additional explanations for the relative prominence of broken homes in the backgrounds of female delinquents could be offered, but the main point here is that the early patterns which emerged in the data collected by official agencies captured the attention of sociologists to an inordinate degree, leaving other equally important issues relatively untouched. Our knowledge about male and female delinquents is far more complete than our knowledge of middle and working class delinquency, and the contribution of family disorganization to delinquency is more thoroughly understood than that of community unsolidarity.

In order to help redress the balance, therefore, this paper will attempt to identify some of the respective characteristics of delinquents residing in urban, village, or rural communities. Much of the information currently available concerning rural and urban delinquency deals with either the relative delinquency rates in these two areas or the degree of sophistication displayed by rural and urban delinquents.[6]

[1] Monahan, *Family Status and the Delinquent Child: A Reappraisal and Some New Findings,* 35, Social Forces 250–58 (1957).

[2] Nye, FAMILY RELATIONSHIPS AND DELINQUENT BEHAVIOR (1958).

[3] Toby, *The Differential Impact of Family Disorganization,* 22 Am. Soc. Rev. 505 (1957).

[4] Block & Flynn, DELINQUENCY; THE JUVENILE OFFENDER IN AMERICA TODAY, 185 (1956).

[5] Toby, *supra* note 3, at 512.

[6] See, e.g., Wier, ECONOMIC FACTORS IN MICHIGAN DELINQUENCY (1944); Lentz, *Rural-Urban Differentials and Juvenile Delinquency,* 47 J. Crim. L., C. & P.S. 331 (1956); Clinard, *The Process of Urbanization and Criminal Behavior,* 48 Am. J. Soc. 202 (1942).

Our knowledge of the offense patterns or the social background of rural and urban delinquents is negligible, but such information, it would seem, is indispensable if we are to resolve our image of rural and urban delinquents to the same clarity that characterizes our picture of male and female delinquents.

To this end the Michigan Department of Social Welfare made available to the writer all the data routinely collected from the juvenile courts of Michigan in 1960. Over the years the Department of Social Welfare has become the clearing house to which all the juvenile courts in Michigan, except the Wayne County courts serving Detroit, send information about their delinquency experience. Each court is supplied by the Department of Social Welfare with a standard form upon which it records a wide range of information about each child it receives. This report is subsequently returned to the Department of Social Welfare.

The information in these reports is gathered by the courts in the course of their social investigation into each child's case, and since many unofficial cases are subjected to this procedure, the reports describe both official and unofficial cases. Indeed, in 1958, 29.8 percent of the cases reported to the Department of Social Welfare were handled unofficially by the courts in Michigan.[7] After the Department of Social Welfare had processed the reports of the several courts, a copy of the assembled data was turned over to the writer for this investigation.

In analyzing this information, it was decided to compare the social characteristics of delinquents living in urban, village, and rural communities. There is good reason to suspect that the social organization of these three types of communities is sufficiently different to affect the style or manner in which deviant behavior is expressed. And accordingly the data were first broken down into three categories defined in terms of the offender's place of residence. In order to identify these three community types in Michigan, information supplied by the United States Census Bureau about each of the 83 counties in Michigan was utilized. The individuals living in a county were considered as living in rural areas if, according to the Census Bureau, less than 15 percent of the inhabitants lived in urban places, between 40 and 60 percent lived in rural, non-farm residences, and more than 40 percent lived on farms. Under these criteria 11 counties were identified as rural counties in Michigan, none of which had a settlement with more than 6,000 inhabitants.

The individuals living in a county were considered as living in villages if between 32 and 40 percent lived in urban places, between 16 and 40 percent lived in rural, non-farm residences, and between 16 and 48 percent lived on farms. The 15 counties identified in this manner contained only two settlements between 20,000 and 25,000 in population; four with between 10,000 and 20,000 inhabitants; and 14 with less than 10,000 but more than 6,000 inhabitants.

The two counties that include Flint and a part of Detroit were taken as the urban counties, and together they had less than 6 percent of their population living on

[7] Mich. Dep't of Social Welfare, Michigan Juvenile Court Reporting (1959).

farms in 1950, less than 25 percent living in rural, non-farm residences, and more than 72 percent living in urban places.

Although these three categories were defined arbitrarily and some overlap in two dimensions could not be avoided, they did permit us to identify the 11 counties in Michigan with the greatest percentage of farm residents and the smallest percentage of urban residents; the 15 counties with moderate percentages of both farm and urban residents; and the two counties with the highest percentage of urban population. The remaining 55 counties in Michigan were not so unimodal in their character.

Once the rural, village, and urban delinquents had been identified in this manner, they were broken down further in terms of their sex, their offense patterns, and their family structure. Two types of offense patterns were defined in the following way: first, those delinquents who committed the offense of Auto Stealing, Other Stealing, Damage to Property, Carelessness, or Mischief were considered to be property offenders; while those who were Truant, Incorrigible, Disobedient, or had Run Away were considered as offenders against authority. Non-white were not included in this investigation because they were concentrated in the urban counties almost exclusively.

The results of the analysis to be presented below suggest several major conclusions. First, as the community type becomes more urban, family disorganization becomes increasingly more prominent in the history of male property delinquents. Male offenders against authority and female offenders, however, fail to exhibit this same pattern.

Second, many of the differences between male and female offenders stem largely from the different mix of delinquent types they include and not from any intrinsic differences the two sexes may exhibit. Third, there is a clear preference of rural delinquents, both male and female, for property offenses, while the delinquencies of urban offenders are more evenly balanced between property offenses and offenses against authority. These, then, are the major findings to be reported below.

In order to get a more detailed picture of the results, however, let us turn directly to the findings. In Table 1 male delinquents are analyzed in terms of their community type and family structure, and a strong positive relationship between urbanization and the percentage of delinquents from voluntarily broken homes is apparent. Moreover, the significance of the father in the rural household seems to be considerably greater than in the urban home, since the percentage of families broken by the death of the father in rural areas is more than double that in urban areas. This finding may suggest that while the father in rural families plays a key role in forestalling delinquent behavior among his sons, in urban areas he is not quite so indispensable in this regard. These findings are supported and extended somewhat by the results reported in Tables 2 and 3. Here we see that the relationships exhibited in Table 1 are almost entirely due to the characteristics peculiar to the property offender. The relationship between family disorganization and community type is specific to the property offender only. Moreover, the father of the property offender is more likely to be absent through death in rural areas than in urban areas, while among offenders against authority this pattern does not emerge at all. In addition, the mother seems to assume a slightly greater significance in preventing delinquency in the families of urban property offenders since her absence through death is somewhat more common there than among the families of rural property offenders. As before, this pattern does not appear in the data describing male offenders against authority.

TABLE 1. Male Juvenile Offenders According to the Marital Status of the Parents and Community Type[a]

Community Type	*Marital Status of Parents*									
	Married & Together		*Separated, Divorced, or Deserted*		*Mother Dead*[b]		*Father Dead*[b]		*Total*	
	%	*N*	%	*N*	%	*N*	%	*N*	%	*N*
Rural	65.8	127	19.2	37	2.0	4	13.0	25	100.0	193
Village	70.3	295	21.4	90	1.4	6	6.9	29	100.0	420
Urban	63.6	432	25.9	176	4.4	30	6.0	41	99.9	679
All Groups	66.0	854	23.5	303	3.1	40	7.3	95	99.9	1292

[a]The frequency matrix yields a chi-square of 23.68 with 6 degrees of freedom and a probability less than .01. Yates' correction for continuity was applied where appropriate.

[b]The matrix of these two columns above yields a chi-square of 10.71 with 2 degrees of freedom and a probability less than .01.

TABLE 2. Male Juvenile Offenders Against Property According to the Marital Status of the Parents and Community Type[a]

Community Type	*Marital Status of Parents*									
	Married & Together		*Separated, Divorced, or Deserted*		*Mother Dead*[b]		*Father Dead*[b]		*Total*	
	%	*N*	%	*N*	%	*N*	%	*N*	%	*N*
Rural	67.0	120	17.9	32	1.7	3	13.4	24	100.0	179
Village	72.0	262	19.2	70	1.4	5	7.4	27	100.0	364
Urban	67.4	348	22.7	117	4.3	22	5.6	29	100.0	516
All Groups	68.9	730	20.7	219	2.8	30	7.6	80	100.0	1059

[a]The frequency matrix yields a chi-square of 21.14 with 6 degrees of freedom and a probability less than .01. Yates' correction for continuity was applied where appropriate.

[b]The matrix of these two columns above yields a chi-square of 13.57 with 2 degrees of freedom and is significant beyond .01.

TABLE 3. Male Juvenile Offenders Against Authority According to the Marital Status of the Parents and Community

Community Type	*Marital Status of Parents*									
	Married & Together		*Separated, Divorced, or Deserted*		*Mother Dead*		*Father Dead*		*Total*	
	%	*N*	*%*	*N*	*%*	*N*	*%*	*N*	*%*	*N*
Rural	50.0	7	35.7	5	7.1	1	7.2	1	100.0	14
Village	59.0	33	35.7	20	1.8	1	3.6	2	100.0	56
Urban	51.5	84	36.2	59	4.9	8	7.4	12	100.0	163
All Groups	53.2	124	36.1	84	4.3	10	6.4	15	100.0	233

[a]The frequency matrix yields a chi-square that is not significant.

In general, then, it would seem that the incidence of offenses against property among males is associated with a complex relationship between family disorganization and community organization. In rural areas, male property offenders are more likely to derive from families broken by the death of the father, but conversely in urban settings they are likely to be from families broken voluntarily by separation, divorce, or desertion or by the death of the mother.

The male offender against authority, however, does not seem to be so responsive to changes in the social organization of his environment. Although he is more likely to be found in disorganized families than the property offender, this likelihood is fairly constant for all types of family disorganization regardless of the surrounding community.

In order to examine the relationship between these same variables in a different context, it was decided to extend our analysis to female delinquents. Accordingly, female offenders were broken down in terms of their place of residence and type of offense, and the family structure of each examined. Unfortunately the number of cases was too few in some instances to enable even rather sharp trends to be statistically significant. The pattern that emerges, however, is quite distinctive and deserves further comment.

First of all, it is apparent from an examination of Tables 4, 5, and 6 that the summary data on female delinquents presented in Table 4 below fails to exhibit any regular trends primarily because it combines data on 78 property offenders who do exhibit some interesting tendencies, with data on 240 offenders against authority who do not. The property offenders were not sufficiently numerous nor their characteristics sharply enough drawn to counterbalance the lack of regular trends in the offenders against authority.

TABLE 4. Female Juvenile Offenders According to the Marital Status of the Parents and Community Type[a]

Community Type	*Marital Status of Parents*									
	Married & Together		*Separated, Divorced, or Deserted*		*Mother Dead*		*Father Dead*		*Total*	
	%	*N*	*%*	*N*	*%*	*N*	*%*	*N*	*%*	*N*
Rural	56.3	18	31.2	10	–	–	12.5	4	100.0	32
Village	59.6	53	29.2	26	1.1	1	10.1	9	100.0	89
Urban	55.3	109	33.0	65	1.5	3	10.2	20	100.0	197
All Groups	56.6	180	31.8	101	1.2	4	10.4	33	100.0	318

[a]The frequency matrix yields a chi-square that is not significant.

One relationship that does manifest itself in Table 4, however, is the relationship between the sex of the delinquent and the manner in which the family structure was ruptured by death. If we compare Table 4 with Table 1, we see that 10.4 percent of the female delinquents came from families in which the father was removed through death, while 7.3 percent of the male delinquents were exposed to similar circumstances in their families. In contrast, 3.1 percent of the males and 1.2 percent of the females came from homes in which the mother had died. Apparently the death of the father prejudices the girl's chances of avoiding delinquency more so than the boy's, while conversely the death of the mother is more significant in this

TABLE 5. Female Offenders Against Property According to the Marital Status of the Parents and Community Type[a]

Community Type	*Marital Status of Parents*									
	Married & Together		*Separated, Divorced, or Deserted*		*Mother Dead*		*Father Dead*		*Total*	
	%	*N*	*%*	*N*	*%*	*N*	*%*	*N*	*%*	*N*
Rural	61.0	11	27.9	5	–	–	11.1	2	100.0	18
Village	62.8	22	25.8	9	–	–	11.4	4	100.0	35
Urban	68.0	17	16.0	4	4.0	1	12.0	3	100.0	25
All Groups	64.1	50	23.1	18	1.3	1	11.5	9	100.0	78

[a]The frequency matrix yields a chi-square that is not significant.

regard for the boy than the girl. When these two patterns were compared statistically, the chi-square was 5.46 with 1 degree of freedom and a probability of having occurred by chance of less than 2 percent. It should be noted here, however, that abstracting columns from separate tables and comparing them statistically is likely to capitalize on chance fluctuations and, hence, does not always yield reliable estimates.

TABLE 6. Female Offenders Against Authority According to the Marital Status of the Parents and Community Type[a]

Community Type	*Marital Status of Parents*									
	Married & Together		*Separated, Divorced, or Deserted*		*Mother Dead*		*Father Dead*		*Total*	
	%	*N*	*%*	*N*	*%*	*N*	*%*	*N*	*%*	*N*
Rural	50.0	7	35.7	5	–	–	14.3	2	100.0	14
Village	57.4	31	31.5	17	1.9	1	9.3	5	100.1	54
Urban	53.5	92	35.5	61	1.2	2	9.9	17	100.1	172
All Groups	54.1	130	34.6	83	1.3	3	10.0	24	100.0	240

[a]The frequency matrix yields a chi-square that is not significant.

In Tables 5 and 6, the characteristics of the female property offender and the female offenders against authority are given. Although these tables reveal no statistically significant patterns, they do exhibit some interesting trends. For example, the percentage of property offenders from voluntarily broken homes tends to decline as the community type becomes more urbanized. The offenders against authority, however, exhibit no such trend. The difference between the types of offenders in this regard is statistically significant, giving a chi-square of 10.03 with 2 degrees of freedom and a chance probability of less than 1 percent, although, for reasons outlined above, we may not conclude definitely that the differences cited are reliable.

Female offenders against authority, like their male counterparts, exhibit no relationship between family disorganization and community type, although family disorganization generally is a much more important factor in their background than in the background of female property offenders.

It is important to note, while comparing male and female delinquents, that in spite of any difference that may exist in the way in which family structure and community organization interact to influence property offenders, the summary data on property and authority offenders is in quite close agreement for both male and female delinquents. The percent of property offenders from homes broken voluntarily, i.e., through separation, divorce, or desertion, was 20.7 and 23.1 respectively for males and females. These same statistics for male and female offenders against authority were 36.1 percent and 34.6 percent, respectively. Clearly the differences between property offenders and offenders against authority are greater than those between male and female offenders. This consistency between the sexes corroborates the finding reported by Weeks in which the commonly reported differences in the family backgrounds of male and female delinquents nearly disappears when only those male and female delinquents who have committed similar offenses are compared.[8]

The difference in family background between the sexes that appears when we compare Tables 1 and 4, therefore, is largely based on the fact that 82.0 percent of the male delinquents but only 24.5 percent of the female delinquents were property offenders. It should also be noted that the heavy predominance of male delinquency over female delinquency–i.e., 4.1 male offenders for every female offender–is entirely due to the large number of male property offenders. Offenders against authority appear with nearly equal frequency among male and female delinquents, as Tables 3 and 6 indicate.

The final analysis in this study compares the offense patterns displayed by delinquents in rural, village, and urban communities. In Table 7 the ratio of property offenders to offenders against authority is presented according to community type, family structure, and sex. Although there is considerable variation in the magnitude of the ratio, it decreases markedly as the community becomes more urbanized for nearly every type of delinquent. In other words, the number of offenses against authority generally increases much faster than the number of property offenses as urbanization proceeds. It would seem, therefore, that property offenses are nearly typical of rural delinquents, but that urban delinquents are more inclined to commit both types of offenses.

TABLE 7. The Ratio of Property Offenders to Offenders Against Authority According to the Marital Status of the Parents and Community Type for Male and Female Delinquents

Community Type	*Marital Status of Parents*									
	Married & Together		*Separated, Divorced, or Deserted*		*Mother Dead*		*Father Dead*		*Total*	
	Male	*Female*	*Male*	*Female*	*Male*	*Female*	*Male*	*Female*	*Male*	*Female*
Rural	17.1	1.57	6.4	1.00	3.0	–	24.0	1.00	12.8	1.13
Village	7.9	.67	3.5	.53	5.0	–	13.5	.80	6.5	.65
Urban	4.1	.18	2.0	.07	2.7	.50	2.4	.18	3.2	.15
All Groups	5.9	.39	2.6	.22	3.0	.33	5.3	.37	4.5	.32

[8] Weeks, *Male and Female Broken Home Rates by Types of Delinquency*, 5 Am. Soc. Rev. 601 (1940).

In sum, then, these findings suggest that the family structure of male and female property offenders is likely to vary considerably, depending on the nature of their community. Male and female offenders against authority, however, are not so variable in this regard. There does not seem to be any general hypersensitivity on the part of females to family disorganization, since male and female delinquents who have committed similar offenses tend to resemble each other also in the likelihood of their coming from broken homes. Male delinquents, however, appear to be peculiarly allergic to the death of the mother, while the death of the father seems to be particularly traumatic for female delinquents. And finally, delinquents in rural areas seem to be predisposed to commit property offenses, while urban delinquents are relatively more inclined to commit offenses against authority.

The pattern of these findings suggest several hypotheses regarding the nature of delinquency. First, it would appear that property offenders and offenders against authority constitute two rather distinctive types of delinquents. Property offenders, for example, are somewhat less likely to have experienced family disorganization than offenders against authority. When it does appear in his environment, however, the significance of family disorganization is much more closely conditioned by his place of residence and sex than with authority offenders. All of this probably indicates that property offenders, as a type, have become delinquent largely through their experiences in extra-family groups, i.e., as a result, perhaps, of an intensive exposure to a delinquent subculture or a subjection to systematic class discrimination. It would seem that if they had lived in a beneficent, conventional environment, many of them might have avoided delinquency altogether.

We do not mean to imply that property offenders all follow similar paths in their development nor that the same constellation of factors is operative in the history of every property offender. We are asserting, however, that in most cases the family has performed its function of shaping the child's personality in a reasonably adequate way and that if it is deficient in any regard, it has failed primarily to insulate the child sufficiently from external, deleterious influences.

The offender against authority, however, probably presents a rather different etiology. First, his offense is directed at persons and institutions that are ubiquitous and irresistible as far as he is concerned, i.e., his parents and the public school system. This fact suggests that the likelihood of detection and ultimate punishment carries little weight in affecting the child's course of action; he must register his protest against authoritarian structures no matter what the cost. It would seem, therefore, that offenses against authority express rather deep-seated antipathies for conventional social structures and that these attitudes are supported by motive structures integrally woven into the personalities of the children involved. We might suggest, then, that offenses against authority signal fairly severe personality disturbances when they appear in delinquents.

Secondly, the fact that family disorganization in one form or another appears in the history of nearly half the authority offenders suggests that the source of the severe disturbance centers right in the home. The relationships between the parents apparently were not sufficiently wholesome to enable even an adequate socialization of the child. Thus, while the property offender's difficulties may arise as a result of the inability of the family to protect him from delinquency pressures in the community, the offender against authority probably could not avoid some form of antisocial activity even in the most healthful of community environments.

Using this typology and the assumptions underlying it, we can explain several other relationships that appeared in this investigation. For example, the fact that authority offenses are much more common among urban delinquents is consistent with what we know about the incidence of family disorganization in urban and rural areas. There is considerable evidence that divorce, separation, and desertion are somewhat more common among urban families than among families in villages or rural areas.[9] Apparently, the greater incidence of offenders against authority in urban areas is a reflection of the fact that seriously disorganized families, which are unable to socialize their children adequately, are more likely to appear there. It should be noted that this interpretation supplements the view commonly held that delinquency is largely an urban phenomenon because delinquent values and techniques have taken root in some adolescent groups which in turn sponsor its spread through their success in recruiting new members.

This typology would also suggest that, although characteristic differences in the incidence of homes broken voluntarily should distinguish property offenders and offenders against authority, homes broken through death should occur with equal frequency among the two types of deliquents. Presumably death strikes the families of both types of delinquents with approximately the same frequency. The data supplied in Tables 2, 3, 5, and 6 indicate that 10.6 percent of the property offenders came from homes in which one parent had been removed by death, while 11.0 percent of the offenders against authority came from similar homes. This in spite of the fact that 20.0 percent of the property offenders but 35.3 percent of the offenders against authority came from homes broken voluntarily by separation, divorce, or desertion. Apparently the mere fact of a disrupted family is not enough to induce the children to defy authority; rather the circumstances under which the family was disrupted seem to be the crucial factor.

One finding reported above, however, that defies explanation in terms of this typology, at least, is the fact that the percentage of voluntarily broken homes among property offenders increases among males but appears to decrease among females as the community type becomes more urban.

This finding may simply reflect the fact that separation, divorce, and desertion generally are more common among urban populations. Thus, male property offenders in this instance may be just mirroring trends implicit in the larger population. If this explanation is correct, however, we should note that there are some rather strong counter-pressures operating on these same data to swing them in the opposite direction. For example, we have already noted that fathers in rural families play an instrumental role in training and disciplining their children. Hence, when

[9] Cannon, *Marriage and Divorce in Iowa*, 1940–1947, 9 Marriage and Family Living 81 (1947).

divorce or death removes the father, his loss in rural areas is keenly felt and is probably reflected in the fact that 13.4 percent of the male property offenders residing in rural areas, but only 5.6 percent of those in urban areas, had lost fathers through death. In this case this factor apparently was not sufficiently strong to counterbalance the fact that considerably more disorganized families are available in urban communities to produce property offenders than in rural areas.

This interpretation, however, could not explain why female property offenders fail to exhibit the same pattern. It may be, however, that the slight trend depicted in Table 5 is a reflection of nothing more than accidental factors and, hence, not worthy of serious consideration.

In conclusion, then, we have attempted in this study to provide some information concerning some questions that are relatively unexplored in the study of delinquency. We have demonstrated that delinquents who commit property offenses and delinquents who commit offenses against authority exhibit two distinctive sets of characteristics. We have shown that urban and rural delinquents also tend to differ systematically in the offense patterns they display. And, finally, we have suggested that male and female delinquents tend to differ principally in the frequency with which they elect offenses against property and that their overall differences stem mainly from this fact.

We have based these observations entirely on data generously supplied by the Michigan Department of Social Welfare and, consequently, any inaccuracies or distortion that official data suffer from probably affect these data, too. These biases are well known and need not be described here. One difficulty, however, which this researcher felt acutely that has not been so widely commented upon is the fact that in working with official data, the investigator has no access to the individuals represented by the data cards, and hence is completely cut off from the kind of firsthand involvement that often provides the most insightful and sophisticated hypotheses. Thus, when paradoxes appear in the data, there is no experience from which pregnant hunches might be drawn.

Section III

Interaction Processes: Linking the Individual to Criminal and Delinquent Groups

Introductory Remarks

Let us momentarily assume that sociocultural forces do not contribute to an explanation of criminal and delinquent behavior, and that explanation is solely psychological. Then it is to be expected that crimes and criminals and delinquencies and delinquents would be evenly distributed throughout the population and localities. This is to be anticipated, since it has not been found that any one group of the population is in sole possession of the psychopathologies or holds in common specific kinds of psychogenic traits. Therefore, on this basis we would expect a number of predictable relationships. For example, we would expect about half the offenders to consist of females; we would expect all age categories to be somewhat equally represented in offender rates; we would expect offensive behavior of these individuals to persist in time; we would expect that all those psychologically maladjusted would choose illegal behavior and none would choose conventional solutions; and we would not expect that the extent and the type of offenses would be related to social, demographical, and ecological characteristics.

That this expectation is not a reality has been initially suggested in the articles of Section II dealing with the variations in forms and patterns of criminal and delinquent behavior which exist within different sociocultural structures. Furthermore, in other ways this expectation directly conflicts with the most consistent data available. Although the available data have serious limitations, there is sufficient consistency in the variations found from diverse sources, in different time periods, and with varied methods to warrant their consideration. It is interesting to note that if all suspected limitations of data were assumed to be limitations and taken into account, significant relationships would still persist between certain offenses and offenders.

A limited presentation of this data follows.

Data on Offenses

1. Police arrests of adults and juveniles for offenses involving no direct victim (e.g., drunkenness, disorderly conduct, gambling) usually average about 70% of the total number of arrests for the 28 offenses (data collected yearly by the F.B.I.) The remaining police arrests deal with offenses against property, usually around 21%, and offenses against person, usually around 9%. If our analysis is focused not on arrests, but on the F.B.I. Index (Part I) of the seven serious offenses (against person: criminal homicide, forcible rape, robbery, aggravated assault; and against property: burglary, larceny $50 and over, motor vehicle theft) reported to police, then property *offenses generally are about 87% of all serious offenses and offenses against person are approximately 13%.*[1]

2. There are some indications that the general delinquency rate increases during war and prosperity and that the general adult crime rate decreases during war and prosperity.

3. Very briefly stated, nonrandom variations exist in this nation, as in other nations, by and within regions; between and within rural and urban areas; and by size, by type, and within areas of cities for offenses in general, as well as for specific offenses. Many social circumstances play a part in accounting for this variation.[2]

Data About Offenders

1. Although females constitute roughly half our population, close to 90% of all arrested offenders are males. However, the ratio over the years has continued to narrow. The great overrepresentation of males persists in all localities (e.g., nations, communities), ages, and types of offenses except those that are uniquely female.

Yet the ratio between males and females varies greatly by social circumstances. Thus, the ratio varies between and within nations, by types of communities and neighborhoods, by time in history, by types of offense by age categories, by social position of each sex within societies, by race, by nationality, and by socioeconomic class.

2. The adolescent and young adult age categories contribute an unusually high proportion of those arrested for certain types of offenses. The vast majority of serious property offenses and a great overrepresentation of serious offenses against person are committed by persons in the 15–24 year age category. Offenders over age 24 are in the great majority for offenses without a direct victim (e.g., drunkenness, vagrancy, gambling), plus fraud, embezzlement, and offenses against family. This is not surprising, since these offenses take a longer period in which to emerge.

There is a steady decrease in the rates of offenders against property and person as age increases. As a matter of fact, in general, the most effective tool of reformation is progressive physical and social maturation. However, the younger a person is at first conviction the more likely he will continue to commit offenses over a longer period. Yet, a good share of persistent older offenders are not convicted before 17 years of age and many not before 21.

The relationships of crime and delinquency to specific ages are affected by variations in social circumstances. Thus, the relationship of both the extent of crime and delinquency and the specific type of offense to age varies by type of locality (e.g., nation, community, neighborhood), time (i.e., a much younger offender group in the United States today compared to that of the past), sex, nationality, socioeconomic class, and so on.

3. As compared to other classes a disproportionately high ratio of arrested offenders come from lower socioeconomic classes. Although this relationship could be somewhat exaggerated by differentials in detection and handling, the lower socioeconomic classes are, nevertheless, vastly overrepresented in institutions that collect the more persistent and patterned offenders.

Yet the rate for the lower socioeconomic groups varies with social circumstances.

[1] See the introduction of this reader for more detailed information on the volume of offenses and for information on unreported offenses and victims of crimes. Materials on "hidden" delinquency are included in Section II, Article No. 15.

[2] See Section II, particularly Article 9.

This relationship is affected by place of residence (e.g., rural versus urban, size and type of community, neighborhood), by ethnic identification, and by nations.

4. In the period (1930's) following great migrations to this country, the rates of delinquencies for children of foreign-born parents of some groups for certain types of offenses exceeded those for children of native-born parents; whereas, the rates in general and for specific types of delinquencies were less for children of foreign-born parents of some groups than for children of native-born parents.

In these past years the blacks (approximately 11% of the population) have had excessively higher rates of arrests for all 28 F.B.I. (Parts I and II) offenses than the remaining population. However, the rate currently for any specific offense varies from 10 or more times to roughly 1/6 greater the rate for the remaining population. In general for the 7 serious Index offenses (Part I), the arrest rate is now about 4 times the rate for the remaining population. For some offenses (i.e., gambling, murder, robbery, aggravated assault) arrests of the blacks often exceed the actual number of arrests in the remaining population for any one of the above offenses. For all 28 F.B.I. (Parts I and II) offenses the arrest rate for the blacks now exceeds the rate for the remaining population by about 3 times. The arrest rates for blacks are particularly greater for those over 18 years of age than under 18 as compared to those for the remaining population group. Second offenses are also found more frequently among blacks.

The differences in rates between these two populations are reduced or increased depending on social circumstances. Thus, these great differences are affected by region of the country, by type of community, by type and place of neighborhood, by socioeconomic class, by sex, by period in time, by recency of migration, and so on.

5. The best available data indicate that delinquent orientation does not last long. Most juveniles committing delinquent acts, who are not only detected but referred and adjudicated by juvenile court, do not move into serious criminal activities in adult years. The majority do not come to the court's attention for further delinquencies after appearing in juvenile court once. Of those who persist, the greater share cease coming to the attention of the authorities by age 25.

The great majority of delinquents not only associate with other delinquents but also accomplish their delinquent acts with the aid and encouragement of companions.

6. No psychogenic traits of the personality consistently distinguish criminals and delinquents from comparable nonoffender populations. Stated differently, persons holding common personality traits are found to engage in diverse activities, and persons holding diversities in personality traits are found to engage in common activities. However, many specialists agree that overt aggression is displayed by many offenders, although they disagree on its source and depth. Explanations for this aggression range from an inborn quality to psychogenic traits of the personality established in early life to an attitudinally (sociogenically) sustained behavior pattern acquired from and reflecting position in sociocultural arrangements. Others point out that this aggressiveness is the same attribute possessed by a number of police officers, military personnel, businessmen, and athletes. Some note that an individual's overt aggression may not be diffused to all settings but is particularized (e.g., in correctional setting, school setting).

It is the unexpected variation found in data of this kind for which there must be an accounting in any explanation of crime and delinquency. And the approaches that strive to separate the general group of criminals and delinquents from comparable nonoffender populations by attempting to uncover distinctions of psychopathologies or psychogenic traits fail to acknowledge the unexpected variability in the existing data.

Sociology has contributed to our understanding of the forms and patterns of criminal and delinquent behavior and their nonrandom distribution. There remains, however, the unresolved problem of why some possessing the most susceptible attributes (e.g., minority group status, age, sex, social class, neighborhood) do not express criminal and delinquent behavior patterns. What are the processes that foster the development of these behavior patterns, and what are the processes that cause them to be rejected? We must account for the differences in behavior today between this person and another, and the similarity in behavior of both in the days that follow. An explanation is needed for the observation that the common vehicle of association leads to conformity of some to conventional groups, and of others to nonconventional groups.

Sociology has derived the data given above from its studies of sociocultural phenomena. However, these sociocultural phenomena are sustained and are a reflection of a most elementary and dynamic social phenomenon: social interaction. Of late, more attention is being given to the interactional perspective as a contributor toward explanation. This perspective reflects the view that forms and patterns of criminal and delinquent behavior located within sociocultural structures arise and are sustained through processes of interaction. With this focus psychogenic traits of the personality alone are not viewed as ensuring continuance of criminal and delinquent behavior of most offenders. Nor are they predictive in determining choice of legal or illegal solutions to common problems. This is evident when one considers the fact that common goals, impulses, motives, as well as traits of insecurity, anxiety, neuroticism, aggression, hostility, and inferiority are found not only among criminals and delinquents, but also among the general population (e.g., teachers, students, union members, housewives, soldiers).

The interactional perspective does not view criminal and delinquent roles as permanent qualities of most people, but rather, it views significant shifts in social roles as induced through variations in the web of interaction.[3] *Therefore, those of the interactional persuasion focus on those processes of interaction within groups which have nurtured or are nurturing and sustaining criminal and delinquent behavior.*

[3] For contributions of the interactionist perspective toward explaining the criminality of "loners" see Donald R. Cressey and David A. Ward, *Delinquency, Crime, and Social Process,* Harper & Row, Publishers, 1968, pp. 1043–1128.

17. Social Roles: Linking Individuals to Criminal and Delinquent Behavior

Richard R. Korn and Lloyd M. McCorkle

The Critical Need for Intervening Variables in a Theory of Behavior

The obvious error in any attempt to relate an individual's personality directly to his overt activities is the failure to realize that certain other factors may intervene between his inner state of mind and his ultimate responses–factors which may change those responses radically. A factor intervening between a causal or *independent variable* and an end effect or *dependent variable* is technically known as an *intervening variable.* A theory which ignores these intervening factors is incapable of dealing with findings that different people behave similarly–and similar people behave differently.

The concept of *role* profoundly clarifies these universal but otherwise baffling findings.. The similar activities of dissimilar personalities clearly seem related to the fact that these different personalities are involved in a similar role. Conversely, the dissimilar activities of relatively similar personalities may be accounted for by the fact that each is behaving with reference to a different role.

It is true that individual reasons for the same role involvement may vary widely. It is equally true that different people play the same roles in different ways, and with different consequences. Nevertheless, though individual differences color the manner and affect the consequences of role-playing, the uniformities imparted by the role itself may often transcend these idiosyncratic factors. Caruso and Peerce may sing *I Pagliacci* in different ways–but the role is still Canio.

Application of the Role Concept to the Problematical Data of Crimes and Criminals. Because *roles* simultaneously have subjective, interpersonal, and social-structural aspects, they are capable of definitions which relate to any one or a combination of these referents. For our purposes the most adequate definition is that

Reprinted from Chapter 14, "Toward the Clarification of Criminological Theory," from *Criminology and Penology* by Richard R. Korn and Lloyd W. McCorkle.

which most comprehensively relates the psychological, interactional, and sociological components in a single formulation. Accordingly, a role may be defined as a *socially standardized and socially transmitted configuration of reciprocal attitudes and activities which organizes selective aspects of the actor's total behavior with reference to certain goals pursued by means of certain interactions with the occupants of other roles.* In order to evaluate the appropriateness of the role concept for criminological theory, we may test its "fit" against the requirements of the *problematical data....*

...

1. The Selective Distribution of Criminal Roles Among the Sexes. Two general findings must be anticipated and accounted for: (1) the disproportionate percentage of males involved in crime and delinquency; and (2) the wider range of crimes and delinquency encountered among males.

The Sex-Linked Character of Many Social Roles. Many legitimate social roles, activities and vocations are differentiated on the basis of sex. For many of these membership in one sex is a virtual requirement–and membership in the other a virtual disqualification. Even in an era which has seen the unprecedented appearance of the lady wrestler there are still certain activities from which the gentler sex is barred. (By the time this text is a few years old the number of these exclusively male activities will probably have decreased.) Most activities requiring heavy physical labor, physical danger, or violence are still restricted to males. (The policewoman is a recent exception to this general rule; the female mugger is still rare.)

Differences in the Role Aspirations and Role Preparations of Boys and Girls. The play activities of children are universally related to preparations and aspirations for the later assumption of socially defined adult roles. In this sense, play activities are themselves an essential aspect of preparation. Certain contrasts in the preparations and aspirations of boys and girls are relevant to the later development and division of various roles among the two sexes.

There is a greater degree of continuity in the role preparations of girls as contrasted with boys. In their play activities girls generally prepare for roles which will be realistically available to them as adults. They play at keeping house, at tending children, at cooking, etc. Their mothers and other female relatives provide models and examples for these roles. *Boys tend to play at roles which will be less realistically available to them as adults.* Margaret Mead has written: "In peacetime the small boy's heroes, whether his own father keeps a grocery store or is president of a bank, are policemen, firemen, flyers, cowboys, and baseball-players..."[1]

The role aspirations and preparations of girls are not only more conventional but *more limited and less variable than those of boys,* a condition anticipating their less variable role activities as adult females. Thus, girls learn early to restrict their aspirations within more realistic limits. In contrast, boys must face the frustration of

[1] Margaret Mead, *Male and Female* (New York: The New American Library of World Literature, 1955), p. 230.

giving up their earlier, more heroic images in exchange for less active, less exciting conventional pursuits structured around earning a living. They will be expected to be earners, fathers, husbands–roles that hardly preoccupied the fantasies of their youth.

Acceptable and unacceptable ways of deviation and rebellion vary for boys and girls. The culture which sets certain limits on role and activity alternatives for the two sexes tends also to surround these limits with a pale of acceptable and unacceptable deviation. There are highly significant differences in both of these areas for boys and girls. In the first place, even the rebellious activity of girls is largely related to their demands for the perquisites of conventional female roles at ages considered premature by society. The girls demand to be allowed to wear lipstick, to smoke, to stay out late on dates–rights which are the prerogatives of older females. Thus the girl frequently rebels by insisting on playing conventional roles earlier than she is permitted to, and her rebellion often takes the form of carrying out these roles in behavior considered intolerable not because of its content but because of its precocity. In contrast, *the rebellion of boys is frequently related to a rejection of the activities of conventional adult males.* Unlike the girl, who dreams of exchanging the uncertain life of waiting and dating for the security of the role of wife, the young man may be less willing to surrender his freedom as the unfettered lover for the role of steady husband and father. Unlike the little girl, who dreams of puttering around the kitchen and taking care of the baby, he is less likely to dream of a day in the office or the factory and an evening at home with the wife and kids.

To a considerable extent society recognizes the realities of the young male's greater frustrations by tolerating less deviation and rebellion by girls–and more by boys. These differences are mirrored in the peer-group traditions of each. Among the girls, successful conformity to adult conduct rules–good manners, neat dressing, etc.–are ways of obtaining status among peers. *Among the boys, a too-yielding conformity to adult conduct rules is cause for lowered status.* For the girl, the role of teacher's pet is a desirable goal; for the boys, the mere accusation may be a deadly insult. Thus the traits for which girls learn they will be liked are charm, prettiness, gentleness, cooperation, *compliance.* Boys, on the contrary, will be admired for being courageous, combative, competitive, and, within limits, *noncompliant.*

The Activity Alternatives Open to Boys and Girls. Boys are encouraged by their peers to engage in competitive activities, to master manipulative skills, to fight, to be independent, to remove obstacles by direct aggressive action. Girls are encouraged to be–or at least to behave as if they were–more dependent, to rely on the boys for help. A girl who is too independent, who defends herself too effectively, who competes, who wants to "show the boys up," is less likely to be popular among the boys. *Therefore she is also less likely to be popular among the girls, among whom status is highly related to the ability to attract and hold males.* The greater initiative, the greater aggressiveness, the greater insistence on abilities of self-help and self-defense among the boys serve as preparations for the presumably greater rigors of the male's destined part in life.

As it turns out, the actual performance for which these heroic rehearsals are presumably the preparation may fall short of the expectations of the aspiring actors. And herein lies a point that need not be labored at any greater length than the sentence required to state it: *For the modern boy growing up in a conventionalized, routinized, and increasingly immobile adult society, the more liberal tolerance of deviation may serve as an increasingly inadequate preparation for conventional adult roles–and as an increasingly efficient preparation for unconventional pursuits.* The endemic rise in juvenile delinquency and the increasing involvement of boys at all class levels may be related to this longer-term trend.

2. The Disproportionate Involvement of the Young in Delinquency and Crime. Many of the relevant relations of role selection and role behavior to the age distribution of offenders have already been anticipated in the previous discussion. The increase in nonproductive leisure, especially among urban youth, the longer postponement of adult responsibilities, the decreased contact with visible models of working adults, the greater dependency on peers for models, the wider range of activity alternatives open to the unemployed but money-hungry adolescent–each of these factors tends to increase the possibility of experimentation in unconventional activities. Although the organization of these experimental activities into delinquent role patterns may require the intervention of additional factors, the activities themselves provide raw material potentially available for criminal exploitation.

The proportionately greater criminal involvement of the young is, of course, a direct function of the comparatively lesser involvement of older adults. Patterns of role involvement typically change as a function of increasing age. This fact suggests a basis for understanding differential age-rates of criminality. Where the late teenager and the twenty-year-old is still likely to be single and not yet strongly tied to an occupational career, the man in his late twenties and early thirties is likely to be married, to be raising a family, and to be heavily engaged in earning the living necessary to fulfilling the responsibilities contingent on his roles of husband and father. These roles, and the increasingly conservative, security-conscious attitudes they engender, are less compatible with the occupational and social hazards of crime.

3. The Disproportionate Incidence of Crime and Delinquency in Urban Localities. As before, the previous discussion has anticipated many of the ideas relevant to the present subject. Leisure is largely an urban invention. The prolonged childhood and unproductivity of the urban adolescent contrasts sharply with the earlier vocational maturity of his country cousin, at work with his father or his neighbors in the fields. In addition to his greater involvement in gainful activities, the rural child is confronted with far fewer activity alternatives and fewer opportunities for diversion. Living and working side by side with adult behavior models, he is less dependent and less involved with a peer society which concentrates on personal consumption to the relative neglect of personal productivity.

... In summary, it is evident that the urban, as contrasted with the rural, setting presents a wider range of both conventional and unconventional role alternatives and a greater possibility of role conflicts. This occurs, moreover, in a situation where the powerful influences of informal social control are vitiated and diluted by the impersonality and isolation characteristic of big-city life.

4. The Disproportionate Involvement of Members of the Lower Socioeconomic Classes. Few sociological conclusions have been more convincingly confirmed than the conclusion which states that the distribution of social roles is largely a function of social class. Members of the lower socioeconomic strata have less access to the educational and vocational perquisites of the more desirable social roles. Beginning at a lower rung of the status ladder, the extent of their climb is highly conditioned by their original starting point. The lower-class child requires talent and perserverance to reach a point that, in many cases, is lower than the level from which the more privileged child will start as a matter of course. Moreover, many of the economic and social obstacles confronting the lower-class child will be unknown to middle- and upper-class children. The occupants of the less desirable vocational roles have gained less by their social conformity—and stand, consequently, to lose less if they cease to conform. To the sophisticated lower-class child who is able to contrast the lot of his hard-working parents with that of the neighborhood racketmen, the doctrine that honesty is its own reward may cease to be persuasive. In any case, the vivid contrast between legitimate and illegitimate alternatives presents the lower-class youth with role conflicts that are much less likely to confront the children of more privileged parents.

The Differential Involvement of Certain Racial and Ethnic Groups in Crime. The situation of certain racial and ethnic groups may be considered as a special case of social deprivation, with resulting exposure to the same limited range of less desirable role alternatives confronting members of the lowest social classes. Among the findings supporting this conclusion is the evidence that the small percentage of minority-race members who, for one reason or another, have escaped entrapment in the lowest economic stratum contribute little to the statistics of crime. Like the middle-class members of the majority race, they tend to occupy roles antagonistic to involvement in criminal activities.

The Explanatory Function of the Role Concept in Criminology.

The Role as an Intervening Variable Between the Person and the Act. One of the most significant contributions of the role concept is the way in which it resolves the dilemma of relating personal traits, needs, and problems to criminal behavior. As was previously pointed out, individual psychological factors were, by themselves, incapable of differentiating between the variety of legal and illegal ways these factors might express themselves in actual behavior. What was clearly called for was a factor intermediate between the personality and the response. The concept of *multiple roles* makes it possible to retain the idea of personality as a relatively stable and distinctive structure while at the same time accounting for the variability of responses under different conditions and in different relationships. Thus, the professional pickpocket, after a day devoted to the highly specialized activities and relationships called for in his occupation, may board the train with other commuters and return to his family to spend a highly conventional evening in his roles of husband, father—and, like as not, good neighbor.

The Role as an Intervening Variable Between the Social Group and the Person. One of the dilemmas of a sociological account of criminality was the problem of explaining how similar cultural values or exposure to similar social conditions was related to a wide range of different legitimate and illegitimate activities. The role concept provides a plausible basis for dealing with this critical problem of different responses to the same social factors. Roles, on the one hand, are the media through which society distributes its functions—its major and minor chores—among different members. On the other hand, for the members themselves, roles provide alternate routes (of varying difficulty and desirability) to the attainment of similar social values and goals. Moreover, just as society creates roles to fulfill its acknowledged needs, so it creates others to satisfy its unacknowledged needs. (The roles of prostitute, racketeer, and gambler are examples of roles that fulfill unacknowledged social demands, just as the roles of physician, teacher, and businessman are examples of those through which the group carries out various acknowledged needs.)

Thus the role concept serves sociological theory as a *distributor* of different social functions. At the same time, it serves psychological theory as a *unifying* factor, channeling diverse individual trends into recognizable patterns of behavior. In this latter aspect, roles function as instruments of social control, bringing about the predictable uniformities essential for group living.

Linking the Individual to the Criminal Role. So far, in our attempt to build a negotiable bridge of intervening variables between the individual and his criminal act, we have suggested one structural concept that partly spans the gap: the idea of *role.* The sequence of concepts might now be ranged as follows: Instead of relating the person directly to the criminal act, we speak of the *person,* the *person's role,* and the *activity* which is attached to the role. In effect, the act has now been detached from its direct link with the individual and attached, instead, to a given role—one among many—which he might occupy. We must now deal with the question: What links the person to the role?

At this point it becomes apparent that the thorny question of individual motivation has merely been postponed. If the role concept relieves psychological theory of the task of finding a separate "personal" significance behind every single activity performed by the individual, it may have done no more than defer the identical problem to the next level of analysis. Even if it is granted that the individual's choice of activities is largely determined by his choice of roles, the question still remains, *What determines his choice of roles?*

Before proceeding further, it should be noted that this way of putting the question is not the only way the question can conceivably be put. On closer examination it becomes evident that this formulation begs a question—actually two questions. In the first place it assumes that individuals *choose* their roles—that role involvement is, in one way or another, a matter of personal motivation. The second unquestioned assumption derives from the first. It suggests that the individual's range of alternatives is unlimited.

Ignored by these assumptions is the possibility that a person's role alternatives may frequently be limited by factors beyond his control, that many of them may be imposed rather than chosen, that many may frustrate rather than satisfy his personal needs. Nevertheless, these possibilities are actualities in many areas of human experience. Consider the following commonplace situation.

Enforced Politeness Toward a Relative One Dislikes

In a typical family gathering a group of the younger people, animatedly chatting, are suddenly broken in upon by a senile and garrulous relative whom each of the young people heartily dislikes. If the older man had approached any one of them individually, they would have quickly moved off, brushing him aside. But now they are trapped and condemned to listen to one more version of the old man's interminable stories.

What traps them? It is not the old man himself; he would not have been able to corner them had he found them alone. It is clearly not their own desires; every one of them would be glad to find a pretext to leave. What keeps them there is something entirely "social," as contrasted with anything "individual" or "personal." Each one of the young people is immobilized by a felt need to conform to a certain social expectation which might be called *"the duty to act attentively toward an old relative no matter how bored you are."* This obligation is, of course, very weak, and could be evaded without guilt if it were not for the fact that the young people have been caught in a group. Thus, they are actually trapped and immobilized by each other.

In a theoretical sense this situation is highly interesting, for the following reasons: (1) The behavior of the young people is in conflict with the private desires of each. (2) Nevertheless, it can be accounted for entirely without reference to conditions in the personal field of the actors and with reference only to forces related to the interpersonal or social field. In other words, in order to understand this behavior, it is not necessary to know the personal characteristics or wishes of the actors—except insofar as they contribute to a forced commitment to a certain social value.

The significance of the interpersonal context of motivation is underscored by the next example to be cited. In his classic work, *The Gang*, Thrasher writes about a group of college students, who, one night, for reasons which none of them could explain, suddenly decided to rob a post-office. Thrasher presents the story in the form of a verbatim report by one of the participants.

The Reluctant Robbers

We three college students—Mac, Art, and Tom—were rooming together while attending V———University, one of the oldest colleges in the South. On the day of our crime all three of us spent over three hours in the library—really working. That was on Sunday and our crime was committed at 1:30 that night (or rather Monday morning).

The conversation began with a remark about the numerous recent bank failures in the state, probably stimulated by one of us glancing at a map of the state. It then shifted to discussion of a local bank that had closed its doors the day before. Tom, who worked at the post-office occasionally as special mail clerk, happened to mention that a sack containing a large amount of money had been received at the post-office that afternoon, consigned to a local bank that feared a run.

The conversation then turned to the careless way in which the money was handled at the office—a plain canvas sack thrown into an open safe. We discussed the ease with which a thief could get into the building and steal the money. Tom drew a plan showing the desk at which the only clerk worked and the location of the only gun in the office. At first the conversation was entirely confined to how easily criminals might manage to steal the money. Somehow it shifted to a personal basis: as to how easily we might get the money. This shift came so naturally that even the next morning we were unable to decide when and by whom the first vital remark had been made.

A possible plan was discussed as to how we might steal the package. Tom could go to the office and gain admittance on the pretense of looking for an important letter. Then Art and I, masked and armed, could rush in, tie Tom and the clerk, and make off with the package. We had lost sight of the fact that the package contained money. We were simply discussing the possibility of playing an exciting prank with no thought of actually committing it. We had played many harmless pranks and had discussed them in much the same way before; but the knowledge that there was danger in this prank made it a subject to linger over.

After about an hour and a half of talk, I started to take off my shoes. As I unlaced them, I thought of how it looked as if I were the one to kill our interesting project. I foolishly said something to the effect that if Tom was going down town, I would write a letter that was already overdue. Tom was anxiously awaiting a letter that should be in that night. He suggested that I go down also as it was a very decent night. I consented and Art decided to join us. I sat down and wrote the letter—meanwhile we continued our talk about the money package.

My letter finished, something seemed to change. We found further inaction impossible: we had either to rob the post-office or go to bed. Tom brought out his two guns; I hunted up a couple of regular plain handkerchiefs, and Art added some rope to the assortment. At the time we were still individually and collectively playing a game with ourselves. Each of us expected one of the other two to give the thing the horse laugh and suggest going to bed and letting the letters wait till morning. But it seemed that we forgot everything—our position in school, our families and friends, the danger to us and to our folks. Our only thought was to carry out that prank. We all made our preparations more or less mechanically. Our minds were in a daze.

Putting on our regular overcoats and caps, we left the rooms quietly. On the way down town we passed the night patrolman without any really serious qualms. Tom entered the post-office as was his usual custom, being a sub-clerk, and Art and I crept up to the rear door. Tom appeared at a window with his hat, a signal that there were no reasons why our plan would not be effective. At the door, in full illumination of a light, we arranged our handkerchiefs over our faces and took our guns out of our pockets. We were ready.

"Have you enough guts to go through with this thing?" I asked, turning to Art, who was behind me.

"If you have," he answered.

Frankly I felt that I had gone far enough, but for some unknown reason I did not throw out a remark that would have ended it all then and there. And Art didn't. He later said that he was just too scared to suggest anything. We were both, it seems, in a sort of daze.

Tom opened the door and we followed our plan out to the end. There was no active resistance by the regular night man.

Then after we left the office with thousands of dollars in our hands we did not realize all that it meant. Our first words were not about getting the money. They were about the fact that our prank (and it was still that to us) had been successful. When we reached our rooms, having hidden the money in an abandoned dredger, the seriousness of the thing began to penetrate our minds. For an hour or so we lay quietly and finally settled on a plan that seemed safe in returning the money without making our identity known. Then I went to sleep.[2]

This incident, reported by one of the participants, describes a cooperative group activity directed toward a criminal object. What is interesting about the incident is that none of the participants was a criminal, that each was secretly opposed to the undertaking, and that all were personally disinterested in the goal. Why, then, did they do it?

The narrative suggests several clues. In the first place, each was reluctant to occupy the humiliating role of the one who "backs out." Apparently, then, though each was afraid, the prospect of humiliation was more threatening. Moreover, in order to avoid the appearance of reluctance, each found it necessary to keep up the pretense of his own willingness—at the same time nourishing the secret hope that *somebody else* would realize that things were going too far and back out. At this point it is probable that each still felt that the others were merely testing him, and that nobody really intended to go through with it. Then, as preparations advanced, the security of this belief began to wane and each boy began to believe that the others might not be fooling after all. This served to isolate each in the intolerable position of the only one who would be chicken-hearted. When the illusion of group daring reaches this level of mutual deception, there could be no turning back. In this manner, with the need to conceal their mounting anxiety forcing them to shows of increased bravado, the boys literally pushed each other over the threshold of fantasy into the criminal act.

Thus there arose a situation of group motivation, based on an illusion and contrary to the actual wishes of each participant. A condition of group motivation exists *when each member is behaving in accordance with the same interpretation of what is expected of him*—whether or not this is in accord with his own wishes and regardless of the correctness of the interpretation. Each of the unwilling bandits was behaving *as if* the others were expecting him to participate. (Actually, they were hoping he would back out.) The illusion went further: though each personally dreaded participating, each was eventually convinced that the others were willing. The curious thing was that none of the group, at any point, put any direct pressure on the others to go along. Each was coerced by a similar image of what the others expected and each dreaded an imagined group reaction.

What was it that committed each to conform to this imaginary expectation in violation of his own wishes? A tentative answer might be that conformity involved certain psychological rewards; nonconformity, certain penalities. Apparently, in the mutual roles in which they found themselves *the way each boy felt about himself was dependent on how he imagined the others were feeling about him.*

Here again, the group authority was exercised by each member over himself. The strength of this authority was related to the extent to which each one's self-evaluation

[2] Frederic M. Thrasher, *The Gang* (Chicago: The University of Chicago Press, 1936) pp. 300–303.

was open to influence by the real or imagined attitudes of the others. Each was intent on fulfilling the expectations of his role, on conforming to its conceived requirements. The behavioral requirements of the role were, as it turned out, secondary, since none of the boys actually desired to engage in the activity itself. Thus the commitment was not to the *act* or to the *goal* of the act (the money), but rather to the *group expectations*–which, in the given situation, ordained that each take the role of a fearless, daring character. In another situation the usages of this group might have cast the members in different roles, ordaining different responses.

Conformity: The Need to Fulfill a Group Expectation

The companionate character of the overwhelming majority of delinquent activities underscores the significance of conformity as a transcendent motivation. *Conformity* may be defined as *a global motive on the part of an individual committed to a group to fulfill the expectations of the group regarding his attitudes and behavior.* The frequent salience of this motive over the most fundamental personal needs and wishes is a matter of universal experience. Soldiers going into battle with the clearest knowledge of the risks, and with strong personal desires to avoid danger, report that the thing that kept them going was the fear of "letting the other guys down." In studies of the behavior of front-line soldiers, the feeling of commitment to "other guys in the outfit" was found to be the strongest single factor in the maintenance of individual combat morale.[3] Apparently the same process works with equal effectiveness in the maintenance of anti-social morale.

A recently reported juvenile gang incident illustrates this point. A neighborhood boy was assaulted and killed by a juvenile gang. On examination it was discovered that the victim had been stabbed many times. The explanation for the multiple wounds was not apparent until, on questioning, it was found that each member of the gang had personally struck him. When individually questioned by the police, several of the boys were able to convince the police that they had actually not wanted to participate in this ritualistic wounding but had gone along because they were afraid of "being called chicken."

A reporter present throughout the trial of these delinquents has recorded his impressions of one of the defendants as the youth was called to the witness stand:

> As he mumbled his name, there was a sudden shock of recognition of how exactly alike these children are. Vincent Pardon was like every other ward of the Children's Court we have seen over the last seven days. He had, as an instance, the same hair, drawn back with some care with a wide-toothed comb, and then splattered at the forelock with concentrated devotion.
>
> These children even talk the same way. There is a voice of 152d St. and Broadway which is different from the voice further up on the Heights. It is a voice without reference to ethnic origin. Children named Lago, O'Kelly and Pardon have the same precise inflection. They say "cluck" for "clock," and "Reeversyd" for "Riverside."

[3] See: S. A. Stouffer, *The American Soldier,* Studies in Social Psychology in World War II, Volumes I and II, (Princeton: Princeton University Press, 1949).

It makes no difference whether their parents be Irish or Spanish; they do not talk like their parents. It is as though they did not learn to talk from parent or teacher, but from other children; as though they had no homes, but only streets called Amsterdam or Broadway.[4]

Commitment: The Process of Personal Involvement with a Group

In our search for concepts capable of dealing with the variability of criminal behavior, we have consistently proceeded in one direction: from the overt or "outward" activities backward or, rather, "inward" toward the person. Thus we found that the otherwise confusing multiplicity of individual activities could be organized meaningfully by the concept of *role.* Coming closer to the person, we found that many aspects of role-playing might be accounted for by a global, unifying, and transcending motive or need to *conform to the expectations of certain groups.* We must now deal with the question, What psychological processes link or "tie" the person to the groups to which he conforms? Why do certain individuals slavishly conform, others less rigorously or totally—others only up to a certain point, beyond which they will not go? Why do certain people conform to certain groups and not to others? How is membership in certain groups related to alienation toward (and by) other groups?

These questions raise issues central not only to criminological theory but to virtually every other field of interpersonal behavior. Needless to say, an adequate description of the subtle and complex processes determining individual involvements in groups has yet to be evolved. Nevertheless, there are at least three reasons a concept standing for the end-result of these processes can serve a useful theoretical function. In the first place, this end-result can be recognized and differentiated—even if only on a descriptive level. It is possible to compare two members of a group and to make the statement, *"A is more (or less) involved and differently involved than B."* Secondly, a comprehensive description of the range and character of the individual's total group involvements has meaningful implications for an understanding of many aspects of his behavior. Finally, there is highly suggestive evidence that *the extent to which the individual conforms to the requirements of any given group is significantly related not merely to the character of his involvement in that specific group but to the character and range of the totality of his group relationships.* Putting it in terser terms, the manner in which A behaves as a member of Group X is meaningfully related to the character of his membership in Groups Y and Z. For a variety of reasons, including the lack of a more precisely adequate term, we have suggested the word *commitment* to identify certain global characteristics of the kind of personal involvement we have in mind.

A Working Definition of Commitment. For our purposes, a person may be said to be *committed* to the extent that his self-evaluation is critically dependent on the evaluations of a person or a group with which he is involved. Psychological commitments have at least two describable dimensions: *intensiveness* and *extensiveness.*

[4] Murray Kempton, the *New York Post,* February 21, 1958.

A person is *intensively committed* when his feelings about himself and his behavior more or less precisely reflect the group's feelings about him. He is less *intensively committed* when his self-evaluation is less open to influence by the evaluations of the group. (Thus we may say: "The group strongly disapproved of John and Frank today. John was very upset, but Frank was merely irritated; he looked as if it didn't bother him very much.") An *extensive* commitment to a group refers to an involvement in which a large proportion of the individual's total activities are in some way dependent on his membership in that group. A vivid example of this subtle and manifold penetration of the influence of commitment is given by Whyte in his *Street Corner Society.*

> ... One Saturday night I stumbled upon one of my most exciting research experiences in Cornerville. It was the night when the Nortons were to bowl for the prize money; the biggest bowling night of the whole season. I recall standing on the corner with the boys while they discussed the coming contest. I listened to Doc, Mike and Danny making their predictions as to the order in which the men would finish. At first, this made no particular impression upon me, as my own unexpressed predictions were exactly along the same lines. Then, as the men joked and argued, I suddenly began to question and take a new look at the whole situation. I was convinced that Doc, Mike and Danny were basically correct in their predictions, and yet why should the scores approximate the structure of the gang? Were these top men simply better natural athletes than the rest?...Then I remembered the baseball game we had had a year earlier against the younger crowd on Norton Street. I could see the man who was by common consent the best baseball player of us all striking out with long, graceful swings and letting the grounders bounce through his legs.... I went down to the alleys that night fascinated and just a bit awed by what I was about to witness. Here was the social structure in action right on the bowling alleys. It held the individual members in their places—and I along with them. I did not stop to reason then that, as a close friend of Doc, Danny and Mike, I held a position close to the top of the gang and therefore should be expected to excel on this great occasion. I simply felt myself buoyed up by the situation. I felt my friends were for me, had confidence in me, wanted me to bowl well. As my turn came and I stepped up to bowl, I felt supremely confident that I was going to hit the pins that I was aiming at. I have never felt quite that way before—or since. Here at the bowling alley I was experiencing subjectively the impact of the group structure upon the individual. It was a strange feeling, as if something larger than myself was controlling the ball as I went through my swing and released it toward the pins.
>
> When it was all over, I looked at the scores of all the other men. I was still somewhat bemused by my own experience, and now I was excited to discover that the men had actually finished in the predicted order with only two exceptions that could readily be explained in terms of the group structure.[5]

It seems likely that *intensiveness* and *extensiveness* are rather highly correlated. In the sense that the self may be said to be expressed in the totality and configuration of a person's roles, the *dispersion* or *concentration* of these roles among various group memberships provides some basis for estimating the person's dependency on

[5] William F. Whyte, *Street Corner Society,* 2d. ed. (Chicago: The University of Chicago Press, 1955), pp. 318–319.

each. An individual whose personally significant roles are concentrated within the confines of a single group is likely to be highly dependent on that group and, therefore, intensely committed to it. In a sense, he is carrying all his eggs in one basket. On the other hand, a person whose major roles are *dispersed* among a variety of groups is less likely to be dependent, less likely to be intensely committed to any one of them. In this sense, a person who has the significant roles of *father* in one group, *son* in another, *employer* in a third, and *clandestine lover* in still another relationship is less likely *and less able* to be committed to any one of these roles than the childless, kinless, and jobless wife whose total life activities are concentrated in her marital relationship.

The Constricting Effect of Delinquent versus Nondelinquent Commitments. Should the relationship between the *dispersion* of commitments and their *intensity* prove valid, it might offer a plausible basis for interpreting many aspects and variations of delinquent behavior. It seems obvious that membership in certain groups tends to increase or decrease the practical possibility of membership in other groups. Mr. X, who is already a member of the exclusive Country Club, will probably have an easier time becoming a member of the equally exclusive Yacht Club than Mr. Y, whose only other group affiliation is the Delancey Street Bowling and Billiard Association. Membership in a delinquent group is likely to have a constricting effect on the possibility of nondelinquent group membership for the self-evident reason that delinquent groups are typically in conflict with more conventional groups. The persistent delinquent, who is also likely to be a persistent truant, may find himself thrown out of school, thrown out of the "better" neighborhood social clubs, kept away from the "nicer" girls—and not asked to join the choir. As the number of groups among which he might have distributed his activities shrinks, he is forced more and more to depend on his delinquent associations for his personally significant experiences. The vicious circle of *constricted commitment leading to intenser commitment* is thus set in motion. The earlier the age at which this process begins, the tighter the circle from the beginning.

Contrast, now, the situation of two children—one born in a deteriorated urban slum area, the other in a highly integrated middle-class residential neighborhood. Awaiting the more privileged child are a variety of potential memberships, all or most of which serve as entrees to other groups. From the well-supervised nursery school he will proceed to the well-supervised kindergarten and elementary school. In the summers he will go to the country with his parents—or to the summer camp. At every stage his leisure and his associates will be evaluated, controlled—and, if necessary, changed by adult intervention. His earlier group commitments will constantly be pointed toward later commitments. As a member of the Cub Scouts he will look forward to the time when he can be a Boy Scout. As a new Boy Scout he will associate with his more recent acquaintances in the troop. He will tend to leave his Cub Scout friends—"those kids"—behind him. Thus, his newer commitments will frequently have the effect of terminating his dependency on earlier ones.

For the child emerging on the slum street the situation will be different, the range of alternatives narrower. Like his neighbor across the tracks, he will have play as the main business of his life. Unlike his neighbor, he will play the game with a different pack of cards—a pack with more deuces than aces.

Competition for Control of the Commitment Process. In most modern urban communities the child effectively emerges onto the street somewhere between the ages of four and seven. In the street he finds other children, doing a variety of things. If the street happens to be located in an exclusive section of New York or Boston or Paris, the activities of the other children will be different from the activities going on in a street located in a slum section of any of these cities. On both streets it is likely that the children are trying to have fun. In the better residential sections, this fun will be rather carefully watched and supervised. Unacceptable group activities will tend to be nipped in the bud: control by the adult world, sternly or benignly exercised, will be the rule.

The upper-or middle-class residential neighborhood is not the optimal locus of a juvenile gang. The children lack the extreme autonomy necessary for the existence of such a group. This contrast suggests a dimension of comparison. As the purveyors of activity-alternatives for the child, peer groups differ in the extent of their autonomy from adult control. The extent of the autonomy may be measured—as it is realistically measured—by the effective limits set upon its activities by adults. These limits become defined when the initiatives of the peer group encounter obstacles from adults. They emerge as resolution of conflict over who will control the child in the given instance—the group or the adults.

The Juvenile Gang Versus Parents and Other Authorities. The typical gang forces the choice between who will control the individual child—the peer group or the parent—in a very decisive and dramatic manner, and virtually as a matter of course. In no other child group is the conflict-forcing situation so marked and so inevitable. It happens in the most natural manner. A new boy, recently moved into the neighborhood, has made friends with some of the gang, has tested and been tested by the other children, and is in a fair way toward acceptance and social success. He is invited to go along on a gang activity—an activity that may not in itself be delinquent but that may keep the boys out late and take them some distance away. More likely than not, a particular evening's program would not be approved by the new boy's parents. The issue is clearly drawn: *Will he go along with the rest, or show himself up as a Mama's boy?* If he refuses to go along, he is socially ruined. If he defies his parents, he will have to maintain this defiance until they "give in"—or "give up." *All the advantages are on the side of the gang.* By forcing the child to make a decision that emphasizes his independence of parental control, the gang is strongly encouraging a trend toward autonomy, which is one of the most necessary features of adolescent development. In effect, the gang is on the side of the maturation process. From a purely psychological point of view, anything that enables the child to achieve independence of the parents—within certain limits, and other things being equal—is fulfilling an increasingly felt need of the child.

Thus, again from a psychological point of view, the peer group becomes the device through which adolescents break out of their dependency and subservience to the parent. This is true regardless of the activities of the peer group. It may be a delinquent gang or a Boy Scout troop.

There is one extremely important distinction, however. The Boy Scout troop, as a new allegiance of the child, does not demand the sharp break with parental values and wishes that the gang demands. The transfer of allegiance is in this case peaceful, willing, and not in conflict with older allegiances. There is no war or revolution, no final break. Moreover, even though the locus of the child's important commitments is now transferred to a new source of control, there is mutual accommodation rather than conflict. In the gang, the reverse is true: the new boy is either "with us" and "against his old man"–or "with his old man," and "finished with us."

The familial rupture created by "going with the gang" is likely to be followed by other ruptures with other figures of authority. The gang may find it fashionable to play hooky often: again the conflict; again the more or less inevitable choice on the "with us or against us" pattern. The gang may want to cut a few capers among the "faggots" (sissies) in the playground or on the sand-lot. Some children may be roughed up. Complaints rain down on parents. Again the ultimatum: Stop going with the gang. And again defiance–and the tacit confession of parental helplessness in the face of the tidal attraction of the gang. Thus, one by one, the gang and its members test the limits posted by the adult world, and find that these limits are flimsy. Successful defiance becomes a sport, a mark of distinction–a competition. Instead of Who can hit more home runs?, it is Who can get away with more without getting stopped? Again, this works hand in hand with the maturational need for self-direction–which is operationally defined as freedom from adult direction, since the gang is actually almost tyrannical in its control.

Thus the activity-alternatives presented by the peer group have, in the natural course of events, produced at least two proto-delinquent results: incorrigibility and truancy. The next move is up to the adults. *Their* alternatives are either to yield or to call in official authority. Calling in the punitive authority of the State may entail a final break with the child–as well as a stigma.

Assuming that neither the parents nor the truant officers use their alternative–what next? The initiative then passes to the street. What else is going on? Gang fights? Petting parties? Promiscuity? Drinking? Drugs? Joy-riding in "borrowed" cars? Junking? Flunkying for older gangs? Shoplifting? Whatever is going on in the the street, it is likely the gang will get into it. The initiative is now in the hands of the street.

The Progressive Shrinking of Alternatives. In the last several pages we have been concerned with the individual's access to alternate routes of personal and social development. Alternatives, like roads, are of two kinds: those that lead to wider vistas and those that lead to dead ends. The period between adolescence and young manhood is normally one of rapidly broadening alternatives; at each successive stage of his growth and education, the young person stands at a wider threshold of possibility. During the early years of adulthood the individual normally commits himself to one of the routes that his earlier preparation has opened up, and from this point on the alternatives tend to narrow. Somewhere in the thirties the possibilities tend to converge to a point where the person's future alternatives can often be predicted in advance, given his occupational status, his family status, and a few other actuarial data.

The early periods are critical. In a sense, the adolescent is taking roads that lead to other roads, while the adult is traveling roads that lead to destinations: places where the roads stop. In a highly competitive and relatively open society the period of wide-open alternatives is alarmingly brief. The riders on the merry-go-round have only a few chances to snatch for the brass rings; after a few turns have gone by, the supply for that particular group of riders is exhausted. The young men and women who fail to qualify in the marriage competition shortly find themselves alone, in the company of others left behind in the race. Those who fail in the job market may face a life-long struggle against poverty and the threat of being swept into the occupational sewers.

There is another difference that sharply distinguishes the free and easy era preceding adulthood from the period quickly to follow. During childhood and adolescence the individual is offered many helping hands. His parents must support him, his community will send him to school—he is cheered on and encouraged, if not lulled, by the prospect of the good future. He has time to loaf and experiment. But this period is brief, and when he is finally launched into the economic arena, the situation is drastically changed. Now he must compete, not only with the newcomers but with those who already occupy the desirable seats. And he has little room for experiment and less time for loafing. To drift now is to drift downward. Thus the society that brought him to the threshold of adult achievement may offer him little help in getting over it—and many opportunities to be moved aside and sifted down. Moreover, at each lower level the competition may become keener, the available jobs scarcer, the space at the bottom more crowded.

The Occupational Hospitality of Crime. We come now to a curious distinction between the occupational opportunities available in legitimate and illegitimate pursuits. The criminal world has always had room for the psychological and occupational misfits who failed in conventional pursuits, provided they were willing to trade risks for chances. The friendless, isolated teen-age bully who waited in ambush for the unaccompanied boy coming home from school has had scant psychological preparation for the social requirements of conventional living. The criminal syndicate, on the other hand, has good opportunities for those whose inability to form friendships can be relied on: the hired gunman must not permit sentimental attachments for other criminals to get in the way of his job.

Crime offers similar opportunities for the occupationally handicapped or retarded. In the legitimate world the field of the unskilled laborer is crowded, insecure, unrewarding. But the lower echelons of crime and vice require little in the way of occupational skill from their apprentices and hired hands. For the uneducated, unskilled, unemployed, or unemployable girl, prostitution may offer occupational solutions which the legitimate world is unwilling or unable to duplicate.

There is a further distinction. In the conventional world one's social status is often no more secure than one's job. The community of successful merchants, the fraternity of successful salesmen, may have no particular interest in the continued good fortune of any one of their number; under certain circumstances they may have a vested interest in his failure. In conventional pursuits, continuance in a given status tends to depend on continued performance; the man who "loses his grip" or has a run of bad luck may find himself deprived not only of his livelihood but of an essential inner prop of his self-image.

No similar threat surrounds the status of the criminal. Once "in the rackets," his role as a criminal is relatively secure—frequently so secure that even reformation cannot shake it. *In this specific sense, his social status is not dependent on his performance.* Not only his associates but those in the legitimate world will tend to regard him in a relatively fixed way no matter what he does. Once he is officially tagged as a lawbreaker, the legitimate alternatives tend to narrow to the vanishing point, and his chances to actualize himself in conventional roles virtually disappear while he maintains his known identity.

These considerations have a direct bearing on the questions of role fixation and the strength or intensity of personal commitments. When a young man flirts with the possibility of becoming an aviation engineer or a stockbroker, when he sees himself in these roles and "tries them on for size," the adult world may smile indulgently, may help him toward the threshold—and then leave him there to shoulder his own way through. When a young person flirts with delinquency, when he commits a few violations in the course of a similarly tentative trying-on of roles, the official and unofficial authorities in the community tend to take his experiments very seriously, especially if they result in damage to persons or property. Since the process of self-definition is intimately related to definition by others, the fact that delinquent experimentation tends to produce a relatively powerful and definite social definition may be decisive in resolving a personal commitment that is still tentative and ambiguous. In this sense, society may "help" the person become and remain a delinquent much more effectively than it helps other young people in their legitimate careers.

18. The Sociology of the Deviant Act: Anomie Theory and Beyond

Albert K. Cohen

My concern in this paper is to move toward a general theory of deviant behavior. Taking "Social Structure and Anomie"[1] as a point of departure, I shall note some of the imperfections and gaps in the theory as originally stated, how some of these have been rectified, some theoretical openings for further exploration, and some problems of relating anomie theory to other traditions in the sociology of deviance. It is not important, for my purposes, how broadly or narrowly Merton himself conceived the range of applicability of his anomie theory. Whatever the intention or vision of the author of a theory, it is the task of a discipline to explore the implications of a theoretical insight, in all directions. Many of the points I shall make are, indeed, to be found in Merton's work. In many instances, however, they either appear as leads, suggestions, or *obiter dicta,* and are left undeveloped, or they appear in some other context and no effort is made systematically to link them with anomie theory.[2]

The Anomie Theory of Deviant Behavior

Merton's theory has the reputation of being the pre-eminently *sociological* theory

Reprinted from *American Sociological Review,* **30**:1 (February 1965), 5–14, by permission of The American Sociological Association and the author.

[1] Robert K. Merton, "Social Structure and Anomie," *American Sociological Review,* 3 (October, 1938), pp. 672–682, *Social Theory and Social Structure,* Glencoe, Ill.: The Free Press, 1957, Chs. 4 and 5, and "Conformity, Deviation, and Opportunity-Structures," *American Sociological Review,* 24 (April, 1959), pp. 177–189; Richard A. Cloward, "Illegitimate Means, Anomie, and Deviant Behavior," *American Sociological Review,* 24 (April, 1959), pp. 164–176; and Robert Dubin, "Deviant Behavior and Social Structure: Continuities in Social Theory," *American Sociological Review,* 24 (April, 1959), pp. 147–164.

[2] I am not here concerned with empirical applications and tests of anomie theory, on which there is now a large literature. In view of the sustained interest in anomie theory, its enormous influence, and its numerous applications, however, it is worth noting and wondering at the relatively slow and fitful growth of the substantive theory itself. It is of some interest also that, with respect to both substantive theory and its applications, there has been little follow-up of Merton's own leads relative to the implications of anomie theory for intersocietal differences in deviant behavior. Almost all of the work has been on variations in deviance within American society.

of deviant behavior. Its concern is to account for the distribution of deviant behavior among the positions in a social system and for differences in the distribution and rates of deviant behavior among systems. It tries to account for these things as functions of system properties—*i.e.*, the ways in which cultural goals and opportunities for realizing them within the limits of the institutional norms are distributed. The emphasis, in short, is on certain aspects of the culture (goals and norms) and of the social structure (opportunities, or access to means). The theory *is*, then, radically sociological. And yet, as far as the formal and explicit structure of Merton's first formulation is concerned, it is, in certain respects, atomistic and individualistic. Within the framework of goals, norms, and opportunities, the process of deviance was conceptualized as though each individual—or better, role incumbent—were in a box by himself. He has internalized goals and normative, regulatory rules; he assesses the opportunity structure; he experiences strain; and he selects one or another mode of adaptation. The bearing of others' experience—their strains, their conformity and deviance, their success and failure—on ego's strain and consequent adaptations is comparatively neglected.

Consider first the concept of strain itself. It is a function of the degree of disjunction between goals and means, or of the sufficiency of means to the attainment of goals. But how imperious must the goals be, how uncertain their attainment, how incomplete their fulfillment, to generate strain? The relation between goals as components of that abstraction, culture, and the concrete goals of concrete role incumbents, is by no means clear and simple. One thing that is clear is that the level of goal attainment that will seem just and reasonable to concrete actors, and therefore the sufficiency of available means, will be relative to the attainments of others who serve as reference objects. Level of aspiration is not a fixed quantum, taken from the culture and swallowed whole, to lodge unchanged within our psyches. The sense of proportionality between effort and reward is not determined by the objective returns of effort alone. From the standpoint of the role sector whose rates of deviance are in question, the mapping of reference group orientations, the availability *to others* of access to means, and the actual distribution of rewards are aspects of the social structure important for the determination of strain.[3]

Once we take explicit cognizance of these processes of comparison, a number of other problems unfold themselves. For example, others, whom we define as legitimate objects of comparison, may be more successful than we are by adhering to legitimate means. They not only do better than we do, but they do so "fair and square." On the other hand, they may do as well as we or even better by cutting corners, cheating, using illegitimate means. Do these two different situations have different consequences for the sense of strain, for attitudes toward oneself, for subsequent adaptations? In general, what strains does deviance on the part of others create for the virtuous? In the most obvious case ego is the direct victim of alter's deviance.

[3] See, for example, how Henry and Short explicitly incorporate reference group theory and relative deprivation into their theory of suicide. Andrew Henry and James F. Short, Jr., *Suicide and Homicide*, Glencoe, Ill.: The Free Press, 1954, pp. 56–59.

Or ego's interests may be adversely but indirectly affected by the chicanery of a competitor—unfair trade practices in business, unethical advertising in medicine, cheating in examinations when the instructor grades on a curve. But there is a less obvious case, the one which, according to Ranulf,[4] gives rise to disinterested moral indignation. The dedicated pursuit of culturally approved goals, the eschewing of interdicted but tantalizing goals, the adherence to normatively sanctioned means—these imply a certain self-restraint, effort, discipline, inhibition. What is the effect of the spectacle of others who, though their activities do not manifestly damage our own interests, are morally undisciplined, who give themselves up to idleness, self-indulgence, or forbidden vices? What effect does the propinquity of the wicked have on the peace of mind of the virtuous?

In several ways, the virtuous can make capital out of this situation, can convert a situation with a potential for strain to a source of satisfaction. One can become even more virtuous letting his reputation hinge on his righteousness, *building his self out of invidious comparison to the morally weak.* Since others' wickedness sets off the jewel of one's own virtue, and one's claim to virtue is at the core of his public identity, one may actually develop a stake in the existence of deviant others, and be threatened should they pretend to moral excellence. In short, another's virtue may become a source of strain! One may also join with others in righteous puritanical wrath to mete out punishment to the deviants, not so much to stamp out their deviant behavior, as to reaffirm the central importance of conformity as the basis for judging men and to reassure himself and others of his attachment to goodness. One may even make a virtue of tolerance and indulgence of others' moral deficiencies, thereby implicitly calling attention to one's own special strength of character. If the weakness of others is only human, then there is something more than human about one's own strength. On the other hand, one might join the profligate.

What I have said here is relevant to social control, but my concern at present is not with social control but with some of the ways in which deviance of others may aggravate or lighten the burdens of conformity and hence the strain that is so central to anomie theory.

The student of Merton will recognize that some of these points are suggested or even developed at some length here and there in Merton's own writing. Merton is, of course, one of the chief architects of reference group theory, and in his chapter on "Continuities in the Theory of Reference Groups and Social Structure," he has a section entitled "Nonconformity as a Type of Reference Group Behavior."[5] There he recognizes the problems that one actor's deviance creates for others, and he explicitly calls attention to Ranulf's treatment of disinterested moral indignation as a way of dealing with this problem.[6] In "Continuities in the Theory of Social

[4] Svend Ranulf, *Moral Indignation and Middle-Class Psychology: A Sociological Study,* Copenhagen: Levin and Munksgaard, 1938.

[5] *Social Theory and Social Structure, op. cit.,* pp. 357–368.

[6] *Ibid.,* pp. 361–362.

Structure and Anomie," he describes how the deviance of some increases the others' vulnerability to deviance.[7] In short, my characterization of the earliest version of "Social Structure and Anomie" as "atomistic and individualistic" would be a gross misrepresentation if it were applied to the total corpus of Merton's writing on deviance. He has not, however, developed the role of comparison processes in the determination of strain or considered it explicitly in the context of anomie theory. And in general, Merton does not identify the complexities and subtleties of the concept strain as a problem area in their own right.

Finally, in connection with the concept strain, attention should be called to Smelser's treatment of the subject in his *Theory of Collective Behavior.*[8] Although Smelser does not deal with this as it bears on a theory of deviance, it is important here for two reasons. First, it is, to my knowledge, the only attempt in the literature to generate a systematic classification of types of strain, of which Merton's disjunction between goals and means is only one. The second reason is Smelser's emphasis that to account for collective behavior, one must *start with* strain, but one's theory must also specify a hierarchy of constraints, each of which further narrows the range of possible responses to strain, and the last of which rules out all alternatives but collective behavior. If the "value-added" method is sound for a theory of collective behavior, it may also be useful for a theory of deviance, starting from the concept strain, and constructed on the same model.

Now, *given strain,* what will a person do about it? In general, Merton's chief concern has been with the structural factors that account for variations in strain. On the matter of choice of solution, as on other matters, he has some perceptive observations,[9] but it has remained for others to develop these systematically. In particular, in the original version of his theory each person seems to work out his solution by himself, as though it did not matter what other people were doing. Perhaps Merton assumed such intervening variables as deviant role models, without going into the mechanics of them. But it is one thing to assume that such variables are operating; it is quite another to treat them explicitly in a way that is integrated with the more general theory. Those who continue the anomie tradition, however–most notably Merton's student, Cloward–have done much to fill this gap. Cloward, with Ohlin,[10] has accomplished this in large part by linking anomie theory with another and older theoretical tradition, associated with Sutherland, Shaw and McKay, and Kobrin–the "cultural transmission" and "differential association" tradition of the "Chicago school." Cloward and Ohlin also link anomie theory to a more recent theoretical development, the general theory of subcultures, and especially the aspect of the theory that is concerned with the emergence and development of new sub-

[7] *Ibid.,* pp. 179–181.

[8] Neil J. Smelser, *Theory of Collective Behavior,* New York: The Free Press of Glencoe, 1963. esp. Ch. 3.

[9] *Social Theory and Social Structure, op. cit.,* p. 151.

[10] Cloward, *op. cit.,* and Richard A. Cloward and Lloyd E. Ohlin, *Delinquency and Opportunity, A Theory of Delinquent Gangs,* Glencoe, Ill.: The Free Press, 1960.

cultural forms.[11] What these other theories have in common is an insistence that deviant as well as nondeviant action is typically not contrived within the solitary individual psyche, but is part of a collaborative *social* activity, in which the things that other people say and do give meaning, value, and effect to one's own behavior.

The incorporation of this recognition into anomie theory is the principal significance of Cloward's notion of illegitimate opportunity structures. These opportunity structures are going social concerns in the individual's milieu, which provide opportunities to learn and to perform deviant actions and lend moral support to the deviant when he breaks with conventional norms and goals.

This is the explicit link with the cultural transmission–differential association tradition. The argument is carried a step farther with the recognition that, even in the absence of an already established deviant culture and social organization, a number of individuals with like problems and in effective communication with one another may join together to do what no one can do alone. They may provide one another with reference objects, collectively contrive a subculture to replace or neutralize the conventional culture, and support and shield one another in their deviance. This is the explicit link to the newer theory of subcultures.[12]

There is one more step in this direction that has not been so explicitly taken. Those who join hands in deviant enterprises need not be people with like problems, nor need their deviance be of the same sort. Within the framework of anomie theory, we may think of these people as individuals with quite variant problems or strains which lend themselves to a common solution, but a common solution in which each participates in different ways. I have in mind the brothel keeper and the crooked policeman, the black marketeer and his customer, the desperate student and the term paper merchant, the bookie and the wire services. These do not necessarily constitute solidary collectivities, like delinquent gangs, but they are structures of action with a division of labor through which each, by his deviance, serves the interests of the others. Theirs is an "organic solidarity," in contrast to the "mechanical solidarity" of Cloward and Ohlin's gangs. Some of Merton's own writing on functionalism—fox example, his discussion of the exchange of services involved in political corruption—is extremely relevant here, but it is not explicitly integrated into his anomie theory.[13]

The Assumption of Discontinuity

To say that anomie theory suffers from the assumption of discontinuity is to imply that it treats the deviant act as though it were an abrupt change of state, a leap from a state of strain or anomie to a state of deviance. Although this overstates the weakness in Merton's theory the expression, "the assumption of discontinuity," does have

[11] *Ibid.*

[12] Albert K. Cohen, *Delinquent Boys, The Culture of the Gang,* Glencoe, Ill.: The Free Press, Ch. 3, and Merton, *Social Theory and Social Structure, op. cit.,* p. 179.

[13] *Social Theory and Social Structure, op. cit.,* pp. 71–82.

the heuristic value of drawing attention to an important difference in emphasis between anomie theory and other traditions in American sociology, and to the direction of movement in anomie theory itself. Human action, deviant or otherwise, is something that typically develops and grows in a tentative, groping, advancing, backtracking, sounding-out process. People taste and feel their way along. They begin an act and do not complete it. They start doing one thing and end up by doing another. They extricate themselves from progressive involvement or become further involved to the point of commitment. These processes of progressive involvement and disinvolvement are important enough to deserve explicit recognition and treatment in their own right. They are themselves subject to normative regulation and structural constraint in complex ways about which we have much to learn. Until recently, however, the dominant bias in American sociology has been toward formulating theory in terms of variables that describe initial states, on the one hand and outcomes, on the other, rather than in terms of processes whereby acts and complex structures of action are built, elaborated, and transformed. Notable exceptions are interaction process analysis,[14] the brand of action theory represented by Herbert Blumer,[15] and the descriptions of deviance by Talcott Parsons[16] and by Howard Becker.[17] Anomie theory has taken increasing cognizance of such processes. Cloward and Merton both point out, for example, that behavior may move through "patterned sequences of deviant roles" and from "one type of adaptation to another."[18] But this hardly does justice to the microsociology of the deviant act. It suggests a series of discontinuous leaps from one deviant state to another almost as much as it does the kind of process I have in mind.

Responses to Deviance

Very closely related to the foregoing point is the conception of the development of the act as a feedback, or, in more traditional language, interaction process. The history of a deviant act is a history of an interaction process. The antecedents of the act are an unfolding sequence of acts contributed by a set of actors. A makes a move, possibly in a deviant direction; B responds; A responds to B's responses, etc. In the course of this interaction, movement in a deviant direction may become more explicit, elaborated, definitive—or it may not. Although the act may be socially ascribed to only one of them, both ego and alter help to shape it. The starting point of anomie theory was the question, "*Given* the social structure, or ego's milieu, what will ego do?" The milieu was taken as more-or-less given, an independent variable

[14] Robert F. Bales, *Interaction Process Analysis: A Method for the Study of Small Groups,* Cambridge: Addison-Wesley, 1950.

[15] Herbert Blumer, "Society as Symbolic Interaction," in Arnold M. Rose (ed.), *Human Behavior and Social Processes,* Boston: Houghton, Mifflin, 1962, pp. 179–192.

[16] Talcott Parsons, *The Social System,* Glencoe, Ill.: The Free Press, 1951, Ch. 7.

[17] Howard S. Becker, *Outsiders: Studies in the Sociology of Deviance,* New York: The Free Press of Glencoe, 1963, esp. Ch. 2.

[18] Merton, *Social Theory and Social Structure, op. cit.,* p. 152, Cloward, *op. cit.,* p. 175; Cloward and Ohlin, *op. cit.,* pp. 179–184; Merton, "Conformity, Deviation, and Opportunity-Structures," *op. cit.,* p. 188.

whose value is fixed, and ego's behavior as an adaptation, or perhaps a series of adaptations, to that milieu. Anomie theory has come increasingly to recognize the effects of deviance upon the very variables that determine deviance. But if we are interested in a general theory of deviant behavior we must explore much more systematically ways of conceptualizing the *interaction* between deviance and milieu.[19] I suggest the following such lines of exploration.

If ego's behavior can be conceptualized in terms of acceptance and rejection of goals and means, the same can be done with alter's responses. Responses to deviance can no more be left normatively unregulated than deviance itself. Whose business it is to intervene, at what point, and what he may or may not do is defined by a normatively established division of labor. In short, for any given role—parent, priest, psychiatrist, neighbor, policeman, judge—the norms prescribe, with varying degrees of definiteness, *what* they are supposed to do and *how* they are supposed to do it when other persons, in specified roles, misbehave. The culture prescribes goals and regulates the choice of means. Members of ego's role set can stray from cultural prescriptions in all the ways that ego can. They may overemphasize the goals and neglect the normative restrictions, they may adhere ritualistically to the normatively approved means and neglect the goals, and so forth. I have spelled out the five possibilities on alter's side more fully elsewhere.[20] The theoretical value of applying Merton's modes of adaptation to responses to deviant acts is not fully clear; yet it seems worthy of exploration for at least two reasons.

First, *one* determinant of ego's response to alter's attempts at control, and of the responses of third parties whom ego or alter might call to their aid, is certainly the perceived legitimacy of alter's behavior. Whether ego yields or resists, plays the part of the good loser or the abused victim, takes his medicine or is driven to aggravated deviance, depends in part on whether alter has the right to do what he does, whether the response is proportional to the offense, and so on.

Normative rules also regulate the deviant's response to the intervention of control agents. How the control agent responds to the deviant, after the first confrontation, depends on his perception of the legitimacy of the deviant's response *to him,* and not only on the nature of the original deviant act. For example, this perceived legitimacy plays an important part in police dispositions of cases coming to their attention.

This approach also directs attention to strain in alter's role, the adequacy of *his* resources relative to the responsibilities with which he is charged by virtue of his role, and the illegitimate opportunities available to *him.* A familiar example would be the normative restrictions on the means police may consider effective to do the

[19] Dubin, *op. cit.,* esp. p. 151, and Merton's remarks on "typology of responses to deviant behavior," in his "Conformity, Deviation, and Opportunity-Structures," *op. cit.,* pp. 185–186.

[20] Albert K. Cohen, "The Study of Social Disorganization and Deviant Behavior," in Robert K. Merton, Leonard Broom, and Leonard S. Cottrell, Jr. (eds.), *Sociology Today,* New York: Basic Books, 1959, pp. 464–465.

job with which they are charged, and variations in the availability to them of various illegitimate means to the same end.

The disjunction between goals and means and the choice of adaptations depend on the opportunity structure. The opportunity structure consists in or is the result of the actions of other people. These in turn are in part reactions to ego's behavior and may undergo change in response to that behavior. The development of ego's action can, therefore, be conceptualized as a series of responses, on the part of ego, to a series of changes in the opportunity structure resulting from ego's actions. More specifically, alter's responses may open up, close off, or leave unaffected legitimate opportunities for ego, and they may do the same to illegitimate opportunities. The simplified table [Table 1] reduces the possibilities to four.

TABLE 1. Responses of the Opportunity Structure to Ego's Deviance

	Legitimate Opportunities	*Illegitimate Opportunities*
Open up	I	II
Close off	III	IV

I. Open Up Legitimate Opportunities. Special efforts may be made to find employment opportunities for delinquents and criminals. On an individual basis this has long been one of the chief tasks of probation officers. On a mass basis it has become more and more prominent in community-wide efforts to reduce delinquency rates.

Black markets may sometimes be reduced by making more of the product available in the legal market or by reducing the pressure on the legal supply through rationing.

Several years ago the Indiana University faculty had a high rate of violation of campus parking regulations, in part because of the disjunction between the demand for parking spaces and the supply. The virtuous left early for work and hunted wearily for legitimate parking spaces. The contemptuous parked anywhere and sneered at tickets. One response to this situation was to create new parking lots and to expand old ones. Since the new parking spaces were available to all, and not only to the former violators, this provides a clear instance where the virtuous—or perhaps the timid—as well as the deviants themselves are the beneficiaries of deviance.[21]

II. Open Up Illegitimate Opportunities. Alter, instead of fighting ego, may facilitate his deviance by joining him in some sort of collusive illicit arrangement from which both profit. The racketeer and the law enforcement officer, the convict and

[21] William J. Chambliss, *The Deterent Influence of Punishment: A Study of the Violation of Parking Regulations,* M.A. thesis (sociology), Indiana University, 1960.

the guard, the highway speeder and the traffic policeman, may arrive at an understanding to reduce the cost of deviance.

Alter, whether he be a discouraged parent, a law enforcement official, or a dean of students, may simply give up efforts systematically to enforce a rule and limit himself to sporadic, token gestures.

An important element in Cloward and Ohlin's theory of delinquent subcultures is that those who run the criminal syndicates are ever alert for promising employees, and that a certain number of those who demonstrate proficiency in the more juvenile forms of crime will be given jobs in the criminal organization.

III. Closing off Legitimate Opportunities. The example that comes most readily to mind is what Tannenbaum calls the "dramatization of evil."[22] A deviant act, if undetected or ignored, might not be repeated. On the other hand, others might react to it by publicly defining the actor as a delinquent, a fallen woman, a criminal. These definitions ascribe to him a social role, change his public image, and activate a set of appropriate responses. These responses may include exclusion from avenues of legitimate opportunity formerly open to him, and thus enhance the relative attractiveness of the illegitimate.

IV. Closing off Illegitimate Opportunities. This is what we usually think of first when we think about "social control." It includes increasing surveillance, locking the door, increasing the certainty and severity of punishment, cutting off access to necessary supplies, knocking out the fix. These measures may or may not achieve the intended effect. On the one hand, they make deviance more difficult. On the other hand, they may stimulate the deviant, or the deviant coalition, to ingenuity in devising new means to circumvent the new restrictions.

The table is a way of conceptualizing alter's actions. The same alter might respond simultaneously in different cells of the table, as may different alters, and these responses might reinforce or counteract one another. Responses might fall in different cells at different stages of the interaction process. In any case, as soon as we conceive of the opportunity structure as a dependent as well as an independent variable, this way of thinking suggests itself as a logical extension of the anomie schema.

Parsons' paradigm of social control is in his opinion applicable not only to deviance, but also to therapy and rehabilitative processes in general. According to this paradigm, the key elements in alter's behavior are support, permissiveness, denial of reciprocity, and rewards, judiciously balanced, and strategically timed and geared to the development of ego's behavior.[23] To exploit the possibilities of this and other paradigms of control, one must define more precisely these categories of alter's behavior, develop relevant ways of coding ego's responses to alter's responses, and investigate both theoretically and empirically the structure of extended interaction processes conceptualized in these terms.

Finally, the interaction process may be analyzed from the standpoint of its conse-

[22] Frank Tannenbaum, *Crime and the Community,* New York: Ginn, 1938, Ch. 7.
[23] *Op. cit.,* pp. 297–325.

quences for stability or change in the normative structure itself. Every act of deviance can be thought of as a pressure on the normative structure, a test of its limits, an exploration of its meaning, a challenge to its validity. Responses to deviance may reaffirm or shore up the normative structure; they may be ritual dramatizations of the seriousness with which the community takes violations of its norms. Or deviance may prompt re-examination of the boundaries of the normatively permissible, resulting in either explicit reformulation of the rule or implicit changes in its meaning, so that the deviant becomes redefined as nondeviant, or the nondeviant as deviant. Thus deviance may be reduced or increased by changes in the norms.[24] These processes go on within the household, courts of law, administrative agencies, and legislative chambers, but also in the mass media, the streets, and the other forums in which "public opinion" is shaped. Although these processes may be punctuated by dramatic, definitive events, like the passage of a new law or the promulgation of a new set of regulations on allowable income tax deductions, the pressure of deviance on the normative structure and the responses of the normative structure to deviance constitute continuing, uninterrupted, interaction processes. One goal of deviance theory is to determine under what conditions feedback circuits promote change and under what conditions they inhibit change in the normative structure.

In this connection, one of Merton's most perceptive and fruitful distinctions is that between the "nonconformist" and other types of deviant.[25] Whereas the criminal and others typically *violate* the norms in pursuit of their own ends, but in no sense seek to *change* those norms (though such change might very well be an unanticipated consequence of their cumulative deviance), the nonconformist's objective is precisely to change the normative system itself. This distinction suggests, in turn, the concept of the "test case" (which need not be limited to the context of legal norms and the formal judicial system)–*i.e.,* the act openly committed, with the intention of forcing a clarification or redefinition of the norms. What we must not overlook, however, is that *any* deviant act, whatever its intention, may, in a sense, function as a test case.

Deviance and Social Identity

There is another piece of unfinished business before anomie theory, and that is to establish a more complete and successful union with role theory and theory of the self. The starting point of Merton's theory is the means-ends schema. His *dramatis personae* are cultural goals, institutional norms, and the situation of action, consisting of means and conditions. The disjunction between goals and means provides the motive force behind action. Deviance is an effort to reduce this disjunction and re-establish an equilibrium between goals and means. It issues from tension; it is an

[24] Theodore M. Mills, "Equilibrium and the Processes of Deviance and Control," *American Sociological Review,* 24 (October, 1959), pp. 671–679.

[25] Merton, *Social Theory and Social Structure, op. cit.,* pp. 360–368; Robert K. Merton and Robert A. Nisbet, *Contemporary Social Problems,* New York: Harcourt, Brace, 1961, pp. 725–728.

attempt to reduce tension. Roles figure in this theory as a locational grid. They are the positions in the social structure among which goals, norms and means are distributed, where such disjunctions are located and such adaptations carried out.

Another starting point for a theory of deviant behavior grows out of the social theory of George Herbert Mead. This starting point is the actor engaged in an ongoing process of finding, building, testing, validating, and expressing a self. The self is linked to roles, but not primarily in a locational sense. Roles enter, in a very integral and dynamic way, into the very structure of the self. They are part of the categorical system of a society, the socially recognized and meaningful categories of persons. They are the kinds of people it is possible to be in that society. The self is constructed of these possibilities, or some organization of these possibilities. One establishes a self by successfully claiming membership in such categories.[26]

To validate such a claim one must know the social meaning of membership in such roles: the criteria by which they are assigned, the qualities or behavior that function as signs of membership, the characteristics that measure adequacy in the roles. These meanings must be learned. To some degree, this learning may be accomplished before one has identified or even toyed with the roles. Such learning Merton has called anticipatory socialization. To some degree, however, it continues even after one has become more or less committed to a role, in the process of presenting one's self, experiencing and reading the feedback, and correcting one's notion of what it is to be that kind of person. An actor learns that the behavior signifying membership in a particular role includes the kinds of clothes he wears, his posture and gait, his likes and dislikes, what he talks about and the opinions he expresses—everything that goes into what we call the style of life. Such aspects of behavior are difficult to conceptualize as either goals or means; in terms of their relation to the role, at least, their function is better described as expressive or symbolic. But the same can be said even of the goals one pursues and the means one employs; they too may communicate and confirm an identity.

Now, *given* a role, and *given* the orientations to goals and to means that have been assumed because they are part of the social definition of that role, there may be a disjunction between goals and means. Much of what we call deviant behavior arises as a way of dealing with this disjunction. As anomie theory has been formally stated, this is where it seems to apply. But much deviant behavior cannot readily be formulated in these terms at all. Some of it, for example, is directly expressive of the roles. A tough and bellicose posture, the use of obscene language, participation in illicit sexual activity, the immoderate consumption of alcohol, the deliberate flouting of legality and authority, a generalized disrespect for the sacred symbols of the "square" world, a taste for marijuana, even suicide—all of these may have the primary function of affirming, in the language of gesture and deed, that one is a certain kind

[26] George Herbert Mead, *Mind, Self, and Society,* Chicago: University of Chicago Press, 1934; Erving Goffman, *The Presentation of Self in Everyday Life,* New York: Doubleday Anchor, 1959, and *Stigma, Notes on the Management of Spoiled Identity,* Englewood Cliffs: Prentice-Hall, 1963.

of person. The message-symbol relationship, or that of claim and evidence, seems to fit this behavior better than the ends-means relationship.

Sexual seduction, for example, may be thought of as illicit means to the achievement of a goal. The point is, however, that the seduction need not be an adaptation to the insufficiency of other means, a response to disjunction. One may cultivate the art of seduction because this sort of expertise is directly significant of a coveted role. Indeed, the very value and meaning of the prize are conferred by the means employed. One could, of course, say that the expertise is itself the goal, but then it is still a goal that expresses and testifies to a role. Finally, one could say that the goal of the act is to validate the role, and all these kinds of behavior are means to this end. I think this statement is plausible and can be defended. If it is the intent of anomie theory, then the language of tension reduction does not seem to fit very well. The relation I have in mind, between deviant act and social role, is like the relation between pipe and elbow patches and the professorial role. Like the professor's behavior, it is not necessarily a *pis aller,* a means that one has hit on after others have failed. It commends itself, it is gratifying, because it seems so right—not in a moral sense, but in the sense that it fits so well with the image one would like to have of oneself.

One important implication of this view is that it shifts the focus of theory and research from the disjunction and its resolution to the process of progressive involvement in, commitment to, and movement among social roles, and the processes whereby one learns the behavior that is significant of the roles. One may, like the child acquiring his sex identity, come to accept and identify with a role before he is quite clear what it means to be that sort of person, how one goes about being one. But once one has established the identity, he has an interest in learning these things and making use of that learning. Thus Howard Becker's dance band musicians arrive at that estate by various routes. For many of them, however, it is only as this identity is crystallizing that they fully learn what being a musician means within the world of musicians. They discover, so to speak, what they are, and what they are turns out to be highly unconventional people.[27] We seek roles for various reasons, some of them having little to do with tension reduction, and having found the role, come into unanticipated legacies of deviant behavior.

The same processes operate in movement in the other direction, toward restoration to conformity. They are most dramatically illustrated in religious conversion. As the sinner is born again, with a new identity fashioned out of new roles, whole bundles of behavior, not all of them deviant, are cast aside, and new bundles are picked up. Relatively little may be learned by examining, one at a time, the items these bundles contain, the sense in which they constitute means to ends, and their adequacy to their respective goals. The decisive event is the transformation of self and social identity. At that moment a wholesale transformation of behavior is determined.

Anomie theory is, perhaps, concerned with *one* structural source of deviance, while

[27] Howard S. Becker, *op. cit.,* Ch. 5.

the ideas just presented are concerned with another. Neither one need be more faithful to reality than the other, and the defense of one need not be a challenge to the other. But those who are interested in the development of a general theory of deviance can hardly let matters stand at that. Is it possible to make any general statements about the kinds of deviance that may be attributed to anomie and the kinds that may be attributed to role validation through behavior culturally significant of membership in the role? Or may two instances of *any* sort of deviant behavior, identical in their manifest or "phenotypic" content, differ in their sources or "genotypic" structure?

Ultimately, however we must investigate the possible ways in which the two kinds or sources of deviance interact or interpenetrate. For example, does role symbolism function as a structural constraint on the choice of means, and instrumental or means-ends considerations as a structural constraint on the choice of expressive symbolism? Does behavior that originates as a characteristic adaptation to the anomie associated with a particular role, come in time to signify membership in that role and thereby to exercise a secondary or even independent attraction or repulsion, depending on one's orientation toward the role itself? Finally, is it possible that in any instance of deviant behavior, or, for that matter, *any* behavior, both processes are intertwined in ways that cannot be adequately described in terms of presently available modes of conceptualization? I suggest that we must bring the two schemes into more direct and explicit confrontation and try to evolve a formulation that will fuse and harness the power of both.

19. Differential Association

Edwin H. Sutherland and Donald R. Cressey

The following paragraphs state...a genetic theory of criminal behavior on the assumption that a criminal act occurs when a situation appropriate for it, as defined by the person, is present. The theory should be regarded as tentative, and it should be tested by the factual information....

Genetic Explanation of Criminal Behavior

The following statement refers to the process by which a particular person comes to engage in criminal behavior.

1. *Criminal behavior is learned.* Negatively, this means that criminal behavior is not inherited, as such; also, the person who is not already trained in crime does not invent criminal behavior, just as a person does not make mechanical inventions unless he has had training in mechanics.

2. *Criminal behavior is learned in interaction with other persons in a process of communication.* This communication is verbal in many respects but includes also "the communication of gestures."

3. *The principal part of the learning of criminal behavior occurs within intimate personal groups.* Negatively, this means that the impersonal agencies of communication, such as movies and newspapers, play a relatively unimportant part in the genesis of criminal behavior.

4. *When criminal behavior is learned, the learning includes (a) techniques of committing the crime, which are sometimes very complicated, sometimes very simple; (b) the specific direction of motives, drives, rationalizations, and attitudes.*

5. *The specific direction of motives and drives is learned from definitions of the legal codes as favorable or unfavorable.* In some societies an individual is surrounded by persons who invariably define the legal codes as rules to be observed, while in others he is surrounded by persons whose definitions are favorable to the violation of the legal codes. In our American society these definitions are almost always mixed, with the consequence that we have culture conflict in relation to the legal codes.

6. *A person becomes delinquent because of an excess of definitions favorable to violation of law over definitions unfavorable to violation of law.* This is the principle of differential association. It refers to both criminal and anti-criminal associations and has to do with counteracting forces. When persons become criminal, they do so because of contacts with criminal patterns and also because of isolation from anti-criminal patterns. Any person inevitably assimilates the surrounding culture unless other patterns are in conflict; a Southerner does not pronounce "r" because other Southerners do not pronounce "r." Negatively, this proposition of differential association means that associations which are neutral so far as crime is concerned have little or no effect on the genesis of criminal behavior. Much of the experience of a person is neutral in this sense, e.g., learning to brush one's teeth. This behavior has no negative or positive effect on criminal behavior except as it may be related to associations which are concerned with the legal codes. This neutral behavior is important especially as an occupier of the time of a child so that he is not in contact with criminal behavior during the time he is so engaged in the neutral behavior.

7. *Differential associations may vary in frequency, duration, priority, and intensity.* This means that associations with criminal behavior and also associations with anti-criminal behavior vary in those respects. "Frequency" and "duration" as modalities of associations are obvious and need no explanation. "Priority" is assumed to be important in the sense that lawful behavior developed in early childhood may persist throughout life, and also that delinquent behavior developed in early childhood may persist throughout life. This tendency, however, has not been adequately demonstrated, and priority seems to be important principally through its selective influence. "Intensity" is not precisely defined but it has to do with such things as the prestige of the source of a criminal or anti-criminal pattern and with emotional reactions related to the associations. In a precise description of the criminal behavior of a person these modalities would be stated in quantitative form and a mathematical ration be reached. A formula in this sense has not been developed, and the development of such a formula would be extremely difficult.

8. *The process of learning criminal behavior by association with criminal and anti-criminal patterns involves all of the mechanisms that are involved in any other*

learning. Negatively, this means that the learning of criminal behavior is not restricted to the process of imitation. A person who is seduced, for instance, learns criminal behavior by association, but this process would not ordinarily be described as imitation.

9. *While criminal behavior is an expression of general needs and values, it is not explained by those general needs and values since non-criminal behavior is an expression of the same needs and values.* Thieves generally steal in order to secure money, but likewise honest laborers work in order to secure money. The attempts by many scholars to explain criminal behavior by general drives and values, such as the happiness principle, striving for social status, the money motive, or frustration, have been and must continue to be futile since they explain lawful behavior as completely as they explain criminal behavior. They are similar to respiration, which is necessary for any behavior but which does not differentiate criminal from non-criminal behavior.

It is not necessary, at this level of explanation, to explain why a person has the associations which he has; this certainly involves a complex of many things. In an area where the delinquency rate is high, a boy who is sociable, gregarious, active, and athletic is very likely to come in contact with the other boys in the neighborhood, learn delinquent behavior from them, and become a gangster; in the same neighborhood the psychopathic boy who is isolated, introverted, and inert may remain at home, not become acquainted with the other boys in the neighborhood, and not become delinquent. In another situation, the sociable, athletic, aggressive boy may become a member of a scout troop and not become involved in delinquent behavior. The person's associations are determined in a general context of social organization. A child is ordinarily reared in a family; the place of residence of the family is determined largely by family income; and the delinquency rate is in many respects related to the rental value of the houses. Many other aspects of social organization affect the kinds of associations a person has.

The preceding explanation of criminal behavior purports to explain the criminal and non-criminal behavior of individual persons. As indicated earlier, it is possible to state sociological theories of criminal behavior which explain the criminality of a community, nation, or other group. The problem, when thus stated, is to account for variations in crime rates and involves a comparison of the crime rates of various groups or the crime rates of a particular group at different times. The explanation of a crime rate must be consistent with the explanation of the criminal behavior of the person, since the crime rate is a summary statement of the number of persons in the group who commit crimes and the frequency with which they commit crimes. One of the best explanations of crime rates from this point of view is that a high crime rate is due to social disorganization. The term "social disorganization" is not entirely satisfactory and it seems preferable to substitute for it the term "differential social organization." The postulate on which this theory is based, regardless of the name, is that crime is rooted in the social organization and is an expression of that social organization. A group may be organized for criminal behavior or organized against criminal behavior. Most communities are organized both for criminal and anti-criminal behavior and in that sense the crime rate is an expression of the differential group organization. Differential group organization as an explanation of variations in crime rates is consistent with the differential association theory of the processes by which persons become criminals.

...

The differential association statement, similarly, is a "principle of normative conflict" which proposes that high crime rates occur in societies and groups characterized by conditions that lead to the development of extensive criminalistic subcultures. The principle makes sense of variations in crime rates by observing that modern societies are organized for crime as well as against it, and then observing further that crime rates are unequally distributed because of differences in the degree to which various categories of persons participate in this normative conflict. Sutherland invented the principle of normative conflict to account for the distribution of high and low crime rates; he then tried to specify the mechanism by which this principle works to produce individual cases of criminality. The mechanism proposed is differential association:

> The second concept, differential association, is a statement of [normative] conflict from the point of view of the person who commits the crime. The two kinds of culture impinge on him or he has association with the two kinds of cultures and this is differential association.[1]

The Value of Differential Association

As an organizing principle, normative conflict makes understandable most of the variations in crime rates discovered by various researchers and observers, and it also focuses attention on crucial research areas.[2] ... The principle of normative conflict does not make good sense out of all the facts, but it seems to make better sense out of more of the facts than do any of the alternative theories.

On the other hand, it also seems safe to conclude that differential association is not a precise statement of the process by which one becomes a criminal. The idea that criminality is a consequence of an excess of intimate associations with criminal behavior patterns is valuable because, for example, it negates assertions that deviation from norms is simply a product of being emotionally insecure or living in a broken home, and then indicates in a general way why only some emotionally insecure persons and only some persons from broken homes commit crimes. Also, it directs attention to the idea that an efficient explanation of individual conduct is consistent with explanations of epidemiology. Yet the statement of the differential

[1] Edwin H. Sutherland, "Development of the Theory," in Albert K. Cohen, Alfred R. Lindesmith and Karl F. Schuessler, editors, *The Sutherland Papers* (Bloomington: Indiana University Press, 1956), pp. 20–21.

[2] Cf. Llewellyn Gross, "Theory Construction in Sociology: A Methodological Inquiry," Chapter 17 in Llewellyn Gross, editor, *Symposium on Sociological Theory* (Evanston: Row, Peterson, 1959), pp. 548–555. See also Donald R. Cressey, "Crime," Chapter 1 in Robert A. Nisbet, editor, *Social Problems and Social Disorganization* (New York: Harcourt, Brace, 1961), pp. 30–44; and Donald R. Cressey, "The State of Criminal Statistics," *National Probation and Parole Association Journal*, 3:230–241, July, 1957.

association process is not precise enough to stimulate rigorous empirical test, and it therefore has not been proved or disproved....

It is important to observe, however, that the "individual conduct" part of the theoretical statement does order data on individual criminality in a general way and, consequently, might be considered a principle itself. Thus, "differential association" may be viewed as a restatement of the principle of normative conflict, so that this one principle is used to account for the distribution of criminal and non-criminal behavior in both the life of the individual and in the statistics on collectivities. In this case, both individual behavior data and epidemiological rate data may be employed as indices of the variables in the principle, thus providing two types of hypotheses for testing it.[3] Glaser has recently shown that differential association makes sense of both the predictive efficiency of some parole prediction items and the lack of predictive efficiency of other items.[4] In effect, he tested the principle by determining whether parole prediction procedures which could have proven it false actually failed to prove it false. First, he shows that a majority of the most accurate predictors in criminology prediction research are deducible from differential association theory while the least accurate predictors are not deducible at all. Second, he shows that this degree of accuracy does not characterize alternative theories. Finally, he notes that two successful predictors of parole violation–type of offense and non-criminal employment opportunities–are not necessarily deducible from the theory, and he suggests a modification that would take this fact into account.

[3] I am indebted to Daniel Glaser for calling this point to my attention.

[4] "Differential Association and Criminological Prediction," *op. cit.* See also Daniel Glaser, "A Reconsideration of Some Parole Prediction Factors," *American Sociological Review,* 19:335–341, June, 1954; and "The Efficiency of Alternative Approaches to Parole Prediction," *American Sociological Review,* 20:283–287, June, 1955; and Daniel Glaser and Richard R. Hangren, "Predicting the Adjustment of Federal Probationers," *National Probation and Parole Association Journal,* 4:258–267, July, 1958.

20. Delinquent Drift

David Matza

Some men are freer than others. Most men, including delinquents, are neither wholly free nor completely constrained but fall somewhere between. The general conditions underlying various positions along a continuum from freedom to constraint may be described. Viewed in this way, determinism loses none of its heuristic value. We may still act as if all were knowable, but we refrain at least temporarily from an image of the delinquent that is tailored to suit social science. The image of the delinquent I wish to convey is one of drift; an actor neither compelled nor committed to deeds nor freely choosing them; neither different in any simple or fundamental sense from the law abiding, nor the same; conforming to certain traditions in American life while partially unreceptive to other more conventional traditions; and finally, an actor whose motivational system may be explored along lines explicitly commended by classical criminology–his peculiar relation to legal institutions.

The delinquent is casually, intermittently, and transiently immersed in a pattern of illegal action. His investment of affect in the delinquent enterprise is sufficient so as to allow an eliciting of prestige and satisfaction but not so large as to "become more or less unavailable for other lines of action."[1] In point of fact, the delinquent is available even during the period of optimum involvement for many lines of legal and conventional action. Not only is he available but a moment's reflection tells us that, concomitant with his illegal involvement, he actively participates in a wide variety of conventional activity. If commitment implies, as it does, rendering oneself presently and in the future unavailable for other lines of action, then the delinquent is uncommitted. He is committed to neither delinquent nor conventional enterprise. Neither, by the canons of his ideology or the makeup of his personality, is precluded.

Drift stands midway between freedom and control. Its basis is an area of the social structure in which control has been loosened, coupled with the abortiveness of adolescent endeavor to organize an autonomous subculture, and thus an independent

Reprinted from "The Positive Delinquent" from *Delinquency and Drift* by David Matza (New York: John Wiley & Sons, Inc., 1964), pp. 1, 27–30, by permission of John Wiley & Sons, Inc.

[1] William Kornhauser, "Social Basis of Commitment: A Study of Liberals and Radicals," in Arnold M. Rose, ed., *Human Behavior and Social Processes* (Boston: Houghton Mifflin, 1962), pp. 321–322.

source of control, around illegal action. The delinquent *transiently* exists in a limbo between convention and crime, responding in turn to the demands of each, flirting now with one, now the other, but postponing commitment, evading decision. Thus, he drifts between criminal and conventional action.

To be loosened from control, conventional or delinquent, is not equivalent to freedom, and, thus, I do not propose a free or calculating actor as an alternative to constraint. Freedom is not only the loosening of controls. It is a sense of command over one's destiny, a capacity to formulate programs or projects, a feeling of being an agent in one's own behalf. Freedom is self-control. If so, the delinquent has clearly not achieved that state. The sense of self-control, irrespective of whether it is well founded, exists to varying degrees in modern man. Those who have been granted the potentiality for freedom through the loosening of social controls but who lack the position, capacity, or inclination to become agents in their own behalf, I call drifters, and it is in this category that I place the juvenile delinquent.

Drift is motion guided gently by underlying influences. The guidance is gentle and not constraining. The drift may be initiated or deflected by events so numerous as to defy codification. But underlying influences are operative nonetheless in that they make initiation to delinquency more probable, and they reduce the chances that an event will deflect the drifter from his delinquent path. Drift is a gradual process of movement, unperceived by the actor, in which the first stage may be accidental or unpredictable from the point of view of any theoretic frame of reference, and deflection from the delinquent path may be similarly accidental or unpredictable. This does not preclude a general theory of delinquency. However, the major purpose of such a theory is a description of the conditions that make delinquent drift possible and probable, and not a specification of invariant conditions of delinquency.

In developing an alternative picture, it should be obvious that not all delinquents correspond to the drifter here depicted. By hypothesis, most delinquents, although perhaps not most criminals, approximate the model. The delinquent as drifter more approximates the substantial majority of juvenile delinquents who do not become adult criminals than the minority who do. Some delinquents are neurotically compulsive and some in the course of their enterprise develop commitment. These flank the more ordinary delinquent on either side, and during situations of crisis prehaps play crucial leadership roles. Partially because he is more sensational and dramatic, the extraordinary delinquent has received greater attention in both mass media and criminological theory. The mundane delinquent is the exemplary delinquent in that he personifies, more fully than the compulsive or the committed, the spirit of the enterprise. The delinquent drifter is less likely to command our attention and we have partially ignored him. However, the drifter is not less a problem than the compulsive or committed delinquent even though he is far less likely to become an adult criminal. Though his tenure is short, his replacements are legion. Though his ideology does not make violations of personal and property rights mandatory, under certain conditions it condones them....

21. Family Integration and Police Contact

William R. Larson and Barbara G. Myerhoff

Three major tasks are undertaken in the present paper: 1. the identification and transcendance of some methodological traditions which the authors regard as unfortunate in studies of the relationships between family disturbances and antisocial behavior of children; 2. the development of two indices of family integration and the relationship of these indices to undesirable social behavior on the part of children; 3. the presentation of a paradigm of four types of family organization and the relationship of these types to two kinds of undesirable social behavior on the part of children.

Perhaps more than most areas of sociological inquiry, delinquency research is carved by deep ruts and well traveled paths which often draw investigation away from other potentially more fruitful approaches. Three closely related methodological traditions in studies of the relationship between attributes of family life and antisocial juvenile behavior are of particular concern to us.

The first of these may be called the "broken home" cliché, which refers to studies of the effects on children of a missing parent—for example, working mothers, absent fathers, and female-dominated households. A glance at the literature on this subject reveals a seemingly inexhaustible concern about this situation shared by laymen, social scientists, and workers in action intervention programs.[1] Such studies are likely to postulate simple, direct, causal relationships between two relatively complex and abstract conditions (broken homes and delinquency). Although this procedure is not logically erroneous, it is frequently misleading. Both conditions may be thought of as outcome criteria of prior processes and the connection between them must be supplied by vague and tenuous inferences. The part played by in-

[1] See, for example, Section V, "Social Values and Social Structure: Theoretical Analyses," pp. 211–318, and Section VI, "The Family Setting," pp. 319–52, in Marvin Wolfgang, Leonard Savitz, and Norman Johnston, eds., *The Sociology of Crime and Delinquency* (New York: John Wiley & Sons, Inc., 1962); James H. S. Bossard and Eleanor S. Boll, *Family Situations* (Philadelphia: University of Pennsylvania Press, 1943); Sheldon and Eleanor Glueck, *Unraveling Juvenile Delinquency* (Cambridge, Mass.: Harvard University Press, 1950).

tervening or mediating variables is largely overlooked. A more desirable procedure would be one in which delinquency is first related to more simple and unidimensional components or indices of family organization, and only after that, to more abstract, complex conditions.

The second tradition we have called the "phenomenological oversight." It occurs as a result of investigators' neglect of the meaning of broken homes to the actors in the situation. This often comes about in spite of the fact that it is a commonplace observation that a family may remain intact though riddled with strife. The mere presence or absence of a parent does not reveal what Shaw and McKay[2] have called "the conflicts, tensions, and attitudes which contribute to family disorganization" and which may cause children to become delinquent irrespective of external and visible family disruptions. Indeed, social scientists are demonstrating a growing concern with the damaging and pathological bonds which may tie a family together as tightly as or more tightly than positive forces.[3]

The concept of the "psychologically broken home" suggested by Wolfgang, Savitz, and Johnston[4] represents an attempt to overcome the common neglect of the *meaning* of a family's life to its members, and thus goes beyond consideration of only visible, crude outcome measures of family disruption, such as parental presence or absence. While such measures are by no means without value, they cannot serve as substitutes for phenomenological indicators of family disturbance.

The third tradition may be called the "psychology is deep and sociology is broad" fallacy. This tradition rests on the assumption that sociology perforce deals with relatively numerous, general, and crude variables, and psychology with fewer, less generalizable, and more precise variables. It is too often the case that after completing a survey-like description of the phenomena in question, the sociologist turns his findings over to the psychologist, implying, as it were, that greater precision is not within the purview of sociology. A preferable alternative open to him is to tighten his focus on his subject matter while continuing to ask *sociological* questions and attempting to develop more precise and refined measures of intra-organizational attributes. Certainly there is no logical reason why intra-organizational variables cannot be as specific, deep, and sharply defined as are intro-personal variables.

Let us now turn to our second task, the development of finer indices of family integration which, we feel, is a step away from the three traditions we have identified. (What other unfortunate traditions we may now be establishing is a matter to be reckoned with by others.)

The indices we have developed are based on data gathered in the course of an

[2] Clifford R. Shaw and Henry D. McKay, *Social Factors in Juvenile Delinquency* (Washington, D.C.: National Commission of Law Observance and Enforcement, Report No. 13, Vol. II, 1931), 275–76.

[3] See, for example, "Family and Personality," in Norman W. Bell and Ezra F. Vogel, eds., *A Modern Introduction to the Family* (New York: Free Press of Glencoe, Inc., 1960), Part IV, pp. 499–649.

[4] Wolfgang, Savitz, and Johnston, *op. cit.*, p. 319.

ongoing study of family socialization of adolescent boys.[5] The sample consisted of 150 adolescent boys, their mothers and fathers in a southern California city. One of the major foci of the study is the identification of various types of family organitions and their relationships to two kinds of outcome criteria–undesirable social behavior on the part of the son 1. in school and 2. in the community. It should be kept in mind that this process results in the development of only *one* index of integration, pertaining to the child. School behavior has been appraised on the basis of teachers' and deans' evaluations, sociometric tests, grades, and school records. For the analysis presented in the present paper, only two categories of school adjustment are employed–successful and unsuccessful. The latter category includes both underachieving and aggressive boys. Community behavior has been defined by the presence or absence of police contacts. A "contact" here means an arrest on record.

The data used as the basis of these indices represent a fraction of the total information gathered during four-hour interviews with the boys and their families. Further, only fifty of the 150 families in the sample have been considered in this preliminary and exploratory paper–twenty-five families whose sons have had police contacts and twenty-five whose sons have not had such contacts. That part of the interview used to develop these indices involved questions pertaining to the family's goals and values for the son, and questions pertaining to the family's perceptions of serious problems concerning the son.

Each member of the family was presented with 110 specific items describing presumably socially desirable behaviors and attitudes referring to the son, and was first asked to rate the importance of each item on a seven point scale. The results of this inquiry comprise the first index of family integration: the extent of agreement between family members as to relative importance of certain values, goals, and beliefs pertaining to the son's activities and feelings. This technique provides an external indicator of family integration–that is, one which is determined by *outsiders.* The second index was obtained by asking each of the family members to designate which of the items constituted serious problems to anyone in the family. The extent of the seriousness of these problems was rated by family members to a seven point scale. This measure is a phenomenological one, for it taps the member's own evaluations of the extent of family disturbance concerning particular items. For example, mothers, fathers, and sons were asked to rate the extent to which they felt it was important that the son obey even those laws which most people ignored. They were then asked to rate the extent to which they felt this issue comprised a serious problem in their family. The same technique was applied to an additional 109 items concerning the son's behaviors and feelings.

The indices of family integration so obtained are but two of a great many parameters of family organization. They serve as a useful point of departure for characterizing the differential ability of various families to successfully socialize children.

[5] The study referred to is entitled "Critical Factors in Adolescence: Intra-Family Relations and Differential School Adjustment," and is supported by U.S. Office of Education (Grant No. 1353).

The indices, we feel, overcome the three methodological objections raised earlier. First, they are simple, unidimensional components of family organization which can be related directly to outcome criteria without requiring elaborate inferences as to intervening mechanisms. Thus, they avoid the "broken home" cliche. Second, the phenomenological oversight is remedied by the employment of a perceptual measurement of family disturbance—namely, the frequency with which serious problems occurred. Finally, the emphasis on an organizational variable, such as the extent of agreement in the family, allows for greater depth than is usually characteristic of such studies, and achieves it without shifting the focus from group to individual attributes. This emphasis makes it possible for us to ask the question, "What kinds of family *organizations,* defined by these two parameters, are most likely to produce children who engage in antisocial behavior?" rather than "What kinds of *individuals* are found in families whose children are engaged in antisocial behavior?" The question so put is precise and thoroughly sociological. A paper by Professor Hughes illustrates the thinking involved here—that the "structural" and the "psychological" perspectives are in need of further study as to their utility when considered in combination.[6]

In working toward answers to the question as to what kinds of family organizations are associated with antisocial children, it can be seen that a paradigm of four ideal family types is implicit in this research. A family may be high on the extent of agreement on expectations and goals (the importance attributed to the items) and low on the number of perceived problems designated. Such a family might be regarded as *maximally integrated;* all the members agree on which of the son's behaviors and attitudes are highly important and feel that few difficulties accrue in these areas.

At the other extreme, a family may agree but little on the importance of the items and may identify a very large number of serious problems. This family can be called *minimally integrated,* for members do not share common values and expectations, and they experience much discomfort and distress concerning aspects of the son's behaviors and attitudes. Further, a family may have a very high level of agreement as to the importance of various items and may indicate numerous serious problems concerning the items. In this type of family, the members seem to share common values and expectations but cannot seem to work out satisfactory ways of implementing them. There is a suggestion in this situation of a distressed and worried group of people whose anxieties are not mitigated by the fact that everyone agrees on what is desirable. This type of family we have called *oversocialized.*

Finally, a family may be characterized by very little agreement among members and very few problems which they describe as serious. This might mean that the family members share few common definitions but are not distressed about this state of affairs and do not regard their family life as troubled. We have labeled such a family *anomic,* because of the normlessness suggested by a situation in which members do not see eye to eye but do not particularly care.

[6] Everett C. Hughes, "The Structural and Psychological Perspectives: Mutually Exclusive or Integrative?" paper presented at the Society for the Study of Social Problems meetings in Los Angeles, August, 1963.

With these four types in mind, it is now possible to hypothesize their various relationships to the outcome criteria—the absence of antisocial behavior in the school and the community.

Common sense alone would lead one to the first two hypotheses regarding both extreme types of family organizations, the maximally and the minimally integrated. It was hypothesized that 1. maximally integrated families will be more likely than not to produce children who *will not* engage in antisocial behavior in school and in the community, and 2. minimally integrated families will be more likely than not to produce children who *will* engage in antisocial behavior in school and in the community. The outcomes of children in the remaining two types of families are not immediately apparent and it is necessary to speculate on the basis of findings and observations of others rather on the basis of common sense alone. It has been stated by Wrong[7] and Bronfenbrenner[8] that oversocialized people are more likely than others to be anxious, dependent, and conforming. This would lead one to the third hypothesis, that 3. children from oversocialized families would not be as likely to engage in antisocial behavior in the community (no police contacts), nor as likely to be successful in school, because the school criteria included grades, demonstration of leadership, independence, and initiative.

Finally, concerning the anomic family, we base our suppositions regarding the connection between normlessness and antisocial behavior on the relationships indicated in such compilations of delinquency research as that of Moles, Lippitt, and Withey.[9] In many of the works they cite, the condition of normlessness figures prominently in the etiology of antisocial behavior. Empirical evidence of this relationship can be found in A. W. McEachern's[10] study of adolescents on probation. Therefore, it was hypothesized that 4. children from anomic families will be more likely to engage in antisocial behavior in the community. There is no reason or evidence to suppose, however, that they will be more or less likely to have difficulty at school.

Table 1 shows the hypothesized relations between the two indices, disagreement and problem perception, as well as the relationship between these indices and the school and community outcome criteria.

Ideally, in the development of sets of independent variables which one wants to relate in some patterned way to dependent criteria, one strives for measures which are themselves uncorrelated, but which bear strong relationship to the chosen criteria. In this case, the two measures approach this ideal, in that a very low chi-square (.38, 1 df, corrected for continuity) was found with both measures as dichotomized.

[7]Dennis Wrong, "The Oversocialized View of Man," *American Sociological Review,* XXVI (April 1961), 183–93.

[8]Urie Bronfenbrenner, "The Changing American Child: A Speculative Analysis," *Journal of Social Issues,* XVII (1961), 6–17.

[9]Oliver Moles, Ronald Lippitt, and Stephen Withey, *A Speculative Review of Research and Theory in Delinquency* (Ann Arbor, Mich.: Institute for Social Research, University of Michigan, Document Series No. 2, September 1959).

[10]A. W. McEachern *et. al., Views of Authority: Probationers and Probation Officers, Los Angeles*: Youth Studies Center, University of Southern California, 1962).

TABLE 1. Hypothesized Relations Between Problem Indices and Outcome Criteria

	[*Criteria as Hypothesized*]			
Family Type	*Disagreement*	*Problem Perception*	*Police Contact*	*School Adjustment*
Integrated	Low	Low	No	Successful
Oversocialized	Low	High	No	Unsuccessful
Anomic	High	Low	Yes	Successful
Disintegrated	High	High	Yes	Unsuccessful

To evaluate the data as to their conformity with the hypotheses, the following procedures were carried out.

The composite measures of school adjustment, developed in previous research by Fred J. Shanlen and his staff at the Youth Studies Center,[11] were used to define two groups—those making successful and unsuccessful adjustments.

Police contact information was also dichotomized, separating those with no record of arrest from those with one or more. The range of arrests in this latter group was from one to eleven.

The family variables were dichotomized on the basis of scores above and below the median score for each variable. High problem families, then, are those in which the number of perceived problems exceeds the median number perceived by the total group of fifty families. The division of families on the disagreement variables was done in the same manner.

With the score dichotomized, the frequency of families within each category is as shown in Table 2. The probability of obtaining cell differences by chance has been determined by a binomial test of the differences between relevant cells as predicted. A 50/50 or chance model was used, reflecting the null hypothesis of "no difference" between frequencies.

In the body of the table the underlined numbers indicate the location of hypothesized high frequencies. These frequencies should be compared with the adjacent value. Of eight relations, five attain statistical significance at or beyond the .10 level in the direction predicted; two are equivocal, and there is one statistically significant reversal. It can be seen that for the integrated and disintegrated family types, the model predicted the distributions accurately for both school and police criteria. Such success was not obtained for the other two types, however. Although the school criterion shows the expected relation for the oversocialized family (seven not successful, zero successful), the police criterion shows a reversal of the direction anticipated (six with contact, one without).

[11] Fred J. Shanley *et. al.*, *Comparative Study of Factors Influencing the School Adjustment of Adolescents—A Preliminary Report* (Los Angeles: Research Paper No. 2, Youth Studies Center, University of Southern California, 1961).

TABLE 2. Police and School Success Criteria as Related to Family Type

	Police Criterion		*School Criterion*	
Family Type	*Contact*	*No Contact*	*Successful*	*Successful*
Integrated	3	16 $p = .016$	1	18 $p < .001$
Oversocialized	6	1 $p = .05$	7 $p = .008$	0
Anomic	6 $p > .10$	5	7	4 $p > .10$
Disintegrated	10 $p = .035$	3	9 $p = .087$	4

The data for the anomic family show little difference on the police criterion, although the direction of difference is as predicted. A reversal from expectation is seen for the school criterion. Neither of the divisions for the anomic family represent significant departures from an even split using a binomial test.

All in all, the conceptual scheme presented here would seem to be moderately successful, particularly considering limitations accruing as a result of the extremely small sample used. Although the literature and previous findings do not allow clear-cut bases for predictions for the anomic and oversocialized families, the model presented here distinguishes well between the more often discussed integrated and disintegrated families.

More importantly, even the small amount of data presented here can serve as a basis for further speculation and study. A considerable amount of refinement is needed in the measurement of the criteria used. Antisocial behavior should be measured in more discriminating units than mere presence or absence of police contact or arrest data. On the basis of the anomic family type, one could speculate, for example, that the boy who is anxious, dependent, and given to overconformity could easily be led into illegal activities by more dominant boys, particularly in gang-ridden neighborhoods. Sutherland, and more lately Cloward and Ohlin,[12] have discussed this very situation, although in somewhat different terms.

In our future work with these data, we hope to make the kinds of additions mentioned above as well as to extend the analysis to the other one hundred families in our sample. At the same time, we will more fully specify the relations between the two variables, disagreement and problem perception, and will develop a

[12] Richard A. Cloward and Lloyd E. Ohlin, *Delinquency and Opportunity* (New York: Free Press of Glencoe, Inc., 1960).

model according to principles of axiomatic theory. Using this model and the enlarged sample, we have to continue to explore the fertile conceptual area of the family as a social organization. Only by such investigation will the differential effects of the family as a socializing agent become more fully understood.

22. Social Processes in the Act of Vandalism

Andrew L. Wade

Method of Study

The data in this study are from interviews with 50 boys from 13 to 17 years of age who had been referred to the Kansas City, Missouri, Police Department's Youth Bureau or to the Jackson County Juvenile Court in that city for the act of vandalism. They were interviewed by the author, then a research fellow with Community Studies, Inc., as soon as possible after the act occurred. The interviews lasted from three quarters of an hour to about an hour and a half, depending on the level of rapport established as well as on the fluency of the adolescent interviewed. In all cases the subjects were assured that the information furnished would be held in strict confidence and would not reach the police, the juvenile court, or the probation officer.

There was no way to verify the boy's story as to what "really did happen" other than by an inspection of the arresting officer's report or possibly by a talk with the boy's probation officer. In some cases a subject's account would be checked with that given by his companions in the same act of vandalism. There were a number of such instances. However, there was no reason to doubt the general truthfulness of the subjects. None expressed unwillingness to talk about vandalism as a social act. Since all of the interviews were conducted by a person in a nonofficial capacity and in private except in three instances, it is reasonable to assume that the adolescent had little to gain from not giving an accurate account of what happened. Furthermore, the fact that most of them were willing to talk about this type of behavior rather than about the offenses for which they were then on probation, in detection, or committed to the institution, was in itself indicative of the general indifference with which vandalism was often regarded by many of these juveniles.

The Setting for Vandalism

When conformity with peer group pressures takes the form of participation in an act of vandalism, the social interaction is complex. First of all, several norms function in the action. They help determine when the behavior is to take place, which are the "proper" objects to be vandalized, who are the "acceptable" victims to suffer from the destructive actions, and what situations are "acceptable" for the behavior. The participant's self-image is also of prime importance. This includes his definition of the act of vandalism as essentially a "prank" or a "good joke" on the victim or victims. Certain rationalizations are utilized to make possible this self definition. These tend to neutralize any guilt feelings present as a consequence of the internalization of the cultural norms governing the sanctity and worth of personal and public property. Also included are the overall attitudes the adolescent has toward himself, toward juvenile behavior in general, and toward the reactions of peers to deviant behavior in particular.

The *situational and cultural variables* cited above are functionally interrelated with the values and norms of the boy's effective reference system. This system is, in turn, related to the class system within which he received his basic socialization. As a part of the overall socialization pattern, the influence of the adolescent subculture is also important to the process of socialization.

In addition to the above variables, there are certain *functional variables* operating. These are actually analytical concepts but are utilized in this study as variables. One of these has been designated as the "opportunity structure."[1] This is a situation which, when present, makes possible the fulfillment of a deviant act. In the context of vandalism an obvious opportunity structure would be the time of Halloween itself, a time when such acts are more or less expected and tolerated by the community at large. Other obvious opportunity structures would be such situations as abandoned houses with broken windows, buildings under construction where doors are left unlocked and water pipes and electrical wires exposed, or a closed school building in a secluded area.

Another analytical concept employed here as a variable has been described elsewhere as the "learning structure."[2] In some of the more complicated forms of criminal activity, such as pickpocketing and confidence games, any elaborate set of techniques or body of knowledge must be mastered prior to the commission of the act if results are to be successful. The underlying assumption is that regardless of how

[1] Richard A. Cloward, "Illegitimate Means, Anomie and Deviant Behavior," *American Sociological Review*, 24 (April 1959), p. 168.

[2] Cloward, p. 168.

often an opportunity structure may occur, its potentialities are not recognized and exploited unless the actor has learned to identify such situations as containing intrinsic rewards he has been trained to seek.

This generalization may also be applied to the act of vandalism. However, the learning structure variable is probably not as imposing as in other forms of delinquent behavior such as the act of "hot-wiring" an automobile for the purpose of "joy riding." On the other hand, some indirect learning does take place even in vandalism. This occurs through the recitation of Halloween escapades and similar destructive acts by parents and adults in the presence of children or by juveniles telling one another of exploits involving vandalism.

There is a third variable present in the interaction underlying participation in an act of property destruction, the *"operating invention."*[3] This is primarily a behavioral innovation assuring the fulfillment of the potential behavior possible within the limits established by the institutional norms. The act of vandalism may be regarded as an operating invention within the normative structure of the gang or deviant peer group. The particular institutional norms involved in this context are those of solidary relations and internal competition among members for status. When the whole group engages in property destruction, it does so with the expectation that its activities will be solidary. The participant in vandalism responsible for suggesting or instigating the activity and its direction does so in the hope of raising his status in the eyes of his fellow participants. Obviously, the act must fall within the normative structure of the group in order to function as an acceptable status-conferring device for the innovator.[4] The fact that the overwhelming percentage of teenagers think it vitally important to act the way other people (their peers) expect[5] makes the possibilities of status-conferring actions by the adolescent seem almost limitless. Any hesitancy on his part to participate in what may seem to him a nonacceptable or delinquent act is generally overcome by the neutralization or rationalization techniques he learns from his peers and which help him to reconcile pressures of the peer group and the normative standards of society.[6]

Stages in the Act of Vandalism

The variables discussed above imply that participation in an act of property destruction is far more complicated than the simple decision so often assumed. There is an involved set of processes underlying this decision which move from one stage to another until the act of vandalism takes place. Viewed in terms of the broader perspective of deviant behavior, these processes constitute the most perplexing issue in the

[3] Robert Dubin, "Deviant Behavior and Social Structure: Continuities in Social Theory," *American Sociological Review,* 24 (April 1959), p. 152.

[4] Dubin, p. 153.

[5] H. H. Remmers and D. H. Radler, *The American Teenager,* Indianapolis: The Bobbs-Merrill Company, Inc., 1957, p. 254.

[6] Sykes and Matza, "Techniques of Neutralization: A Theory of Delinquency," *American Sociological Review,* 22 (December 1957), p. 669.

contemporary theory of deviant behavior.[7] Vandalism as a social act may be thought of as a sequence of behavior which has some meaning in terms of a goal or end result.[8] This sequence implies a series of steps or stages which are considered herein as social processes. An act of vandalism may be (1) a deliberately planned event, (2) one that takes place fortuitously as part of a larger social action, such as the play situation, or (3) one that functions as a catalyst for a series of unplanned additional acts as the element of mutual excitation takes hold of the participants. Since the deliberately planned act is rare, the emphasis here is upon vandalism as spontaneous deviant acts.

Structuring the Act. Participation in any social activity usually involves an evaluation by the actor of the imminent action in light of how his reference group will regard the act. If this group is "deviant-prone," delinquent behavior is more likely to occur than if the reverse is true. On the other hand, one's reference group may be "deviant-opposed" but the enveloping situation fraught with deviant opportunity structures. For this person to choose the deviant opportunity suggests the intervention of an additional variable, perhaps the rejection of the reference group itself. In some instances, the choice may involve the substitution of the authority of another reference group:

> Each situation presents its own variety of problems. A boy out on a window-breaking spree "for fun" may assess the relative weight of conflicting directives: "My mother (or teacher) says this is not the thing to do, but hell, she's only a woman. The kids in my gang say to do it, so I guess I better."[9]

How pressure is applied on the motivational system of the actor will vary as the function of the kind of pattern with which he is expected to conform. The resulting behavior is itself a function of the nature of the situation in which the individual finds himself.

In an act of vandalism there are usually five stages: (1) waiting for something to turn up, (2) removal of uncertainty: the exploratory gesture, (3) mutual conversion, (4) joint elaboration of the act, (5) aftermath and retrospect.

Stage I: "Waiting for something to turn up." Preliminary to the act is the situation from which the suggestion or innovating behavior develops. Much of the juvenile's free time outside school and in other unsupervised contexts is spent in unstructured situations. This free time is characterized by him as "messing around." What is often interpreted as aimless activity by the untrained observer and even the participants themselves has in actuality a subtle pattern. Much of it centers about and emanates from a particular location serving a vital function in the emotional

[7] Cf. Clarence Ray Jeffrey, "An Integrated Theory of Crime and Criminal Behavior," *Journal of Criminal Law, Criminology and Police Science,* 49 (March-April 1959), pp. 533–552.

[8] Theodore M. Newcomb, *Social Psychology,* New York: Holt, Rinehart and Winston, Inc., 1950, p. 77.

[9] William C. Kvaraceus and Walter B. Miller, *Delinquent Behavior: Culture and the Individual,* Washington, D.C.: National Education Association, 1959, pp. 112f.

life of the adolescent.[10] These are the kinds of situations utilized by the innovator. The actors are poised, ready for an action-provoking suggestion. As one boy defined a similar situation:

> Well, we were all at the cafe; we didn't have anything to do. We were all sitting, talking. When we didn't have anything else to do, we'd go over there to the cafe and sit down. The guys who were old enough would play the pinball machine.

"An opportunity structure" is present. The aimless talk and "bull sessions" provide the chance for gossip. The talk concerns what other juveniles have done and the escapades of their contemporaries. Such talk might never get started if these seemingly purposeless get-togethers did not occur. One interviewee summed up the situation when he said, "Things get around, boy to boy."

The play situation is another general type of context out of which vandalism may develop. The destructive activity may itself be a form of play or it may be a spontaneous outgrowth of the play situation. The two forms are often inextricably bound together by the nature of the play activity itself. The following account illustrates how vandalism may take the form of a play activity:

> There were these lights in the apartment house; they stand on a stand, have a globe on the outside. There were three others besides me; we'd been messing around. We went walking around—went down, got a cup of coffee. We came up; we broke that light bulb. Gene picked it up and threw it on the sidewalk. He just acted like he was bowling and threw.

Vandalism as play generally takes the shape of a game of skill. As such, either the quantity or the quality of the destruction is stressed. The following account shows how the quantity aspect is emphasized, although not originally intended as the goal of the play activity:

> The first time we did vandalism, me and my brother and another boy down at the garage, we were smoking and playing cards. They had some old cars in the back; we played around there. We cleaned them out one day. Swept out the broken glass—busted windshields—rolled down the windows so we wouldn't cut ourselves. This one guy threw a whiskey bottle up on the roof; threw another. It hit the side of the window. We just started throwing at the windows. When we were through, we had broken twenty-seven of them. We saw who could break out the most. There wasn't anything else to do. We finally got tired and just left. They didn't catch us until the next day. We returned to see what had happened; we were out there playing cards and smoking again.

On other occasions the destruction is subordinate. What primarily counts is one's ability to hit a target with a BB gun, pellet gun, a stone, or some other object. The target chosen is something easily broken since a hit is more visible or audible. A competitive situation ensues with destruction resulting:

[10] Herbert A. Bloch and Arthur Niederhoffer, *The Gang: A Study in Adolescent Behavior,* New York: Philosophical Library, Inc., 1958, p. 178.

About seven years ago I was shooting out switch lights on a rail road track with an air rifle. There were three of us, and each of us had guns. We were looking for pigeons. One of them said, "See that switch light up there?" He shot and missed it, and the other boy shot and missed it. I shot and missed it. So we kept on shooting until we hit it.

Oh, I broke out a few windows—see who was the straighter shot. I had a pellet pistol. See, we'd aim for the center. If you hit the center, then the window wouldn't break, only have a little hole with some small cracks. We tried to shoot through the same hole.

Once the spirit of destructive activity takes hold, massive destruction may result and the "game" quality of the activity heightens. There is a spontaneous eruption of wholesale vandalism:

This last July my parents were out of town. Me and these other kids went on a hay ride. We got home about eleven o'clock. Well, we were walking around; we were going to stay up all night—just something to keep us awake. We went out and broke windows and ran—just for excitement. We would just walk by and someone would pick up a rock and throw it and everyone would start running. We broke about fifty windows. We went around all night till it got light. We ended up walking quite a ways from our neighborhood.

As the interview data show, vandalism is sometimes the inadvertent result of ordinary play activity. Sometimes it may even be an accidental result. For example, several boys gained entry to a feed mill one weekend in order to play tag on the stacks of feed bags. The original objective soon changed as a number of motorized forklifts were discovered, and the boys began having fun driving them. The resulting destruction was rationalized as accidental:

Some of us drove the lifts. I found out I couldn't drive, so I didn't drive after about five minutes. I rode with someone else. (Did any of the guys deliberately drive into the feed bags?) They weren't doing that on purpose; sometimes they'd hit them but never on purpose. We didn't know how to drive. They were piled in huge stacks. You'd try to turn around or something; you know the back wheels are supposed to turn. They'd spin too fast; we'd hit the sack. We didn't do all the damage anyway. We weren't the first ones in there.

Stage II: Removal of Uncertainty (the Exploratory Gesture). The unstructured situation as the general context from which vandalism may develop undergoes a significant change when an action-provoking suggestion is made by one of the actors. It is generally in the form of an "exploratory gesture,"[11] This is a suggestion, sometimes cautiously, sometimes boldly, broached to effect action from a group. It functions to change the ongoing interaction and to interject a focus to the interest and conversation of the hangers-on. The prevailing boredom begins to disappear as interest develops in the exploratory gesture:

[11] Albert K. Cohen, *Delinquent Boys: The Culture of the Gang,* New York: The Free Press of Glencoe, 1955, p. 26.

> We were just sitting on the corner talking. Each boy had a different idea, but this boy had a funny idea. He told of wanting to break a window—of about a big crash: I didn't want to do it; I told him that a couple of times. But he called me "chicken." Like the Y (another place where he had committed vandalism), just riding around thinking of something to do—get an idea in their heads about causing trouble.

At times the exploratory gesture meets with little or no resistance. This is usually the case when the suggestion involves a play activity having a decided element of excitement. The original suggestion may not be that the group do property damage but that it participate in an activity challenging individual daring. The resulting vandalism is often a by-product of the situation but may also become the substitute activity:

> This one guy came up to us and said, "Let's go down to the bottom (basement) of Hilliard's (a local new car dealer) and drive around the cars." So we went and started driving around. I think it was on a Saturday. One of the salesmen came down and chased us out. We went down to this cafe and played the pinball machine. I was telling about it, so one of the guys got the bright idea that we go back there. We drove them around, scratched some of them.

The exploratory gesture may also be in the form of an overt act. In this case the act is an event of vandalism. It may be deliberate or spur-of-the-moment behavior. The episode is taken as a cue by others to commit similar ones, and a series of destructive acts may result. The following interviews illustrate this cue-taking sequence of behavior:

> Well, me and a couple of boy friends and a girl got in a car we had taken. We were going to stay there that night. She asked me if I had a knife. I said, "Yeah." So she started cutting up the upholstery, ceiling and everything. After she quit cutting up, Joe got out of the car and went to the drugstore. I locked the door and wouldn't let him back in. So Raymond kicked out the window on the right side of the driver's seat. So Joe put his foot through the same window. Then I bent up the gear shift—took out the speedometer. Joe, he took the glove compartment, took it all apart. If I'd known she was going to cut it up, I wouldn't have given her the knife. I just took it away from her and started cutting up myself. So did Joe and Raymond. I cut up the driver's seat. We didn't want to go home that night—just wanted to stay out.

Obviously, the exploratory gesture that the group participate in an act of vandalism may be rejected. No attempt is made here to determine why, when, or how such a suggestion is refused further elaboration. However, the following section has implicit propositions considered as suggestive clues to an explanation of why some adolescents will engage in vandalism while others shy away from such behavior.

Stage III: Mutual Conversion. In most instances vandalism is a group type of activity. Some degree of agreement, therefore, must be present among the prospective participants in order for the act to materialize. Prefacing this agreement is a period of mutual exploration as discussed above. As a stage in the ongoing sequence of the act, it may be very incidental and of short duration. On the other hand, a series of exploratory gestures may be made and discarded over a relatively long period of time before the process of "mutual conversion" to the idea takes place. The acceptability of an idea to oneself depends upon its acceptability to others. "Converting the other is part of the process of converting oneself."[12]

A number of pressures operate, causing the individual to accede to the implications of the exploratory gesture. In general, these challenge or threaten the person's self-concept as an acceptable peer. One of the most obvious is the dare to commit the act of vandalism. It functions as a device to measure the boy's courage and manliness before the critical audience of his peers. This form of mutual conversion is illustrated below:

I came home from doing three lawns, ate dinner. These boys waited for me till I ate dinner. This boy had some BB's and said, "Why don't you get your gun?" So I got the gun and we walked down the street. Just pointed the gun at it and shot the window. Well, when we started, I thought we were just going over to Larry's house to play cards or mess around. No reason to pick that house (to shoot the window). I think they said, "Bet you can't hit that window." It was just about eight by ten inches. After shooting the window we ran.

There are occasions when the dare involves a particularly danger-charged challenge. But one may enhance his status within the peer group if he accepts the dare even though the chances of getting away with the act are negligible. As an example:

Ronny was stupid for kicking that neon sign in front of the funeral parlor. He knew he was going to get caught. I wouldn't have done it. The cops were standing down the street not more than ten feet away. He was going along; anything he saw he was hitting. One of the boys dared him to do it. Then we tried to run, and we didn't make it.

Usually, the dare is reinforced by an epithet in current vogue among juveniles. The one most often used is "chicken." Whether applied in earnest or in jest, this appellation is taken seriously by the adolescent. It is a threat to his status in the eyes of his peers, especially when it is an overt challenge to test his courage. If the pressure toward conformity is too great, he will react as he thinks others in this reference group would react to a similar challenge. An inner struggle results between what he knows to be the right response in keeping with the internalized norms of the larger social system and the demands of loyalty to the peer group or friendship clique.[13] If he sacrifices the demands of larger society for those of the smaller social group, he does so at the risk of violating the law. When the decision is made in favor of the peer group, the process of mutual conversion has taken place.

Continued peer pressure to conform for the promise of psychological rewards, primarily that of being an accepted member of a favored group, will be too much for some juveniles. They eventually accede, and the act of property destruction is consummated:

[12] Cohen, p. 61.
[13] Sykes and Matza, p. 669.

One of the kids I ran around with and I were walking around one night, and we came to the Motor Company. He just picked up a rock and threw it. He didn't tell me he was going to do it. Those were $150 windows, something like that. He picked up a nice, big, juicy rock. He came back and said, "Now it's your chance." Of course, the guys I ran around with, they call you "chicken." One guy dares another—calls him "chicken." Some guys can't take that. I took it as long as I could until I got into it. They said if you want to belong to our club, you got to break a window. We broke about eight windows that night. Usually it started by someone calling you "chicken." If you get in the gang, you got to break a window if you want to get in our club. So we stopped, found some rocks, and threw them. Happened in a minute and sped off. We thought it was kind of funny.

It is obvious from the story that there is a tendency on the part of these boys to minimize the damage they have done and to excuse their participation in such acts on the basis of an inability to face the scorn of peers if they refuse to commit vandalism. The very fact they do eventually submit to the pressure is indicative of the importance of being accepted as a worthy peer. However, occasionally a boy will find himself included in an act of vandalism without his prior consent. The conversion stage of the act is circumvented as is the preliminary stage of the exploratory gesture. Loyalty to friends prevents him from "ratting" on them:

Yeah, one of my friends got me in some vandalism. Put a cherry bomb in a toilet stool. We were taking boxing then. A kid came in there where I was, told me all about it. We left and came back there. Police picked us up. He threw the cherry bomb in the toilet stool; I guess to have fun. I was with him when they picked him up. A lady knew he was in the rest room—she suspected him anyway. She called the cops on him. Blew it all to bits. They didn't have any proof that he did it, but he did it. I didn't say anything about it to him, I just said he was crazy (to have done that). I asked him why he came in there (into the gym). He said, "Be quiet, I'll tell you about it." He said, "Let's leave." I said I was fixing to leave. So we left anyway.

The time that it takes before the conversion process reaches fulfillment is dependent upon many factors. The more obvious of these is the seriousness of the proposed action as defined by the prospective participants. Many juveniles who already have a history of delinquencies such as theft are not likely to consider vandalism as a particularly serious offense. Little mutual exploration is necessary preliminary to participation in property destruction by these boys. On the other hand, some juveniles might define vandalism as "kid stuff." No amount of inducement short of financial reward or release from boredom would effect conversion to the idea. But most probably for these boys property destruction would be an incidental and initial phase to the "breaking and entering" of a business establishment for the purpose of burglary.

The mutual conversion process is also effected more quickly in a group in which the configuration of past experiences of the interacting individuals is very similar or strongly related. Little exploration of feelings of fellow members of a delinquent group need be made when past natural histories of their careers indicate predispositions to any behavior hinting of excitement, danger, and even malice.

Parsons[14] indicates still another factor in his discussion of the effect of the uncertainty of alter's reaction to the exploratory gesture. This uncertainty tends to create an indefiniteness in the requirements of the normative pattern, which in turn influences the interactive relationship between alter and ego. As a consequence, the time necessary for the conversion process to be completed will be affected by how quickly the uncertainty is removed as to how alter or alters will react to ego's suggestions. A case in point is the Halloween situation. There is less indefiniteness at this time than at others during the year relative to property destruction. Not only is there more definite expectation as to how alter will react to an exploratory gesture, but the conversion process is more quickly consummated. The unstructuredness of the situation is soon removed because the uncertainty as to what the normative pattern itself requires is less than at other times.

Stage IV: Joint Elaboration of the Act. In this stage of the social act there is likely to be large-scale property destruction. There is a spontaneous eruption of wholesale vandalism once the spirit of the activity takes hold of the participants. For example, breaking one window may lead to extensive damage to others. Occasionally, the participants become so stimulated by the first few acts of destruction that a veritable orgy of vandalism takes place.

One time ... four or five of us went to an apartment just being built, took a whole wall of cement down. We took a chisel and knocked down hundreds of cinder blocks, just mischievous. We went to old houses, broke windows ... In one house we found a big Victrola. We threw it down the stairs, we pushed down the bannister, we broke the chandelier. We didn't steal anything, just broke things ... I had to do it so they wouldn't call me chicken.[15]

It was indicated in the previous section dealing with the conversion stage in the act of vandalism that the tolerance threshold of some adolescents is much lower than that of others. The effects of family and class socialization patterns need to be temporarily removed in order for some of these boys to participate in such an act. Pressure from peers to conform also makes this condition possible. The pressuring takes place within a group situation in which members interact with each other and upon each other in both direct and indirect ways. Mutual testing with exploratory gestures takes place. Calling each other's bluff through the use of epithets is often the device to complete the process of securing conformity from the individual.

Contributing to the elaboration of an act of vandalism is the element of mutual excitation. The play situation is often responsible for generating this type of excitement. This is especially true if there is a competitive event involved. Such a situation may develop into a destructive race between contestants to see who can do the most or the best damage. Underlying the event is a kind of "group psychological intoxi-

[14] Talcott Parsons, *The Social System*, New York: The Free Press of Gencoe, 1951, p. 278.

[15] Benjamin Fine, 1,000,000 *Delinquents*, Cleveland: The World Publishing Company, 1955, pp. 36f.

cation."[16] One participant's behavior serves as the model for another's. Present is a "behavioral contagion" denoted by the spontaneous pickup or imitation by the other individuals of a behavior initiated by one member of the group.

In analyzing collective behavior, Blumer has suggested the term "circular reaction."[17] By this is meant a type of interstimulation in which the response of one individual tends to produce the stimulation for another. When the stimulation is reflected back to the first person, it is reinforced. This is the general result in a group contagion situation. Social psychological research has shown that in a situation of stress where the members of a group have a common need or mood, the most impulsive person–the one who first reacts in a manner representative of the shared feeling–is most likely to evoke a chain of contagion.[18] There are, of course, varying individual thresholds for participation in such group reactions.

The functional nature of mutual excitation or group contagion is of particular importance in vandalism. A primary function of this element is the tendency for the individual to lose his feeling of self-identity in the prevailing group interaction. This temporary *loss of identity* is especially significant because it helps make possible his participation in vandalism and any resulting elaboration of the act. The very fact that property destruction is generally a group act functions to reduce individual feelings of fear and guilt. The dilution of such feeling in the peer association operates as a sort of "guilt insurance."[19] The peer group inadvertently furnishes a sense of security in numbers which functions to reduce feelings of individuality and responsibility. The belief is present that when the act is committed by a group, the authorities will find it difficult, if not impossible, to single out the specific instigators.

This *feeling of security* is enhanced by the additional belief that vandalism is one of the less serious delinquencies. Particularly is this the case when the adolescent interprets his destructive behavior as a prank or "just being mischevious." This interpretation also functions as a rationalization of the activity and as an attempt to neutralize whatever guilt feelings he may have from participation in vandalism.

There is still another result of the functional nature of the element of mutual excitation. The apparent loss of individuality and responsibility obtained from anonymity operates to bring into the group interaction patterns the more cautious individuals. When this occurs, the range of anonymity is further expanded. An *impression of universality* is created, giving the appearance of group solidarity. On some occasions, especially when the participating group is large, there will be found on the fringes of the group action the supportive individuals who cannot be stampeded

[16] This is a term suggested by Dr. Fritz Redl and quoted in Martha M. Eliot, "What Is Vandalism?" *Federal Probation,* 18 (March 1954); p. 4.

[17] Herbert Blumer, "Collective Behavior," *New Outline of the Principles of Sociology,* Alfred McClung Lee (ed.), New York: Barnes & Noble, Inc., 1951, p. 170.

[18] Harold H. Kelley and John W. Thibaut, "Experimental Studies of Group Problem Solving and Processes," *Handbook of Social Psychology,* Gardner Lindzey (ed.). Reading, Mass.: Addison-Wesley Publishing Company, Inc., 1954, II, p. 752.

[19] Herbert A. Bloch and Frank T. Flynn, *Delinquency: The Juvenile Offender in America Today,* New York: Random House, Inc., 1956, p. 198.

into actual participation in the act. Although they do not oppose the group, they tend to draw the line at joining in the "fun." However, these persons are not averse to enjoying the ensuing action. The ultimate effect of these "fringes" is to add to the already created impression of universality, the impression that everyone is "in on the act."[20]

The resulting destructive behavior is extemporaneous. The participants are precipitated into it by the fast-rising events of the situation over which they have had little control. Once the action begins, apparently little can be done to prevent it from gathering momentum. The interview data tend to show that few, if any, of the participants offered strong objections to engaging in vandalism. Group pressure and mutual excitation combined to smother any protestations which arose. Not until the destruction was completed or the participants were chased from the scene did the activity halt.

Stage V: Aftermath and Retrospect. The fifth stage is of particular importance in terms of the meaning of the acts to the participant. The motive for the act will largely determine the evaluation the actor makes of the destructive behavior. The fact that nothing is stolen during most acts of vandalism tends to reinforce the vandal's conception of himself as merely a prankster and not a delinquent. In fact, this would appear to indicate that vandalism is nonutilitarian. Actually, many acts do have some meaning and utility for the participants even though not defined explicitly by them. Some property destruction appears to function for the adolescent as a protest against his ill-defined social role and ambiguous status in the social structure. Other meanings are more specific. If a boy has suffered frustration, he may express his resentment by a revengeful act of destruction:

Well, he accused us of stealing some stuff out of his joint. He didn't come right out and say it was us, but the way he talked he made it sound like it, particularly us. We were kidding him about an old rifle he had in there, about ninety years old. And he wanted $15 for it, and the stock on it was all cracked up and everything. And we kept kidding his mother—she's in there (the store) with him—and we kept kidding her. And old Gay (the store owner) himself came over there and started raising the devil, blowing off steam and everything. We didn't like it too well. We left and came back later. I told him (his companion), "Let's go down and break those windows." He said, "Okay," and we went down there and picked up some rocks along the way. We got down there and stood in front of the place till there weren't any cars very close to us, and we threw the rocks and ran.

If a boy is apprehended in the act, the destructive activity will still give him considerable satisfaction. This may be so because he has the feeling of group solidarity and support for his actions:

The cops hauled us in a couple of times out at Cow Town (a teenage dance hall hangout). I kicked in a sign at a funeral home. See, we were all drunk up there (at Cow Town), starting trouble, and they kicked us out. We were all mad. One

[20] Roger W. Brown, "Mass Phenomena," in Gardner Lindzey (ed.), *Handbook of Social Psychology*, Reading, Mass.: Addison-Wesley Publishing Company, Inc., 1954, p. 847.

of my buddies was ahead of me and was going to kick the sign. I ran ahead of him and beat him to it. The cops came running out, chasing us, and we took off down the street. They got Clyde, he was coming out behind us and he was drunk. The cops caught some of us. Boy, when they started chasing us, some of them (his companions) got sober awful quick! They could hardly run, weaving down the street. They took us down to the station in the paddy wagon. What was funny (laugh), we got down to the station, and Clyde raised his head and said, "Make a run for it, boys, I'll hold them off." Boy, we laughed and laughed!

When the act embodies a certain amount of satisfaction, the delight is keen enough for the participants to gloat over what has happened to the victim's property. As one boy described the aftermath of such an act, "Sometimes they do that (vandalism) just before somebody comes out; and when they come out, they will be behind the house killing themselves laughing," This malicious enjoyment of the victim's distress and anger is further illustrated in the following:

We went over to this one girl's house we didn't like. We threw rotten eggs all over the porch, inside the door—everywhere. Boy, did it stink around there! We went by the next day and said, "What happened?" The windows on the second floor were all up, the house and the lawn all covered. She said, "You know what happened." "Prove it," I said. Boy, did it stink! About 300 eggs we used. That place was an odorous mess! After that (the night of the vandalism) we retired to a friendly drugstore, had a couple of malts; went home to bed. Terrific!

Whatever guilt may be felt is usually neutralized by the convenient rationalizations motivating the behavior. Such rationalizations may or may not represent the "real" reason: they do reconcile the conflict between legal norms and the acts of vandalism: *Prejudice* is one source of these rationalizations. Both the majority and the minority groups engaging in such behavior find justification for it in prejudice. As an example:

The neighborhood was old and filled with all kinds of people ... Mexicans and niggers came and everything changed. Niggers and an Indian family lived next door to us and we fought them all the time because we didn't like niggers. The boys would break their windows, holler in their doors, and throw tin cans into their house ...[21]

The minority's justification for vandalism is usually interpreted as a protest against the prejudice and discrimination shown toward it by the majority group. For example, testimony before the Senate subcommittee investigating juvenile delinquency revealed that in Denver three or four significant gangs which were identified by the police as causing a great deal of vandalism were Spanish-American boys.[22] A study of vandalism in that city some time ago tended to substantiate this view.[23] The

[21] Clifford R. Shaw and Henry D. McKay, *Social Factors in Juvenile Delinquency: Report on the Causes of Crime,* National Commission on Law Observance and Enforcement, Vol. II; Washington, D.C.: Government Printing Office, 1931, p. 117.

[22] Subcommittee of the Senate Committee on the Judiciary, *Interim Report, Juvenile Delinquency,* 83d Cong., 2d Sess., 1954, p. 48.

[23] Raymond Gordon, "Vandalism," Letters to the Editor, *Federal Probation,* 18 (September 1954), p. 50.

investigating committee found a similar situation when it met in Boston.[24] It has also been maintained that much of the vandalism participated in by the Puerto Rican youth of New York is due to ethnic prejudice shown them by the majority group.[25]

The act is also justified under the rationalization that "they had it coming to them." This is designated by Sykes and Matza as a technique of neutralization labeled "the denial of the victim."[26] The boy insists that what he has done is justifiable in the light of the circumstances. For example, the damage committed is regarded as a form of rightful *retaliation* or punishment:

> I know of some friends of mine who went over to school and we decided to break some of Mr. X's windows for the simple reason that we absolutely despise this teacher. There were about four or five of us.

> Many windows are broken in our school. In one room in particular in which one unpopular teacher holds classes, about twenty-five panes a year have to be replaced. The vandals believe that this is a way to "get back at" a teacher.[27]

Goldman has also pointed out that additional attitudes such as boredom and desire for *status achievement* motivate students to damage school buildings.[28] Such vandalism is generally motivated by feelings of frustration as a result of the child's academic position in the classroom, his status among his peers, and his relationships with his teachers.

In his *retrospective view of the act,* the participant sometimes redefines his behavior from the original definition of "fun" to a negative one. There are indications of mixed feelings on the part of these boys as they look back upon such behavior. It is a mixture of rebellion, guilt, and malicious delight. This process of redefinition and revision of self attitudes has been designated by Faris as the "retrospective act."[29] Usually, the apprehension and detention experiences are significant in fostering this change in the definition of the act: "But at the time we thought it was fun until the police came and then that was all."

Another element causing a change in the original definition of the act is the realization that it caused "trouble." This is interpreted in personal terms, that is, being brought down to the police station or to the juvenile court or being involved in a

[24] *Interim Report,* p. 59.

[25] Helen L. Witmer (ed.), *Parents and Delinquency,* Department of Health, Education and Welfare, Social Security Administration, Children's Bureau; Washington, D.C.: Government Printing Office, 1954, pp. 9f.

[26] Sykes and Matza, p. 668.

[27] These two accounts are taken from the exploratory study by Nathan Goldman, "Attitudes towards Vandalism: A Preliminary Report of Research," revision of a paper presented at the annual meetings of the American Sociological Association in Seattle, Wash., August 29, 1958, p. 9. (Dittoed.)

[28] Goldman, pp. 8–12.

[29] Ellsworth Faris, "The Retrospective Act," *Journal of Educational Sociology,* 14 (October 1950), pp. 82 and 87.

disagreeable family situation. Comments such as these are indicative: "We didn't think about getting caught; we were thinking about having fun. I'm sorry I did it—more trouble than it was fun." "It didn't seem like then that it would amount to this much." "I didn't think it would cause so much trouble."

Although the primary aspect of the guilt is that of apprehension, there is also present a feeling that this kind of behavior might have resulted in something more serious, such as an injury. It is particularly true in cases where damage was done to automobiles by throwing rocks or using slingshots. Attitudes expressive of such guilt feelings are: "I could have hurt someone in the car." "It's bad; it could have caused an accident."

Further indicative of the guilt which some held concerning their behavior is a feeling of relief at having been apprehended. This tends to represent how effectively the conventional norms are internalized. The internalization, although not complete enough to forestall deviation from property norms, was still effective enough to provoke guilt feelings. It also led to the realization that vandalism was contrary to parental expectations and "good sense":

> First place, we shouldn't have been over there. Second place, one of us might have got killed. Third place, I'm glad we got caught because we'd do more damage and more damage—be hard on our parents. Fourth place, that was an awful place to go play in, the (feed) mill.

Also present on occasion in the retrospective assessment of the act is the boy's conclusion that vandalism is "senseless." To some extent this represents a feeling of shame with the implication that one's behavior should have reason and utilitarian ends to it. Inherent is the idea that one ought to have good sense to think ahead and weigh the consequences of the act. It also represents a certain amount of chagrin at not having met expectations internalized relative to evaluating consequences before acting.

Although there are these feelings of guilt and shame at having been a participant in vandalism, some express a malicious delight at having been a party to the act. This is especially true if the victim is known to the individual and has been defined in negative terms. In some instances it is an attempt to justify the act to oneself.

By engaging in this kind of retrospective activity the vandal is taking the role of the other. In doing so, a changed conception of self begins to form. It is also conceivable that this same process helps to inhibit certain forms of vandalism as well as encourage still other types.[30] However, whether or not such a redefinition takes place will greatly depend upon the individual's "normative reference group." This

[30] Tamotsu Shibtani, *Society and Personality: An Interactionist Approach to Social Psychology*, Englewood Cliffs, N.J.: Prentice-Hall, Inc., 1961, pp. 70–79, for a discussion of the blockage of social acts and resulting secondary adjustments.

is especially true of the deviant's choice of behavior responses to begin with in the interactional process.[31]

Since the individual gets much of his self-definition from the way others treat him and talk to him, the roles of law enforcement authorities and other significant adults are important in effecting the retrospective act on the part of the juvenile vandal with the end result of a changed self-image. As mentioned above, his apprehension often leads the boy to re-evaluate the act. This re-evaluation in terms of guilt or shame is probably more true in the case of the boy who has never been arrested before than of the adolescent who is a familiar face to authorities. The adolescent's peers who also function as significant others, are also highly important in fostering his self-conception, as well as revising it to conform with their perceived expectations of him. Obviously, much depends upon how significantly the actor has identified himself with the normative reference group in question.[32]

Self-Image

The juvenile's conception of the act of vandalism is a clue to his self-image. If he construes the event as "just a joke" or "just having fun," it implies that he thinks of himself as a "prankster" and not specifically as a delinquent. This construction, however, does not also exclude a conception of his actions as "bad" or "wrong" since concurrently he is able to deny responsibility for his actions by a favorable definition of the situation as an acceptable one for vandalism. This denial of responsibility functions to reduce the disapproval of self and others as a restraining influence.[33]

The interview data bear out the vandal's self-definition of being a prankster. Also included on occasion are elements suggesting that this self-image is flexible when the juvenile frames the act from the standpoint of the evaluator rather than the participant. A person who commits property destruction is thus considered "mean" or "ornery." On the other hand, in his efforts to protect his self-image as that of "prankster" or "mischievous" boy, the juvenile will resort to various rationalizations. These include the idea that there are no "good" boys but only "lucky" ones who have never been caught, that the possessions of certain persons or at particular places are appropriate or acceptable targets for vandalism, and that those who disapprove of such acts are hypocrites and even deviants in disguise.

Conclusions

In this study juvenile vandalism has been analyzed by viewing it as a social act. Be-

[31] Albert K. Cohen, "The Study of Social Disorganization and Deviant Behavior," *Sociology Today: Problems and Prospects*, Robert K. Merton, *et al.* (eds.), New York: Basic Books, Inc., 1959, pp. 468–473.

[32] Martin R. Haskell, "Toward a Reference Group Theory of Juvenile Delinquency," *Social Problems*, 8 (Winter 1960–1961), pp. 220–230.

[33] Sykes and Matza, p. 667.

cause each behavioral act has a career and is built up in a succession of responses,[34] using this approach has the advantage of bringing into focus the social processes growing out of group interaction. It also emphasizes the definitions held by the actor of himself and of the behavioral act; the two are found to be functionally interrelated.

Within such a framework vandalism is revealed to be spontaneous behavior and the outgrowth of the social situations in which group interaction takes place. There is an observable movement as a result of this interaction. The initial inertia begins to give way as a series of successive interactional responses change the emotional climate of the social situation. Each interactive response builds upon the preceding until a focus develops and a solidary relationship results among the participants.

The act of vandalism functions as a means of ensuring group solidarity. Conformity to the peer group occurs because involvement tends to satisfy the adolescent's need dispositions for status, recognition, and response. Identification with societal property norms becomes subordinate to the demands of the peer group. The adolescent will thus participate in acts of property destruction in order not to appear "chicken." In other words, he can through this involvement maintain a satisfying self-definition and avoid becoming a marginal member of the group. Even though he may recognize the act to be "wrong" or "delinquent," he finds some comfort through the guilt-assuaging rationalizations present in the subculture of the peer group.

Further research is needed in this important area of changing self-definitions. The preceding study pointed out that these redefinitions have a definite relationship to the situational context. The arrest experience is only one such context within which this redefinition takes place. Obviously, there are other significant situations effecting such change. It may occur at the time the participant is involved in a social act, such as, for example, when the boy is with a group on the verge or in the process of committing vandalism.

How easily the redefinition of self takes place may have a real relationship to the ease with which positive changes in treatment programs can be actuated. It may also have important bearing on efforts to formulate a typology of deviants when one of the important elements in the classification is the development within the behavior system of the individual's self-concept.[35]

[34] Shibutani, pp. 69 f.

[35] Cf. John W. Kinch, "Self-Conceptions of Types of Delinquents," *Sociological Inquiry*, 32 (Spring 1962), pp. 228–234.

23. Boy's Story: Entering and Leaving Gang Life*

David Dressler

Beginnings of Street Life

[*Q.*] *How did you first start hanging out, do you remember?*

[*A.*] You wouldn't believe it, but when I was nine, ten, I used to be bashful. I just didn't want to go nowhere. We didn't even have no television then, but I'd just lay around by the radio, listen to that all night. 'Till time to go to bed. Or I'd read. Fiction. True stuff. All them old books, like *Smoke Blows West, Daniel Boone,* westerns, stuff like that. Mysteries. Football stories. Baseball stories. Comics once in awhile. You couldn't get me out of the house. My ma would say, "For Pete's sake! Why don't you go outside and play?"

I was about eleven, twelve, when I commenced going out a little. There was these guys I went to school with. We'd ride home together on our bike. One of us would say, "Where you going tonight?" "Where you going?" "Well," he'd say, "let's go over and get Johnny. He'll go riding with us." So we'd go get him. There'd be three, four guys that way. There wasn't nothing else to do. You don't want to stay home all the time.

After awhile it wasn't just bike riding. We'd maybe go to a show. Or we'd get together some money and go to Ferry's [a concession park], ride the roller coaster.

Hanging out happens gradual. You don't realize you're starting a gang. You feel jittery at home. You don't know what to do with yourself. You know the other guys will be on a certain corner. Or a malt shop. You say, "Hell! I haven't nothing better to do. I'll just walk over and kick it around a little with the fellows." You get so you head for that spot 'most every night.

Then, from hanging around, you commence cutting up now and then. When I was twelve, thirteen, we used to think it was smart to walk past a newsstand and when the guy turned his back we'd snatch a bunch of papers. If he seen us we'd throw them in his face and run. We just did it to be ornery. You did what the others did.

Reprinted from "Gang Boy" from David Dressler, *Readings in Criminology and Penology* (New York: Columbia University Press, 1964), pp. 153–155, 161–163, by permission of Columbia University Press.

*[Editor's Note: This is part of a tape recorded by David Dressler of an unemployed (not in school) 18-year-old youth living in a community of 100,000 in the west.]

The first thing I ever took to amount to anything was when I was twelve. Me and Sloppy started out to make a night of it. Well, that night seemed awful long, boy, once you got in the middle of it! We didn't have nothing to do. We was kind of sleepy, we wanted to keep going, so naturally, we was going to find something to do.

We was sitting around, and we seen this bicycle parked up on a lawn, right in front. It was a real keen deal, one of them English makes. The guy left it out there where it had no business being, so we jumped on it and took off. Sloppy was driving it. I hung on the back. We hadn't had it no more than a couple of hours, when zooooom! The juvenile officers come around the corner in a car. We tried to get away but we hit some gravel and slid and fell, ass over tea kettle. We busted out a couple of spokes. They took us downtown and called our folks to come down. The guy that owned the bike come down, too. He was a grown guy. The cops told him they didn't think we realized how serious it was, what we done—and we didn't, at the time. So they let us go after our folks paid for the damage.

By this time we had quite a few fellows that was hanging around regular. There was never any meetings. Just: "You going to be in the malt shop tonight?" "Yeah!" There was nothing else you could do.

[*Q.*] *What about that Boys' Club about a mile away from your house? Ever go there when you had nothing else to do?*

[*A.*] You can't go to no Boys' Club. There was probably some kids that went there, to shoot pool or something, but we didn't go. A club, you want to be taken for what you are. You don't want to have to keep your hands clean and do this and don't do that. That's what gets some guys down. They just don't go for stuff like that. These sissy places, a couple guys go there, and they're shooting pool, say. And the cue slips, and one of them says, "Oh, shit!" That's all, boy! Out! They throw you out.

So we kept on hanging out. And the trouble commenced. Picked up for hitching rides. Picked up for curfew. A couple of us was feeling ornery one night, didn't have nothing to do, so we went over and let the air out of some guy's tires. Quite a few times we got picked up for drinking. We got throwed in jail a couple times for fighting at a party. We wasn't fighting, we was arguing. You know, you get a couple, three deals like that and you get so you haven't got a bit of use for cops.

There's another thing. They lock us up for having beer in the car. Why don't they do something about the grownups that sell us the stuff? They're more at fault than we are. If they wasn't to sell it to us we wouldn't be getting drunk, would we?

It's gone on and on like that. I been downtown maybe 125 or 150 times. They just suspended my license, for drunk driving. I run into the side of a house. I got 30 days, license suspended, and now I have to drive without a license.

[*Q.*] *Hank, were there any guys your age, when you started hanging out, who found other things to do? Who didn't hang out?*

[*A.*] Oh, yeah! I'll tell you why that is. Everybody wants to hang out when he's a certain age, because he's got to get away from the monotony. Some *don't* hang out because they're scared. They hear you get put in jail if you belong to a gang.

[*Q.*] *You mean there's nobody at all that age who just wouldn't care to belong to a street gang?*

[*A.*] Oh, them! They're scared the group wouldn't accept them. They're the studious type, book worms. What do they do for fun? They go to the show. Make popcorn at home. Cook fudge or something.

[*Q.*] *Well, why would this fellow want to do that while you fellows want to be on the street?*

[*A.*] I don't know what would make you want to hang out. Maybe just one night you went out and had some fun at a party or something and kept on going like that. Maybe you think that's more fun than making fudge. I for damn sure don't care to make fudge!

• • •

The Gang and Crime

Most of the stuff me and the gang get into is just fun, raising hell, or orneriness. You wouldn't call it crime. But I guess we've done things you could. There ain't a kid that hasn't stolen something–cigarettes or a can of beer or a comic. Hub caps.

I remember there was three Chevvies sitting out there on Marlin Boulevard once, where the aircraft plant is. Well, three of our gang had Chevvies. We all went down there one night and when we was through, good God! We had all them cars stripped down to bare metal. We took the engines, wheels, dashboard equipment, steering wheels, every goddamn thing but the shell. You should have seen them silly things sitting there after we left!

I might roll a drunk, maybe get in a robbery. Snatch me some hubcaps. But certain things I wouldn't do, gang or no gang. Shaking down fags–that's dirty business. I wouldn't peddle dope. And I wouldn't commit one of them sex offenses, messing with little girls. I've got absolutely no use for that and I wouldn't give the time of day to any bastard that would do a thing like that. There's a limit.

About Cops

I don't hate all cops. The cops that kids hate earn it. Figure it out. I'll bet there isn't but three out of every ten people in the country that hasn't been pinched at least once. Now, that's a lot of people. If there's one bad cop, there's a lot of people hating him. Cops should think of that.

There's some decent cops. Let you get away with stuff. Dixville isn't too bad that way, as long as you're not living in the bad part of town, where we live. That's where you get the lousy cops.

What I mean by a good cop is he don't look to be hauling you in right away. Say you're under age, you're drinking. A cop is supposed to run you in. A decent cop won't run you in just for drinking. A cop you could get along with would be one, he'd say, "Well, as long as you fellows are only drinking beer, go ahead." I'd rather see kids sitting around with a can of beer than I would with a marijuana cigarette!

I've got nothing against cops or judges or probation officers, so long as they're decent. I just don't like to be robbed.

Good Deeds

Why do people only tell about the bad things? Why don't they mention that gangs do good? If a guy has a blowout, you help him fix it. If you're working in a gas station and one of your buddies is broke, you let him drive his car in and give him a couple gallons of gas when the boss isn't around. Many a kid that wasn't living home, got kicked out, I've taken out, bought hamburgers for, fed him in the morning. You never hear them college professors tell about the good things gangs do.

Leaving the Gang

[*Q.*] *Sooner or later, you're going to move out of the gang, aren't you? You don't expect to be around the same bunch the rest of your life?*

[*A.*] Oh, yeah! You give it up after a while. I'm about ready to quit this kind of life. Get me a job. Settle down.

[*Q.*] *Is that what happens to most of the fellows you know about? They get a little older and settle down?*

[*A.*] Oh, yeah! They wisen up and begin to see their mistakes. I guess you wouldn't call it mistakes. It's just you look back and see what you had done before. When you was a kid.

[*Q.*] *Hank, you talk about kids a lot. When does a fellow stop being a kid and become a man, settle down, take responsibilities, work, make a living, support a family, things like that?*

[*A.*] I'd say when you get married.

[*Q.*] *You're a kid until you get married?*

[*A.*] Yeah. Because until you get married you're going to keep on doing the same things.

Summing Up

[*Q.*] *Hank, if someone were going to do a character sketch of you, describe what you're like, say "Hank's a good fellow, Hank's a bad fellow," this, that. If you were describing yourself, what would you say?*

[*A.*] Oh, I don't know. Just a kid that lives on the worst side of town in terms of where to live. Likes to go out with girls. Interested in cars all the time. That's about the main interests. Cars and women.

[*Q.*] *Is this fellow a good sport?*

[*A.*] Oh, yeah!

[*Q.*] *Is he honest?*

[*A.*] Yeah. With his friends.

[*Q.*] *Is he a good citizen?*

[*A.*] What do you mean by that?

[*Q.*] *Works, supports his family, helps keep his community decent. And so on. Being a good citizen might mean you carry your own freight.*

[*A.*] Oh, yeah! I say yes to that. He's a good citizen, this guy.

[*Q.*] *Suppose a young fellow—a kid—came to you and asked if it would be a good thing, a smart thing, for him to get in with a gang something like yours. Imagine he asks your advice. What would you tell him?*

[*A.*] Knowing what I know, I'd tell young guys to kind of hold it down a little bit. Go with the gang, but don't be so damn wild as I was, because when you're as wild as I was, it's hard on your folks, they worry a lot. I'd just hold it down to a mild roar if I had it to do all over again. But I sure as hell wouldn't advise him to make fudge. But books, there's no harm in reading books. I read books myself. But I don't go overboard with it. I'd advise him to finish high school. If he has a chance, go to college.

[*Q.*] *Do you ever worry about the way you've been going, up to now?*

[*A.*] Yeah. I was always worried one of these days I'm going to end up in the can for a long, long time.

[*Q.*] *But still, that hasn't stopped your hanging out.*

[*A.*] No, but it's made me stop and think for quite a bit. I'm going to show my will power very shortly.

24. Professional Thief: Processes in Selection and Tutelage

Edwin H. Sutherland

The professional thief is one who steals professionally. This means, first, that he makes a regular business of stealing. He devotes his entire working time and energy to larceny and may steal three hundred and sixty-five days a year. Second, every act is carefully planned. The selection of spots, securing of the property, making a getaway, disposing of the stolen property, and fixing cases in which he may be pinched (arrested) are all carefully planned. Third, the professional thief has technical skills and methods which are different from those of other professional criminals. Manual skill is important in some of the rackets, but the most important thing in all the rackets is the ability to manipulate people. The thief depends on his approach, front, wits, and in many instances his talking ability. The professional burglar or stickup man (robber with a gun), on the other hand, uses violence or threat of violence even though he may on occasion use soothing language in order

Reprinted from Chapter 1, "The Profession," and Chapter 9, "Interpretation," from *The Professional Thief–By a Professional Thief* by Edwin H. Sutherland (Chicago: The University of Chicago Press, 1937), pp. 3–4, 209–228, by permission of The University of Chicago Press.

to quiet people. Fourth, the professional thief is generally migratory and may work in all the cities of the United States. He generally uses a particular city as headquarters, and, when two professional thieves first meet, the question is always asked: "Where are you out of?"

In addition to these four characteristics, professional thieves have many things in common. They have acquaintances, congeniality, sympathy, understandings, agreements, rules, codes of behavior, and language in common.

The professional thief has nothing in common with the amateur thief or with the amateur in any other racket. The professional thief will be in sympathy with the amateur's attempt to steal something but will not be interested in him, for they have no acquaintances or ideas of stealing in common. He would talk with an amateur whom he might happen to meet in the can (police lockup) no longer than necessary to find out that he was an amateur. He might offer advice on how to beat the rap (charge), but this would be very rare, for, in addition to the fact that the amateur means nothing in his life, there is danger in telling the intricacies of the fix to someone who may be loquacious.

...

Selection and tutelage are the two necessary elements in the process of acquiring recognition as a professional thief. These are the universal factors in an explanation of the genesis of the professional thief. A person cannot acquire recognition as a professional thief until he has had tutelage in professional theft, and tutelage is given only to a few persons selected from the total population.

Selection and tutelage are continuous processes. The person who is not a professional thief becomes a professional thief as a result of contact with professional thieves, reciprocal confidence and appreciation, a crisis situation, and tutelage. In the course of this process a person who is not a professional thief may become first a neophyte and then a recognized professional thief. A very small percentage of those who start on this process ever reach the stage of professional theft, and the process may be interrupted at any point by action of either party.

Selection is a reciprocal process, involving action by those who are professional thieves and by those who are not professional thieves. Contact is the first requisite, and selection doubtless lies back of the contacts. They may be pimps, amateur thieves, burglars, or they may be engaged in legitimate occupations as clerks in hotels or stores. Contacts may be made in jail or in the places where professional thieves are working or are spending their leisure time. If the other person is to become a professional thief, the contact must develop into appreciation of the professional thieves. This is not difficult, for professional thieves in general are very attractive. They have had wide experience, are interesting conversationalists, know human nature, spend money lavishly, and have great power. Since some persons are not attracted even by these characteristics, there is doubtless a selective process involved in this, also.

The selective action of the professional thieves is probably more significant than the selective action of the potential thief. An inclination to steal is not a sufficient explanation of the genesis of the professional thief. Everyone has an inclination to steal and expresses this inclination with more or less frequency and with more or less finesse. The person must be appreciated by the professional thieves. He must be appraised as having an adequate equipment of wits, front, talking ability, honesty, reliability, nerve, and determination. The comparative importance of these several characteristics cannot be determined at present, but it is highly probable that no characteristic is valued more highly than honesty. It is probably regarded as more essential than mental ability. This, of course, means honesty in dealings within their own group.

An emergency or crisis is likely to be the occasion on which tutelage beings. A person may lose a job, get caught in amateur stealing, or may need additional money. If he has developed a friendly relationship with professional thieves, he may request or they may suggest that he be given a minor part in some act of theft. He would, if accepted, be given verbal instructions in regard to the theory of the racket and the specific part he is to play. In his first efforts in this minor capacity he may be assisted by the professional thieves, although such assistance would be regarded as an affront by one who was already a professional. If he performs these minor duties satisfactorily, he is promoted to more important duties. During this probationary period the neophyte is assimilating the general standards of morality, propriety, etiquette, and rights which characterize the profession, and he is acquiring "larceny sense." He is learning the general methods of disposing of stolen goods and of fixing cases. He is building up a personal acquaintance with other thieves, and with lawyers, policemen, court officials, and fixers. This more general knowledge is seldom transmitted to the neophyte as formal verbal instructions but is assimilated by him without being recognized as instruction. However, he is quite as likely to be dropped from participation in further professional activities for failure to assimilate and use this more general culture as for failure to acquire the specific details of the techniques of theft.

As a result of this tutelage during the probationary period, he acquires the techniques of theft and consensus with the thieves. He is gradually admitted into differential association with thieves and given tentative status as a professional thief. This tentative status under probation becomes fixed as a definite recognition as a professional thief. Thereby he enters into the systematic organization which constitutes professional theft.

A person who wished to become a professional thief might conceivably acquire some knowledge of the techniques and of the codes by reading the descriptions of theft in newspapers, journals, and books. Either alone or in the company of two or three others he might attempt to use these techniques and to become a self-made professional thief. Even this, of course, would be tutelage. Aside from the fact that hardly ever is the technique of a theft described in such manner that it can be applied without personal assistance, this part of the skill of the thief is only a part of the requirements for a successful career. This person would not have that indefinite body of appreciations which is called "larceny sense," nor would he have the personal acquaintances with and confidence of fences, fixers, and policemen which are necessary for security in professional theft. He would quickly land in prison, where he would have somewhat better opportunity to learn how to steal.

A person who is a professional thief may cease to be one. This would generally result from a violation of the codes of the profession or else from inefficiency due to age, fear, narcotic drugs, or drink. Because of either failure he would no longer be able to find companions with whom to work, would not be trusted by the fixer or by the policemen, and therefore he would not be able to secure immunity from punishment. He is no longer recognized as a professional thief, and therefore he can no longer be a professional thief. On the other hand, if he drops out of active stealing of his own volition and retains his abilities, he would continue to receive recognition as a professional thief. He would be similar to a physician who would be recognized as a physician after he ceased active practice. ...

25. Becoming a Marihuana User*

Howard S. Becker

The use of marihuana is and has been the focus of a good deal of attention on the part of both scientists and laymen. One of the major problems students of the practice have addressed themselves to has been the identification of those individual psychological traits which differentiate marihuana users from nonusers and which are assumed to account for the use of the drug. That approach, common in the study of behavior categorized as deviant, is based on the premise that the presence of a given kind of behavior in an individual can best be explained as the result of some trait which predisposes or motivates him to engage in the behavior.[1]

Reprinted from *The American Journal of Sociology,* **59**:3 (November 1953), 235-242, by permission of The University of Chicago Press and the author.

*Paper read at the meetings of the Midwest Sociological Society in Omaha, Nebraska, April 25, 1953. The research on which this paper is based was done while I was a member of the staff of the Chicago Narcotics Survey, a study done by the Chicago Area Project, Inc., under a grant from the National Mental Health Institute. My thanks to Solomon Kobrin, Harold Finestone, Henry McKay, and Anselm Strauss, who read and discussed with me earlier versions of this paper.

[1] See, as examples of this approach, the following: Eli Marcovitz and Henry J. Meyers, "The Marihuana Addict in the Army," *War Medicine,* VI (December, 1944), 382-91; Herbert S. Gaskill, "Marihuana, an Intoxicant," *American Journal of Psychiatry,* CII (September, 1945), 202-4; Sol Charen and Luis Perelman, "Personality Studies of Marihuana Addicts," *American Journal of Psychiatry,* CII (March, 1946), 674-82.

This study is likewise concerned with accounting for the presence or absence of marihuana use in an individual's behavior. It starts, however, from a different premise: that the presence of a given kind of behavior is the result of a sequence of social experiences during which the person acquires a conception of the meaning of the behavior, and perceptions and judgments of objects and situations, all of which make the activity possible and desirable. Thus, the motivation or disposition to engage in the activity is built up in the course of learning to engage in it and does not antedate this learning process. For such a view it is not necessary to identify those "traits" which "cause" the behavior. Instead, the problem becomes one of describing the set of changes in the person's conception of the activity and of the experience it provides for him.[2]

This paper seeks to describe the sequence of changes in attitude and experience which lead to *the use of marihuana for pleasure.* Marihuana does not produce addiction, as do alcohol and the opiate drugs; there is no withdrawal sickness and no ineradicable craving for the drug.[3] The most frequent pattern of use might be termed "recreational." The drug is used occasionally for the pleasure the user finds in it, a relatively casual kind of behavior in comparison with that connected with the use of addicting drugs. The term "use for pleasure" is meant to emphasize the noncompulsive and casual character of the behavior. It is also meant to eliminate from consideration here those few cases in which marihuana is used for its prestige value only, as a symbol that one is a certain kind of person, with no pleasure at all being derived from its use.

The analysis presented here is conceived of as demonstrating the greater explanatory usefulness of the kind of theory outlined above as opposed to the predispositional theories now current. This may be seen in two ways: (1) predispositional theories cannot account for that group of users (whose existence is admitted)[4] who do not exhibit the trait or traits considered to cause the behavior and (2) such theories cannot account for the great variability over time of a given individual's behavior with reference to the drug. The same person will at one stage be unable to use the drug for pleasure, at a later stage be able and willing to do so, and, still later, again be unable to use it in this way. These changes, difficult to explain from a predispositional or motivational theory, are readily understandable in terms of changes in the individual's conception of the drug as is the existence of "normal" users.

The study attempted to arrive at a general statement of the sequence of changes in individual attitude and experience which have always occurred when the individual has become willing and able to use marihuana for pleasure and which have not

[2] This approach stems from George Herbert Mead's discussion of objects in *Mind, Self, and Society* (Chicago: University of Chicago Press, 1934), pp. 277–80.

[3] Cf. Roger Adams, "Marihuana," *Bulletin of the New York Academy of Medicine,* XVIII (November, 1942), 705–30.

[4] Cf. Lawrence Kolb, "Marihuana," *Federal Probation,* II (July, 1938), 22–25; and Walter Bromberg, "Marihuana: A Psychiatric Study," *Journal of the American Medical Association,* CXIII (July 1, 1939), 11.

occurred or not been permanently maintained when this is not the case. This generalization is stated in universal terms in order that negative cases may be discovered and used to revise the explanatory hypothesis.[5]

Fifty interviews with marihuana users from a variety of social backgrounds and present positions in society constitute the data from which the generalization was constructed and against which it was tested.[6] The interviews focused on the history of the person's experience with the drug, seeking major changes in his attitude toward it and in his actual use of it and the reasons for these changes. The final generalization is a statement of that sequence of changes in attitude which occurred in every case known to me in which the person came to use marihuana for pleasure. Until a negative case is found, it may be considered as an explanation of all cases of marihuana use for pleasure. In addition, changes from use to nonuse are shown to be related to similar changes in conception, and in each case it is possible to explain variations in the individual's behavior in these terms.

This paper covers only a portion of the natural history of an individual's use of marihuana,[7] starting with the person having arrived at the point of willingness to try marihuana. He knows that others use it to "get high," but he does not know what this means in concrete terms. He is curious about the experience, ignorant of what it may turn out to be, and afraid that it may be more than he has bargained for. The steps outlined below, if he undergoes them all and maintains the attitudes developed in them, leave him willing and able to use the drug for pleasure when the opportunity presents itself.

I

The novice does not ordinarily get high the first time he smokes marihuana, and several attempts are usually necessary to induce this state. One explanation of this may be that the drug is not smoked "properly," that is, in a way that insures sufficient dosage to produce real symptoms of intoxication. Most users agree that it cannot be smoked like tobacco if one is to get high:

> Take in a lot of air, you know, and...I don't know how to describe it, you don't smoke it like a cigarette, you draw in a lot of air and get it deep down in your system and then keep it there. Keep it there as long as you can.

Without the use of some such technique[8] the drug will produce no effects, and the user will be unable to get high:

[5] The method used is that described by Alfred R. Lindesmith in his *Opiate Addiction* (Bloomington: Principia Press, 1947), chap. i. I would like also to acknowledge the important role Lindesmith's work played in shaping my thinking about the genesis of marihuana use.

[6] Most of the interviews were done by the author. I am grateful to Solomon Kobrin and Harold Finestone for allowing me to make use of interviews done by them.

[7] I hope to discuss elsewhere other stages in this natural history.

[8] A pharmacologist notes that this ritual is in fact an extremely efficient way of getting the drug into the blood stream (R.P. Walton, *Marihuana: America's New Drug Problem* [Philadelphia: J. B. Lippincott, 1938], p. 48).

The trouble with people like that [who are not able to get high] is that they're just not smoking it right, that's all there is to it. Either they're not holding it down long enough, or they're getting too much air and not enough smoke, or the other way around or something like that. A lot of people just don't smoke it right, so naturally nothing's gonna happen.

If nothing happens, it is manifestly impossible for the user to develop a conception of the drug as an object which can be used for pleasure, and use will therefore not continue. The first step in the sequence of events that must occur if the person is to become a user is that he must learn to use the proper smoking technique in order that his use of the drug will produce some effects in terms of which his conception of it can change.

Such a change is, as might be expected, a result of the individual's participation in groups in which marihuana is used. In them the individual learns the proper way to smoke the drug. This may occur through direct teaching:

I was smoking like I did an ordinary cigarette. He said, "No, don't do it like that." He said, "Suck it, you know, draw in and hold it in your lungs till you ... for a period of time."

I said, "Is there any limit of time to hold it?"

He said, "No, just till you feel that you want to let it out, let it out." So I did that three or four times.

Many new users are ashamed to admit ignorance and, pretending to know already, must learn through the more indirect means of observation and imitation:

I came on like I had turned on [smoked marihuana] many times before, you know. I didn't want to seem like a punk to this cat. See, like I didn't know the first thing about it–how to smoke it, or what was going to happen, or what. I just watched him like a hawk–I didn't take my eyes off him for a second, because I wanted to do everything just as he did it. I watched how he held it, how he smoked it, and everything. Then when he gave it to me I just came on cool, as though I knew exactly what the score was. I held it like he did and took a poke just the way he did.

No person continued marihuana use for pleasure without learning a technique that supplied sufficient dosage for the effects of the drug to appear. Only when this was learned was it possible for a conception of the drug as an object which could be used for pleasure to emerge. Without such a conception marihuana use was considered meaningless and did not continue.

II

Even after he learns the proper smoking technique, the new user may not get high and thus not form a conception of the drug as something which can be used for pleasure. A remark made by a user suggested the reason for this difficulty in getting high and pointed to the next necessary step on the road to being a user:

I was told during an interview, "As a matter of fact, I've seen a guy who was high out of his mind and didn't know it."

I expressed disbelief: "How can that be, man?"
The interviewee said, "Well it's pretty strange, I'll grant you that, but I've seen it. This guy got on with me, claiming that he'd never got high, one of those guys, and he got completely stoned. And he kept insisting that he wasn't high. So I had to prove to him that he was."

What does this mean? It suggests that being high consists of two elements: the presence of symptoms caused by marihuana use and the recognition of these symptoms and their connection by the user with his use of the drug. It is not enough, that is, that the effects be present; they alone do not automatically provide the experience of being high. The user must be able to point them out to himself and consciously connect them with his having smoked marihuana before he can have this experience. Otherwise, regardless of the actual effects produced, he considers that the drug has had no effect on him: "I figured it either had no effect on me or other people were exaggerating its effect on them, you know. I though it was probably psychological, see." Such persons believe that the whole thing is an illusion and that the wish to be high leads the user to deceive himself into believing that something is happening when, in fact, nothing is. They do not continue marihuana use, feeling that "it does nothing" for them.

Typically, however, the novice has faith (developed from his observation of users who do get high) that the drug actually will produce some new experience and continues to experiment with it until it does. His failure to get high worries him, and he is likely to ask more experienced users or provoke comments from them about it. In such conversations he is made aware of specific details of his experience which he may not have noticed or may have noticed but failed to identify as symptoms of being high:

I didn't get high the first time....I don't think I held it in long enough. I probably let it out, you know, you're a little afraid. The second time I wasn't sure, and he [smoking companion] told me like I asked him for some of the symptoms of something, how would I know, you know.... So he told me to sit on a stool. I sat on—I think I sat on a bar stool—and he said, "Let your feet hang." and then when I got down my feet were real cold, you know.

And I started feeling it, you know. That was the first time. And then about a week after that, sometime pretty close to it, I really got on. That was the first time I got on a big laughing kick, you know. Then I really knew I was on.

One symptom of being high is an intense hunger. In the next case the novice becomes aware of this and gets high for the first time:

They were just laughing the hell out of me because like I was eating so much. I just scoffed [ate] so much food, and they were just laughing at me, you know. Sometimes I'd be looking at them, you know, wondering why they're laughing, you know, not knowing what I was doing. [Well, did they tell you why they were laughing eventually?] Yeah, yeah, I come back, "Hey, man, what's happening?" Like, you know, like I'd ask, "What's happening?" and all of a sudden I feel weird, you know. "Man, you're on, you know. You're on pot [high on marihuana]." I said, "No, am I?" Like I don't know what's happening.

The learning may occur in more indirect ways:

> I heard little remarks that were made by other people. Somebody said, "My legs are rubbery," and I can't remember all the remarks that were made because I was very attentively listening for all these cues for what I was supposed to feel like.

The novice, then, eager to have this feeling, picks up from other users some concrete referents of the term "high" and applies these notions to his own experience. The new concepts make it possible for him to locate these symptoms among his own sensations and to point out to himself a "something different" in his experience that he connects with drug use. It is only when he can do this that he is high. In the next case, the contrast between two successive experiences of a user makes clear the crucial importance of the awareness of the symptoms in being high and re-emphasizes the important role of interaction with other users in acquiring the concepts that make this awareness possible:

> [Did you get high the first time you turned on?] Yeah, sure. Although, come to think of it, I guess I really didn't. I mean, like that first time it was more or less of a mild drunk. I was happy, I guess, you know what I mean. But I didn't really know I was high, you know what I mean. It was only after the second time I got high that I realized I was high the first time. Then I knew that something different was happening.
>
> [How did you know that?] How did I know? If what happened to me that night would of happened to you, you would've known, believe me. We played the first tune for almost two hours–one tune! Imagine, man! We got on the stand and played this one tune, we started at nine o'clock. When we got finished I looked at my watch, it's a quarter to eleven. Almost two hours on one tune. And it didn't seem like anything.
>
> I mean, you know, it does that to you. It's like you have much more time or something. Anyway, when I saw that, man, it was too much. I knew I must really be high or something if anything like that could happen. See, and then they explained to me that that's what it did to you, you had a different sense of time and everything. So I realized that that's what it was. I knew then. Like the first time, I probably felt that way, you know, but I didn't know what's happening.

It is only when the novice becomes able to get high in this sense that he will continue to use marihuana for pleasure. In every case in which use continued, the user had acquired the necessary concepts with which to express to himself the fact that he was experiencing new sensations caused by the drug. That is, for use to continue, it is necessary not only to use the drug so as to produce effects but also to learn to perceive these effects when they occur. In this way marihuana acquires meaning for the user as an object which can be used for pleasure.

With increasing experience the user develops a greater appreciation of the drug's effects; he continues to learn to get high. He examines succeeding experiences closely, looking for new effects, making sure the old ones are still there. Out of this there grows a stable set of categories for experiencing the drug's effects whose presence enables the user to get high with ease.

The ability to perceive the drug's effects must be maintained if use is to continue;

if it is lost, marihuana use ceases. Two kinds of evidence support this statement. First, people who become heavy users of alcohol, barbiturates, or opiates do not continue to smoke marihuana, largely because they lose the ability to distinguish between its effects and those of the other drugs.[9] They no longer know whether the marihuana gets them high. Second, in those few cases in which an individual uses marihuana in such quantities that he is always high, he is apt to get this same feeling that the drug has no effect on him, since the essential element of a noticeable difference between feeling high and feeling normal is missing. In such a situation, use is likely to be given up completely, but temporarily, in order that the user may once again be able to perceive the difference.

III

One more step is necessary if the user who has now learned to get high is to continue use. He must learn to enjoy the effects he has just learned to experience. Marihuana-produced sensations are not automatically or necessarily pleasurable. The taste for such experience is a socially acquired one, not different in kind from acquired tastes for oysters or dry martinis. The user feels dizzy, thirsty; his scalp tingles; he misjudges time and distances; and so on. Are these things pleasurable? He isn't sure. If he is to continue marihuana use, he must decide that they are. Otherwise, getting high, while a real enough experience, will be an unpleasant one he would rather avoid.

The effects of the drug, when first perceived, may be physically unpleasant or at least ambiguous:

> It started taking effect, and I didn't know what was happening, you know, what it was, and I was very sick. I walked around the room, walking around the room trying to get off, you know; it just scared me at first, you know. I wasn't used to that kind of feeling.

In addition, the novice's naive interpretation of what is happening to him may further confuse and frighten him, particularly if he decides, as many do, that he is going insane:

> I felt I was insane, you know. Everything people done to me just wigged me. I couldn't hold a conversation, and my mind would be wandering, and I was always thinking, oh, I don't know, weird thing, like hearing music different.... I get the feeling that I can't talk to anyone. I'll goof completely.

Given these typically frightening and unpleasant first experiences, the beginner will not continue use unless he learns to redefine the sensations as pleasurable:

> It was offered to me, and I tried it. I'll tell you one thing. I never did enjoy it at all. I mean it was just nothing that I could enjoy. [Well, did you get high when

[9] "Smokers have repeatedly stated that the consumption of whiskey while smoking negates the potency of the drug. They find it very difficult to get 'high' while drinking whiskey and because of that smokers will not drink while using the 'weed'" (cf. New York City Mayor's Committee on Marihuana, *The Marihuana Problem in the City of New York* [Lancaster, Pa.: Jacques Cattell Press, 1944], p. 13).

you turned on?] Oh, yeah, I got definite feelings from it. But I didn't enjoy them. I mean I got plenty of reactions, but they were mostly reactions of fear. [You were frightened?] Yes. I didn't enjoy it. I couldn't seem to relax with it, you know. If you can't relax with a thing, you can't enjoy it, I don't think.

In other cases the first experiences were also definitely unpleasant, but the person did become a marihuana user. This occurred, however, only after a later experience enabled him to redefine the sensations as pleasurable:

[This man's first experience was extremely unpleasant, involving distortion of spatial relationships and sounds, violent thirst, and panic produced by these symptoms.] After the first time I didn't turn on for about, I'd say, ten months to a year....It wasn't a moral thing; it was because I'd gotten so frightened, bein' so high. An' I didn't want to go through that again, I mean, my reaction was, "Well, if this is what they call bein' high, I don't dig [like] it."... So I didn't turn on for a year almost, accounta that....

Well, my friends started, an' consequently I started again. But I didn't have any more, I didn't have that same initial reaction, after I started turning on again.

[In interaction with his friends he became able to find pleasure in the effects of the drug and eventually became a regular user.]

In no case will use continue without such a redefinition of the effects as enjoyable.

This redefinition occurs, typically, in interaction with more experienced users who, in a number of ways, teach the novice to find pleasure in this experience which is at first so frightening.[10] They may reassure him as to the temporary character of the unpleasant sensations and minimize their seriousness, at the same time calling attention to the more enjoyable aspects. An experienced user describes how he handles newcomers to marihuana use:

Well, they get pretty high sometimes. The average person isn't ready for that, and it is a little frightening to them sometimes. I mean, they've been high on lush [alcohol], and they get higher that way than they've ever been before, and they don't know what's happening to them. Because they think they're going to keep going up, up, up till they lose their minds or begin doing weird things or something. You have to like reassure them, explain to them that they're not really flipping or anything, that they're gonna be all right. You have to just talk them out of being afraid. Keep talking to them, reassuring, telling them it's all right. And come on with your own story, you know: "The same thing happened to me. You'll get to like that after awhile." Keep coming on like that; pretty soon you talk them out of being scared. And besides they see you doing it and nothing horrible is happening to you, so that gives them more confidence.

The more experienced user may also teach the novice to regulate the amount he smokes more carefully, so as to avoid any severely uncomfortable symptoms while retaining the pleasant ones. Finally, he teaches the new user that he can "get to like it after awhile." He teaches him to regard those ambiguous experiences formerly defined as unpleasant as enjoyable. The older user in the following incident is a per-

[10] Charen and Perelman, *op. cit.,* p. 679.

son whose tastes have shifted in this way, and his remarks have the effect of helping others to make a similar redefinition:

A new user had her first experience of the effects of marihuana and became frightened and hysterical. She "felt like she was half in and half out of the room" and experienced a number of alarming physical symptoms. One of the more experienced users present said, "She's dragged because she's high like that. I'd give anything to get that high myself. I haven't been that high in years."

In short, what was once frightening and distasteful becomes, after a taste for it is built up, pleasant, desired, and sought after. Enjoyment is introduced by the favorable definition of the experience that one acquires from others. Without this, use will not continue, for marihuana will not be for the user an object he can use for pleasure.

In addition to being a necessary step in becoming a user, this represents an important condition for continued use. It is quite common for experienced users suddenly to have an unpleasant or frightening experience, which they cannot define as pleasurable, either because they have used a larger amount of marihuana than usual or because it turns out to be a higher-quality marihuana than they expected. The user has sensations which go beyond any conception he has of what being high is and is in much the same situation as the novice, uncomfortable and frightened. He may blame it on an overdose and simply be more careful in the future. But he may make this the occasion for a rethinking of his attitude toward the drug and decide that it no longer can give him pleasure. When this occurs and is not followed by a redefinition of the drug as capable of producing pleasure, use will cease.

The likelihood of such a redefinition occurring depends on the degree of the individual's participation with other users. Where this participation is intensive, the individual is quickly talked out of his feeling against marihuana use. In the next case, on the other hand, the experience was very disturbing, and the aftermath of the incident cut the person's participation with other users to almost zero. Use stopped for three years and began again only when a combination of circumstances, important among which was a resumption of ties with users, made possible a redefinition of the nature of the drug:

It was too much, like I only made about four pokes, and I couldn't even get it out of my mouth, I was so high, and I got real flipped. In the basement, you know, I just couldn't stay in there anymore. My heart was pounding real hard, you know, and was going out of my mind; I thought I was losing my mind completely. So I cut out of this basement, and this other guy, he's out of his mind, told me, "Don't, don't leave me, man. Stay here." And I couldn't.

I walked outside, and it was five below zero, and I thought I was dying, and I had my coat open; I was sweating, I was perspiring. My whole insides were all..., and I walked about two blocks away, and I fainted behind a bush. I don't know how long I laid there. I woke up, and I was feeling the worst, I can't describe it at all, so I made it to a bowling alley, man, and I was trying to act normal, I was trying to shoot pool, you know, trying to act real normal, and I couldn't lay and I couldn't stand up and I couldn't sit down, and I went up and laid down where some guys that spot pins lay down, and that didn't help me, and I went down to a doctor's office.

I was going to go in there and tell the doctor to put me out of my misery ... because my heart was pounding so hard, you know.... So then all week end I started flipping, seeing things there and going through hell, you know, all kinds of abnormal things....I just quit for a long time then.

[He went to a doctor who defined the symptoms for him as those of a nervous breakdown caused by "nerves" and "worries." Although he was no longer using marihuana, he had some recurrences of the symptoms which led him to suspect that "it was all his nerves."] So I just stopped worrying, you know; so it was about thirty-six months later I started making it again. I'd just take a few pokes, you know. [He first resumed use in the company of the same user-friend with whom he had been involved in the original incident.]

A person, then, cannot begin to use marihuana for pleasure, or continue its use for pleasure, unless he learns to define its effects as enjoyable, unless it becomes and remains an object which he conceives of as capable of producing pleasure.

IV

In summary, an individual will be able to use marihuana for pleasure only when he goes through a process of learning to conceive of it as an object which can be used in this way. No one becomes a user without (1) learning to smoke the drug in a way which will produce real effects; (2) learning to recognize the effects and connect them with drug use (learning, in other words, to get high); and (3) learning to enjoy the sensations he perceives. In the course of this process he develops a disposition or motivation to use marihuana which was not and could not have been present when he began use, for it involves and depends on conceptions of the drug which could only grow out of the kind of actual experience detailed above. On completion of this process he is willing and able to use marihuana for pleasure.

He has learned, in short, to answer "Yes" to the question: "Is it fun?" The direction his further use of the drug takes depends on his being able to continue to answer "Yes" to this question and, in addition, on his being able to answer "Yes" to other questions which arise as he becomes aware of the implications of the fact that the society as a whole disapproves of the practice: "It is expedient?" "Is it moral?" Once he has acquired the ability to get enjoyment out of the drug, use will continue to be possible for him. Considerations of morality and expediency, occasioned by the reactions of society, may interfere and inhibit use, but use continues to be a possibility in terms of his conception of the drug. The act becomes impossible only when the ability to enjoy the experience of being high is lost, through a change in the user's conception of the drug occasioned by certain kinds of experience with it.

In comparing this theory with those which ascribe marihuana use to motives or predispositions rooted deep in individual behavior, the evidence makes it clear that marihuana use for pleasure can occur only when the process described above is undergone and cannot occur without it. This is apparently so without reference to the nature of the individual's personal makeup or psychic problems. Such theories assume that people have stable modes of response which predetermine the way they will act in relation to any particular situation or object and that, when they come in contact with the given object or situation, they act in the way in which their makeup predisposes them.

This analysis of the genesis of marihuana use shows that the individuals who come in contact with a given object may respond to it at first in a great variety of ways. If a stable form of new behavior toward the object is to emerge, a transformation of meanings must occur, in which the person develops a new conception of the nature of the object.[11] This happens in a series of communicative acts in which others point out new aspects of his experience to him, present him with new interpretations of events, and help him achieve a new conceptual organization of his world, without which the new behavior is not possible. Persons who do not achieve the proper kind of conceptualization are unable to engage in the given behavior and turn off in the direction of some other relationship to the object or activity.

This suggests that behavior of any kind might fruitfully be studied developmentally, in terms of changes in meanings and concepts, their organization and reorganization, and the way they channel behavior, making some acts possible while excluding others.

[11] Cf. Anselm Strauss, "The Development and Transformation of Monetary Meanings in the Child," *American Sociological Review,* XVII (June, 1952), 275–86.

Section IV

Identities: Social Labeling and Self-labeling

Introductory Remarks

In Section III, it was pointed out that a specific personality trait does not distinguish offenders from nonoffenders. Criminal and delinquent behavior does not arise directly from psychogenic traits. This may be the case, however, for some "lone-wolf" offenders possessing severe psychic pressures and idiosyncratic motives; but sociological perspective sees this as not applying to the large majority expressing criminal and delinquent behavior.

The sociological perspective views commitments to behavior as arising from and through interaction with others. It further views changes in behavior induced by this same process of interaction. We find, therefore, that some careers in criminality end in the juvenile years, and others have their genesis in the adult years. There are still others who alternate from periods of criminal behavior to periods of conventional behavior.

Commitments to behavior are sustained through identities and motives acquired by internalizing the role expectations and judgments of others through processes of social interaction occurring in a social life organization. Identities and motives presently held, however, are subject to modifications by significant changes in social life organization.

The degree of susceptibility to deviance, therefore, with presently held personality traits is modulated by the intensity and the range of identities and of roles held and those to be held. Yet there are many, particularly youth, who are experimenting with incongruent roles and identities and who are not as yet intensely committed to one core identity or another. There are also others who, even though possessing congruencies of roles and identities, secretly satisfy desires through the risks and joys a deviance brings. In both cases the commission of deviant acts does not reflect a fixation to this identity.

We cannot look only toward the act to reveal the total identity of the offender. That is, the acts of individuals may well be similar; but self-labels, motives, and core commitments may indeed vary (e.g., the experimenting or chance deviant versus the career deviant). To understand the progression toward deviance it is most important to detect the effects on identity of others knowing and reacting to the initially visible deviance. The reactions of others in interaction with the offender may contribute both materials toward a core identity and restrictions in the future directions of his social participation.

We therefore arrive at another crucial element to be included in any explanation of criminal and delinquent behavior. We must ask to what extent the reactions of others (formal and informal agents) in processes of interaction may contribute to an increase or a decrease in deviant self-labeling, other than what would have existed. In short, the sources (physiological, psychological, sociocultural, situational) that initially led to the undetected deviances may now combine with or be superseded by the reactions of others (social labeling) in determining progressive commitment to deviance. To what extent do the reactions of others influence the personality? Which potentials of the personality will become nurtured in the relational setting? In fact, to what extent could reactions of others increase personality maladjustments, thereby introducing an increased necessity for intensive individualized treatment?

We shall view in a limited way the renewed focus in sociology: the processes of interaction between offenders and their "conventional judges."

26. The Dramatization of Evil

Frank Tannenbaum

In the conflict between the young delinquent and the community there develop two opposing definitions of the situation. In the beginning the definition of the situation by the young delinquent may be in the form of play, adventure, excitement, interest, mischief, fun. Breaking windows, annoying people, running around porches, climbing over roofs, stealing from pushcarts, playing traunt–all are items of play, adventure, excitement. To the community, however, these activities may and often do take on the form of a nuisance, evil, delinquency, with the demand for control, admonition, chastisement, punishment, police court, truant school. This conflict over the situation is one that arises out of a divergence of values. As the problem develops, the situation gradually becomes redefined. The attitude of the community hardens definitely into a demand for suppression. There is a gradual shift from the definition of the specific acts as evil to a definition of the individual as evil, so that all his acts come to be looked upon with suspicion. In the process of identification his companions, hang-outs, play, speech, income, all his conduct, the personality itself, become subject to scrutiny and question. From the community's point of view, the individual who used to do bad and mischievous things has now become

Reprinted from Frank Tannenbaum, "The Dramatization of Evil," from *Crime and Community* (New York: Columbia University Press, 1938), pp. 17–20, by permission of Columbia University Press.

a bad and unredeemable human being. From the individual's point of view there has taken place a similar change. He has gone slowly from a sense of grievance and injustice, of being unduly mistreated and punished, to a recognition that the definition of him as a human being is different from that of other boys in his neighborhood, his school, street, community. This recognition on his part becomes a process of self-identification and integration with the group which shares his activities. It becomes, in part, a process of rationalization; in part, a simple response to a specialized type of stimulus. The young delinquent becomes bad because he is defined as bad and because he is not believed if he is good. There is a persistent demand for consistency in character. The community cannot deal with people whom it cannot define. Reputation is this sort of public definition. Once it is established, then unconsciously all agencies combine to maintain this definition even when they apparently and consciously attempt to deny their own implicit judgment.

• • •

The first dramatization of the "evil" which separates the child out of his group for specialized treatment plays a greater role in making the criminal than perhaps any other experience. It cannot be too often emphasized that for the child the whole situation has become different. He now lives in a different world. He has been tagged. A new and hitherto non-existent environment has been precipitated out for him.

The process of making the criminal, therefore, is a process of tagging, defining, identifying, segregating, describing, emphasizing, making conscious and self-conscious; it becomes a way of stimulating, suggesting, emphasizing, and evoking the very traits that are complained of. If the theory of relation of response to stimulus has any meaning the entire process of dealing with the young delinquent is mischievous in so far as it identifies him to himself or to the environment as a delinquent person.

The person becomes the thing he is described as being. Nor does it seem to matter whether the valuation is made by those who would punish or by those who would reform. In either case the emphasis is upon the conduct that is disapproved of. The parents or the policeman, the older brother or the court, the probation officer or the juvenile institution, in so far as they rest upon the thing complained of, rest upon a false ground. Their very enthusiasm defeats their aim. The harder they work to reform the evil, the greater the evil grows under their hands. The persistent suggestion, with whatever good intentions, works mischief, because it leads to bringing out the bad behavior that it would suppress. The way out is through a refusal to dramatize the evil. The less said about it the better. The more said about something else, still better.

The hard-drinker who keeps thinking of not drinking is doing what he can to initiate the acts which lead to drinking. He is starting with the stimulus to his habit. To succeed he must find some positive interest or line of action which will inhibit the drinking series and which by instituting another course of action will bring him to his desired end.[1]

[1] John Dewey, *Human Nature and Conduct,* p. 35. New York, 1922.

The dramatization of the evil therefore tends to precipitate the conflict situation which was first created through some innocent maladjustment. The child's isolation forces him into companionship with other children similarly defined, and the gang becomes his means of escape, his security. The life of the gang gives it special mores, and the attack by the community upon these mores merely overemphasizes the conflict already in existence, and makes it the source of a new series of experiences that lead directly to a criminal career.

In dealing with the delinquent, the criminal, therefore, the important thing to remember is that we are dealing with a human being who is responding normally to the demands, stimuli, approval, expectancy, of the group with whom he is associated. We are dealing not with an individual but with a group.

27. The Concept of Secondary Deviation

Edwin M. Lemert

In an earlier book[1] I proposed the concept of secondary deviation to call attention to the importance of the societal reaction in the etiology of deviance, the forms it takes, and its stabilization in deviant social roles or behavior systems. Sympathetic reception of the idea by a number of reputable sociologists and by unheralded teachers in the field has encouraged me to undertake further clarification of the concept to articulate it with some of the newer ideas which have come out of sociological studies of deviance.

The notion of secondary deviation was devised to distinguish between *original* and *effective* causes of deviant attributes and actions which are associated with physical defects and incapacity, crime, prostitution, alcoholism, drug addiction, and mental disorders. Primary deviation, as contrasted with secondary, is polygenetic, arising out of a variety of social, cultural, pychological, and physiological factors, either in adventitious or recurring combinations. While it may be socially recognized and even defined as undesirable, primary deviation has only marginal implications for the

From Edwin M. Lemert, *Human Deviance, Social Problems, and Social Control,* ©1967. Reprinted by permission of Prentice-Hall, Inc., Englewood Cliffs, New Jersey.

[1] Edwin M. Lemert, *Social Pathology* (New York: McGraw-Hill Book Company, 1951), pp. 75 f.

status and psychic structure of the person concerned. Resultant problems are dealt with reciprocally in the context of established status relationships. This is done either through *normalization,* in which the deviance is perceived as normal variation—a problem of everyday life—or through management and nominal controls which do not seriously impede basic accommodations people make to get along with each other.

Secondary deviation refers to a special class of socially defined responses which people make to problems created by the societal reaction to their deviance. These problems are essentially moral problems which revolve around stigmatization, punishments, segregation, and social control. Their general effect is to differentiate the symbolic and interactional environment to which the person responds, so that early or adult socialization is categorically affected. They become central facts of existence for those experiencing them, altering psychic structure, producing specialized organization of social roles and self-regarding attitudes. Actions which have these roles and self attitudes as their referents make up secondary deviance. The secondary deviant, as opposed to his actions, is a person whose life and identity are organized around the facts of deviance.

Parenthetically it needs comment that all or most persons have physical attributes or histories of past moral transgressions, even crimes, about which they are sufficiently self-conscious to have developed techniques for accepting and transforming, or psychologically nullifying degrading or punitive societal reactions. Recognition of this compromised state of mankind led Goffman in his sensitive analysis of stigma to hold that secondary deviation is simply the extreme of a graded series of moral adaptations, found among "normal" persons as well as those with socially obtrusive stigma.[2] I believe, however, that this overlooks the fact that stigma involves categorical societal definitions which depict polarized moral opposites, and also that self definitions or identities are integral in the sense that individuals respond to themselves as moral types.

Moreover, whereas Goffman addresses himself to the question of how persons manage stigma and mitigate its consequences, secondary deviation concerns processes which create, maintain, or intensify stigma; it presumes that stigma may be unsuccessfully contained and lead to repetition of deviance similar or related to that which originally initiated stigmatization. Also, it does not exclude the possibility that stigmatized deviance may be strategic, willful, or readily accepted as a solution to problems of the person standing in a stigmatized position.

The way in which a person presents himself in public encounters, particularly in an attenuated, pluralistic society, does much to direct the kinds of reactions others make to him and by such means he protects cherished aspects of his identity. However, to dwell upon the cognitive, dramatic details of face-to-face interaction is to grapple with only part of the thorny question of secondary deviance. Over and beyond these are macrocosmic, organizational forces of social control through which public and private agencies actively define and classify people, impose punishments,

[2] Erving Goffman, *Stigma* (Englewood Cliffs, N.J.: Prentice-Hall, Inc., 1962), p. 127.

restrict or open access to rewards and satisfactions, set limits to social interaction, and induct deviants into special, segregated environments.[3]

Although the ideas of personal adaptation and maladaptation rest uneasily in a kind of sociological limbo, the conception of primary and secondary deviance inclines thought in their direction, or at least toward some comparable terms. Their consideration makes it clear that awareness of unenviable features of the self is a complex rather than a simple reciprocal of societal insults to identity, and, further, that adaptations can turn into maladaptations on the person's own terms.[4] This comes to light where efforts at validating the self are complicated by distinct feelings of hopelessness, entrapment, or loss of control over actions presumed to be volitional. These can be observed in certain forms of deviance best described as self-defeating; their peculiar, illogical manifestations speak of underlying difficulty or dilapidation in the communication process by which self and other are constituted.

The Societal Reaction

The societal reaction is a very general term summarizing both the expressive reactions of others (moral indignation) toward deviation and action directed to its control. In broad purview the societal reaction often presents a paradox in that societies appear to sustain as well as penalize actions and classes of people categorized as immoral, criminal, incompetent, or irresponsible. The tendency of societies to sustain deviance was recognized quite early by Durkheim and by Marx, and recently in more explicit statements by Dentler and Erikson, and Coser.[5] Their line of thought emphasizes the functional necessity of deviance for promoting group solidarity, differentiating what is moral or goal-worthy, and for keeping society's defense mechanisms at standby readiness. Their propositions are commendable as general orientations to the study of deviance, but in my estimation do not account for secondary deviance and its variable emergence at different times and places. Explanations of the latter call for more detailed formulation of the processes by which societies create moral problems for deviants, define, and punish or reward the individual deviant's attempts to deal with such problems in a configuration of general life problems.

Stigmatization

Stigmatization describes a process attaching visible signs of moral inferiority to persons, such as invidious labels, marks, brands, or publicly disseminated information.

[3] John Kitsuse and Aaron Cicourel, "A Note on the Uses of Official Statistics," *Social Problems,* 11 (1963), 131–39.

[4] On this point see Messinger's criticism of Goffman Sheldon Messinger, "Life as a Theatre," *Sociometry,* 25 (1962), 98–109.

[5] Emile Durkheim, *The Division of Labor in Society* (New York: Free Press of Glencoe, Inc., 1949), pp. 99–103; Robert Dentler and Kai Erikson, "The Functions of Deviance in Groups," *Social Problems,* 7 (1959), 98–107; Lewis Coser, "Some Functions of Deviant Behavior and Normative Flexibility," *American Journal of Sociology,* 68 (1962), 172–81. The reference to Marx is found in Coser's article.

However, it defines more than the formal action of a community toward a misbehaving or physically different member. Degradation rituals, such as drumming the coward out of the regiment, administering the pauper's oath, diagnosing the contagious illness, and finding the accused guilty as charged may dramatize the facts of deviance, but their "success" is gauged less by their manner or enactment than by their pervailing consequences.[6] The point is commonly illustrated by the initial court appearance of the errant juvenile. The ancient ceremonial there may strike him with awe and fear, but if nothing much happens as a consequence, the memory fades or is retrospectively rationalized. Whatever the deviance, it remains primary.

An assertion, by no means new, is that for stigmatization to establish a total deviant identity it must be disseminated throughout society. Lecky spoke strongly on this point, contending that the solid front of public opinion against the "slightest frailty" among women in mid-nineteenth century England did much to add to the ranks of habitual prostitutes. To his view the "terrible censure" of opinion and the deep degradation of unchaste women caused the status of the prostitute to be irrevocable, and likewise contributed heavily to the associated crime of infanticide.[7]

Much the same thought was voiced by G. H. Mead, who first approximated a theory of criminal stigma in terms of the amount and kind of punishments inflicted upon law violators. His thesis, generically similar to Durkheim's, stressed the function of punishments in preserving group cohesion, but went further to show that deterrent punishments, conjoined with pursuit, detection, and prosecution, are incompatible with reinstatement of the criminal in society. Such a system, by suppressing all but aggressive attitudes toward the lawbreaker, effectively destroys communication and generates hostility in the criminal. Mead's conclusion, clearly a partial recognition of secondary deviance, was that a system of deterrent punishments not only fails to repress crime but also "preserves a criminal class."[8]

The Sense of Injustice

When scrutiny is narrowed to uncover the finer ways in which stigmatization fixes deviance and subjectively incorporates a deviant version of the self, the notion of total stigma gives some difficulties. Mead held that impartiality, maximization, and the *consistent* application of punishment, expressed in the "fixed attitude towards the jailbird," provoked intransigeance and hostility in the criminal. He seemed to take it for granted that such reactive antagonism led to further crime. To emphasize this interpretation he cited the individualized justice of the newly developed juvenile court as an example of alternative corrective procedure most suited to avoid stigma-

[6] Garfinkel's article on the subject, while a succinct discussion of the requirements for successful denunciation of deviants, does not consider what happens or must happen afterwards. Harold Garfinkel, "Conditions of Successful Degradation Cerominies," *American Journal of Sociology*, 61 (1956), 420–24.

[7] William Lecky, *History of European Morals* (New York: George Braziller, Inc., 1955), pp. 282–86.

[8] George H. Mead, "The Psychology of Punitive Justice," *American Journal of Sociology*, 23 (1928), 577–602.

tization and the recidivism otherwise likely to flow from deterrent punishments.

Standing in contrast if not opposition to Mead's conception of stigma are the views of later writers who assert that *inconsistent* imposition of punishments is the prime factor which sets youth in criminal careers, largely through the arousal of a natural sense of injustice. This idea was originally brought forward in obscure reports appended to some of the numerous crime surveys carried out in American cities between 1920 and 1930. Pound, Osborne, Chaffee, Jr., Stern, and Pollak severally and jointly noted the prevalent confusion in jurisdictions, procedures, and philosophies within or between law administering agencies, and they concluded that this could be vital in diverting occasional youthful offenders into habitual crime, primarily through engendering a sense of unfairness.[9]

> Not to be overlooked is the effect of unfairness upon the accused. Even if he is guilty there may be degrees of criminality which he may not have reached...but... if he feels deeply and justly that society...has behaved tyranically and brutally ... the natural effect of this emotion is to alienate him still further from the community and make him regard his criminal associates as the only ones who treat him decently. In consequence he may leave prison a bitter enemy of society, more willing than before to continue a criminal career.

Recent writers such as Cloward and Ohlin, and Matza, pursue much the same thought, but also show how "undue deprivation" and the sense of injustice support or reinforce a subcultural ideology of delinquency.[10] Matza holds the thesis, directly contradictory to Mead's that juvenile court procedure amounts to inconsistent punishment, that its very precept of individualized justice, when coupled with judicial arbitrariness and shifting group pressures reflected in court decisions, becomes from phenomenological perspective an affront to the charged youth's sense of the just.

The apparent contradiction that both consistency and inconsistency in the administration of punishments conduce to secondary deviance dissolves if several dimensions of inconsistency or, better, incommensurability, in punishments are recognized: (1) inconsistency or disproportion between stigma or punishments and the deviant attributes or actions toward which they are directed; (2) inconsistent applications of stigma or penalties to the same person at different times or places; and (3) inconsistent penalties or stigma applied to persons in the same jurisdiction or by the same law officials.

The definition of stigmatization as a collective process which necessarily misrepresents what a person has done and attacks his integrity permits the deduction that

[9] See Roscoe Pound's summary in the *Cleveland Crime Survey*, (Cleveland: Cleveland Foundation, 1922), pp. 585–ff; also Alfred Bettman, "Confusion of Concepts," *National Commission on Law Observance and Enforcement: Report of the Prosecution* (Washington, D.C.: Government Printing Office, 1931), pp. 161–66; the excerpt is from Zechariah Chaffee, Jr., Walter Pollak, and Carl Stern, "Unfairness in Prosecutions," ibid., p. 268.

[10] Richard Cloward and Lloyd Ohlin, *Delinquency and Opportunity* (New York: Free Press of Glencoe, Inc., 1960), pp. 117–21; David Matza, *Delinquency and Drift* (New York: John Wiley & Sons, Inc., 1964), Chap. 4; see also Allen Barton and Saul Mendlovitz, "The Experience of Injustice as a Research Problem," *Journal of Legal Education*, 13 (1960), 24–39.

it "naturally" arouses feelings of injustice.[11] The fact that a wide variety of deviants–the physically handicapped, stutterers, homosexuals, drug addicts, alcoholics, mental patients, as well as delinquents and criminals–express such feelings turns empirical support to this hypothesis. But whether in fact a felt sense of unjust treatment at the hands of society in itself leads on to renewed deviance requires an order of assumptions many sociologists would be unwilling to make. Perhaps it is best regarded as a precipitating factor in some but not all forms of secondary deviance. It becomes one of the problems imposed by the societal reaction. More important is the expression and structuring of such feelings, and their reception by others. While sub-groups and subcultural ideologies assume obvious importance here, I believe such subjective reactions are most profitably studied in a larger context of organized social control.[12]

...

Process and Secondary Deviance

The most general process by which status and role transitions take place is socialization. As it has been applied to the study of deviants the concept has been further circumscribed to designate such processes as criminalization, prisonization, "sophistication," "hardening," pauperization, addiction, conversion, radicalization, professionalization, and "mortification of self." All of these speak in varying degrees of a personal progression or differentiation in which the individual acquires: (1) morally inferior status; (2) special knowledge and skills; (3) an integral attitude or "world view;" and (4) a distinctive self-image based upon but not necessarily coterminous with his image reflected in interaction with others.

The earliest descriptions of deviant socialization current in sociology came from Shaw's documents on delinquent careers. These were likened to natural histories and so titled, but their descriptive content was derived from the delinquent's "own story," as related to an interviewer.[13] From a present-day perspective these studies appear to have been colored by Shaw's unconcealed interest in reform and the probable interest of the respondent in supporting Shaw's views. Valuable as the stories

[11] For a discussion which derives the sense of injustice from natural law see Edmond Cahn, *The Sense of Injustice* (New York: New York University Press, 1949); whether natural laws need to be invoked is debatable. It is equally plausible to argue that a sense of justice is learned in primary group experiences, or that it reflects one of what Cooley called the primary group values.

[12] It may be that the sense of distrust or that one is a distrusted person, cuts across a wider population of deviants, and does more to explain their alienation. It indicates to the stigmatized person the ominous magnitude of his problem, not only the large number of social positions from which he is likely to be excluded, but also his difficulties of normalizing interaction.

[13] Clifford Shaw, *The Jack Roller* (Chicago: University of Chicago Press, 1930). Goffman uses the concept "moral career" as a broad orientation to changes over time basic and common to persons in a social category. He regards it as a two-sided perspective which shifts back and forth between the self and its significant society. Erving Goffman, "The Moral Career of the Mental Patient," *Psychiatry,* 22 (1959), 123–42.

were and still are for certain purposes, they carried unavoidable overtones of nineteenth-century entrepreneurial ideology in reverse, resembling "sad tales," or reminiscent of Hogarth's rake's progress, or early moral propaganda tracts which portray prostitution as the "road to ruin."

The deviant career concept also has been linked with or partly derived from an occupational model, examples of which are found in the descriptions of criminal behavior systems, such as thieving, and the marginal deviance of dance musicians.[14] The occupational parallel, of course, can be demonstrated in the professionalization of some types of thieves, prostitutes, political radicals, vagrants, bohemians (beatniks), beggars, and to some extent the physically handicapped. In contrast to these, however, there is little indication of an occupational orientation among alcoholics, mentally disordered persons, stutterers, homosexuals, and systematic check forgers.

Closer examination of the career concept suggests that its application to deviance should be guarded. I doubt, for example, that the notion of "recruitment" of persons to most kinds of deviance can be any more than a broad analogy. While learning specialized knowledge from other deviants is a condition of some deviance, it is not so for all, and the notion that deviants serve an "apprenticeship" may be more figurative than literal where it is applicable. A career denotes a course to be run, but the delineation of fixed sequences or stages through which persons move from less to more serious deviance is difficult or impossible to reconcile with an interactional theory. Furthermore, no incontrovertible evidence has yet been marshaled to justify the belief that prodromal signs of deviance exist—either in behaviors or in personality syndromes such as "predelinquent," "prepsychotic," or "addiction-prone." The flux and pluralism of modern society make concepts of drift contingency, and risk far more meaningful in deviance than inevitability or linear progress.

A more defensible conception of deviant career is that of recurrent or typical contingencies and problems awaiting someone who continues in a course of action, with the added notion that there may be theoretically "best" choices set into a situation by prevailing technology and social structure. There is some predictive value of a limited or residual nature in concepts like "turning points" or "points of no return," which have been brought into the sociological analysis of careers. These allow it to be said that persons having undergone certain changes will not or cannot retrace their steps; deviant actions act as social foreclosures which qualitatively change meanings and shift the scope of alternatives within which new choices can be made.[15] Even here a caveat is necessary, for alcoholics, drug addicts, criminals, and other

[14] E. H. Sutherland, *The Professional Thief* (Chicago: University of Chicago Press, 1937); Howard Becker, *Outsiders* (London: Free Press of Glencoe, 1963), Chaps. 5, 6; C. Cambor, Gerald Lesowitz, and Miles Miller, "Creative Jazz Musicians: a Clinical Study," *Psychiatry,* 25 (1960), 1–15; Raymond Mack, "The Jazz Community," *Social Forces,* 38 (1960), 211–22.

[15] See Lemert *Social Pathology,* Chap. 4; also Becker, *op. cit.,* Chap. 2; for a careful evaluation and critique of attempts to predict delinquency; see Jackson Toby, "An Evaluation of Early Identification and Intensive Treatment Programs for Predelinquents," *Social Problems,* 13 (1965), 161–75.

deviants do sometimes make comebacks in the face of stigma, and an early history of deviance may in some instances lead to success in the conventional world.

Drift, Contingency, and Discovery

While some fortunate individuals by insightful endowment or by virtue of the stabilized nature of their situations can foresee more distant social consequences of their actions and behave accordingly, not so most people. Much human behavior is situationally oriented and geared to meeting the many and shifting claims which others make upon them.[16] The loose structuring and swiftly changing facade and content of modern social situations frequently make it difficult to decide which means will insure ends sought. Often choice is a compromise between what is sought and what can be sought. Finally, even more important, situations and the actions involved often are defined after they occur, or late in the course of interaction when formal social controls intrude. Where deviance is a possible contingency, delayed definition is more likely than early.

All of this makes me believe that most people drift into deviance by specific actions rather than by informed choices of social roles and statuses. Each of such actions has its consequence and rationale and leaves a residual basis for possible future action depending on the problems solved or the new problems brought to life. From the societal side, repetition of deviant action may be ignored or normalized by those who are thereby threatened, or it may be compounded through patronage of associates who have something to gain from it. The pimp may encourage his new female conquest in her belief that she is entertaining men for pay because she "loves him so." The family of the heavy-drinking man erects perceptual defenses against seeing his action as alcoholism because they, like him, are distressed by this ascription of meaning. The ideological gulf between stereotypes of good and bad, acting in concert with prevalent medical conceptions of deviance as the symptom of a defective or "sick" personality strengthens such normalizing tendencies by inhibiting recognition of similarities between the primary deviant and stigmatized persons. Meantime they allow the drift to deviance to go on.

This may proceed from one of two kinds of psychological states: in one the individual has no prior awareness that such actions are defined or definable as deviant; he must learn or must apply the definitions to his attributes or actions.[17] In the other the person already has learned the definitions but progressively rationalizes

[16] The concept of drift comes from Matza, *op. cit.*, Chap. 1, esp. pp. 27–30.

[17] Lindesmith, of course, has held that opiate addiction depends upon learning that withdrawal symptoms can be alleviated by taking more opiates. Alfred Lindesmith, *Opiate Addiction* (San Antonio, Tex.: Principia Press, 1947). A study of teen-age drug users in New York found that lack of deterrent information was a factor in willingness to try heroin. However, shift to regular use was explained on the basis of a need. In some cases youths began regular use after one shot, saying in effect, "This is what I have been waiting for all my life." While such a person might be "hooked" in a figurative sense, the full social and physiological implications of addiction come later when he becomes a "frantic junkie." Isidor Chein, Donald Gerard, Robert Lee, and Eva Rosenberg, *The Road To H* (New York: Basic Books, Inc., 1964), Chap. VI.

or dissociates them from his actions. Unequivocal perception of a deviant self comes when the person enters new settings, when supportive (normalizing) interaction with intimates becomes antagonistic, or when contact is made with stigmatizing agencies of social control. In other cases internal changes or changes in the feedback of meanings from the actions themselves bare the new self.[18]

Whether the imputation of self-characteristics, or "labeling" in itself initiates or causes deviant acts is something of a moot point. The possibility cannot be arbitrarily ruled out, but it moves onto questionable grounds where social reality is made coterminous with ideas and symbolic representations. Erik Erikson, not to be designated as an idealist, speaks of changes from positive to negative identities which result from societal diagnosis by the "balance of us." This is illustrated by the mother who constantly berates her daughter as "immoral," "no good," or "tramp." The girl in time may yield to the derogatory self-image because it is nearest and "most real" to her. Yet Erikson is careful to say that this may be only a final step in the acquisition of a negative self-image, and he also refers to the necessity of confirming changes in identity.[19] I take this to be a way of saying that there must be some basis for validating a degrading self-conception in prior acts, to which I would add that it also needs subsequent overt acts to clothe it with social reality. Such acts may be fortuitous or they may be deliberate in origin, but in any case they conclude with some manner of interpersonal involvement or commitments. More complete data collected in actual cases similar to the hypotehtical case in question often disclose that the girl takes some precipitant action, such as running away from home, is then arrested and handled in a way to confirm the mother's expectation. Even more tangible confirmation transpires if, as may happen, she is picked up by strange men who take her in charge and exploit her sexually.

While an abiding deviant self demands validation and reinforcement in social interaction, it overdraws the social to insist that self-discovery always has immediate antecedents in participant social interaction dramatizing good and evil. Revelations may be little more than solitary moments of disenchantment, points at which a fabric of rationalizations collapses in the face of repeated contradictions from cumulative experiences. The alcoholic looks at his dirty clothes, shabby hotel room with a

[18] Tannenbaum, whose early ideas came close to a statement of secondary deviance, believed that delinquency was the outcome of a hardening process observable in conflict of youthful gangs with police and with other gangs. In the process, new definitions get placed on their actions. This, of course, was a forerunner of the subcultural, learning conception of delinquency. Frank Tannenbaum, *Crime and The Community* (New York: Columbia University Press, 1957), esp. pp. 19–22; More recent views, such as those of Sykes and Matza, direct attention to the coexistence of conventional as well as criminal values, in the delinquent youth, his ambivalence, and resolutions of the ambivalence through a process of neutralization. Gresham Sykes and David Matza, "Techniques of Neutralization: A Theory of Delinquency," *American Sociological Review,* 22 (1957), 664–70; David Matza and Gresham Sykes, "Juvenile Delinquency and Subterranean Values," *American Sociological Review,* 26 (1961), 712–19.

[19] Helen Witmer and Ruth Kotinsky, eds. *New Perspectives on Delinquency*, Washington, D.C.: U.S. Department of Health, Education, and Welfare, No. 56 (1956), pp. 1–23.

scattered array of empty bottles, and realizes the pretense that he is "between jobs," or still the best auto salesman in town is just pretense and nothing more. The check forger finally throws away a book listing his victims and with it the idea that he will some day repay the sums he has carefully noted by their names. The form of the deviance, the situation, and the flow of meaning in face-to-face interaction undoubtedly have great importance in normalizing action and supporting perceptual defenses against the slow stain of deviation, but the logic of self-discovery is an inner one.

The Secondary Deviant

Devaluation of the self on society's terms ordinarily has a sequel of internal or psychic struggle, greatest where the sense of continuity of the self is massively threatened. Some persons never move beyond this state, overtly striving to conform at times, at others entangling themselves with deviance. Terms like "unorganized" or "transitional" deviance may be apt descriptions of their actions for certain purposes. Assuming that the person moves further toward deviance, the abatement of his conflicts usually follows discovery that his status as deviant, although degraded is by no means as abysmal as represented in moral ideologies. The blinded war veteran learns that blindness is not a stark tragedy but more like a "damned nuisance," and that life is possible, particularly if a lot of "charitable" people would leave him alone. The prostitute soon realizes that her new life is sometimes rough and unpredictable, and that arrest is a hazard, but it is not a life of shame. Having discovered the prosaic nature of much of his life under a new status, the deviant, like other people, usually tries to make out as best he can.[20] What happens will be conditioned by several factors:[21] (1) the clarity with which a role or roles can be defined; (2) the possession or acquisition of attributes, knowledge, and skills to enact, improvise, and invent roles; and (3) the motivation to play his role or roles.

A great deal can be said, mostly illustrative, about the first two items. Confidence men, for example, have clearly defined occupational roles in a criminal world, but not many persons are recruited to the roles because they lack the requisite skills and knowledge for this exacting form of thievery. In decided contrast, there are few or no specialized roles available to stutterers, save perhaps that of a clown or an entertainer. Fashioning their own roles is difficult because effective speech is a requirement for most social roles. Consequently they are reduced to filling conventional occupational roles usually below their educational or skills level, becoming, in a figurative sense, ridiculous or strangely silent hewers of wood and haulers of water.

[20] This may be likened to playing a game with new and not very favorable rules. Tannenbaum described it in connection with the professional criminal; "After a while he accepts it (the game) as a matter of course. He bargains upon the amount of freedom he may have, hopes for escape, for total freedom from arrest, but bargains with fate and gives hostages to freedom, calculates his chances and accepts the inevitable with stoicism." Frank Tannenbaum, The Professional Criminal, *op. cit.*, p. 584.

[21] I am indebted for these ideas to William Robinson who some years ago in a seminar at UCLA suggested them as a parsimonious summary of Leonard Cottrell's article, "The Adjustment of the Individual to His Age and Sex Roles," *American Sociological Review*. 7 (1942), 617-620.

Somewhere between the two extremes of confidence men and stutterer is the drug addict, most of whom in our society are excluded from conventional occupations and tend to be excluded from professional or organized criminal pursuits. However, they may elect to be petty thieves, burglars, prostitutes, hustlers, stool pigeons, or choose to peddle drugs to other addicts.

While the social roles available to deviants vary in number, kind, and degree of stigmatization there is always some basis for adaptation or a modus vivendi open to the deviant. Moreover, attributes can be faked or concealed and some measure of skills and knowledge learned, whether they be means of filling the leftover, low-status roles of conventional society or those more explicitly defined as immoral or criminal. Such conclusions furnish the more pertinent one that secondary deviance to a large extent becomes a phenomenon of motivation.

Motivation and learning

If motivation to exploit the possibilities of degraded status and to play a deviant role are critical aspects of transition to secondary deviance, then analysis is pushed toward some form of learning theory, preferably one which accounts for the variable social meanings of satisfactions, rewards, and punishments. This enters an area little trod by sociologists and to some extent looked upon as an alien if not sterile preoccupation of psychologists. Yet notwithstanding the criticism that the laws of learning have been largely formal and devoid of content, the outlook is less bleak than sometimes pictured—particularly where efforts have been made to bring together dynamic personality theory and ego-psychology with newer formulations of the learning process.

If nothing else, common sense dictates that some variant of the law of effect be made part of the explanation of secondary deviance. This is true even in the face of the formidable task of specifying what is rewarding or punishing to human beings, whose actions in contrast to those of the rest of the animal world are complicated by symbolic learning and delayed gratification. Restated and applied to deviance, the law of effect is a simple idea that people beset with problems posed for them by society will choose lines of action they expect to be satisfactory solutions to the problems. If the consequences are those expected, the likelihood that the action or generically similar action will be repeated is increased. If the consequences are unsatisfactory, unpleasant, or make more problems than they solve, then the pattern of action will be avoided.[22] The fact that anticipation of satisfactions or expectation of punishments is a cognitive process based upon symbolic learning as well as experience does not vitiate the principle of effect; it only reasserts the longstanding need to show how individuals evaluate their own responses in a world where the accommodations of others become means to ends. The absence of any well worked-out

[22] The law of effect was originally stated by the psychologist, E. L. Thorndike. For a discussion of his principle and learning theory in general, see O. Hobart Mowrer, *Learning Theory and Behavior* (New York: John Wiley & Sons, Inc., 1960), Chap. I.

theory for doing this leaves the field open to several propositions which may be suitable for further study of the process of evaluation connected with secondary deviance.

1. Defining one's self as deviant is instrumental in seeking out means of satisfaction and mitigating stigmatization. The redefinition of self leads to reinterpretation of past experiences, which in turn reduces inner tensions and conflict. Ends and means are more easily sorted out, and personal accommodations established necessary to utilize available alternatives.
2. The value hierarchy of the degraded individual changes, in the process of which ends become means and means become ends. Conventional punishments lose their efficacy with loss of status. Experiences at one time evaluated as degrading may shift full arc to become rewarding. The alcoholic is an example; deeply ashamed by his first stay in jail, he may as years go by come to look upon arrest as a means of getting food, shelter, and a chance to sober up.
3. Persons who renounce higher status are less affected by the promise of remote satisfactions and more by those within their immediate ken. This is related to the degree of degradation, and also to incarceration or hospital sojourns which determine the point in personal life cycles at which evaluations are made. Deprivation and long experience with highly specific systems of sanctions within control institutions reinforce a world view of the attainable over the achievable.
4. Once deviance becomes a way of life the personal issue often becomes the costs of making a change rather than the higher status to be gained through rehabilitation or reform. Such costs are calculated in terms of the time, energy, and distress seen necessary to change.

28. Secrecy and Presentation of Self

*Howard S. Becker**

The analysis is based on fifty intensive interviews with marihuana users from a variety of social backgrounds and present position in society.**

...

Marihuana use is limited .... to the extent that individuals actually find it inexpedient or believe that they will find it so. This inexpediency, real or presumed, arises from the fact or belief that if non-users discover that one uses the drug, sanctions of some important kind will be applied. The user's conception of these sanctions is vague, because few of them seem ever to have had such an experience or to have known anyone who did. Although he does not know what specifically to expect in the way of punishments, the outlines are clear: he fears repudiation by people whose respect and acceptance he requires both practically and emotionally. That is, he expects that his relationships with non-users will be disturbed and disrupted if they should find out, and limits and controls his behavior accordingly.

This kind of control breaks down in the course of the user's participation with other users and in the development of his experience with the drug, as he comes to realize that, though it might be true that sanctions would be applied if non-users found out, they need never find out. At each level of use, there is a growth in this realization which makes the new level possible.

For the beginner, these considerations are very important and must be overcome if use is to be undertaken at all. These fears are challenged by the sight of others–more experienced users–who apparently feel there is little or no danger and appear to engage in the activity with impunity. If one does "try it once," he may still his fears by observations of this kind. Participation with other users thus furnishes the beginner with the rationalizations with which first to attempt the act.

Reprinted from "Marihuana Use and Social Control," *Journal of Social Problems,* 3:1 (July 1955), 35, 36, 38–41, by permission of The Society for the Study of Social Problems and the author.

*The research on which this paper is based was done while I was a member of the staff of the Chicago Narcotics Survey, a project done by the Chicago Area Project, Inc., under a grant from the National Mental Health Institute. I wish to thank Eliot Freidson, Erving Goffman, Anselm Strauss, and R. Richard Wohl for reading and commenting on an earlier version.

**Most of the interviews were done by me. I wish to thank Solomon Kobrin and Harold Finestone for allowing me to make use of interviews done by them.

Further participation in the marihuana use of these groups allows the novice to draw the further conclusion that the act can be safe no matter how often indulged in, as long as one is careful and makes sure that non-users are not present or likely to intrude. This kind of perspective is a necessary prerequisite for occasional use, in which the drug is used when other users invite one to join them. While it permits this level of use, such a perspective does not allow regular use to occur for the worlds of user and non-users, while separate to a degree allowing the occasional use pattern to persist, are not completely segregated. The points where these worlds meet appear dangerous to the occasional user who must, therefore, confine his use to those occasions on which such meetings does not seem likely.

Regular use, on the other hand, implies a systematic and routine use of the drug which does not take into account such possibilities and plan periods of "getting high" around them. It is a mode of use which depends on another kind of attitude toward the possibility of non-users finding out, the attitude that marihuana use can be carried on under the noses on non-users, or, alternatively, on the living of a pattern of social participation which reduces contacts with non-users almost to the zero point. Without this adjustment in attitude, participation, or both, the user is forced to remain at the level of occasional use. These adjustments take place in terms of two categories or risks involved: First, that non-users will discover marihuana in one's possession and second, that one will be unable to hide the effects of the drug when he is "high" while with non-users.

The difficulities of the would-be regular user, in terms of possession, are illustrated in the remarks of a young man who unsuccessfully attempted regular use while living with his parents:

> I never did like to have it around the house, you know. (Why?) Well, I thought maybe my mother might find it or something like that. (What do you think she'd say?) Oh, well, you know, like...well they never do mention it, you know, anything about dope addicts or anything like that but it would be a really bad thing in my case, I know, because of the big family I come from. And my sisters and brothers, they'd put me down the worst. (And you don't want that to happen?) No, I'm afraid not.

In such cases, envisioning the consequences of such a secret being discovered prevents the person from maintaining the supply essential to regular use. Use remains erratic, since it must depend on encounters with other users and cannot occur whenever the user desires.

Unless he discovers some method of overcoming this difficulty, the person can progress to regular use only when the relationship deterring use is broken. People do not ordinarily leave their homes and families in order to smoke marihuana regularly. But if they do, for whatever reason, regular use, heretofore proscribed, becomes a possibility. Confirmed regular users often take into very serious account the effect on their drug use of forming new social relationships with non-users:

> I wouldn't marry someone who would be belligerent if I do (smoke marihuana), you know, I mean, I wouldn't marry a woman who would be so untrusting as to

think I would do something...I mean, you know, like hurt myself or try to hurt someone.

If such attachments are formed, use tends to revert to the occasional level:

(This man had used marihuana quite intensively but his wife objected to it.) Of course, largely the reason I cut off was my wife. These were a few times when I'd feel like...didn't actually crave for it but would just like to have had some. (He was unable to continue using the drug except irregularly, on those occasions when he was away from his wife's presence and control.)

If the person moves almost totally into the user group, the problem ceases in many respects to exist, and it is possible for regular use to occur except when some new connection with the more conventional world is made.

If a person uses marihuana regularly and routinely it is almost inevitable–since even in urban society such roles cannot be kept completely separate–that he one day find himself "high" while in the company of non-users from whom he wishes to keep his marihuana use secret. Given the variety of symptoms the drug may produce, it is natural for the user to fear that he might reveal through his behavior that he is "high," that he might be unable to control the symptoms and thus give away his one secret. Such phenomena as difficulty in focusing one's attention and in carrying on normal conversation create a fear that everyone will know exactly why one is behaving in this way, that the behavior will be interpreted automatically as a sign of drug use.

Those who progress to regular use manage to avoid this dilemma. It may happen, as noted above, that they come to participate almost completely in the subculture group in which the practice is carried on, so that they simply have a minimal amount of contact with non-users about whose opinions they care. Since this isolation from conventional society is seldom complete, the user must learn another method of avoiding the dilemma, one which is the most important method for those whose participation is never so completely segregated. This consists in learning to control the drug's effects while in the company of non-users, so that they can be fooled and the secret successfully kept even though one continues participation with them. If one cannot learn this, there exists some group of situations in which he dare not get "high" and regular use is not possible:

Say, I'll tell you something that just kills me, man, I mean it's really terrible. Have you ever got high and then had to face your family? I really dread that. Like having to talk to my father or mother, or brothers, man, it's just too much. I just can't make it. I just feel like they're sitting there digging (watching) me, and they know I'm high. It's a horrible feeling. I hate it.

Most users have these feelings and move on to regular use, if they do, only if an experience of the following order occurs, changing their conception of the possibilities of detection:

(Were you making it much then, at first?) No, not too much. Like I said, I was a little afraid of it. But it was finally about 1948 that I really began to make it strong. (What were you afraid of?) Well, I was afraid that I would get high and not be able to op (operate), you dig, I mean, I was afraid to let go and see what would happen. Especially on jobs. I couldn't trust myself when I was high. I was afraid I'd get too high, and pass out completely, or do stupid things. I didn't want to get too wigged.

(How did you ever get over that?) Well, it's just one of those things, man. One night I turned on and I just suddently felt real great, relaxed, you know, I was really swinging with it. From then on I've just been able to smoke as much as I want without getting into any trouble with it. I can always control it.

The typical experience is one in which the user finds himself in a position where he must do something while he is "high" that he is quite sure he cannot do in that condition. To his surprise, he finds that he can do it and can hide from others the fact that he is under the drug's influence. One or more occurrences of this kind allow the user to conclude that his caution has been excessive and based on a false premise. If he desires to use the drug regularly he is no longer deterred by this fear, for he can use such an experience to justify the belief that non-users need never know:

(The suggestion was made that many users find it difficult to perform their work tasks effectively while high. The interviewee, a machinist, replied with the story of how he got over this barrier.)

It doesn't bother me that way. I had an experience once that proved that to me. I was out on a pretty rough party the night before. I got pretty high. On pot (marihuana) and lushing, too. I got so high that I was still out of my mind when I went to work the next day. And I had a very important job to work on. It had to be practically perfect—precision stuff. The boss had been priming me for it for days, explaining how to do it and everything.

(He went to work high and, as far as he could remember, must have done the job, although there was no clear memory of it since he was still quite high.)

About a quarter to four, I finally came down and I thought, "Jesus! What am I doing?" So I just cut out and went, home. I didn't sleep all night hardly, worrying about whether I had f..ked up on that job or not. I got down the next morning, the boss puts the old "mikes" on the thing, and I had done the f..kin' job perfectly. So after that I just didn't worry any more. I've gone down to work really out of my mind on some mornings. I don't have any trouble at all.

This problem is not equally important for all users, for there are those whose social participation is such that it cannot arise; all their associates know they use marihuana and none of them care, while their conventional contacts are few and unimportant. In addition, some persons achieve idiosyncratic solutions which allow them to act "high" and have it ignored:

They (the boys in his neighborhood) can never tell if I'm high. I usually am, but they don't know it. See, I always had the reputation, all through high school, of being kind of goofy, so no matter what I do, nobody pays much attention. So I can get away with being high practically anyplace.

In short, persons limit their use of marihuana in proportion to the degree of their fear, realistic or otherwise, that non-users who are important to them will discover that they use drugs and react in some punishing way. This kind of control breaks down as the user discovers that his fears are excessive and unrealistic, as he comes to conceive of the practice as one which can be kept secret with relative ease. Each level of use can occur only when the person has revised his conception of the dangers involved in such a way as to allow it.

29. Encounters and Outcomes: The Case of the Young Shoplifter

Mary Owen Cameron

Shoplifting, as the data show, is disproportionately a crime of young people. The data also seem to indicate that noncommercial shoplifting continues until the experience of arrest forces the shoplifter either to abandon the practice or to reconsider the attitudes he will have toward the maintenance of a respectable social status. This naturally leads us to wonder whether private police practices do not have within them a general preventive potential insofar as the younger offender is concerned. If so, could it be realized in a practical way?

Apprehension for shoplifting is a very frequent first brush with the law for young people. The experience often has a traumatic impact that may have real significance in their lives. If the young shoplifter can believe that he has a great deal to lose by continuing to steal, he stops stealing just as the older shoplifter does. His belief, however, must be grounded in reality, and many young people are necessarily confused as to where their status lies. If the young pilferer has a family which, in effect, gathers around him and says, "You didn't *have* to steal things; we like you just as you are," and if by implication, the family adds "but never do this again or you'll be in real trouble, you'll have a police record and you'll never get a job or be able to finish high school or do any of the things we had hoped you'd be able to do," these reactions represent for the younger as well as for the adult pilferer a kind of unexpected support which will help to keep him from repeating his offense. Whether or not family-type punishments short of total rejection add to or detract from the

Reprinted with permission of The Macmillan Company from Chapter 8, "The 'Respectable' Criminal and the Young Offenders," from *The Booster and the Snitch: Department Store Shoplifting* by Mary Owen Cameron. Copyright by The Free Press of Glencoe, a Division of The Macmillan Company, 1964.

preventive value of the arrest experience is at present a matter of pure conjecture. The young person with firm middle-class status aspiration is, we can surmise, little different in this respect from his older counterpart and behaves in a similar way.

Not every young person, however, has a *real* status which is threatened by arrest. Many children and adolescents reared in the "underprivileged" areas of cities have, in their own eyes, *no* status at all; and they have strong reasons to reject the conventional channels to success. In their own world two value structures compete for their allegiance They have seen examples of adults in their own neighborhoods who have achieved considerable "success" in the criminal rackets. Such examples are inescapable in slum areas where the well-dressed local man in a fine, new car is almost sure to be someone who is engaged in a criminal career, and the best dressed and most attractive young women are likely to be call girls. They have also seen the economic and personal difficulties which beset the lives of relatives and neighbors who are honest, hard working and law abiding citizens.

Career choices are not, of course, made on a calculated rational basis, but a realistic appraisal of the prospects for success and upward mobility can hardly lead the slum boy or girl to a firm conviction that crime does not pay when, in fact, it sometimes pays rather well. Crime as an occupation, moreover, does not require a college degree or even a high school diploma.

Nevertheless young people also know something of the risks and deprivations involved in extra-legal success and they have observed successful aspirants to respectability (teachers, social workers, civil servants, police, nurses, lawyers, doctors, etc.). The career decision which has to be made by the slum-reared young man or woman is thus of greater moment than that of his middle-class contemporary who can, still, be thrown into a minor panic when he must choose between law and dentistry. Bloch and Niederhoffer say:

> The lower-class boy... absorbs dominant middle-class values which set goals for him, but sees on every hand that he is unable to pursue these ends. To many a lower-class boy socially approved objectives for desired manhood are so far-fetched, so unattainable, that they constitute a sort of chimera, a never-never land about which he can dream but actually not hope to achieve. The patterns of living of his father and other adult male figures in his environment appear to offer testimony as to the futility of achieving goals which the popular cult of American success so stridently affirms in the classroom, the movies, TV, and other popular channels of mass enlightenment. What models are offered in the lives of parents and others in his environment, who are closely bound to a limited and constricted routine of seemingly unrewarded toil, appear uninspired and, for many youths, hardly worth the effort. Recognizing the limitations on his strivings, the values of the working-class youth may be an actual negation of the very things which the calculated prudence of the middle-class hopes to foster among its own young.[1]

In spite of the seeming attractiveness of a criminal career, most young people (slum-reared or otherwise) chose the lesser risk by conforming to conventional de-

[1] Block, Herbert and Arthur Niederhoffer. *The Gang: A Study in Adolescent Behavior.* (New York, 1958), p. 109.

mands; although this conformity for many slum-reared children leads only to one dreary and difficult job after another rather than into a spiral of increasing responsibilities, increasing status, and increasing rewards. Sometimes they are rejected by criminal in-groups as lacking the initiative, trustworthiness, and cunning needed for a criminal career.

The slum-reared boy or girl in his initial encounters with law enforcement agencies is apt to be balanced on a tightrope:

> These early acts of deviance are in effect tentative steps toward the adoption of norms in competition with the official rules. At this stage the deviant needs all the encouragement and reassurance he can muster to defend his position. He finds these by searching out others who have faced similar experiences and who will support one another in common attitudes of alienation from the official system. The deviant who is unable to mobilize such social support will have great difficulty in establishing firm grounds for his defiance of the official system, for he requires not only justifying beliefs but also social validation of the appropriateness of his deviant acts.
>
> The initial contest between the individual and the authorities over the legitimacy of certain social norms and the appropriateness of certain acts of deviance sets in motion a process of definition that marks the offender as different from law-abiding folk. His acts and his person are defined as "evil," and he is caught up in a vicious cycle of norm-violation, repression, resentment, and new and more serious acts of violation. The process of alienation is accelerated, and the chasm between the offender and those who would control and reform him grows wider and deeper. In such circumstances he becomes increasingly dependent on the support of others in his position. The gang of peers forms a new social world in which the legitimacy of his delinquent conduct is strongly reinforced.[2]

Although motivated initially by the same acquisitive desires as his middle-class peers, the slum-reared adolescent may, however, respond to arrest for shoplifting not by tearful imploring but by a show of hardness and cynicism which invites further retribution. The store detective has been hired to protect merchandise. It seems perfectly obvious to him that the "young tough" of both sexes need to be taught a lesson and that only public officials are equipped to teach this lesson. A store protection official thus tends to push the prosecution in such cases as hard as it can be pushed. Commitment to a reform institution or jail is frequently the outcome.

Having been able to enjoy the benefits of a juvenile penal institution, however, the "young tough" indeed learns a number of lessons. He (or she) learns to stay away from "kid stuff" like pilfering and "get wise" to the real rackets. He learns where merchandise can be sold; and where stolen merchandise can be pawned. He learns the kinds of things to take and, he learns to hate and fear all legal authority. In short, he learns to be a "booster" or to follow some other criminal trade.

> The firm dramatization of the "evil" which separates the child out of his group for specialized treatment plays a greater role in making the criminal than perhaps any other experience. It cannot be too often emphasized that for the child the whole

[2] Cloward and Ohlin, *Delinquency and Opportunity.* (New York, 1960), pp. 126–127.

situation has become different. He now lives in a different world. He has been tagged. A new and hitherto nonexistent environment has been precipitated out for him.

The process of making the criminal, therefore, is a process of tagging, defining, identifying, segregating, describing, emphasizing, making conscious and self-conscious; it becomes a way of stimulating, suggesting, emphasizing, and evolving the very traits that are complained of. If the theory of relation of response to stimulus has any meaning, the entire process of dealing with the young delinquent is mischievous in so far as it identifies him to himself or to the environment as a delinquent person.[3]

When the process of identifying the child to himself and to his environment as a delinquent simultaneously equips him with the attitudes and skill of an extra-legal trade that has immediate rewards and the possibility of increasing "success," he is well set on a career that is difficult or impossible to reverse.

[3] Tannenbaum, Frank. *Crime and the Community.* (New York, 1938), pp. 19–20.

30. The Function of Social Definitions and Self-definitions in the Development of Delinquent Careers

Carl Werthman

The moral career of the lower class juvenile gang boy often begins at age 6, 7, or 8 when he is defined by his teachers as "predelinquent" for demonstrating to his friends that he is not a "sissy," and it ends between the ages of 16 and 25 when he either takes a job, goes to college, joins the Army, or becomes a criminal.[1] Although much of his behavior during this period can be seen and is seen by him as a voluntary set of claims on one of the temporary social identities available to him as a lower class "youth," his final choice of an "adult" identity will depend in large measure on the way his moral character has been assessed, categorized, and acted upon by his parents, teachers, and officials of the law as well as on the attitudes and actions he has chosen in response. How the boys embrace these identities, how adults tend to define and treat them for doing so, and how the boys respond to these definitions and treatments is thus the subject of this paper.[2]

Reprinted from "The Function of Social Definitions in the Development of Delinquent Careers," *Task Force Report: Juvenile Delinquency and Youth Crime,* a Report by The President's Commission on Law Enforcement and Administration of Justice (Washington: Government Printing Office, 1967), Appendix J, pp. 155–159, 166–170.

[1] The concept of a moral career has been defined by Erving Goffman as "the regular sequence of changes that career entails in the person's self and in his framework of imagery for judging himself and others." See Erving Goffman, "The Moral Career of the Mental Patient," in "Asylums" (New York: Doubleday & Co., Inc., 1961), p. 128.

[2] The data on which this study is based consists of taped interviews with 56 "core" members of 11 "delinquent" gangs or "jacket clubs" plus observations and more informal conversations involving over 100 members of these 11 gangs. The boys were drawn from the clientele of a delinquency-prevention program in San Francisco called Youth For Service, and the research was conducted largely out of their offices for a 2-year period. Of the 56 boys interviewed on tape, 37 were Negro, 11 were Mexican, and 8 were Caucasian. This report is thus based primarily on a sample of Negro gang boys.

The Identity Materials of the Delinquent

...

In the adult world, occupations are the major source of social identity. The jobs themselves are used to classify and rank, while the norms governing performance are the principal criteria by which competence and character are judged. In the world inhabited by youth, however, identities must be constructed from other materials; and on the whole, these materials are limited to the activities that take place in schools and those engaged in and around them.[3] The school provides a number of instrumental training roles for those who wish to pursue them, but if a student is neither academically nor politically inclined, these roles are likely not to have much meaning. Particularly in elementary and junior high schools, it is not so much what you *do* that counts but rather what you *are*, since everyone tends to be doing about the same things.

In the absence of occupational titles, a rich vocabulary of identity categories tends to emerge, a vocabulary that often includes referents to physical or anatomical features, clothing styles, places, possessions, special membership groups, and a general relationship to the administration of schools.[4] In addition, each of these categories tends to be associated with certain skills and attributes of character as well as with the activities in which these skills and character traits are generally displayed.

As Erving Goffman has elegantly made clear, however, there are certain skills and attributes of character, particularly those most prized by gang boys, that can only be claimed by aspirants to them in social situations where something of consequence is risked; and since the school facilities available for nonacademic character construction are generally limited to games, it is not surprising that boys who wish

[3] Although the family can be seen as an important source of emotional support for the various contests that go on outside it, there is little important contribution it can make to the genesis of public identities since most young people do not spend time together in the same home.

[4] Just prior to the completion of this study, for example, the high school population of San Francisco had divided itself into four major groups. The lower and working class Negroes, Spanish-speaking minorities, and whites were referred to as "bloods," "barts," and "white shoes," respectively, while the fourth group, the "Ivy Leaguers," contained the middle and lower middle class segments of all three races. The relationship to schools implicit in this vocabulary is obvious, and all four groups were easily identifiable by uniform. The "bloods," "barts," and "white shoes" were further broken down into gangs by districts and each gang had its own jacket. Moreover, the district and gang distinctions took precedence over race in racially integrated districts so that the lower class Negroes and whites living in predominantly Spanish-speaking areas wore the "bart" uniform and were referred to by members of their own race as such.

In the city of Albany on the other side of the San Francisco Bay, the vocabulary adopted by the students in the all-white high school is devoid of ethnic references but certainly no less to the point: the students who congregate during recess on plots of land in the middle of the school have been entitled the "quadrangles;" the students who meet in the parking lot outside the school are called just that, "parking lots;" and the remainder of the student body is referred to as "uncommitted," presumably because they occupy the territory between the parking lot and the quadrangle that surrounds the school on four sides.

to play for higher stakes tend to use each other, the law, and sometimes even school officials in order to demonstrate their claims.[5]

• • •

Yet if someone with an adult status actually decides he desires "action," there is always Las Vegas or a risky job, while a lower class gang boy is more or less forced to create his own. If he wishes to prove that he is autonomous, courageous, loyal, or has "heart," not only must he take a chance, he must also construct the situation in which to take it; and for most gang boys this means that risky situations must be made from whatever materials happen to be available on the streets and at schools.[6]

On the streets, the various activities defined by law as "thefts" provide perhaps the best examples of the way gang boys use laws to construct and claim identities. In order to become usable as identity materials, however, the situations in which laws against theft are broken must be carefully selected to insure that sufficient risk is present. Unlike the professional thief who takes pride in knowing how to minimize the occupational risks of his trade, most younger gang boys create risks where none need be involved.[7] Joyriding, for example, is ideally suited for this purpose since "cool" is required to get a stolen car started quickly; and once started, the situation contains the generous though not overwhelming risk of detection. Moreover, given the wide range of risky activities that can be engaged in once the cars are stolen, joyriding is viewed as an abundant source of the anxiety, excitement, and tension that accompanies the taking of risks for its own sake, a complex of emotions often referred to as "kicks."

• • •

As the members of a gang get older, their perception and use of theft become increasingly instrumental; and if they are still in the gang after graduating or getting expelled from high school, theft turns into a particular version of the "hustle." These hustles still involve risks, but the risks are no longer incurred exclusively for what can be demonstrated about the self by taking them. The possible sanctions faced are much more serious than they were in junior high school. Moreover, the boys now need the money. Without it they would find themselves hard pressed to sustain a daily round of socializing with ease. Thus, their relationship to the risky situation changes as both positive and negative outcomes become more consequential; and as this shift takes place, the actual thefts themselves are talked about less and less. Where a boy happens to be getting his money becomes his own private business,

[5] I am indebted to a recent unpublished paper by Goffman for much of the analysis of gang activity that follows. See Erving Goffman, "Where the Action Is: Or, Hemingway Revisited," Center For the Study of Law and Society, University of California, Berkeley, 1965.

[6] It was largely on the basis of an argument such as this that Norman Mailer suggested "medieval jousting tournaments in Central Park" and "horse races through the streets of Little Italy" as delinquency prevention programs for the City of New York. See Norman Mailer, "The Presidential Papers" (New York: Bantam Books, 1964), p. 22.

[7] See Edwin H. Sutherland, "The Professional Thief" (Chicago: The University of Chicago Press, 1937).

a policy that gradually evolves as attempts are made to cut down the probability of detection.

Yet the boys still do not see themselves as professional thieves, even after they have graduated from high school. As long as they can rely on their parents for room and board, the hustle is viewed as a transitory, impermanent, and part-time way of simply getting by. It is not conceived of as "adult" training role, even though it is an instrumental relationship to the economic world. On the other hand, if the boys remain on the streets after 18, they are no longer stealing for "kicks."

The laws against theft are not the only materials used by gang boys to demonstrate moral character. On the streets, they also tend to use each other for this purpose, activities that Goffman has called "character games."

• • •

Goffman further suggests that a claim to possess "honor" is what initiates most character games, honor defined as "the property of character which causes the individual to engage in a character contest when his rights have been violated and when the likely cost of the contest is high."[8] Like other forms of "action," then, character games are played at some risk but also presumably for some reward.

As Short and Strodtbeck have pointed out, fighting is perhaps the classic example of a gang activity that is best understood with this model.[9] After observing gang boys in Chicago for a number of years, these authors concluded that most fights take place either when a "rep" for toughness is suddenly challenged by a situation that the gang boy cannot avoid confronting or when a challenge to within-group rank appears, either from inside or outside the gang. In the first instance, the gang boy is handed a chance to appear "honorable," perhaps even a chance he did not want; while in the second instance, the boy will provoke a character contest to reaffirm or reclaim his status in the gang after it is challenged by a streetworker or another boy, sometimes during an absence in jail.

• • •

In addition to fighting, there are also other activities in which gang boys use each other to claim and construct identities. The behavior described by Miller as "verbal aggression," also known variously as "ranking," "capping," or "sounding," seems to involve some of the same principles found in fights.[10] As Matza has pointed out, this activity amounts essentially to a process of testing status by insult, and thus honor is the quality of moral character at stake.[11] Goffman has called these encounters "contest contests," situations in which someone forces someone else "into a contest

[8] Erving Goffman, "Where the Action Is: Or Hemingway Revisited," Center for the Study of Law and Society, University of California, Berkeley, 1965, p. 63.

[9] James F. Short, Jr., and Fred L. Strodtbeck, "Group Process and Gang Delinquency" (Chicago: The University of Chicago Press, 1965), pp. 248–264; also J. Short and F. Strodtbeck, "Why Gangs Fight," "Trans-Action," 1, 1964.

[10] W. B. Miller, H. Geertz, and S. G. Cutter, "Aggression in a Boy's Street-Corner Group," "Psychiatry" (November 1961), pp. 283–298.

[11] David Matza, "Delinquency and Drift" (John Wiley & Sons, 1964), pp. 42–44.

over whether or not there will be a contest."[12] Like fighting, it involves risk and can thus have a bearing on status. Unlike fighting, however, it is not engaged in to demonstrate toughness or courage but rather to display a type of verbal agility that gang boys call "smart."

...

The gang boy thus aspires to an identity that puts him in a special relationship to risk. When he is around his friends, he often creates the situations in which he chooses to exist, an act of creation that involves selecting out certain features of the social environment and then transforming them into the conditions that allow him to define a self. In part, these risks are taken for their own sake since a reputation can be built on this capacity alone and the emotional reward is a "kick." In part, there are also honor, courage, and loyalty involved, special attributes of moral character that can only be demonstrated in situations of risk. Taken together, however, these risks seem to represent a set of special claims to the status of "men," a status they are culturally and structurally forbidden to occupy until the "delinquent career" comes to an end....

The Genesis of Autonomy

...A gang boy's career as a "delinquent" in the schools is thus a somewhat problematic affair. It begins in earnest around the fourth or fifth grade when he comes to the attention of his teachers for paying no attention to them, beating up other students, and forcing his colleagues to surrender their lunch money. During junior high school the fights are better organized and the posture adopted towards teachers turns from unconcern to insolence. And in the last years of high school, the boys either graduate or depart, usually at the school's request. For most of these years, the school regards him as hopeless, and they suspend him regularly for his activities in the presence of other boys as well as for his attitude towards the authority of the school itself. Most of this behavior, however, is designed to claim an identity that the school itself cannot stamp out. What the boys do on the streets with one another is beyond the scope of their control although they punish it severely when it happens to take place on school grounds.

Whether the boys are given the chance to engage in character contests with teachers, however, is directly affected by the school itself since what is made of an act depends almost entirely on how it is defined and evaluated by the teacher, including the issue of whether or not the act is a violation of the basic authority rule. The boy is using the teacher to define himself as autonomous, and, like his behavior on the streets, he often creates or provokes the situation in which he then defends his honor. Yet if a teacher is willing to concede the fact that school is meaningless to some boys and therefore that other activities besides "teaching and learning" will necessarily go on in class, and if he is willing to limit the scope of his jurisdiction to the activity of "teaching and learning" itself, then his authority is likely to remain

[12] Goffman, *op. cit.*, p. 68.

intact, regardless of how much it may be "tested." Whether or not he wishes to persuade the boys to join the learning process is another matter, but it is precisely at this point that we see the merits of defining authority, after Bertrand de Juvenel, as "the faculty of gaining another man's assent."[13]

The Delinquent and the Police

... In many cases, the gang boy responds to patrolmen the same way he responds to schoolteachers who subtly or not so subtly cast aspersions on his moral character. By acquitting himself with a straightforward nonchalance of indifference and refusing to proffer the expected signs of deference that typically denote respect, he challenges the authority of the policeman who then must either arrest the boy, use his "billy club," or withdraw from the encounter by saving face as best he can. Once again, the gang boy takes a risk in a social situation, only this time the situation is one he did not construct. When he chooses to challenge the authority of the patrolmen, he is defending his pride, his honor, and his social self respect. He does this at a risk, however, since his "rap sheet" includes field interrogation reports and thus continues to grow.

...

Although the age of the offender, his family situation, his prior arrest record, and the nature of his offense all enter into the dispositions made by juvenile officers, recent students of the police suggest that perhaps the most important factors affecting dispositions are related to *demeanor.* Cicourel found that the decisions made by juvenile officers were strongly influenced by the style and speed with which the offender confessed.[14] If a boy confesses to his misdeeds immediately, or at least immediately after being offered lenient treatment by the officer for doing so, this act is taken as a sign that the boy "trusts" adults, in which case it is further assumed that his attachment to the basic authority rule is both sound and intact. On the other hand, if the boy proves to be a "tough nut to crack," he is viewed with suspicion. It is said that he is "hardened," does not "trust" authority, and is therefore probably "out of control." Piliavin and Briar also report that boys who appear frightened, humble, penitent, and ashamed are also more likely to go free.[15] Like the test for "trust," these indicators are used to measure respect for the authority of the law. Similarly, in a study of the differential selection of juvenile offenders for court appearances, Nathan Goldman reports that "defiance on the part of a boy will lead to juvenile court quicker than anything else."[16]

The juvenile officer, like the probation officer, thus seems to make arrest decisions

[13] Bertrand de Juvenel, "Sovereignty: An Inquiry Into the Political Good," translated by J. F. Huntington (Chicago: The University of Chicago Press, 1957), p. 29.

[14] Aaron V. Cicourel, "The Social Organization of Juvenile Justice," MS.

[15] Irving Piliavin and Scott Briar, "Police Encounters with Juveniles," "American Journal of Sociology," LXXX, 1964.

[16] Nathan Goldman, "The Differential Selection of Juvenile Offenders for Court Appearances," National Council on Crime and Delinquency, 1963, p. 106.

on the basis of a more or less complete gestalt. A series of minor brushes with the law, when added to a negative school report, a "bad" family situation, and suspicious associates, often does the same damage to imputed moral character as the insolent behavior that gets a "bright boy" from a "good family" defined by the juvenile officer as a "punk."

• • •

Like the facts of his situation as determined by the police, his relationship to this sanction system affects the fatefulness of his acts. A boy who knows that the California Youth Authority awaits him if he is caught for theft or joyriding one more time can demonstrate possession of more courage for the same act than the boy who has never been caught. To the extent that boys do not drop out of gangs as they move through this sanction system, the fatefulness of their acts increases, and they tend to constitute an increasingly select elite. In the identity system of the gang world, reputation increases with the fatefulness of the situation in which a boy is willing to take a risk, and thus the boys who have been sent to the more important prisons can flaunt this fact as evidence that they have paid and were willing to pay a more significant price for maintaining an identity on the streets.

• • •

The second effect of the sanction system concerns the use of the rules themselves. If a boy is ordered by the court not to associate any more with his friends, the court has in effect created a rule that allows the boy to demonstrate greater loyalty to them. He has the opportunity to prove himself an even better comrade than he could ever have proved before, and thus again the sanction system can function in two quite different ways.

Third, there is the fact that the courts sometimes create their own special rules to judge the "improvement" of a boy, but when these rules are violated, there is a sense in which they have artificially created the very rules by which the boy is then condemned. Consider, for example, the following conversation between this researcher and a 12-year-old boy who had just run away from his foster home. He had been living with "Uncle Eddie," his mother's brother, essentially because his older brothers were in jail, his father deserted the family some years ago, and, as a result of these actions by other members of the family, his mother was declared "unfit" and Danny was forced to leave home.

(Why did you stay away from school yesterday?) I felt like comin' to San Francisco to see my mother. (Didn't you go back last night?) Yeh, but my cousin Darlene said they was lookin' for me, you know, my probation officer. He came to visit me in school and couldn't find me. I got scared so I came back up here. (Where did you stay last night?) I slept in a friend of mine's car. I figured I better not go home. I don't want to get my mother in dutch. They'll call her and if she says I'm home that'll get her in trouble. (What do you think your probation officer will do when he finds you?) He told me he was going to send me to C.Y.A. like Billy if I got into any trouble down there, you know, at my Uncle Eddie's. I don't want to go to C.Y.A.

(Well what do you plan to do now?) I don't know. I figure I could keep running. I could stay with my brother up in Tahoe, but it's tough bein' on the run. What do you think I should do? (I don't know either. Let's discuss it. You're the one that has to make the decision. How do you like living down at your Uncle Eddie's?) I don't like it. They talk about me behind my back, and they say bad things about my mother. And Eddie's no good. He won't even buy me gym clothes. They told me at school I can't go to gym class unless I got the clothes, and he won't get them. He said he already bought me some and I lost 'em but he's lyin'. He never bought me no gym clothes. (Would you rather live somewhere else?) Yeh, but they won't let me come home. They say I got too many friends up there and the school won't let me back. But all my friends have left, and I could go to a different school. I know I could make it. But they won't let me. I know they're going to send me to C.Y.A.

(Well, it looks to me like you have two choices. You could either keep running and take your chances on getting caught, or go back and take your chances on getting sent to C.Y.A.) [After a long silence.] Well maybe C.Y.A. wouldn't be so bad after all. [He tries hard to fight back tears and succeeds.]

This is a good example of what can happen with probation restrictions. A boy is sent to a foster home because he comes from a broken one and then plays hookey in order to come back. The truancy is produced by the desire to see his mother, and the terms of his probation make this act an offense unless it is properly approved. The boy is thus in danger of being sent to the California Youth Authority for committing an offense that was actually created by the courts themselves.

Yet the fact remains that boys who *do* remain on the streets to face increasingly serious sanctions *do* take more serious risks than other boys; and in terms of the logic underlying the identity system itself, they at least can see themselves as more committed than others to this round of life. The most serious change in their situation occurs, however, when the police finally decide to "crack down." The boys are warned to "stay off the streets or else."...

This sudden escalation of the risks involved in remaining on the streets as well as the fact that these risks are present in a large area of space can have a decisive and damaging effect on a gang boy's identity as a "delinquent." During most of the years he spends in a gang, he uses a great many objects to demonstrate his courage and autonomy in situations of risk. As suggested above, there are laws, school rules, teachers, girls, and rival gangs as well as the police. When the police make this final move, however, they effectively surround or encompass him with one source of identity material. Practically everywhere he goes, he is in a situation of risk that is defined by the police; and if this goes on for a long enough time, this identity begins to leave a permanent impact on a boy's conception of himself. His only choice is either to leave the streets or define himself exclusively in relation to the police. Although most boys still leave the streets rather than surrender to this identity as a permanent or "adult" way of life, there are some who begin losing the capacity to imagine themselves as anything else; and when this happens, there is a chance that the boy will graduate into adulthood as a self-defined criminal.

Contingencies, Risks, and Opportunities

There is some evidence to suggest that most gang boys have a conception of how and when their careers as "delinquents" will end. As Short and Stordtbeck have recently reported, most look forward to becoming stable and dependable husbands in well-run households, despite their reluctance to voice these expectations around one another and despite the fact that some become fathers out of wedlock along the way.[17] Similarly, although about half the boys interviewed by Short and Strodtbeck anticipate problems in securing "good paying honest jobs," their images of family life make it clear that the great majority expect to be holding down some kind of conventional occupation when they become "adults."[18] During most of the years spent in gangs, however, these occupational concerns are neither salient nor relevant. The boys understand that as long as they are defined and define themselves as "youth," they are not the people they will someday become; and for this reason they have little difficulty identifying with two apparently conflicting sets of attitudes, values, and behavior patterns.

As we have seen, the issue of whether a particular career will come to the expected conventional end is often resolved in large measure by how a boy deals with a host of contingencies that arise before the end of the career arrives, particularly those associated with the way he is defined and acted upon by parents, teachers, policemen, probation officers, and judges of the juvenile court. At the early stages of the career, it is often difficult for the boys to make objective assessments of the risks they run in defining themselves since the implications of these acts for the way moral character is defined, evaluated, and acted upon are only known "after" the acts themselves have taken place. This is particularly true in the case of the police where many more rules are invoked to pass judgment on the offender than were actually involved in the offense, particularly since these judgments are often made on the basis of how he behaves in four different institutions at once. As Howard Becker has suggested, "deviance is not a quality of the act a person commits, but rather a consequence of the application by others of rules and sanctions to an 'offender';"[19] and there are many instances in which the criteria used to reconstitute moral character are simply seen by gang boys as arbitrary, unfair, or outright illegitimate.

Yet regardless of how a boy feels about the rules that have been used to judge him, these judgments often alter the objective fact of his situation, and this requires him to make new decisions. He must decide, for example, whether to use his probation restrictions as an excuse to leave the gang or as a new and riskier source of identity material, just as he must decide how he feels about the fact that his parents may no longer trust him. By viewing the "delinquent career" as a more or less stable sequence of acts taken in risky social situations in order to claim an identity or define a self, often followed by changes in the rules and judgments that make up these situations, and followed again by new choices of the self in response to these changes,

[17] Short and Strodtbeck, "Group Process," *op. cit.*, n. 9, pp. 25–46.

[18] See James F. Short, Jr., Ramon Rivera, and Ray A. Tennyson, "Opportunities, Gang Membership, and Delinquency," "American Sociological Review" (February 1965), p. 60; see also Delbert S. Elliott, "Delinquency and Perceived Opportunity," "Sociological Inquiry" (Spring, 1962), pp. 216–228.

[19] Howard S. Becker, "Outsiders" (New York: The Free Press of Glencoe, 1963), p. 9.

it is possible to see how a gang boy could arrive at the age of 18 or 21 to find that his situation makes it costly, painful, or difficult for him to take the conventional job that he always expected to take, particularly if the boy has come to view the conventional world as a place full of the kinds of people who have labeled him a "delinquent."[20]

This process can be seen quite clearly in the schools where the initial payoff in female acclaim for fights and risky character contests slowly vanishes during high school. The "big men" in 7th grade often become school rejects in the 10th or 11th, and thus they do pay a price for their early notoriety, only this price cannot always be foreseen.

Once a gang boy gets beyond the age of 18, moreover, his situation changes rather dramatically. Whether he likes it or not, he now has a choice to make about what identity system to enter. He could get married, get a job, and assume the status of a full-fledged "adult;" he could decide to postpone this decision in legitimate ways such as joining the Army and going to school at night; or he could decide to remain for a few more years as an elder statesman on the streets, in which case he will continue to make use of the identity materials available to youth.

The decision he makes at this point in his career will depend in part on his situation. If he managed to graduate from high school, he may well decide to go on to college; but if he was expelled from high school, he may feel either bitter or reluctant about going back to night school to get the high school degree. He knows that he has been administratively reborn in the eyes of the law, and thus the risks he takes by staying in the streets increase considerably since he now may be processed by the courts as an adult. On the other hand, if his status in the gang world is still high, he may not want to trade it right away for a low-paying blue-collar job; and he knows he will be rejected by the Army if he has a jail record of any kind.

In short, it is at this point in his career that the "opportunities" available to him will affect his behavior, his attitudes, and the decisions he makes about his life.[21] If there are no legitimate options that at best would not make him suffer a sudden decrease in status and at worst would allow him not to face his ultimately dismal status-fate as an adult, then he may well decide to stay on the streets, despite the greater consequences involved in taking risks. He may adopt a "hustle," and he may also adopt a full-blown ideology along with it. Since he now views the conventional world as a place he is expected to enter, he tends to develop a "position" on it. Jobs become "slaves"; going to school becomes "serving time"; and in some cases the assumptions about marriage and getting a conventional job are replaced by fan-

[20] This process has been described in somewhat different terms by Lemert as a transformation from "primary" to "secondary" deviance. See Edwin M. Lemert, "Social Pathology" (New York: McGraw Hill Book Co., 1951), p. 75.

[21] This view suggests that the various processes discussed by Cloward and Ohlin tend to effect outcomes of the transition between youth and adult status at the end of the delinquent career. See Richard A. Cloward and Lloyd E. Ohlin, "Delinquency and Opportunity" (Glencoe: The Free Press, 1960).

tasies about the quick and big "score." These are no longer the "delinquent boys" described by Cohen.[22] They are the self-styled aristocrats described by Finestone and Sykes and Matza.[23] They have an answer to everything, and they always "know the score."

After a few years of this existence, these boys are really at the end of their "delinquent" careers. Some get jobs, some go to jail, some get killed, and some simply fade into an older underground of pool rooms and petty thefts. Most cannot avoid ending up with conventional jobs, however, largely because the "illegitimate opportunities" available simply are not that good.

Note: The research on which this paper is based was initiated by the Survey Research Center at the University of California in Berkeley on a grant from the Ford Foundation and was later moved to the Center for the Study of Law and Society on the Berkeley campus, where funds were made available under a generous grant from the Office of Juvenile Delinquency and Youth Development, Welfare Administration, U.S. Department of Health, Education and Welfare, in cooperation with the President's Committee on Juvenile Delinquency and Youth Crime.

[22] Albert K. Cohen, "Delinquent Boys," (Glencoe: The Free Press, 1965).

[23] Harold Finestone, "Cats, Kicks, and Colors," "Social Problems," vol. 5 (July 1957), pp. 3-13; G. M. Sykes and David Matza, "Techniques of Neutralization: A Theory of Delinquency," "American Sociological Review," vol. 22 (December 1957), pp. 664-670.

31. Two Studies of Legal Stigma

Richard D. Schwartz and Jerome H. Skolnick

From a sociological viewpoint, there are several types of indirect consequences of legal sanctions which can be distinguished. These include differential deterrence, effects on the sanctionee's associates, and variations in the degree of deprivation which sanction imposes on the recipient himself. First, the imposition of sanction, while intended as a matter of overt policy to deter the public at large, probably will vary in its effectiveness as a deterrent, depending upon the extent to which potential offenders perceive themselves as similar to the sanctionee. Such "differential deterrence" would occur if white-collar anti-trust violators were restrained by the convic-

Reprinted from *Social Problems,* **10**:2 (Fall 1962), 133–140, by permission of The Society for the Study of Social Problems and the authors.

tion of General Electric executives, but not by invocation of the Sherman Act against union leaders.

The imposition of a sanction may even provide an unintended incentive to violate the law. A study of factors affecting compliance with federal income tax laws provides some evidence of this effect.[1] Some respondents reported that they began to cheat on their tax returns only *after* convictions for tax evasion had been obtained against others in their jurisdiction. They explained this surprising behavior by noting that the prosecutions had always been conducted against blatant violators and not against the kind of moderate offenders which they then became. These respondents were, therefore, unintentionally educated to the possibility of supposedly "safe" violations.

Second, deprivations or benefits may accrue to non-sanctioned individuals by virtue of the web of affiliations that join them to the defendant. The wife and family of a convicted man may, for instance, suffer from his arrest as much as the man himself. On the other hand, they may be relieved by his absence if the family relationship has been an unhappy one. Similarly, whole groups of persons may be affected by sanctions to an individual, as when discriminatory practices increase because of a highly publicized crime attributed to a member of a given minority group.

Finally, the social position of the defendant himself will serve to aggravate or alleviate the effects of any given sanction. Although all three indirect consequences may be interrelated, it is the third with which this paper will be primarily concerned.

Findings

The subject studied to examine the effects of legal accusation on occupational positions represented two extremes: lower-class unskilled workers charged with assault, and medical doctors accused of malpractice. The first project lent itself to a field experiment, while the second required a survey design. Because of differences in method and substance, the studies cannot be used as formal controls for each other. Taken together, however, they do suggest that the indirect effects of sanctions can be powerful, that they can produce unintended harm or unexpected benefit, and that the results are related to officially unemphasized aspects of the social context in which the sanctions are administered. Accordingly, the two studies will be discussed together, as bearing on one another. Strictly speaking, however, each can, and properly should, stand alone as a separate examination of the unanticipated consequences of legal sanctions.

Study 1. The Effects of a Criminal Court Record on the Employment Opportunities of Unskilled Workers. In the field experiments, four employment folders were prepared, the same in all respects except for the criminal court record of the applicant. In all of the folders he was described as a thirty-two year old single male of unspecified race, with a high school training in mechanical trades, and a record of

[1] Richard D. Schwartz, "The Effectiveness of Legal Controls: Factors in the Reporting of Minor Items of Income on Federal Income Tax Returns." Paper presented at the annual meeting of the American Sociological Association, Chicago, 1959.

successive short term jobs as a kitchen helper, maintenance worker, and handyman. These characteristics are roughly typical of applicants for unskilled hotel jobs in the Catskill resort area of New York State where employment opportunities were tested.[2]

The four folders differed only in the applicant's reported record of criminal court involvement. The first folder indicated that the applicant had been convicted and sentenced for assault; the second, that he had been tried for assault and acquitted; the third, also tried for assault and acquitted, but with a letter from the judge certifying the finding of not guilty and reaffirming the legal presumption of innocence. The fourth folder made no mention of any criminal record.

A sample of one hundred employers was utilized. Each employer was assigned to one of four "treatment" groups.[3] To each employer only one folder was shown; this folder was one of the four kinds mentioned above, the selection of the folder being determined by the treatment group to which the potential employer was assigned. The employer was asked whether he could "use" the man described in the folder. To preserve the reality of the situation and make it a true field experiment employers were never given any indication that they were participating in an experiment. So far as they knew, a legitimate offer to work was being made in each showing of the folder by the "employment agent."

• • •

Some deception was involved in the study. The "employment agent"—the same individual in all hundred cases—was in fact a law student who was working in the Catskills during the summer of 1959 as an insurance adjuster. In representing himself as being both an adjuster and an employment agent, he was assuming a combination of roles which is not uncommon there. The adjuster role gave him an opportunity to introduce a single application for employment casually and naturally. To the extent that the experiment worked, however, it was inevitable that some employers should be led to believe that they had immediate prospects of filling a job opening. In those instances where an offer to hire was made, the "agent" called a few hours later to say that the applicant had taken another job. The field experimenter attempted in such instances to locate a satisfactory replacement by contacting an employment agency in the area. Because this procedure was used and since the jobs involved were of relatively minor consequence, we believe that the deception caused little economic harm.

• • •

[2] The generality of these results remains to be determined. The effects of criminal involvement in the Catskill area are probably diminished, however, by the temporary nature of employment, the generally poor qualifications of the work force, and the excess of demand over supply of unskilled labor there. Accordingly, the employment differences among the four treatment groups found in this study are likely, if anything, to be *smaller* than would be expected in industries and areas where workers are more carefully selected.

[3] Employers were not approached in preselected random order, due to a misunderstanding of instructions on the part of the law student who carried out the experiment during a three and one-half week period. Because of this flaw in the experimental procedure, the results should be treated with appropriate caution. Thus, chi-squared analysis may not properly be utilized ....

Of the twenty-five employers shown the "no record" folder, nine gave positive responses. Subject to reservations arising from chance variations in sampling, we take this as indicative of the "ceiling" of jobs available for this kind of applicant under the given field conditions. Positive responses by these employers may be compared with those in the other treatment groups to obtain an indication of job opportunities lost because of the various legal records.

Of the twenty-five employers approached with the "convict" folder, only one expressed interest in the applicant. This is a rather graphic indication of the effect which a criminal record may have on job opportunities. Care must be exercised, of course, in generalizing the conclusions to other settings. In this context, however, the criminal record made a major difference.

From a theoretical point of view, the finding leads toward the conclusion that conviction constitutes a powerful form of "status degradation"[4] which continues to operate after the time when, according to the generalized theory of justice underlying punishment in our society, the individual's "debt" has been paid. A record of conviction produces a durable if not permanent loss of status. For purposes of effective social control, this state of affairs may heighten the deterrent effect of conviction—though that remains to be established. Any such contribution to social control, however, must be balanced against the barriers imposed upon rehabilitation of the convict. If the ex-prisoner finds difficulty in securing menial kinds of legitimate work, further crime may become an increasingly attractive alternative.

Another important finding of this study concerns the small number of positive responses elicited by the "accused but acquitted" applicant. Of the twenty-five employers approached with this folder, three offered jobs. Thus, the individual accused but acquitted of assault has almost as much trouble finding even an unskilled job as the one who was not only accused of the same offense, but also convicted.

...

...The courts have done little toward alleviating the post-acquittal consequences of legal accusation. One effort along these lines has been employed in the federal courts, however. Where an individual has been accused and exonerated of a crime, he may petition the federal courts for a "Certificate of Innocense" certifying this fact.[5] Possession of such a document might be expected to alleviate post-acquittal deprivations.

Some indication of the effectiveness of such a measure is found in the responses of the final treatment group. Their folder, it will be recalled, contained information on the accusation and acquittal of the applicant, but also included a letter from a judge addressed "To whom it may concern" certifying the applicant's acquittal and reminding the reader of the presumption of innocence. Such a letter might have had a boomerang effect, by reemphasizing the

[4] Harold Garfinkel, "Conditions of Successful Degradation Ceremonies," *American Journal of Sociology,* 61 (March, 1956), pp. 420–24.

[5] 28 United States Code, Secs. 1495, 2513.

legal involvement of the applicant. It was important, therefore, to determine empirically whether such a communication would improve or harm the chances of employment. Our findings indicate that it increased employment opportunities, since the letter folder elicited six positive responses. Even though this fell short of the nine responses to the "no record" folder, it doubled the number for the "accused but acquitted" and created a significantly greater number of job offers than those elicited by the convicted record. This suggests that the procedure merits consideration as a means of offsetting the occupational loss resulting from accusation. It should be noted, however, that repeated use of this device might reduce its effectiveness.

...The differences in outcome found...indicate that various types of legal records are systematically related to job opportunities. It seems fair to infer also that the trend of job losses corresponds with the apparent punitive intent of the authorities. Where the man is convicted, that intent is presumably greatest. It is less where he is accused but acquitted and still less where the court makes an effort to emphasize the absence of a finding of guilt. Nevertheless, where the difference in punitive intent is ideally greatest, between conviction and acquittal, the difference in occupational harm is very slight. A similar blurring of this distinction shows up in a different way in the next study.

Study II: The Effects on Defendants of Suits for Medical Malpractice. As indicated earlier, the second study differed from the first in a number of ways: method of research, social class of accused, relationship between the accused and his "employer," social support available to accused, type of offense and its possible relevance to occupational adequacy. Because the two studies differ in so many ways, the reader is again cautioned to avoid thinking of them as providing a rigorous comparative examination. They are presented together only to demonstrate that legal accusation can produce unanticipated deprivations, as in the case of Study I, or unanticipated benefits, as in the research now to be presented. In the discussion to follow, some of the possible reasons for the different outcomes will be suggested.

The extra-legal effects of a malpractice suit were studied by obtaining the records of Connecticut's leading carrier of malpractice insurance. According to these records, a total of 69 doctors in the State had been sued in 64 suits during the post-World War II period covered by the study, September, 1945, to September, 1959.[6] Some suits were instituted against more than one doctor, and four physicians had been sued twice. Of the total of 69 physicians, 58 were questioned. Interviews were conducted with the approval of the Connecticut Medical Association by Robert Wyckoff, whose extraordinary qualifications for the work included possession of both the M.D. and LL.B. degrees. Dr. Wyckoff was able to secure detailed response to his inquiries from all doctors contacted.

Twenty of the respondents were questioned by personal interview, 28 by telephone,

[6] A spot check of one county revealed that the Company's records covered every malpractice suit tried in the courts of that county during this period.

and the remainder by mail. Forty-three of those reached practiced principally in cities, eleven in suburbs, and four in rural areas. Seventeen were engaged in general practice and forty-one were specialists. The sample proved comparable to the doctors in the State as a whole in age experience, and professional qualifications.[7] The range was from the lowest professional stratum to chiefs of staff and services in the State's most highly regarded hospitals.

Of the 57 malpractice cases reported, doctors clearly won 38; nineteen of these were dropped by the plaintiff and an equal number were won in courts by the defendant doctor. Of the remaining nineteen suits, eleven were settled out of court for a nominal amount, four for approximately the amount the plaintiff claimed and four resulted in judgment for the plaintiff in court.

The malpractice survey did not reveal widespread occupational harm to the physicians involved. Of the 58 respondents, 52 reported no negative effects of the suit on their practice, and five of the remaining six, all specialists, reported that their practice *improved* after the suit. The heaviest loser in court (a radiologist), reported the largest gain. He commented, "I guess all the doctors in town felt sorry for me because new patients started coming in from doctors who had not sent me patients previously." Only one doctor reported adverse consequences to his practice. A winner in court, this man suffered physical and emotional stress symptoms which hampered his later effectiveness in surgical work. The temporary drop in his practice appears to have been produced by neurotic symptoms and is therefore only indirectly traceable to the malpractice suit. Seventeen other doctors reported varying degrees of personal dissatisfaction and anxiety during and after the suit, but none of them reported impairment of practice. No significant relationship was found between outcome of the suit and expressed dissatisfaction.

A protective institutional environment helps to explain these results. No cases were found in which a doctor's hospital privileges were reduced following the suit. Neither was any physician unable later to obtain malpractice insurance although a handful found it necessary to pay higher rates. The State Licensing Commission, which is headed by a doctor, did not intervene in any instance. Local medical societies generally investigated charges through their ethics and grievance committies, but where they took any action, it was almost always to recommend or assist in legal defense against the suit.

Discussion

Accusation has different outcomes for unskilled workers and doctors in the two studies. How may these be explained? First, they might be nothing more than artifacts of research method. In the field experiment, it was possible to see behavior directly, i.e., to determine how employers act when confronted with what appears to them to be a realistic opportunity to hire. Responses are therefore not distorted

[7]No relationship was found between any of these characteristics and the legal or extra-legal consequences of the lawsuit.

by the memory of the respondent. By contrast, the memory of the doctors might have been consciously or unconsciously shaped by the wish to create the impression that the public had not taken seriously the accusation leveled against them. The motive for such a distortion might be either to protect the respondent's self-esteem or to preserve an image of public acceptance in the eyes of the interviewer, the profession, and the public. Efforts of the interviewer to assure his subjects of anonymity–intended to offset these effects–may have succeeded or may, on the contrary, have accentuated an awareness of the danger. A related type of distortion might have stemmed from a desire by doctors to affect public attitudes toward malpractice. Two conflicting motives might have been expected to enter here. The doctor might have tended to exaggerate the harm caused by an accusation, especially if followed by acquittal, in order to turn public opinion toward legal policies which would limit malpractice liability. On the other hand, he might tend to underplay extra-legal harm caused by a legally insufficient accusation in order to discourage potential plaintiffs from instituting suits aimed at securing remunerative settlements and/or revenge for grievances. Whether these diverse motives operated to distort doctors' reports and, if so, which of them produced the greater degree of distortion is a matter for speculation. It is only suggested here that the interview method is more subject to certain types of distortion than the direct behavioral observations of the field experiment.

Even if such distortion did not occur, the results may be attributable to differences in research design. In the field experiment, a direct comparison is made between the occupational position of an accused and an identical individual not accused at a single point in time. In the medical study, effects were inferred through retrospective judgment, although checks on actual income would have no doubt confirmed these judgments. Granted that income had increased, many other explanations are available to account for it. An improvement in practice after a malpractice suit may have resulted from factors extraneous to the suit. The passage of time in the community and increased experience may have led to a larger practice and may even have masked negative effects of the suit. There may have been a general increase in practice for the kinds of doctors involved in these suits, even greater for doctors not sued than for doctors in the sample. Whether interviews with a control sample could have yielded sufficiently precise data to rule out these possibilities is problematic. Unfortunately, the resources available for the study did not enable such data to be obtained.

A third difference in the two designs may affect the results. In the field experiment, full information concerning the legal record is provided to all of the relevant decision makers, i.e., the employers. In the medical study, by contrast, the results depend on decisions of actual patients to consult a given doctor. It may be assumed that such decisions are often based on imperfect information, some patients knowing little or nothing about the malpractice suit. To ascertain how much information employers usually have concerning the legal record of the employee and then supply that amount would have been a desirable refinement, but a difficult one. The alternative approach would involve turning the medical study into an experiment in which full information concerning malpractice (e.g., liable, accused but acquitted, no record of accusation) was supplied to potential patients. This would have permitted a comparison of the effects of legal accusation in two instances where information concerning the accusation is constant. To carry out such an experiment in a field situation would require an unlikely degree of cooperation, for instance by a medical clinic which might ask patients to choose their doctor on the basis of information given them. It is difficult to conceive of an experiment along these lines which would be both realistic enough to be valid and harmless enough to be ethical.

Section V

Institutional Arrangements and Collective Violence

Introductory Remarks

In this section we turn our attention to law-violating acts that are collective in participation, large scale in effect, and short term in process. Collective violence in the broad usage (assaults, killings, destruction of property, occupying property by force, etc.) does not differ greatly from the acts perpetrated by traditional offenders. Nor does it differ in another sense. Its distribution is also subject to sociocultural variations.

Nevertheless, collective violence is distinct in one sense in that it opens to question not only the "righteousness" of the existing institutional arrangements but the ability or intent of those institutions to cope with the problems the collective action reflects as well; whereas, the acts of traditional offenders do not explicitly question the generalized "righteousness" of institutional arrangements. Instead, these offenders rely on segmented rationalizations to support their own immediate self-interests.

Placing aside acts of violence by individuals and small groups and focusing on these same crimes perpetrated by large collectivities requires that we especially view the nature of intergroup relations and institutional arrangements.

Collective violence is hardly a new phenomenon, for it characterizes our past history (labor-management violence ideological violence, white-originated race riots) as it does our present circumstances.[1] *To be sure, in the present as in the past there exist societal consensuses and interdependencies promoting a degree of cohesiveness among members of American society. Nevertheless, the increased complexity of societal processes and interaction can and has led to dissensus and dissociation.*

American society continues its commitment to democracy and free enterprise and continues to place stress on individual self-determination in competing and achieving goals. However, it also continues to weave an impersonal bureaucratic structure and the characteristics of the mass society. Thus, one man's destiny lies as much with the bureaucratic structure as it does with his merits. At the same time we witness increased agreement in the expectations of fulfilling certain goals (e.g., material gain, equality, justice, opportunity).

Since one man can hardly move the structure for his own ends, this process has increasingly necessitated that those with like minds collectively organize (i.e., teachers, laborers, businessmen, students, police, blacks, homosexuals) in order to communicate problems and to influence action by other parts of the bureaucratic structure.

Thus, there exist, governed by a loose set of norms, avenues of communication and influence interconnecting various groups within the larger bureaucratic structure. It is, then, the linkage of a subgroup to the larger bureaucratic structure which somewhat increases the possibility of greater involvement of the parts of the larger structure in the solution of problems and objectives of other groups. In a sense, to the degree that both rewards and costs can be experienced by all groups in these interdependencies and coalitions, there is a degree of normative control and regulation achieved as each subgroup pursues its own ends.

However, it does not necessarily follow that those groups in the initial stages of collective awareness possess equal access to and influence through the conventional means of communication within bureaucratic structures. This is particularly the case with groups occupying statuses outside the already established hierarchy of power, influence, and interaction (e.g., students, blacks, the poor). It is less likely that these groups, without previously achieved power and influence, can easily effect change through existing conventional means.

[1] The National Commission on the Causes and Prevention of Violence summarizes the extent of group violence connected with protest behavior during the past five years:

> 370 civil rights demonstrations have occurred, involving more than a million participants; 80 counter-demonstrations have been held in opposition to civil rights demonstrators and school integrations; confrontation between demonstrators and police and between opposing groups has often led to violence.
>
> Some 200 private acts of violence toward Negroes and civil rights workers have caused more than 20 deaths and more than 100 injuries. (These figures are derived only from those incidents reported in the New York Times Index; many others may also have occurred.)
>
> Nearly every major city in the United States has experienced riots and civil disorder, arising, as the Commission on Civil Disorders found, from widespread Negro discontent and frustration over the conditions of life in the black ghetto; 239 violent urban outbursts, involving 200,000 participants, have resulted in nearly 8,000 injuries and 191 deaths, as well as hundreds of millions of dollars in property damage and economic losses.
>
> Hundreds of student demonstrations have occurred on campuses across the land; some of the conflicts arising between demonstrators and authorities have resulted in seizure of university facilities, police intervention, riot, property damage, and even death, and several institutions have been brought to a temporary halt.
>
> Anti-war and anti-draft protests have involved some 700,000 participants in cities and on campuses throughout the country: some of these protests either were violently conducted or resulted in a violent official response; some were marked by violence on both sides.
>
> (Progress Report of the National Commission on the Causes and Prevention of Violence, Washington: Government Printing Office, January 1969, p. A-11).

Under these circumstances it is likely that these newly formed expressive groups, possessing little power and influence and therefore less commitment to the prescribed conventional procedures, develop alternate means usually at little social costs. And as some alternate means (i.e., sit-ins, strikes, freedom rides) not only prove ineffective but generate frustration and hostility as well, increased manifestations of collective violence are resorted to by some, both to call attention to the problems and to forcibly secure positions within the linkages of power and influence.

It is equally true that to the extent that emerging groups acquire rapid social, political, and economic progress which is not only visible but is also viewed to be acquired at the direct expense of others who are established or who are attempting to be established in the hierarchy of power and influence, potentialities for expressions of violence continued to exist. In another sense, the greater the hostility and fears of other community groups, and also the lack of ability or unwillingness of institutional representatives to cope with both the violence and the problems that it reflects, the more so police and other institutional groups resort to extreme measures in counterreaction (e.g., violence, sophisticated weapons, punitive legislation). Similarly, the initial instigators of collective violence shift to new strategies in counterreaction.

The reader should be cautioned that a more extensive treatment, which is beyond the scope of this section, would dwell more on historical and social psychological forces as contributors to collective violence.[2] *However, special stress on institutional arrangements illustrate well the social processes underlying the recent activities by the blacks, the young, and the poor.*

[2] See the following sources:

"Violence in America: Historical and Comparative Perspectives," Volumes 1 and 2. A Report to the National Commission on the Causes and Prevention of Violence, U.S. Government Printing Office, Washington, D.C., June, 1969.

"The Politics of Protest-Violent Aspects of Protest and Confrontation." A Report to the National Commission on the Causes and Prevention of Violence, U.S. Government Printing Office, Washington, D.C., June, 1969.

32. The Search for Power and Participation: Youth, Negroes, and the Poor

Marvin E. Wolfgang

We have said that to speak generically of youth overlooks variability in a pluralistic society, and we have drawn attention to some notable variations between middle-class and lower-class youth. There are, however, many more versions of the concatenation of variables that differentiate youth. Being young, middle class, white, and from an economically secure family generates a quite different image from being young, lower class, poor, and Negro. In sheer absolute numbers, more young people are located in the former group than in the latter and probably suffer fewer strains from culture contradictions, anomie, and psychological deprivation than do the latter. There is likely to be greater conformity to parental prescriptions in the former, more familial transmission of group values, more cohesiveness of the family. The Negro, lower-class youth drop out of school and drift into delinquency in greater proportions than do white middle-class youth. Class is probably a stronger factor contributing to value allegiance and normative conduct than is race, which is to say that Negro and white middle-class youth are more alike than are Negro middle- and lower-class or white middle- and lower-class youngsters.

Yet, with all the variabilities that might be catalogued in an empirically descriptive study of youth, there are characteristics of the life stage, status, and style of youth in general which are shared by the status of poverty and the status of being Negro in American society. All may be described as possessing a kind of structural marginality[1] that places them on the periphery of power in our society. When the multiple probabilities of being young, Negro and poor exist, the shared attributes are more than a summation. The force of whatever problems they represent is more of a multiplicative than an additive function.

Reprinted from *The Culture of Youth* by Marvin E. Wolfgang (Washington: Government Printing Office, Office of Juvenile Delinquency and Youth Development, Welfare Administration, U.S. Department of Health, Education, and Welfare, 1967), pp. 20–23, 29.

[1]Tamme Wittermans and Irving Kraus, "Structural Marginality and Social Worth," *Sociology and Social Research* (April 1964) 48:348–360. For an excellent summary of theory and research on lower-class family life, see the recent work of Suzanne Keller, *The American Lower Class Family,* Albany: New York State Division for Youth, 1965.

Youth, Negroes, and the poor have subcultural value systems different from, yet subsidiary to the larger culture. They often share many features, such as being deprived of certain civil rights and liberties, barred from voting, and denied adequate defense counsel and equality of justice. Their current statuses are frequently subject to manipulation by an enthroned elite and their power to effect change in their futures may be minimal. They tend to have common conflicts with authority and to be dominated by females in the matriarchal structure of their own social microcosms.

All three groups know the meaning of spatial segregation, whether voluntary or compulsory. For youth, it is in schools, clubs, seating arrangements, occupations, forms of entertainment, and leisure pursuits. For the poor and for Negroes, it may be all of these as well as place of residence and other alternatives of work, play, and mobility opportunities. There are similarities in their subordinate and dependency status, and in having poor, inadequate, or irrelevant role models. The values and behavior of the dominant culture and class in American society, as adopted by Negroes, often reveal a pathetically compulsive quality; the poor have been denied access to the ends to which they subscribe, and youth is, at best, a power-muted microculture. For all three, norms seem to shift and change with more than common frequency or are not clearly designated. All three groups tend to be more romantic, nonrational, impulsive, physically aggressive, more motivated toward immediacy and directness than their counterparts in the dominant culture. There is among youth, Negroes, and the poor more deviant and criminal behavior, and a greater disparity between aspiration and achievement. At times their revolt against authority erupts into violence for which they feel little guilt or responsibility.

Increasingly they are self-conscious, aware of their own collectivities as subcultural systems, partly because their revolt is today a greater threat to the systems which have been established to control, govern, or manipulate them. The poor are being asked for the first time what they want and what they would like to do to help themselves or have done for them. Negroes are acting as advisers and consultants on Federal policy, and young people are being heard when they speak about Vietnam, restrictions on passports, college curricula, faculty appointments, and new notions of freedom and sexual morality.

With more clarity and conscience, the three groups are searching for meaningfulness, identity, and social justice. They are articulating their protest against powerlessness, are seeking participation in decision-making processes that affect their own life conditions. That some retreat into drugs, alcohol, and other symptoms of alienation is now viewed as dysfunctional by their own majorities as well as by the establishment. That some resort to violence, whether in Watts or in Hampton Beach,[2] is episodic, meant to display boredom with their condition, blatant protest, and latent power. As achievement, as a danger signal, and as a catalyst, violence for them may

[2]See the Hampton Beach Project, Paul Estaver, Director, Project Director's Report, Hampton Beach, New Hampshire: Hampton Beach Chamber of Commerce, n.d.

serve the social functions outlined by Lewis Coser.[3] But their use of violence is end-oriented and cannot be viewed as a cultural psychopathology. They desire to be recognized, not to be forgotten, because they now see themselves for the first time. They are seeking what Edmund Williamson,[4] dean at the University of Minnesota, calls the most important freedom of all—to be taken seriously, to be listened to.

One of the interesting things about American youth today, especially the older student segment, is its activistic character and increasing identification with the poor and with the civil rights movement.* There is an intense morality and a demand for clear commitments. In many cases young people are directly involved in working in neighborhoods of poverty or in the Negro struggle in the South, whether in song, march, or litigation. Moreover, the idealism of youth and this identification with the process toward participation in power are being fostered by Federal support of the Peace Corps program, both foreign and domestic, and by much governmental concern and protection of young civil rights workers in the South. But the reference here to identification is not to these overlapping involvements; it is to the means for communicating their lack of participation in formulating the rules of life's games. Impatience, discontent, and dissatisfaction with the state of American society[5] become healthy reflections of a new commitment, a commitment to the desire for change and for participating in the direction of change.

Obviously, there are also differences among the three groups, the most striking of which is the fact that youth is a temporary stage in a life cycle and that ultimately the structural marginality and status deprivation are overcome for many by the passage of time. The representatives of the subculture of youth are mobile, eventually leave the subculture, and with age, birth cohorts socially fold into one another. But the status designation of Negro is, except for race crossings, permanent, and the poor commonly have oppressive generational continuity. That youth in its temporariness shares with the major minority groups certain attributes of being and of the struggle for becoming is itself noteworthy, even if the youth were less affected by and conscious of their mutual interests, means, and goals. Perhaps the short sample of time represented by youth will one day be viewed in the long perspective as symbolic of the longer, but also temporary, state of depriviation and disenfrachisement of being poor or of having the status of Negro in American society.

The identity of youth with the protestation process, whether similar to or in common with the poor and the Negro, is, of course, not universal and may not even be a cultural modality. Its expression is, nonetheless, vigorous and viable. It has entered the arena of public attention and functions as a prodder for its concepts of

[3] Lewis A. Coser, "Some Social Functions of Violence," in Marvin E. Wolfgang (ed.), "Patterns of Violence," *The Annals of the American Academy of Political and Social Science* (March 1966) 364:8–18.

[4] *The New York Times,* November 21, 1965, p. 72.

[5] On this point, see Talcott Parsons, "Youth in the Context of American Society," in Erik H. Erikson, *The Challenge of Youth,* 1965, pp. 110–141.

Editor's Note: Recent activities among college students would also indicate deep concern with the militaristic domination of the political and economic affairs of the nation since 1950.

progress. With this identity, the youth of today are unlike the "flaming youth" in the frenetic milieu of the twenties, the youth associated with the political left and the proletarian cult of the thirties, the uniformed youth of the forties, or the passive youth of the fifties. And yet, even with this identity they are without a systematic ideology. Despite the fact that they have come to realize the advantages of collective drives that prick the giants of massive and lethargic organization into action, they have developed no political affiliation. Perhaps the closest these young groups come to a focal concern is in their alerting their peers and adults to the ethical conflicts and issues embraced by society's increasing ability to reduce individual anonymity and to manipulate lives. In one sense it could be said that they jealously guard the constraints a democratic society ideologically imposes on overcontrol, invasion of privacy, and overreaction to deviancy.

There are fringes to most movements, and there are parasites attached to the youth we have been describing as healthier segments of society. Frequently the fringe looms larger than the core in the public image of youth and an excessive degree of rebelliousness is conveyed. The bulk of our youth are not engaged in a rebellion against adults, and the degree of dissimilarity between the generations has often been overstressed, as some authors have recently asserted.[6] Rather than rejecting most parental norms, the majority of those in the youth subculture are eager to participate in the larger society. Individuals resisting specific authority patterns do not constitute group rejection of dominant social norms.

Moreover, except for those suppressed beyond youth by their status of being poor of being Negro, achievement comes with aging and that convergence often leads to the collapse of a once fiery, romantic drive. And, as Peter Berger[7] has eloquently remarked, with success prophets become priests and revolutionaries become administrators. The gravity of time pulls hard on our muscles and ideals and too often the earlier triumph of principle gives way to the triumph of expedience. The once lambent minds of youth are frequently corroded by conformity in adulthood and a new flow of youth into the culture is needed to invoke their own standards of judgement on our adult norms.

[6] Robert C. Bealer, Fern K. Willits, and Peter R. Maida, "The Myth of a Rebellious Adolescent Subculture: Its Detrimental Effects for Understanding Rural Youth," in Lee G. Burchinal (ed.), *Rural Youth in Crisis,* Proceedings of a National Conference on Rural Youth in a Changing Environment, Stillwater, Oklahoma, 1963, Washington, D.C.: U.S. Government Printing Office, 1965.

[7] Peter Berger, *An Invitation to Sociology: A Humanistic Perspective,* New York: Doubleday and Co., Anchor Book, 1963.

33. Riots and Crime–Historical Backround

The President's Commission on Law Enforcement and Administration of Justice

Violent racial conflict is not a new phenomenon in America. Perhaps the most atrocious riots that ever occurred in this country were the 1863 draft riots in New York. For about 4 days white mobs controlled much of the city, during which they looted stores, burned Negro dwellings, and beat or lynched those Negroes they got their hands upon. Before the State militia restored order there were about 2,000 casualites. The draft riots are notable for more than their extreme savagery. They were the archetype of most of the racial clashes that took place before the summer of 1964. They occurred during a time of national tension and anxiety, the Civil War. They occurred at a time when Negroes appeared to be on the verge of making a major social advance, emancipation. They were a response by predominantly working class white citizens to a requirement that they assist this Negro advance by making personal sacrifices and by serving in the Army. They consisted of offensive action by white mobs against the persons of Negroes, and defensive action by Negro mobs and individuals against the persons of whites, with looting and property destruction as by-products of those actions. They were not confined to any one part of the city, but involved raids and incursions, attacks and counterattacks. They lasted longer than they might have because of the reluctance of officials to invoke full military or police force against them promptly, and because of the more or less open sympathy of many members of the military or the police with the rioters. They were, in sum, actions by members of the majority against the presumably threatening minority.

All the bloodiest riots of the 20th century, until Watts, conformed to this pattern. The very bloodiest took place in East St. Louis, Ill., on July 3 and 4, 1916, during the First World War, slightly a week after the first American troops landed in France; 39 Negroes and 9 whites were killed, hundreds of people were injured or wounded, and 244 buildings, mostly Negro homes, and 44 railroad cars were destroyed by fire. This riot was the culmination of a long period of racial tension provoked by a massive influx of southern Negroes into East St. Louis, and their subsequent use as

Reprinted from "Riots and Crime," *Task Force Report: Crime and Its Impact–An Assessment,* a Report by The President's Commission on Law Enforcement and Administration of Justice (Washington: Government Printing Office, 1967), ch. 9, pp. 117–120.

strikebreakers in some of the city's aluminum and steel plants. The incident that precipitated the riot was the shooting of two plainclothes detectives as they drove through the Negro district of the city in an unmarked car on the night of July 2. The blood-stained car was displayed in front of the police station the following morning. An angry crowd gathered, and soon broke into bands of roving toughs, armed with stones, clubs, and guns. These bands assaulted Negroes on the streets, and set fire to more than 200 homes in "Black Valley," a Negro slum; snipers shot the residents as they attempted to flee the flames, and the efforts of fireman to save the houses were resisted by the mobs. The rioting continued for 24 hours, largely because the 12 National Guard companies that were sent to put it down were late in arriving; there were strong indications that this tardiness was due to their sympathy with the rioters.

Twenty-three Negroes and 15 whites were killed, and more than 500 people were injured, in the course of the riot that raged in Chicago from July 27 to August 2, 1919, at the depth of the economic depression that accompanied the country's transition from a wartime to a peacetime economy. Chicago's Negro population had increased by almost 150 percent since 1910, and there was acute competition both for jobs and for housing; no new housing, of course, had been built during the war. The trouble started on July 27 at a southside beach, one end of which was used by whites, the other by Negroes. A brawl broke out as the result of the alleged crossing of the imaginary dividing line by some Negroes. It escalated rapidly. A Negro boy who had drifted opposite the white beach was stoned, and presently he drowned; whether or not he had been hit by a stone was never determined. The Negro bathers became enraged, and as the news of the drowning spread to a nearby Negro neighborhood, they were joined by hundreds of other Negroes. A policeman who refused to arrest a white man the Negroes charged with the boy's death was attacked. A Negro was shot by another policeman, also a Negro. That night the rioting spread to other sections of the city, and continued sporadically until the end of the week. It was aggravated by a transit strike that began Monday night and that forced both whites and Negroes to walk to and from work through hostile neighborhoods. Throughout the week bands of both whites and Negroes roamed the streets searching for and attacking stragglers of the other race. In the Loop gangs of white servicemen attacked Negroes. On the southside a gang of Negroes attacked an apartment house, and the police fired into the crowd and killed four of its members. There were automobile forays, ambushes, and rooftop sniping. The National Guard was not put into action until Wednesday, although it had been ready for action on Monday. The rioting was finally ended conclusively on Friday by a heavy rainstorm

Between the early evening of June 20, 1943 (also a Sunday) and the early morning of June 22, 24 Negroes and 9 whites were killed, and 933 people were injured in a riot in Detroit. Once again, the general background was wartime. Large numbers of Negroes had come to the city to work in the defense plants, with the resulting pressure on housing. Federal regulations prescribed equal employment standards in defense industries, and so Negroes were being upgraded in their jobs. The tension was so obvious that a year earlier Life magazine had published a feature article about it, entitled "Detroit is Dynamite." Characteristically enough, the riot started at the Belle Isle Amusement Park with a fight whose precise nature never was discovered. Within an hour, rioting was taking place in many parts of the city. Negroes began looting white-owned stores in the Paradise Valley ghetto. Whites attacked Negroes emerging from all-night movie theaters in the downtown district. The next evening the pattern of raids, ambushes, and sniping began to take shape. The Detroit police were unable to handle the situation; several well-documented accounts indicate that they were unwilling to because of their prowhite sympathies. The Governor had been reluctant to call in the National Guard, but by midnight Monday he was compelled to, and order was quickly restored.

Those three riots were the most violent of a dozen or more that followed similar courses during the first half of this century. While many factors contributed, they seemed to be the outcome of white resistance to social and economic progress by Negroes, and Negro response to that resistance. It is accurate to call them race riots. Their basic design was the infliction of personal injury by whites on Negroes and by Negroes on whites. People and homes were the important targets. However, there were two major riots during this period, the 1935 and 1943 riots in America's oldest, most famous Negro ghetto, Harlem in New York City, whose design was considerably different. They foreshadowed the ghetto riots of 1964, 1965, and 1966.

Neither of the Harlem riots were precipitated by an interracial clash on some piece of neutral ground, or by a white attack on Negroes. Both were set off by law enforcement incidents in the ghetto itself. On the afternoon of March 19, 1935, near the bottom of the great depression, a Negro boy was caught shoplifting in a five-and-tencents store. He was taken by store employees to the back of the store for questioning and to await the arrival of the police, but when he became hysterical he was released through a back door into an alley. However, the shoppers in the store believed that he was being beaten, and their anger and alarm were heightened by the grim coincidence that a hearse happened to be parked in the alley. Within a half hour there was a large and vociferous picket line in front of the store. A crowd assembled to watch. A policeman arrested a picketer, and the crowd began throwing rocks and bottles at the police. By early evening, several thousand Negroes were roaming around Harlem breaking store windows. Looting began after dark, and continued until the police restored order late the next day. Foodstores were a particular target of the looters. There was much hunger in Harlem at the time; 70 percent of the population was on relief. In addition there was much resentment over the unwillingness of white merchants to employ Negroes.

On the evening of August 1, 1943, a Negro soldier was shot and wounded by a white policeman in a Harlem hotel lobby. A false rumor that the soldier had been shot in the back and killed spread through the neighborhood. A crowd gathered in front of the hospital where the wounded man had been taken. No one bothered to tell the crowd the true state of affairs, and it soon rampaged up the street, smashing store windows. Presently looting began. By dawn a stretch of 40 city blocks was under attack. By the following night, when the New York and the military police restored order, 1,234 stores had been looted. Almost all were white-owned. Of course, the large majority of Harlem stores were (and are) white-owned, but the best evidence available about the selection of stores to attack is that in 1943 the looters spared whatever Negro-owned stores there were. Several hundred people were injured more or less seriously in each of the Harlem riots, but by comparison with race riots like those in East St. Louis, Chicago, and Detroit, fatalities were few–two Negroes and two whites in 1935 and five Negro looters in 1943–and property damage was great–it ran over $5 million in 1943. These riots were confined to the ghetto, and commercial establishments and the goods in them, rather than persons or homes, were the chief targets of the rioters.

The seven riots that astonished America during the summer of 1964 conformed in almost all respects the Harlem pattern, although in all of them there was the additional element of furious mob hostility toward the police. Each one was precipitated by a police incident, only the first of which was serious; in New York by the fatal shooting of a 15-year-old Negro boy by an off-duty police lieutenant; in Rochester 6 days later by the attempt of a policeman to arrest a drunk and disorderly Negro adolescent at a street dance; in Jersey City the following week by the arrest of a Negro couple for disorderly conduct; in Paterson and Elizabeth a week after that by similar arrests; in the Dixmoor area just south of Chicago 3 days later by the arrest of a Negro woman for stealing a bottle of gin from a liquor store; in Philadelphia 2 weeks later by an altercation that arose between a policeman and a Negro couple whose car had stalled in the middle of a busy intersection. There were few fatalities: The boy in New York and four people in Rochester, three of whom were civilian defense workers who were killed when the helicopter from which they were observing the movements of the mobs, got out of control and crashed. Property damage was extensive, particularly in New York (541 shops damaged), Rochester (204), and Philadelphia (225).

Watts

The 5-day riot that began on Wednesday, August 11, 1965, in the South Central Los Angeles ghetto (the area of which the Watts neighborhood is a small part) has probably been more carefully examined than any riot that has ever occurred....

The Watts riot was, of course, different from the other riots of the last three summers in several ways; no two riots are exactly alike. The most striking difference was its extreme violence and destructiveness. Thirty-four people were killed and 1,032 injured. Two hundred buildings were burned to the ground and 720 more looted or damaged; the total property loss was estimated at $40 million. The resources of the Los Angeles Police Department, the Los Angeles Fire Department, the Los Angeles County Sheriff's Department, and the California Highway Patrol were so overtaxed that 13,400 troops of the California National Guard were finally committed to controlling the riot.

However, there is no evidence that Watts lasted so long and caused so much damage because the Los Angeles ghetto is unique. What was unique in Los Angeles was a conjunction of topographical, organizational, jurisdictional, and operational circumstances that made controlling the riot exceptionally difficult. The area in which rioting occurred is big (46.3 square miles) and flat, and so preventing the riot from spreading required a large number of men. The Los Angeles Police Department had only about 5,000 officers to police a city that is the country's largest in area and second largest in population. Three-quarters of the riot area is in the city of Los Angeles and the rest is in Los Angeles County, which is under the jurisdiction of the county sheriff, and the two departments had done an insufficient amount of joint planning to meet a major emergency. In addition both city and State authorities hesitated for about 2 days to seek the help of the National Guard; when the Guard was deployed, some 52 hours after the first rioting began, the situation rapidly improved, although another 2 days were needed to restore order completely....

Certainly the spark that ignited Watts was feeble and random. At about 7 p.m. on August 11, a day on which the temperature reached 94°, a Negro driving a pickup truck in a portion of South Central Los Angeles that is outside the city limits called the attention of a white California highway patrolman to the reckless way in which an old gray Buick was being driven north (toward the city limits) on Avalon Boulevard. The patrolman followed the Buick on his motorcycle and determined that it was going 50 miles an hour in a 35-mile-an-hour zone. He turned on his red light and siren, pulled alongside the car and ordered the driver to the curb. The driver, a 21-year-old Negro named Marquette Frye, obeyed at once and without demur. He was evidently drunk and he did not have a driver's license. The patrolman told him he was under arrest and radioed for his backup officer and a transport car to come and help him place Frye in custody. Both arrived promptly. Meanwhile 20 or 30 passersby and residents of nearby buildings had gathered to watch the scene apparently purely for entertainment. There was no sign of trouble. The patrolman was friendly and polite. Frye was good humored, even jocular.

Suddenly the situation changed. Vociferously and belligerently Frye refused to get into the transport car. The officers attempted to handcuff him. He resisted. The spectators became sullen and hostile. The officers radioed for more help. Frye's stepbrother, who had been riding in the car, and his mother, who owned the car and who had hastened to the scene when a neighbor told her what was happening, came to Frye's assistance. More highway patrolmen and members of the Los Angeles Police Department arrived. The size of the crowd increased. Frye was forcibly subdued, and put in the car. The spectators who by then numbered several hundred, hurled abuse at the police, who by then numbered about 50. Finally the police, with the three Fryes as prisoners, managed to disengage themselves from the crowd and leave the scene, under a shower of rocks and bricks and bottles. In the course of doing so they made another arrest, of a young woman who, according to the police, was spitting and cursing at them and, according to herself, was doing nothing more than talking and giggling. She was a barber and was wearing her professional smock, which gave rise to an impression that the police had manhandled a pregnant woman; a report of this instance of "police brutality" spread through the ghetto area, and as it spread it became a rumor that the police had beaten and kicked Frye's pregnant mother. The crowd did not disperse after the police left. On the contrary, it stayed on Avalon Boulevard, which is a main thoroughfare through South Central Los

Angeles, and bombarded passing motorists with whatever missiles were available. Meanwhile angry groups began assembling in other parts of the ghetto. The riot was on.

What is most suggestive—and alarming—about the events that began the Watts riot is the chain of accident and chance. The highway patrolman, responding to a complaint by a Negro citizen, had more than sufficient cause to arrest Frye, and he went about his business with efficiency and propriety. The act for which Frye was arrested, driving drunkenly and recklessly on a main city thoroughfare, could not possibly be interpreted as either a harmless lapse or as a gesture of protest, conscious or unconscious, against white oppression. Frye was not an agitator or a militant; there is not even reason to believe that he was an especially aggrieved young man. The people who first gathered to watch the scene were not looking for trouble, but for amusement. The particular police force against which there was the most antagonism in South Central Los Angeles was not the California Highway Patrol but the Los Angeles Police Department. If the highway patrolmen doing what they did could precipitate a catastrophe like Watts, it is surely safe to say that almost anything might have precipitated it. South Central Los Angeles was ready and willing—and perhaps even eager—to run amok.

34. Profiles of Disorders

National Advisory Commission on Civil Disorders

The summer of 1967 again brought racial disorders to American cities, and with them shock, fear and bewilderment to the nation.

The worst came during a two-week period in July, first in Newark and then in Detroit. Each set off a chain reaction in neighboring communities.

On July 28, 1967, the President of the United States established this Commission and directed us to answer three basic questions:

What happened?
Why did it happen?
What can be done to prevent it from happening again?

Reprinted from "Summary of Report," a Report by the National Advisory Commission on Civil Disorders (Washington: Government Printing Office, 1968), pp. 1–7.

To respond to these questions, we have undertaken a broad range of studies and investigations. We have visited the riot cities; we have heard many witnesses; we have sought the counsel of experts across the country.

This is our basic conclusion: Our nation is moving toward two societies, one black, one white—separate and unequal.

Reaction to last summer's disorders has quickened the movement and deepened the division. Discrimination and segregation have long permeated much of American life; they now threaten the future of every American.

This deepening racial division is not inevitable. The movement apart can be reversed. Choice is still possible. Our principal task is to define that choice and to press for a national resolution.

To pursue our present course will involve the continuing polarization of the American community and, ultimately, the destruction of basic democratic values.

The alternative is not blind repression or capitulation to lawlessness. It is the realization of common opportunities for all within a single society.

This alternative will require a commitment to national action—compassionate, massive and sustained, backed by the resources of the most powerful and the richest nation on this earth. From every American it will require new attitudes, new understanding and, above all, new will.

The vital needs of the nation must be met; hard choices must be made, and, if necessary, new taxes enacted.

Violence cannot build a better society. Disruption and disorder nourish repression, not justice. They strike at the freedom of every citizen. The community cannot—it will not—tolerate coercion and mob rule.

Violence and destruction must be ended—in the streets of the ghetto and in the lives of people.

Segregation and poverty have created in the racial ghetto a destructive environment totally unknown to most white Americans.

What white Americans have never fully understood—but what the Negro can never forget—is that white society is deeply implicated in the ghetto. White institutions created it, white institutions maintain it, and white society condones it.

It is time now to turn with all the purpose at our command to the major unfinished business of this nation. It is time to adopt strategies for action that will produce quick and visible progress. It is time to make good the promises of American democracy to all citizens—urban and rural, white and black, Spanish-surname, American Indian, and every minority group.

Our recommendations embrace three basic principles:

- To mount programs on a scale equal to the dimension of the problems:
- To aim these programs for high impact in the immediate future in order to close the gap between promise and performance;
- To undertake new initiatives and experiments that can change the system of failure and frustration that now dominates the ghetto and weakens our society.

These programs will require unprecedented levels of funding and performance, but they neither probe deeper nor demand more than the problems which called them forth. There can be no higher priority for national action and no higher claim on the nation's conscience.

We issue this Report now, four months before the date called for by the President. Much remains that can be learned. Continued study is essential.

As Commissioners we have worked together with a sense of the greatest urgency and have sought to compose whatever differences exist among us. Some differences remain. But the gravity of the problem and the pressing need for action are too clear to allow further delay in the issuance of this Report.

Profiles of Disorder

The report contains profiles of a selection of the disorders that took place during the summer of 1967. These profiles are designed to indicate how the disorders happened, who participated in them, and how local officials, police forces, and the National Guard responded. Illustrative excerpts follow:

Newark ... It was decided to attempt to channel the energies of the people into a nonviolent protest. While Lofton[1] promised the crowd that a full investigation would be made of the Smith incident[2] the other Negro leaders began urging those on the scene to form a line of march toward the city hall.

Some persons joined the line of march. Others milled about in the narrow street. From the dark grounds of the housing project came a barrage of rocks. Some of them fell among the crowd. Others hit persons in the line of march. Many smashed the windows of the police station. The rock throwing, it was believed, was the work of youngsters; approximately 2,500 children lived in the housing project.

Almost at the same time, an old car was set afire in a parking lot. The line of march began to disintegrate. The police, their heads protected by World War I-type helmets, sallied forth to disperse the crowd. A fire engine, arriving on the scene, was pelted with rocks. As police drove people away from the station, they scattered in all directions.

A few minutes later a nearby liquor store was broken into. Some persons, seeing a caravan of cabs appear at city hall to protest Smith's arrest, interpreted this as evidence that the disturbance had been organized, and generated rumors to that effect.

However, only a few stores were looted. Within a short period of time, the disorder appeared to have run its course.

* * *

... On Saturday, July 15, [Director of Police Dominick] Spina received a report of snipers in a housing project. When he arrived he saw approximately 100 National Guardsmen and police officers crouching behind vehicles, hiding in corners and lying on the ground around the edge of the courtyard.

Since everything appeared quiet and it was broad daylight, Spina walked directly down the middle of the street. Nothing happened. As he came to the last building of the complex, he heard a shot. All around him the troopers jumped, believing themselves to be under sniper fire. A moment later a young Guardsman ran from behind a building.

[1]Editor's Note: Oliver Lofton, administrator of the Newark Legal Services Project.

[2]Editor's Note: Refers to alleged brutality by police toward Negro cab driver, John Smith, accused of "tailgating" and driving the wrong way on a one-way street.

The Director of Police went over and asked him if he had fired the shot. The soldier said yes, he had fired to scare a man away from a window; that his orders were to keep everyone away from windows.

Spina said he told the soldier: "Do you know what you just did? You have now created a state of hysteria. Every Guardsman up and down this street and every state policeman and every city policeman that is present thinks that somebody just fired a shot and that it is probably a sniper."

A short time later more "gunshots" were heard. Investigating, Spina came upon a Puerto Rican sitting on a wall. In reply to a question as to whether he knew "where the firing is coming from?" the man said:

"That's no firing. That's fireworks. If you look up to the fourth floor, you will see people who are throwing down these cherry bombs."

By this time truckloads of National Guardsmen had arrived and troopers and policemen were again crouched everywhere looking for a sniper. The Director of Police remained at the scene for three hours, and the only shot fired was the one by the guardsman.

Nevertheless, at six o'clock that evening two columns of National Guardsmen and state troopers were directing mass fire at the Hayes Housing Project in response to what they believed were snipers....

Detroit ... A spirit of carefree nihilism was taking hold. To riot and destroy appeared more and more to become ends in themselves. Late Sunday afternoon it appeared to one observer that the young people were "dancing amidst the flames."

A Negro plainclothes officer was standing at an intersection when a man threw a Molotov cocktail into a business establishment at the corner. In the heat of the afternoon, fanned by the 20 to 25 m.p.h. winds of both Sunday and Monday, the fire reached the home next door within minutes. As residents uselessly sprayed the flames with garden hoses, the fire jumped from roof to roof of adjacent two-and three-story buildings. Within the hour the entire block was in flames. The ninth house in the burning row belonged to the arsonist who had thrown the Molotov cocktail....

* * *

... Employed as a private guard, 55-year-old Julius L. Dorsey, a Negro, was standing in front of a market when accosted by two Negro men and a woman. They demanded he permit them to loot the market. He ignored their demands. They began to berate him. He asked a neighbor to call the police. As the argument grew more heated, Dorsey fired three shots from his pistol into the air.

The police radio reported: "Looters, they have rifles." A patrol car driven by a police officer and carrying three National Guardsmen arrived. As the looters fled, the law enforcement personnel opened fire. When the firing ceased, one person lay dead. He was Julius L. Dorsey...

* * *

... As the riot alternately waxed and waned, one area of the ghetto remained insulated. On the northeast side the residents of some 150 square blocks inhabited by 21,000 persons had, in 1966, banded together in the Positive Neighborhood Action Committee (PNAC). With professional help from the Institute of Urban Dynamics, they had organized block clubs and made plans for the improvement of the neighborhood....

When the riot broke out, the residents, through the block clubs, were able to organize quickly. Youngsters, agreeing to stay in the neighborhood, participated in detouring traffic. While many persons reportedly sympathized with the idea of a rebellion against the "system," only two small fires were set—one in an empty building.

* * *

... According to Lt. Gen. Throckmorton and Col. Bolling,[3] the city, at this time, was saturated with fear. The National Guardsmen were afraid, the residents were afraid, and the police were afraid. Numerous persons, the majority of them Negroes, were being injured by gunshots of undetermined origin. The general and his staff felt that the major task of the troops was to reduce the fear and restore an air of normalcy.

In order to accomplish this, every effort was made to establish contact and rapport between the troops and the residents. The soldiers—20 percent of whom were Negro—began helping to clean up the streets, collect garbage, and trace persons who had disappeared in the confusion. Residents in the neighborhoods responded with soup and sandwiches for the troops. In areas where the National Guard tried to establish rapport with the citizens, there was a smaller response.

New Brunswick...A short time later, elements of the crowd—an older and rougher one than the night before—appeared in front of the police station. The participants wanted to see the mayor.

Mayor [Patricia] Sheehan went out onto the steps of the station. Using a bull-horn, she talked to the people and asked that she be given an opportunity to correct conditions. The crowd was boisterous. Some persons challenged the mayor. But, finally, the opinion, "She's new! Give her a chance!" prevailed.

A demand was issued by people in the crowd that all persons arrested the previous night be released. Told that this already had been done, the people were suspicious. They asked to be allowed to inspect the jail cells.

It was agreed to permit representatives of the people to look in the cells to satisfy themselves that everyone had been released.

The crowd dispersed. The New Brunswick riot had failed to materialize.

Patterns of Disorder

The "typical" riot did not take place. The disorders of 1967 were unusual, irregular, complex and unpredictable social processes. Like most human events, they did not unfold in an orderly sequence. However, an analysis of our survey information leads to some conclusions about the riot process.

In general:

- The civil disorders of 1967 involved Negroes acting against local symbols of white American society, authority and property in Negro neighborhoods—rather than against white persons.
- Of 164 disorders reported during the first nine months of 1967 eight (5 percent) were major in terms of violence and damage; 33 (20 percent) were serious but not major; 123 (75 percent) were minor and undoubtedly would not have received national attention as "riots" had the nation not been sensitized by the more serious outbreaks.
- In the 75 disorders studied by a Senate subcommittee, 83 deaths were reported. Eighty-two percent of the deaths and more than half the injuries occurred in Newark and Detroit. About 10 percent of the dead and 38 percent of the in-jured were public employees, primarily law officers and firemen. The overwhelm-

[3] Editor's Note: Commanders of the Federal troops.

ing majority of the persons killed or injured in all the disorders were Negro civilians.

- Initial damage estimates were greatly exaggerated. In Detroit newspaper damage estimates at first ranged from $200 million to $500 million; the highest recent estimate is $45 million. In Newark early estimates ranged from $15 to $25 million. A month later damage was estimated at $10.2 million, over 80 percent in inventory losses.

In the 24 disorders in 23 cities which we surveyed:

- The final incident before the outbreak of disorder, and the initial violence itself, generally took place in the evening or at night at a place in which it was normal for many people to be on the streets.
- Violence usually occurred almost immediately following the occurrence of the final precipitating incident, and then escalated rapidly. With but few exceptions, violence subsided during the day, and flared rapidly again at night. The night-day cycles continued through the early period of the major disorders.
- Disorder generally began with rock and bottle throwing and window breaking: Once store windows were broken, looting usually followed.
- Disorder did not erupt as a result of a single "triggering" or "precipitating" incident. Instead, it was generated out of an increasingly disturbed social atmosphere, in which typically a series of tension-heightening incidents over a period of weeks or months became linked in the minds of many in the Negro community with a reservoir of underlying grievances. At some point in the mounting tension, a further incident—in itself often routine or trivial—became the breaking point and the tension spilled over into violence.
- "Prior" incidents, which increased tensions and ultimately led to violence, were police actions in almost half the cases; police actions were "final" incidents before the outbreak or violence in 12 of the 24 surveyed disorders.
- No particular control tactic was successful in every situation. The varied effectiveness of control techniques emphasizes the need for advance training, planning, adequate intelligence systems, and knowledge of the ghetto community.
- Negotiations between Negroes—including your militants as well as older Negro leaders—and white officials concerning "terms of peace" occurred during virtually all the disorders surveyed. In many cases, these negotiations involved discussion of underlying grievances as well as the handling of the disorder by control authorities.
- The typical rioter was a teenager or young adult, a lifelong resident of the city in which he rioted, a high school dropout; he was, nevertheless, somewhat better educated than his nonrioting Negro neighbor, and was usually underemployed or employed in a menial job. He was proud of his race, extremely hostile to both whites and middle-class Negroes and, although informed about politics, highly distrustful of the political system.
- A Detroit survey revealed that approximately 11 percent of the total residents of two riot areas admitted participation in the rioting, 20 to 25 percent identified themselves as "bystanders," over 16 percent identified themselves as "counter-rioters" who urged rioters to "cool it," and the remaining 48 to 53 percent said they were at home or elsewhere and did not participate. In a survey of Negro males between the ages of 15 and 35 residing in the disturbance area in Newark, about 45 percent identified themselves as rioters, and about 55 percent as "non-involved."
- Most rioters were young Negro males. Nearly 53 percent of arrestees were between 15 and 24 years of age; nearly 81 percent between 15 and 35.

- In Detroit and Newark about 74 percent of the rioters were brought up in the North. In contrast, of the noninvolved, 36 percent in Detroit and 52 percent in Newark were brought up in the North.
- What the rioters appeared to be seeking was fuller participation in the social order and the material benefits enjoyed by the majority of American citizens. Rather than rejecting the American system, they were anxious to obtain a place for themselves in it.
- Numerous Negro counter-rioters walked the streets urging rioters to "cool it." The typical counter-rioter was better educated and had higher income than either the rioter or the noninvolved.
- The proportion of Negroes in local government was substantially smaller than the Negro proportion of population. Only three of the 20 cities studied had more than one Negro legislator; none had ever had a Negro mayor or city manager. In only four cities did Negroes hold other important policy-making positions or serve as heads of municipal departments.
- Although almost all cities had some sort of formal grievance mechanism for handling citizen complaints, this typically was regarded by Negroes as ineffective and was generally ignored.
- Although specific grievances varied from city to city, at least 12 deeply held grievances can be identified and ranked into three levels of relative intensity:

First Level of Intensity

1. Police practices
2. Unemployment and underemployment
3. Inadequate housing

Second Level of Intensity

4. Inadequate education
5. Poor recreation facilities and programs
6. Ineffectiveness of the political structure and grievance mechanisms

Third Level of Intensity

7. Disrespectful white attitudes
8. Discriminatory administration of justice
9. Inadequacy of federal programs
10. Inadequacy of municipal services
11. Discriminatory consumer and credit practices
12. Inadequate welfare programs

- The result of a three-city survey of various federal programs—manpower, education, housing, welfare and community action—indicate that, despite substantial expenditures, the number of persons assisted constituted only a fraction of those in need.

The background of disorder is often as complex and difficult to analyze as the disorder itself. But we find that certain general conclusions can be drawn:

- Social and economic conditions in the riot cities constituted a clear pattern of severe disadvantage for Negroes compared with whites, whether the Negroes lived in the area where the riot took place or outside it. Negroes had completed fewer years of education and fewer had attended high school. Negroes were twice as likely to be unemployed and three times as likely to be in unskilled and service jobs. Negroes averaged 70 percent of the income earned by whites and were more than twice as likely to be living in poverty. Although housing cost Negroes relatively more, they had worse housing—three times as likely to be overcrowded and substandard. When compared to white suburbs, the relative disadvantage is even more pronounced.

A study of the aftermath of disorder leads to disturbing conclusions. We find that, despite the institution of some postriot programs:

- Little basic change in the conditions underlying the outbreak of disorder has taken place. Actions to ameliorate Negro grievances have been limited and sporadic; with but few exceptions, they have not significantly reduced tensions.
- In several cities, the principal official response has been to train and equip the police with more sophisticated weapons.
- In several cities, increasing polarization is evident, with continuing breakdown of inter-racial communication, and growth of white segregationist or black separatist groups.

35. Institutional Arrangements as Underlying Conditions of Race Riots

*Stanley Lieberson and Arnold R. Silverman**

...Using both "hard" and "soft" data, employing journalistic accounts as well as census data, we consider in a somewhat more systematic fashion the influence of diverse factors suggested as causes of riots in sociological case studies and texts on collective behavior.[1] Riots, as distinguished from lynchings and other forms of collective violence, involve an assault on persons and property simply because they are part of a given subgroup of the community. In contrast, lynchings and other types of violence are directed toward a particular individual as a collective response to some specific act. In practice, this distinction is sometimes difficult to apply, particularly in deciding when a localized racial incident has become a riot.[2] We have excluded some of the housing "riots" from our analysis because they were directed specifically at Negroes attempting to move into an area rather than at Negroes *per se* or some other more generalized target.

...

Reprinted from "The Precipitants and Underlying Conditions of Race Riots," *American Sociological Review,* **30:6** (December 1965), 887, 891-898, by permission of The American Sociological Review and the authors.

*The comments of Alma and Karl Taeuber, and David Heise are gratefully acknowledged.

[1] Herbert Blumer, "Collective Behavior," in Alfred McClung Lee (ed.), *New Outline of the Principles of Sociology,* New York: Barnes and Noble, 1951, pp. 165–222; Chicago Commission on Race Relations, *The Negro in Chicago,* Chicago: University of Chicago Press, 1922, pp. 1–78; Allen D. Grimshaw, "Three Major Cases of Colour Violence in the United States," *Race,* 5 (1963), pp. 76–86 and "Factors Contributing to Colour Violence in the United States and Britain," *ibid.,* 3 (May, 1962), pp. 3–19; Allen D. Grimshaw, "Urban Racial Violence in the United States: Changing Ecological Considerations," *American Journal of Sociology,* 66 (1960), pp. 109–119; Kurt Lang and Gladys Engel Lang, *Collective Dynamics,* New York: Thomas Y. Crowell, 1961; Alfred McClung Lee and Norman Daymond Humphrey, *Race Riot,* New York: Dryden Press, 1943; Elliott M. Rudwick, *Race Riot at East St. Louis, July 2, 1917,* Carbondale: Southern Illinois University Press, 1964; Neil J. Smelser, *Theory of Collective Behavior,* New York: Free Press of Glencoe, 1963; Ralph H. Turner and Lewis M. Killian, *Collective Behavior,* Englewood Cliffs, N. J.: Prentice-Hall, 1957; Ralph H. Turner and Samuel J. Surace, "Zoot-Suiters and Mexicans: Symbols in Crowd Behavior," *American Journal of Sociology,* 62 (1956), pp. 14–20.

[2] Lynchings, for example, are sometimes followed by riots. No doubt we would have included some of these events and excluded others had more detail been available.

Underlying Conditions

Applying Durkheim's typology, we observe that many of the immediate precipitants were acts that call for repressive sanctions, that is, they "consisted essentially in an act contrary to strong and defined states of the common conscience."[3] Repressive sanctions are normally administered under penal law by courts in the U.S. For example, murder, rape, and other acts of physical violence are strongly disapproved and severely punished in our society. Many, though not all, of the violations of segregation taboos in the period studied were also punishable through law enforcement, but in these instances, at least some members of either or both racial populations were unable to accept the institutions normally used for handling such offenses. Instead a riot occurred, involving, by definition, a generalized response directed at a collectivity rather than the offender–indeed, the actual offender was often untouched.

Although the immediate precipitants were highly inflammatory, we may still ask why a riot occurred rather than the normal processes of arrest, trial, and punishment, for interracial friction occurs far more often than the small number of occasions that erupted into race riots indicates. Why did violence break out where it did rather than at other places where similar incidents occurred? Or to put it another way, the types of violation described earlier probably occur almost daily, yet in most instances they do not lead to collective violence. Are there special circumstances that increase or decrease the chances of a riot ensuing?

One possible interpretation of the location and timing of riots is simply that riots are randomly distributed. Any precipitating incident of this type increase the chances of a riot, but there is no systematic reason why riots occur when and where they do, other than possible differences among cities in the frequency of precipitating incidents. A second approach is based on the notion that certain social conditions in the community increase the probability that a precipitating incident will lead to a riot. From this perspective, we can ask whether cities experiencing riots differ from other cities with regard to the institutional conditions suggested as increasing the chances of a riot.

Poisson Distribution. To evaluate the first interpretation, that is, whether riots are randomly distributed in time and place, we used the Poisson distribution, which the low frequency of race riots (1.5 per year between 1913 and 1963) makes appropriate for comparing the actual frequency of riots with what would be expected in a random distribution.[4] Columns 2 and 3 of Table 1 show, respectively, the actual and expected number of riots per year in the 51 years from 1913 through 1963. Inspection indicates that the Poisson distribution yields a poor fit. For example,

[3] Emile Durkheim, *The Division of Labor in Society*, Glencoe, Ill.: Free Press, 1933, p. 105.

[4] For discussions of the application of the Poisson distribution, see G. Udny Yule and M. G. Kendall, *An Introduction to the Theory of Statistics*, London: Charles Griffin, 1950, pp. 189–194; M. J. Moroney, *Facts From Figures*, Harmondsworth, Middlesex: Penguin Books, 1951, Ch. 8.

in 26 of the years no riot was reported though the theoretical distribution would lead us to expect only 11 such years. Applying the appropriate chi-square test for goodness of fit, we conclude that we cannot accept the assumption that the probability of riots is equal each year.[5]

TABLE 1. Race Riots: Actual and Expected Frequencies

By Year			*By City*		
Riots per Year (1)	*Observed Frequency (2)*	*Poisson Frequency (3)*	*Riots per Year (4)*	*Observed Frequency (5)*	*Poisson Frequency (6)*
0	26	11.4	0	300	281.2
1	10	17.1	1	25	47.2
2	7	12.8	2	3	4.3
3	2	6.4	3	3	0.3
4	1	2.4	4	1	0.0
5	0	0.7	5–14	1	0.0
6	0	0.2			
7	2	0.0			
8	1	0.0			
9	1	0.0			
10	0	0.0			
11	1	0.0			
Total Years	51	51.0	Total Cities	333	333.0

In similar fashion, we can consider the concentration of riots in cities. Restricting ourselves to the 333 cities with 50,000 or more population in 1960, we have compared the actual and expected frequencies of cities experiencing a specified number of riots. There are more cities without any riots, and more with several, than would be expected on the basis of the Poisson distribution (columns 5 and 6): riots occurred in only 33 of these cities. The goodness-of-fit test confirms our impression that the theoretical distribution does not fit the actual distribution of riots in cities.

Two types of sampling bias may have influenced these results. First, newspapers probably fluctuate in their propensity to report riots, so that the frequency of riots at a given point in time increases the probability that riots occurring shortly afterwards will be reported. This is analogous to the tendency of newspapers to make the frequency of rapes or other events into a crime wave when in fact the major variable is the frequency of reporting such events.[6] A second possible bias arises from the fact that our primary source is the *New York Times.* Milder forms

[5] Our computation of chi-square is based on the adjustments suggested in Helen M. Walker and Joseph Lev, *Statistical Inference,* New York: Henry Holt, 1953, pp. 105–107.

[6] See, for example, Nahum Z. Medalia and Otto N. Larsen, "Diffusion and Belief in a Collective Delusion: The Seattle Windshield Pitting Epidemic," *American Sociological Review,* 23 (1958), pp. 180–186.

of racial violence in metropolitan New York and the Mid-Atlantic area are more likely to be covered than riots of equivalent severity elsewhere. This would lead to a distribution of repeated riots different from that expected on the basis of the Poisson formula. Also, note that our test refers only to riots, not to precipitating incidents *per se.* Therefore we can reach no conclusions with respect to the distribution of precipitants by time or place. These difficulties notwithstanding, the results give us no reason to think riots are random with respect to time and place.

A Comparative Analysis

Since the type of event that precipitates riots is far more common than actual riots, we ask whether this form of collective violence is due to underlying conditions that keep at least one segment of the population from accepting the normal institutional response to a provocative incident. From this perspective, precipitants are a necessary but not sufficient cause of riots.

A rather wide-ranging array of interpretations have been advanced after the occurrence of riots in particular communities. Such factors as rapidly expanding Negro population, economic hardships, police brutality, job ceilings, Negro competition with whites, slums, unsympathetic city officials, contagion, communist elements, agitators, warm weather, unruly elements, and others have figured in popular and semi-popular interpretations of race riots. Although case studies of race riots are extremely valuable where they provide an accurate description of events before and during a riot, obviously it is impossible to determine which factors are critical on the basis of one city's experience.

When we move from the presentation of *plausible* reasons to a systematic empirical test of the actual importance of various attributes in increasing the chances of riots, we encounter serious difficulties. Not only do we have a plethora of independent variables, but their actual significance is very difficult to test. Quantitative data on many of these characteristics are scarce, and in any case it is difficult to know how much causal significance to attribute anyway. For example, a riot may occur in a city containing a Negro slum area. The cruel truth is that housing conditions for Negroes are inferior in virtually every city in the U.S. To infer a casual link, one must determine not whether Negro slums exist in the riot city, but whether that city is worse in this respect than others where no riots occurred. Similarly, in any large city unemployed whites and Negroes might respond to an opportunity for a racial riot. Again the question is whether an unusually large number of such people live in one community compared with another.

Our requirements for quantitative data covering at least part of a 50-year span limit the causal hypotheses we can test. For the most part we have relied on U.S. censuses of the past six decades for data bearing on some of the propositions encountered in case studies and popular interpretations of race riots. This part of our study, therefore, necessarily has a certain *ad hoc* quality.

Method. To examine the influence of variables others have suggested as underlying causes of race riots, we used a paired-comparison analysis. Each city experiencing a riot was compared with a city as similar as possible in size and region which had no riot in the ten years preceding or following the riot date.[7] Preference was given to the city in the same state closest in population size, with the provision that it have at least half but no more than twice the population of the riot city. Where no such city existed we selected the city closest in size in the same subregion or region.[8] We compared the very largest cities, such as New York, Chicago, and Los Angeles, with other leading centers in the nation closest in population, regardless of region.

Using the nonparametric sign test, we evaluated the extent to which riot cities differ from their control cities in the direction hypothesized. When a given city experienced more than one riot, it was included as many times as the number of riots. Because census data by size of place and decade were not always available, our "N" in most cases is considerably less than the 76 riots discussed earlier. For convenience in presentation, we have divided the hypotheses into four major categories: population growth and composition; work situation; housing; and government.

Demographic Factors

The rapid influx of Negroes and sometimes whites into cities is certainly one of the most frequently cited reasons for the occurrence of race riots. Although large-scale migration is not usually viewed as a sufficient cause for a riot, it is commonly considered important because rapid influx disrupts the on-going social order and creates various problems in the Negro community. For 66 riots we could determine the growth of the Negro and white populations between the census years preceding and following the race riot, for each riot city and for a comparable community selected at the beginning of the decade. We thus have data for 66 pairs of cities, each pair consisting of a riot city and a control city.

In about half the cases, percentage increases in both total and white population were smaller in the riot cities than in the non-riot cities. Moreover, in 56 per cent of the comparisons the control cities experienced greater percentage increases in Negro population than the riot cities did. Our results clearly fail to support the contention that rapid population change accompanies riots. For the years between 1917 and 1921–a period marked by both Negro migration and numerous riots–we found no sizable difference between riot and control cities in their percentage gains in Negro population during the decades. Also contrary to expectation are the differences in racial composition of riot and control cities. Again for 66 pairs, we find that in exactly half the comparisons, the proportion of Negroes is smaller in the riot city than in its control city.

Since this comparative approach is used with succeeding hypotheses, we should consider briefly the implications of these findings. First, we draw no conclusions

[7] For the most recent riots we could not apply the ten-year limit into the future in selecting control cities, but such cities were included in our analysis.

[8] See U.S. Bureau of the Census, *U.S. Census of Population: 1960. Selected Area Reports, Standard Metropolitan Statistical Areas.* Washington, D.C.: U.S. Government Printing Office, 1963, pp. xvi–xvii.

about whether Negro population growth in riot cities differs from its growth elsewhere in the U.S. Riot cities have experienced more rapid growth than the remainder of the nation simply because Negro population movement has been largely from rural to urban areas. Similarly, since our method is designed to compare riot cities only with other cities similar in size and region, we make no inferences about differences between riot cities and all other U.S. cities. What we do conclude is that riot cities do not differ from non-riot cities of the same size and region in their rates of population increase, and therefore that increases in population fail to explain the occurrence of outbreaks in one city rather than another.[9]

Work Situation

Traditional Occupations. The occupational world of Negroes is far more restricted than that of whites. In particular, certain occupational pursuits have been more or less "traditional" for urban Negroes. These are generally lower in both status and income. Accordingly, wherever possible we determined the proportion of Negro men in the labor force who are employed either as laborers or in domestic and service occupations. Needless to say, we were forced to use some rather crude measures as well as broad categories which undoubtedly include some occupations outside the "traditional" rubric. A serious difficulty is created by contradictory hypotheses that depend on which group appears to be the aggressor. On the one hand, we might expect greater antagonism on the part of Negroes in cities where they are relatively restricted in occupational opportunities, i.e., where most Negroes are in traditional pursuits. On the other hand, we might well expect that where Negroes fare relatively well in their efforts to break through the job restrictions, whites' hostility might be greater and hence riots more likely to ensue.

For 43 riots we were able to determine the Negro occupational distribution in both the riot and control city during the closest census period. In 65 per cent of these paired comparisons (N=28), the percentage of Negro men holding traditional occupations is lower in the riot city.[10] This suggests that riots are due to the relative threat to whites where Negroes are less concentrated in their traditional pursuits. If such were the case, then we might expect the white and Negro percentages in these occupations to be more alike in the riot city than in the control city. This is precisely what we find: in 30 of the 43 paired comparisons, the *difference* between whites and Negroes, in proportions engaged in laboring, domestic, and service occupations, is smaller in the riot city.[11] The encroachment of Negroes in the white occupa-

[9] See Robin Williams, Jr., in collaboration with John P. Dean and Edward A. Suchman, *Strangers Next Door,* Englewood Cliffs, N.J.: Prentice-Hall, 1964, pp. 135–137. In a study based on a nationwide sample of cities, they find the general level of race conflict and tension no higher in cities with rapid population growth and high mobility than in those with relatively stable population. In short, our method gets at the question of why riots occur in the particular cities they do, rather than in comparable urban centers.

[10] Using a two-tailed test, $p = .0672$.

[11] $p = .0073$, single-tailed test.

tional world evidently tends to increase the chances of a riot, although we must also consider the possibility that Negro militancy increases as Negroes move out of their traditional niche.

Store Owners. A more specific occupational factor sometimes associated with riot–particularly ghetto riots–is the low frequency of store ownership in Negro areas and the consequent resentment of white store owners in these areas. We are unable to get at these data directly. If we assume, however, that virtually all Negro store owners are located in the ghetto, then we can simply examine the percentage of employed Negro men who are self-employed in various facets of retail trade, such as store, restaurant, or tavern owners. Although differences between riot and control cities tend to be slight, nevertheless in 24 of 39 riots, the percentage of Negroes who are store owners is larger in the non-riot city.[12] Results might be even stronger had it been possible to subcategorize riots. For instance, the absence of Negro store owners would presumably contribute to Negroes' rioting but would contribute relatively little to white assaults.

Unemployment. As was the case for traditional occupations, unemployment presents contradictory possibilities, so that we might well expect riots when either Negroes or whites have relatively high unemployment rates. Our analysis is even cruder here, since unemployment is far more volatile from year to year, and we are able to use data only for the closest census year.[13] First, the white unemployment rate appears to have no influence on the likelihood of a riot. In 12 comparisons white unemployment rates were higher in the city experiencing the riot, and in 13 cases, higher in the control city. For Negro unemployment, results tend to run counter to what we might expect. Negro unemployment is higher in the control than in the riot city in 15 out of 25 comparisons. And Negro-white *differences* are lower in the riot than in the control city in 15 out of 25 comparisons.[14]

These results do not confirm our expectations: high white unemployment apparently does not increase the chances of a riot, nor is high Negro unemployment associated with riots in the direction expected. On an aggregate basis, the number of riots during the Great Depression of the thirties was not unusually large. In view of the weakness of the data–particularly the fact that we do not have unemployment rates for the specific year in which the riots take place–all we can conclude is that we have failed to confirm the hypothesis, not that we have disproved it.

Income. Since the influence of income on riots may reflect either group's position, our problem is similar to that discussed in connection with Negro occupational composition. Median income data are available for only 12 riots and their controls. In six comparisons Negro income is higher in the control city and in the other six it is higher in the riot city. In 11 of the 12 cases, however, white income in the riot city

[12] These differences are significant at the .10 level.

[13] Although data are available for other years, to our knowledge none can be obtained by race for specific cities.

[14] $p = .212$, single-tailed test.

is lower than in the control.[15] The *difference* between Negro and white income was larger in the city without a riot in ten of the 12 cases.[16] The small number precludes analysis of these findings in greater detail, but we can observe that riots tend to occur in cities where white income is lower than that of whites in comparable areas. The lower white income also means that Negro-white differences tend to be smaller in these cities than in the control areas. Thus, the results, though extremely limited in time and place, do not support the notion that race riots are a consequence either of low Negro income or of relatively large Negro-white discrepancies in income.

Housing

Ghetto riots in particular are often attributed to the poor housing conditions of Negroes, but our data fail to disclose any tendency whatsoever for housing to be of lower quality in cities that have experienced riots. For 20 paired comparisons we could determine which city had a larger percentage of Negro families in sub-standard housing (using the census categories of "dilapidated" in 1950 and 1960 and "needing major repairs" in 1940). In ten cases the non-riot city had poorer Negro housing than the riot city. Although obviously not all riots could be considered ghetto riots, surely we should find some tendency for Negroes in cities experiencing riots to have poorer dwellings than they do in cities without riots, if it were true that poorer housing quality increases the likelihood of a race riot. Very likely, Negro housing is poor in so many locales that it cannot distinguish cities experiencing riots from those that do not.

Government

Police. Local government is one of the most important institutions to consider in an analysis of race riots. Municipal policies, particularly with respect to police, can greatly influence the chances of a race riot. Earlier, we observed that many of the precipitating incidents involve white police behavior toward Negroes, and adequate police training and tactics often prevent incipient riots from developing.[17] Moreover, police activities reflect the policies, sympathies, and attitudes of the local municipal government.

One often-cited factor in race riots is the lack of Negro policemen. First, one major complaint on the part of Negroes is that of white police brutality. So far as the police are Negroes, actual brutality will probably not arouse strong racial feelings. Second, police in some riots have encouraged or tolerated white violence toward Negroes, so that we might expect stronger police control where the force is mixed, as well as greater confidence in police protection among Negroes. Finally, since the number of Negro policemen is for the most part controlled by the city administra-

[15] $p < .01$, single-tailed test.

[16] $p = .038$, two-tailed test.

[17] Joseph D. Lohman, *The Police and Minority Groups*, Chicago: Chicago Park District, 1947, pp. 80–93; Smelser, *op. cit.*, pp. 261–268.

tion, the representation of Negroes is an indicator of city policies toward race relations in general.

Data are hard to obtain and for 1950 and 1960 we have been obliged to use census reports for entire metropolitan areas. Also, for some decades policemen are not reported separately from closely related occupations such as sheriffs and marshals. Nevertheless, of 38 pairs of cities, in 24 the city without the riot had more Negro policemen per thousand Negroes than did the matched city that experienced a riot.[18] Although differences between riot and control cities are rather slight, these results do suggest that police force compositions influences the likelihood of a riot.

City Council. We hypothesize that the manner in which councilmen are elected and the relative size of the city council will influence the occurrence of riots. Our reasoning is based on several assumptions. The election of councilmen-at-large gives numerically smaller groups a greater handicap in expressing their interests than they encounter in communities where councilmen are elected directly from spatial districts.[19] In cities where the average size of a councilman's constituency is small, we assume that representatives are more responsive to the wishes of the population and therefore that members of the community have a more adequate mechanism for transmitting their interests and concerns. This implies that more diverse interests will be expressed in the city's governing body.

Our hypothesis is that the more direct the relation between voter and government the less likely are riots to occur. A more responsive government makes riots less likely because it provides regular institutional channels for expressing grievances. Small districts provide more responsive government than large districts, and large districts, more than elections at large. In comparisons between a city with a city-wide election system and one where councilmen are elected both at large and by district, we classified the latter situation as the less likely to lead to riots. Where both cities have the same form of election, we computed the mean population per councilman. (Comparisons involving Deep South cities were based on the white population only.) Thus, we gave form of election priority over size of constituency in our causal hypothesis.

In 14 of 22 pairs, population per councilman was larger in the city experiencing the riot than in the control city, or elections at large were used in the riot city and direct election of representatives in the control city.[20] Considering our inability to take into account the degree of gerrymandering in cities with direct representation, these results offer an encouraging degree of support for our hypothesis.

Discussion

...Going beyond our data and trying to place our findings in a broad framework, we suggest that riots are more likely to occur when social institutions function inadequately, or when grievances are not resolved, or cannot be resolved under the

[18] $p = .07$, single-tailed test.

[19] James Q. Wilson, *Negro Politics*, Glencoe, Ill.: Free Press, 1960, pp. 25–33.

[20] Though p is not significant (.143), the relationship is in the predicted direction.

existing institutional arrangements. Populations are predisposed or prone to riot; they are not simply neutral aggregates transformed into a violent mob by the agitation or charisma of individuals. Indeed, the immediate precipitant simply ignites prior community tensions revolving about basic institutional difficulties. The failure of functionaries to perform the roles expected by one or both of the racial groups, cross-pressures, or the absence of an institution capable of handling a community problem involving inter-racial relations will create the conditions under which riots are most likely. Many riots are precipitated by offenses that arouse considerable interest and concern. When members of the victimized race are dubious about the intention or capacity of relevant functionaries to achieve justice or a "fair" solution, then the normal social controls are greatly weakened by the lack of faith in the community's institutions.

Our evidence supports the proposition that the functioning of local community government is important in determining whether a riot will follow a precipitating incident. Prompt police action can prevent riots from developing; their inaction or actual encouragement can increase the chances of a race riot. Riot cities not only employ fewer Negro policemen, but they are also communities whose electoral systems tend to be less sensivitive to the demands of the electorate. Local government illustrates the possibility that riots occur when a community institution is malfunctioning, from the perspective of one or both racial segments.

Our finding that Negroes are less likely to be store owners in riot cities illustrates the problem arising when no social institution exists for handling the difficulties faced by a racial group. Small merchants require credit, skill and sophistication in operating and locating their stores, ability to obtain leases, and so on. To our knowledge no widely operating social institution is designed to achieve these goals for the disadvantaged Negro. Similarly, our finding that riots are more likely where Negroes are closer to whites in their proportions in "traditional" Negro occupations, and where Negro-white income differences are smaller, suggests that a conflict of interests between the races is inherent in the economic world.

Our use of significance tests requires further comment. Many of the relationships are in the direction predicted but fail to meet the normal standards for significance. Several extenuating circumstances help account for this. First, many of our hypotheses refer to specific types of riots: for example, some riots are clearly "white-riots;" others, equally clearly, are Negro; and many are both, in the sense that extensive attacks are directed at both groups. Were the data in an ideal form, we could separate the ghetto riots, the white assaults, and the inter-racial warfare into separate categories, and then apply our hypothesis to specific subsets of riots. Because our sample is small and the accounts of many riots are very scanty, we are prepared to accept these weaker associations as at least consistent with our approach to the underlying conditions of race riots.

Several implications of our results are relevant to riots elsewhere. Racial and ethnic incidents in other parts of the world are also frequently precipitated by physical violence. Dahlke's description of the Kishinew pogrom in Russia ascribes considerable importance as a precipitant to the widespread legend that Jews annually kill Christian children, as a part of their religious rites.[21] The extensive riots in Ceylon in 1958 included a number of highly provocative rumors of inter-ethnic violations. For example, "a Sinhalese baby had been snatched from its mother's arms and immersed in a barrel of boiling tar."[22] The Durban riots of 1949 were precipitated by an incident in which an African youth was knocked over by an Indian trader.[23]

A number of other riots, however, are precipitated by violations of symbols rather than persons or taboos. The burning of an American flag by Negroes triggered a race riot in the United States. Our impression is that this type of precipitant is more common in some other parts of the world. Riots in Kashmir, West Bengal, and East Pakistan in late 1963 and early 1964, for example, were precipitated by the theft of a hair of the prophet Mohammed from a Mosque in Kashmir.[24] One of the precipitants of the Chinese-Thai riots of 1945, the Yaorawat Incident, was the Chinese tendency to fly Chinese flags without also flying the Thai flag of the nation.[25] Jews tore down the czar's crown from the town hall and damaged portraits of various rulers prior to Kiev's pogrom in 1905.[26]

Our results also suggest that race riots are frequently misunderstood. We have encountered a number of accounts in the popular literature attributing riots to communist influence, hoodlums, or rabble-rousers. Although lower-class youths and young adults are undoubtedly active during riots, potential participants of this type are probably available in almost any community. What interests us is the community failure to see the riot in terms of institutional malfunctioning or a racial difficulty which is not met—and perhaps cannot be—by existing social institutions. Many riots in other parts of the world revolve about national political institutions such that a disadvantaged segment is unable to obtain recognition of its interests and concerns through normal political channels. While this type of riot is not common in the U.S., the same basic conditions exist when either whites or Negroes are unable to use existing institutions to satisfy their needs and interests.

[21] H. Otto Dahlke, "Race and Minority Riots—A Study in the Typology of Violence," *Social Forces,* 30 (1952), p. 421.

[22] Tarzie Vittachi, *Emergency '58: The Story of the Ceylon Race Riots,* London: Andre Deutsch, 1958, p. 48.

[23] Anthony H. Richmond, *The Colour Problem* (rev. ed.), Harmondsworth, Middlesex: Pelican Books, 1961, p. 123.

[24] *New York Times,* January 16, 1964, p. 17; January 19, p. 6; January 20, p. 6; January 24, p. 2; January 26, p. 15.

[25] G. William Skinner, *Chinese Society in Thailand: An Analytical History,* Ithaca, N.Y.: Cornell University Press, 1957, p. 279.

[26] From the diary of Shulgin, in *Source Book for History 2.1,* Vol. 2, "History of Western Civilization," Brooklyn, N.Y.: Brooklyn College, Department of History, 1949, Ch. 31.

36. Why a Rebellion at Columbia was inevitable

Ellen Kay Trimberger

The student demonstrations at Columbia University in the spring of 1968 caused a very serious institutional crisis–involving the disruption of the university for two months, the arrest of more than 800 students, the injuring of almost 250 students and faculty, and the prospect of continuing conflict. To explain why, one must first understand how the institutional weakness of the university and the politicization of students in recent years led to confrontations between students and the administration.

Starting in 1966, students resorted to direct action against the administration to protest against university policies toward the community and its cooperation with the military, the C.I.A., and the Selective Service. The administrators responded first with concessions, and later with repression, but they failed to re-examine their basic policies–or to make any reforms in the way the university's policies were determined. In fact, the public policies of the university (as opposed to its internal academic issues) were being decided by only a few administrators, after little or no consultation with the faculty, let alone the students.

This combination of a remote and unaccountable administration, a politicized and dissatisfied group of students, and a virtually powerless faculty was explosive. Add to it the unhappiness of the faculty and students over the declining educational

Reprinted from *Trans*-action, Vol. 5, No. 9, September, 1968 by permission of the publisher and the author.

*Editor's Note: During the 1969 student spring offensive violent protest has occurred at a number of institutions, some of which are: Harvard, University of Chicago, Columbia, Dartmouth, Howard, City College of New York, University of California at Berkeley, Agricultural and Technical College (black) of North Carolina, Cornell, Southern University (black), La., Stanford, and Kent State University, Ohio.

The academic year: 1969-70 has begun. The major issues as the basis for past confrontations at Columbia and other institutions remain. Many college officials are attempting to reduce grievances. At the same time many are taking tougher positions (e.g., in strengthening of college police, through the rewriting of policies and procedures). Many states have enacted "control" legislation aimed directly at college officials and students. Whether student radicals can muster student support (instead of student opposition) for on-campus confrontations or will turn to confrontations and organizing off-campus remains to be seen.

quality and reputation of a great university, as well as the absence of effective ways to seek change, and you have a highly overdetermined "revolutionary" situation. (A survey by Allen Barton—"Student and Faculty Response to the Columbia Crisis," Bureau of Applied Social Research, Columbia University, June 1968—found a strong link between student and faculty dissatisfaction with the university and their support of the demonstrators. Thus, 57 percent of the most-dissatisfied faculty and 56 percent of the most-dissatisfied students thought that the sit-ins were justified, compared with only 12 percent of the most-satisfied faculty and 30 percent of the most-satisfied students. In the university as a whole, only 66 percent of the students and only 58 percent of the faculty were satisfied with Columbia's educational quality.)

Background

For more than 20 years two extremely weak presidents have ruled Columbia, with little contact and rapport with faculty and students. Since the retirement of President Nicholas Murray Butler in 1945 until very recently, Columbia's administration had also been very decentralized. Each school and division had a good deal of academic and administrative autonomy, even to the extent of raising its own funds. What this meant was that the core of the university—the undergraduate colleges and the graduate faculties in arts and sciences—declined, both financially and in educational quality. The pay scales and the teaching loads of these faculties did not stay in line with those of other major universities, and the educational ratings of many of Columbia's famous departments dropped (surveys by Hayward Keniston of the University of Pennsylvania, 1957, and the American Council on Education, 1966).

Several years ago, the Columbia administration launched a massive campaign to stem the university's decline. Their reform plan called for a centralized fund drive, as well as for the physical expansion of the university into Morningside Heights. But these plans for expansion brought Columbia into conflict with the residents of the neighborhood, with city and state officials, and with Harlem leaders (Harlem is next to Morningside Heights, and its residents especially objected to Columbia's plans to build a gymnasium in an adjoining park). Thus Columbia, like other metropolitan universities, was drawn into the urban crisis. But because of its stagnation for the past 20 years, even in construction and in fund-raising, Columbia was in more desperate straits than most other universities, and its officers and trustees were more likely to think not of the public's needs but of the university's narrow self-interest.

At the same time, Columbia students were becoming more and more involved in social-action work with the poor who surround the university. (Since 1966, the largest and most active student organization has been the Citizenship Council, whose 1100 members take part in a variety of community-action projects.) The students' work with the poor brought them into direct opposition to the administration's community policies. Even more important, many students were politicized by the Vietnam war, and became antagonized by the university's contribution to military research.

The students, however, lacked effective channels within the university to express their discontent and to influence administration policy. Student structures are weak at Columbia, and those organizations that have tried to use legitimate channels to reach the administration usually have failed. In Columbia College, the students voted more than six years ago to abolish the student government. The all-university student council is not respected by most students, primarily because it is so powerless. For example, its resolutions in the past two years—on class ranks for the draft, military recruiting on campus, indoor demonstrations, the gym in Morningside Park, and the tuition increase—had no influence on administration policy. Nor did the administration formally or informally consult the student council. In fact, several months before the demonstrations both the president and vice-president of the student council resigned, saying that it was completely ineffective.

Moreover, students were unable to get effective faculty support for their grievances, because of the weakness of faculty organization. At Columbia there is no faculty government. The university council is composed of two elected faculty members from each school, the deans, and a number of administrators, but it is chaired and run by the administration; it meets only three times a year; and it deals almost exclusively with technical and routine matters. Of the arts and sciences faculties, only the small faculty of Columbia College has a formally constituted body that meets often and sometimes takes stands on policy matters. In recent years, a few active and concerned faculty members have used regular committees, or set up ad-hoc ones, to investigate controversial subjects with policy implications. But their reports (in 1967, on student affairs, on reporting class ranks to draft boards, on university civil-rights policies, and on faculty housing) generally were disregarded by the administration. Last year a member of the only standing committee of the university faculty admitted in public that his committee had very little power, and charged: "The present system of government at Columbia is similar to that of Tsar Nicholas II."

Faced with an unresponsive administration and a powerless faculty, student activists turned to direct action. In 1966 and 1967, a coalition of moderate and radical student leaders, with wide undergraduate support, won important concessions from the administration after mass demonstrations and threats to strike. These concessions included:

- a university policy of witholding class ranks from the draft boards;
- the establishment of a special tripartite commission (student, faculty, and administration) to try students who had demonstrated against the C.I.A. Most students saw such a judicial commission as setting a precedent toward greater due process, and as moving away from the traditional methods of student discipline at Columbia, where students were accused, judged, and punished by the dean's office.
- The cancellation of army recruiting on campus and of the annual Naval Reserve Officers Training Corps ceremony.

At the end of the school year in 1967, the student newspaper, *The Columbia Spectator,* wrote (March 17):

"Within the last 12 months, student organizations—enjoying the general sympathy of the student body as a whole—made demands on the university which are of unprecedented nature. And, in turn, the university has given unprecedented response to these demands. The confrontation between the two has developed into what may be a revolution in the role of the student at Columbia.... The greatest single phenomenon on the campus in the last 12 months has been the shift to radicalism, the development of the feeling that the usual, slow-moving methods of change are inadequate, and the growing attraction of more forceful action."

But for all the success of student power at Columbia, the administration did nothing to give permanency to the student voice, or to foster reforms in general. The clearest clue to the administration's disinclination to consider reform was President Grayson Kirk's refusal to implement, or even release, the Student Life Report submitted to him in August 1967.

This report was the result of two years of study by five administrators, five faculty members, and five students, all appointed by the president after the first student demonstration in May 1965. Four of the five student members issued a minority report rejecting the majority opinion as "too little and too late." But even the implementation of the majority's recommendations might have been sufficient to prevent the student revolt in April 1968.

The majority recommended that demonstrations inside buildings be allowed as long as they did not disrupt the normal functioning of the university. They proposed the establishment of judicial bodies, composed of students, faculty, and administrators, to impose and review discipline. They also recommended formation of student advisory committees on academic affairs in all departments and schools, and a university tripartite committee on student interests to advise the president.

The four students writing the minority report stated (with what now appears as unusual foresight):

"We believe a tripartite committee on administrative policy should instead be created to decide important matters of non-academic policy, subject to the veto of the president or trustees. It would not make most policy or operating decisions within the university. That is quite properly the responsibility of the administrator. But it should deal with major questions which are of concern to all the elements of the university community. Such recent decisions as whether to involve Columbia in the business of promoting cigarette filters, whether to continue tuition deferment, and where or whether to build a gymnasium and how to allocate its facilities, serve as examples of the scope of the committee. Such matters as the physical expansion of the university, the university's relations with governments, and major policies of student conduct vis-a-vis the rest of the university community would be in the purview of the tripartite committee and its decisions would be policy unless vetoed by the president or trustees."

In September 1967, disregarding this Student Life Report, President Kirk banned all indoor demonstrations. Vice-President David Truman explained, "The administration will not tolerate efforts to make the university an instrument of opposition to the established order." Yet, in order to avoid a free-speech controversy, the administrators later interpreted the rule liberally (and often arbitrarily). They considered two indoor demonstrations early in the year as only "near demonstrations," and the participants were not punished. It was only in early April 1968 that the administration began to enforce the rule. At the same time, the president declined to follow either his own precedent of the year before, or the recommendations of the Student Life majority, by refusing to appoint a tripartite judicial body to try students accused of breaking the rule against indoor demonstrations.

The Great Confrontation

This new ban—following the administration's concessions in 1967 and in the absence of effective channels for student grievances—helped discredit the administration's authority and helped legitimate direct-action tactics in the eyes of the students. Meanwhile, Students for a Democratic Society and other radical groups had formed coalitions with moderate student groups. This was possible because, from March 1967 until Mark Rudd became president in March 1968, S.D.S. was run by moderates, who temporarily rejected direct-action techniques in favor of "research" to expose the administration and "education" to gain the allegiance of moderate students. The student radicals, therefore, had a broad base to mobilize for a student revolt.

In brief, the escalation of confrontation between students and administration from April to June 1968 consisted of:

- a student sit-in at Hamilton Hall, the classroom and administration building of Columbia College, and the detention of a dean for 24 hours;
- the occupation and barricading of five university buildings for five days by about 800 students;
- the administration's calling of 1000 policemen to remove the demonstrators from the buildings, which resulted in the arrest of about 700 students and the injuring of 150 students and faculty;
- a massive strike by 5000 active students;
- the administration's "lock-out" to counter the strike—its canceling of formal classes and exams for the remainder of the school year;
- the start of disciplinary action against the student activists, which led to a second student sit-in at Hamilton Hall;
- the arrest of about 200 more students and the injuring of another 68 in a second police action;
- violence by students during this second police action; and
- the university's suspending of about 75 students.

The occupation of the five buildings and the subsequent student strike mobilized wide student support. Many of the official student leaders supported all of the demands of the occupation forces and even were leaders in the strike. While initially opposed to the barricading of buildings, these moderates saw the confrontation as an opportunity to win the student voice they had so long and fruitlessly sought. As they said later, two days at the barricades would probably accomplish more than years of work through legitimate channels. The moderates' prior use of direct-action techniques also conditioned them to accept more radical tactics.

Throughout the revolt there was solidarity between radical and moderate activists, despite disagreements and tensions. Moderates worked with the radical leaders of the Steering Committee that coordinated the occupation of four of the buildings (the black demonstrators maintained their separate leadership); this coalition continued in the Stike Steering Committee. This solidarity encouraged the moderates to accept the occupation, the demand for amnesty, and the strike.

Later on, the radicals also accepted some of the moderates' stands on tactics and issues—the organization of the Strike Committee along representative lines, and an increased emphasis on the internal restructuring of the university. One reason for the trust between moderates and radicals was their interaction and coalition in former years; but more important was their common alienation from the administration and isolation from the faculty.

As the confrontation escalated, many students previously unaffiliated and politically inactive suddenly became involved, either in support of or in opposition to the sit-in. The strike that followed the police intervention generated more organization and solidarity among students, in the form of "liberated" classes and strike constituencies. In addition, ad-hoc student groups arose to proclaim grievances and make demands for change.

The specific events that propelled increasing numbers of students into confrontation with the administration can now be traced more closely.

In late March of 1968, S.D.S. Sponsored a march to President Kirk's office to present a petition signed by 1700 students requesting the university's separation from the Institute of Defense Analyses. The President's response was to put six leaders of S.D.S. on probation for violating his ban on indoor demonstrations. The six students thereupon requested an open hearing before a tripartite judicial board, and were refused. On April 23, S.D.S. held a noon rally to organize a peaceful march into Low Library, the administration building, to present President Kirk with a demand for open hearings for the six students. This march, like the previous one, would deliberately defy the ban on indoor demonstrations. The April rally also repeated demands for the university to cut all ties with I.D.A. and to stop building a gym. Thus, this student movement simultaneously criticized the internal procedures of the university and its public policies.

When the demonstrators reached Low Library, they found the door locked. In much confusion, between 200 and 300 students decided to march to the gym site a few blocks away. After trying to rip down a wire fence and being confronted by police, they returned to campus and voted to sit-in at Hamilton Hall. That night the black students decided to occupy the building by themselves, and asked the whites to leave. Humiliated, white radicals decided spontaneously to break into and occupy the president's office. During the next two days, three additional buildings were occupied. The most militant acts—the detention of the college dean for 24 hours, the occupation of the president's office, and the inspection of his files—alienated many students. On the other hand, moderate students were mobilized by the reorganization of Hamilton Hall under black students and by the occupation of Avery Hall by architecture students and of Fayerweather Hall by graduate social-sicence students.

After the Student Afro-American Society took over Hamilton Hall it erected barricades at the doors, an act that was to become symbolic of all the "liberated" buildings. This act was probably inspired by the Harlem radicals in the building who were not students. But during the next two days, the course of events inside Hamilton

Hall was moderated. The black students became highly organized; they evicted the non-students and allowed outsiders (like Rap Brown and Stokely Carmichael) to visit only for a short time; they released the dean; they cleaned the building and maintained it in good condition; they were open to visits and suggestions from professors, city officials, and Negro leaders; and they held numerous negotiations.

The graduate students took over Avery and Fayerweather somewhat haphazardly, but soon became organized. The architecture students had not been political in the past, but recently they had become resentful over university policies toward the community. Earlier in the year, the students and faculty of the School of Architecture had petitioned the administration to reconsider building the gym. Similarly, many of the graduate students in social science had never taken political action before, at least at Columbia, but had become more and more critical of the university's public policies.

Many students soon joined in the occupation of Avery and Fayerweather, and others visited the buildings (through the windows) to discuss the issues and give their support. Most of these students were not radicals and could not have seen themselves doing such a thing two days earlier. These occupations generated feelings of moral exhilaration and solidarity; the buildings were transformed into "communes" where the students engaged in lengthy political discussions.

Failure of Negotiations

Student support of the demonstrations was not limited to those willing to occupy buildings: The *Columbia Spectator* endorsed all the demands of the occupation—the end of university ties with I.D.A., no construction of a gym, the ending of probation for the six students, amnesty for all demonstrators in the occupation, and open hearings for all future disciplinary proceedings. A referendum held by undergraduate honor societies during the occupation, in which 5500 students voted, showed large majorities supporting the goals of the demonstrators, though not their tactics. Ten student leaders, including the president and vice-president of the university student government, came out in support of all the demonstration's demands, including amnesty. They also urged major university reform—including the establishment of faculty-student legislative and judicial bodies. Up to 800 students held vigils to support the rebels. (About 250 students opposed to the sit-ins tried to prevent students and food from reaching the demonstrators holding the president's office.)

After the police action, according to the Barton survey 42 percent of all students (and probably a much larger percentage of the undergraduates) supported a general boycott of all classes. A strike steering committee was formed of about 70 delegates, each representing 70 constitutents. Thus, almost 5000 students were actively organized, and many others boycotted classes. The Strike Committee supported all the original demands of the occupation and went on to demand a restructuring of the university.

The massive and militant student demonstrations immobilized the administration at first, but then were countered by the use of massive police force. The confrontation jarred part of the faculty into a belated, and ultimately unsuccessful, attempt to intervene between the students and the administration.

The great confrontation at Columbia did not lead to a successful negotiation between the students and the administration. In fact, bargaining never really began, for the administration and students could never agree on a basis for negotiation. Indeed, the administration did not seriously seek to negotiate. On the second day of the occupation, the administrators did present a proposal to the black students in Hamilton Hall, but when this was rejected they did not try again. The administration never presented a proposal for negotiating to the white students in the other four buildings. (According to the Barton survey, 50 percent of the faculty and 58 percent of the students thought the administration negotiated too little.)

It was ultimately the organizational weakness of Columbia that prevented any effective negotiations.

- The administration, because of its isolation and lack of supporting structures, became fixated upon upholding its own authority. To negotiate would have accorded some legitimacy to students' grievances, and the administration found this too threatening.
- The faculty, because of its weak organization and lack of experience in university government, could not counter the administration-student polarization.

The administration made every effort to discredit the demonstrators, but this served only to confirm the views of the most radical students and to strengthen their leadership.

Here were the students sitting in a few "liberated" buildings, with no weapons and with flimsy barricades of furniture, citing slogans of Che Guevara and Mao. But then the administration said that they *were* revolutionaries—"an unscrupulous bunch of revolutionaries out to destroy the university." The students said they would shut down the university; the administration did it for them. Four buildings and a president's office do not constitute a university, but the administration never tried to reschedule classes or to keep the university operating. A radical black leader kept saying that Harlem was marching up to Columbia to burn it down. Immediately the administration closed down the university and then sealed it off. It soon became a standing joke to ask, "When is the community coming?," for not more than 80 to 100 people from Harlem ever showed up.

Here were 800 student demonstrators, supported by all the moderate and legitimate student leaders. But the administration saw only a small minority of radical students organized by outside agitators. Even when Vice President Truman admitted that there was increasing student support of amnesty, he said it was only because the "students don't understand what the fundamental issue is and they want to get on back to work."

Some of the radicals used vulgar language and obscenities in attacking the administration. Vice-President Truman in turn charged the activists with a "total lack of morality." Personal attacks upon President Kirk were countered with personal attacks upon the radical student leaders. Thus, Vice-President Truman said of Mark Rudd: "He is totally unscrupulous and morally very dangerous. He is an extremely capable, ruthless, cold-blooded guy. He's a combination of a revolutionary and an adolescent having a temper tantrum....It makes me uncomfortable to sit in the same room with him."

The radicals pictured Columbia University, its president and its trustees, as part of the American power structure. And the administrators acted so as to seemingly confirm their dependence upon external groups rather than upon students and faculty. During the crisis, the administrators were isolated from all the students and most of the faculty. They remained cloistered in Low Library, consulting almost exclusively with trustees, Mayor Lindsay, and other outside advisers. The president and vice-president never talked directly and publicly to the demonstrators or to other students. Only once did they meet personally (but secretly) with several of the student leaders.

This approach to the students helped solidify their distrust of the administration and their determination to resist its authority. The issue of amnesty became the focus of distrust between students and administrators. From the first day of the occupation, the students demanded amnesty as a prerequisite to negotiation on the other issues. From the first, the administration refused to consider amnesty.

The student demonstrators sought amnesty as a confirmation of their position. In the words of the Strike Committee:

"Our demand for amnesty implies a specific political point. Our actions are legitimate; it is the laws, and the administration's policies which the laws have been designed to protect, that are illegitimate. It is therefore ridiculous to talk about punishment for students. No one suggests punishment for the administration, who in fact must assume the guilt for the present situation. To consider discipline against the students is thus a political position."

In addition, the activists did not trust the administration to radically change its policies, and therefore they sought to protect the students from even a relatively light punishment, like probation. (A student "on probation" could be suspended for slight infractions during future demonstrations.)

Conversely, the administration saw the granting of any form of amnesty as a capitulation that would undermine its authority. Vice-President Truman said later: "We couldn't give on the amnesty thing at all. Not only would we be destroying the whole position of this university, with that one we'd have been destroying every other university in the country." (It seems that the presidents of Stanford, Northwestern, and France were not listening, for during subsequent weeks they granted amnesty to *their* student rebels.) Hence, during the first days of the occupation the administration told the radical leaders, with great emotion and vehemence, that they would be expelled.

Not only did the administration refuse amnesty for students, but they also rejected a compromise designed by an ad-hoc faculty group. This faculty group proposed light and equal punishments for all demonstrators, to be imposed by new forms of due process. (The Barton survey found that 78 percent of the students and 69 percent of the faculty believed that all judicial decisions on student discipline should be made in open hearings by a committee of students and faculty.) But the administration twice refused this compromise, and instead resorted to police force.

Twelve hours before using the police the first time in April, President Kirk had accepted the "spirit" of the faculty proposal, but had rejected most of its substance. Among other things, he refused to give up his authority to make the final decision on student discipline; and he refused to agree beforehand to uniform penalties for all the demonstrators. When the students also refused to accept the ad-hoc faculty's compromise, the administration cited the "intransigence" of the demonstrators as justifying their own resort to police force.

Again in May, the president refused to give final authority on discipline to the then-operating Joint Committee on Discipline. After a huge outcry from the faculty, and pressure behind the scenes from both faculty and trustees, he retreated somewhat, but still refused to accept any specific long-range limitations on his authority. The Joint Committee on Discipline also recommended that the university not undertake disciplinary action while criminal charges against certain students were pending in the courts. But one week later the administration called four student leaders to the dean's office for a closed hearing. Most student leaders interpreted these summonses as an attempt to reestablish the former disciplinary procedures behind a thin facade of reform. The four students, therefore, did not appear (both to protect their legal rights in court and to protest the administrators' action), but sent their parents and lawyers instead. This was unacceptable to the administrators, who immediately suspended the four students.

These suspensions seemed deliberately provocative to the demonstrators, and were countered by a second student sit-in. This time the administration announced that it would call the police that same evening, and that anyone arrested would be immediately suspended. Again, the administration, in threatening automatic suspensions, made no reference to the new disciplinary committee or to new judicial procedures. Thus, as the *Columbia Spectator* stated on May 22: "The administration and the strikers yesterday engaged in a test of strength where there was no buffer of faculty intermediaries and no chance of a compromise settlement. Both groups were committed to holding the line against what they regarded as the illegitimate opposition of the other."

There is some evidence that both the administration and the radical student leaders *wanted* the use of the police, at least the first time. The activists believed that the use of the police to clear the buildings would radicalize the campus, and bring many more students and faculty to their side. This did happen after the first police action. (According to the Barton survey, faculty support for the sit-ins increased by 17 percent and student support by 19 percent.) The administration, on the other hand, believed that the police were needed to restore its authority. Vice-President Truman said that "there were only two alternatives: either to give in or to bring in the police."

The result of the police intervention was to create an atmosphere of violence, contempt, and hatred. It was during the second police action that students for the first time became violent—throwing bricks at the police, smashing windows, and perhaps starting fires in several buildings. Apolitical, nonviolent students were enraged at seeing policemen beat their friends, many of whom were only spectators. Apolitical, nonviolent professors were enraged by the burning of a professor's research papers and by fires set in university buildings. After both police actions, the mood on campus was one of outrage.

Yet the administration maintained its confrontation mentality and became even more committed to a strategy of force and repression. Vice-President Truman commented to the press in May that the most important lesson he had learned from the Columbia crisis was to call the police immediately to oust student demonstrators. In June, President Kirk suspended 75 students for their part in the second sit-in. At the same time, the president continued to maintain that there was nothing fundamentally wrong with the university, and that no positive changes were possible in a crisis atmosphere. In response, the student activists—even the moderates—vowed to continue mass action against the university.

The long history of disorganization and withdrawal of the Columbia faculty members prevented them, at first, from taking any stand on the student demonstration. No faculty faction was organized to directly support the students. Nor was there any effectively organized support for the administration. The one attempt by the administration to organize faculty support was to call an unprecedented meeting of the Joint Faculties on Morningside Heights. Two meetings were convened—one right before the first police action and one right after. In both cases, the assembly passed mild, noncommittal statements, which neither condemned not supported the administration. The meetings were presided over by the president and vice-president, thereby attesting to the faculty's lack of an independent role in university government. Because this body had no independence, no experience, and no leaders, it was unable to seek a solution to the confrontation.

The Faculty Response to Confrontation

During the first part of the crisis, only an ad-hoc faculty group was active. The original organizers of this group included 34 tenured professors, 38 assistant professors, and 84 teachers below that rank. Its membership grew to an active core of about 200. Members of the ad-hoc faculty had many different positions and views on the crisis, but they tended to be more sympathetic to the students than were other faculty members. Many (especially those from Columbia College) had close personal relations with their students, including some of the demonstrators, and some in the past had been among the few faculty activists on university issues. The younger teachers, especially, to a great degree shared the ideals, political frustrations, and disaffection from the university that had propelled the students into the buildings. (Barton's survey of 769 faculty members showed that tenured faculty members were most conservative on all issues, and instructors most favorable to the demonstrations. For example, 12 percent of assistant professors, and 48 percent of lecturers and instructors.) The one purpose that did unite the ad-hoc faculty was a strong stand against the use of the police to resolve the dispute. For five days, members sought a basis for negotiation in order to prevent police action.

From its beginning, the ad-hoc faculty recognized the fierce antagonism between the administration and the demonstrators. And because it had so little active support from the senior faculty and no constitutional status, the ad-hoc group itself was propelled into the politics of confrontation in attempting to persuade the antagonists to accept its efforts at compromise. Its first statement, which shocked many faculty members, made two threats to the administration:

(1) "Should the students be willing to evacuate the buildings on the basis of our proposals, we will not meet classes until the crisis is resolved along these lines."
(2) "Until the crisis is settled, we will stand before the occupied buildings to prevent forcible entry by police or others."

The motive behind these threats was to win credibility from the students and administration, without taking a stand on amnesty. It worked—for a while.

On the third day of the confrontation, Vice-President Truman came to the ad-hoc faculty's meeting to announce that the president had called the police. The faculty present arose in indignation, with shouts of "Shame!" A few of the leaders rushed to the president's office; the rest went and stood in front of the occupied buildings. After several faculty members were physically attacked by a small contingent of policemen seeking entry to the administration building, the president ordered the police to withdraw. He thus granted the ad-hoc faculty a little more time to seek a negotiated settlement.

The ad-hoc faculty, in trying to find a basis for negotiation between the administration and student demonstrators, sought to apply pressure on both sides without itself taking a clear stand on the issues. While strongly disagreeing with the administration's position (and with some of the student actions), the leaders of the ad-hoc faculty never clearly broke with the administration. Nor did they try to organize the senior faculty members and win their active support for the group's proposals. In the Joint Faculties meeting called by the administration, the ad-hoc faculty declined to ask for a vote on its proposal for arbitration. Even though the ad-hoc faculty's leaders believed they could have won a small majority, they did not want to split the faculty, or risk the possibility of being rebuffed by the trustees.

On only one occasion—the day before the first police action—did the ad-hoc faculty try to bolster its position by mobilizing mass support. On that day it obtained 800 faculty and 3000 student signatures, and the support of some city and state political leaders. But these supporters were not an organized constituency that could be mobilized for action. Thus, when both students and administration refused to accept its compromise settlement, the ad-hoc faculty had no alternative plan to check the polarization between administration and students or to block the police action. Even at the zero hour, when both the president and the students had rejected their proposals and they knew that police intervention was immanent, the ad-hoc faculty members could only frantically vote to call on either Governor Rockefeller or Mayor Lindsay to arbitrate the dispute.

It was this reluctance of the faculty to adopt a clear position, rather than trying to find a compromise, that most alienated the student protestors. This was especially true in view of the fact that the faculty institutions were so weak and faculty members had been so inactive in the past. The students did not believe that the ad-hoc faculty could really influence the administration without its taking a stronger stand.

organization from below—for discussion in private by experts, rather than open deliberation and debate.

In the general outrage after the first police action, the ad-hoc faculty group held an extraordinary meeting. Its steering committee introduced a strong resolution to its members (and to many other faculty members present) that expressed no confidence in the administration and supported the student strike. The resolution obviously would have passed, but during the debate the chairman withdrew the resolution and, along with the steering committee, left the meeting. What happened was that these faculty members began to fear that their resolution was too radical and that it might further polarize the faculty and university community. Later the same day, the leaders of the ad-hoc faculty supported a resolution in the Joint Faculties meeting calling for the establishment of an executive committee of the faculty to propose university reforms. Half of the ad-hoc faculty's leaders were appointed to this committee of 12, and the ad-hoc faculty group was thus dissolved.

The new Executive Committee of the Faculty (in contrast to the ad-hoc faculty group) had ready access to the trustees and enjoyed the confidence of the administration, but it had neither a constituency nor any clear mandate. The ad-hoc faculty had begun, at least, to build a participating constituency. Although the Executive Committee could call meetings of the Joint Faculties, it never did. Its work was done behind closed doors, and as a group it became invisible to most of the campus. During the second police action, and on the arguments over discipline, it publicly supported the administration, and worked only secretly to pressure the president and vice-president to adopt a more conciliatory stand. Such procedures did not gain it the confidence and support of the students.

Moreover, in its first month of work (to the end of the academic year), the Executive Committee failed to formulate any principles for restructuring the university that could have been publicly debated, but simply organized a series of study groups for the summer. Students and faculty were asked to join the paid staff of these committees, but no campaign was undertaken to actively recruit such members. In any case, most concerned students viewed such committees as an inadequate response to the crisis. Even the moderate students most committed to restructuring the university feared being coopted through their participation in such efforts. Another new faculty group, the Independent Faculty, formed out of the remaining 15 leaders of the ad-hoc faculty, also failed to organize a real constituency.

The student organizations pressing for reform were much different. Representation on the Steering Committee to lead the strike was based upon constituencies. Any group of 70 students could elect a member to the Strike Steering Committee. Subsequently, the Steering Committee split, about half of its members withdrawing to form their own organization, Students for a Restructured University. This new organization wanted to give primary emphasis to the internal reform of the university; the Strike Committee was more concerned with political conflicts of the larger society, and with the relationship of the university to these political issues. Both groups continued to support the original demands of the sit-ins, and to vigorously oppose the administration. Both continued to organize students. The two

Right before the first police intervention, some of the more moderate students occupying Avery and Fayerweather hinted that they were ready to talk about alternatives to complete amnesty, as suggested by the ad-hoc faculty's proposals. But then they decided that they had to stay with the amnesty demand because the ad-hoc faculty did not seem to them to be sufficiently dependable.

The morning after the first police action, the ad-hoc faculty group dissolved in chaos. It was completely alienated by the administration's resort to force. (Many of these faculty members had witnessed the police action and some were injured by the police.) But the group was unable to agree on a common strategy towards the administration. Successive faculty groups also failed to change the administration's stand on discipline and its reliance upon the use of force, nor did they gain the trust and support of the students.

The faculty thus failed to check the escalating polarization and confrontation between students and administration. This failure shocked the faculty into a recognition of the need for fundamental institutional reform.

Restructuring the University

Even before the first police action, some students and faculty members recognized that one result of the conflict would have to be major changes in the university. After the police action, the predominant issue became the restructuring of the university. But student and faculty reformers held different conceptions of how this restructuring would occur and of the ends to be achieved. (The Barton survey found a relatively small difference in answers given by students and faculty on the issues of the crisis, except on items dealing with the relative power of students and faculty in a restructured university. Here the differences were greater than 20 percent.)

The student activists believed that real change in the university could be obtained and institutionalized only if the crisis continued. Faculty reformers argued that important institutional restructuring could occur only slowly, after careful study in a less stressful atmosphere. The latter envisioned *reform* of the university from above, through the work of a few appointed *committees*. The students desired a *change* from below, through the participation of *constituencies*. Faculty members viewed both the process and results of university reform in *professional* terms; that is, decisions should be made by those with the most relevant expertise. To improve Columbia's educational quality and institutional effectiveness, what was needed, they believed, was a new *rational-legal* organization (more and better committees and courts, and a more progressive administration). The students, on the other hand, wanted the university to divorce itself from existing centers of power and to contribute to the solution of major social and human problems. The students recognized that the professional competence of professors and even administrators would prevail on many technical and academic issues, but they insisted that students as well as faculty must *participate* in setting the university's general public and educational policies.

One incident during the faculty's early efforts at reform illustrates the preference of faculty leaders for change from above by committee, rather than by participatory groups also united on special issues, and both remained suspicious of faculty organizations. In addition to these two student groups, caucuses arose in many school and graduate departments to press for educational and institutional reform. This proliferation of student groups backing the reform of the university was in sharp contrast to the lack of faculty participation.

At present, the faculty committees are in extremely weak positions vis-a-vis the administration and trustees. Within the Faculty Executive Committee, there is probably a powerful minority that supports the administration and wants only minimal change. Moreover, the Executive Committee does not have the support of most students. Even more troublesome is the extent of the faculty's division over whether students should take part in university decision-making. About half of the faculty are willing to grant students some decision-making power, according to Barton, but the others favor only regular consultation with them.

It thus seems evident that it is only through organizing constituencies that the faculty committed to reform at Columbia will be able to achieve real change in the university, or even to recreate its basic cohesion. Faculty reform leaders will have to assert organized pressure to gain ascendency and to make sure that new university committees, judicial bodies, and legislative organs are not just appointed from above, but receive general consent. Yet it is still questionable whether faculty leaders will arise and make the attempt. Columbia, therefore, faces more polarization, confrontation, and probably repression.

In Conclusion

It was the great and increasing polarization between administrators, students, and faculty that prevented a solution to the Columbia student revolt. In this polarization the moderate positions were destroyed: Student moderates became radicalized, administration moderates became rigid and conservative, faculty moderates failed in attempts to mediate and became alienated from both sides. The weakness of the moderates was a result of the institutional weakness of Columbia–the archaic and isolated nature of administrative authority, the lack of effective faculty and student governments, and the attenuation of faculty-student relations. These institutional weaknesses led to a general lack of administrative and faculty responsiveness to student grievances and to the students' attempt to compel response by dramatic action.

A critical problem of Columbia, then, is to strengthen all components of the university in order to render them more responsive to one another. Even the administration requires strengthening–not, however, apart from students and faculty, but by new links to them. The forging of multiple institutional relations *within* the university can increase the interdependence of students, faculty, and administration, and simultaneously decrease dependence upon external forces (especially for the administration, but also for the faculty and even for the students).

Only then can the university fully develop its own capacities for intellectual and moral excellence, and independently determine its social responsibilities.

37. Violence in the Streets: Its Context and Meaning

Joseph Lohman

I cannot refrain from accepting the challenge of the Dean of the Law School in his reference to the Milquetoast attitude of the Berkeley campus. My answer is by way of expressing a problem which has been set forth in the discussions at this point. The discussions have been concerned with a revolution and the violence in the context of that revolution. A good deal of the concern with that revolution indicates that the term "violence" has to be employed with reservation—even insofar as to suggest that much of what is unwittingly associated with violence in these times and calls for action by various authorities is really behavior which is nonviolent in character. But even out of that there has been engendered some measure of the violence which we are addressing. Not all of it is considered as such only from the standpoint of the reactionary elements, because what invites violence quite often escalates into a mutual system of violence. It does no good to speak in terms of blame or finding a guilty party—reserving for ourselves some kind of security from such reference to one or the other of the parties.

Because I suspect I shall have some difficulty in communicating in the degree which I should like, I am reminded of the story which is told of the man who went to hunt lions. We must not be in the situation which came upon him when his gun jammed and he saw the lion coming at him. He went to his knees and shut his eyes in prayer. When he opened his eyes, he saw that the lion was also kneeling in prayer. In obvious relief, he raised his hands to the heaven above and shouted, "Alleluia, alleluia, we both believe in the same, true, ever-loving God! We are praying! We can talk this thing over!" And the lion replied, as lions occasionally will, "I don't know what you've been praying about, but I've been saying grace."

I suspect that there are some of us who, in the course of the discussion, will be seen as saying grace and others as praying for deliverance. We are all praying, and the dilemma which confronts us now as to the problem of violence depends, in some respects, upon who is using violence. It must be remembered that not all violence is necessarily bad; there are some forms of violence which are indeed legitimate in our society. Thus, we must concern ourselves with the problem of hostility and violence through a value-laden approach. There is a proper question as to the

Reprinted from *Notre Dame Lawyer,* **40**:5 (1965), 517–526, by permission of the publisher and Mrs. Joseph D. Lohman, Executrix of the Estate.

desirability of overhostility and the resulting violence. But wherever one may stand, he must admit that violence is sometimes necessary to smash a brittle, resistant social order. At the same time the police have been endowed with the thought that, in order to make an arrest in the face of resistance, they are under law permitted to exercise that degree of violence necessary to effect the arrest under such conditions. While police reluctance to use this power is in itself a problem, its existance complicates the problem of violence more than is commonly assumed. The importance and necessity of such a power must be recognized. Yet sometimes it adds to an engendered situation of violence in a very aggravating and dangerous way, ultimately contributing to social chaos. If this is kept in mind, it is possible to examine more critically the conditions of violence. The problem may be expressed another way.

Much in vogue today are accounts of the so-called revolution of the Negro population. The revolution of our times is more considerable, however, than that portion of it represented by the explosion in the area of race. The problem is best expressed in what may seem a curious rhetorical statement. We must address the problem of our view of our view of violence, rather than directly view violence as a problem. Contemporary America faces a revolution which is really the dilemma posed in addressing the problem of violence. There is not only, as is quite apparent, the revolt of the Negro. There is an equally portentous revolt, the revolt of youth. The incident on the Berkeley campus was a manifestation of that revolt, however aggravated and complicated the revolt may become by expression in the mounting of action with reference to the civil rights question off campus. Another aspect of the revolution may be found in the revolt of the clients of the institutionalized professional structure of the times. The revolution has been characterized as a revolt of the people who were the objects of social service, of some kind of mental health program or of the employment placement apparatus of the country. At the moment, in mounting the war on poverty, concern centers upon an insurgent expression of the clientele as the means of implementing the program. This recognition of the necessity for working for the poor, through the poor, represents an anticipation of more serious aspects of revolt in that area than have been generally identified. Still other aspects of the revolution are the revolt of the aged, mounted at the moment with reference to legislation but expressed in other areas as well, the revolt of the urbanized population, the revolt of the blue-collar workers, and the revolt of the teachers. The dilemma posed by each of these has been expressed in recent times by spokesmen of these particular groups.

The problem is also identified by the popular views of the crises of today: the crisis in civil rights in the confrontation of states' rights and that system with the rights guaranteed under the Constitution and enforced under federal authority; the crisis of our educational institutions, not only those institutions of higher learning, but the public schools of the country; the crisis of our welfare institutions; the crisis of the cities, in terms of the problem of reapportionment which is plaguing most of the states after the recent decisions of the Supreme Court. What these crises, these manifestations of revolt, the growing organization of these distressed elements and groups has produced is a series of physical confrontations in which violence is more frequent today than in the past. This has raised a serious question as to the means of repressing deprivation or despair,[1] means which will answer the lament effectively and yet which will perserve the essential meaning and purpose of our democracy in such a context.

There is a structural deficiency becoming apparent which is conducive to over-expressions of hostility in American society.[2] It takes several forms, each of which should be considered. Most Americans are unaware that the structure of responsible management under situations of stress is so weak and so impaired as to permit violence which is uncontrollable under the circumstances. Some notable instances of this structural deficiency are the government of a state in the southern regions of this country, the police departments or the sheriffs' offices. Similar agencies have a very considerable responsibility for law enforcement in the North and throughout the rest of the United States. This deficiency results in the failure to act and the blaming of troublemakers rather than the exhibition of a capacity to act and the acceptance of responsibility for the accepted procedures of initiating a dialogue, entertaining the complaints of grievances and, indeed, the redressing of grievances. These deficiencies create a condition under which a confrontation results in what is called in desperation an overt assertion or act, nothing less than violence, nothing less than going through the barricades.

Recently on the Berkeley campus, it has been an instructive experience for those of us on the faculty and the administration to have students tell us, "Yes, the dialogue is all right, but nothing happens, nothing comes out, nothing develops. But when we sit down, and when we persist, or when we block your action, then something does happen." This is a commentary not upon them so much as a commentary upon the structure of responsibility on the part of the agencies and institutions which are presumably more or less, less in this instance, adequately prepared to address strain, since it is a condition of our life.

The second structural condition that has encouraged and is encouraging even greater hostility and overt violence is the absence of effective channels for expressing grievances. In the first place, there is the "waitness" of the channels; nothing happens in them; they are pale representations. As a way of absorbing this problem and hoping that it will pass by, authorities are tolerant, even permissive, of individuals who go outside the channels to extralegal means. Since I have been a police officer and identify with the police even as an academic, I cannot forget the situation on the Berkeley campus in the first days of that revolt (and I happen to be one of those who believe the students had much merit in their grievances). When an action was taken by the administration involving an arrest, the students seized a squad car with a policeman and a prisoner in it. The disposition of this incident on the part of the administration was to wait them out, to let them have the policeman and car for

[1] See Goldin, *Violence: The Integration of Psychiatric and Sociological Concepts,* 40 Notre Dame Lawyer 508 (1965).

[2] See Smelser, *Theory of Collective Behavior*, (New York: Free Press of Glencoe, 1963).

a while. The students held them for thirty-nine hours. They did not know how to let go of them, and under the circumstances the administration did not know how to get them back. This was a kind of permissiveness of authority which in that situation aggravated the continuing attitude of objection and exception to authority which reach in some measure into the present time.

What are the legtimate means of protest? What are their perimeters? Although the channels for expressing grievances are extraordinarily slow and even conflict with each other, this was not the time to be permissive. This is true particularly since the police action was not initiated by the police themselves but was mounted at the instance of a civilian complaint. The police were acting only in an instrumental capacity. And yet they were not supported, so that people have reason to believe that police intervention can be ignored with impunity–one can prevail upon those who stand above them not to support them. Under these circumstances, chaos is indeed entertained. A further invitation to chaos is the willingness to act upon the assumption that a problem will go away if those in authority wait long enough. This assumption suggests that if anything does happen, it will happen fortuitously, and because it happens fortuitously, one will simply have to be circumspect and proper and in that fact the problem will be managed.

The notable illustration of what was happening in Philadelphia[3] cannot be given as an instance of the innocence of the police simply because they did not provoke it or initiate the action. For the condition of the community was such that a riot could be triggered at any time, in any place and in almost any way. This was known to the police, and the beginning of wisdom is to know that in that circumstance the police will be recognized as an instrument of the white group, even though they are not disposed to represent themselves in that role. Because they will be recognized as such, permissiveness and unwillingness to act may dominate the situation and result in an impossible situation at a later date.

The third structural consideration of importance is the empirical condition of violence as it confronts us today. That condition is the possibility of those who are aggrieved actually being in touch and in a new and extraordinary relationship with each other. The ecology of violence commands our attention. The proximity and accessibility of individuals of common plight and conditions, and their involvement in this system of social relationships which places them (to use the euphemism of the day) in the form of a subculture, constitutes a condition of violence which there has been no occasion to address seriously in the past.[4]

These observations should be related to the more general problems of life in a revolution. The revolution has presented a picture of society, not as some refer to it, as decadent, but as divided in new ways which create a condition of almost automatic violence when there is effective confrontation and no mechanism for mediating these new centers of power.

[3] See Leary, *The Role of the Police in Riotous Demonstrations,* 40 Notre Dame Lawyer 499 (1965).

[4] Joseph Lohman, *Police and Minority Groups,* Chicago Park District, 1947.

The problem of violence caused by structural deficiencies in a society undergoing revolution can also be expressed by reference to the general problem of crime. Violence commands attention as an unlegal and unwarranted measure in resolving issues. In this sense it is a criminal act, and in the last analysis the men that have been captured in Alabama will be taken before a court and tried for the commission of crime. The problem of violence relates to the changes taking place in the general crime problem, which are manifested in terms of the structural conduciveness referred to above. The problem of violence is part of the larger relation of the crime problem to the general changes in social and communal life. The community is in transformation. The best evidence of this is found by studying crime, which has been called the lengthened shadow of the community. Conversely, if the community has changed, these changes can be studied in terms of the perceivable changes in the crime problem. First, perhaps the most challenging feature about today's trends in crime is the youthfulness of the criminal offender. Last year, 60 per cent of the serious, "part-one" crimes reported in the nation by the Uniform Crime Reports were committed by persons 18 years of age and under. These are crimes of violence, taking of property, action against persons. It is interesting to note the average age of criminal offenders for each of the past twenty years. Twenty years ago, the average age for serious part-one crimes was in the twenties, *i.e.*, 50 per cent of these crimes were committed by persons 24 years of age and over. In each year thereafter the average age has gone perceptively down. Now 60 per cent of the serious part-one crimes are committed by persons 18 years of age and under. What are the changes? What transformations are taking place in our community life that makes the criminalgenic process strategically focussed within the younger generation? What is this condition which makes deviates in general and crime in particular a phenomenon in the time of youth? In what sense are they apart from the common life of the community so as to become an identifiable representation of values and norms which are at odds with those of the general community? I will just leave that as a question. Let us look at a second aspect of crime.

Organized crime is not new but is distinguished from the predatory orders of crime in its mode of assertion. It is a crime of marketing various services, such as the vices, narcotics, sex and labor management relations. These are services provided for the community and paid for by individuals who need an organizer to supply the service. Organized crime has developed so that it is at present the number-one crime problem of the nation and coincident with the development and emergence of the metropolitan community in the transistion from rural to not only urban but metropolitan distribution.

The third aspect of the crime problem which is increasingly in focus is with reference to groups that are at the moment the marginal groups of the society, those which are marginal in terms of race, ethnic origin, income or class status. They happen to be at this time the Negro, the Mexican-American and the people who live in the pockets of poverty and who are removed from the common life of the community. These pockets geographically simulate the same conditions of deprivation, denial and exclusion which are represented by groups closer to the urban centers but are nevertheless excluded from the common life on the basis of race or ethnic origin.

These developments in the crime problem suggest interesting developments in our society as a whole. These are the collective experiences which take the form of associated life and its subcultural content. These are, in some respects, unprecedented in terms of their numbers and in terms of their specification in our previous history. We speak knowingly and meaningfully today about an adolescent subculture. We speak about the subcultures of race, of the aged, of those chronically serviced and indigent and of the automated blue-collar worker. We have modified and, in some instances, corrected the too literal references to some of these groups as culturally deprived by noting that their subcultures have positive content as well as the absence of middle class values which distinguishes them. Because of nationwide legislative programs—even though the government answers are weak and timid, somewhat in the manner of Casper Milquetoast—continuously we have occasion to recognize the necessity of attending to the problems created by this phenomenon. We also must recognize that there are confrontations between people who are racially differentiated, and who exhibit varied subcultures of the races, and who are at the same time economically differentiated, consequently possessing a culture developed as an answer to their poverty. A complicating factor is the dilemma of youth in the sense of its estrangement and alienation from the common stream of life. The centers of power which have existed or have been developed have called for the mounting of answers to those centers of power. To a large extent these answers have been an anticipation of the problem in basic terms because the anguish, anger, hostility, bitterness and violence attendant upon the confrontations have given to many of us an early recognition of what truly confronts society. The point is that there are pronounced cleavages in American society today, not only in terms of religion but in terms of ethnic origin, wealth, power, prestige and age. These cleavages are a challenge superior to our structural capacity to contain violence. This, in short, is why it is necessary at this juncture to examine our administrative apparatus and the police function with a view of giving it competency to afford the time necessary to address seriously the contexts out of which confrontations have developed.

An important generalization may be made at this point. Our structural apparatus has been for the most part committed to the protection of the overriding, defined, established interests. The police, as frequently as not, enforce not only the law but, as has been seen pervasively in the South, custom as well, which is not the province of the police. The police have also enforced the power structure established apart from the law, and they have enforced the interests and beliefs of the power enforcing group itself, the bureaucracy of law enforcement. They have done this, rather than repair singularly and exclusively to the law as the condition of their operation. The great lesson of the distinguished sheriff in Alabama is that even within law enforcement areas under the official organized administrative apparatus of the community there is an answer to abuse and excess by that officialdom. The policeman, under the Constitution, is required to enforce the law, not the directives of special interest or power holding groups in the community, not merely his own fraternal group. The concept of law enforcement in this society is far removed from those of the authoritarian social systems. In America, the police officer is no more than the professional citizen. The use of that phrase suggests that because he knows what a citizen's obligation is, even better than a citizen does, he is a policeman. The term means that he enforces law under no different conditions and with no different prerogatives and with no different ends than does every citizen under law. Both are bound by due process, which is the canon of our society and democratic way of life.

The time has come to mount quickly and seriously a program under which the structural competency of the apparatus will be increased in order to deal with pools of hostility and violence. This cannot be done without some clarification of the issues outlined above. Were it not for limitations of time, a word about youth would be in order. In focussing on race with reference to violence, we may fall into the error of equating violence exclusively with the confrontation on the basis of race. I offer this illustration of the broad context in which violence in the streets is to be understood. Race is but one aspect of this context, which in itself included the problems of youth and poverty stricken people confronting the elder generation.

Most thoughtful students of the problems of young people are quick to assess their difficulties in the light of changing social and economic conditions. This is true particularly as the socioeconomic scene may complicate and even aggravate the central concern of all self-sustaining individuals, namely, the realization of oneself in one's lifetime tasks or work. Paul Goodman, at the University of Wisconsin, stated the issues succinctly when he wrote, "It's hard to grow up when there isn't enough men's work."[5] Goodman further noted that men have always done drudging work in order to produce necessary food and shelter, secure in the idea that it was justified and worthy of a man to do it, although sometimes feeling that the social conditions under which the work was performed were not worthy of a man. This is not the whole of the problem, however. Material security is important but, under normal conditions, greater security is derived from knowing that one's contribution is useful and unique–that one is needed.

These remarks are more than truisms. They indicate a fundamental problem, for every young person wants to know and needs to know whether he can make a useful and valuable contribution. Often he is afraid that he cannot be useful and that he will not be wanted as a person. This is one of the questions that confronts us in the public school system, for whole masses of children see themselves as apart from the "others" in precisely these terms.

In the United States, the adults of earlier generations needed youth because often the very life of the family–the bread on the table or the coal in the kitchen stove–depended on their making a contribution by doing chores. The word "chore" has lost its former meaning: fifty years ago performing a chore meant filling a responsible role. Today a chore is regarded as an irksome invasion of childish freedom.

In many foreign countries today, youths have specific roles to play in society and are regarded by their elders as successors to the roles of the elders. The elders know that only the young can carry on the task of shaping and building a new and better

[5] See Goodman, *Growing Up Absurd,* (New York: Random House, 1960).

society. In many of the emerging nations of Asia and Africa, only youth is free from ancient tribal custom and only youth can lead society from tribal confusion and anarchy toward lasting economic independence in a unifying democracy. When adults and young people recognize the need for each other, there is less tension, less estrangement of the generations. The generations need each other, not alone for the economic survival of the society, but for the maintenance of its very integrity as a moral order. Without such mutual recognition there is no sense of being needed; without the sense of being needed there is no corresponding commitment by the younger generation to the maintenance of society.

It is a sad fact that in the United States the older generation, for economic and technological reasons, no longer needs the younger generation. To great extent youth has become an economic liability rather than an economic asset. A child represents an income tax deduction, but this by no means makes up the difference. The prolongation of childhood, the child labor laws, the effect of automated technology, the cost of bringing up and educating youth for possibly fifteen to twenty years—these are the economic grounds which have caused the mutuality of the generations to disappear in recent years. The economic obligations and responsibilities, the rewards and particularly the power relations between young and old are merely shadows of the past. The powers and responsibilities of the generations today are tenuous and unclear.

The same factors which are threatening youth's sense of importance and meaningfulness and its sense of being needed are also threatening many adults. Automation is threatening all too many able-bodied men with a future of chronic indigence or insecurity, and this affects both the generations. An adult, insecure as a worker, cannot be secure as a parent; his insecurity as a parent is certain to be visited as a secondary and confirming deprivation upon his children who are already suffering from the lack of meaning and purpose in life, and thus the process comes full circle. It is at this point that the awesome negative impact of a generation of deprived and alienated youth becomes apparent. Many youths see themselves as the avenging angels of their parents since they hold the power to prove their parents' success or failure as parents. Young people in a society which no longer depends on them for economic survival are tempted to use the power conferred upon them by the reversal between generations to act as the accuser and the judge of their parents. In this regard, the whole society stands accused to a certain extent. We are all in *loco parentis* as we witness the ubiquitous pattern of rebelliousness of presentday youth which is manifest in a plurality of deviant patterns ranging from one end of the spectrum to the other.

We are, in the current crises, becoming aware of the existence of a plurality of subcultures produced by the problem-solving tendency of human groups when confronted by specific and recurrent problems. These subcultures are a reflection of both the broadly encompassing and the narrowly specific changes in the socioeconomic system which confronts young people in general, and young people who are members of different cultural, economic and racial groups in particular. Leaders of the society also have begun to recognize that poverty is a factor which must be dealt with, for the subcultures as collective entities have a power potential which they are beginning to express in the streets and in the elections.

I have attempted in my remarks today to call attention to the changes in the social order which are structuring the new collective entities. I have pointed out that we have so far failed to engage the new collective entities except through the agency of the individual who comes from them. When we engage such individuals, we tend to separate them from their experiences, to ignore their experiences or to regard them as valueless. In my judgment, the degree to which we do this is the measure of our failure to affect such persons. Instead of producing a desirable effect, we generate through our patronizing attitude a hostility which can prove a serious threat to the workings of the democratic society. We can effectively engage the members of subcultures only after close re-examination of the problem and a reconstruction of our view.

I will conclude with an observation about the general posture of our society. Throughout the nineteenth century, America was a complex of hyphenated Americans who came to this melting pot world and attempted, through institutions which were tailored to their condition, to effect a transition from their old world condition to the American scene—to wit, the German-Americans, the Italian-Americans, the Irish-Americans. The Settlement House taught them English, vocational schools gave them skills to use in the economic interdependence of the new society. It is interesting to note what has happened to such institutions as the Settlement House and vocational education since that day. The traditional vocational education is today regarded as obsolescent and even pointless in the light of technological change. The Settlement House is seen as ill-adapted to the transition of the new immigrant populations. Their methods are not appropriate to their condition as they come to the city and metropolitan areas of the North in present times. In the nineteenth and early part of this century, American culture exhibited a centripetal tendency. Immigrant groups came out of other social worlds into one world, with a drive toward a common definition. The common denominator was the American melting pot. The common aim was the acquisition of the one new language and the acquisition of a skill to gain a place in the American scene. Now, since World War I, we are witnessing a reverse tendency. The social process is elaborating a complex of subcultures in American society which are driving us apart in local communities and groups which are interacting among themselves and producing their own distinctive norms and values. These are the current subcultures of youth, of race, of suburbia and of income, high and low. It is the reality of their subcultures which are so confounding to our established institutional structures. It is not that there is a culture of crime; it is that there is such a plurality of subcultures that the problem of the individual's adjustment to commonly accepted norms is confounded, and deviance is generated as a matter of course. Crime and delinquency are its logical accompaniment. We must develop means for modifying and preparing personnel to play new and meaningful roles.

It is a paradox of the new metropolitan development that we are constantly moving toward self-defeating extremes in our desperate and uninformed efforts to keep abreast of the changing community. The heartlands of our great metropolitan centers are becoming the provinces of the new minorities. These groups are potential threat that may express themselves in the traditional patterns of organized crime. They have come out of a segregated discriminatory experience, in search of freedom and opportunity, into a social environment which in many respects is as restrictive as the older pattern. It is not only crime which becomes the abortive fruit of our failure to understand this changing community.

The unwitting processes of the middle-class "suburban drift" and the transformation of vast areas of the central city into an enormous racial slum have profound political implications. In many of our major cities it is affecting a change in the balance of political power. We must recognize the coincidence of the development of these great racial blocs with the traditional organization and location of the urban political machines. The traditional alliances between crime and politics have focused on the immigrant community and the slum. We may be ushering in a new era of unprecedented political conflict between the cities and their suburbs with aggravating overtones of race tension and conflict as an additional feature of organized crime. To ignore the social, economic and cultural disabilities under which these populations labor and to try to contain their volcanic eruptions by the expedient of repressive and antiquated police measures can only have the effect of force-feeding the fires which are smoldering at the core of our metropolitan communities.

In short, many of the problems which confront us stem from the failure of the public to know and to understand the new dimensions and ramifications of community life. Our success in controlling the crime problem in general, and organized crime in particular, will depend upon our understanding of the complexities of the newly emerging communal life and the problems which it has engendered. An effective law enforcement function must be familiar with and equal to its target.[6]

The changing patterns of crime are a projection of the far-reaching changes in American community life. The police and the courts, the machinery of punishment and corrections, are also projections of the community. It is not likely that we will be successful in controlling crime without seriously changing the organization and administration of criminal justice. The ultimate answer is to see crime and violence not only as problems in law enforcement but as problems in education, family organization, employment opportunity and housing. These are the structures which incubate deviance and hence crime, delinquency and violence. It is a myth that man's behavior can be changed directly. It can be changed only by altering the conditions which underlie his behavior. We must learn to treat the causes, not only the effects, of crime and violence.

We are at a critical juncture in the history of American community development. The resettlement of the American community and the emergence of the metropolitan community is not merely a change in the size of our population nor in its geographic location. It is something of far greater importance, namely, the modification and, indeed, creation of a whole new set of human relations.

[6] See Lohman, *New Dimensions in Race Tension and Conflict*, 30 The Police Chief No. 7 (1963).

Section VI

Processes in Law Enforcement and the Courts

Introductory Remarks

This section is concerned with the institutional structures for the apprehension and adjudication of the accused. Several articles cannot fully deal with the complexities of the problems and practices that characterize law enforcement and the courts today. Furthermore, no analysis can fully capture the unique problems and practices that characterize a specific community.

For example, all agencies of the criminal justice control system operate under criminal and juvenile codes that are similar from state to state, but differ in many aspects from one state to another. Also, between communities within the same state the application of laws is affected both by the quality and by the extent of organization, and by the differences in enforcement and interpretation of laws by each police and court agency. In addition, differences in the application of laws by these agencies are influenced to some extent by variations in expectations, public involvement, power structures, and the availability of other means of social service and control existing in each community. The extent of apprehending and adjudicating offenders as well as the actual amounts and forms of deviance which thrive in a particular community are partly influenced by the forces mentioned above.

Nevertheless, these numerous agencies have been delegated similar responsibilities, have experienced common problems, and have developed similarities in practices. Accordingly, we can focus on the common aspects that more or less characterize all criminal justice control systems.

These agencies have been assigned the function of apprehending the accused, thereby reducing and controlling violations. The agencies are crucial in preserving order, ensuring the safety of the people and their property, and protecting what is considered the preferred moral climate. In recent times these agencies have been increasingly relied on to preserve the social order. Indeed, it is the extent of dependency on these formal agencies and the practices evolved in fulfilling this mandate which reflect the quality of the social life in a free society. This reliance has been strongly supported by the progressive complexity and impersonality of our social life which is reflected in increased uncertainties of the citizen role, normative and functional differentiations, divisional conflicts, rising expectations, and freedom from informal controls.

An additional function is expected of these agencies. This expectation has been encouraged by an increasing emphasis on justice, humanitarianism, and the scientific approach in the handling of social problems. Thus, the function of differential handling of offenders by these agencies is expected and recognized as potentially supportive of the concepts of rehabilitation and individual justice. We witness the increased use of means other than institutionalization (e.g., fines, referral to social agencies, probation). We also observe the enactment of discretionary powers in sentencing. Also to be recognized is continued tolerance of the extensive discretionary practices (e.g., warn and release, decision to arrest, dismissal of charges, allowance of pleas of guilty for reduction of charges) informally developed by police and court personnel. Particularly are the rights of the accused forfeited in the name of individualized handling and treatment in juvenile court settings.[1]

One last function expected of these agencies is the adjudication of a continuous heavy stream of cases, particularly in our large cities. Therein lies a dilemma in our criminal justice control system. The dilemma is that restrictive legal procedures make it necessary to resort to informally developed practices in handling these vast caseloads. These informal practices are used from the initial selection of offenders to expediting the adjudication of the large numbers of accused offenders before the courts. Seeking organizational efficiency may therefore result in the use of practices serving differential handling (warn and release, reduction of charges, dismissal of charges, etc.) being used to a greater extent for the benefit of police operations and to clear the court's calendar than to serve the functions of individualized handling or to protect the community through apprehension and adjudication of offenders.

In recent years attention has been drawn to these incongruencies of law enforcement and court agencies' functions and practices. The agencies have now become the center of increased controversy in American society. The quality of justice and fairness versus the evolved practices in administrating justice has now been reopened for study.

One of the more important factors contributing to controversy is that the actions of individuals representing these agencies become collectively visible through improved communicative networks (i.e., police handling of public demonstrations). Also, police organizational practices enhance structural isolation (e.g., from foot patrol to motor patrol). Another is the increasing solidarity among many minority group members who interpret police-court practices toward them as reflecting and sustaining structural arrangements favorable to white power groups. The greatest factor, of course, has been the recent Supreme Court's decisions governing "due process of law" for adults and juveniles.[2] *These series of decisions have demanded increasingly high and consistent standards in assuring that the guarantees of individual rights as expressed by the U.S. Constitution and Bill of Rights be equally available in various stages in the criminal justice process for all accused persons. Yet it is these decisions that bring to the surface the conflicts in functions assigned the police and to the courts in a free society.*[3]

These being the central issues, our major concern is to view these formal agencies of control in terms of their commitment toward and their effectiveness in achieving these functions. Problems, processes, and structural arrangements affecting the achievement of the responsibilities mentioned above will be the concern of this section.

[1] The "due process" procedures that govern the handling of adults generally do not apply to juveniles. See the footnote 2 on Supreme Court decisions in this introduction.

[2] *Escobedo vs. Illinois* (1964): ruled that a suspect, when he is arrested, has a constitutional right to counsel if he so desires and must be advised of his right to remain silent; *Maranda vs. Arizona* (1966): forbids the interrogation of a suspect in custody without counsel present unless the suspect expressly waives his right to counsel; *Mapp vs. Ohio* (1961): evidence obtained through searches and seizures committed with absence of warrant or probable cause is inadmissible in both state and federal courts; *McNabb-Mallory rule* (1947 and 1957): held confessions are invalid if made during illegal detention, and includes the requirement to bring the suspect to a hearing officer (U.S. Commissioner) promptly. This ruling applies only to federal cases, but has had an effect in discouraging both illegal arrests and coerced confessions in state courts; *Gideon vs. Wainwright* (1963): ruled that regardless of financial capacity, all felony defendants possess the right to have the presence and assistance of counsel at trial and on appeal; *Kent vs. U.S.* (1966): requires that juvenile courts hold hearing on question of waiving its jurisdiction so that child can be tried as adult, as well as providing counsel for child and making available the child's juvenile court records to counsel; *In the Matter of the Application of Gault* (1967): for those youth subject to juvenile proceedings which could lead to commitment extends the right to be sufficiently notified of charges so as to permit preparation of a defense, and to be informed of rights to remain silent, to counsel, and to confront and cross-examine adverse witnesses.

[3] Some of the developments these decisions have encouraged are:

(1) In practice as well as theory constitutional rights are more available to minority and lower-class groups.

(2) They have increased the necessity for law enforcement agencies to move toward professional skills of investigation.

(3) Much of the population with increasing concern and emotion view these decisions as an excessive imbalance of justice in favor of accused offenders. Recent Supreme Court appointments as this is written would suggest future constitutional interpretations in this area will tend to be more conservative.

38. America's System of Criminal Justice

The President's Commission on Law Enforcement and Administration of Justice

America's System of Criminal Justice

The system of criminal justice America uses to deal with those crimes it cannot prevent and those criminals it cannot deter is not a monolithic, or even a consistent, system. It was not designed or built in one piece at one time. Its philosophic core is that a person may be punished by the Government if, and only if, it has been proved by an impartial and deliberate process that he has violated a specific law. Around that core layer upon layer of institutions and procedures, some carefully constructed and some improvised, some inspired by principle and some by expediency, have accumulated. Parts of the system—magistrates' courts, trial by jury, bail—are of great antiquity. Other parts—juvenile courts, probation and parole, professional policemen—are relatively new. The entire system represents an adaptation of the English common law to America's peculiar structure of government, which allows each local community to construct institutions that fill its special needs. Every village, town, county, city, and State has its own criminal justice system, and there is a Federal one as well. All of them operate somewhat alike. No two of them operate precisely alike.

Any criminal justice system is an apparatus society uses to enforce the standards of conduct necessary to protect individuals and the community. It operates by apprehending, prosecuting, convicting, and sentencing those members of the community who violate the basic rules of group existence. The action taken against lawbreakers is designed to serve three purposes beyond the immediately punitive one. It removes dangerous people from the community; it deters others from criminal behavior; and it gives society an opportunity to attempt to transform lawbreakers into law-abiding citizens. What most significantly distinguishes the system of one country from that of another is the extent and the form of the protections it offers individuals in the process of determining guilt and imposing punishment. Our system of justice deliberately sacrifices much in efficiency and even in effectiveness in order to

Reprinted from "The Challenge of Crime in a Free Society: Introduction," *The Challenge of Crime in a Free Society,* a Report by The President's Commission on Law Enforcement and Administration of Justice (Washington: Government Printing Office, 1967), Ch. 1, pp. 7, 10–14.

preserve local autonomy and to protect the individual. Sometimes it may seem to sacrifice too much. For example, the American system was not designed with Cosa Nostra-type criminal organizations in mind, and it has been notably unsuccessful to date in preventing such organizations from preying on society.

•••

...the criminal process, the method by which the system deals with individual cases, is not a hodgepodge of random actions. It is rather a continuum–an orderly progression of events–some of which, like arrest and trial, are highly visible and some of which, though of great importance, occur out of public view. A study of the system must begin by examining it as a whole.

•••

The popular, or even the lawbook, theory of everyday criminal process oversimplifies in some respects and overcomplicates in others what usually happens. That theory is that when an infraction of the law occurs, a policeman finds, if he can, the probable offender, arrests him and brings him promptly before a magistrate. If the offense is minor, the magistrate disposes of it forthwith; if it is serious, he holds the defendant for further action and admits him to bail. The case then is turned over to a prosecuting attorney who charges the defendant with a specific statutory crime. This charge is subject to review by a judge at a preliminary hearing of the evidence and in many places if the offense charged is a felony, by a grand jury that can dismiss the charge, or affirm it by delivering it to a judge in the form of an indictment. If the defendant pleads "not guilty" to the charge he comes to trial; the facts of his case are marshaled by prosecuting and defense attorneys and presented, under the supervision of a judge, through witnesses, to a jury. If the jury finds the defendant guilty, he is sentenced by the judge to a term in prison, where a systematic attempt to convert him into a law-abiding citizen is made, or to a term of probation, under which he is permitted to live in the community as long as he behaves himself.

Some cases do proceed much like that, especially those involving offenses that are generally considered "major": serious acts of violence or thefts of large amounts of property. However, not all major cases follow this course, and, in any event, the bulk of the daily business of the criminal justice system consists of offenses that are not major–of breaches of the peace, crimes of vice, petty thefts, assaults arising from domestic or street-corner or barroom disputes. These and most other cases are disposed of in much less formal and much less deliberate ways.

The theory of the juvenile court is that it is a "helping" social agency, designed to prescribe carefully individualized treatment to young people in trouble, and that its procedures are therefore nonadversary. Here again there is, in most places, a considerable difference between theory and practice. Many juvenile proceedings are no more individualized and no more therapeutic than adult ones.

What has evidently happened is that the transformation of America from a relatively relaxed rural society into a tumultous urban one has presented the criminal justice system in the cities with a volume of cases too large to handle by traditional methods. One result of heavy case-loads is highly visible in city courts, which process many cases with excessive haste and many others with excessive slowness. In the interest both of effectiveness and of fairness to individuals, justice should be swift and certain; too often in city courts today it is, instead, hasty or faltering. Invisibly, the pressure of numbers has effected a series of adventitious changes in criminal process. Informal shortcuts have been used. The decision making process has often become routinized. Throughout the system the importance of individual judgement and discretion, as distinguished from stated rules and procedures, has increased. In effect, much decision making is being done on an administrative rather than on a judicial basis. Thus, an examination of how the criminal justice system works and a consideration of the changes needed to make it more effective and fair must focus on the extent to which invisible, administrative procedures depart from visible, traditional ones, and on the desirability of that departure.

The Police. At the very beginning of the process—or, more properly, before the process begins at all—something happens that is scarcely discussed in lawbooks and is seldom recognized by the public: law enforcement policy is made by the policeman. For policemen cannot and do not arrest all the offenders they encounter. It is doubtful that they arrest most of them. A criminal code, in practice, is not a set of specific instructions to policemen but a more or less rough map of the territory in which policemen work. How an individual policeman moves around that territory depends largely on his personal discretion.

That a policeman's duties compel him to exercise personal discretion many times every day is evident. Crime does not look the same on the street as it does in a legislative chamber. How much noise or profanity makes conduct "disorderly" within the meaning of the law? When must a quarrel be treated as a criminal assault: at the first threat or at the first shove or at the first blow, or after blood is drawn, or when a serious injury is inflicted? How suspicious must conduct be before there is is "probable cause," the constitutional basis for an arrest? Every policeman, however complete or sketchy his education, is an interpreter of the law.

Every policeman, too, is an arbiter of social values, for he meets situation after situation in which invoking criminal sanctions is a questionable line of action. It is obvious that a boy throwing rocks at a school's window is committing the statutory offense of vandalism, but it is often not at all obvious whether a policeman will better serve the interests of the community and of the boy by taking the boy home to his parents or by arresting him. Who are the boy's parents? Can they control him? Is he a frequent offender who has responded badly to leniency? Is vandalism so epidemic in the neighborhood that he should be made a cautionary example? With juveniles especially, the police exercise great discretion.

Finally, the manner in which a policeman works is influenced by practical matters: the legal strength of the available evidence, the willingness of victims to press charges and of witnesses to testify, the temper of the community, the time and information at the policeman's disposal. Much is at stake in how the policeman exercises this discretion. If he judges conduct not suspicious enough to justify intervention, the chance to prevent a robbery, rape, or murder may be lost. If he overestimates the seriousness of a situation or his actions are controlled by panic or prejudice, he may hurt or kill someone unnecessarily. His actions may even touch off a riot.

The Magistrate. In direct contrast to the policeman, the magistrate before whom a suspect is first brought usually exercises less discretion than the law allows him. He is entitled to inquire into the facts of the case, into whether there are grounds for holding the accused. He seldom does. He seldom can. The more promptly an arrested suspect is brought into magistrate's court, the less likelihood there is that much information about the arrest other than the arresting officer's statement will be available to the magistrate. Moreover many magistrates, especially in big cities, have such congested calendars that it is almost impossible for them to subject any case but an extraordinary one to prolonged scrutiny.

In practice the most important things, by far, that a magistrate does are to set the amount of a defendant's bail and in some jurisdictions to appoint counsel. Too seldom does either action get the careful attention it deserves. In many cases the magistrate accepts a waiver of counsel without insuring that the suspect knows the significance of legal representation.

Bail is a device to free an untried defendant and at the same time make sure he appears for trial. That is the sole stated legal purpose in America. The Eighth Amendment to the Constitution declares that it must not be "excessive." Appellate courts have declared that not just the seriousness of the charge against the defendant, but the suspect's personal, family, and employment situation, as they bear on the likelihood of his appearance, must be weighed before the amount of his bail is fixed. Yet more magistrates than not set bail according to standard rates: so and so many dollars for such and such an offense.

The persistence of money bail can best be explained not by its stated purpose but by the belief of police, prosecutors, and courts that the best way to keep a defendant from committing more crimes before trial is to set bail so high that he cannot obtain his release.

The Prosecutor. The key administrative officer in the processing of cases is the prosecutor. Theoretically the examination of the evidence against a defendant by a judge at a preliminary hearing, and its reexamination by a grand jury, are important parts of the process. Practically they seldom are because a prosecutor seldom has any difficulty in making a prima facie case against a defendant. In fact most defendants waive their rights to preliminary hearings and much more often than not grand juries indict precisely as prosecutors ask them to. The prosecutor wields almost undisputed sway over the pretrial progress of most cases. He decides whether to press a case or drop it. He determines the specific charge against a defendant. When the charge is reduced, as it is in as many as two-thirds of all cases in some cities, the prosecutor is usually the official who reduces it.

In the informal, noncriminal, nonadversary juvenile justice system there are no "magistrates" or "prosecutors" or "charges," or, in most instances, defense counsel. An arrested youth is brought before an intake officer who is likely to be a social worker or, in smaller communities, before a judge. On the basis of an informal inquiry into the facts and circumstances that led to the arrest, and of an interview with the youth himself, the intake officer or the judge decides whether or not a case should be the subject of formal court proceedings. If he decides it should be, he draws up a petition, describing the case. In very few places is bail a part of the juvenile system; a youth whose case is referred to court is either sent home with orders to reappear on a certain date, or remanded to custody. This decision, too, is made by the screening official. Thus, though these officials work in a quite different environment and according to quite different procedures from magistrates and prosecutors, they in fact exercise the same kind of discretionary control over what happens before the facts of a case are adjudicated.

The Plea and the Sentence. When a prosecutor reduces a charge it is ordinarily because there has been "plea bargaining" between him and a defense attorney. The issue at stake is how much the prosecutor will reduce his original charge or how lenient a sentence he will recommend, in return for a plea of guilty. There is no way of judging how many bargains reflect the prosecutor's belief that a lesser charge or sentence is justified and how many result from the fact that there may be in the system at any one time ten times as many cases as there are prosecutors or judges or courtrooms to handle them, should every one come to trial. In form, a plea bargain can be anything from a series of careful conferences to a hurried consultation in a courthouse corridor. In content it can be anything from a conscientious exploration of the facts and dispositional alternatives available and appropriate to a defendant, to a prefunctory deal. If the interests of a defendant are to be properly protected while his fate is being thus invisibly determined, he obviously needs just as good legal representation as the kind he needs at a public trial. Whether or not plea bargaining is a fair and effective method of disposing of criminal cases depends heavily on whether or not defendants are provided early with competent and conscientious counsel.

Plea bargaining is not only an invisible procedure but, in some jurisdictions, a theoretically unsanctioned one. In order to satisfy the court record, a defendant, his attorney, and the prosecutor will at the time of sentencing often ritually state to a judge that no bargain has been made. Plea bargaining may be a useful procedure, especially in congested urban jurisdictions, but neither the dignity of the law, nor the quality of justice, nor the protection of society from dangerous criminals is enhanced by its being conducted covertly.

In the juvenile system there is, of course, no plea bargaining in the sense described above. However, the entire juvenile process can involve extra-judicial negotiations about disposition. Furthermore, the entire juvenile process is by design invisible. Though intended to be helpful, the authority exercised often is coercive; juveniles, no less than adults, may need representation by counsel.

An enormously consequential kind of decision is the sentencing decision of a judge. The law recognizes the importance of fitting sentences to individual defendants by giving judges, in most instances, considerable latitude. For example the recently adopted New York Penal Code, which will go into effect in autumn of 1967, empowers a judge to impose upon a man convicted of armed robbery any sentence between a 5-year term of probation and a 25-year term in prison. Even when a judge has presided over a trial during which the facts of a case have been carefully set forth and has been given a probation report that carefully discusses a defendant's character, background, and problems, he cannot find it easy to choose a sentence. In perhaps nine-tenths of all cases there is no trial; the defendants are self-confessedly guilty.

In the lower or misdemeanor courts, the courts that process most criminal cases, probation reports are a rarity. Under such circumstances judges have little to go on and many sentences are bound to be based on conjecture or intuition. When a sentence is part of a plea bargain, which an overworked judge ratifies perfunctorily, it may not even be his conjecture or intuition on which the sentence is based, but a prosecutor's or a defense counsel's. But perhaps the greatest lack judges suffer from when they pass sentence is not time or information, but correctional alternatives. Some lower courts do not have any probation officers, and in almost every court the caseloads of probation officers are so heavy that a sentence of probation means, in fact, releasing an offender into the community with almost no supervision. Few States have a sufficient variety of correctional institutions or treatment programs to inspire judges with the confidence that sentences will lead to rehabilitation.

• • •

The Foundations of a Crime Control Program

In the ensuing chapters of this report, the Commission's specific recommendations for improvements in the criminal justice system are set forth in detail. Here a brief identification of the general needs of the system is sufficient.

Resources. The many specific needs of the criminal justice system—for manpower, for equipment, for facilities, for programs, for research, for money—are interlocking. Each one must be filled with the others in mind. Equipment cannot be operated, facilities manned, programs initiated or research conducted without personnel of many different kinds. It would be useless to seek to recruit more and better personnel if there were not more and better jobs for them to do. Programs cannot be conducted without equipment and facilities, and cannot be conducted effectively without research. Money is needed for everything. This discussion of the system's needs assumes that every need is dependent on the others.

The problem of personnel is at the root of most of the criminal justice system's problems. The system cannot operate fairly unless its personnel are fair. The system cannot operate swiftly and certainly unless its personnel are efficient and well-informed. The system cannot make wise decisions unless its personnel are thoughtful. In many places—many police departments, congested urban lower courts, the understaffed county jails, the entire prison, probation and parole apparatus—more manpower is needed. Probably the greatest manpower need of all, in view of the increasing—and overdue—involvement of defense counsel in all kinds of cases, is for lawyers who can handle criminal cases. Everywhere more skilled, better trained, more imaginative manpower is needed. Some positions are hard to fill. Often the pay is bad and the working conditions are difficult. In addition, an odd and injurious notion is widespread that there is something disreputable about being a policeman or a criminal lawyer or a prison guard. The fact is that there are few fields in which people have more opportunities to do important and responsible work than the criminal justice system. Recruiting such people in large numbers, training them fully and giving them the pay, the opportunities for advancement and the responsibility they deserve is a matter of great urgency.

Too much of the system is physically inadequate, antiquated or dilapidated. This condition goes beyond the obvious obsolescence of many correctional institutions and the squalor and congestion of many urban lower courts, which make it difficult to treat defendants or convicts humanely. The system's personnel often must work with poor facilities: recordkeeping systems that are clumsy and inefficient, communications equipment that makes speedy action difficult, an absence of all kinds of scientific and technological aids. Furthermore, in few States is there the variety of correctional facilities that could make a variety of correctional programs possible. Most institutions are almost entirely custodial in a physical sense–with high walls, locked gates, and barred windows. New kinds of institutions, less forbidding in character and situated within reach of the community, are an immediate and pressing need.

Probably the single greatest technical limitation on the system's ability to make its decisions wisely and fairly is that the people in the system often are required to decide issues without enough information. A policeman who has just set out in pursuit of a speeding and suspicious looking car should be able to get immediate information as to whether or not the car is wanted; a judge about to sentence a criminal should know everything about him that the police know; and the correctional authorities to whom that criminal is delivered should know everything about him that the judge knows. When they make dispositional decisions, judges and corrections officials should be able to draw on the experience of the system in dealing with different offenders in different ways. Existing procedures must be made more efficient; and new procedures must be devised, so that information can flow more fully and swiftly among the system's many parts.

Finally, the nature of crime and the means of controlling it are subjects about which a surprisingly small amount of research has been done. What "deterrence" really means and involves, how different kinds of criminals are likely to respond to different kinds of treatment, what the objective effects of making various kinds of marginal behavior criminal have been, how much of the juvenile justice system's informality can be preserved without sacrificing fairness–and a multitude of other abstruse questions of this kind–are almost totally unanswerable today. There is almost as great a lack of operational knowledge. It is impossible to state accurately, for example, what proportions of police time are spent on the different sorts of police work, or how large a proportion of the drunks that come before lower courts are chronic offenders, or what personal characteristics best qualify a man to be an effective correctional official.

This lack of firm data of almost every kind has been the greatest obstacle to the Commission's work, in many instances requiring it to base its recommendations on fragmentary information, combined with the experienced judgment of those who have worked in this field. The process of change cannot await all the answers the

Commission would like to have had. The criminal justice system is faced with too urgent a need for action to stand back for a generation and engage in research. At the same time self-education is one of the system's crucial responsibilities. Only by combining research with action can future programs be founded on knowledge rather than on informed or perceptive guesswork. Moreover, once knowledge is acquired, it is wasted if it is not shared. An east coast city must be able to draw on a west coast city's experience, a judge on a policeman's. Scattered about the country today are many individuals and groups with special knowledge about one aspect or another of law enforcement and the administration of justice. Often no one else in the system knows that these individuals and groups know anything. Sometimes these individuals and groups are themselves not aware, through lack of contact with the rest of the system, that they know something no one else knows. The system must devote itself to acquiring and diffusing knowledge, with special emphasis on exploring ways in which the criminal justice system and the universities can work together.

...

A Willingness to Change. The inertia of the criminal justice system is great. More than 30 years ago the Wickersham Commission described the scandalous way in which justice was being administered in many of the country's "lower" courts, and urged that they be abolished; few of them have been abolished and many of the remaining ones are still a scandal. For centuries the imposition of money bail has discriminated against poor defendants, but only in the last few years has the movement to eliminate money bail for most defendants gained any momentum, and even so money bail is still used for almost everyone in the overwhelming majority of courts. State prisons that were built before 1850 and became obsolete before 1900 are still in operation. Police departments continue to insist that all policemen start their careers at the bottom and rise through the ranks slowly, despite the clearly damaging effect this has on the recruitment and effective use of able personnel. A third of the arrests and convictions in America every year are for drunkenness, though for many years almost everyone in the criminal justice system and out of it has recognized that the criminal process is an irrational means of dealing with drunks. The list of examples could extend for pages.

Many of the criminal justice system's difficulties stem from its reluctance to change old ways or, to put the same proposition in reverse, its reluctance to try new ones. The increasing volume of crime in America establishes conclusively that many of the old ways are not good enough. Innovation and experimentation in all parts of the criminal justice system are clearly imperative. They are imperative with respect both to entire agencies and to specific procedures. Court systems need reorganization and case-docketing methods need improvement; police-community relations programs are needed and so are ways of relieving detectives from the duty of typing their own reports; community-based correctional programs must be organized and the pay of prison guards must be raised. Recruitment and training, organization and management, research and development all require reexamination and reform.

The Commission believes that the first step toward improvement is for officials in all parts of the system to face their problems. The lower courts never will be reformed if their officials do not grapple with the hard fact that the quality of justice that is dispensed in them is disgracefully low. Any program to rehabilitate prisoners must begin with the acknowledgement of the fact that most prisons today do not even try to do this job. Until the police recognize that they exercise great discretion about whom they arrest and how they investigate, no effort to ensure that that discretion is exercised wisely can be made. It is futile to consider ways of making plea negotiation an open, regular procedure as long as prosecutors and defense attorneys state ritually to judges that pleas are not negotiated.

39. The Juvenile Court in Its Relationship to Adult Criminality: A Replicated Study

Mildred R. Chaitin and H. Warren Dunham

This research is the exact replication of a study which Mary E. Knauer carried out in 1952 and which was subsequently reported in the pages of this journal.[1] In that study Knauer worked out the percentage of juvenile delinquents who had been processed through the Wayne County Juvenile Court and who subsequently became registered with the police for adult offenses, for a series of years between 1920 and 1940. By this procedure Knauer provided empirical data to show that the rates of juvenile court offenders who entered adult criminality have remained relatively constant for a period of two decades. She predicted that under the conditions of (1) the time required to mold a skillful criminal, (2) a relatively constant crime rate, and (3) an absence of successful therapy in the juvenile court this constancy of rate for juvenile offenders who entered adult crime would continue on into future years. It has been the intent of the present research to provide data that would serve as a test of this prediction.

Reprinted from *Social Forces,* 45:1 (September 1966), 114–119, by permission of The University of North Carolina Press.

[1] Mary E. Knauer, "A Study of Alleged Juvenile Delinquents as Recruits for Adult Criminality," master's thesis, Wayne State University, 1952. Published in *Social Forces,* H. Warren Dunham and Mary E. Knauer, "The Juvenile Court in Its Relationship to Adult Criminality," 32 (March 1954), pp. 290–296.

Design of the Experiment

As we have indicated the design of the current study was an exact replication of Knauer's procedure in 1952. However, we will repeat it briefly here so that the reader will understand clearly what is to follow.

I. *Operational Definitions Utilized in the Study*

1. Juvenile delinquents are those persons who have a court record at the Juvenile Court.
2. Adult offenders are those persons over 17 years of age who are registered with police on arrest tickets.

II. *Criteria for Selection of Juvenile Delinquents*

1. Only male delinquents.
2. Those between the ages of ten and 17.
3. First offenders in the years in which the samples were drawn.

III. *Selection of Samples*

1. One hundred offenders were drawn from each of six sample years, 1941, 1944, 1946, 1948, 1950, and 1952,[2] utilizing Tippett's random numbers.
2. Exposure period of adult crime—An exposure period of five years was allotted to each delinquent in our sample in order to assure an equality of the rates between the years. Since a juvenile delinquent is released from the jurisdiction of the juvenile court on his seventeenth birthday each of the sample cases would have completed his twenty-first birthday by the time the additional five year exposure time had terminated. Since the study was conducted in 1964, 1952 had to be the last sample year because a boy of ten years of age in the 1952 sample would not have completed his twenty-first year until 1962.

IV. *Data Abstracted from Juvenile Court Records*

1. First offense and date.
2. All subsequent offenses and dates.
3. Age and birth date.
4. Identifying information such as name, color, nativity, names of parents, nativity of parents, and all past addresses.

V. *Data Abstracted from Bureau of Records, Detroit Police Department*

All arrests, charges, and dates of commission of any offense recorded within five years of the time the person left the jurisdiction of the juvenile court.[3]

[2] L. H. C. Tippett, *Tracts for Computers No. XV: Random Sampling Numbers* (London: Cambridge University Press, 1927).

[3] In the tabulation of our data we have included as adult offenders only those juvenile delinquents whose identification could be made beyond any reasonable doubt. Therefore, the percentage of registration with the police may be recorded as lower than it actually is in each sample. However, we can state with assurance that although the percentages from each sample may be higher than those which we shall indicate, they are certainly not lower. In addition, it should be noted that we have excluded from our count of adult offenses traffic warrants, disorderly conduct due to drunkenness, and detention by the police under the golden rule drunk ordinance. This ordinance makes it possible for the police to detain an intoxicated person who, in the judgment of the police, is incapable of assuming responsibility for his own safety.

Juvenile Delinquents as Adult Offenders

As we have already indicated, Knauer, in her study, demonstrated a constancy in the percentage of juvenile delinquents who subsequently became registered with the police as adult offenders in five selected years between 1920 and 1940. Knauer established this constancy by pointing to the fact that the difference between the lowest percentage in 1925 and the highest percentage in 1940 which was a difference of 13 percent gave a critical ratio of 2. On the basis of this critical ratio she accepted the null hypothesis and argued that the true percentage in the universe of years are more likely to be approximately equal than to indicate an upward trend. On the basis of this evidence Knauer predicted that if the same conditions as indicated above would continue to operate in the future the rates, representing the percentage of those juveniles registered with the police, would continue to be constant for subsequent years. Chaitin, then, has proceeded to test this prediction with the same research design for the years between 1941 and 1952. If her findings permit her to accept the null hypothesis that no significant differences exist between the percentage of juvenile delinquents registered with the police in the sample years, then she would be in a position to conclude that these rates have indeed remained relatively constant, and thus confirm Knauer's findings.

Table 1 shows the percentage of juvenile delinquents from each sample year who were registered with the police as adult offenders within the five years of the time they were released from the jurisdiction of the juvenile court, and the confidence limits for these percentages. For purposes of comparison, the data from Knauer's study are also shown. From this comparison of these two studies it does indeed seem likely that there has been an upward trend among juveniles who have been recruited into adult criminality, although the total number of cases comprising the universe of cases handled by the court has remained relatively constant from 1920 to 1952. In fact, it is perhaps interesting to note that on the average the court processed just 182 fewer cases in the 1941–1952 period as contrasted to the 1920–1940 period. Further, Knauer reports as an overall percentage 30.6 juvenile offenders were registered with the police while Chaitin reports an overall percentage of 40.2. Are we dealing here with significant differences? And does this actually indicate an upward trend? We proceeded to answer this question by comparing the lowest percentage (37 percent in 1952) with the highest percentage (47.0 percent in 1948). The difference between these two extreme percentages was ten percent and this yielded a critical ratio of only 1.43. Since this greatest observed difference between the percentages of any two sample years is not statistically significant further comparisons are not necessary. On the basis of this analysis, therefore, we conclude that the percentage of juvenile delinquents who were registered with the police remained relatively constant for the period 1941 to 1952 and that these findings confirm those of the Knauer study.

However, we carried our analysis one step further by examining the combined data of both the original and the repeat studies. Thus, the comparisons of the 11 sample years, taken two at a time, entailed computations for 55 combinations and provided us with 55 critical ratios with their corresponding P values. From these results we observed that only 12 of the 55 combinations yielded critical ratios of 2 or more and only two of these 12 provided critical ratios which exceeded 3. We also noted that 11 of these critical ratios were influenced by the low percentage years of 1925 (24.0%) and 1930 (25.0%). While one was affected by the high percentage year of 1948 (47.0%), the remainder of our comparisons between sample years showed no significant differences in percentage of juvenile delinquents who were registered with the police as adult offenders. The low percentages found for 1925 and 1930 no doubt reflect fluctuations that are present in any sampling procedure. We thereby concluded that the percentage of juvenile delinquents who were registered with the police for adult offenses remained relatively constant for the period 1920 to 1952.

TABLE 1. Percentage of Juvenile Delinquents Registered with Police as Adult Offenders by Sample Year

Sample Year	Number in Universe	Number in Sample	Percent Registered with Police	Confidence Limits
Knauer Study				
1920	1,029	100	33	±9.24
1925	1,771	100	24	±8.40
1930	1,785	100	25	±8.50
1935	1,264	100	34	±9.29
1940	1,127	100	37	±9.47
Total	6,976	500	30.6	±4.05
Chaitin Study				
1941	1,122	100	39	±9.56
1944	1,323	100	39	±9.56
1946	1,255	100	38	±9.51
1948	965	100	47	±9.78
1950	1,216	100	41	±9.64
1952	1,396	100	37	±9.46
Total	7,277	600	40.2	±3.92

However, the examination of the observable trend in the percentages over the years could point to a different conclusion. We note that 1940, the last year of Knauer's study, contained the highest percentage of delinquents and this upward trend tended to continue in the Chaitin study, but with a drop to 37 percent in 1952. If such an upward trend could be substantiated it might seem to indicate that the social controls to prevent illegal behavior were considerably weaker during the latter period as compared with the former and that the social situation of the latter period provided a more certain access to the criminal culture than did that of the earlier period.

The position that an upward trend in percentages has taken place is strengthened when we compare both studies in terms of total sample percentages of juvenile delinquents who were registered with the police as adult offenders. We have noted that 30.6 percent of Knauer's total sample of 500 were registered for adult offenses, whereas 40.2 percent of the 600 sample delinquents in the present study became adult offenders. From our computations, we find that this difference of 9.6 percent gives a critical ratio of 3.31 and has a P value of .00097. Since a difference as great as this is likely to occur by chance only 97 times in 100,000, we conclude that it is a significant one not attributed to chance. Therefore, our data indicate an increase in percentages, for the period 1941 to 1952 over those from 1920 to 1940, of juvenile delinquents who were subsequently registered with police on arrest tickets.

In interpreting our findings, we would be inclined to argue that there has occurred a trend toward increasing percentages of juvenile delinquents who subsequently enter adult crime. Albeit such a trend is not revealed by year to year comparisons, it is possible that the cumulative effect of higher incidences, for the six sample years from 1941 to 1952, represents ascending rates. We tend to accept this interpretation in view of the fact that the crime rates, for the country as a whole, have been increasing over the last decade.[4] Since Knauer specified a relatively constant crime rate as one condition under which relatively constant percentages of juvenile delinquents would be recruited into adult crime, it is consistent with our theoretical framework that, under the changed condition of an increasing crime rate, increasing percentages of juvenile delinquents will enter adult criminality.

From the analysis of our data, we conclude that the rates of juvenile delinquents who were registered with the police as adult offenders remained constant for the years 1941 to 1952. On the other hand, when we consider these percentages over

[4] *Uniform Crime Reports for the United States and Its Possessions* (Washington, D.C.: United States Government Printing Office, 1950–1963). Using 1950 as a base, the relationship between crime and population increases has been as follows:

Years	*% Major Crime Increase*	*% Population Increase*	
1950–1953	20	5%	(Vol. 24, January 1954, p. 67)
1950–1954	26.7	7	(Vol. 25, January 1955, p. 67)
1950–1955	26	9	(Vol. 26, January 1956, p. 67)
1950–1956	43	11	(Vol. 27, Annual Bulletin, 1956)
1950–1957	56.2	13	(Vol. 28, Annual Bulletin, 1957)

In 1958 a New Crime Index was adopted, and as a result subsequent totals were not comparable to those of prior years.

1958–1963 Crime Increase, 40%, Population Increase, 8%, *Uniform Crime Report,* 1963, p. 1.

a period exceeding one-third of a century, there is evidence that an upward trend occurred during the time period which was covered by our present inquiry.

Juvenile Recidivists as Adult Offenders

Knauer, in her study, adhering to the differential association theory of crime,[5] and further attempting an evaluation of the juvenile court's achievement in dealing with delinquent behavior investigated the relationship of juvenile recidivism to adult behavior.

The differential association theory, as is well known, posits that adult criminal behavior flows from attitudes and behavior patterns acquired from other law violators during the preadolescent and/or adolescent years and is reinforced by repeated delinquent acts that are undertaken in the course of this learning period. On the basis of this theory, it is reasonable to expect that more juvenile recidivists would be registered with the police as adults than would juvenile single offenders. Knauer, by her analysis, substantiated this prediction. We thought that a similar examination of the data in the repeat study would provide further support for the theoretical position which stresses the relationship of cumulative delinquent experiences at the juvenile level to adult criminality.

Table 2 shows the percentage of juvenile single offenders and juvenile recidivists who were registered with the police as adult offenders for our total sample of 600 delinquents. It can be noted that 31.9 percent of all single offenders were subsequently registered with the police as adults, whereas 54.3 percent of all recidivists became adult offenders. Our computations show that this difference in percentages yields a critical ratio of 5.4, which indicates that the difference we found between single offender and recidivist police registration is a significant one.

TABLE 2. Juvenile Single Offenders and Juvenile Recidivists Registered with the Police as Adult Offenders

	Juvenile Single Offenders		*Juvenile Recidivists*		
	Number	*Percentage*	*Number*	*Percentage*	*Total*
Registered with Police	121	31.9	120	54.3	241
Not Registered with Police	258	68.1	101	45.7	359
Total	379	100.0	221	100.0	600

Again, our results confirm Knauer's finding and support the view that repeated delinquency during the adolescent years provides an adequate training ground for entrance into adult criminality. Perhaps, it is interesting to note that our percentage of juvenile recidivists is somewhat in excess of Knauer's (54.3% to 46.0%).

[5] Edwin H. Sutherland, *Criminology* (3d ed.; Chicago: J. B. Lippincott Co., 1939), chap. 1.

However, the differences in both sets of data between the percentage of recidivists and single offenders police registrants are identical.

Interpretation of Results

It should be recalled that a study prior to Knauer's established the fact that it cost five and one-half times more money to process a child through the juvenile court in 1945 than it did in 1920.[6] The increased costs were practically all accounted for by the increase in professional staff. Thus, the Knauer study was undertaken to provide some kind of measure for determining if the increased costs of the court meant that it was more effective in arresting the delinquent tendencies of juveniles.

In addition, the theoretical orientation of the juvenile court from the beginning has focused upon the idea of helping the child. That is, since its inception, and written into all juvenile court laws, was the conception that the child, because he is a minor, cannot commit a crime. It followed that because he could not be lawfully charged with a criminal offense that his basic problem was one of adjustment and the court took upon itself to determine for any child brought before it what the maladjustment was and how this maladjustment might be remedied. In the course of this attitude, the court has made wide and extensive use of social workers, psychologists, and in recent decades, psychiatrists, all working together to try to understand the child's maladjustment, and to lay plans for its treatment. Thus, over the years, various psychological theories have been utilized in order to understand and correct the maladjustment of delinquent youth. However, as the Knauer study shows, and now the Chaitin study has confirmed, there seems to be little evidence that the court through its various professionals, is any more successful in arresting delinquency than it was at its inception.

While we have attempted to sharpen up this *impasse* that the court has reached we are well aware that this does not tell the entire story. For the juvenile court, regardless of its lofty aim and dedicated concern for the welfare of the child, has another very important function to perform within the community. Here, we are referring to its function as an agency for social control. For the court, along with numerous other institutions in the community, has not only its manifest but also its latent functions. And one of its latent functions is, of course, to represent that arm of the social structure which attempts to regulate and control the activities of certain youth who for various reasons find it difficult to be fitted into the more conventional styles of life in the society. Thus, one could make a case for the position that the increasing cost of the juvenile court has been responsible for moving in the direction of a greater humanitarianism. However, this humanitarianism, when linked to the theory under which juvenile courts operate, has tended to soften and to confuse the social control function of the court.[7]

[6] Marilyn A. Blake, "A Study of the Relationship Between Costs and Complaints of the Wayne County Juvenile Court, 1920–1945," master's thesis, Wayne State University, 1948.

[7] H. Warren Dunham, "The Juvenile Court: Contradictory Orientations in Processing Offenders," *Law and Contemporary Problems*, 3 (Summer 1958), pp. 508–527.

In recent years, the court has experienced a number of critical attacks. These attacks have emphasized that the legal rights of the child have been abrogated by the court, that there is no determination of guilt or innocence with respect to a specific act, and that the principle of individualized justice to which the court adheres makes unclear the reasons for a given disposition. One recent critic has succinctly described the consequences of utilizing individualized justice in the handling of juvenile delinquents in place of concentrating entirely upon the offense that has been committed:

> Spokesmen for individualized justice do not suggest the offense is irrelevant; rather that it is one of many considerations that are to be used in arriving at a sound disposition. Offense, like many other forms of behavior, is to be taken as an indication or symptom of the juvenile's personal and social disorder. The principle of individualized justice suggests that disposition is to be guided by a full understanding of the clients personal and social character and by his individual "needs"...(It) results in a frame of relevance that is so large, so all-inclusive, that any relation between the criteria of judgment and the disposition remains obscured....Its consequence has been that hardly anyone, and least of all the recipients of judgment, ...is at all sure what combination of the widely inclusive relevant criteria yield what sorts of specific disposition.[8]

On our part we take the position that the Knauer findings and the confirmation provided by the Chaitin study, provide some empirical evidence for critically examining the principle of individualized justice as practiced by the juvenile court. The evidence clearly indicates that in spite of the addition of numerous highly paid and qualified professionals, the court has no better results in arresting juvenile delinquency today than it did 30 years ago. In fact, there is some evidence to indicate that it has lost ground, which is not so much a criticism of the court as it is possibly a general reflection of the changes and upheavals that have taken place in American society, particularly since the end of World War II. It is perhaps, not so much a matter that individualized treatment never works but rather a reflection of the inadequacies of our knowledge concerning those cases where it might be effective and those cases where it cannot be effective. If this knowledge does not exist one can hardly expect that the juvenile court can make this distinction because the court, as an institutional structure within the larger society, merely reflects and absorbs the prevailing theories and conflicting ideas that are present in the larger community. Then, too, it can be questioned, particularly on the basis of the evidence presented here, as to whether the court, in its long historical development, has not made a mistake with respect to its true function. Here, we are suggesting that whatever the merits or demerits may be of individualized treatment of maladjusted youth, such practices should not be tied to the court but should be lodged in other agencies to which the court might refer cases. The court, then, not having the obligation to treat the child as well as control him, could return to its more important function, namely, social control and this would then become its true manifest and not its latent function.

[8] David Matza, *Delinquency and Drift* (New York: John Wiley & Sons, 1964), pp. 114-115.

40. The Juvenile Court—Quest and Realities

Edwin M. Lemert

Roscoe Pound called the juvenile court one of the great social inventions of the 19th century. But the enthusiasms heralding its birth and early history have dampened considerably with the slow stain of passing time. Its later years have been those of unmet promise and darkened with growing controversy. Evidence that it has prevented crime or lessened the recidivism of youthful offenders is missing, and dour sociological critics urge that it contributes to juvenile crime or inaugurates delinquent careers by imposition of the stigma of wardship, unwise detention, and incarceration of children in institutions which don't reform and often corrupt. The occasional early voice of the dissenting judge and of the frustrated lawyer has grown to a heavy swell of modern contention that the juvenile court under the noble guise of humanitarian concern and scientific treatment of the problems of children too often denies them the elements of justice and fair play.

Even more impressive than the mounting volume of polemic literature and responsible criticism arraigning the court are the concrete actions taken by a number of leading States, such as New York and California, Minnesota, and indeed, the State of its origin, Illinois, which in years immediately past have substantially or drastically revised their laws dealing with the form and operation of the juvenile court. Other States have seen the appointment of committees of inquiry and new legislation introduced to amend significant aspects of their juvenile or family courts. Events as well as the literature of protest compel thoughtful persons to a searching reconsideration of the makeup and purposes of the juvenile court in a society dominated by large-scale social organization, aggressive public welfare ideologies, and mass-produced justice.

The Philosophy and Function of the Juvenile Court

Much has been said of the philosophy of the juvenile court and little that is definitive can be added to it, other than to note that the very preoccupation with its philosophy sets it apart from other courts. In general, American courts created for children were given broad grants of power by legislatures to protect and help

Reprinted from *Task Force Report: Juvenile Delinquency and Youth Crime,* a Report by The President's Commission on Law Enforcement and Administration of Justice (Washington: Government Printing Office, 1967), Appendix D, pp. 91–97.

children, depart from strict rules of legal procedure, and utilize kinds of evidence ordinarily excluded from criminal and civil adjudication. There have been attempts by some writers to discover historical continuity between the juvenile court and courts of equity or chancery following guardianship proceedings. But these have been held to be dubious exercises at best, and in the words of a wry English judge, little more than spurious justifications for the sometimes "highhanded methods of American judges." As he and others have noted, equity procedure clearly requires evidentiary findings within specifiable limits conspicuously lacking in our early juvenile court statutes.

It is less profitable to speculate on the philosophy of the juvenile court than to examine its historical development and the variety of its adaptations to regional and local necessities. Such an examination will benefit by heuristically distinguishing the official goals of the court from its functions, particularly those which sociologists call unintended or unanticipated consequence of purposeful action. In so doing it becomes apparent that the functions of the juvenile court in reality are several, indicated by its peculiar sociolegal characteristics. Thus while it is well known to sociologists of law that regular courts may serve a number of extralegal or nonlegal ends, such as, for example, an action for damages brought solely to embarass a business competitor, the anomalous design of the juvenile court has made its extraneous, nonlegal functions paramount.

In historical retrospect the juvenile court has the look of an agency of social control directed to raising and maintaining standards of child care protection and family morals, a purpose currently reinforced by its close association with social welfare organizations. At the same time the juvenile court by virtue of its inescapable identity as a court of law is an agency of law enforcement seeking to reduce and prevent crime, but also protecting legal rights. Finally, it serves purposes derived from its essentially local nature as an arena of conflict resolution, in which conflicts within and between families, between individuals, and between organizations (not excluding those within the court itself) are aired, dramatized, and sometimes turned into cold war compromises.

Despite their insular character and the cloak of independence given juvenile courts by their connection with the regular courts, they tend to reflect patterns of values and power alignments within the community or areas they service. When this is joined with the fact that there are 50 federated States, these States having from 5 to 58 more or less autonomous juvenile courts each, it is painfully clear that efforts to outline the distinctive philosophy and function of the juvenile court are feckless. It is, however, possible to state that juvenile courts in action generally reveal variations in the order in which values falling within the three areas of function of the court are satisfied. This permits questions to be raised as to whether and how the juvenile court should be restructured so that certain value orders do not occur, or further, so that some of the values currently satisfied will be excluded from its decisions and patterns of action.

There are some social science propositions which can serve well enough as guides for those seeking to install new forms and methods in the juvenile court. A salient one is that the family, even though badly attenuated or disturbed by conflict, morally questionable, or broken by divorce or death, continues to be the institution of choice for the socialization of children. Neither the Spartan gymnasuim, nor the Russian creches, nor the Israeli Kibbutz nurseries, nor scientifically run childrens' homes have been found to successfully duplicate the sociopsychological mystique which nurtures children into stable adults. Explicit recognition of this might very well preface the juvenile court codes and statutes of the land. At the same time it would be well to delete entirely from such laws pious injunctions that "care, custody and discipline of children under the control of the juvenile court shall approximate that which they would receive from their parents," which taken literally becomes meaningless either as ideal or reality. Neither the modern state nor an harassed juvenile court judge is a father; a halfway house is not a home; a reformatory cell is not a teenager's bedroom; a juvenile hall counselor is not a dutch uncle; and a cottage matron is not a mother. This does not mean that the people referred to should not be or are not kindly and dedicated, but rather that they are first and foremost members of organizations, bound by institution controls and subject to its exigencies; they are enforcers of superimposed rules. Where conflicts arise between the interests of a youth and those of the organization to which these functionaries are bureaucratically responsible there is no pattern of action which can predict that they will observe an order of value satisfaction favorable to the youth's interest.

Stigma

Social scientists familiar with the juvenile court and its problems in the main agree that one of the great unwanted consequences of wardship, placement, or commitment to a correctional institution is the imposition of stigma. Such stigma represented in modern society by a "record," gets translated into effective handicaps by heightened police surveillance, neighborhood isolation, lowered receptivity and tolerance by school officials, and rejections of youth by prospective employers. Large numbers of youth appearing in juvenile court have lower class status or that of disadvantaged minorities, whose limited commitments to education already puts them in difficulties in a society where education increasingly provides access to economic opportunity. Given this, the net effect of juvenile court wardship too often is to add to their handicaps or to multiply problems confronting them and their families.

Lest these seem like animadiversions or imprecise charges, consider the hard facts that social welfare agencies can be identified which as a matter of policy, without delving into the facts of the case, arbitrarily refuse to accept as clients youth who have been wards of the juvenile court. The reality of stigma due to wardship is also borne home by the firmed policy of the Armed Forces, which may make it the grounds for rejection, or most certainly the bar to officer candidacy. The paradoxical expression of stigma often colors the statements of probation and correctional officers, even judges, who at certain stages of a youth's progress through juvenile court and beyond, openly label him as a type destined for failure.

Proposals, laws, and administrative action to preserve the anonymity of juvenile court proceedings through closed hearings, sealing case records, and expunging records are probably worthy moves, but it is vain to expect them to eliminate the stigma of wardship and contacts with the juvenile court. In smaller communities, as one judge observed. "Everyone knows about juvenile court cases anyway." In larger communities strongly organized police departments can be expected to resist rigorous controls over delinquency records detrimental to their efficiency, and will search for ways to circumvent them. Employers denied information from juvenile courts often get the desired facts from the police.

Expunging records is not the simple operation it may seem. In California it requires initiative from the party concerned and usually the assistance of an attorney; the procedure necessitates a hearing, and it may be complicated or impossible if a person has been a juvenile ward in more than one county. Private and public organizations can and do protect themselves by including questions about a juvenile record on application forms for employment or for occupational licenses, indicating that perjured replies will be grounds for rejection. The applicant has the unpleasant "damned if you do, damned if you don't" choice of lying or revealing damaging facts about himself. Finally, it is doubtful whether total anonymity of juvenile court hearings and records is in the public interest.

While the successful management of stigma by individuals is not impossible, the necessary insights and social skills are not given to many people, least of all immature youth or those struggling with other status handicaps. A number of social psychologists, including the author, believe that social rejections provoked by such stigma may reinforce a self-image held by the individual that he is no good or that he can't make it on the outside. They may feed a brooding sense of injustice which finds expression in further delinquency, or they may support, strengthen, and perpetuate ideological aspects of delinquent subcultures. In this sense the juvenile court may become a connecting or intervening link of a vicious circle in which delinquency causes delinquency.

Preventing Delinquency

The indiscriminate way in which stigma embraces juvenile court wards raises the most serious questions about an important part of the rationale for state intervention into the lives of youth and parents through the juvenile court. Reference here is to the idea that delinquency can be or will be thereby prevented. This belief rests upon uncritical conceptions that there are substantive behaviors, isometric in nature, which precede delinquency, much like prodromal signs of the onset of disease. The viability of these ideas probably can be traced to their lineal ties with older, repressive Puritan philosophy; they received new life from early 20th century propaganda of the mental hygiene movement, which helped to birth child guidance clinics, school social work, and establish juvenile courts in many areas. Quaint examples of these views were the 19th century convictions that smoking or drinking by youth, shining shoes, selling newspapers, or frequenting poolrooms insidiously set them on a downward path toward a life of crime. Their contemporary survivals can be seen in unproved concepts like predelinquent personality, or delinquency prone, and in laws of a number of States which make truancy, running away from home, or refusal to obey parents or school officials jurisdictional bases for juvenile court control.

Social science research and current theory in social psychology refute the idea that there are fixed, inevitable sequences in delinquent or criminal careers. As yet no behavior patterns or personality tendencies have been isolated and shown to be the antecedents of delinquency, and it is unlikely that they will be. Furthermore, youthful actions conventionally regarded as delinquent tendencies in a number of jurisdictions, such as truancy, curfew violations, incorrigibility, and running away from home on close examination are found to correspond to no behavior entities, but rather to arbitrary definitions by school authorities, parents, and police. Truancy is defined variously, depending on the area, by anywhere from 3 to 10 days of unexplained absences. An older New York investigation into a large number of cases of truancy disclosed little or no similarity in the contingencies associated with school absences. Indeed, to a degree they were simply a measure of the willingness or availability of parents to write excuses for their children. Runaways found in juvenile court cases cover departures from home ranging from a few hours to 2 months, and incorrigibility may mean anything from refusing a mother's order not to see a boy friend to attacking a parent with a knife. While curfews are useful administrative devices for policing communities, there are attorneys who argue that the associated ordinances are questionable law because they leave violations incapable of definition.

The allegation of incorrigibility often is difficult to distinguish from that of parental neglect or unfitness, and both kinds of allegations at times arise in a welter of accusations and counteraccusations which are quieted by arbitrary fixing of the blame by a probation officer assigned to investigate the case.

The brave idea that the juvenile court can prevent delinquency is further deflated or even reduced to absurdity by sociological studies of unreported or hidden delinquency. These have brought to light that the majority of high school and college students at some time or another engage in delinquencies, not excluding serious law violations. The main difference which emerged from comparisons of delinquencies by college students and those by youths who had been made wards of juvenile courts was the greater recidivism of the latter group. While these data admit of several interpretations, on their face they demand explanation as to why the large population of youth committing delinquent acts and made court wards commit more rather than fewer delinquencies. The conclusion that the court processing rather than the behaviors in some way helps to fix and perpetuate delinquency in many cases is hard to escape.

There are other data which suggest that formal efforts by the juvenile court to shape the course of childhood and adolescent development away from hypothetically dire directions in the large may be gratuitous or self-defeating. The reference is to facts or common knowledge that most youth pass through epochs in their lives when they engage in activities definable in other than their contexts as delinquency. Children normally play hookey, help themselves to lumber from houses under construction, snitch lipstick or other items from 10-cent stores, swipe some beer, get a little drunk, borrow a car, hell around, learn about sex from an available female or prostitute, or give the old man a taste of his own medicine. Transitional deviance not only is ubiquitous in our society but universal to all societies, especially among boys turning into men—Margaret Mead's droll observations on adolescence in the south seas to the contrary notwithstanding.

Most youth phase out of their predelinquency, so-called, and their law flaunting; they put away childish things, ordinarily as they become established in society by a job, marriage, further education, or the slow growth of wisdom. Maturation out of the deviance of adolescence is facilitated by a process of normalization in which troublesome behavior, even petty crimes, are dealt with by parents, neighbors, and law people as manifestations of the inevitable diversity, perversity, and shortcomings of human beings—in other words, as problems of everyday living calling for tolerable solutions short of perfection. This means the avoidance whenever possible of specialized or categorical definitions which invidiously differentiate, degrade, or stigmatize persons involved in the problems. The costs of "muddling through" with children who become problems have multiplied with the rising plateau of mass conformities needed for a high-energy society but they must be absorbed in large part where the alternatives are even more costly.

The 3-Minute Children's Hour

The ideology of delinquency prevention is much more urban than rural. Handling problems of youthful disorders and petty crime in rural areas and small towns, characteristically by sheriffs' deputies, town police, the district attorney, and probation officer in the past and even yet today in many places has been largely informal. Sharp distinctions are drawn between less consequential moral and legal infractions—"mickey mouse stuff"—and serious delinquencies, with no implications that one conduces to the other. This is reflected in the reluctance of elective officials and those beholden to them to make records of their action, but at the same time for action in serious misdemeanors and crimes by youth to be swift and punitive. The juvenile court usually reserves formal action for real problems of families and the community; the functional context of youthful misconduct ordinarily can be realistically gauged and its consequences dealt with in a number of different situations.

A major difficulty in the large bureaucratic urban juvenile court is that the functional context of child problems directed to it easily gets lost; it has to be reconstructed by bits and pieces of information obtained through investigations and inquiries conducted under highly artificial circumstances, and communicated in written reports which easily become stereotyped as they pass from person to person. There is little or no direct community feedback of criticism and reaction which might put individual cases into a commonsense context which would encourage normalization. This plus the rapidity with which cases are heard in large courts (3 minutes per case in Los Angeles circa 1959) explains why the distinction between mild and serious child problems breaks down or disappears. A notorious illustration of the tendency came to light in Orange County, Calif., in 1957 when a private attorney put his own investigator to work on a case of an 8- and 9-year-old boy and girl accused of sex crime against a 7-year-old girl. It was discovered that the probation officer presenting the case in court had not even investigated, and the private investigator's report swiftly pared down the charge to an imputed incident witnessed by no one and reported 2 days after it supposedly occurred.

While it would push facts too far to insist that the ideology of preventing delinquency is used deliberately by juvenile courtworkers and judges to justify slipshod operations which bring cases of benign youthful misbehavior before them under the duress of formal allegations, nevertheless it has allowed them to change the basis of jurisdiction from one problem to another. The practice is baldly indicated in the statement of a California judge arguing for retention under juvenile court jurisdiction of simple traffic violations by juveniles:

> Moreover it seems to have been demonstrated that the broad powers of the juvenile court can be helpfully invoked on behalf of children whose maladjustment has been brought to light through juvenile traffic violations. A girl companion of a youthful speeder may be protected from further sexual experimentation. Boys whose only amusement seems to be joyriding in family cars can be directed to other more suitable forms of entertainment before they reach the stage of borrowing cars when the family car is unavailable.

Police and Community Delinquency Prevention

The ideology of delinquency prevention and statutes incorporating special laws for regulating the conduct of children have not been ill adapted to the needs and problems of police in large cities, and to some extent have been their outgrowth. It needs to be emphasized, however, that police generally are less concerned with the prevention of delinquency in individual cases than in its prevention and control as a communitywide problem variously manifested in gang violence, disturbances of public order, a rise in crime rates, or mounting property losses. The special utility to police of specious legal categories describing delinquent tendencies is most obvious when they seek to break up youthful gang activity, quell public disturbances, such as occur at drive-ins or public parks, gain access to witnesses or sources of information to solve a crime series or to recover stolen property. While the arrest and detention of youth to clear up other crimes may be efficient police tactics, abuses may arise at the expense of individual youths if such methods can be pursued under diffuse charges. Unfortunately there have been and are judges willing to allow juvenile detention to be used for these purposes. It was for reasons such as these that the Juvenile Justice Commission of California, following a statewide survey, in 1960 recommended legislation to encourage the use of citations for minor offenses by juveniles, and to require that detention hearings be held within specified time limits to act as a check on overzealous police action.

Lest a picture be left of police as ruthless manipulators of juveniles of law enforcement ends, be it noted that in a number of areas they have sought to aid juveniles avoid clashes with the law through setting up recreation programs, Big Brother assignments, informal probation, and even police social work. However, such undertakings have declined in recent years and tend to be looked upon as too widely divergent from essential police functions. This may also point to growing disillusionment with more generalized or communitywide delinquency prevention programs. Police in some cities sharply disagree with community organizers of such projects over the issue of maintaining the autonomy of neighborhood gangs; they tend to take a jaundiced view of proposals and attempts to divert such groups from law breaking into more compliant pursuits.

Research assessments of community programs to prevent delinquency, such as the Chicago area project, the Harlem project, and the Cambridge-Somerville youth study, have been disappointing; results either have been negative or inconclusive. Possible exceptions are community coordinating councils, especially in the Western United States where they originated. However, they seem to work best in towns between 2,000 and 15,000 population; it remains unclear whether they can be adapted successfully to large urban areas. Significantly, they work chiefly by exchanging agency information, and referrals of cases to community agencies, with full support and cooperation of the police. In effect they represent concerted action to bypass the juvenile court, and it might be said that their purpose if not function is prevention of delinquency by preventing, wherever possible, the adjudication of cases in the court.

Treatment of Child Problems and Delinquency

Much of what has already been said about preventing delinquency by means of juvenile court intervention is equally applicable as criticisms of intervention by the court to treat youth problems and delinquency by therapeutic means. The ideal of therapeutic treatment found its way into juvenile court philosophy from social work and psychiatry, its pervasiveness measurable by the extent to which persons educated and trained in social work have indirectly influenced the juvenile court or moved into probation and correctional officer positions. An underlying premise of therapeutic treatment of children is that scientific knowledge and techniques exist making possible specific solutions to individual and family problems. It seeks to impose the positivism of hard science upon individual behavior.

Scientific social work, whose tenets were originally laid down by Mary Richmond in her early work, "Social Diagnosis," eventually came to lean heavily upon theories of Freudian psychiatry, taking over its psychobiological orientation and the medicinal idea that childhood problems and delinquency are symptoms of unresolved Oedipal conflicts. Updated versions of socially applied psychoanalysis conceive of delinquency as an acting out of repressed conflicts in irrational, disguised forms. Accent in treatment is laid upon the internal emotional life rather than upon external acts; the social worker or the psychiatrist is a specialist who understands the problems while the client does not; the specialist knows best, studies, analyzes and treats, much in the manner of the authoritative medical practitioner.

A divergent, competing line of thought in social work repudiates scientific treatment in favor of a more simple conception of its task as essentially a helping process, in which problems are confronted in whatever terms the child or youth presents them; responsible involvement of the client is a sine qua non of success in this process. Needless to say, this conception of the nature of social work is much more compatible with a philosophy of democracy.

Generally speaking, social workers advocate a more curtailed dispositional function for the juvenile court and advocate assigning to other agencies many of the tasks it has assumed. Some social workers seriously doubt whether the helping process can be carried on in an authoritarian setting, and to emphasize their stand refuse as clients children who have been wards of the court. Other social workers believe that judges go beyond their competence, and should use their power solely for adjudication, after which determination of treatment should pass on to social work agencies. A smaller number of social workers hold to a more sanguine view of reconciling personal help and authority within the role of the probation officer. Finally, there are some social workers who are not beyond using juvenile court power as a tool for getting access to clients, or prolonging their contacts with them because they will benefit from treatment. Experience showed that this pattern became aggravated in Utah during the period when juvenile courts there were under the administration control of the State department of welfare.

A long-standing, ubiquitous problem of social workers and psychiatrists of whatever theoretical persuasion has been that of the noninvolvement of their clients or patients. Clients are either disinclined to seek their services or they break off contacts after they have been established, or they respond superficially without showing interest in changing their personal values or life styles. Much of the difficulty stems from the identification of social workers with middle-class values and the invidious moralistic implications of imputing defective personalities to those they try to assist. As a result, barriers to communication often become insurmountable.

Actually, comparatively few juvenile court cases are referred to social workers for treatment and many juvenile court judges and probation officers are inhospitable toward social workers. According to a U.S. Children's Bureau study some years ago, the most frequent disposition of juvenile court cases was dismissal, followed by informal or formal supervision under a probation officer. Dismissals can scarcely be called treatment even though the associated court appearance before an admonitory judge may have a chastening effect upon some youths. At most, such cases have a brief exchange with an intake or investigating officer who asks some questions, issues a stern warning, and says he hopes he will not see the boy again.

The consequences of supervision of delinquents by probation officers either in parental homes or in foster homes have been little studied and the outcome, even when successful, little understood. Probation practices with juveniles have little in common if the Nation is taken as a whole, and often they consist of a bare minimum of office interviews and phone or mail reports. The frequent claim of probation officers that they could give more help to their charges if they had more time for supervision must be scouted as an occupational complaint rather than an accurate prediction of treatment possibilities. What little research there is on the subject has shown that mere reduction of the size of caseloads of probation and parole officers does not in itself lower rates of recidivism of those supervised.

If the results of probation supervision of delinquents on the whole are disappointing or inconclusive, even less can be said in behalf of the treatment of juvenile offenders undertaken under institutional commitments. Sociological analysis and evaluations of correctional programs in institutional settings tend to be uniformly negative, with some writers taking a position that the goals of correctional programs in prisons and reformatories are inherently self-defeating. This follows from the very fact of incarceration, which by necessarily posing a series of problems of personal deprivation for inmates, generates a more or less antithetical subculture which negates and subverts formal programs of rehabilitation. The logistics of processing delinquents or criminal populations brings large numbers of recidivists to the institutions, where they control informal communication and face-to-face interaction which importantly shapes the course of inmate socialization.

The problems of correctional institutions for delinquents have been highlighted in the popular press and literature as those of poor physical plants, niggardly appropriations and underpaid, undereducated personnel, but to the social scientist they lie far deeper. At this writing it remains doubtful whether the generously funded and well-staffed California Youth Authority has neared its original purpose of providing individualized treatment for youthful offenders. This has not been due to a lack of dedication of its leadership, but rather has resulted from having to assume the task of institutional administration, in which sheer numbers of commitments, contingencies, conflicting values of staff and custody people, and organizational inertia daily conspire to defeat the purpose of treatment. The top people of CYA have not been unaware of its dilemmas, which accounts for recent moves to establish large-scale community treatment projects and a probation subsidy program devised to stimulate local innovations in the supervision or treatment of juveniles as alternatives to commitment.

The less-than-sanguine remarks here directed to the ideology of delinquency treatment do not exclude the possibility that clinically trained and humanly wise people cannot help youth solve problems which have brought them athwart the law. Rather the intent is to leaven professional contumely with humility, to place the notion of treatment into a more realistic perspective, and to point out denotative differences between dealing with problems of human relationships and treatment as it has evolved in the practice of medicine. The treatment of delinquency is best regarded as a kind of guidance, special education, and training, much more akin to midwifery than medicine, in which hopeful intervention into an ongoing process of maturation is undertaken. Objective criteria for the use of methods of intervening, and controlled conditions necessary for predictable outcomes are neither present nor likely to be. Hence the actions of a judge, probation officer, correctional counselor, or an institutional psychiatrist at most can be small influences brought to bear among many simultaneously affecting child development and emergence of youth into adulthood. Although the power and the authority of the juvenile court can determine that certain intervenings will take place in a prescribed order in the process of socialization they cannot control the meanings and values assigned to such occurrences.

Judicious Nonintervention

The aims of preventing delinquency and the expectation of definitively treating a profusion of child and parental problems have laid an impossible burden upon the juvenile court, and they may be seriously considered to have no proper part in its philosophy. If there is a defensible philosophy for the juvenile court it is one of judicious nonintervention. It is properly an agency of last resort for children, holding to a doctrine analogous to that of appeal courts which require that all other remedies be exhaused before a case will be considered. This means that problems accepted for action by the juvenile court will be demonstrably serious by testable evidence ordinarily distinguished by a history of repeated failures at solutions by parents, relatives, schools, and community agencies. The model should be derived from the conservative English and Canadian juvenile courts, which in contrast to the American, receive relatively few cases.

This statement of juvenile court philosophy rests upon the following several propositions:

1. Since the powers of the juvenile court are extraordinary, properly it should deal with extraordinary cases.
2. Large numbers of cases defeat the purpose of the juvenile court by leading to bureaucratic procedures antithetical to individualized treatment (guidance).
3. The juvenile court is primarily a court of law and must accept limitations imposed by the inapplicability of rule and remedy to many important phases of human conduct and to some serious wrongs. Law operates by punishment, injunction against specific acts, specific redress, and substitutional redress. It cannot by such means make a father good, a mother moral, a child obedient, or a youth respectful of authority.
4. When the juvenile court goes beyond legal remedies it must resort to administrative agents, or itself become such an agency, which produces conflicts and confusion of values and objectives. Furthermore, it remains problematical whether child and parental problems can be solved by administrative means.

It may be protested that the conception of the juvenile court adumbrated here is so narrow as to emasculate it or take away any distinctive purpose. However, if it can be accepted that many acts termed delinquent in reality are not equitable with adult crimes, and that many situations called dangerous for youth on close examination turn out to be functions of moral indignation by persons and groups who, to paraphrase Maitland, "Screw up standards of reasonable ethical propriety to unreasonable heights," then organized nonintervention by the juvenile court assumes a definite protective function for youth. It has become equally or more important to protect children from unanticipated and unwanted consequences of organized movements, programs and services in their behalf than from the unorganized, adventitious "evils" which gave birth to the juvenile court. America no longer has any significant number of Fagans, exploiters of child labor, sweatshops, open saloons, houses of prostitution, street trades, an immoral servant class, cruel immigrant fathers, traveling carnivals and circuses, unregulated racetracks, open gambling, nor professional crime as it once existed. The battles for compulsory education have long since been won and technological change has eliminated child labor—perhaps too well. The forms of delinquency have changed as the nature of society has changed; social and personal problems of youth reflect the growth of affluence in one area of society and the growth of hostility and aggression in a nonaffluent sector. Current sociological theories of delinquency stress drift and risktaking as causes on one hand and on the other deprivation and dilapidated opportunity structures.

The basic life process today is one of adaptation to exigencies and pressures; individual morality has become functional rather than sacred or ethical in the older sense. To recognize this at the level of legislative and judicial policy is difficult because social action in American ways has been heavily laden with moral purpose. However, if the juvenile court is to become effective, its function must be reduced to enforcement of the ethical minimum of youth conduct necessary to maintain social life in a high energy, pluralistic society. Given this lower level of function, it can then proceed to its secondary task of arranging the richest possible variety of assistance to those specially disadvantaged children and youth who come under its jurisdiction.

41. The Adversary System

Abraham S. Blumberg

The Dissonance of Principles and Practice

The ideals of due process when translated into procedural regularities, as we have seen, are calculated to redress the disparate balance between an accused person and his accuser. Granted that we have developed the most libertarian rules of criminal justice of any nation. Nevertheless, the rules themselves do not actually define or limit the operations of the police, the prosecution, and the courts, who are responsible for their enforcement. These agencies rework the rules for organizationally prescribed ends which are consistent with values of efficiency, high production, and maximizing individual careers. The formal rules of due process generate a state of tension between due process ideals and practice. One of the major functions of formal organization or bureaucracy is to reduce the uncertainties of the environment. The rules of due process introduce elements of chance into the organizational environments of the enforcement agencies. "Bureaucratic due process" represents the "practice" which they have devised to reduce the elements of chance in their respective work milieus.

The rules of due process, as expanded and strengthened by the Supreme Court, are predicated on the existence of an adversary system of criminal justice. The rules envision a "combative" procedural system wherein prosecution and defense (who are admittedly possessed of unequal resources) will clash. After the dust has settled, the data which determine guilt or innocence will have emerged. Unfortunately, this model of criminal justice does not exist in fact. At each stage of the process a tacit but erroneous assumption is made. It is assumed that the accused will ultimately have "his day in court." Oversights, mistakes of judgment, and the capricious behavior of enforcement officials will be carefully reviewed–by the next higher authority. The sort of individualization necessitated by due process introduces special complications in the daily work of the enforcement agencies, interfering with organizational values of efficiency and maximum production. As a result, all the screening agencies in the system of criminal justice move in a case along toward a trial–which seldom occurs.

Police officials, the prosecution, and grand juries provide little real protection for accused persons because of the rather superficial standards of proof of guilt they require in order to move a case along to the next step in the criminal screening process.[1] Although prosecution agencies are bound by arrest standards of "probable cause" in connection with felonies (a reasonable belief that a crime has been committed and that the accused is the perpetrator), pressures of administrative efficiency too often resolve any doubts in favor of the organization. Police see little danger in this practice because they feel that any legal or factual irregularities will be unearthed in the trial court (the mansion). But as a practical matter there is widespread resentment among police of judges and courts, which they think seek to "handcuff" them through stricter rules of due process. Police "efficiency" is thereby threatened, and as a consequence strategies of evasion of rules are perfected which tend to support the validity of a given arrest and charge. "Probable cause" as an arrest standard is at best not necessarily enough evidence to charge a defendant. But prosecutors are too often ready, because of their own organizational requirements, to prosecute. Grand juries, through their indictment power, become too readily the willing handmaidens of a sytem of justice which has been called by Jerome Skolnick a system of "justice without trial."

Under these circumstances of mass administration of criminal justice, presumptions necessarily run to regularity and administrative efficiency. The negation of the presumption of innocence permeates the entire system of justice without trial. All involved in the system, the defense attorneys and judges, as well as the prosecutors and policemen, operate according to a working presumption of the guilt of persons accused of crime. As accused after accused is processed through the system, participants are prone to develop a routinized callousness, akin to the absence of emotional involvement characterizing the physician's attitude toward illness and disease. That the accused is entitled to counsel is an accepted part of the system, but this guarantee implies no specific affirmation of "adversariness" in an interactional sense. Indeed, the most respected attorneys, prosecuting and defense alike, are those who

[1] Abraham S. Goldstein, *"The State and the Accused: Balance of Advantage in Criminal Procedure," op. cit.*, p. 1163.

can "reasonably" see eye to eye in a system where most defendants are guilty of some crime.[2]

In a recent study of the guilty plea practices in the United States, it was estimated that when all pleas to both felonies and misdemeanors are combined, the total guilty plea convictions rate may be almost 95 percent. When felony cases alone are used as the basis for the calculation of guilty pleas, the total is estimated to be 70 to 85 per cent.[3] In another study, sponsored by the American Bar Foundation, of a representative sample of counties in all fifty states, the median percentage of guilty pleas in felony cases was 69 during the year studied, 1962.[4] Conclusions drawn from the foregoing data are in general affirmed by the data drawn from Metropolitan Court over a period of fifteen years, from 1950 to 1964 inclusive, at the felony level.

Table 1 shows the total number of accused persons who pleaded guilty in a given calendar year without completing the formal process of a trial, and the total number of cases processed or disposed of during the given year, expressed in absolute terms and as a percentage relationship. By "processed or disposed of" is meant all those persons who were either convicted by plea or trial, dismissed, or acquitted–in other words, concluded cases awaiting formal sentence.

While the American Bar Foundation data include many cases of individuals who were not represented by counsel, *every* accused person in the Metropolitan Court data was furnished counsel either privately or through an elaborate legal-aid defender

TABLE 1. Volume of Cases Pleading Guilty Before Trial in Metropolitan Court (1950–1964)

Year	*Cases Processed*	*Pleaded Without Formal Trial*	*Per Cent Pleading Guilty*
1950	2498	2287	91.55
1951	2905	2666	91.77
1952	3220	3034	94.22
1953	3390	3185	93.95
1954	3762	3436	91.33
1955	3391	3190	94.07
1956	3140	2859	91.05
1957	3356	3130	93.26
1958	3926	3692	94.04
1959	3923	3732	95.13
1960	4639	4416	95.19
1961	4002	3785	94.58
1962	4363	4070	93.28
1963	4953	4616	93.19
1964	5030	4673	92.90

[2] Jerome H. Skolnick, *Justice Without Trial,* New York, 1966, p. 241.

[3] Donald J. Newman, *Conviction: The Determination of Guilt or Innocence Without Trial,* Boston, 1966, p. 3.

[4] Lee Silverstein, *Defense of the Poor,* Chicago, 1965, p. 90.

system. Nevertheless, the results over a fifteen-year period indicate a consistently high conviction rate by way of plea before trial—considerably higher than the aforementioned national median rate of 69 per cent.

An even more definitive omen of the administrative, non-adversary character of "bureaucratic due process" is expressed in the Table 2, in which the same years are examined. The universe with which we begin each calendar year is the total number of persons indicted by grand jury. Since so much attention and regard is lavished upon the institution of trial by jury as a procedural safeguard in our system of jurisprudence, the data take on added significance and meaning.[5]

TABLE 2. Volume of Cases Disposed of by Trial in Metropolitan Court (1950–1964)

Year	*Indictments Found by Grand Jury*	*Total Cases Disposed of by Trial*	*Per Cent Disposed of by Trial*
1950	2676	113	4.22
1951	3217	137	4.25
1952	3638	127	3.49
1953	3532	131	3.70
1954	3934	112	2.84
1955	3235	102	3.15
1956	3159	114	3.60
1957	3524	115	3.26
1958	3772	107	2.83
1959	4314	104	2.41
1960	4750	116	2.44
1961	4319	142	3.28
1962	4392	162	3.68
1963	4997	150	3.00
1964	5073	145	2.85

Of course, although the actual criminal process does not reflect the textbook version of a trial (there being so few actual trials), the system is not in imminent danger of collapse. Nor have the participants withdrawn sentiments supporting its legitimacy. Further, we are *not* suggesting that many of those who plead guilty are innocent of any crime. Quite the contrary is true in all probability, and in many instances those who have been able to negotiate a lesser plea have done so willingly, even eagerly, in order to obtain the benefits of a more favorable disposition. Indeed, *the system of justice by negotiation, without trial, probably tends to serve better the interests and requirements of the guilty.* As compensation for his acquiescence and participation, having observed the prescriptive etiquette in compliance with what is expected of

[5] "...Under our system of justice the most elemental concepts of due process of law contemplate that an indictment be followed by a trial, in an orderly courtroom, presided over by a judge, open to the public, and protected by all the procedural safeguards of the law." *Massiah vs. United States,* 377 U.S. 201 (1964), at p. 204.

the defendant, he is rewarded. But an innocent person is confronted with the same role prescriptions, organizational features, and structural alternatives, with few of the accompanying possibilities of assuagement.

The central fact is that accused persons shun jury trials and prefer to alleviate the onerous burdens of their defendant status through a negotiated lesser plea. To risk a jury trial poses an obviously great statistical probability of conviction, often of far more serious charges than those administratively available in the bargained-for plea. The threat of a jury trial is one of the subtleties employed by the prosecution to reduce a defendant's resistance. Jury trials are discouraged in any event, because they are time consuming, expensive, and introduce an altogether cumbersome dimension into a system which is otherwise characterized by regularity, supreme rationality, and efficiency. Indeed, at the time of sentence, whether one was convicted after a trial or by way of a plea becomes a basis for invidious comparison. Prosecution and defense will often stress, by way of mitigation for the accused, that he has not caused the state to go to the expense of a time-consuming trial. The defendant who has been convicted after trial receives rather less generous treatment than one who has negotiated.

It would appear at least tentatively that once one is caught up in the system as an accused (indicted) individual, there is little chance of escaping conviction. This is so whether one pleads guilty or actually proceeds with a trial. As the results in Table 3 indicate, the jury trial conviction rate is also quite formidable.

TABLE 3. Conviction Rates in Cases Disposed of by Trial in Metropolitan Court (1950–1964)

Year	*Total Cases Disposed of by Trial*	*Convictions, Number and Per Cent*	*Acquittals*	*Disagreements (Hung Juries)*
1950	113	92 (81.41)	21	15
1951	137	103 (75.18)	34	12
1952	127	95 (74.80)	32	22
1953	131	101 (77.09)	30	18
1954	112	88 (78.57)	24	8
1955	102	82 (80.39)	20	7
1956	114	94 (82.45)	20	11
1057	115	81 (70.43)	34	8
1958	107	90 (84.11)	17	8
1959	104	96 (92.30)	8	21
1960	116	104 (89.65)	12	6
1961	142	127 (89.43)	15	9
1962	162	142 (87.65)	20	8
1963	150	127 (84.66)	17	6
1964	145	123 (84.82)	14	8

Disagreements which resulted in hung juries and therefore produced no disposition are not included in the total cases disposed of by trial. Thus, for example, in 1950 there were actually 128 trials, but only 113 resulted in an actual disposition of a case.

One social critic expresses the view, probably shared by many, that the criminal court in America is "inefficient, corrupt, and archaic."[6] While these appellations have somewhat value-laden character, to call the court system "inefficient" may be inaccurate. It seems to have articulated structures of a highly "rational" character, calculated to achieve maximum production and near maximum rates of conviction. If these are the ends to be pursued, then the criminal court is highly "efficient."

The Role of Ideology

How then can the court's functionaries and the clients it serves continue to defend as legitimate such a negatively evaluated, oppressive social arrangement? Partly the answer lies in the concept of ideology—the fact that "man does not live by bread alone," that he must seek to develop an ideology to justify, reinforce, and give meaning to interests he pursues. These ideologies and their elaborate rationales become as real and consequential as the material interests. Every regime, in all epochs involving varied groups and political systems, has sought to claim legitimacy by employing "political myths" or "formulas." The "divine right of kings"; *"liberté, égalité, fraternité"*; "justice under law"; "due process"; "all men are created equal"—these are prominent examples of the political myth. Ideologies need not be and often are not the weapons of a conspiracy of rulers to keep the ruled submerged or to falsify a given state of affairs. On the contrary, they are often nurtured and subscribed to by all strata, rulers and ruled alike, to resolve the inevitable discordancies and incompatibilities of belief systems and behavior or action systems.

One ideological aspect of due process, as we have seen, is the concealment of the emergence of justice without trial, the system of justice by negotiation. Another and probably more significant aspect of the ideological rationale which makes the criminal court palatable to all involved is the almost universal belief on the part of accusers and accused alike in two other basic suppositions:

(1) A defendant in a criminal court is really beaten by the deprivations and limitations imposed by his social class, race, and ethnicity. These in turn preclude such services as bail, legal counsel, psychiatric services, expert witnesses, and investigatory assistance. In essence, the concomitants of poverty are responsible for the fact that due process sometimes produces greatly disparate results in an ill-matched struggle.[7] Further, if these disabilities of the accused were alleviated, then the traditional principles of due process would function to make "justice" available to all. Due process is revered and believed in as the normatively established, time-honored means for obtaining justice, but its lack of vitality is explained away by sociological inequities.

Largely ignored in this argument is the institutional structure—the organizational characteristics and requirements of the criminal court itself. It mediates between

[6] Max Lerner, *America as a Civilization,* New York, 1957, p. 433.

[7] Justice Arthur Goldberg, "Equal Justice for the Poor, Too," *New York Times Magazine,* March 15, 1964, p. 24. See also a most recent volume in this vein, Arnold S. Trebach, *op. cit., passim; Report of The Attorney General's Committee on Poverty and the Administration of Federal Criminal Justice,* Washington, 1963.

the rules as they have been elaborated and the accused person, who has been presented to the court for disposition by still other organizational structures–the police and the district attorney.

The organizational variable affects the values and ideals of normatively established procedures of due process and produces outcomes other than those intended. The *élan vital* of the organization itself has a thrust, purpose, and direction of its own, at variance too often with the stated values of due process. We can tentatively state at least seven elements in the organizational variable which tend to deflect it from its prescribed goals:

(a) Occupational and career commitments and drives generate priorities which have a higher claim than the stated organizational goals.

(b) Empire building.

(c) Organizational goals of maximum production, which in their implementation are inconsistent with due process and rule of law.

(d) Institutionalized evasions of due process requirements.

(e) A routine of idiosyncratic and deviant solutions–which are denied on an overt level–to organizational problems of production.

(f) Secrecy and relative immunity from scrutiny.

(g) Individual pathology meeting its needs and finding its satisfactions while cloaked in organizational authority and under cover of the activities of the organization.

(2) The second basic ideological rationale which supports the legitimacy of the criminal court is the ameliorative-therapeutic model of the court, the origin of which is to be found in the Positivist school of criminology and serves to cast the criminal in the role of a "sick" person. The court then becomes something more than a legal structure; it is also a clinical way station in the long process of individualization of "treatment" of offenders.[8]

For judges, lawyers, probation personnel, and accused persons, the psychiatrist not only has a place in the court setting but tends to validate legal judgments in terms of medical "science." In fact, psychiatry becomes the theology by which legal procedures and pronouncements are interpreted and their legitimacy reinforced for all of the foregoing categories of persons, the accusers and the accused alike. In addition, the charismatic quality of the various occupational roles, even as routinized in the court setting, tends to overwhelm the court's clients, who continue to believe sufficiently in the efficacy, justification, and intentions of psychiatry, probation, and law as "helping" disciplines.

Positivist criminology simply rejects a legal definition of crime and postulates the idea that "punishment" should be replaced by "scientific treatment" of crime. Almost from its inception as a special discipline in medicine, psychiatry has had a role in the administration of the criminal law. As psychiatry developed its theories and

[8]The basic proposition asserted here is reiterated in its classic version in Franz Alexander and Hugo Staub, *The Criminal, the Judge and the Public: A Psychological Analysis,* revised ed., New York, 1962, and in Philip Q. Roche, *The Criminal Mind,* New York, 1958.

made contributions to the study of human behavior, especially in the deviant and the criminal, it also became more powerful socially and politically. Psychiatry has greatly affected the ideas of those who deal with offenders administratively in courts and prisons—as well as in the more remote sphere of human organization in the corporation, shop, factory, and office. Every bureaucracy now has a psychiatric practitioner on tap to deal with the maverick or cantankerous employee—or for that matter anyone—who appears to have "gotten out of line."

But the connection between psychiatry and the court's ameliorative-therapeutic concept is best understood in terms of psychiatry's objectives. Basic to psychiatry as an intellectual effort is its attempt to understand the nature of human behavior and its development, and to control its direction and purpose by manipulating the individual and his enviroment. Psychiatry, through research and evaluation, claims to develop indices of predictability about human conduct, making possible controlled results for the greater felicity of man and society. But instead, psychiatry, through what one of its most distinguished practitioners in the criminal courts has termed its "psychoauthoritarianism,"[9] has become in many instances a *threat* to offenders, because psychiatrists are called upon to participate in virtually every stage of a criminal proceeding. As a consequence, that which another prominent authority in the field, in an unflattering comparison with wire tapping, has termed "mind tapping,"[10] is employed without the consent or cooperation of the accused. The practical effect is often to deprive him of certain elements of due process, including the privilege against self-incrimination or ultimately even the right to a trial. For once a psychiatrist has determined that a person is "mentally ill" or "sick" and unable to stand trial, he is more than likely to spend a much longer time behind bars in a mental hospital than if he had been simply convicted of a crime in the first place.[11]

Despite strong evidence (the data are now fairly overwhelming) that "criminals" and "delinquents" do not possess personality characteristics significantly different from the rest of the population, and that the prevalence of psychoses, neuroses, and other disturbances among them is not significantly different from similarly matched samples of the rest of the population, psychiatrists still exert an extremely strong influence in the criminal courts.[12] Because of their ideological utility and charismatic

[9] Frederick Wertham, "Psychoauthoritarianism and the Law," *University of Chicago Law Review,* XXII, at p. 338.

[10] Thomas S. Szasz, *Law, Liberty and Psychiatry,* New York, 1963, pp. 161–165.

[11] *Ibid.,* pp. 165–169.

[12] Karl F. Schuessler and Donald R. Cressey, "Personality Characteristics of Criminals," *American Journal of Sociology,* LV (March 1950), 476–484; S. R. Hathaway and Elio D. Monachesi, *Analyzing and Predicting Delinquency with the MMPI,* Minneapolis, 1953; Arthur P. Volkman, "A Matched Group Personality Comparison of Delinquent and Nondelinquent Juveniles," *Social Problems,* VI (Winter 1959), 238–245. For example, Guttmacher and Weihofen assert: "The authors are completely out of sympathy with those who maintain that all criminals are sick people and should be treated as such." M.S. Guttmacher and Henry Weihofen, *Psychiatry and the Law,* New York, 1952, p. 87. See also the following critiques of the psychiatric position: Barbara Wooton, *Social Science and Social Pathology,* London, 1959; Michael Hakeem, "A Critique of the Psychiatric Approach to Crime and Correction," *Law and Contemporary Problems,* XXIII (Autumn 1958), 650–682.

character of their profession, they are simply too useful to dispense with in the administration of the criminal law.

The nosologies, the jargon, and the values of psychiatry, as they are embodied in the ameliorative-therapeutic model which is used in the criminal court, help to disguise and falsify the reality of what occurs. The most analogous situation is the custodial-mental hospital setting, where what is for all practical purposes a prison, presents a therapeutic façade.

The heart of the matter, however, is that in its relationship with other institutions, publics, and its clients, the court uses the language of therapy to justify such varied phenomena as the juvenile court, the indeterminate sentence, the sexual offender laws and civil commitment of the mentally ill, and the use of psychiatric reports before guilt or innocence is determined. Even judges speak the language when imposing sentence.

In practice, measures and techniques that tend to deprive a person of liberty under the guise of an exercise in therapeutic method are seen as punishment, and psychiatry has been seriously criticized on that account. The most strenuous objectors have indicated, in effect, that psychiatry has lent itself to questionable enterprises, and its affirmations of helping through punishment virtually amounts to the discipline being unable to perceive the real nature of its role.[13]

Metropolitan Court has in fact reached the ideal-typical goal in personnel and structure. In its arrangements for bail, counsel, and elaborate psychiatric and probation services, it represents what all who have had serious concern with the criminal court have hoped for. But the court which serves as the universe of this case study produces an administrative result in which the overwhelming majority of defendants simply plead guilty. The idealized version of due process is not translated into social action. The administrative instruments and resources are co-opted in behalf of the court organization to deal more effectively with a large caseload of defendants, by processing them toward a guilty plea.

An observer of the Soviet legal system has called the Soviet criminal trial "an appeal from the pre-trial investigation." In the Soviet Union the "trial" is simply a recapitulation of the data collected by the pre-trial investigator. Notions of a trial being a "tabula rasa" and presumptions of innocence are wholly alien to Soviet notions of justice. How closely does "bureaucratic due process" and its accompanying non-adversary system pose a discomforting parallel to the Soviet system, wherein "the closer the investigation resembles the finished script, the better, ..."?[14]

[13]David Matza, *Delinquency and Drift,* New York, 1964, Chapter 4; Francis A. Allen, "Criminal Justice, Legal Values and the Rehabilitative Ideal," *Journal of Criminal Law, Criminology and Police Science,* L., No. 3 (September-October 1959), 226–232; Thomas S. Szasz, *op. cit., passim,* Lewis Diana, "The Rights of Juvenile Delinquents: An Appraisal of Juvenile Court Procedures," *Journal of Criminal Law, Criminology and Police Science,* XLVII, No. 5 (January-February 1957), 561–569; Luis Kutner, "The Illusion of Due Process in Commitment Proceedings," *Northwestern University Law Review,* XLVII, 383–399; see also Thomas Szasz, *Psychiatric Justice,* New York, 1965.

[14]George Feifer, *Justice in Moscow,* New York, 1965, p. 86.

42. Systems Analysis and the Criminal Justice System

Alfred Blumstein

When the National Crime Commission first formed its Science and Technology Task Force,[1] and directed it to look into the question of how science and technology could help in the control of crime, the Task Force was faced with the typical problem of today's prolific technology: a rapidly changing environment, a plethora of alternatives, with no clear indication of how to choose among them. A small police department wants to know whether to invest in more automobiles or in portable radios for its patrolmen. A large department must choose between installing an automatic patrol-car locator or an automated command-and-control system. Every department must decide where, when, and how to assign its personnel and material resources. Even more fundamentally, decision-makers need to have estimates of the consequences and implications of any of the actions they may be contemplating.

These are the kinds of questions which have led to the development of that branch of endeavor must commonly known as "systems analysis."[2] Systems analysis has been used most extensively on military problems,[3] largely because of the rapid changes in military technology in the last three decades, the larger variety of choices being made available, and the generally close relationships that have developed between the Defense Department and the scientists qualified to perform such analyses. Furthermore, until very recently, the Defense Department has been almost alone in

Reprinted from *The Annals of the American Academy of Political and Social Science,* 374 (November 1967), 93–100, by permission of the American Academy of Political and Social Science and the author.

[1] For the basic background material behind this paper, see U.S., President's Commission on Law Enforcement and Administration of Justice, *Task Force Report: Science and Technology* (Washington, D.C.: U.S. Government Printing Office, 1967).

[2] Similar work is often labeled "operations research," "systems engineering," or "systems research." Among these, *systems analysis* usually emphasizes the quantiative relationships between cost and effectiveness in comparing alternative ways to design and operate systems. *Operations research* is usually concerned with reallocation of existing resources to improve performance through changes in operating procedures. *Systems engineering* is usually concerned with alternatives which involve significant technological aspects. *Systems research* is usually more concerned with simply unearthing the relationships among parts of a system and its operating performance.

[3] See, for example, Charles J. Hitch and Roland N. McKean, *The Economics of Defense in the Nuclear Age* (Cambridge, Mass.: Harvard University Press, 1960); and E. S. Quade, *Analysis for Military Decisions* (Chicago: Rand-McNally, 1964).

government in having the discretionary resources to worry about where to spend them and to purchase assistance in such worries.

Basic Concepts of Systems Analysis

The primary concepts of systems analysis have been with us for a long time. The important novelty in their current application is the extent to which they have been applied in such subject areas as military operations, transportation, and social systems.

A systems analysis focuses successively on:

1. A particular *system*—a collection of people, devices, and procedures intended to perform some function.
2. The *function* of the system—the job it is supposed to perform.
3. *Measures of effectiveness* by which one can measure or calculate how well alternative system designs perform the function.
4. *Alternative* system designs to be compared.
5. A *mathematical model* with which one can calculate the measures of effectiveness associated with each alternative system design.

Its functional emphasis is the primary feature of systems analysis. For the criminal justice system—the agencies of police, prosecution, adjudication, and correction and the legal framework within which they operate—the focus is on controlling crime. The system may also serve other functions, such as meting out punishment for criminal acts beyond that intended to provide a measure of deterrence. Examining the system in such other contexts would provide a very different picture and raise different issues than those raised by the crime-control context considered here.

The use of mathematical models is the most significant contribution of systems analysis. A mathematical model is an abstract representation of some real-world system such that it "behaves" like its real-world counterpart in some limited respects. The behavioral correspondence implies that changes in the system in the model world would produce changes in the calculated measures of effectiveness that are comparable to what would be measured in the real world if the operating system were subjected to the same changes. The validity of the model, of course, depends on the comparability between the real and model worlds. But the comparability need extend only over the range of conditions for which change is contemplated. A model can be identical to its real-world counterpart in all respects only by duplicating the real world, and this, of course, would defeat the purpose of using the model.

The model finds its value because the real system is, in most respects, inaccessible for experimentation or manipulation. Whether for reasons of cost, time, political sensitivity, or legal constraints which may ultimately be removed, the real criminal justice system is often unavailable for experimentation. To the extent that experimentation is an inherent part of successful innovation, some means must become available for experimentation and analysis without disrupting the ongoing operations. The abstract model provides such an opportunity. With it, one can gain a first estimate of the consequences of any manner of change. The validity of the estimate is, of course, only as good as the theory and data underlying the model.

There are many forms such a model might take. One might create a simulated environment in which people are asked to make decisions just as they might in a real environment: war games or mock trials are illustrations. One might describe in a computer simulation program the sequence of events and decisions that occur in a system's operation. This has been done for a court[4] and a state criminal justice system.[5]

The growth of systems analysis in recent years has been a natural consequence of the increasing complexity of government decisions. In parallel, there have been significant developments in methodological tools for handling the large numbers of variables inherent in such problems and the computing tools for manipulating these complex models and their data demands in an efficient way.

In its pure form, systems analysis is supposed to provide quantitative comparisons of the consequences of alternative decisions, in terms of both cost and effectiveness. These comparisons, however, are rarely sufficient for making most decisions, since the qualitative value considerations are usually at least as important as those that can be quantified. But by putting numbers on the measurable aspects of a question, the debate no longer need center on those questions, as it now so often does. Then the public debate and the administrative decisions can focus on the critical questions involved in the weighing of conflicting social values.

The Total Criminal Justice System

One basic tenet of the systems approach is that important but seemingly narrow questions be viewed in a sufficiently broad system context. By looking beyond the immediate narrow question, issues that were formerly ignored ("that is someone else's problem") or blindly accepted ("we only do our job") become open to question: What is the impact of higher arrest rates on the corrections process and on future crimes? What is the impact of community-based corrections on both the near- and long-range crime rates? What is the impact of nonbail release on the rate of guilty pleas and on court work-load? Would it be more economical to add court resources to cut the court backlog and reduce the cost of detention while awaiting trial? What will be the effect of providing free counsel more widely on correctional work-loads? These questions all involve interactions among various parts of the criminal justice system, and they can only be examined by considering the total system.

Any such attempt to deal with the larger system is limited by its inherent complexity. Every system can be viewed as a subsystem within some larger system. The smallest systems are too trivial to be of much interest. The largest ones are too complex or involve considerations too qualitative to treat analytically. Part of the

[4]See, for example, Joseph A. Navarro and Jean G. Taylor, "Data Analyses and Simulation of the Court System in the District of Columbia for the Processing of Felony Defendants," *Task Force Report: Science and Technology, op. cit.*, Appendix I.

[5]See, for example, "Prevention and Control of Crime and Delinquency in California–Final Report," Space-General Corporation, July 29, 1965; *Task Force Report: Science and Technology, op. cit.*, chap. v, pp. 53–67.

art of systems analysis is finding the level in this hierarchy of systems that is amenable to analysis.

The Apprehension Process

In the work of the Science and Technology Task Force, for instance, this led to the definition of an "apprehension process" describing the activities of the police in apprehending a suspect.

The description was reached by first considering how the criminal justice system acts to reduce crime. Upon further consideration, it became clear that even this was an insufficiently broad view of the system's function. Crime could be reduced, for instance, by very intense policing. This led to the recognition of the broader measure of effectiveness, "social disutility," with two components–one resulting from crime and one resulting from actions taken for crime control. As crime-control efforts are increased, the first goes down but the second goes up. These disutilities might involve invasions of privacy and erroneous arrest, as well as simple economic cost. Thus, there may be an "optimum" level of crime control which minimizes the sum of these two disutilities. More control would lead to too much oppressiveness and less control to too much crime.

Clearly, there are very difficult but basic value questions involved in trying to relate these two components through a common disutility scale. It is also very difficult, and perhaps even more complicated, to assess the two disutilities associated with any contemplated action such as doubling the police patrol force, lengthening maximum prison sentences, or precluding the use of confessions obtained without the presence of counsel. Despite the difficulty of precise quantification, these concepts must be weighed in considering any system changes.

Even when considering only the problem of controlling crime, the difficulties are considerable. Very little is now known of the impact on crime of any action that might be taken by the criminal justice system. Do the rigors of imprisonment deter a man in the future, or do they teach him antisocial values? Does intensified police patrol in an area reduce crime, displace it to adjoining areas, or have no effect whatsoever? And for what kinds of crimes and what groups of people? Who can be rehabilitated, by what kind of correctional treatment?

The problem can be reduced further by identifying the means by which the criminal justice system controls crime. These include:

1. rehabilitation of identified offenders.
2. removal from society of identified offenders, and
3. deterrence of potential offenders.

The most complicated of these mechanisms, and the one whose effect is most difficult to assess, is deterrence. What people are deterred from committing what crimes by what actions of the criminal justice system? Although this question is central to much of the operation of the criminal justice system, and especially to police operations, there has been no systematic attempt to answer it. The one exception might be in the area of capital punishment, and the continuing confusion there is well known.

Thus, the basic question of what deters whom from doing what must also remain unanswered. Rather, one might make the assumption that where deterrence applies, it involves a weighing of benefits from a crime against the risk in committing it. The threat of apprehension then enters as the primary factor on the risk side of that equation, and that factor is under the control of the criminal justice system. Since it is the threat rather than the actuality that deters, various nonfunctional approaches might be considered: for example, public relations programs, overplaying the image of police effectiveness, and the like.

Since the threat must eventually be related to the actuality, however, it is important to consider how the true apprehension capability can be improved. This is much more amenable to quantitative analysis. First, the factors relating to successful apprehension can be developed from police crime and arrest reports. Data from Los Angeles,[6] for instance, indicated that naming of the suspect, either through apprehension at the crime scene or identification by a victim or witness, was almost essential to solution of a crime. Less than 12 per cent of the cases without these named suspects were solved by the police. The named-suspect cases, comprising only 18 per cent of the crime cases, accounted for 62 per cent of the clearances.

This effect is closely related to the other observation in these data—that the chance of arrest was appreciably higher when the police responded more rapidly—62 per cent for responses of one minute and only 44 per cent for all cases of fourteen minutes or less.

With this indication that response time was a significant factor in apprehension, one can examine alternative ways to reduce response time: more public telephones to speed the public's access to the police; more police telephone clerks to shorten the delay before a call is answered; automated procedures for handling messages in the police communications center; car-location devices in the street to find the available car closest to a crime scene; and more cars in the street to shorten the average travel distance.

Comparison of these alternatives is relative straightforward. One can formulate a model which calculates the average delay reduced each time one of these resources is invoked and the frequency with which each is called on. This provides an estimate of the annual time-saving associated with possible investment to be related to the additional annual operating cost associated with each. This permits comparing the alternatives to find which is most "cost-effective."

In a particular case examined,[7] a hypothetical city typical of cities of about a half-million population, it turned out that computer automation in the police communications center was the best investment.

Having identified the best investment, this could then be followed by detailed design of the hardware system, including such considerations as car-locator equip-

[6] See Herbert H. Isaacs, "A Study of Communications, Crimes, and Arrests in a Metropolitan Police Department," *Task Force Report: Science and Technology, op. cit.*, Appendix B, pp. 88–106.

[7] *Task Force Report: Science and Technology, op. cit.*, pp. 10–12.

ment, displays in the communications center and in the patrol cars, car-to-computer inquiry capability, and other technological aspects of the command-and-control system.

Similar analytical techniques can be used to improve efficiency of management throughout the system. A computer simulation was prepared to describe the processing of persons arrested for felonies through the District of Columbia court system.[8] Use of the simulation showed that the processing through the grand jury was the critical bottleneck in the pretrial processing. The simulated effect of a second grand jury, sitting part-time, would thus have been to reduce a six-week delay from initial presentment to return of indictment to two weeks. The simulation thus permitted experimentation with various possible changes in the operation of that court system—all without disrupting the critical ongoing operations of the court.

Model of the Criminal Justice System

The use of models extends well beyond consideration of technological or managerial alternatives. They can also be used to explore relationships within the system. To this end, the flow of crimes, arrestees, defendants, and convicted persons through the criminal justice system and back into society was also simulated. At each juncture point in the flow, the routing was described by a set of branching ratios, which describe the proportions that flow along each of the paths out of that point. The feedback into society was characterized by the probability of being arrested again, described as a function of the person's age and the last crime for which he was arrested. For those who are rearrested, the time until rearrest was simulated to represent the actual probabilistic time lag until rearrest. The type of crime subsequently committed is given by a "crime-switch matrix," representing the proportions of people whose successive arrests are for each specified combination of crimes.

This model could then simulate criminal careers of persons arrested for the first time. Considering only the "index"[9] crimes, and using the distribution of juvenile (under 18) arrests as the distribution of first arrests, 1,000 criminal careers beginning at age 16 were simulated. In this simulation, these 1,000 individuals were arrested for over 3,000 subsequent index crimes. The simulation indicated that murder, rape, and robbery accounted for only 4 per cent of the initial arrests, but for 19 per cent of the later arrests. Auto theft and larceny of $50 or over, on the other hand, accounted for 68 per cent of the initial arrests but for only 35 per cent

[8]Navarro and Taylor, *op. cit.*

[9]The "index" crimes, used by the Federal Bureau of Investigation (FBI) to calculate an annual "index of crime" are willful homicide, forcible rape, aggravated assault, robbery, burglary, larceny of $50 and over, and auto theft. See U.S., Federal Bureau of Investigation, *Crime in the United States: Uniform Crime Reports* (Washington, D.C.: U.S. Government Printing Office, 1930——[annually]), 1958——. [Editor's Note: See the Introductions to the present book and to Section II where this is covered.]

of the subsequent arrests. This apparent escalation of seriousness over a criminal career, although still tentative because of poor data, raises the question of why successive arrests appear to be for more serious crimes. This phenomenon may be due to the aging of the individuals, to the development of antisocial attitudes in being processed through the criminal justice system, or possibly even to negative reactions to treatment. A question to be explored is whether the rearrest probabilities and the crime-type distributions become worse for those who are processed further through the system. If that is the case, it may be that the system processes further those who are least susceptible to rehabilitation, or it may be a consequence of the treatment itself. Unfortunately, the data to examine such basic questions do not yet exist, and a significant new research program is needed to provide the answers.

The contribution of the model with regard to these basic questions is in providing a systems context in which they are raised and in identifying the specific data required to close in on the answers—"close in" rather than "resolve" because definitive controlled experiments that isolate cause and effect are almost impossible to perform.

Arrest Probability

One side-effect of the operation with such models and the data needed to feed them is the generation of basic analytical questions. In our examination of the data on rearrest probabilities, the question of what proportion of people ever get arrested arose, initially as a matter of casual curiosity. Making such a projection requires data for each age group on: population (available from the United States Bureau of the Census); the annual number of arrests (available from the FBI's *Uniform Crime Reports*[10]); and the proportion of arrests represented by people who have never before been arrested.[11] The last item is the most difficult to estimate, since it must rely ultimately on the completeness of arrest records. Any incompleteness of arrest records would tend to overestimate the virgin proportion, and hence to overestimate the arrest probabilities. To compensate for this effect, the virgin proportions used were those estimated for a 1965 sample of referred juveniles and convicted male adult felons in the District of Columbia.[12] Their prior records were developed from investigations by the probation department. The characteristics of being convicted felons (and presumably with more extensive criminal histories than misdemeanants and nonconvicted felony defendants) and in the District of Columbia (where the arrest rate is higher than in the nation at large) would probably compensate for any residual unrecorded arrests.

For the juveniles, it was found that about 39 per cent of those referred to the juvenile court had no prior referrals. For the adults, 8 per cent of the Negroes and

[10] *Crime in the United States: Uniform Crime Reports, op. cit.*

[11] See Ronald Christensen, "Projected Percentage of U.S. Population with Criminal Arrest and Conviction Records," in *Task Force Report: Science and Technology, op. cit.*, Appendix J. pp. 216–228.

[12] Based on data in U.S., President's Commission on Crime in the District of Columbia, *Report* (Washington, D.C.: U.S. Government Printing Office, 1966), Appendix.

15 per cent of the whites had no record of prior arrests. Other data and analyses showed that in a year there are about 25 per cent[13] more juvenile arrests than the number of different juveniles arrested. For adults, 70 per cent of the arrests are accounted for by men previously arrested that year.

Putting these results together leads to an estimate of an average of one new offender in eight arrests. With this estimate, one can approximate the probability of an American boy's being arrested. The *Uniform Crime Reports* reports 4,431,000 male arrests in its 1965 sample population, or an equivalent of 6,420,000 for the total United States; one-eighth of these, or about 800,000, would have been new arrestees. One can assume, for simplicity, that all first arrests occurred at a specific age, say, sixteen. Since there were about 1,710,000 sixteen-year-old boys in the United States in 1965, their arrest probability is thus calculated to be about 47 per cent, or, conservatively, at least 40 per cent. More detailed calculations, correcting for race and residence (city, suburban, and rural), show that a city male's chances of being arrested for a nontraffic offense some time in his life are about 60 per cent, about 50 per cent for a United States male in general, and that they may be as high as 90 per cent for a Negro city male. These results are based on 1965 arrest rates, and arrest rates have been increasing in recent years.

Despite the surprising magnitude of these numbers, they were not contradicted by the two data points found. In both Philadelphia, Pennsylvania, and Fayette County, Kentucky, as of 1961, about 21 per cent of the boys had been referred to juvenile courts before reaching age 18. This is somewhat lower than the projection that about 27 per cent[14] of today's young boys will have been arrested by age 18. Part of this small difference can be accounted for by the increase in arrest rates since 1955–1960, when most of these boys experienced their arrests.

It should be pointed out that these projections are not literal predictions of the future. Rather, they are projections of current trends–trends that could well be reversed by changes in the operation of the criminal justice system. Furthermore, they are estimates based on limited available data, which may turn out to be somewhat in error. It appears very unlikely, however, that their basic import will be significantly altered. Intervention by the criminal justice system appears to be far more pervasive than has previously been recognized. The implications of this intervention are important to consider and debate. Is the criminal sanction being employed too widely in cases where it is ineffective, thus debasing its effectiveness where it might be more applicable? Is a man without an arrest record more or less deterred than one with an arrest record? How long should arrest records be maintained, especially when they are used, either directly or indirectly, in screening applicants for jobs? These are merely some of the basic questions that arise out of some analysis with the limited available data. Having the analyses permits a quantification of some aspects of these questions.

[13]Based on data from the *52nd Annual Report of the County Court of Philadelphia,* 1965, pp. 111 and 131.

[14]Christensen, *op. cit.,* Figure J–7, p. 222.

The basic value consideration will still have to be invoked, but perhaps in a more enlightened way, when some of the data are available.

Conclusions

This paper has reported on some of the ways in which the National Crime Commission's Science and Technology Task Force has used a variety of quantitative approaches to study the operation of the criminal justice system. These have been undertaken with a view both to improving the system's crime-control effectiveness and to gaining insight into its operation. Clearly, there are many more possibilities: Models of the total system can be used to provide first estimates of the consequences in terms of numbers, crimes, costs, and resource requirements (courtrooms, judges, probation officers, and the like) associated with contemplated changes in the system's operation (for example, providing free counsel more widely, bail reform, community-based correction treatment, and automatic fingerprint recognition).

Models oriented to the crime-control function identify the data required for improving decisions throughout the system, and can help to structure a research program and identify statistics to be collected. The data most immediately needed are those which embody the consequences in terms of crime of the various actions taken by the criminal justice system.

In the future, it would be reasonable to expect that such analyses would be conducted first at research institutions closely coupled to, but independent of, operating criminal justice agencies. Their work would involve explorations into fundamental questions underlying crime in society and the operation of the criminal justice system. They would be expected to provide the major methodological advances, including new and more refined models and innovative studies using sophisticated analytical techniques, and to validate their developments by a small number of pilot studies.

Other groups, more closely tied to operating agencies, would follow these developments closely and adapt them to the needs of their individual organizations. The infusion of such approaches can provide a valuable complement to the traditional approach of making decisions based only on professional judgment, prejudice, or hunch.

43. Recent Trends: Deviant Behavior and Social Control*

David J. Bordua

The very title of this subdivision of sociology—deviant behavior and social control—indicates that the two parts are separable but interrelated. It further indicates that a wide variety of specific subject matters can be subsumed under either part. Deviant behavior can, after all, range from public nose-picking to treason. Social control can range from the refusal to reciprocate a dinner invitation to public execution.

To add to the complexity and confusion, several more specific areas of inquiry which at least semantically fall under the heading of deviant behavior have long histories of rather independent status—study of crime and delinquency, for example.

If we were to adopt the notion that the field of deviant behavior and social control is simply the summation of all the special studies of norm-violating behavior, a summary report would be impossible. If, on the other hand, we were to focus on some special area much at the forefront of current attention, we would run the risk of ignoring significant developments elsewhere. Moreover, the specific empirical research done in any period will heavily reflect social interest in specific forms of deviance as evidenced by the availability of public and private research funds, and may not either reflect or foreshadow significant intellectual developments.

We have tried, therefore, to select a limited set of areas of recent work which constitute new theoretical orientations of likely future interest, which bear on older theoretical developments which are still undergoing evaluation, or which indicate changes in the social objects of research.

The most basic trend in the recent past has been a shift toward more interest in the social control half of the deviance and social control field. This renewed interest has a number of sources and takes a number of forms not all of which can be reviewed here. Broadly speaking, attention has shifted from a focus on the sources and etiology of deviance to the analysis of processes of social control. This separation is, however, tied together by the idea that social control processes are them-

Reprinted from *The Annals of the American Academy of Political and Social Science* (January 1967), 149–163, Vol. 57, No. 4, by permission of The American Academy of Political and Social Science and the author.

*The help of John P. Clark is gratefully acknowledged. Other commitments prevented us from carrying out our original plan to write the paper jointly.

selves importantly involved not only in the more or less successful suppression of deviance, but in the very processes of defining and producing deviance.

Because of this close interconnection, distinctions within the larger social control emphasis are likely to be arbitrary–and specific labels even more so. Yet some division does exist between recent studies that focus on organized agencies of social control themselves and other work which focuses on the nature and effects of social control in the generation and perpetuation of deviance. Purely for present convenience, we can discuss work on organized agencies, as such, under the heading of social control agencies, and the work on the definition and perpetuation of deviance under the heading of the societal reaction to deviance.[1] One point of contact between these two areas is study of the decision-making processes in formal social control agencies.

If we may be granted this rather arbitrary terminology, the discussion will be divided into two major sections. In the first, we discuss recent work on the societal reaction to deviance. In the second, we focus on study of formal agencies of social control, with main attention to studies of the hitherto neglected police.

Societal Reaction to Deviance

There is a long tradition in the sociology of deviance that focuses on the consequences of social control processes for the development of deviance. Indeed, sociologically influenced policy innovations such as the juvenile court were based on the notion that traditional control procedures were not only inhumane but even productive of greater deviance. Given the existence of this tradition, it is rather difficult to properly give credit where it is due. Nevertheless, it seems appropriate to cite the work of Edwin M. Lemert as especially relevant in inspiring more recent developments. This is especially the case as the more recent writers constitute themselves as something of a "school" and acknowledge greater or lesser debt to Lemert.[2]

It is useful to begin presentation of the "societal reaction" school by consideration of a recent book by Kai T. Erikson.[3] Building upon Durkheim's ideas of the functions of deviance in societies, Erikson develops an approach to deviance which stresses the functions of deviance and deviance-definition as central to the maintenance of social boundaries and community identity. A people know whom and what they are by whom and what they condemn. It follows then that a continuing group identity requires a continuing condemnation.

Erikson then applies the perspective to three deviance-defining and (in his interpretation, at least) boundary-maintaining sets of events in the history of the Puritan Commonwealth of Massachusetts Bay. The three examples are the Antinomian con-

[1] This distinction is not likely to be of more than temporary value. Thus, the Department of Sociology at the University of Illinois has a training program with the title, "Research on Operations and Effects of Agencies for Reaction to Behavioral Deviance."

[2] See especially Edwin M. Lemert, *Social Pathology* (New York: McGraw-Hill, 1951).

[3] Kai T. Erikson, *Wayward Puritans* (New York: John Wiley & Sons, 1966). See also an earlier paper by the same author, "Notes on the Sociology of Deviance," *Social Problems,* 9 (Spring 1962), pp. 307–314.

troversy involving Anne Hutchinson, the Quaker "invasion," and the witchcraft persecutions. These are cases where either the "norms" were ambiguous or where there was ambiguity about the conforming or deviant status of particular acts and persons, even if norms themselves were more or less clear.

Erikson's discussion of these examples may stand for a general characteristic of the "societal reaction" perspective—it focuses on problems of social ambiguity. Two closely related but separable definitional processes are involved. In the first situation, that of "normative ambiguity," the process of deciding whether a behavior is deviant involves the creation of new norms or the recasting of old norms. A model here is the Common Law. In the second situation, that of "behavioral ambiguity," where norms are more clear, the definitional process determines whether an individual or group action is, in fact, that proscribed by the norms.

Where the behavior is fairly ambiguous, a stereotyping process may develop which can in extremes convince not only the conformers but also—to a degree— the "deviants" that they are, in fact, deviant. Thus, in the case of the witchcraft prosecutions not only were observers convinced that the accused were witches, but the accused seemed convinced also. The witchcraft accusations came to have less and less defining criteriality, however, as the finger was pointed at persons eminent about whom the accusations made much less "sense"—persons whose eminence, we might suppose, provided them not only with social protection from the accusation but also self-protection. They seem to have had sufficient self-esteem to refuse to entertain any self-doubt.

This problem of the behavioral ambiguity of deviance is of especial interest whenever the deviant behavior is attributed to a "condition" of the person whose behavior is under scrutiny, or where the condition, as such, is defined as of basic social concern and the behavior is only an indicator or "symptom" of the condition. This distinction between "conditions" and "acts" is central to much of the societal reaction perspective, especially since social control responses predicated on the idea that there is a "condition" to be discovered in the person may create something like the very condition search for which set off the social control process in the first place.

Because of the interest in the social definitions of conditions rather than merely of acts the societal reaction perspective has led to a few studies of stereotypes and stereotyping processes, essentially a search for the patterns of inference used to assess the existence of deviant "conditions."

There are two levels on which this problem of inference can be approached—on the level of popular stereotypes and on the level of formal or official decision-making. Studies of popular or interpersonal stereotyping of deviants are rare, as compared, for example, with the elaborate literature on ethnic or racial stereotypes. Two recent studies have appeared which indicate beginnings in that direction.[4]

At the level of official decision-making, more work has been done. Some of this

[4] John I. Kitsuse, "Societal Reactions to Deviant Behavior: Problems of Theory and Method," *Social Problems,* 9 (Winter 1962), pp. 247–256; J. L. Simmons, "Public Stereotypes of Deviants," *Social Problems,* 13 (Fall 1965), pp. 223–232.

will be discussed later in connection with studies of police decision-making with juveniles. Perhaps the most interesting of the recent studies of official decision-making in the context of the societal-reaction approach are in papers by Scheff and by Sudnow.[5]

The study by Scheff is particularly relevant to the raging controversy over the modes of defining illness and the appropriate uses of state power in coercing "treatment." Insofar as deprivation of liberty is involved, the ordinarily applicable apparatus is the court, and the ordinary decision-rule is that it is better to err in letting people go who "should" be confined than to confine people who should be let go.

However, insofar as the decision to confine is contingent upon a medical diagnosis, another procedure and another decision-rule may operate. In medical diagnosis it is better to err on the side of illness than of health. If a person who is really healthy is labeled ill, the usual cost of the error is expense and inconvenience. If however, an ill person is labeled healthy, then the cost may be more serious illness or even death.

Thus, the "judicial" and the "medical" decision-rules are quite opposed. Moreover, procedurally, judicial and medical decision-making differ.[6] In what is by now a quite famous study of psychiatric diagnosis involved in the decision to commit to a state hospital, Scheff discovered that examinations were often perfunctory, conducted in a manner clearly indicating that the decision preceded the examination, and included no mechanisms whereby the patient could reasonably refute the "charge."[7]

Whether the results of Scheff's study would obtain elsewhere is not known. He himself cites a procedure in another state which is legally rather than medically dominated and was a model of due process and careful investigation.[8]

[5] Thomas J. Scheff, "The Societal Reaction to Deviance: Ascriptive Elements in the Psychiatric Screening of Mental Patients in a Midwestern State," *Social Problems,* 11 (Spring 1964), pp. 401–413. Thomas J. Scheff, "Social Conditions for Rationality: How Urban and Rural Courts Deal with the Mentally Ill," *American Behavioral Scientist,* 7 (March 1964), pp. 21–24. Scheff's work can be more easily assessed in a recent book, *Being Mentally Ill: A Sociological Theory* (Chicago: Aldine, 1966). David Sudnow, "Normal Crimes: Sociological Features of the Penal Code in a Public Defender's Office," *Social Problems,* 12 (Winter 1965), pp. 255–276.

[6] Thomas J. Scheff, *Being Mentally Ill, ibid.,* chap. 4. The problem of explicit as opposed to implicit decision-rules is the subject of elaborate statistical and mathematical discussion. For a relatively nontechnical discussion relevant to deviant behavior see David J. Bordua, *Prediction and Selection of Delinquents* (Washington, D.C.: United States Children's Bureau, 1961).

[7] Thomas J. Scheff, "The Societal Reaction to Deviance: Ascriptive Elements in the Psychiatric Screening of Mental Patients," *op. cit.*

[8] *Ibid.* The due-process implications of substituting professional for judicial decision-making are receiving a great deal of attention not only in the area of mental illness but in general. See Francis Allen, *The Borderline of Criminal Justice: Essays on Law and Criminology* (Chicago: University of Chicago Press, 1964).

It is interesting that as the traditionally legitimated discretionary authority of medical practitioners and others is increasingly called into question, the long-standing but condemned *de facto* discretionary decision-making of the police is becoming more visible and perhaps more legitimated. Cf. Wayne R. LaFave, *Arrest: The Decision to Take a Suspect into Custody* (Boston: Little, Brown, 1965).

What seems like such slipshod procedure—not to speak of diagnostic arrogance—in the one study is partly due to the presumption on the part of psychiatric and legal decision-makers (the latter rubber-stamping the decisions of the former) that "mental illness" is really an illness like physical conditions, that it will "get worse" if not treated, that effective treatment is possible, and that involuntary treatment is at worst neutral but not harmful. Scheff points out that these presumptions are not necessarily held by many psychiatrists and that they are increasingly being questioned.[9] These presumptions along with the basic medical decision-rule that it is better to make illness-errors constitute a model of one kind of decision process in the handling of deviance. It is perhaps, better to call it an implicit model since decision-makers may be consciously aware of only parts of it.

Scheff calls these presumptions into question by developing a theory of "being mentally ill." This theory—because it is the clearest presentation in the "societal reaction" school of the etiology of a form of deviance—deserves more extended presentation as an example of the approach. Moreover, presentation of the propositions of the theory coupled with more general discussion of the "societal reaction" approach will help show how the theories of etiology relate to theories of decision-making process.

One is, of course, always tempted to see "schools" where they may not exist, for example, in this loosely akin set of viewpoints which characterizes the work of men like Lemert, Kai Erikson, and John Kitsuse, to which we have already referred as well as the work of Howard Becker and, to some degree, of David Matza. They may not all accept the labeling label however.[10]

Scheff defines mental illness as "residual rule-breaking," that is, violation of rules which are fundamental to social interaction but not codified. His propositions are as follows.

1. Residual rule-breaking arises from fundamentally diverse sources: organic, psychological, situations of stress, volitional acts of innovation or defiance.
2. Relative to the rate of treated mental illness the rate of unrecorded residual rule-breaking is extremely high.
3. Most residual rule-breaking is "denied" and is of transitory significance.
4. Stereotyped imagery of mental disorder is learned in early childhood.
5. The stereotypes of insantiy are continually reaffirmed, inadvertently, in ordinary social interaction.
6. Labeled deviants may be regarded for playing the stereotyped deviant role.
7. Labeled deviants are punished when they attempt the return to conventional roles.
8. In the crisis occuring when a residual rule-breaker is publicly labeled, the deviant is highly suggestible, and may accept the label.
9. Among residual rule-breakers, labeling is the single most important cause of careers of residual deviance.

[9] Thomas J. Scheff, *Being Mentally Ill, op. cit.,* p. 151.

[10] Howard S. Becker, *Outsiders* (New York: Free Press of Glencoe, 1963). David Matza, *Delinquency and Drift* (New York: John Wiley & Sons, 1964). For a critique of the labeling school see Jack P. Gibbs, "Conceptions of Deviant Behavior: New and Old," *Pacific Sociological Review* (Spring 1966), pp. 9–14.

It is impossible to present the theory in more detail here. The propositions are discussed and supporting evidence presented in two entire chapters of the book covering seventy-two pages. In any event it is not our concern to evaluate the theory as a theory of mental illness.

The theory displays the basic elements of the "labeling" school approach: an assumption of widespread deviance which is reponded to in a variety of ways. Given certain kinds of response the deviance can become stabilized into a deviant role or "career." A few criticisms rather generally applicable to the school can be pointed out.

First, it assumes an essentially empty organism or at least one with little or no autonomous capacity to determine conduct. The process of developing deviance seems all societal response and no deviant stimulus. Second, in the case of mental illness and the Scheff theory specifically, there is no attempt to differentiate the varieties of mental illness. Third, and perhaps most significantly, it locates the fate of the deviant, and indeed his very development, in the acts of the reactors, especially, of course, reactors in positions of power. The labeling perspective need not, but often does, become an ideology of the underdog. Finally, in practice, though not necessarily in principle, there is a strong tendency to look at the visible end of the selection process, that is, at those cases where the societal reaction seems to be involved in the development of stabilized "career" deviance. Rarely are the successes of social control observed or discussed. As a theory of the etiology of stabilized deviance or as a base for social policy, the "labeling" perspective will be extremely weak, if not positively misleading, until it solves the vexatious methodological problems of longitudinal analysis, taking account of those cases which do *not* develop into "career" deviants.

In order to do so successfully, the approach will have to pay more attention to variables locatable in the deviant himself or in his prereaction social history.

Sociologists have traditionally served the overdog by providing a sympathetic link to various underdogs, but the details change from period to period. The deviant as underdog seems to be coming into his own, and, correlatively, "due process" seems to be replacing earlier welfare-oriented shibboleths. In any event, it seems easy for this perspective to turn into a kind of witchhunt in reverse—the witches now being the decision-makers rather than the deviants. In the next section our examination of police decision-making with delinquents will indicate how complex matters can be.

We have already mentioned that the most central intellectual ancestor of the "labeling" approach is Edwin M. Lemert. It was he who developed the core concepts of primary and secondary deviance and held out for a view of norm-creating and deviance-labeling that stressed the lack of normative integration of modern society and the opportunity for many diverse and "self-interested" organizations to impose special moral and legal standards on behavior.[11]

[11] Edwin M. Lemert, *Social Pathology, op. cit.* For a more recent and more concise statement of Lemert's views, see Edwin M. Lemert, "Social Structure, Social Control and Deviation," in Marshall B. Clinard (ed.), *Anomie and Deviant Behavior* (New York: Free Press of Glencoe, 1964), pp. 57–97.

In some ways there is a West Coast school (many of whose members were trained elsewhere) and an East Coast school in the analysis of deviance and social control. The Eastern approach, centering on people like Parsons, Merton, and Homans, tends to begin with a model of social order and pose the problem of why there is violation of norms and to be mainly concerned with the problem of social control as part of the interest in the conditions of persistence or equilibrium of social systems. A recent volume of papers, related to Merton's theory of anomie and deviant behavior, reviews—for the most part critically—the relevance of one of the Eastern perspectives on the sociology of deviance.[12] The differences between these schools are not large, and, indeed, except for Lemert, the "labeling" theorists seem to have decided to honor what we have called the Easterners by almost entirely ignoring them. Among the viewpoints that do not differentiate these loose groups is the issue of whether deviance is somehow to be located in the individual rather than in social process and social structure. The almost hysterical insistence among the "labeling" theorists that this is a key matter differentiates them largely from some psychiartrists—mainly old-fashioned ones. At least this issue does not differentiate sociologists from each other on principle. As David Matza has pointed out, however, some of the research strategy of sociological positivists implies a view of deviance such as that criticized by the "labelers."[13]

Earlier we presented our view that the "societal reaction" approach concerns itself mainly with areas of ambiguity. We used the term behavioral ambiguity to refer to situations where the norms were relatively clear but there was difficulty in determining whether a particular act was prohibited. The societal reaction approach has also called attention to the nature and consequences of normative ambiguity and especially to the processes whereby norms are created in modern society.[14]

Ours is an age, of course, of conscious norm-making, through law mainly, but also heavily through rules of formal organizations. Ours is also an age of pressure politics, and norm-making through law is often the consequence of successful use of the lawmaking process by pressure groups.

Howard S. Becker has coined the term "moral entrepreneurs" to denote persons or groups who take on themselves—for whatever motives—the task of securing the prohibition of particular behaviors.[15] Such moral entrepreneurs may be either public or private groups. Becker describes the elaborate and successful campaign of the Federal Bureau of Narcotics to secure passage of the Marijuana Tax Act. The campaign included not only the usual lobbying and testimony before congressional com-

[12] Marshall B. Clinard (ed.), *Anomie and Deviant Behavior* (New York: Free Press of Glencoe, 1964). This volume is also very useful for other theoretical discussions, an excellent bibliography, and reviews of recent research on gang delinquency, mental disorder, drug addiction, and alcoholism. Talcott Parson's classic statement is in his, *The Social System* (Glencoe, Ill.: Free Press, 1951), chap. vii. George C. Homans' most succinct discussion is in his, *The Human Group* (New York: Harcourt Brace, 1950), chap. 11.

[13] David Matza, *Delinquency and Drift* (New York: John Wiley & Sons, 1965), esp. chap. 1.

[14] They are by no means alone or even prominent in doing so. At least as significant has been the dramatic development of interest in the sociology of law in American sociology in the last decade. See Jerome H. Skolnick, "The Sociology of Law in America: Overview and Trends," in *Law and Society*, a supplement to *Social Problems*, 13 (Summer 1965), pp. 11–39.

[15] Howard S. Becker, *The Outsiders* (New York: Free Press of Glencoe, 1963), chap. 8.

mittees, but also a program of propaganda designed to inflame public opinion against "dope fiends."[16]

Social Control Agencies: The Police

The police, of course, make many decisions in the processing of deviants–juvenile and adult. It is useful to focus discussion of recent studies of the police by taking up a branch of research closely related to the decision-making studies emphasized by Scheff and others. Considerable attention has been paid recently to studies of police decision-making with juveniles, and it is to this material that we will soon turn. Decision-making with respect to juveniles–as complex as it turns out to be–is, however, only one of the kinds of decisions made by police. In a recent book on a municipal police department, Jerome H. Skolnick analyzes a variety of law-enforcement situations.[17]

Police discretion is of concern not only to the sociologist of deviance or the sociologist of legal process, but also to the newly social-research-oriented legal scholar. The recent work of LaFave represents the most thorough and valuable work from the side of sociolegal scholarship.[18] These studies have been of discretionary decision-making by the municipal police. Only one comparable study exists of a state police unit, and it is valuable not only because of its attention to problems of decision-making in a context not covered in other studies–highway traffic control–but also because it presents an analysis of a quite differently organized kind of police unit.[19] The Preiss and Ehrlich analysis proceeds from a complex version of role theory which in itself need not concern us, but the perspective led to a discussion of the relations of organizational structure, and processes of recruitment and training to decision-making.

The relationship of police and community and links to police organization are the focus of a recent comparative study of Scottish and American police by Michael Banton.[20] Public attitudes toward police and police response thereto have also been the subject of a number of studies. A recently published one compares British survey results with surveys in three middle-sized American cities.[21]

[16] *Ibid.*, pp. 135–146.

[17] Jerome H. Skolnick, *Justice Without Trial: Law Enforcement in Democratic Society* (New York: John Wiley & Sons, 1966).

[18] Wayne R. LaFave, *Arrest: The Decision to Take a Suspect into Custody* (Boston: Little, Brown, 1965).

[19] Jack J. Preiss and Howard J. Ehrlich, *An Examination of Role Theory: The Case of the State Police* (Lincoln: University of Nebraska Press, 1966).

[20] Michael Banton, *The Policeman in the Community* (New York: Basic Books, 1965).

[21] John P. Clark, "Isolation of the Police: A Comparison of the British and American Situations," *Journal of Criminal Law, Criminology and Police Science,* 56 (1965), pp. 307–319. Two classic articles are William A. Westley, "Violence and the Police," *American Journal of Sociology,* XLIX (August 1953), pp. 34–41; and the same author's "Secrecy and the Police," *Social Forces,* XXXIV (March 1956), pp. 254–257. The most elaborate opinion survey is British. See Royal Commission on the Police, "Relations Between the Police and the Public," Appendix IV to the Minutes of Evidence. Prepared by R. Morton Williams (London: Her Majesty's Stationary Office, 1962). For an insightful comparison of British and American public attitudes as they relate to police culture see Jerome H. Skolnick, *op. cit.,* chap. 3.

These and other topics—police decision-making, the relations of police organization to community environment, the development of modern police, changes in the organization and internal control of police departments, and the police role as it relates to recruitment and training—are dealt with in a collection of essays on the police scheduled to appear in early 1967.[22]

Of particular significance for the sociology of police are the problems of variations among police departments and changes in police organization over time. These have been the focus of two especially influential papers by James Q. Wilson, one published and the other soon to appear.[23] Both change and variation involve significant differences in the processes of command and control in police departments. These processes are the subject of a recent article which examines them in the context of police modernization, police deployment patterns, occupational culture, and variations in the structure of civilian control over the police.[24] Police bureaucratization as it relates to the legal and political structures of different societies, the sensitivity of regimes to politicized violence, and the capacity of the police to behave legally in conditions of community conflict is treated in an article in the forthcoming new edition of the *International Encyclopedia of the Social Sciences.*[25] In another paper Allan Silver deals with the establishment of modern police in Britain with especial attention to the need for a nonmilitary body to intervene between threatened elities and the "dangerous classes."[26]

Decision-Making with Juveniles

While there has been considerable speculation over the years as to the criteria used by police in making disposition decisions with juveniles, it was not until a study by Nathan Goldman in four communities near Pittsburgh, orginally conducted in 1950, that any serious empirical work was done.[27] Since that time a number of other studies

[22] David J. Bordua (ed.), *The Police: Six Sociological Essays* (New York: John Wiley & Sons, in press).

[23] The published paper is James Q. Wilson, "The Police and Their Problems: A Theory," *Public Policy,* XII (1963), pp. 189–216. The unpublished paper by the same author is "The Police and the Delinquent in Two Cities." It is scheduled to appear in a volume on delinquency control, edited by Stanton W. Wheeler, to be published by John Wiley & Sons.

[24] David J. Bordua and Albert J. Reiss, Jr., "Command, Control and Charisma: Reflections on Police Bureaucracy," *American Journal of Sociology,* 72 (July 1966), pp. 68–76. See also Albert J. Reiss, Jr. and David J. Bordua, "Organization and Environment: A Perspective on the Municipal Police," in David J. Bordua (ed.), *The Police: Six Sociological Essays, op. cit.*

[25] David J. Bordua, "Police," *International Encylopedia of the Social Sciences* (forthcoming).

[26] Allan Silver, "On the Demand for Order in Civil Society," in David J. Bordua (ed.), *The Police: Six Sociological Essays, op. cit.*

[27] Nathan Goldman, *The Differential Selection of Offenders for Court Appearance* (Washington, D.C.: National Research and Information Center and National Council on Crime and Delinquency, 1963).

directly on the subject have appeared.[28] In addition, at least two studies have appeared which included considerable related material.[29]

Goldman's early study was mainly concerned with discovering sources of bias in criminological statistics rather than with the decision-making process itself. It also showed a concern with the problem of socioeconomic bias in police decision-making. We shall not follow out the interest in criminal statistics but will revert to the theme of socioeconomic bias.

In his later interpretation of the study results, Goldman arrived at the following conclusions. Decision-criteria close to the contact situation which seemed to affect dispositions were seriousness of the offense and race, age, and sex of the offender. Negroes and older boys and girls were more likely to be referred to court. Goldman also points out that these criteria interact. Thus, differential referral of Negroes seems confined to minor offenses.

Goldman also was able to analyze variations among the communities studied. Among the most interesting findings was the fact that court referral rates varied from 9 per cent to 71 per cent. Looked at in terms of release rather than referral—a perspective we shall employ later—the police departments in Goldman's study let go from 29 per cent to 91 per cent of the juveniles they took into custody.

McEachern and Bauzer found that offense seriousness, length of previous record, ethnic origin, sex, age, intactness of family, and probation status were all related to police dispositions. There were important interactions between these variables so that when offense is held constant the effects of family intactness, ethnicity, and sex are eliminated, and the effects of previous record and probation status are reduced. The effect of age remains the same.

Controlling for the effects of offense category increased the effects of the year in which the police contact occured, of department differences, and of differences in court referral rates between individual officers.[30]

In his study in Syracuse, Bodine discovered an even more complex picture. He

[28] A. W. McEachern and Riva Bauzer, "Factors Related to Disposition in Juvenile Police Contacts," in Malcom W. Klein and Barbara G. Meyerhof (eds.), *Juvenile Gangs in Context: Research, Theory, and Action,* University of Southern California Youth Studies Center, 1963 (Mimeo.); Irving Piliavin and Scott Briar, "Police Encounters with Juveniles," *American Journal of Sociology,* LXX (September 1964), pp. 206–214; George E. Bodine, "Factors Related to Police Dispositions of Juvenile Offenders," Syracuse University Youth Development Center (Paper read at the annual meeting of the American Sociological Association, Montreal, Canada, August 31, 1964); Robert M. Terry, *The Screening of Juvenile Offenders: A Study in the Societal Reaction to Deviant Behavior* (Unpublished Ph.D. Dissertation, University of Wisconsin, 1965).

[29] Charles R. Guthrie, *Law Enforcement and the Juvenile: A Study of Police Interaction with Delinquents* (Unpublished Ph.D. Dissertation, University of Southern California, 1963); William W. Wattenberg and Noel Bufe, "The Effectiveness of Police Youth Bureau Offices," *Journal of Criminal Law, Criminology, and Police Science,* 54 (December 1963), pp. 470–475.

[30] A. W. McEachern and Riva Bauzer, "Factors Related to Disposition in Juvenile Police Contacts," *op. cit.*

was particularly concerned with the relationship of income area to type of disposition. After a fairly complex multivariate analysis, the findings included the following:

1. A relationship between arrest history and disposition.
2. A relationship between arrest history and income level.
3. An interrelationship such that juveniles from low income areas committed a disproportionate share of those offenses likely to lead to referral (theft offenses).
4. After arrest history and offense type were taken into account, age was not a discernible factor in dispositions.
5. Variation between income areas was not due to race.

Bodine further concludes:

> Juveniles from low income areas have a higher referral rate to court than juveniles from high income areas for two reasons: low income youth are more often apprehended as repeating offenders, and repeating offenders have a referral rate which is twice as great as the rate for initial offenders; low income youth have a higher arrest rate for petty theft and petty thieves in general, and low income petty thieves in particular, have a higher court referral rate.[31]

One reason for the peculiar significance of petty theft in Bodine's findings was that this offense category included thefts from parking meters, which were invariably referred to court. Juveniles from low-income areas committed a large number of these offenses.

If we put together the findings of McEachern and Bauzer and of Bodine we find that offense type, arrest record, probation status, age, department, and officer all seem to affect disposition. Of the factors common to these studies and also in Goldman's, offense and previous record seem most securely established.

In a more recent study in Racine, Wisconsin, Terry found that offense, previous record, and age held up as correlates of disposition-decision out of twelve factors studied. Terry points out that his results imply a rather "legalistic" handling of juveniles and also that the much claimed socioeconomic bias of the police simply does not appear.[32]

Terry further makes the interesting observation that:

> the police appear to be remarkably lenient with juvenile violators. Even for the most serious types of offenses, the juvenile stands a relatively good chance of being released without further action.[33]

Armed with at least one version of the societal reaction perspective—which often carries with it an ideology favoring the deviant underdog—Terry seems surprised to discover leniency rather than severity, legality rather than bias. He should, perhaps, not have been surprised. Over the study period (1958-1962) the Racine police released in 88.8 percent of the offenses.[34] Surely, in order for socioeconomic bias

[31] George E. Bodine, "Factors Related to Police Dispositions of Juvenile Offenders," *op. cit.*, p. 14.

[32] Robert M. Terry, *The Screening of Juvenile Offenders: A Study in the Social Reaction to Deviant Behavior, op. cit.*, pp. 104-106.

[33] *Ibid.*, pp. 105-106.

[34] *Ibid.*, p. 72.

to appear, it would have to be monumental since after all the police must pay *some* attention to the law.

The studies by McEachern and Bauzer, Bodine, and Terry are the best available, and with some differences in detail they add up to what Terry calls a "legalistic" picture with little or no evidence of socioeconomic bias. These studies are, however, all statistical, all carried on at the "juvenile bureau" level of decision-making, all deal with formal records and, finally, all represent at least fairly high-caliber police departments.

Another study, by Piliavin and Briar, attacks the problem from a different vantage point. The authors stress the significance of the demeanor of juveniles as a set of cues used by police to make decisions. The authors conclude that demeanor is especially important in cases of first or minor offenders. Racial imbalance in the severity of police decisions is attributed to the fact that Negro boys often behave in such a way that police are more likely to be strict. While the authors do not systematically say so, it seems that a large part of their observations were of street behavior rather than of decisions at the juvenile bureau level. Only sixty-six cases are reported, and it is not possible to assess the over-all significance of the demeanor-variable in the total of decisions made by the police. Nevertheless, this study does provide some indication that, at the street-patrol level, other factors quite different from those previously discussed may be important.[35]

The patrol police differ from juvenile officers in at least three main respects. They are more offense-oriented, especially toward offenses constituting forms of public disorder. They are more often charged with the job of maintaining pressure on suspected offenders in high crime areas under police doctrines of aggressive patrol. Most significantly, they must maintain respect for police authority even when dealing with gang boys whose morale may derive largely from successful baiting of the police.[36] Juvenile officers tend to be offender-oriented and, indeed, perform a quasijudicial role not unlike that of state's attorney.

Some of the disagreement among the studies reviewed may be due to stage in the decision chain on which the research concentrates. Police decision making at different stages in the chain operate under different role pressures.

A quite provisional clue that some of the "on-street" factors may operate at the disposition stage, however, is available from an as yet incomplete study of disposition decisions in Detroit. Officers in the Detroit Youth Bureau filled out a form on

[35] Irving Piliavin and Scott Briar, "Police Encounters with Juveniles," *American Journal of Sociology,* LXX (September 1964), pp. 206–214. See also Charles R. Guthrie, *Law Enforcement and the Juvenile: A Study of Police Interaction with Delinquents, op. cit.,* for evidence that poor demeanor on the part of the juvenile may be induced by the language and manner of the officer.

[36] In another report from the same research project, gang boys are described as being aware that the patrol police may take them in for what amounts to inappropriate demeanor toward officers only to have the juvenile officer release them. See Carl Werthman and Irving Piliavin, "Gang Members and the Police," in David J. Bordua (ed.), *The Police: Six Sociological Essays, op. cit.*

first offenders which included an item called "Attitude Toward Officer." The categories and percentage on whom court petitions were filed are: Honest, 67 per-cent; Responsive, 70 per cent; Evasive, 78 per cent; Anti-Social, 80 per cent.[37]

Concern for stage in the decision chain leads naturally to concern for the ways in which the decision chain is organized and variations between departments and over time in the same department. As previously mentioned, McEachern and Bauzer have reported important variation in court referral rates in Santa Monica over a twenty-year period. Figures for Detroit for the period 1951-1964 show a steady increase in rates of referral to court from 44 per cent in 1951 to 80 per cent in 1964.

Not only are there dramatic changes in at least some departments over time, but great variation among departments. A review of studies covering some thirteen communities or groups of communities reveals a range of court referral rates by police running from a low of 9 per cent in what Goldman calls Manor Heights to the 80 per cent figure for Detroit in 1964.

In addition to the problem posed by decision stage, this amount of organizational variation indicates that understanding of police decision-making is not likely to be furthered as much by more microscopic studies of decisions within single departments as by attempts to deal with the organizational variation directly. In a study just getting under way, an attempt is being made to relate differences in juvenile release ratios initially to variations in the social characteristics of communities and later to variations among departments.

Individual police agency data secured from the Uniform Crime Reports Section of the Federal Bureau of Investigation indicate that the degree of variation observed in published studies holds true when a much larger number of departments is considered.[38]

Elements of an interpretive scheme for analyzing organizational variation are available in Goldman's discussion of differences between the communities he studied, in a paper by James Sterling, and most importantly in the as yet unpublished paper by James Q. Wilson previously cited.

In commenting upon the variations reported by Goldman, Sterling suggested that the presence or absence of a specialized juvenile bureau with an organizational existence, definition of mission, and *esprit* of its own would account for the differences.[39]

[37]The study involves a sample of 10,000 contacts with boys over the period 1952–1961 and is being conducted by David J. Bordua and James W. Harris. The concern for organizational variation which has developed out of the study is discussed in "Police Decision-Making with Juveniles," read before the Midwest Sociological Society, Madison, Wisconsin, April 22, 1966.

[38]The study is being carried out by Robert E. Ford. In reports for 1965 on 2,369 police agencies, 385 release fewer than 5 per cent of juveniles taken into custody, while at the other extreme 60 agencies release more than 95 per cent. Every other 5 per cent interval contains at least 57 agencies.

[39]James W. Sterling, "The Juvenile Offender from Community to Court: Two Stages of Decision," paper read before the Illinois Academy of Criminology, November 31, 1962. Lieutenant Sterling is with the Youth Division, Chicago Police Department.

Wilson's paper goes much farther and constitutes the most promising perspective currently available. In comparing what he calls Western City and Eastern City, Wilson summarized several departmental characteristics under the typological labels "professional" and "fraternal." Briefly put, the professional Western City department is highly centralized and staffed largely by nonresidents with high levels of education. Its juvenile officers are organized in a single central bureau and have much interaction among themselves and little with outsiders. The fraternal Eastern City department is "old style." It is markedly decentralized. Juvenile officers are part of the precinct complement and may spend their entire careers in the same precinct–it may, indeed, be the precinct in which they grew up.

In Western City the professional officers invoke universalistic criteria, arrest a larger share of the juveniles they process, and release 53 per cent. Moreover Wilson's data indicate no selective bias on socioeconomic grounds. In Eastern City the fraternal officers arrest fewer of the juveniles they process and release 70 per cent. Moreover, the gross referral rate for Negroes is 43 per cent as compared to 16 per cent for whites. This difference persists when offense is controlled, though the sample of cases is small.[40]

Wilson's analysis is too complex to pursue further, but it seems clear that the combination of community and organizational characteristics is even more complicated than his paper states. It also seems clear that the meaning of specific correlates of police disposition decisions will vary greatly from place to place and from time to time.

Police Dispositions and the Societal Reaction School

From the material on police decisions with juveniles it is possible to draw some further implications for the societal reaction or "labeling" approach to deviance. In doing so it will be useful to look at a few additional figures from Detroit.

For the year 1964 the Detroit Police Department reported 106,000 total "encounters" with juveniles. The Youth Bureau reported 34,109 "interviews" with boys. The Youth Bureau recorded 9,445 "official contacts" with Detroit boys. These official contacts involved 5,282 individuals. Of the 34,109 interviews conducted by Youth Bureau officers 10,157 were with boys not involved in delinquency but interviewed in the course of investigating complaints.[41]

Raw figures of this sort are, of course, notoriously difficult to understand. They do, however, indicate at least plausibly several things. First, the Detroit police do *not* seem eager to "pull kids in." Indeed, it is their stated policy to avoid involving juveniles in the legal apparatus whenever possible. Second, given the volume of business with juveniles, it is just as plausible to suppose that it is the level and frequency of deviance which determines the degree of police processing rather than the reverse. This is at least compatible with the findings thus far with respect to youth

[40] James Q. Wilson, "The Police and the Delinquent in Two Cities," *op. cit.*

[41] The data on Youth Bureau Operations are from Detroit Police Department Youth Bureau, *Annual Report for 1964.* The figure for department encounters was provided in a personal communication by then Inspector Robert Potts.

officers' decisions to refer to court.

Third, the idea that deviance is definable only in terms of societal reaction should be distinguished from the idea that deviants are defined by societal processes. This distinction between norm-making, deviance-defining, and deviant-labeling, not always made by the societal reaction school, is closely related to our earlier distinction between normative and behavioral ambiguity.[42]

Finally, such figures lead to an obvious problem which tends to be scanted by the societal reaction people. Is not the typical funnel-shaped selection process illustrated by these Detroit figures a consequence of the fact that social control efforts that work with most fail with a few? Is it not plausible to look at these figures as showing not or at least not only that the social control process is producing deviance by developing stabilized deviants but that it is also reducing deviance through the deterrent effect of control efforts?

The societal reaction approach as we have mentioned pays little attention to the successes of social control, only to the failures—if by success we mean either the prevention or reversal of deviant careers or the reduction of behavioral deviance through the symbolic effects of the way in which more serious deviants are treated. The processes which produce stabilized deviants may be precisely the ones which reduce deviance in the population as a whole. This is, of course, an old idea and is implicit in Erikson's argument about boundary maintenance. Boundary maintenance may be effective to the degree that it creates the "outsiders" with whom Becker is concerned. Thus, the functionalism of Erikson accords ill with the antifunctionalism of others in the labeling tradition. The contradictions are not clear, however, until one complements the "career"-oriented labeling perspective with the social-system-oriented perspective more apparent in others.

It is not necessary to argue that the decision process *necessarily* (though it may) makes ritual scapegoats out of a few more or less randomly chosen norm violators.

All of this is not intended to urge a pollyanna perspective on police decision-making. Nevertheless, it does serve to highlight weak points in the general labeling orientation which should be considered along with its strength.

Broadly speaking, a police juvenile unit with a selective process such as that illustrated by the Detroit figures or by Terry's report of Racine seems to operate on the basis of what might be called a "well intentioned punishment" model. The police believe in punishment as the proper response to crime but define it as unpleasant and something a large part of the juvenile population should be spared. The basic principle according to which specialized juvenile units were originally organized was that keeping juveniles out of the legal apparatus was much to be desired. Further work on such implicit or explicit models of the decision process would seem a promising avenue of future development.[43]

[42] See Jack P. Gibbs, "Conceptions of Deviant Behavior: The Old and the New," *op. cit.*, for a critique which takes up some of these same points from a somewhat different perspective.

[43] See David Sudnow, "Normal Crimes: Sociological Features of the Penal Code in a Public Defender's Office," *op. cit.*

This kind of analysis of variation both in decision ideologies and also in the effects of different ways decision processes are organized would help correct some of the ideological one-sidedness apparent in the labeling perspective. One can hardly fault a concern for social justice, yet some of these writers not only seem in a state of continual outrage, but also seem about to substitute a naive view of justice derived from eighteenth-century legal theory for the naive "therapeutic" views which they criticize.[44]

Thus, Terry's study in Racine is marred not only by the failure to think through the implications of the 89 per cent release rate, but by the failure to consider until after the data were in and analyzed that the police in Racine might be playing the game straight. Indeed the penchant for criticism (perhaps especially of the police who have never been the symbolic favorites of sociologists) can be so great that decision-makers are damned whatever they do. When he discovers that the juvenile officers seem to behave rather "legalistically," Terry criticizes them by invoking more "therapeutic" standards derived from statements of the United States Children's Bureau.[45] He seems unaware that being more "therapeutic" would necessarily introduce many of those elements of doubtfully legitimate selectivity that he failed to find in Racine.

The labeling perspective can, under at least some circumstances, lead to a naive perspective on the great human problem of the balance between order and justice. Some of the recent work by sociologists on the police is couched in terms of this dilemma.[46]

Jurisprudence constitutes, however, the largest reservoir of thought on such matters, and it may not be amiss to conclude this brief paper with a quotation indicative of a view more balanced than some we have considered.

Where the early surveys (of the administration of justice) seemed to assume that the ideal system was one in which all suspects are arrested, prosecuted, convicted, and sentenced, we assume that the ideal is one where intelligent and consistent decisions are made as to who, among even the clearly guilty, will be arrested, prosecuted, convicted and sentenced. The aim is not, in other words, statistically measurable efficiency but rather a more difficult to measure, intelligent and responsible exercise of discretion.[47]

[44] David Matza's highly regarded discussion of the sense of injustice as it relates to the subculture of delinquency should be read in this light. See David Matza, *Delinquency and Drift, op. cit.*, chap. 4.

[45] Robert M. Terry, "The Screening of Juvenile Offenders: A Study in the Societal Reaction to Deviant Behavior," *op. cit.*, p. 105.

[46] See Jerome H. Skolnick, *Justice Without Trial: Law Enforcement in Democratic Society, op. cit.*, esp. chap. 1. Also see David J. Bordua (ed.), *The Police: Six Sociological Essays, op. cit.*, especially the chapter by Albert J. Reiss, Jr. and David J. Bordua, "Environment and Organization: A Perspective on the Municipal Police," and the chapter by John H. McNamara, "Uncertainties in Police Work: The Relevance of Recruits' Backgrounds and Training."

[47] Frank J. Remington, in Editor's Foreword to Wayne R. LaFave, *Arrest: The Decision to Take a Suspect into Custody, op. cit.*, p. xvii.

Section VII

Treatment: Corrections and Prevention

Introductory Remarks

To what extent the higher rates of crime and delinquency are a reflection of an actual increase in lawbreaking behavior and to what extent they reflect an increase in the willingness to observe and report that which has previously been ignored or handled informally are unknown. Nevertheless, what motivates people to act and react, whether based on fact and/or fiction, is what is felt to be real.

From this perspective, crime and delinquency are generating fear, hostility, and disgust among the American people.[1] *It is this mood that has contributed to favoring the maximum use of correctional resources, particularly imprisonment. The public may be under the delusion that what passes for corrections today, if resorted to fully, will assure its safety, will deter, and will correct. The public's attention, therefore, is focused more on apprehension and judicial activities than it is on the activities within the correctional experience.*

However, today's correctional experiences (i.e., probation, parole, jails, prisons, training schools) cannot be viewed as a comprehensive *and* sequential *process of instituting individual and sociocultural changes that prepare the offender for the inevitability of self-determination. Because of public sentiments, existing facilities, nature of personnel, and extremely heavy caseloads, in actual fact correctional personnel dominantly resort either to repression and punishment as tools of control (in institutions) or to an unbelievable superficiality in supervising offenders (probation and parole). Furthermore, controls that characterize the correctional experience disappear once the offender completes his correctional assignment. Practices that are both* comprehensive *and* individualized *are the exceptions to the statement above.*

The sources (e.g., traditions, collective sentiments, sociocultural arrangements) that contribute to these practices do not concern us here. For whatever the sources, the results do not satisfy our favored cultural criteria: effectiveness and practicality. The available historical-empirical evidence does not indicate that the practices are effective–it does provide evidence that they are harmful both to offenders and to communities.

For example, in spite of our severe sentences for those adults who are incarcerated and in spite of the increasing numbers of juveniles who are institutionalized, about 95 percent will eventually be released back into the community. Considering com-

[1] See the Introduction to the present book.

munity safety and the limits of correctional resources, we can ill afford to continue to experience a return engagement of most of these offenders. Furthermore, assuming that decision-makers had the courage and the determination to fully implement a repressive-punitive ideology by indefinitely incarcerating all offenders, we certainly do not have the means (i.e., laws, public consensus, correctional personnel, facilities, monies) within our existing social economic and political framework to do so.

Therefore, from the viewpoint of efficiency and practicality, the reliance either on lax supervision or on repression and punishment results in not preparing the offender for life in the community, and in the final analysis, in not protecting the community.

Because of greater awareness of the ineffectiveness and impracticality of the old ideology and because of moral sentiments, nonpunitive settings incorporating innovative techniques in the treatment of offenders and in the prevention of delinquency are gradually being stressed as a more favored alternative. This is occurring not only in theory, but also in practice. A host of these innovative techniques are being utilized in correctional treatment and in prevention with individuals and within group settings. There is no final evidence that this emerging alternative is more effective than the old or that the old should be totally discarded for all offenders. However, evidence that aspects of this approach have been successful with certain offenders warrants continued experimentation.

In addition, the new ideology, unlike the old, does reflect more fully some of the accumulated knowledge in the behavioral sciences concerning the nature of man in society. However, the introduction of the new ideology has just begun. Its domination may not be realized in the immediate years to come. There are a number of reasons that account for the wide gap between correctional practices and available knowledge in the behavioral sciences. One reason is that theory cannot always be easily translated into practice. Another is that legislative controls governing correctional practices and expenditures in some states are heavily molded by certain population groups (e.g., rural, union, industry). Neither is it expected that jurisdictions with difficulties in taking care of their children, their ill, and their aged (particularly counties) will divert a noticeable part of their funds derived from their limited tax bases to the treatment of offenders.

Nor is it by any means a simple task to challenge the traditionally-bound power groups dominating many settings. Thus, the new warden or social worker with his innovative, rehabilitative ideas may soon have to face the fact that the guards may indeed run the prison. It is also difficult to encourage probation personnel, as it is with other vested interest groups (e.g., social workers, school personnel, police), to experiment with lay people operating as assistant probation counselors. In addition, although there is great variation in the personal qualities and training of corrections personnel, many of the personnel do not come close to possessing the qualities and training considered necessary to fully implement nonpunitive, rehabilitative programs. Neither should we forget that the introduction of innovative approaches requires not only significant changes in practices but also extensive reorganization and substitution of existing facilities and personnel.

44. Corrections

The President's Commission on Law Enforcement and Administration of Justice

The American correctional system is an extremely diverse amalgam of facilities, theories, techniques, and programs. It handles nearly 1.3 million offenders on an average day; it has 2.5 million admissions in the course of a year; and its annual operating budget is over a billion dollars.* Correctional operations are administered by Federal, State, county, and municipal governments. Some jurisdictions have developed strong programs for the control and rehabilitation of offenders. But most lack capacity to cope with the problems of preventing recidivism—the commission of further offenses. Some fail even to meet standards of humane treatment recognized for decades....

Corrections remains a world almost unknown to law-abiding citizens, and even those within it often know only their own particular corner....

•••

Correctional Institutions

There are today about 400 institutions for adult felons in this country, ranging from some of the oldest and largest prisons in the world to forestry camps for 30 or 40 trusted inmates. Some are grossly understaffed and underequipped—conspicuous products of public indifference. Overcrowding and idleness are the salient features of some, brutality and corruption of a few others. Far too few are well organized and adequately funded. Juvenile institutions tend to be better, but also vary greatly. The local jails and workhouses that handle most misdemeanants are generally the most inadequate in every way.

Reprinted from "American Corrections: An Overview and Directions for the Future" from *Task Force Report: Corrections,* a Report by The President's Commission on Law Enforcement and Administration of Justice (Washington: Government Printing Office, 1967), pp. 1-16.

*Editor's note: The statistics from the 1965 National Survey of Corrections indicate nearly a third of 1.3 million offenders represent juvenile offenders. A breakdown of the figure of 1.3 million offenders (juveniles and adults) indicate 95 percent were males; 426,000 (one-third) offenders were incarcerated; and 857,000 were undergoing supervision in the community. The average operating cost for each incarcerated offender was for juveniles: $3,613 and for adults: $1,966. The average operating cost for each offender supervised in the community was for juveniles: $328 and for adults: $198. These operating costs do not include misdemeanant corrections.

Although most inmates of American correctional institutions come from metropolitan areas, the institutions themselves often are located away from urban areas and even primary transportation routes. The original reasons for such locations were diverse and, to a large extent, now outdated: interest in banishing dangerous persons to a remote locale; belief that a rural setting is salutary for slum-reared delinquents; the desire of rural legislators to create public employment among their constituents. Remoteness interferes with efforts to reintegrate inmates into their communities and makes it hard to recruit correctional staff, particularly professionals.

Prisons designed for secure custody typically have been built of stone, steel, and concrete. They are noteworthy for their endurance. Sixty-one prisons opened before 1900 are still in use. In the juvenile field, 16 percent of the living units in State training schools are at least 50 years old.

There are still many large maximum-security prisons operating in the United States today. The directory of the American Correctional Association showed a 1965 average population of over 2,000 inmates in 21 prisons. Four of these had well over 4,000 inmates each: San Quentin in California; the Illinois State Prison complex at Joliet and Stateville; the Michigan State Prison at Jackson; and the Ohio State Penitentiary at Columbus.

Rehabilitative services for the adult offender are most likely to be available in correctional facilities for felons. Very few jails, where misdemeanants are confined, have advanced beyond the level of minimum sanitation and safety standards for inmates and guards. The net result is that only a small fraction of the adult offenders who were incarcerated in jails in 1965 were receiving any correctional services except restraint.

The picture is somewhat brighter for juveniles. In 1965 there were 220 State-operated facilities for juveniles, with a total capacity of 42,423. In addition, there were 83 locally operated institutions for juveniles, with a total capacity of 6,634. Many of these institutions were well staffed and equipped.

Juvenile institution programs have been the subject of considerable attention. Although many principles are generally agreed to—including the importance of using small units, relatively brief periods of confinement, and stress on remedial education—there still remains much difference of opinion concerning the type of rehabilitation required for the young offender. Some institutions emphasize discipline and strict conformity to the rules. Others focus on psychiatrically oriented programs administered by clinical personnel. Still others seek to achieve a "therapeutic community" in which the total milieu of institutional life itself becomes a medium of change. And this enumeration is not exhaustive.

Community Treatment

While most offenders now under correctional control—some two-thirds, including those on parole after institutionalization—are in the community, the "treatment" afforded them is more illusion than reality. Impressive probation and parole operations do exist here and there around the country. Some experimental projects have built up evidence for particular techniques and documented their superiority to penal confinement for reducing recidivism. But the United States spends only 20 percent of its corrections budget and allocates only 15 percent of its total staff to service the 67 percent of offenders in the corrections workload who are under community supervision.

Probation and parole officers have too much to do and too little time in which to do it. Over 76 percent of all misdemeanants and 67 percent of all felons on probation are in caseloads of 100 or over, though experience and available research data indicate an average of 35 is about the highest likely to permit effective supervision and assistance. At best, they receive cursory treatment from overworked probation officers who must also spend typically half of their time preparing presentence investigations for the court. In addition, their efforts often are held suspect by employers, police, school officials, and other community figures whose help is essential if the offender is to be fitted into legitimate activities.

The statistics from the National Survey of Corrections make clear the enormity of the community treatment task and the smallness of the resources available to accomplish it. They do not, however, convey the everyday problems and frustrations which result from that disparity. These incidents are only examples:

A probation officer has arranged a meeting with a 16-year-old boy, on probation for car theft for the past 2 months. The boy begins to open up and talk for the first time. He explains that he began to "slip into the wrong crowd" a year or so after his stepfather died. He says that it would help to talk about it. But there isn't time; the waiting room is full, and the boy is not scheduled to come back for another 15-minute conference until next month.

A parole officer feels that a 29-year-old man, on parole after serving 3 years for burglary, is heading for trouble. He frequently is absent from his job and there is a report of his hanging around a bar which has a bad reputation. The parole officer thinks that now is a critical time to straighten things out—before it is too late. He makes a couple of calls to find his man, without success, then considers going out to look for him. But he decides against it. He is already far behind in dictating "revocations" on parolees who have failed and are being returned to prison.

A young, enthusiastic probation officer goes to see his supervisor and presents a plan for "something different," a group counseling session to operate three evenings a week for juvenile probationers and their parents. The supervisor tells him to forget it. "You've got more than you can handle now, getting up presentence reports for the judge. Besides, we don't have any extra budget for a psychiatrist to help out."

In each of these situations the offender is denied the counseling and supervision that are the main objects of probation and parole. Because the officer is too overworked to provide these services, the offender is left on his own. If he does not succeed, he loses and the community loses too.

• • •

Directions for the Future

In several senses corrections today may stand at the threshold of a new era, promising resolution of a significant number of the problems that have vexed it throughout its development. At the very least, it is developing the theory and practical groundwork for a new approach to rehabilitation of the most important group of offenders—those, predominantly young and lower-class, who are not committed to crime as a way of life and do not pose serious dangers to the community.

It is beginning to accumulate evidence from carefully controlled experimentation that may help guide its efforts more scientifically. Its increasing focus on rehabilitation has, according to recent opinion polls, found widespread acceptance among members of the general public. And, sitting as it were at the crossroads of a dozen disciplines—among them law, sociology, social work, psychology, and psychiatry—dealing with problems of poverty, unemployment, education, and morality, corrections has also attracted the interest of increasing numbers of talented people.

•••

Reintegration of the Offender into the Community. The general underlying premise for the new directions in corrections is that crime and delinquency are symptoms of failures and disorganization of the community as well as of individual offenders. In particular, these failures are seen as depriving offenders of contact with the institutions that are basically responsible for assuring development of law-abiding conduct: sound family life, good schools, employment, recreational opportunities, and desirable companions, to name only some of the more direct influences. The substitution of deleterious habits, standards, and associates for these strengthening influences contributes to crime and delinquency.

The task of corrections therefore includes building or rebuilding solid ties between offender and community, integrating or reintegrating the offender into community life—restoring family ties, obtaining employment and education, securing in the larger sense a place for the offender in the routine functioning of society. This requires not only efforts directed toward changing the individual offender, which has been almost the exclusive focus of rehabilitation, but also mobilization and change of the community and its institutions. And these efforts must be undertaken without giving up the important control and deterrent role of corrections, particularly as applied to dangerous offenders.

•••

Increased Use of Community Treatment. The main treatment implication of reintegration concepts is the value of community-based corrections. Most of the tasks that are now carried out by correctional officials would still be required if the goal of reintegration were adopted: diagnosis and classification, counseling, application of necessary controls and sanctions.

But probation and parole would have wider functions than are now usually emphasized within their casework guidance orientation. They would have to take much more responsibility for such matters as seeing that offenders get jobs and settle into responsible work habits; arranging reentry into schools and remedial tutoring or vocational training; giving guidance and counseling to an offender's family; securing housing in a neighborhood without the temptations of bad companions; or getting a juvenile into neighborhood club activities or athletic teams.

•••

While the efforts of corrections to date to alter the operations of community institutions as they affect offenders have not been extensive or highly visible, they have shown that much can be done within the existing frame-work of communities. For example, arrangements have been made with employment service agencies to assign special staff for the placement of offenders in jobs. Schools have developed special counseling and work-study programs for delinquent youth in cooperation with local correctional officials. Some recreation agencies have focused their efforts upon young people referred and supervised by probation departments. Gains have been made in breaking down the legal and administrative procedures which exclude offenders from employment through bonding and licensing requirements and through policies which make them ineligible to compete for many jobs because of a criminal record.

• • •

A somewhat different set of examples of what can be done along these lines are the special community programs that have been established in several places, including New Jersey, California, and Utah, for juveniles so involved in delinquency that they would ordinarily be incarcerated. It has been found in some cases that they can achieve higher rates of success if, instead of being committed to an institution, they are assigned to new types of community facilities where they must report daily for intensive counseling, work, and training, or where they live while working or attending school in the community.

In the sense that they employ residential facilities or themselves provide rehabilitative programs exclusively for offenders, they are pragmatic modifications of the community treatment-reintegration ideal. But their location in cities and their wide use of neighborhood facilities and opportunities avoids the inward orientation and isolated subculture of the conventional institution.

These special community programs also have a major advantage in that they permit staff to become closely aware of the offender's relationships at home, at school, and in community social groups. Their cost in relation to the number of youths handled is generally much higher than the cost of regular probation supervision, but lower than the cost of institutional confinement.

Closer to the model of reintegration through employment of community resources is the Youth Services Bureau proposed and discussed in chapter 3 of the Commission's General Report and in the volume on juvenile delinquency. These facilities would handle not only adjudicated delinquents referred to them by juvenile courts but also youths who had not gotten into trouble but needed various kinds of activities or help to avoid it. The bureaus might themselves provide some of these services—tutoring; after-school, weekend, and vacation jobs; recreation and social contacts; and clinical treatment. Or they might employ the resources of schools, private welfare agencies, and other community institutions. To the extent that, by accepting others than adjudicated offenders, they could avoid labeling those who came to them as delinquents and thus setting them off from normal society, the Youth Services Bureaus would fulfill one of the main aims of reintegrative community treatment.

For even without the addition of new roles for probation and parole in working with community institutions, treatment outside of a prison or training school avoids the breaking down of community ties and labeling that makes rehabilitation doubly difficult. Correctional practice can thus begin, as indeed some progressive jurisdictions already have begun, simply by making maximum use of conventional probation and parole. There have been several recent demonstrations that the proportion of persons on probation or parole can be increased without increasing rates of recidivism. For example, the State of Texas doubled the number of persons placed on parole in the period between 1958 and 1960 and maintained a constant rate of recidivism....

Blurring Lines Between Institution and Community. Closely allied in premise and method to new concepts in community treatment are a variety of attempts to remove some of the isolating effects of institutionalization and to ease the difficult transition back into the community for those who have been confined to prison or training school. Historically, parole itself began in part as such an attempt, and such other means as halfway houses and work-release programs have also been used in a few States for years.

But this report envisions such basic changes as construction of a wholly new kind of correctional institution for general use. This would be architecturally and methodologically the antithesis of the traditional fortress-like prison, physically and psychologically isolated from the larger society and serving primarily as a place of banishment. It would be small and fairly informal in structure. Located in or near the population center from which its inmates came, it would permit flexible use of community resources, both in the institution and for inmates released to work or study or spend short periods of time at home. Its closest existing models are some of the residential centers developed in the special juvenile treatment programs mentioned above, and the halfway houses that have been developed in a number of communities for released prisoners.

This type of institution would perform many functions. It would receive newly committed inmates and carry out extensive screening and classification with them. For those who are not returned quickly to community treatment, the new institutions would provide short-term, intensive treatment before placing them in the community under appropriate supervision. Still other offenders, after careful diagnosis, would be sent to the higher custody facilities required for long-term confinement of more difficult and dangerous inmates. But they might be eventually returned to the small facility as a port of reentry to the community.

The "partial release" programs that such a community-based institution would facilitate can also in many instances be employed in traditional facilities. In recent years the most dramatic increase in programs of graduated release from prisons has been in the area of work release. A work-release program was first introduced in Wisconsin institutions for misdemeanants in 1913 under that State's Huber Act, but for over four decades its use spread slowly. Large-scale extension to adult felons began with North Carolina legislation in 1959. Favorable experience there led to work release for felons in the early 1960's in South Carolina, Maryland, and other States in rapid succession. Work release for Federal prisoners was authorized by the Prisoner Rehabilitation Act of 1965. The record with work release has been predominantly favorable, despite some difficulties inherent in the lack of experience in administering it.

A variant of this program, sometimes called study release, is praticularly appropriate for juvenile and youthful offenders. It is highly developed at several State establishments and at the Federal prerelease guidance centers. Prerelease guidance centers and halfway houses are themselves central to the concept of reintegrating offenders into the community and should be developed as complete alternatives to traditional institutionalization for some offenders. The New York State Youth Board, for example, has several centers consisting of a few apartments within large apartment buildings that serve primarily as an alternative to traditional training school commitment but are also used as prerelease centers.

Such programs permit offenders to cope with release problems in manageable pieces, rather than trying to develop satisfactory home relationships, employment, and leisure-time activity all at once. They also permit staff to carry out early and continuing assessment of individuals' progress under actual stresses.

Maximizing Participation in Treatment. Traditional prisons, jails, and juvenile institutions are highly impersonal and authoritarian. Mass handling, countless ways of humiliating the inmate in order to make him subservient to rules and orders, special rules of behavior designed to maintain social distance between keepers and inmates, frisking of inmates, regimented movement to work, eat, and play, drab prison clothing, and similar aspects of daily life—all tend to depersonalize the inmate and reinforce his belief that authority is to be opposed, not cooperated with. The phrase much heard in inmate circles—"do your own time"—is a slogan which expresses alienation and indifference to the interests of both staff and other inmates. Such an attitude is, of course, antithetical to successful reintegration.

In contrast with this traditional system, a new concept of relationships in correctional institutions, the "collaborative regime," has been evolving during the past few decades. An outstanding feature of this trend is increased communication between custodial staff, inmates, and treatment staff. Custodial staff, by virtue of their number and their close contact with all aspects of an inmate's life, have a great potential for counseling functions, both with inmates and in organized group discussions. Instructors, administrators, and business staff also have been brought into the role of counselors and have been assigned rehabilitative functions in some programs.

Another important dimension of this collaborative concept of institutional life is the involvement of inmates themselves in important treatment functions. Group counseling sessions, particularly, have become settings in some institutions for inmates to help each other, often through hard and insistent demands for honesty in self-examination, demands that cannot be provided with equal force and validity by staff who have not as individuals shared experience in the manipulative world of criminal activity. Group counseling has also been extended with success to community treatment.

...

The Purposes of Corrections

The focus of this volume, as of this chapter, is on rehabilitative treatment, and specifically on methods for reintegrating the offender into the community. Such treatment is often, though not always, less burdensome and unpleasant than traditional imprisonment. Rehabilitation efforts therefore may to some extent conflict with the deterrent goal of the criminal justice system. Rehabilitation has been opposed in the past by some people for these reasons.

But the issue is not simply whether new correctional methods amount to "coddling." The ultimate goal of corrections under any theory is to make the community safer by reducing the incidence of crime. Rehabilitation of offenders to prevent their return to crime is in general the most promising way to achieve this end. Varying degrees and periods of incarceration must be recognized as the most appropriate way to deal with some offenders, and efforts must be made to screen out such persons and treat them accordingly.

Deterrence–both of people in general and offenders as potential recidivists–and, where necessary, control remain legitimate correctional functions. Unfortunately there has been little attempt to investigate by research and evaluation the extent to which various methods of handling offenders succeed in these respects. It is no more logical, however, to suppose that various methods operate with uniform effect in deterrence than to suppose that any sort of rehabilitative treatment will work with all sorts of offenders. Some research has indicated that firm discipline and an authoritarian approach are the most effective ways of handling certain types of offenders, while they are likely only to intensify the antagonism and violence of other types.

Excessively harsh penalties may simply backfire by fostering hostility and despair. Revocation of a driver's license may be a more effective deterrent to vehicle offenses than even a heavy fine. The punitive impact of imprisonment may all lie in the first few months. Simple arrest may be deterrence enough in many cases. For the most part the choice of methods can be made meaningfully only at the level of specific types of offenders and individual cases. And at this level there is in practice frequently no apparent conflict in purposes.

45. The Prison as a Rehabilitation Agency

Donald L. Garrity

Most studies of the prison community have been principally concerned with sociological analysis of the prison as a social system, and they have portrayed the social structure, role systems, normative systems, and value orientations of the inmates.[1] In addition, some attention has been given to the pragmatic implications of the data developed. Clemmer, Schrag, and Sykes have been particularly concerned with the implications of their findings for administrative policy. These and other works have developed propositions concerning the effects of the prison community on both the institutional and post-institutional behavior of prisoners. "Common-sense" observations and statements also have contributed to the knowledge about the impact of the prison upon the individual. Yet little attention has been given to an empirical evaluation of these propositions, which is our objective here.

The research analyses of the prison community have concentrated on examining conditions which sociological theory suggests are important in the functioning of any social system. Most important among the concepts utilized in structuring the research have been "value," "norm," "position," and "role." The prison social system can be described in terms of the important values around which the thought and action of inmates and custodians are oriented. The normative systems of the prison are listings of the social restrictions and expectations which guide behavior. The system of roles and positions places acting people within the value framework and the normative system. It describes how people may actually interact in every-

[1] Hans Reimer, "Socialization in the Prison Community," in *Proceedings of the American Prison Association,* 1937, 151–55; Donald Clemmer, *The Prison Community,* New Edition, (New York: Rinehart, 1958); S. Kirson Weinberg, "Aspects of the Prison's Social Structure," *American Journal of Sociology,* 47 (March, 1942), 217–226; Norman S. Hayner and Ellis Ash, "The Prison as a Community," *American Sociological Review,* 5 (April, 1940), 577–583; and "The Prison Community as a Social Group," *American Sociological Review,* 4 (June, 1939), 762–769; Clarence C. Schrag, *Social Types in a Prison Community* (Unpublished M.A. thesis, University of Washington, 1944); Gresham M. Sykes, *The Society of Captives* (Princeton: Princeton University Press, 1958).

day life situations within the prison. Observers have often pointed out that the prison is divided into two different but interacting systems, the inmate system and the administrative system.

Schrag, Clemmer, Sykes, and others have pointed out that the inmate social system is dominated by a set of values and norms which are largely antisocial and anti-administration. Time, sex, food, health, leisure, etc. are handled by a set of normative restrictions and expectations which encourage an inmate to "do his own time," recognize the virtues of an alcoholic beverage called "pruno," recognize the necessity of merchants and peddlers, etc. The dominant normative system values criminal behavior, is consistent with the criminal subculture and generally disapproves of friendly and cooperative behavior with the administration.

It is within this fabric that inmate behavior occurs. However, there are variations in the degree of "organization" observed among inmates. Clemmer reported that value and normative ingredients of prison culture are essentially as described above, but he did not find any clear-cut social structure among the inmates. He concluded that the prison community is not characterized by consensus among inmates and that by and large, prisoners are isolates:

> Contrary to impressions and writings of other investigators, this study found and reported considerable evidence to indicate that consensus, solidarity, and feeling among prisoners has been previously exaggerated.[2]

Clemmer reported further that the population of his prison was divided into three general and relatively vague aggregates which he called the "elite class," the "middle class," and the "hoosier class." This class division was believed to be important only in determining social distance in a very general way; knowledge of it was not viewed as crucial for understanding the dynamics of the prison community or the behavior patterns of particular inmates.[3]

Sykes, on the other hand, reports from his research that a systematic structure of roles can be observed in the prison community and can be used to describe the general behavior patterns of inmates.[4] He found that prison argot labeled and described the position and role behavior of the inmates, and he described eleven roles which he believes form the basic social structure of the prison community.

Schrag described a social system very similar to the one reported by Sykes. He found that the inmate population of his prison tended to be classified in five major types. This typology describes a broad and generic role system which is predictive of the behaviorial tendencies of the inmates. Schrag's typology appears to be broader than Sykes', and it seems to include the argot roles described by Sykes.[5]

The more recent of the three studies suggest, then, that there is a broadly defined social structure in the prison community. This social structure includes a norma-

[2]Clemmer, *op. cit.,* p. 322.
[3]*Ibid.,* pp. 107–109.
[4]Sykes, *op. cit.,* pp. 84–108.
[5]Schrag, *op. cit.,* pp. 55–97.

tive system which stems from the common problems of adjustment faced by all of the inmates and tends to be dominated by antisocially-oriented offenders.[6]

Set apart from but interacting with the inmate social system, the administrative structure is composed of a set of somewhat contradictory forms. In its simplest form, the administrative social structure is bifurcated into two substructures each with its own role and normative system. Treatment and custody, the two substructures, are joined together by common tasks and responsibilities and a common set of public expectations. The two systems have distinct and separate role and normative systems which specify different and, in many instances, contradictory expectations for employees.[7]

Interaction between inmates and administrators is dominated and controlled by the social system of each. However, a set of common expectations has developed and these common expectations minimize conflict between the two systems and thus maximize the undisturbed continuance of each social system. In the language of inmates, it is basically a "no rap" arrangement. Each group expects the other to refrain from involvement in areas which clearly lie outside its domain. When interaction is necessary, cooperation is expected only to that point where it is fairly certain that little "heat" or displeasure will be incurred from outsiders.

Within social systems defined as loosely as these, it is possible for considerable deviation to occur. Deviations do occur in inmate-inmate, inmate-administration, and administration-administration interaction. However, in all cases the deviation tends to be judged as tolerable or intolerable in terms of a general body of expectations.

Prisons do not uniformly correspond to the description above or to the more detailed descriptions stemming from the formal studies or inmate and administrative social systems. These descriptions seem to be most relevant to maximum security institutions and to apply least adequately to minimum security or open institutions. As the number of institutions increases, as greater selectivity is exercised in assignment of inmates to institutions, and as institutions tend to be organized around relatively new and specialized concepts, the probability that any description will fit all institutions decreases. The diversification of institutions in California may be a case in point. However, the vast majority of prisons do conform within reasonable limits to these descriptions of the prison, and probably they will do so for some time to come.

Impact of the Prison

There is general consensus that prison experience is criminogenic in nature. Prisons breed crime. Some years ago, both Tannenbaum and Gillin wrote that exposing an individual to experience in prison increases the probability that he will engage in criminal behavior:

[6] Clarence C. Schrag, "Leadership Among Prison Inmates," *American Sociological Review,* 19 (February, 1954), 37–42.

[7] See Donald R. Cressey, "Contradictory Directives in Complex Organizations: The Case of the Prison," *Administrative Science Quarterly,* 4 (June, 1959), 1–19.

Every time the apprehension of a child involves throwing him in contact with other young criminals who are confined together there is an increased stimulus in the education for crime.... The institutional experience is thus a concentration of stimuli adapted to develop delinquent interests.[8]

What monuments of stupidity are these institutions we have built—stupidity not so much of the inmates as of free citizens. What a mockery of science are our prison discipline, our massing of social inequity in prisons, the good and the bad together in one stupendous potpourri. How silly of us to think that we can prepare men for social life by reversing the ordinary process of socialization.[9]

In his statement, Gillin identifies the process by which prison experience produces its effects—socialization. Prison experiences, like those of the child in family and peer group, may be sufficient to shape attitudes, values, behavior patterns, etc. Although he did not specifically utilize the concept of socialization, Clemmer developed much the same thesis when he described the process of prisonization.

Prisonization. Clemmer defined prisonization as the process of assimilation of the prison culture by inmates as they become acquainted with the prison world.[10] After the inmate is stripped of most of the symbols of personal identity, he begins to attach new meanings to all the conditions of life which were previously taken for granted. These new meanings are provided by the prison culture. Every inmate, Clemmer claims, is exposed to the "universal factors of prisonization."[11] In addition, conditions which maximize prisonization are:

1. A sentence of many years, thus a long subjection to the universal factors of prisonization.
2. A somewhat unstable personality made unstable by an inadequacy of "socialized" relations before commitment, but possessing, nonetheless, a capacity for strong convictions and a particular kind of loyalty.
3. A dearth of positive relations with persons outside the walls.
4. Readiness and a capacity for integration into a prison primary group.
5. A blind, or almost blind, acceptance of the dogmas and mores of the primary group and the general penal population.
6. A chance of placement with other persons of a similar orientation.
7. A readiness to participate in gambling and abnormal sex behavior.[12]

The conditions which allow for minimum prisonization are the reverse of these.

The over-all effect of prisonization is to produce a person who generally conforms to the prison expectations and whose behavior upon release is contradictory to anti-criminal norms. As Clemmer pointed out:

Even if no other factor of the prison culture touches the personality of an inmate of many years residence, the influence of these universal factors are sufficient to make a man characteristic of the penal community and probably so disrupt his personality that a happy adjustment in any community becomes next to impossible.[13]

[8] Frank Tannenbaum, *Crime and the Community* (Boston: Ginn and Co., 1939), 71.
[9] John L. Gillin, *Taming the Criminal* (New York: Macmillan, 1931), 295–296.
[10] Clemmer, *op. cit.*, p. 299.
[11] *Ibid.*, pp. 299–300.
[12] *Ibid.*, pp. 301–302.
[13] *Ibid.*, p. 300.

A recent study has given added weight to Clemmer's propositions concerning the process of prisonization.[14] Wheeler found that inmate reactions to certain attitudinal and value situations tended to vary with the amount of time served and with other measures of prisonization. However, he did not investigate the post-release effects of prisonization.

Anomie. The prisonization concept stresses the effect of prison culture on inmates. Some observers have emphasized, alternatively, the apparent high degree of unorganization and individualism among inmates. Clemmer found that 80 percent of the prisoners did not feel themselves a part of any group, and hence existed to varying degrees as isolates.[15] Weinberg's research stressed the poverty of interaction among certain types of inmates and the consequent anonymity which follows from lack of interaction.[16] Cressey and Krassowski have shown that this condition exists in Soviet labor camps as well as in American prisons.[17] They found that while most inmates live in social conditions of anomie, strong tendencies toward organization and interdependence are also present; both conditions are valuable to administrators.

The literature of social psychology suggests that relatively stable and continuous points of reference are necessary if a person is to function as a normal social creature.[18] Isolation from any meaningful reference groups, and interaction on only superficial levels, lead to serious personality and social difficulties. An individual who has developed normally and who exhibits relatively stable patterns of behavior may be little effected by relatively short periods of anomie, but prolonged exposure might have important consequences for him. On the other hand, an unstable individual might not be able to withstand the conditions of anomie for even a relatively short period of time. Long periods of exposure to unorganization would be even more serious for the unstable than for the stable personality.

If indeed the prison is a world of anomie for some inmates, continued exposure to such an experience should have a deteriorating effect upon the inmates' abilities to function as normal persons. At a minimum, motivation to participate in any given form of social behavior would be effected. Claims about the effects of physical isolation and solitude in prison form part of the important folk knowledge of corrections.[19] Since a condition of anomie has essentially the same elements as physical isolation, essentially the same consequences might follow. The general predictions from this position would be that prolonged incarceration will result in greater inability to function properly within the prison, and that upon release from the institution numerous adjustment problems will occur. Post-release behavior should be poorer as time spent in the institution increases. We did not specifically test the

[14] Stanton Wheeler, *Social Organization in a Correctional Community* (Unpublished PhD. Thesis, University of Washington, 1958).

[15] Clemmer, *op. cit.,* pp. 116–33.

[16] Weinberg, *op. cit.*

[17] Donald R. Cressey and Witold Krassowski, "Inmate Organization and Anomie in American Prisons and Soviet Labor Camps," *Social Problems,* 5 (Winter, 1957–58), 217–23.

[18] Cf. Robert E. L. Faris, *Social Psychology* (New York: Ronald Press, 1952), 338–49.

[19] George Ives, *History of Penal Methods,* (New York: F. A. Stokes Co., 1914), 186–87.

proposition that anomie has disruptive effects on individual behavior in the institution, but our study does examine the predicted post-institutional consequences of anomie.

Imprisonment and Parole Violation

The concept of prisonization suggests that as time in the prison is extended, prisonization increases. In turn, as prisonization increases the probability of successful adjustment following release decreases. Thus, it is expected that success on parole decreases as time spent in the institution increases, personality becomes less stable, non-prison contacts diminish, the person becomes involved in prison primary groups, tends to accept the norms of the prison, is housed with a cellmate involved in the prison community, and participates in abnormal behavior in the prison.

The concept of prison anomie also leads to the expectation that as exposure to the prison increases the probability of successful adjustment on release decreases.

No study has definitively tested these propositions. Such a test is difficult, if not impossible, because the variables and dimensions of the propositions are not easily operationalized. Empirical analysis can be made only in very general terms, and this was done in a study of a population of inmates released from two Washington prisons over approximately one year.[20] A total of 703 cases were released from one institution and 562 from the other. At the time the data were gathered, all individuals had been on parole for at least one year. In Washington, over 99 percent of all inmates are released on parole. Thus, the parole population studied was almost the total population of releases during the year.

Information on the 1265 men was limited to the data contained in the files of the parole board. These files contain the official records and documents of the board, the institution, and other agencies. They do not contain detailed information concerning the primary associations of the prisoners, measures of his self conception, statements about his role-playing ability, or other facts valuable for research purposes. Although the needs of research and administration may not always coincide, policy and administrative decisions most often deal with the same questions with which the sociologist is concerned. It could be argued that improvement of record systems for research purposes would result in equal improvement for administrative purposes.

The parole performance of each person was recorded. The criterion of adjustment on parole was defined as the issuance or non-issuance of a parole violation warrant.[21]

[20] Donald L. Garrity, *The Effects of Length of Incarceration Upon Parole Adjustment and Estimation of Optimum Sentence: Washington State Correctional Institutions* (Unpublished PhD. thesis, University of Washington, 1956).

[21] There are many disadvantages to this definition of parole success or failure, for actions by individual parole officers weigh heavily in determining whether a warrant is issued. There is an unknown amount of variation between parole officers. It would be preferable to use some measure of the actual behavior of the parolee as a criterion. Even better would be some measure of the parolee's efforts to play the role of law-abiding citizen, a measure of the conditions which the parolee encountered in the free community, and a measure of the "therapeutic" assistance he received. Since such measures were not available, issuance of a warrant was accepted as an approximation. For a discussion of these problems see Garrity, *op. cit.,* pp. 51–52.

If a warrant was issued, the parole adjustment was defined as a failure, whether the person was returned to the institution or not. If no warrant was issued, the parole adjustment was defined as a success. Issuing of a warrant was preferable to return to the institution because some parolees committed new offenses in another jurisdiction and were incarcerated in that jurisdiction, and others absconded and remained at large. In a few cases, a warrant was issued in error and later withdrawn. Such cases were considered successful.

Prisonization Considered. No test of prisonization per se was attempted in this study. Rather, the concern was with the purported effect of prisonization on post-release behavior. As indicated previously, Clemmer and others have indicated that prisonization minimizes the probabilities of successful adjustment on parole, probably because antisocial attitudes are assimilated in the prison community.[22] As Clemmer noted, "The phases of prisonization which concern us most are the influences which breed or deepen criminality and antisociality and make the inmate characteristic of the criminalistic ideology in the prison community."[23]

"Time served" was the principal measure of prisonization. If prisonization increases with time, which seems highly probable, parole-violation rates should show a steady and continuing increase as time served in the institution is extended.

Parole-violation rates were computed for categories of parolees who had served various periods of time. The rates for neither institution conformed to the expected pattern. Among parolees from the institution for younger adults, the violation rates went up until a category of men who had served two years was reached, but then the rates decreased rather steadily. Among parolees from the institution for older offenders, the violation rates were highest if release on parole occurred after less than one year in the prison, and then decreased as length of time in the institution increased.

Since it was not possible to construct any reasonable and reliable measure of prisonization, it was assumed that involvement in criminal activity and prison experiences prior to the current incarceration would be directly correlated with degree of prisonization. This assumption may not be completely warranted. Indeed, Clemmer suggests that prisonization is a complex phenomenon which cannot easily be described in a set of propositions. Thus, the fact that a person has adopted a criminal pattern of behavior, or has been is prison a number of times, or has served a number of years in one institution, might not always mean that he will be prisonized to a great degree or at a high rate upon incarceration. However, when a relatively large population of individuals is observed, a positive correlation between prisonization and previous criminal career and incarceration should appear.

The variables selected as measures of the individual's involvement in criminal behavior were "prior criminal record," "prior penal commitments," "total time in custody prior to current commitment," "type of criminal career," "type of offense for

[22] See the discussion by Edwin H. Sutherland and Donald R. Cressey, *Principles of Criminology,* Sixth Edition, (New York: Lippincott, 1960), 497.

[23] Clemmer, *op. cit.,* p. 300.

current commitment," and "age at arrest for current commitment."[24] The first three variables are obvious measures of involvement in criminal behavior. The variables "type of criminal career" and "type of offense" were added because of the well-known differential arrest, conviction, and incarceration practices for different career types and offenses. For example, an individual who has committed a number of robberies is more likely to have been arrested, convicted, and incarcerated on each offense than an individual who has committed an equal number of check-writing offenses. If such differential risks were not handled in some way in the analysis, low-risk individuals with considerable involvement in crime would be classified with individuals who had little involvement in crime but had committed a high-risk offense. Age also determines the possibility of involvement in criminal activities. Relatively young offenders have not had the same opportunity as older offenders for involvement in criminal activity or for incarceration.

The initial analysis was computation of parole-violation rates, by time served, for each of the logical combinations of these six variables. The matrix of obtained violation rates thus show variations by time served for all the combinations of sub-categories of each of the pairs of items. It was expected that as the previous criminal record became more serious, as the number of prior penal commitments increased, and as the total time in custody prior to the current commitment increased, the total violation rate would increase, and that this rate itself would increase systematically with increasing time served.

It was also expected that a differential in violation rates would exist among offenders in terms of type of offense for current commitment and type of criminal career. The general expectation was that persons convicted of property offenses (burglary, auto theft, grand larceny, etc.) would have higher over-all violation rates than would personal, sex, or other types of offenders. Additionally, it was expected that the violation rates for property offenders would increase markedly with increasing amount of time served, but that the same general pattern of increase would be observed for all types. The same general set of expectations was held for the variable, "type of criminal career." For the variable "age at arrest for current commitment," the expectation was that the most marked increase in violation rates with time served would occur among younger offenders. This, it was believed, would be true because younger offenders are not as committed to any particular system of norms as are older offenders.

In the analysis of pairs of factors, it was expected that each of the above relations would hold, and that the interaction of these factors would clearly indicate the effects of time in the prison community. The analysis was carried out independently for each institution. It was anticipated that the differences in institutional character, if any existed, might show up in differential patterns of post-release success or failure.

Analysis of the variables "type of criminal career" and "previous criminal record" indicated that individuals who had no previous criminal career could nevertheless be classified according to previous criminal record: no record, one misdemeanor,

[24] For a definition of these variables see Garrity, *op. cit.*, pp. 79, 231–42.

and more than one misdemeanor. The individuals with no previous criminal record (and no criminal career) who served short prison terms had very low violation rates, and as the amount of time served increased, the violation rates decreased to zero. For individuals with a prior record of a misdemeanor, the violation rates were initially very low but rose systematically and steadily with length of time served. For the third group, who had a number of previous misdemeanors, the violation rate was very high for men with short terms and decreased with length of time served. Thus, the violation rates of the man with one misdemeanor were consistent with our expectations, but in the other two cases the rates were in the direction opposite of that expected.

Among individuals with a previous criminal career, only the group whose previous criminal careers involved offenses against property conformed to the expectation. For them, the violation rates were relatively high among those who served short prison terms and increased steadily as length of time in prison increased. As previous involvement in criminal activities increased, the violation rates started higher and were systematically higher with increasing time served. The rates for all other types of previous criminal career and previous criminal record were not consistent with the expectations. Although violation rates rose as previous criminal record became more serious, violation rates for all categories decreased as time served increased. Thus, for individuals with previous records of property offenses the expectations developed by utilizing the concept of prisonization appear to hold; in all other cases the data were not consistent with expectations.

These same general findings were obtained when "type of offense for current commitment" and "previous criminal record" were used. Persons convicted of burglary, larceny, forgery, and auto theft have violation rates which tend to increase systematically with time served. As previous criminal record became more serious, the rates were initially higher and the increase in rates more dramatic. However, persons who had committed an offense against the person, sex offense, or other types of offense had violation rates which were generally lower and did not increase with time served.

When "type of offense" and "prior penal commitment" were utilized, the same general patterns were observed. Although violation rates in general tended to be higher if the institution of previous incarceration confined more mature offenders, only in the case of the property offenders did the violation rates increase with increasing length of time served. An analysis utilizing the variable "total time in custody" prior to current commitment revealed that this variable did not discriminate either in terms of violation rates in general or the violation rates following various periods of incarceration.

When the variable "age at arrest for current commitment" was utilized in connection with "type of offense," it appeared to discriminate among offenders. The level of violation rates tended to be highest for younger offenders and to become lower as age increased. However, when "age at arrest" was analyzed in conjuction with each of the other variables, the discriminating power of the variable "age" tended to be lost.

On the basis of the above findings, we selected for analysis the four variables which appeared to have the greatest discriminating power. These were "type of offense," "previous criminal record," "type of criminal career," and "prior penal commitment." A multiple classification table utilizing these variables was constructed. For both institutions, the analysis indicated that systematic increase in violation rates with increasing time served in prison occured only among property offenders with a previous criminal record and career of property offenses, or a combination of offenses and a prior commitment to one or more penal institutions. In all other cases, there was no increase or decrease in violation rates as the time in prison increased.

In short, the data did not clearly support the expectations developed from the prisonization concept. It appears from this analysis that the hypothesized post-institutional effects of prisonization appear among property offenders, and the expected pattern is clearer in this one case if the variables "prior penal commitments," "previous criminal record," and "type of criminal career" are also considered. However, manipulation of these variables did not develop the expected trends among other groups of offenders. The consequences of prisonization for post-institutional behavior are not clear. Our data indicate that if prisonization does occur and each person is affected by it to some degree, the post-institutional consequences of this process are quite variable.

Anomie Considered. As indicated previously, the concept "prison anomie" leads to the expectation that as exposure to prison life is increased the probability of success on parole decreases. Also, it is expected that the effects of the prison experience will vary according to the stability of inmates prior to incarceration. The records used did not permit detailed measurement of the personal stability of each offender. Rather, a measure of the probable stability was attempted by utilizing data relating to the social background, personal history, and clinical evaluation upon admission to the prison. It was assumed that personal-history data crudely indicate the stability of a person and that there is an association between degree of social disorganization in the background of a prisoner and his stability. The variables used as indicators of personal and social stability were "family background and delinquency," "employment record," "military record," "marital history," "previous criminal record," "behavior disorder," and "psychiatric classification."[25] The variable "family background and delinquency" is two-dimensional, for it refers to both the socioeconomic status of the parental family and to misconduct by family members in the form of excessive use of alcohol, habitual immorality, conviction of crime, and other kinds of delinquency. "Employment record" refers to the stability of the subject's work record and the level of performance on the job, and "behavior disorder" refers to the presence of alcoholism or excessive drunkenness, use of drugs, habitual gambling, homosexual behavior, etc. The categories of psychiatric diagnosis used were: psychotic, pre-psychotic, psychopathic without disorder, psychopathic with sex disorder, senile, neurotic, and no abnormality noted.

[25] For a definition of these variables see *ibid.*, pp. 231–42.

Analysis took the form used for prisonization. Pairs of variables were utilized to classify the population, and violation rates were computed according to time served. The results were almost uniformly contradictory to the expectation. When the population of the institution containing younger offenders was classified by "family background and delinquency" and also by "previous criminal record," the violation rates increased as family disorganization increased and the violation rates tended to increase with increasing length of time in prison. This pattern did not appear among parolees from the other institution or among parolees from either institution when other variables were used.

In cases from both institutions it was found that as employment record shows greater instability, the total parole-violation rate tends to go up. However, violation rates computed according to time served were variable. Among men with relatively stable employment records, the violation rates were initially low and remained relatively low no matter how much time was served, but among persons with relatively unstable employment records, the violation rates decreased with increasing time in the prison. Similarly, men with good military records had lower total violation rates than the others, but among the men with poor records, violation rates went down with increasing time in prison, while among the men with better records the violation rate increased with increasing time in prison. Essentially the same results appeared when the populations were classified by behavior disorder and psychiatric category. Men with no observed behavior disorder or psychiatrically-defined abnormality had lower total violation rates than those with behavior disorders and psychiatrically-defined abnormality. But again, the violation rates according to time served increased for the first group and decreased for the second.[26]

In general, the analysis showed positive association between personal and social disorganization or stability and parole violation. However, the expected effects of incarceration on the various categories of offenders did not appear. In only one case did the violation rates increase over time. If anything, the data indicated that the extension of prison experience tended to damage the parole performance of those showing greater stability and help the parole performance of those with greater instability. In general then, the observations tended to be contradictory and the reverse of expectation.

[26] For a detailed discussion of these data see *ibid.*, pp. 134–62.

46. The Misdemeanant in the Correctional System

The President's Commission on Law Enforcement and Administration of Justice

The focus of corrections generally is on felons and juvenile offenders. But misdemeanants form a far larger group than both of the others combined in terms of the number of cases handled by the criminal justice system.

A 12-State study revealed that 93.5 percent of persons arraigned in 1962 in these States for offenses other than traffic violations were charged with misdemeanors.[1] The ratio of misdemeanants to felons showed wide variation from State to State. Iowa had 4 times as many misdemeanants as felons; New Hampshire had 30 times as many.

• • •

Diversity of Misdemeanant Groups

The range and diversity of misdemeanant offenders are far greater than those of the felony and juvenile groups. Some appreciation of this diversity and the problems it poses for corrections is a necessary starting point for any analysis of how improvements could be made.

For one thing, a considerable volume of misdemeanors involve motor vehicle laws. Misdemeanor courts also handle a variety of other regulatory violations in health, housing, safety, and commercial fields. This class of cases seldom reaches corrections, since in most instances such matters are disposed of by fines or license suspensions.

Another very large group consists of drunkenness offenders. The National Survey of Corrections indicated that, excluding traffic offenders, nearly half of all misdemeanants are arrested for public drunkenness or offenses related to drinking....

Another substantial and varied group of misdemeanants have committed offenses generally characteristic of inner-city life, including among others, after-hours liquor

Reprinted from *Task Force Report: Corrections,* a Report by The President's Commission on Law Enforcement and Administration of Justice (Washington: Government Printing Office, 1967), ch. 7, pp. 72–76.

[1] Lee Silverstein, "In Defense of the Poor" (Chicago: American Bar Foundation, 1965), p. 123.

offenses, weapons offenses, and gambling. Some of the offenders in this group can easily become involved in the kinds of crimes with which the mainstream of corrections deals. Indeed, weapons offenses, such as "pointing a gun," suggest the ease with which this may happen and the consequent seriousness of such matters. But many of these offenders are also engaging in behavior which their community does not strongly and generally condemn as an offense. "Playing the numbers," for example, is an established part of life in many slum neighborhoods.

In many such instances, extensive correctional programs may not seem warranted. The cost of successfully changing behavior not strongly condemned by the community is, for one thing, extremely high in comparison to the interest of society in being protected against such offenses. Moreover, it is difficult to justify in other terms and very extensive interference with the liberty or values of persons who have not engaged in crimes directly threatening in any substantial way the person or property of another.

The correctional challenge in those personal and property crime misdemeanors that more resemble felonies is not so unique. As a group, these misdemeanants present the same dangers to the community and the same need and potential for rehabilitation....

In fact many cases are processed initially as felonies and later reduced to misdemeanors, often as the result of negotiation between prosecutor and defense counsel. A housebreaking felony will, for example, be reduced to a petit larcency misdemeanor, a forgery to a "bad check" violation. In the District of Columbia in 1965 more than half of felony arrests were thus disposed of,[2] and this rate is not uncommon.

The less serious nature of misdemeanor property and personal crimes means, of course, that there are likely to be more "casual" offenders and marginal cases than with felonies. Driving a car without the owner's consent can be a relatively innocent frolic of youth, quite different from habitual auto theft or the abandoning, stripping, or selling of stolen cars. Shoplifting, if not habitual, is usually diverted from the criminal justice process at an early stage. Full-scale correctional intervention, whether aimed at deterrence or rehabilitation, does not appear appropriate in most such cases.

But in many of the more serious misdemeanors against property or persons, correctional intervention clearly is just as necessary as in the case of felonies. It is in these cases that the misdemeanor-felony distinction seems least meaningful from the correctional standpoint. This is particularly true since many misdemeanants subsequently commit felonies....

Present Misdemeanant Services

The handling of such diverse groups creates perplexing problems for modern corrections. The classic sentencing alternatives for the wide assortment of acts denom-

[2] Harry Subin, "Criminal Justice in a Metropolitan Court" (Washington: U.S. Government Printing Office, 1966), pp. 33–36.

inated misdemeanors or petty offenses have been a fine and jail, often in the alternative, such as "$30 or 30 days." This sentencing structure provides generally the same alternatives in terms of deterrence and punishment as the felony and juvenile systems; and, as long as the function of corrections centered on these purposes, there was nothing particularly anomalous in the way misdemeanants were treated.

But as the correctional focus has turned with other offenders to rehabilitation, the processes of misdemeanant corrections have become harder to justify. Suspended sentences are widely used in many jurisdictions; but formal probation is much less common, and the supervision offered is rarely more than nominal. Parole is virtually nonexistent. The lack of meaningful rehabilitative intervention in community treatment programs is even more true of jails.

• • •

Moreover, the lack of rehabilitative efforts, with respect to such misdemeanant groups as drunks, has also pointed up the frequent failure of misdemeanant corrections to deter, at least in terms of preventing recidivism. Studies consistently indicate that a large number of misdemeanants are repeatedly convicted of criminal offenses. For example, a survey of 5 county misdemeanant penitentiaries in New York State found, as shown in table 1, that half of the men committed in 1963 had prior commitments and a fifth had been committed 10 times or more.

While it is true that misdemeanants with extensive prior records are most often found among those convicted of a petty offense or for an alcohol-related charge such as disorderly conduct, they do not totally account for all the severely recidivistic groups found in misdemeanant corrections. In a special study, a sample of 1,342 persons sentenced to jail in Los Angeles and San Joaquin Counties, Calif., in 1966 was divided into two categories.[3] Group A included more serious offenses such as assault, burglary, and theft. Group B contained violations considered less serious, including gambling, vandalism, and drunkenness; of these, over 50 percent had 10 or more prior convictions. While the more serious offenders in group A had on the average fewer prior convictions, 18.4 percent of them had 10 or more.

Misdemeanant Institutions. The National Survey of Corrections estimated that there were about 3,500 local institutions for misdemeanants in the Nation in 1965. Three-quarters of the institutions in the 250-county sample were jails, and the remainder were designated as workhouses, camps, farms, or institutions having some of the characteristics of all three. Not only are the great majority of these facilities old, but many do not even meet the minimum standards in sanitation, living space, and segregation of different ages and types of offenders that have obtained generally in the rest of corrections for several decades.

Of one State, a consultant noted:

> This State has 9 jails which confine nearly 25,000 people a year. Five are more than 100 years old, and 3 have been standing for 160 years. In 4 jails, there were 899 cells without sanitary facilities.

[3] Data taken from reports submitted by Malcolm Matheson, a task force consultant who conducted the study and developed other materials for this chapter.

TABLE 1. Number of Times Male Prisoners Committed Have Been Confined, New York County Penitentiaries, 1963

	Counties					*Total*	
	Albany	*Erie*	*Monroe*	*Onondaga*	*Westchester*	*Individuals*	*Percent*
1st time	931	765	715	542	615	3,568	49.62
2nd time	13	243	82	108	247	693	9.64
3rd time	11	141	56	23	177	408	5.67
4th time	3	68	37	20	107	235	3.27
5th time	2	53	40	21	91	207	2.88
6th time		78	28	26	48	180	2.50
7th time		45	30	28	53	156	2.17
8th time		33	29	23	50	135	1.88
9th time		22	25	16	42	105	1.46
10th time and over		342	436	305	421	1,504	20.91
Total	960	1,790	1,478	1,112	1,851	7,191	100.0

SOURCE: Adapted from New York State Commission of Correction, "Thirty-Seventh Annual Report, 1963," p. 485.

Another consultant concluded after covering the jail system of a Western State:

Most counties and cities persist in operating their own jails, nearly all of which are nothing more than steel cages in which people stay for periods of time up to a year. Most of the jails are custody-oriented and supervised by ill-trained, underpaid personnel. In some cases, the institution is not manned except when a police officer on duty can look in once during his 8-hour shift.

Two-thirds of the sample of 215 local correctional institutions covered by the National Survey reported no type of rehabilitative program at all. If consideration were given to facilities handling those sentenced for 30 days or less, not included in the National Survey, the proportion of institutions without such programs would undoubtedly be greater....

Over 19,000 persons were employed to staff jails and local correctional institutions in 1965. The distribution of this staff, by type of assignment, is presented in table 2.

• • •

Community Services. Community treatment programs for misdemeanants suffer from the same lack of resources as do programs for felons and juveniles, but in aggravated form due to even higher average caseloads and generally shorter periods of supervision.

Probation. As the study of misdemeanant sentencing in 8 jurisdictions presented in table 3 shows, formal probation is used relatively infrequently in most jurisdictions....

In 11 states there are no probation services for misdemeanants in any county. None of these States encompasses a very large metropolitan area, and most are not highly urbanized. Only 2 of these 11 jurisdictions were above the median per capita income in 1964, and 6 were in the bottom quarter.

TABLE 2. Personnel in Jails and Other Local Correctional Institutions, 1965, by Type of Position and Ratio of Staff to Inmates

Position	*Number*	*Ratio of Staff to Inmates*
Social workers	167	1:846
Psychologists	33	1:4,282
Psychiatrists	58	1:2,436
Academic teachers	106	1:1,333
Vocational teachers	137	1:1,031
Custodial officers	14,993	1:9
Other	3,701	1:38

SOURCE: National Survey of Corrections.

About one-third of the 250 counties in the National Survey had no probation services for misdemeanants. Eight counties reported having a probation service but no cases; 4 counties did not report; and 59 counties were unable to report the total cases on probation during their last reporting year.

Over the country, then, probation services to misdemeanants are sparse and spotty. Some exceptions are seen in a few States which have combined services to felons and misdemeanants and in large metropolitan areas which have probation departments either exclusively for the misdemeanant or as part of an integrated service for both misdemeanants and felons. Even here caseloads are too high to permit adequate presentence investigations and meaningful supervision of probationers.

TABLE 3. Disposition of Misdemeanors in Selected Lower Courts, 1964, 1965

(In percent)

Jurisdiction	*Disposition*				
	Jail Sentence	*Probation*	*Fine*	*Suspended Sentence*	*Other*
Baltimore	28.6	2.5	15.7	17.8	35.3
Denver	20.6	19.7	31.2	28.5	
Detroit	26.4	5.7	56.6	8.7	2.6
Los Angeles County	32.0	8.9			59.1[a]
New York City	47.6	1.7	18.9	31.8	
San Mateo County, Calif.	66.2	19.6			14.2[a]
Washington, D.C.	63.3	10.0	16.7	10.0	
Westchester County, N.Y.	30.8	2.4	51.3	11.4	10.6

[a] Includes fine and suspended sentence cases.

SOURCES: New York City data from Criminal Court of the City of New York, "Annual Report," 1964; Westchester County data from a special study by the National Council on Crime and Delinquency; San Mateo County data from California Department of Justice; all other data from studies by Commission Consultants.

In 20 States misdemeanant probation is organized nominally on a statewide basis. Some of these programs, however, provide only minimal services. Comments such as "service provided occasionally" or "as the caseload permits" or "will so provide if asked" typify the reports on probation service to misdemeanant offenders in several of these States. In another 20 States, probation services are organized on a city, city-county, county or court district basis. These States contain slightly over half of the Nation's population.

...

As table 4 shows, such high caseloads are the rule in most jurisdictions. A few counties covered by the National Survey reported caseloads in excess of 200, and one county reported 400. Of all misdemeanants on probation, 76 percent were supervised in caseloads of over 100. For the country as a whole, the average caseload was estimated at 114 cases. Added to this workload is an estimated average of 85 presentence reports per officer annually.

Field researchers describe the probation process in high-caseload areas as one in which the client comes to the office once a month, sees his probation officer for a few minutes, and then departs. Probation here is a checking rather than counseling function, and even its checking aspect is so limited as to be of very little value. Other surveys of probation services have concluded that, as a result of inadequate staffing, individuals are jailed when they should be placed on probation, and those who are placed on probation often fail because of inadequate supervision.[4]

TABLE 4. Distribution of Misdemeanant Probationers, 1965, by Size of Caseload in Which Supervised

Caseload Size	*Percentage Supervised*	*Caseload Size*	*Percentage Supervised*
Under 40	0.7	71–80	2.4
41–50	.2	81–90	1.4
51–60	4.2	91–100	10.9
61–70	3.9	Over 100	76.3

SOURCE: National Survey of Corrections.

Parole for Misdemeanants. The use of parole for misdemeanants is extremely limited....The National Survey found a very small number of misdemeanants on parole in 1965. Short sentences undoubtedly contribute to this low rate of parole. However, more significant is the fact that, in a number of jurisdictions, parole for misdemeanants is not even provided by law. Further, many of those States which have statutory provisions for the parole of misdemeanants have very inadequately staffed programs and parole boards often include local law enforcement officials as ex-officio board members, a procedure rejected as poor practice in the parole of felons.

[4]Robert L. Smith, "Probation Study" (Sacramento: California Board of Corrections, Sept. 1965).

47. Custody and Treatment in Juvenile Institutions

Mayer N. Zald and David Street

Correctional organizations, no matter how much they vary in emphasis, must ultimately have the dual purpose of custody and rehabilitation. If one of them attempts to do away with containment and control, the community and relevant officials will build pressure to reinstate controls. On the other hand, given the values of our society and the original definition of the juvenile institution as rehabilitative, even the most custodial institution has to make some effort to reclaim its youth and use *humanitarian* controls. Yet, differences in goals, ranged along a continuum from custody to treatment, have a number of effects on the operation of these organizations.

Organizational analysis, a developing subdiscipline within sociology, directs attention to the broad problems of organizational goals, relations between the organization and its environment, the internal structure of the organization, and relations with and among the clientele. In this article we shall examine the organizational patterns and problems of juvenile correctional institutions, particularly those which have attempted to convert from a custodial to a treatment-oriented type of approach.

Some time ago, we had the opportunity to explore this problem in a comparative study of several institutions for male juvenile offenders.[1] Questionnaires filled in by inmates and staff, historical documents, observations of meetings and organizational practices, extended interviews with executives and others, and consultation with people outside the organization were some of the methods used.

The institutions we studied differed in their goals. Among the four major organizations, one was strongly, even repressively, custodial, emphasizing discipline and hard work; a second was a "moderated custody" institution, beginning to tone down repressive control but not yet committed to a full treatment program; a third emphasized individual treatment; and the last was developing a program of milieu treatment. These institutions, which were located in several states, varied in size—from

Reprinted from *Crime and Delinquency,* **10** (July 1964), 249–256, by permission of the National Council on Crime and Delinquency and the authors.

[1]Detailed findings of the study, which was directed by Robert Vinter and Morris Janowitz, may be found in *The Comparative Study of Juvenile Correctional Institutions: A Research Report* (Ann Arbor: University of Michigan School of Social Work, 1961). The research was supported by grant M-2104 from the National Institute of Mental Health.

400 boys and 180 staff to 75 boys and 40 staff—and were both public and private. In addition, we studied two smaller private institutions which had custodial goals but which were "open" in that they sent their inmates out to ordinary public and parochial schools each day.

Such aspects of organization as departmental structure, balance of power, level and patterns of conflict, staff-inmate relations, and inmate responses to the institutions will be considered both generally and with special reference to those institutions.

Departmental Structure

One striking difference between institutions with more custodial goals and those with more treatment-oriented goals is the case of routinization and coordination of the former. The first reason for this is that inmates in the custodial institutions are rendered more passive by the use of dominating and coercive sanctions, whereas in the treatment institutions staff must be continually adapting to the inmates. Secondly, custodial philosophy provides rules for most situations that will arise, while treatment philosophy requires that each situation be handled in terms of the particular inmate involved. Thirdly, custodial institutions establish programs which hold for large groups of boys, while treatment institutions try to set up programs to meet the needs of each boy. Finally, treatment institutions have continually changing programs which require a great deal of individual coordination of staff and boys. This is in marked contrast to the repetitive programing of the custodial institutions.

These differences in the degree of routinization sharply affect other aspects of the institutions. While in custodial institutions little departmentalization occurs and most personnel report directly to the superintendent or assistant superintendent, in treatment institutions the superintendent's span of control becomes extremely attenuated because he must make so many different kinds of decisions. Thus, the clearly custodial institutions are organized simply, while institutions toward the center of the continuum and institutions utilizing mainly individual treatment have what can be called a "multiple department" structure in which each area of the institution—the school, the cottage, the social service, maintenance, business—operates relatively autonomously. Each has a department head who makes decisions for his own area. Both the moderate custodial and the individual treatment institutions are likely to have this type of structure because the activity in one department seems to have no relevance for another. In contrast, in the correctional institution with a program of milieu treatment, all activity with inmates must correspond to that philosophy; thus, action in the school and cottage, for example, must be as treatment-oriented as action elsewhere in the institution. As a result, milieu institutions are likely to have a dual divisional structure: all activity with inmates is placed under a single division head and is guided and supervised by professional treatment personnel, and all business and maintenance staffs are placed in a separate division.

To illustrate these ideas about departmental structure, let us turn specifically to the institutions in our study. The most custodial was only slightly departmentalized.

Its farm had a departmental structure, but only so as to achieve better production rather than to supervise staff-inmate relations. The superintendent did not feel hard-pressed to make decisions and spent an hour or two each morning reading the political news. The largest institution in our sample, presently a moderated custodial institution with a multiple department structure, was, at an earlier time, more custodial and had fewer departments, though the size was the same. Indeed, it once resembled our most custodial institution, even though it had over one hundred employees. Departmentalization came to this institution when outside pressure groups complained about the autonomy and power of cottage parents in disciplining and treating boys as they wished. In this circumstance, departmentalization helped the executive establish a reasonable span of control so that he could guarantee appropriate behavior from his staff.

Of course, as institutions get larger they require some greater departmentalization, but size alone does not account for departmentalization, as the case of the moderated custodial organization indicates. Similarly, the individual treatment institution had only forty staff and seventy-five boys: yet it was fully departmentalized and the assistant superintendent, who was the key person in running the institution, was under a great deal of pressure. However, departmentalization did not solve all the problems of executive control. The lack of routinization and the fact that the assistant superintendent was chief disciplinarian put him in the position of having to make decisions about many things every day.

Balance of Power

How is power distributed among executives and staff groups in the institutions? What are the orientations and values of the people who hold power?

Looking first at the distribution of power among the executives, we note that as the institution becomes more departmentalized, the superintendent finds it more difficult to control and supervise all personnel: consequently, power must be shared. This sharing of power is especially true, therefore, for the treatment institutions, which are not only departmentalized but also in the public eye, in contrast to custodial institutions, which tend to be relatively isolated and removed from the public. Treatment institutions generally are involved with a wide range of external agencies and, because of their open policies, superintendents must be prepared to defend their institutions against attack and share their power as a means of building support for their relatively expensive programs.

We found that in the most custodial institution only the superintendent was perceived by the staff as having a great deal of influence among the executives. In three of the institutions studied, an "inside-outside" split in the executive role occurred. The assistant superintendent in each of the two treatment institutions was seen as having a great deal of power; in fact, the number of staff who thought *he* had a great deal of influence was larger than the number who felt the superintendent had. In the moderate, or intermediate, custodial institution, where the superintendent was ideologically more committed to a treatment goal but was unable to implement this commitment, the second in command—unofficially—was the head of the cottage parents, who had two mottoes: "We're not in the beating business," and "The community has a right to be protected." Thus, in this institution, a person with primarily nonrepressive custodial attitudes was in command. What is important here is that by giving him power, the superintendent could insure containment and control.

In most of the institutions the values of the chief executive and the assistant superintendent tended to parallel the difference in goals. Only in the moderate custodial institution do we see any marked feeling that program and goals were not up to the standards of the figures in power there. The superintendent, for example, felt he had to compromise his aims in order to meet the restricted budget and lack of public support for a more rehabilitative program.

Among staff groups, power distribution took a fairly predictable course. First, in all institutions the teachers and the principal had very little power, reflecting the fact that the schools were relatively isolated from the major operating problems of the organization. Secondly, as we move from the most custodial to the individual treatment institution we see a decreasing amount of power given to cottage parents. Cottage parents have less and less say over discipline, over when the boy goes home, and over what the boy's program should be like. On the other hand, in the milieu institution, where cottage parents participated in the basic decisions, their power was higher than in any of the other institutions. Thirdly, as we move from custodial to treatment institutions, the social service workers move from a position relatively isolated from internal operations, a position in which they deal mainly with the courts and families to an increasingly central position, in which they make decisions about the boys. He who controls decisions about the boys controls the organization.

Level and Pattern of Conflict

The power balance in an organization is also related to its pattern of conflict. The extent to which the institution is committed to both custodial and treatment goals should be related to the amount or level of conflict there. Many objective observers have noted the apparently irreconcilable conflict among treatment personnel—who tend to be professionals, white-collar workers, and younger people—and the custodial cottage parents over such well-known issues as: Should or shouldn't we lock the doors? Must the boys march? Should boys be allowed to go off grounds? How much should we believe the boys? We made it our job to go beyond mere recognition that institutions are conflict-prone organizations and, instead, attempted to account for differences in their level and pattern of conflict.

Our first notion was that institutions near the middle of the goal continuum, with social service workers in one department and cottage parents in another, should have the highest tension level. Our second was that institutions with custodial goals would have fewer social service workers and, since these few would be isolated from the organization, there would be little conflict. In treatment institutions, we thought that careful selection of cottage parents and the clear dominance of treatment goals and social service workers would lead to a decline in conflict. In other words, we hypothesized that the further away from the end points of the continuum, the more the conflict. We were wrong in this hypothesis because we seriously underestimated the problems of the treatment institution.

First, it is hard to know when one is effective in treating a delinquent–one can only know after his means have proved successful ten years later. In other words, good criteria for what means to use are absent in treatment institutions. In the absence of hard criteria, one can debate endlessly about what constitutes appropriate staff behavior even though there may be a basic agreement on goals. This is not the case in custodial institutions, where there is a clear relationship between the means and the end. Furthermore, because communication and coordination are more important in treatment institutions, the personnel have more of an opportunity to express their differences so that the amount of conflict perceived is higher. Although the conflict may be less virulent and less basic, it nevertheless is likely to exist and to be fairly strong. What we found, then, is that conflict was lowest in our two most custodial institutions and highest in the milieu treatment institution. Of course, idiosyncrasies of the institution may help to account for this, but we would not discount this basic pattern.

What about the *pattern* of conflict–that is, who conflicts with whom–within the institution? In any organization, conflict is most likely to occur between those who control the basic definition of policy and decisions and those who disagree with those policies. Briefly and oversimply, we expected that in the more custodial institutions social service workers and teachers would conflict with cottage parents but not with each other, and that in treatment institutions cottage parents and teachers would conflict with the powerful social service staff but not with each other. In a milieu institution, however, where cottage parents and social service workers are highly integrated, we expected that both would be likely to conflict with teachers but not with each other. These are oversimplified explanations, however, because they make assumptions which are not necessarily met. They assume, for example, that the values of social service workers in a custodial institution will conflict with those of the cottage parents, while in reality institutions may select and train people who can accommodate to the institution. In other words, our predictions would hold true only if these groups did, in fact, have divergent values. Secondly, we had assumed that groups interact and recognize the conflict, but if groups are relatively isolated, the partners to the conflict would not be aware of it.

In general, our model worked. In those cases where it did not, we could see that the institution's selection policies had solved the problem. For instance, in the individual treatment institution, we had expected a great deal of conflict between the cottage parents and the social service workers, but since the cottage parents were all college-educated persons who identified with the professional staff and accepted their professional ideals, this institution effectively by-passed such conflict. This does not mean that the cottage parents failed to experience a large degree of role strain; they did feel pressured, were not sure what they were supposed to be doing and so on. Since they accepted the values of the social service staff, however, they could not come out in open conflict with them. The one case in which we clearly were wrong was the milieu institution: there, cottage parents and social service workers continued to be in conflict even though we had expected them not to be and even though they identified with each other and considered themselves part of the same team. So although they continued to fight, they felt they were fighting on the same side and for the same goals and they attempted to reconcile their differences.

Staff-Inmate Relationships

In testing out some of our common sense assumptions about what relationships of staff to inmates would obtain in different organizations, we found that in custodial institutions staff had a relatively dominating relationship with the inmates, while in treatment institutions staff were less domineering and relied more on manipulation and persuasion to control the inmates. To illustrate, in custodial institutions all staff are called "sir" or "ma'am" by the boys, reflecting the emphasis upon social distance: in treatment institutions friendly–and sometimes not so friendly–nicknames are permitted. In the most custodial institution one of the staff members, who was well-liked by both staff and boys, was ordered to paddle any boy who called him by his nickname–a nickname which all the staff used in front of the boys.

These differences in basic relationship were reflected in the staff attitude toward the inmates. Thus, the staff in the more custodial institutions felt that boys should keep to themselves, should conform, should not make too many friends within the the institution, and should not have close relationships with many people. Staff in the more treatment-oriented institutions wanted boys to make friends with both the staff and the other boys and to express themselves, articulate their needs, and so on. They also stressed the importance of understanding the boys more than did those in the custodial institutions.

Another difference is subtle. In all the institutions studied, staff were preoccupied with two kinds of inmates–the boy who is quiet and the boy who makes himself known. The quiet, withdrawn boy generally does not get too much attention, although the staff in treatment institutions try to encourage this type of child to come out of himself, to start acting up a little, if you will. Custodial institutions tend to ignore this type of boy. The reasoning used by the treatment personnel is that if a boy is just quietly getting by, the institution is not actually teaching him. He is just "doing time."

In all institutions, however, when staff are among themselves, it is not the quiet one they talk about, but the troublemakers and the heroes who, in all the institutions, tended to be the good athletes. But personnel in the treatment and custodial institutions have fundamentally different attitudes toward the troublemakers. Although staff in custodial institutions tend to talk about them with awe, the only problem they worry about is how to stop them. For the staff in the treatment institution, trouble-making reflects underlying disturbance and is not something to be clamped down on immediately. To know what is bothering the inmate, one must almost encourage disturbance.

Inmate Response

How do differences in goal emphasis affect the behavior of the inmates? Instead of stretching our resources to gather data on inmate recidivism, we chose to focus on the attitudes and social relations of the inmates while they were in the institution. Findings in this area, we believe, have implications for the inmates' future adjustment.

We asked the inmates a variety of questions as to whether the institution was a better or worse place than they expected, whether they thought the institution had been of some help to them, whether staff members were fair, and other subjects. From the replies, we found that the atittudes of inmates in custodial institutions were less favorable than the attitudes of the inmates in treatment organizations. Further, we found that among the inmates of custodial institutions, those who were more involved in or who were informal leaders of the inmate group were even more antipathetic toward that type of institution than were the other inmates. By contrast, the more involved inmates and leaders in the treatment institutions had more favorable attitudes than the other boys. Overall, then, the results of our inmate questionnaire showed a consistent pattern of differences in inmate attitudes toward themselves, the institution, and the staff, depending on the type of institutions they were in. In the custodial institutions emphasizing containment and conformity, the inmate group, by stressing covert opposition and "playing it cool," moved toward behavior more consistent with the institutional policy than did inmates in the treatment institutions. The custodial inmates thus made little move to alter their behavior, while the inmate group in the treatment facility seemed to influence its members toward achieving change, at least insofar as change in behavior requires some cooperation with the staff.

Of special interest were our findings on the ways in which the formal organizational structure influences the informal patterns of inmate social relations. The results clearly challenge the frequently held view that the inmate group is inevitably opposed to the goals of the organization. First, the degree of inmate solidarity against the administration in juvenile institutions was nowhere as high as that reported generally for adult prisons. Second, solidarity—the inmates' belief that they should and do stick together—was not necessarily linked to attitudes opposed to the institution and staff. Third, solidarity was high in the treatment institutions, where, as we have suggested, inmate attitude was relatively more favorable than it was in the custodial institutions. Finally, in the custodial organizations the staff's repression of inmate social relations effectively reduced the level of inmate solidarity but at the same time tended to assure that whatever inmate group activity did take place would be oriented against the institution and staff. By contrast, in the treatment institutions, where the inmates were allowed to organize and express hostility overtly, the boys apparently were more day-to-day "trouble" to the staff, but their groupings were less often oriented against the institution and staff and had fewer undesirable effects upon the inmates' attitudes.

Differences between the inmates in the two custodial and two treatment institutions were clear-cut, and our findings for inmates in the two small open institutions paralleled those for the inmates in the treatment institutions. Inmates in these open organizations were almost as favorably disposed to their environment as those in the treatment institutions—a finding which raises the question of whether the great resources used for treatment are really necessary if the same results are produced in an open institution.

This paper is not a prescription for running a correctional institution. Rather, it points to dilemmas which arise from the various goals which institutions set for themselves. Today, professionalization of correctional personnel is leading toward a greater emphasis upon rehabilitation and treatment so that few institutions will be able to cling to predominantly custodial goals in the years ahead. Yet, any executive who wants to move his institution toward treatment goals must be prepared to face conflicts among staff members, higher operating costs, and the need for, and risks in, delegating authority. But the effort, as our study indicated, will be worth it.

48. Correctional Outcome: An Evaluation of 100 Reports*

Walter C. Bailey

This article presents selected results of a content analysis of 100 reports of empirical evaluations of correctional treatment. The reports, which are listed at the end of the article, were systematically selected primarily from those correctional outcome studies published between 1940 and 1960.[1] Within these broad limits, actual selec-

Reprinted from *The Journal of Criminal Law, Criminology and Police Science,* 57:2 (June 1966), 153-160, by permission of the publisher and the author.

*Professor Bailey's article is a modified version of a paper prepared for the California Study of Correctional Effectiveness under grant OM89R from the National Institutes of Health, Public Health Service, U.S. Department of Health, Education, and Welfare. He expresses his sincere appreciation to Dr. Daniel M. Wilner, Director of the California Study of Correctional Effectiveness for his support and encouragement and also to a number of assistants and assistant researchers for their help in collecting materials and annotating the research studies.

[1] A few unpublished papers were included because of availability and some correctional outcome reports published prior to 1940 were included either because of their reputation as "classics" or because of some specific area of relevance. Selection of reports for this analysis was made on the basis of a systematic search through books and monographs, relevant journals, the American Prison Association Index, the International Index to Periodical Literature, the Public Affairs Index, and various government publications. The reports, listed below, comprise the sample upon which this analysis is based. Obviously, they constitute neither an exhaustive nor representative account of the literature. Also, a few represent evaluations of somewhat different aspects of the same general study projects. Nevertheless, the relatively large number of reports included and the selection methods employed, suggest that this sample provides a reasonable basis for tentative judgments regarding the status of correctional outcome research in this country.

tion of reports was guided by three principles: (1) the report must have been based upon empirical data; (2) the treatment evaluated must have been dependent upon the manipulation of some form of interpersonal relations as the independent variable, and (3) the behavior to be corrected must have had a negative value in the sense of being actually or potentially subject to legal sanctions.

Five preliminary questions are explored: (1) What is the relative frequency of various types of correctional outcome reports in terms of research design? (2) What is the relative frequency of various forms of *group* treatment approaches as compared with *individual* forms such as *individual counseling, psychotheraphy,* etc.? (3) What is the relative frequency of occurence of study reports dealing with outcomes of treatment carried out in correctionally administered settings (forced treatment or "treatment at the point of a gun") as compared with treatment carried out in non-correctional settings such as private practice, outpatient clinics, etc. (voluntary treatment)? (4) What kinds of persons, in terms of training and background, conduct correctional outcome research projects? and (5) What kinds of theories of causation of criminal behavior are implicit or explicit in the treatment programs evaluated? Finally, the main question is considered, namely, how effective is correctional treatment?

Frequency of Types of Study Reports

Of the 100 correctional outcome reports evaluated, 22% were classified as describing experimental study designs (those utilizing some form of control group design); 26% were classified as describing systematic-empirical study designs (those using control procedures but no control groups); and 52% were classified as describing nonsystematic empirical study designs (those based upon empirical observations but lacking control procedures). As expected, the more rigorous experimental type study report was the least frequently encountered and the least rigorous, least controlled type of study report, the most plentiful.

Group vs. Other Forms of Correctional Treatment

Since group treatment appears to be one of the most rapidly expanding forms of treatment of emotional and mental disorders generally, one would expect the same trend in correctional treatment.

Of the 100 correctional outcome reports under consideration, we found that 58% of them dealt with an evaluation of the effectiveness of some form of group (as opposed to various kinds of individual) treatment. When treatment form (*i.e.,* whether group or individual) is compared with type of outcome report, we find that roughly 60% of the experimental type involved evaluations of group treatment compared with 58% of the systematic-empirical type, and 59% of the non-systematic-empirical. In other words, consistently throughout the ranges of types of correctional outcome reports considered, the major focus was on evaluation of various forms of group treatment.

Correctional vs. Noncorrectional Settings

It is of interest to compare the frequency of evaluations of correctional treatment programs which are under the legal administration of a correctional agency (*e.g.*, parole, probation, etc.) with the frequency of those studies evaluating correctional treatment or prevention programs carried out in community, private agency, or private practice settings. Here we included in the comparison only those research reports classified as either experimental or systematic-empirical, comprising a total sample of 48 reports. We find that 26 (54%) of these were evaluations of treatment programs under direct correctional administration as compared with 22 (46%) in noncorrectional settings. Thus, a slight majority of those outcome reports describing either experimental or systematic-empirical research designs, involved evaluations of correctional treatment in authoritarian settings where treatment is "forced."

Professional Identification of Researchers

What kinds of persons conduct or direct correctional outcome studies? Here, we restricted our analysis to only the most rigorous type of outcome reports, those describing experimental designs. Ten of the 22 experimental studies (46%) were conducted by psychologists; next were the sociologists with 6 (28%). Ten percent (2) could not be classified. The fields of psychiatry, education, and social work each contributed one study (4% each). On the basis of this sample, it appears that psychologists and sociologists have a monopoly on conducting the experimental correctional outcome studies. Together, they authored 74% of the experimental outcome reports.

Interventional Premises in Correctional Outcome Studies

Treatment figures,[2] we assume, do not make interventions at random. Thus, all correctional treatment procedures and progress are based upon some theoretical frame of reference which, whether implicitly or explicitly formulated, explains the behavior being treated, establishes the goals of treatment, and provides plausible procedural connections between the problem and the goals in the sense that the interventions utilized are viewed as "correct" means to an end (treatment goals).

In this sample of 100 reports there were few attempts to either make explicit the behavioral theory undergirding the treatment approach or the procedural connections between the theory and treatment goals. One of the exceptions, for example, was the Grants' evaluation of group treatment with military offenders. They made a considered effort to spell out the causal theory underlying the criminal behavior and to specify the logical connections between the theory and the treatment procedure.[3]

[2] This term refers to any person or persons in the assigned role of treater. It includes "untrained" lay counselors under certain institutionalized conditions (e.g., parole officer, group counselors) as well as trained clinicians.

[3] Douglas & Grant, *A Group Dynamics Approach to the Treatment of Nonconformists in the Navy*, 322 Annals Am. Acad. Pol. & Soc. Sci. 126 (1959).

Behavioral theories underlying the various types of correctional treatment described in our sample of reports were grouped under two major and two minor headings. The major, or primary type causation theories are those that assume either (1) the sick premise, or (2) the group relations premise.[4] In the former kinds of theories, whether Freudian, neo-Freudian, or whatever, the basic assumption is that the behavior is only a symptom of some underlying psychopathology. From this point of view crime is like a disease, in the medical sense, and can be cured only by alleviating the underlying pathological condition. This may be accomplished, according to the terms of the theory, by *individual psychotherapy, group psychotherapy, psychoanalysis, etc.* This point of view implies that criminality can be treated in the privacy of the "Doctor's office," or in a clinic, or in the "group therapy room of a prison," without recourse to procedures designed to directly modify the person's day-to-day interpersonal associations and group identifications.[5]

The basic assumption of the major competing point of view is that behavior, including deviant and criminal behavior, is primarily a function of the individual's group relations. Major independent variables associated with this approach include social status, role, significant associates, group identifications and the attitudes and values learned through and reinforced in these interpersonal situations. This point of view sees "sickness" as unrelated to criminality as such. A criminal may be suffering from some type of psychopathology which, let us say, is cured. According to strict proponents of the group relations principle, he would then simply be an emotionally stable criminal. Treatment programs based upon this approach attempt to directly manipulate and modify the nature of the individual's group relations, social roles, group identifications, etc., in such a manner that law abiding attitudes and values take precedence over criminal attitudes and values.[6]

The two minor or secondary types of theoretical approaches are those based upon either the *deficit* premise or the *activity* premise. The deficit premise assumes that there is "something missing" in the criminal. In some instances it is possible to replace this "something that is missing." For example, the person has been unable to learn vocational or occupational skills adequate to equip him to compete economically in our society. The "answer" or "cure" is to give such skills and the necessary attitudes and values with which to implement them.[7] Or, he may be lacking in the right kind of religious attitudes and values; or he may simply have been deprived of the opportunity to learn "right" from "wrong."[8] Whatever the content of the theory the treatment approach is implicit in it.

The activity premise simply assumes that there is something "bad" about too much

[4] Cressey, *Changing Criminals: The Application of the Theory of Differential Association,* 61 Am. J. Sociology 116 (1955).

[5] *Ibid.,* p. 116.

[6] *Ibid.,* p. 117.

[7] Chenault, *Education,* Tappan, Contemporary Correction 224–337 (1951).

[8] Edmonds, *The Place of Religion in the Treatment of the Offender,* 15 Federal Probation 14 (1951). Also see Gore, *The Antidote for Delinquency: God-Inspired Love,* 19 Federal Probation 33–36 (1955).

leisure time. It may be subsumed under the old saying, "idleness is the devil's workshop."[9] The "answer" is to provide constructive leisure time activities and supervised recreational programs. Together, these two points of view (deficit plus activity premises) are considered as "minor" because they are almost never employed alone but usually occur in conjunction with one or both of the major assumptions.

When only one type of intervention premise is used in the treatment evaluated, we can speak of a single premise theory of causation. When two are used together we can describe it as a dual premise theory. When two or more of these premises are used in a treatment procedure, one may speak of a multiple premise theory.

In these terms, then, what kinds of explanatory theories of criminal behavior were implicit or explicit in the 100 treatment programs evaluated? Almost one-half (47%) employed the sick premise (single premise approaches). However, a substantial majority (67%) of the treatment programs evaluated in this sample of reports were based upon some form of the sick premise—either singly or in conjunction with one or more other types of conceptual formulations (dual and multiple premise theories). In contrast, only 9% of these programs were based solely on the group relations premise. The finding, previously noted, that well over 50% of the outcome reports described efforts to evaluate some type of group treatment underlines the paradoxical fact that most forms of correctional group treatment are based, not upon the group relations premise, but upon the individualized sick premise.[10]

Effectiveness of Treatment

Finally, how corrective is correctional treatment? Of the total sample of correctional outcome reports evaluated, 10% described effects of the treatment as resulting in either "harm" or "no change" in behavior. Thirty-eight percent of the studies reported "some improvement." Thirty-seven percent reported a statistically significant difference in the direction of improvement for the group treated. Five percent of the reported results were classified as "not relevant" to the outcome problem posed by the study.

Thus, roughly one-half of the outcome reports evaluated concluded considerable improvement[11] in the treatment group. Almost one-fourth of the reports concluded either harmful results or "no change." These results, based upon the reported findings themselves, raise some serious questions regarding the efficacy of correctional treatment.

Reports Describing Experimental Designs. Five of the 22 correctional outcome reports classified as experimental indicated either harmful results or "no change" in the treatment group. This amounts to roughly 23% of the sample of experi-

[9] Conner, *For Satan Finds Some Mischief Still for Idle Hands to Do*, 24 Federal Probation 40 (1960). Also see preface by John Harding to Journal of Social Issues (Therapeutic Camping for Disturbed Youth) 13 (1957).

[10] Cressey, *Contradictory Theories in Correctional Group Therapy Programs*, 17 Federal Probation 22 (1954).

[11] This category includes those reporting "marked improvement" plus those reporting statistically significant improvement at the .05 level or below.

mental studies. Four (17%) reported "some improvement," four reported "marked improvement." Nine of these studies (43%) reported a "positive" statistically significant change in indices of the dependent variable applied to the treatment group.

Again, positive and negative findings are about equal. Roughly 60% ("marked improvement" plus statistically significant) may be classified as reporting successful outcomes. However, only 43% provided statistical evidence that the changes which occurred in the experimental group were not due to chance. On the other hand, roughly one fourth of the experimental reports concluded that the treatment group either became worse, or, there was no statistically significant change in the index of the dependent variable employed.

Reports Describing Systematic-Empirical Designs. Only 3 of the 26 systematic-empirical studies reported harmful results or "no change" (12%). Ten reported "some improvement" (38%). Eleven reported "marked improvement" (42%). Only one reported a statistically significant positive change in the treatment group (4%). Finally, one study finding was considered "not relevant."

Reports Describing Non-Systematic Empirical Designs. At the level of the least rigorously designed correctional outcome studies only 2 of the 52 studies evaluated reported harmful results or "no change" (4%). Twenty-four (46%) reported "some improvement" in the treatment group. Twenty-two (42%) reported "marked improvement." No studies in this category used tests of statistical significance. Finally, 4 (8%) cited findings considered to be irrelevant to the question posed.

Summary

A sample of 100 correctional outcome reports was subjected to a content analysis in an effort to obtain provisional answers to a number of questions relevant to an evaluation of the status of correctional treatment. Results of the analysis indicated that a slight majority of the correctional treatment programs evaluated in the reports was carried out in "forced treatment" settings (prison, parole or probation situations) as compared with correctional treatment programs carried out in "voluntary treatment" settings (private practice, private agencies, etc.) It was also found that psychologists and sociologists seem to have something of a monopoly on conducting this type of evaluative study. In addition, despite the fact that well over one-half of the reports were concerned with some form of group treatment, only a few described treatment procedures conceptually based upon the group relations premise. The most popular approach to explaining criminal or delinquent behavior and conceptualizing treatment goals and procedures involves some form of the sick premise regardless of whether the treatment deals with groups or individuals.

Over one-half of these reports described research designs of questionable rigor (classified as nonsystematic empirical). Roughly one-fourth of the reports dealt with more rigorous designs (systematic empirical). The remaining one-fourth of the reports described experimental designs. However, variations in research design seemed to have exerted little influence on frequency of reported successful treatment outcome. As the rigor of design increases, the frequency of reported treatment success increases (nonsystematic empirical–42%, systematic-empirical–46%, experimental–60%). Although the differences are not marked, the trend is in the unexpected direction. This is clarified somewhat when we note that as the rigor of design increases, the frequency of irrelevant conclusions markedly decreases; and that as the rigor of the design decreases, there is a marked decrease in the frequency of reported "harm" or "no change" in the treatment group (experimental–23%, systematic-empirical–12%, nonsystematic-empirical–4%). In this sample of reports apparently wishful thinking, when not subject to appropriate design controls, tends to be expressed in a resistance to negative results and indulgence in obscure generalities.

Since positive results were indicated in roughly one-half of the total sample of 100 reports analyzed, the problem of interpretation is not unrelated to that of determining "whether the cup is half empty or half full." But, when one recalls that these results, in terms of success or failure of the treatment used, are based upon the conclusions of the authors of the reports, themselves, then the implications of these findings regarding the effectiveness of correctional treatment become rather discouraging. A critical evaluation of the actual design and the specific research procedures described in each instance would substantially decrease the relative frequency of successful outcomes based upon reliably valid evidence. Therefore, it seems quite clear that, on the basis of this sample of outcomes reports with all of its limitations, evidence supporting the efficacy of correctional treatment is slight, inconsistent, and of questionable reliability.

This negative conclusion regarding correctional treatment is in general agreement with those drawn from several reviews of the correctional outcome literature. For example, in 1952 Dalton reported his fairly pessimistic impression of the value of counseling techniques in probation work.[12] In 1954, Kirby reviewed the literature on the effects of treating criminals and delinquents and concluded that "most treatment programs are based on hope and perhaps informed speculation rather than on verified information."[13] Two years later, Witmer and Tufts reviewed the literature on the effectiveness of delinquency prevention programs and concluded that such programs had not been notably effective.[14]

On the positive side there is impressive evidence of an increasing concern with correctional outcome research and progressive improvement in the calibre of the scientific investigations conducted. This is shown in the increasing numbers of experimental and systematic-empirical investigations, the greater involvement of professionally trained researchers and the resulting increase in sophistication and rigor of research designs, and in the growing efforts to more explicitly relate treatment practice to behavioral science theory.

[12] Dalton, *Value and Use of Counseling Techniques in the Work of Probation Officers,* 16 Federal Probation 17 (1952).

[13] Kirby, *Measuring Effects of Treatment of Criminals and Delinquents,* 38 Sociology and Social Research 374 (1954).

[14] Witmer & Tufts, *The Effectiveness of Delinquency Prevention Programs,* Washington: U.S. Department of Health, Education, and Welfare, Government Printing Office, 1954.

But how can we account for the apparent fact that although the operational means and resources of correctional outcomes research have substantially improved, there has been no apparent progress in the actual demonstration of the validity of various types of correctional treatment? There probably could be no one answer to this question which, at least for a period, must remain unanswered. However, one or more of the following "explanations" may be suggestive: (1) there is the possibility that reformative treatment is "really" ineffectual either in its own right or as a consequence of the ambivalence of the "crime and punishment" setting in which it takes place; (2) one may hazard that much of the correctional treatment currently practiced is not corrective and that little of the rehabilitation work being done should be dignified by the term *treatment;* (3) it may be that some types of correctional treatment are "really" effective with some types of individuals under certain conditions, but so far we have been unable to operationally describe the independent variable (treatment), reliably identify in terms of treatment response the type of behavior patterns being treated, adequately control the conditions under which such treatment takes place, or reliably delineate and measure relevant indices of the dependent variable; (4) perhaps much of the reformative treatment currently practiced is based upon the "wrong" theories of delinquent and criminal behavior.

LIST OF THE 100 STUDIES REVIEWED

Experimental

Walter C. Bailey, *Differential Communication in the Supervision of Paroled Opiate Addicts* (Paper read at the 1958 Meeting of the American Sociological Society).

Bertram J. Black and Selma J. Glick, *Recidivism at the Hawthorne-Cedar Knolls School,* Research Monograph No. 2, New York: Jewish Board of Guardians (1952).

Paul Hoover Bowman, *Effects of Revised School Program on Potential Delinquents,* 332 Annals of the American Academy of Political And Social Science (1959).

Roscoe C. Brown, Jr., and Dan W. Dodson, *The Effectiveness of a Boy's Club in Reducing Delinquency,* 332 Annals of the American Academy of Political and Social Science (1959).

Vernon Fox, *Michigan's Experiment in Minimum Security Penology,* 41 Journal of Criminal Law and Criminology 150 (1950).

Vernon Fox, *The Effect of Counseling on Adjustment in Prison,* 3 Social Forces 285 (1954).

Charles Gersten, *Group Therapy with Institutionalized Delinquents,* 80 Journal of Genetic Psychology 35 (1952).

J. Douglas Grant and Marguerite Q. Grant, *A Group Dynamics Approach to the Treatment of Nonconformists in the Navy,* 322 Annals of the American Academy of Political and Social Science (1959).

Joan K. Jackson, *The Seattle Police Department Rehabilitation Project for Chronic Alcoholics,* 24 Federal Probation 36 (1958).

Isaac Joiles, *An Experiment in Group Therapy for Adult Offenders,* 9 Federal Probation 16 (1946).

Ruth Jacobs Levy, *Reductions in Recidivism through Therapy* (1941).

Herbert S. Lewin, *An Experiment in Non-Authoritative Treatment of Juvenile Delinquents,* 1 Journal of Child Psychiatry, 195 (1948).

Arthur Mann, *Group Therapy–Irradiation,* 46 Journal of Criminal Law, Criminology, and Police Science, 50 (1955).

Joan and William McCord, *A Follow-up Report on the Cambridge-Somerville Youth Study,* 322 Annals of the American Academy of Political and Social Science, 89 (1959).

Edwin Powers and Helen Witmer, *An Experiment in the Prevention of Delinquency* (1951).

Ellery F. Reed, *How Effective are Group-Work Agencies in Preventing Juvenile Delinquency?* 22 Social Service Review, 341 (1948).

Melvin Roman, *Reaching Delinquents Through Reading* (1957).

Alfred C. Schnur, *The Educational Treatment of Prison and Recividism,* 54 American Journal of Sociology 143–147 (1948).

Harry M. Shulman, *Delinquency Treatment of the Controlled Activity Group,* 10 American Sociological Review 405 (1945).

Robert S. Wallerstein, *Comparative Study of Treatment Method for Chronic Alcoholism: The Alcoholism Research Project at Winter V.A. Hospital,* 113 American Journal of Psychiatry 228 (1956).

H. Ashley Weeks, *Youthful Offenders at Highfields* (1958).

Robert D. Wirt and James L. Jaconson, *Experimental Studies in Group Psychotherapy with Prisoners; Report N.L. Selected Groups,* Minnesota State Prison Department of Social Welfare (June, 1958) (mimeographed).

Systematic-Empirical

Augusta F. Bronner, *Treatment and What Happened Afterward,* 14 American Journal of Orthopsychiatry 28 (1944).

Morris G. Caldwell, *Review of a New Type of Probation Study Made in Alabama,* 15 Federal Probation 3 (1951).

James F. Chastin, *A Public School Offers Special Courses for Young Probationers,* 22 Federal Probation 37 (1958).

Eric K. Clarke, *Group Therapy in Rehabilitation,* 16 Federal Probation 28 (1952).

David Dressler, *Parole Results,* Proceedings of the American Prison Association (1941) 416–525.

Warren H. Dunham and Mary E. Knauer, *The Juvenile Court in its Relationship to Adult Criminality,* 3 Social Forces 290 (1954).

Warren H. Dunham and LeMay Adamson, *Clinical Treatment of Male Delinquents: A Case Study in Effort and Result,* 21 American Sociological Review (1956).

Albert Ellis, *The Effectiveness of Psychotherapy with Individuals who Have Severe Homosexual Problems,* 20 Journal of Consulting Psychology, 191 (1956).

Ralph England, *A Study of Post Probation Recidivism Among Federal Offenders,* 19 Federal Probation 10 (1955).

Louisve V. Frishie, *The Treated Sex Offender,* 122 Federal Probation 18 (1958).

John M. Gandy, *Preventive Work with Streetcorner Groups: Hyde Park Youth Project, Chicago,* 322 Annals of the American Academy of Political and Social Science 107 (1959).

Lester H. Gliedman, et al., *Group Therapy with Alcoholics with Concurrent Group Meetings of Their Wives,* 17 Quarterly Journal of Studies on Alcohol 665 (1956).

Maxwell Jones, *The Therapeutic Community* (1953).

Sidney Kosofsky, *Directive Therapy with Female Juvenile Delinquents,* 11 Journal of Clinical Psychology 357 (1955).

Gerald R. Ladhoff, *The Contribution of Physical Education in the Prevention of Potential Juvenile Delinquency,* (unpublished Masters Thesis, University of California, Los Angeles, 1956).

R. Lessner, *Psychodrama in Prison,* 3 Group Psychotherapy 77 (1950).

Tom McGee, *Changes in Adjustment During Detention,* Association News, (March 7, 1955).

Walter B. Miller, *The Impact of a Community Group Work Program on Delinquent Corner Groups,* 31 Social Service Review 390 (1957).

Walter B. Miller, *Preventive Work with Streetcorner Groups: Boston Delinquency Project,* 322 Annals of the American Academy of Political and Social Science 97 (1959).

New York City Youth Board, *How They Were Reached: A Study of 310 Children and Their Families Known to Referral Units,* (Youth Board Monograph, No. 2, New York: New York City Youth Board, 1954).

Florence Powdermaker, *Psychopathology and Treatment of Delinquent Girls,* 6 Pastoral Psychology 33 (1955).

George J. Reed, *The Federal Youth Corrections Program,* 22 Social Service Review 340 (1956).

Vin Rosenthal and Edmund Shimberg, *The Program of Group Therapy with Incarcerated Narcotic Addicts,* 49 Journal of Criminal Law, Criminology and Police Science 140 (1958).

Nathaniel Showstack, *Preliminary Report on the Psychiatric Treatment of Prisoners at the California Medical Facility, San Pedro, California,* a paper read at the annual meeting of the American Psychiatric Association, Atlantic City, New Jersey, May 12, 1955 (mimeographed).

Frederic M. Thrasher, *The Boys' Club and Juvenile Delinquency,* 42 American Journal of Sociology 66 (1936).

Lorraine O'Donnell Williams, *Short-Term Treatment of Women: An Experiment,* 21 Federal Probation 42 (1957).

Non-Systematic Empirical

Joseph Andriola, *Success and Failure in the Treatment of Twenty-five Truants at a Child Guidance Clinic,* 13 American Journal of Orthopsychiatry 691 (1943).

Freed Bales, *Types of Social Structure as Factors in "Cures" for Alcoholic Addiction,* 3 Applied Anthropology 1 (1942).

Ernest G. Beier, *Experimental Therapy with a Gang,* 30 Focus 97 (1951).

Howard Bennett, *Successful Treatment of a Sociopathic Personality, Anti-Social Type with Schizoid Trends,* 11 American Journal of Pschotherapy 111 (1957).

Benjamin Boshers, Lee G. Sewall and Mary Koga, *Management of the Narcotic Addict in an Outpatient Clinic,* 113 American Journal of Psychiatry 158 (1956).

Margaretta K. Bowers, M.D., *A Triangle of Treatment,* 30 Focus 161 (1951).

Harry J. Brevis, *Counseling Prison Inmates,* 7 Pastoral Psychology 35 (1956).

Martha Brunner-Orne and Martin T. Orne, *Alcoholics,* Slavson Fields of Group Psychotherapy, Ch. 5 (1956).

Martha Brunner-Orne, *The Utilization of Group Psychotherapy in Enforced Treatment Program for Alcoholics and Addicts,* 6 The International Journal of Group Psychotherapy 272 (1956).

Edward Cass, *Parole Can be Successful,* 31 Journal of Criminal Law and Criminology 7 (1940).

F. C. Cesarman, *Religious Conversion of Sex Offenders During Psychotherapy: Two Cases;* 11 Journal of Pastoral Care 25 (1957).

Jack Chwast, *Casework Treatment in a Police Setting,* 18 Federal Probation 35 (1954).

J. H. Conn, *The Psychiatric Treatment of Certain Chronic Offenders,* 32 Journal of Criminal Law and Criminology 631 (1942).

Raymond J. Corsini, *Psychotherapy with a Hostile Group,* 6 Group Psychotherapy 168 (1954).

Marie Duffin, *Reaching Out to Prevent Delinquency,* 19 Federal Probation 27 (1955).

James R. Dumpson, *An Approach to Antisocial Street Gangs,* 13 Federal Probation 22 (1949).

Albert Eglash, *Adults Anonymous,* 49 Journal of Criminal Law, Criminology and Police Science 237 (1958).

Benjamin B. Ferencz, *Rehabilitation of Army Offenders,* 34 Journal of Criminal Law and Criminology 245 (1943).

Jay W. Fidler, Jr., M.D., *Possibilities of Group Therapy with Female Offenders,* 4 International Journal of Group Psychotherapy 330 (1951).

Maurice Flock, *Use of Fiction or Drama in Psychotherapy and Social Education,* Proceedings of 88th Congress of American Corrections Association 339 (1958).

John P. Fort, *The Psychodynamics of Drug Addiction and Group Psychotherapy,* 5 International Journal of Group Psychotherapy 150 (1955).

Adele Franklin, *The All-Day Neighbor Schools,* 332 Annals of the American Academy of Political and Social Science, 62 (1959).

Antoinette Fried, *A Work Camp Program for Potential Delinquents,* 322 Annals of the American Academy of Political and Social Science 38 (1959).

James M. Hebron, *Study of Parole in Maryland,* (Baltimore Criminal Justice Commission, 1935).

L. Wallace Hoffman, *Can You Trust Them?* 34 Journal of Criminal Law and Criminology 26 (1943).

Isaac Jollcs, *An Experiment in Group Guidance,* 23 Journal of Social Psychology 55 (1946).

W. C. Jones, *Parole: A Five Year Study,* 31 Journal of Criminal Law and Criminology, XXXI (May-June, 1940) 15-21.

Gisela Konopka, *Coordination of Services as a Means of Delinquency Prevention,* 322 Annals of the American Academy of Political and Social Science 30 (1959).

Solomon Korbin, *The Chicago Area Project–A 25 Year Assessment,* 322 Annals of the American Academy of Political and Social Science 19 (1959).

Arthur Lerner, *Self-Evaluation in Group Counseling with Male Alcoholic Inmates,* 5 International Journal of Group Psychotherapy 286 (1955).

James V. Lowry, *Hospital Treatment of the Narcotic Addicts,* 20 Federal Probation 42 (1956).

R. W. Newkirk, *Psychotherapy on Juvenile Delinquents,* 34 Journal of Criminal Law and Criminology 100 (1943).

Clifford V. Oje, *The Air Force Corrections and-Retraining Programs,* 19 Federal Probation 31 (1955).

J. W. Osberg and A. K. Berline, *The Developmental Stages in Group Psychotherapy with Hospitalized Narcotic Addicts,* 6 Journal of Group Psychotherapy 35 (1956).

G. Lewis Penner, *An Experiment in Police and Social Agency Cooperation,* 322 Annals of American Academy of Political and Social Science 79 (1959).

Ethel Perry, *The Treatment of Aggressive Juvenile Delinquents in "Family Group Therapy,"* 5 International Journal of Group Psychotherapy 131 (1955).

Chester D. Poremba, *Group Probation: An Experiment,* 19 Federal Probation 22 (1955).

Margaret G. Reilly and Robert A. Young, *Agency-Initiated Treatment of Potentially Delinquent Boys,* 16 American Journal of Orthopsychiatry 697 (1946).

Dietrich C. Reitzes, *The Effect of Social Environment upon Former Felons,* 46 Journal of Criminal Law, Criminology and Police Science, 226 (1955).

Melitta Schmideberg, *Just Out of Prison,* Focus (January, 1951; Taken from a reprint, no volume or number designation available).

Irving Schulman, *The Dynamics of Certain Reactions of Delinquents to Group Psychotherapy,* 2 International Journal of Group Psychotherapy 334 (1952).

Leon N. Shapiro and Donald H. Russell, *Psychotherapeutic Investigation of Imprisoned Public Offenders,* (part of report on meeting of March 9, 1956 of the Massachusetts Society for Research in Psychiatry), 123 Journal of Nervous and Mental Disease 409 (1956).

E. Preston Sharp, *Group Counseling in a Short-Term Institution,* 23 Federal Probation 7 (1959).

Bernard H. Shulman, *Group Psychotherapy in an Army Post Stockade,* 21 Federal Probations 45 (1957).

Derrick Sington, *Redeeming the Murderer,* 184 Nation 117 (1957).

John C. Spencer and Tadeusz Grygier, *The Probation Hostel in England,* 6 Focus 165 (1952).

Marion Stranahan and Cecile Schwartzman, *An Experiment in Reaching Asocial Adolescents Through Group Therapy,* 322 Annals of Academy of Political and Social Science 117 (1959).

Leon Tec, *A Psychiatrist as a Participant Observer in a Group of "Delinquent" Boys,* 6 International Journal of Group Psychotherapy 418 (1956).

Ruther S. Tefferteller, *Delinquency Prevention Through Revitalizing Parent-Child Relations,* 322 Annals of American Academy of Political and Social Science 69 (1959).

James J. Thorpe and Bernard Smith, *Phases in Group Development in Treatment of Drug Addicts,* 3 International Journal of Group Psychotherapy 66 (1953).

James J. Thorpe and Bernard Smith, *Operational Sequence in Group Therapy with Young Offenders,* 2 International Journal of Group Psychotherapy 24 (1952).

George H. Weber, *The Boy Scout Program as a Group Approach in Institutional Delinquency Treatment,* 19 Federal Probation 47 (1955).

49. Inter-Institutional Conflict as a Major Impediment to Delinquency Prevention

Walter B. Miller

Juvenile delinquency is a major area of concern in the United States today. Although there is evidence of some increase in the actual incidence of juvenile crime, it is equally evident that the intensity of public concern over this issue has increased far more rapidly than the demonstrated statistical increase. This paper will focus, not on juvenile crime as such, but on the larger adult community, and, in particular, on that segment of the community which maintains explicit responsibility in this area.

It is the thesis of this paper that the nature of current concern over juvenile delinquency serves important latent functions for substantial segments of the adult community. If this thesis is true, we would expect to find, as in all areas where a significant discrepancy exists between the overt or recognized aspects of a phenomenon and its covert aspects or latent functions: 1) Discrepancies and contradictions between officially stated policy and actual operating procedure; 2) recurrent failure to follow through on plans whose objectives conform to officially stated positions but whose execution would in fact run counter to the latent function; 3) much conflict over goals and methods both between concerned institutional systems and between sub-units within these systems. The net result of these forces would be to produce action stalemates both through failure to take action and through mutual blocking of efforts to the end that the latently functional status quo is preserved.

That public concern over juvenile delinquency serves *psychological* functions for adults as individuals has been maintained by several investigators. This paper will attempt to show that the nature of current institutional practice regarding delinquency serves important *structural* functions as well; that is, for the great majority of organized institutions which maintain programs directed at juvenile delinquency, the adoption of operating procedures and philosophies which would be effective in reducing juvenile crime would, in fact, pose severe threats to the viability of the institution. The focus here will be on the area of delinquency *prevention* rather

Reprinted from *Human Organization,* 17:3 (Fall 1958), 20-23, by permission of The Society for Applied Anthropology and the author.

than on methods of dealing with the adjudicated delinquent. Since the area of prevention is far less structured and has developed fewer established operating procedures than the area of treatment or disposition, the dynamics of institutional functioning in this area are revealed in much sharper relief.

It has been established that there is far more law-violating behavior by adolescents than is officially acted on; according to one study, the actual number of potentially arrestable delinquents is three times that of those actually arrested. Once an individual is officially apprehended for the commission of a delinquent act or acts, a whole series of established procedures are set into motion; the individual may be released with a warning, put on probation, or sentenced to undergo a variety of corrective measures ranging from a citizenship course through psychiatric treatment to straight confinement. But in the area of "prevention" things are much less well established. There is growing sentiment to the effect that "prevention" of juvenile crime would be a much sounder procedure than attempting to deal with the individual once he has already committed a crime, and would be much more economical in the long run. But then the question becomes–how does one "prevent"? Once something has happened you can take steps as a consequence of that occurrence, but what steps should you take for something that has not happened yet, but which might? Thus, while there are many well-established institutions–courts, police, correctional institutions, psychiatric agencies–whose operating procedures and philosophies are geared to handling individuals who have committed delinquent acts and been apprehended, there are, with a few exceptions, *no* established institutional structures whose major responsibility is delinquency prevention, and whose institutional values and operating philosophies are geared to that objective. Existing organizations undertake prevention, if at all, as a relatively minor adjunct to major institutional responsibilities which lie elsewhere–a fact which has important bearing on the potential effectiveness of prevention programs.

Following sections will describe very briefly the experience of one large eastern city in attempting to institute and maintain a "preventive" program on the community level. In 1950, rising public apprehension over juvenile delinquency in general, and gang violence in particular, produced demands for action from many quarters. Since gang activity was a focus of concern, and much gang delinquency is undetectable or undetected, traditional approaches based on restriction or treatment were seen as unfeasible, and pressures to institute some sort of community-based preventive program were exerted on the major institutional structures with assumed or assigned responsibility in the area of juvenile crime.

I

The city contained scores of intricately interrelated organizations, both public and private, varying widely in size, scope and method of operations, and in assigned or claimed area of jurisdiction or concern with juvenile crime. Of these, about a dozen public and private organizational groupings maintained major responsibility in the area of juvenile crime. The principal public agencies were the municipal government, the recreation department, the police department, the courts, the public schools, and the state youth corrections division. Major private groupings were medical and psychiatric clinics, social work agencies, churches, universities, and various special cause groups, such as ethnic associations and crime prevention societies.

Initial pressures produced a variety of statements as to the desirability of a preventive program, but no action. A complex set of maneuvers was carried on for about three years, usually involving the appointment of special committees which then appointed a study group which turned in a set of recommendations strongly affirming the desirability of a preventive program, and at the same time explaining why such a program was not the responsibility of that particular organization. This continuing stalemate was finally broken early in 1953, primarily through combined pressures from two ethnic groups, the Jews and the Negroes, after a prominent Jewish clergyman had been murdered, allegedly by a Negro teenage gang. The Jews, acting through their organized representative groupings, inferentially charged the Negroes with antisemitism; the Negroes, through their organized groupings, intimated that this charge indicated anti-Negro sentiment on the part of the Jews. Two other groups whose interests were being threatened by gang activity—the public schools and the settlement houses—added their pressures to those of the Jews and Negroes, and, in the spring of 1953, a central delinquency committee was created, comprising representatives of over one hundred youth-concerned groupings in the metropolitan area, including the major groups cited above. At the time this committee was formed, many statements were made by all groupings—police, courts, the municipal administration, churches, private agencies—pledging their fullest mutual cooperation in this enterprise aimed at coping with the city gang problem.

Despite the sense of urgency and crisis which attended the organization of the central committee, no concrete action was taken for more than a year. This year was filled with indecision, groping for direction, and constant mutual blocking and conflict, sometimes veiled, sometimes overt, among the agencies represented on the central committee. A great variety of proposals was forewarded and debated, reflecting many divergent conceptions of the causes and proper treatment of juvenile crime, and the group seemed unable to reach any agreement on a positive course of action. After six months, a sociology professor at a local university was persuaded to accept responsibility for formulating a plan of action, and in June of 1954—four and a half years after the initial moves, and a year and a half after the murder which had broken the stalemate—a special demonstration project in delinquency prevention was set up in one district of the city. By this time, several of the major organizations originally represented on the central committee had terminated active affiliation—principally, the police and the Jewish clergy. The Jews lost interest rapidly when it developed that anti-semitism had played a relatively small role in gang attacks on Jews.

The prevention project, which was to operate for three years, was staffed primarily by social workers, and included three service programs—a program of direct service to selected "delinquogenic" families, a community organization program, and, as a major effort, a program of direct work with delinquent corner gangs. Although it was the creation of the central committee, once project operations actually started, the committee became progressively disenchanted with its off-spring. As the project took action in more definite and visible ways, it became clear that many of its methods and the operating philosophies behind them were in radical conflict with the institutional ideals of the various groups represented on the central committee. This was evidenced in responses ranging from passive non-participation, through withdrawal, to active opposition.

During the three years of the project's existence, the executive board of the central committee became a battleground for its component organizations, with the project and its methods serving as a pawn in these conflicts. After the first meeting, at which a project worker presented a report on his activities, the representative of the Catholic Archdiocese resigned in indignation from the executive board. Following this incident, a watchdog committee was set up to oversee the project; the chairman of this committee was a Protestant clergyman who was strongly opposed to major methods of the project. About a year later the project became involved in direct conflict with the state division of corrections, with enmity reaching sufficient intensity that the corrections division issued an order forbidding its parolees to participate in project activities, and, in fact, jailed one parolee who defied this order. The social agencies initially regarded the program with great suspicion, as did the schools. During the latter part of the program the city recreation department representative on the central committee, incensed by a report issued by the project, demanded that no further reports be issued unless approved by the central committee. During the second year, funds to support the project, which were raised by the central committee, became increasingly difficult to obtain, and about this time the committee's original chairman, who had been active in initiating and supporting the project, was replaced, without his prior knowledge, by another man who was far less assertive.

Shortly after the start of the project's third year, its director resigned, partly because of increasing difficulties in obtaining financing, and no attempt was made to replace him with a person of equivalent status. Before the director left, he formulated a detailed proposal for the establishment of a permanent delinquency prevention agency under state and municipal auspices, using the project's experience as the basis of recommendations. The three-man committee chosen to present this program to the mayor and governor consisted of an amiable but aged chairman and the two most outspoken opponents of the project on the central committee. The recommendations for a state-municipal program presented under these auspices were rejected both by the mayor and governor. Once the program was officially terminated, the central committee appeared eager to forget that it had ever existed. Although federal support for post-project research had been obtained, members of the central committee were most reluctant to permit such continuation and questioned the right of the project to have sought these funds, depite the fact that authorization had been officially voted.

During the period when the project was subject to increasing opposition by its parent organizations on the central committee, these agencies were also engaged in attacking one another both in the arena of central committee meetings and through other media. A judge accused the police of inefficiency in dealing with delinquents and in keeping adequate crime statistics; a police chief accused the social welfare agencies of coddling delinquents; the director of a medical group accused the corrections division of increasing the delinquency of those in their care; a Catholic prelate accused the social work agencies of neglecting religion in their dealings with delinquents; a psychiatric agency head accused the police of harmful advocacy of punitive measures; the Archbishop accused enforcement agencies of politically motivated laxness in prosecuting delinquents; a group of legislators attempted to oust major officials of the youth corrections department over the issue of personnel qualifications. In addition, sub-units within these larger organizations feuded with one another; a judge accused other judges of excessive leniency in dealing with juvenile offenders; a committee of the school department claimed that some teachers were fostering delinquency by being unable or unwilling to cope with school behavior problems; the Police Commissioner castigated and demoted a sizable group of patrolmen, charging them with inefficiency in dealing with juveniles in their area of jurisdiction; a Protestant clergyman claimed that some Protestant sects were failing in the fight against delinquency by remaining too aloof from community involvement.

II

We have, then, a situation which involves these elements: first, a social phenomenon–gang violence–which is universally condemned; a crisis incident which arouses deep feelings and provides a spur to direct action; the mobilization and cooperation of all the major concerned institutional groupings of a major American city, and then–much delay and misdirected energy by these institutions in setting up a project to which they become progressively more hostile; constant interinstitutional conflict over a variety of issues; and finally a virtual stalemate in launching any sort of effective action to cope with the problem. This situation is by no means unique; it is found in many cities faced with similar problems; in particular, conflicts between the police, churches, courts, social agencies, and schools in the New York City gang situation have been widely publicized. This prevalent phenomenon–apparently universal agreement on a basic objective, gang control, coupled with mutual conflict leading to almost complete blocking of action, may be explained by focusing on the *means* proposed to secure the end–means which derive from the operating philosophies of the various concerned organizations. This paper suggests that operating philosphies may be nonfunctional for the purpose of reducing juvenile crime, and that a consequence of differences in institutional philosophies is that a significant proportion of energy potentially directable to delinquency reduction is instead expected in conflict between institutions.

The nature of these differences may be illuminated by specifying six dimensions along which conflict takes place: these relate to differences in conception of the *etiology* of delinquency; of the *disposition* of the delinquent; of the *approach priority;* of the appropriate *organizational method,* and of the proper *status* of *personnel.*

Morality-Pathology: A major difference in assumptions as to the etiology of juvenile crime, as well as other forms of behavior, involves fundamental concepts of human nature. According to one school of thought, deviant or criminal behavior must be viewed in terms of morality and immorality; an individual is morally responsible for his own behavior, and failure to conform to norms and standards represents a triumph of evil forces over good in an inner struggle for which the individual is held personally responsible. The opposing school maintains that deviant or criminal behavior should be viewed in terms of sickness and health; that an individual who violates social and legal norms is, in fact, driven by inner forces over which he has relatively little control, and which have their origins in pathological conditions of the organism.

Individual Locus–Social Locus. A second important difference involving etiological concepts relates to the locus of deviant behavior. One school attributes criminal behavior to forces within the *individual*–moral or physical-psychological–which may be dealt with by corrective measures directed at the individual; the other school finds the significant factors in the nature of the *social milieu,* and sees basic alterations in social conditions as the necessary course of action.

Restriction-Rehabilitation. This dimension relates to the proper method of dealing with offenders. The restrictive school of thought advocates the separation or isolation of the individual from normal social intercourse on the assumption, first, that the *protection of society* is the paramount necessity, and second, that punishment both serves as a deterrent to future violation and is merited in consequence of transgression. This dispositional prescription is generally forwarded by those espousing the morality concept of etiology. The treatment or rehabilitative school, basing procedure on the "pathology" conception of etiology, postulates "cure" or directed efforts to modify behavior patterns of the offending individual as of prime importance, with his restoration to normal social interaction a desired objective.

Action–Research. This dimension relates to consideration of priority in approaching the problem. One school maintains that the urgency of the situation, or the intensity of need, demands immediate action, based on the best knowledge currently available; the other maintains that far too little reliable information exists as to the nature of the involved phenomena and methods of treatment, and that the most productive expenditure of energy can be made by undertaking systematic research to gain essential knowledge.

Localization-Centralization. This dimension concerns the issue of the most desirable method for organizing preventive programs; one school believes that programs should be undertaken within and by the local community, on the grounds that only local people are sufficiently familiar with the special conditions of the local situation for adequate understanding, and that local autonomy must be maintained; the centralization school maintains that the nature and magnitude of the problem demand mobilization of resources which local groups, operating independently, could not afford, and that, to be effective, resources must be pooled and efforts coordinated to avoid duplication and overlap.

Lay-Professional. This dimension relates to the qualifications and status of personnel who are to implement preventive programs. One school holds that only those who manifest characteristics similar to those of the subject population–either through similarities in class or locality status–can be effective, and the attributes essential to effectiveness, such as warmth and sympathy, are independent of training; the other school maintains that work in so difficult an area demands that practitioners be exposed to a course of professional training which both imparts knowledge as to specialized procedures and eliminates those whose personality characteristics would be detrimental to this kind of work.

The various institutional structures related to delinquency tend to maintain characteristic syndromes of these etiological and procedural positions. The described positions are seldom maintained in the "pure" form, since they are presented here as polar extremes which define variable dimensions–and "middle positions," such as equal stress on action and research, may be taken, but most institutions involved do maintain definitely identifiable positions of varying intensity along these dimensions. Conflicts along the varying dimensions take place, both *between* and within, concerned institutions, but intrainstitutional differences are generally concealed from public notice. The most severe conflict occurs between institutions which take extreme opposing positions on all or most of these dimensions; conflict is less severe when there is disagreement on only one or two. For example, the major juvenile court of the city described above strongly supported the "morality" and "individual locus" concepts of etiology: the restrictive dispositional method, action priority, and localized organization. The major child psychiatry clinic supported the "pathology" etiological concept. Rehabilitative treatment method, centralized organization, and use of professional implementary personnel. These positions put the two organizations in direct conflict in four of the six dimensions: in agreement over one–individual etiological locus–and in minor opposition over the action-research issue. Similar comparisons could be made between each set of involved institutions.

Summary

The argument of this paper may be summarized as follows: There is much conflict over the issue of proper procedure among the different groups which maintain varying orders of responsibility for delinquency prevention. This conflict results in a lack of coordination and mutual blocking of efforts leading to a stalemate in reference to a community-supported objective. But these conflicts over method derive from the basic institutional philosophies of the several institutions. Although these philosophies may be effective in facilitating achievement of the stated objectives of the institution, their maintenance is vital to the institution's continued existence and this latent objective has greater priority than the achievement of the institution's explicit objectives, and much greater priority than achieving objectives only peripherally related to the institution's primary explicit aims.

This situation would appear to have important implications for delinquency prevention. It would imply that the major impediment to effectiveness in this field relates more to the nature of relations among the various concerned institutions than to lack of knowledge as to effective procedure. Much is now known about the causes of delinquency and promising ameliorative techniques have been developed. The principal difficulty lies in the *application* of these techniques, and any realistic possibility of such application depends almost entirely on existing institutional structures. This would suggest a shift in emphasis in current research and action efforts, from a primary focus on the relations between implementing institutions and the subject population, to the relationships among the institutions themselves. Both research and action efforts involve severe difficulties since they will touch on areas intimately related to the visibility of the institution—areas all the more charged and sensitive, since they are frequently unconscious or implicit.

50. An Evaluation of Early Identification and Intensive Treatment Programs for Predelinquents*

Jackson Toby

The "early identification and intensive treatment" approach to delinquency control is breathtakingly plausible. A plausible argument is not necessarily correct, as Columbus showed those who believed that the world was flat. "Early identification and intensive treatment," though probably not as erroneous as the flat-world theory, is more a slogan or a rallying cry than a realistic assessment of the difficulties that delinquency control programs must overcome. This paper points out the need for sharper definition of the implicit assumptions of "early identification and intensive treatment" programs and then examines two of the best-known early identification programs in the light of this need.

Early identification programs are based on either of two logically distinct principles: extrapolation or circumstantial vulnerability. The principle of extrapolation assumes that predelinquents are youngsters in the early stages of a delinquent way of life; the principle of circumstantial vulnerability assumes that youngsters who

Reprinted from *Social Problems,* **13**:2 (Fall 1965), 160–175, by permission of The Society for the Study of Social Problems and the author.

*A preliminary version of this paper was published in *Social Work,* 6 (July, 1961), pp. 3–13. The research on which it is based was financed by the Ford Foundation.

have been exposed to circumstances believed to cause delinquency are likely to become delinquent. The Cambridge-Somerville Youth Study emphasized the extrapolative approach to prediction. "Difficult boys" and "average boys" were nominated by teachers and policemen. The expectation of adolescent delinquency was based primarily on quasi-delinquent behavior during preadolescence. Although the three raters on the Cambridge-Somerville research team made a clinical assessment of each case and made predictions on a variety of family and personal circumstances, the great majority of the predictions were that difficult boys would remain difficult and average boys, average.[1] Early identification meant in short that antisocial tendencies would persist and develop further unless checked by outside intervention. This is quite different from identifying potential delinquents by a theory of delinquency which holds that youngsters exposed to certain sociocultural conditions will become delinquent. Yet the latter is also called "early identification." Criminologists Sheldon and Eleanor Glueck claim to be able to predict delinquency on the basis of factors distinct from the child's early behavior: (1) affection of mother for the boy; (2) affection of father for the boy; (3) discipline of boy by father; (4) supervision of boy by mother; and (5) family cohesiveness.[2] The New York City Youth Board has attempted to test this claim by applying the Glueck prediction table to a sample of 223 boys who in 1952 entered the first grade of two New York City schools in high delinquency neighborhoods. Note that the

[1]Professor Robert Stanfield found in his re-analysis of the Cambridge-Somerville data that 81 to 84 per cent of the "difficult" referrals were given a *delinquent* prognosis; 59 to 68 per cent of the "average" referrals were given a *nondelinquent* prognosis. (Personal communication, March 24, 1965.) Nevertheless, the extent to which the raters were influenced by the source and nature of the referrals is not clear. The seeming extrapolations might be accounted for by systematic differences in the environmental circumstances of "difficult" and "average" boys. The three raters themselves claimed to give considerable weight to the nature of the neighborhood and the family situation. See Donald W. Taylor, "An Analysis of Predictions of Delinquency Based on Case Studies," *Journal of Abnormal and Social Psychology,* 42 (January, 1947), pp. 45–46. Recall, however, that the design of the study was such that the raters started with a bimodal universe: boys identified by teachers and policemen as troublesome and boys identified as law-abiding. Although the ratings ranged from minus 5 (most delinquent) to plus 5 (most nondelinquent), comparatively few borderline ratings (zero) were made. In characterizing the predictions as extrapolative, I am assuming that a troublesome boy was predicted to be more or less delinquent depending on his family and neighborhood situation and a law-abiding boy was predicted to be more or less nondelinquent, but troublesome boys did not usually get into the nondelinquent prediction range nor law-abiding boys into the delinquent range by virtue of their family and neighborhood situations. In Tables 1 and 2, any prediction from minus five to minus one was considered a prediction of delinquency, and any prediction from plus five to plus one was considered a prediction of nondelinquency. Zero predictions were eliminated from the analysis. See also the discussion in Edwin Powers and Helen Witmer. *An Experiment in the Prevention of Delinquency: The Cambridge-Somerville Youth Study.* New York: Columbia University Press, 1951, pp. 29–36.

[2]Sheldon and Eleanor Glueck. *Unraveling Juvenile Delinquency,* New York: Commonwealth Fund. 1950: Sheldon and Eleanor Glueck, *Predicting Delinquency and Crime,* Cambridge, Massachusetts: Harvard University Press, 1959; Eleanor T. Glueck, "Efforts to Identify Delinquents," *Federal Probation,* 24 (June, 1950), pp. 49–56.

Cambridge-Somerville approach to prediction is less ambitious than the Youth Board-Glueck approach. One can extrapolate without knowing much about causes. One presumably ought to know a great deal about the causes of delinquency if one hopes to make accurate predictions on the basis of the sociocultural circumstances to which the child is exposed.

This distinction bwteeen an extrapolative prediction and a circumstantial prediction, though clear in theory, is often obscured in practice. Diagnostic interviews or self-rating scales (like the Minnesota Multiphasic Personality Inventory) combine the youngster's reports about his own antisocial behavior and/or attitudes with his reports about his family and neighborhood environment. Thus, in many attempts at early identification, the basis for the prediction of future delinquency is not clear.[3] Of course, it can be contended that a better prediction can be made if it is based *both* on the child's early behavior and on his exposure to known deleterious influences. Possibly so. However, such predictions emerge like sausages from a sausage machine but without real insight into *why* they are correct. The drawback of predictions made without theory becomes all too evident when treatment is attempted. Since the prediction is mechanical and does not imply an understanding of the causes of delinquency, it provides no guidance for treatment. "Treatment" becomes an umbrella word meaning all things to all men. A therapeutic program based on family casework is not the same thing as one based on individual psychotherapy, the improvement of reading skills, participation in organized sports, or vocational counseling.

Predictions made without a theory of delinquency causation can be matched with a treatment program that is similarly eclectic. Sometimes it is very difficult indeed to find out what "intensive treatment" consists of. The therapist may contend that each case is unique and that treatment is tailored to the individual case. One might well be suspicious of such vagueness. Vagueness can conceal two kinds of ignorance: ignorance as to what is causing the antisocial behavior and ignorance of the best strategy of intervention. In any case, most "individual treatment" programs and programs claiming to "co-ordinate" community resources are in practice not genuinely eclectic. They implicitly answer the question, "What kind of treatment?" by selecting resources ideologically congenial to the agency. For example, the same predelinquent child may be treated through casework techniques if he comes to the attention of one agency and through group work techniques if he comes to the attention of another. Presumably the type of treatment selected should be governed by the etiological factor involved in the youngster's predelinquency. The type of treatment selected by practitioners of "individual treatment" seems more closely related to the practitioners' preconceptions than to the child's problems. This is said, not to condemn efforts to treat predelinquency, but to point out that in the present state of knowledge the frequently invoked analogy between medical practice

[3] D. H. Stott, "The Prediction of Delinquency from Non-Delinquent Behavior," *British Journal of Delinquency,* 10 (January, 1960), pp. 195–210.

and delinquency control is misleading. Whereas medical practice aims at precise diagnosis and specific treatment, early identification and intensive treatment of delinquency usually address themselves to an unknown problem with an unproved technique. Is it any wonder that the few treatment programs that have been rigorously evaluated reveal disappointingly small effects? For instance, the Cambridge-Somerville Youth Study offers little support to proponents of "early identification and intensive treatment" as an approach to delinquency control. Whereas 41 per cent of the 253 boys in the treatment group subsequently were convicted of at least one major crime in a state or federal court, 37 per cent of the 253 boys in the control group were so convicted. Considering (a) that treatment began by age 10 for 121 boys and by age 13 for the remaining 132, and (b) that treatment lasted for four years or more for 171 boys, *more* criminality in the treatment group is rather surprising. The McCords point out that only 12 of the 253 boys had intensive therapy (according to their quite reasonable criteria of "intensive"), and they suggest that for this reason intensive treatment was not really tested. Perhaps so. On the other hand, hardly a probation or parole system in the United States gives as intense supervision as was given routinely in the course of the Cambridge-Somerville Youth Study. The case loads of Cambridge-Somerville workers were 34 youngsters per counselor at the beginning of the study and even fewer when the boys grew older.[4]

Tacit Assumptions of Early Identification and Intensive Treatment Programs

Presumably the rationale of early identification is to economize treatment efforts. Otherwise, society would expose all youth to whatever resources are available for delinquency control. But in order to achieve economy, the predictions must be accurate. If delinquency occurs in too many cases where nondelinquency was predicted or *fails* to occur in too many cases where it *was* predicted, economy may not be realized. Once the predictions are found to be sufficiently accurate, greater intensity of treatment efforts is possible because youngsters not in danger of becoming delinquent can be ignored.

The conditions under which accurate predictions may be anticipated are therefore important. For the occurrence of adolescent delinquency to be predicted accurately from either preadolescent behavior or preadolescent circumstances, no crucial etiological factors should make their appearance after the original predictions have been made. For instance, in the New York City Youth Board project, the ratings of the family backgrounds of the 223 boys were made when they were 6 years old. If family relations are the major factor in delinquency and if family relations change appreciably in the course of the study, the predictions

[4]See Powers and Witmer, *op. cit.*, pp. 85, 88; William and Joan McCord, *Origins of Crime: A New Evaluation of the Cambridge-Somerville Youth Study*, New York: Columbia University Press, 1959, pp. 20, 26, 29, 38–39.

ought not to be very accurate.[5] Peer group relations are even more prone to change than family relations. Since studies of adolescent street-corner groups reveal that youngsters who join such groups are more likely to commit delinquent acts than youngsters who do not join such groups and since delinquent groups rarely recruit members younger than 10, preadolescent ratings of school misbehavior or family background ought not to predict delinquency during adolescence very accurately. Of course, if we assume that early childhood experiences are so important that they establish a differential vulnerability for all subsequent experiences, early predictions might be accurate despite later changes in family and peer relations. Freudian psychiatrists subscribe to this assumption of the disproportionate importance of early socialization; sociologists, on the other hand, believe that socialization continues throughout life and that the course of a child's life can be radically changed by subsequent experiences.

Correct identification of youngsters who will ultimately become delinquent is the first step of "early identification and intensive treatment" programs. The second step is to upset these initially correct predictions by an effective treatment program. It is usually assumed by the proponents of "early identification and intensive treatment" that treatment is effective merely by being intensive. This is not necessarily so. The focusing of treatment efforts on youngsters most likely to become delinquent necessarily involves special handling for them. It is extremely difficult for a focused treatment program to avoid stigmatizing the recipients of the "benefits" of the program. Early identification does not necessarily imply early stigmatization, but early *discriminatory* treatment seems to. Thus, it is conceivable that a boomerang effect will occur and that greater intensity of exposure to treatment will be *less* effective than less intense but less discriminatory exposure. Suppose, for instance, that a community has an organized recreational program for *all* children up to the age of 16. Someone convinces the city fathers that organized recreation can prevent delinquency, and the program is changed to focus on identified predelinquents. Instead of 1,000 boys using the facilities occasionally, 200 boys use them frequently. Before leaping to the conclusion that these 200 boys are less likely to become delinquent, let us consider what the impact of their segregation is on "predelinquents." We know from experience with ability groupings in the schools that the evaluations of the adult world cannot be concealed from youngsters. Just as the children in the "dumb" classes know that they are not in the "smart" classes, these 200 boys are unlikely to think of themselves as the pride of

[5] Professor Isidor Chein of New York University suggested that the Youth Board rate the family situations of the 223 boys *again* several years after the original ratings were made. How well would the two sets of ratings correlate with one another? If the later ratings were less closely related to outcome than the earlier ratings, this would tend to support the Glueck hypothesis that the early family situation is the major factor in delinquency. If the later ratings were more closely related to outcome than the earlier ratings, this would suggest that the contemporary situation—familial and extrafamilial—is more important in the genesis of delinquency than the Gluecks think.

the community. It is possible that less intensive recreational participation would have been more effective in arresting their delinquent tendencies than the more intensive—and incidentally more stigmatizing—exposure.[6]

The Cambridge-Somerville Youth Study and the New York City Youth Board Prediction Study did not assess the effect of neighborhood, ethnic background, or socio-economic status on the *accuracy* of their predictions. As a result, they missed an opportunity to clarify the conditions under which predisposing personal or family factors eventuate in delinquency. I propose to examine both studies in the light of these omissions in order to demonstrate that explicit consideration of the social context is necessary for further progress in delinquency *prediction* and ultimately control.

The Cambridge-Somerville Youth Study

Table 1 shows a positive relationship between the original predictions of delinquency or nondelinquency made in 1937-38 and the outcomes as of 1956.[7] Insofar as errors of prediction occurred, they were mainly overpredictions of delinquency. That is, of the 305 boys for whom delinquency was predicted, 191 turned into "good" boys (63 per cent); but only 18 of the 150 for whom *nondelinquency* was predicted subsequently committed offenses (12 per cent). Bear in mind that the Cambridge-Somerville Youth Study assumed that, unless the service program were successful, preadolescent boys who manifested antisocial behavior would con-

TABLE 1. Comparison of Original Predictions and Final Outcomes of Boys in the Cambridge-Somerville Youth Study

	Outcomes		
Predictions	*Delinquent*	*Nondelinquent*	*Total*
Delinquent	114	191*	305
Nondelinquent	18*	132	150
Total	132	323	455

*Errors of prediction.

[6] Proponents of early identification and intensive treatment might argue that stigmatization occurs but that it is helpful in preventing delinquency (by nipping the deviant tendency in the bud). Law enforcement officials sometimes use this argument, but they usually talk in terms of "punishment" rather than "treatment." Social workers and psychiatrists seem unwilling to face the logical possibility that well-intentioned "treatment" can do more harm than good. For an analysis of the comparative consequences of punishment and treatment, see Jackson Toby, "Is Punishment Necessary?" *Journal of Criminal Law, Criminology and Police Science,* 55 (September, 1964), pp. 332-337.

[7] The unpublished tabulations in Tables 1 and 2 were made available to me through the graciousness of Professor William McCord of Stanford University, Professor Gordon W. Allport of Harvard University, Dr. Stanton Wheeler of the Russell Sage Foundation, and Professor Robert Stanfield of the University of Massachusetts. Note that these tabulations include boys from both treatment and control groups. Since the treatment program proved ineffective, the exclusion of treatment cases from the analysis was unnecessary.

tinue such behavior in adolescence. In point of fact, the majority of identified pre-delinquents did *not* persist in their delinquent activities. The obvious question is: Why not?

It might be possible to find out why delinquency was overpredicted and, hopefully, the conditions making for more accurate predictions if the data in Table 1 were partitioned into meaningful subsamples. For example, various ethnic groups are represented in the study population: "Italian," "Other Latin," "Negro," "Eastern European," "Western European," and "Native American."[8] If predictions were more accurate for Italian boys than, say, for native American boys, this might throw light on the relationship between cultural values and delinquency.[9] Similarly, several socioeconomic levels were represented in the study population. If predictions were more accurate for slum-dwelling youngsters than for boys living in better residential neighborhoods, this might throw light on the relationship between social class and delinquency. Table 2 explores the latter question by breaking down the data of Table 1 into subsamples of neighborhoods. What does Table 2 reveal about the effect of the socioeconomic milieu?

TABLE 2. Partition of Cambridge-Somerville Youth Study Cases by Neighborhood of Residence

Predictions	*Outcomes*					
	In Slum Neighborhoods			*In Better Neighborhoods*		
	Delinquent	*Nondelinquent*	*Total*	*Delinquent*	*Nondelinquent*	*Total*
Delinquent	90	126*	216	24	65*	89
Nondelinquent	12*	62	74	6*	70	76
Total	102	188	290	30	135	165

*Errors of prediction.

Facts

1. Predictions of delinquency were more likely to be made in slum neighborhoods than in better residential neighborhoods. Seventy-five per cent of the 290 boys from slum neighborhoods were predicted by the raters to become delinquent as compared with 54 per cent of boys from better neighborhoods.

2. Predictions of delinquency were more likely to be correct in slum neighborhoods than in better neighborhoods. Forty-two per cent of the 216 boys predicted

[8] The ethnic data relating to the study population do not appear in *Origins of Crime* but are found in a second volume, which explored the causes of alcoholism rather than crime. For information on ethnic groupings, see William and Joan McCord, *Origins of Alcoholism,* Stanford, California: Stanford University Press, 1960, p. 38.

[9] See Jackson Toby, "Hoodlum or Business Man: An American Dilemma," in Marshall Sklare, ed., *The Jews,* Glencoe, Ill.: The Free Press, 1958, pp. 542–550, for a discussion of the relationship between ethnic background and delinquency.

delinquent from slum neighborhoods actually became so as compared with 27 per cent of the 89 boys predicted delinquent in better neighborhoods.

3. Predictions of *nondelinquency* were more likely to be correct in better residential neighborhoods than in slum neighborhoods. Ninety-two per cent of the boys predicted nondelinquent from better neighborhoods remained law-abiding as compared with 84 per cent of the boys predicted nondelinquent in slum neighborhoods.

4. The differences between the later delinquency rates of troublesome and conforming preadolescents are striking. In slum neighborhoods, 42 per cent of the troublesome preadolescents, as contrasted with 16 per cent of the conformists, subsequently committed offenses. In the better residential neighborhoods, 27 per cent of the troublesome preadolescents, as contrasted with 8 per cent of the conformists, subsequently committed offenses.

Interpretation

1. Predictions of delinquency could have varied by neighborhood for either one of two reasons (or a combination of both):

a. Because preadolescent misbehavior at school and in the community is more common in slum neighborhoods than in better residential neighborhoods.
b. Because preadolescent misbehavior was likely to be discounted by the Cambridge-Somerville raters on the basis of favorable family situations, and such situations are more frequent in better residential neighborhoods. That is to say, the raters were more likely to predict nondelinquency or to assign an undecided (zero) rating if the troublesome preadolescent came from a "good" neighborhood.

2. The greater tendency of predictions of delinquency to come true and predictions of nondelinquency to be incorrect in slum neighborhoods may be explained by differing neighborhood traditions of delinquency. Precisely how these traditions originate and are sustained is not clear. One relevant factor is a concentration of disorganized families exercising ineffective control over children, especially over adolescent boys.[10] Another is the proliferation of highly visible street-corner groups that are frequently delinquent. Sociologists have suggested that the weakness of family control and the influence of the peer group are different sides of the same coin.[11]

3. The negligible tendency of *conforming* preadolescents to become delinquent in later years—in both slum neighborhoods and in better residential neighborhoods—may mean that boys controlled effectively by their parents in preadolescence continue to be controlled effectively in adolescence and young adulthood. External controls, however, may not be so crucial as the conforming preadolescent develops a nondelinquent self-conception that insulates him from involvement in delinquent

[10] Jackson Toby, "The Differential Impact of Family Disorganization," *American Sociological Review*, 22 (October, 1957), pp. 505–512.

[11] Frederick M. Thrasher, *The Gang*, Chicago: University of Chicago Press, 1927; William Foot Whyte, "Social Organization in the Slums," *American Sociological Review*, 8 (February, 1943), pp. 34–39.

peer groups.[12] Thus, the delinquent peer group is likely to have a quite different impact on troublesome and on conforming preadolescents. Not only were the differences between the delinquency records of the troublesome and the conforming preadolescents substantial in later years. The conforming preadolescents from slum neighborhoods had a less delinquent record than the troublesome preadolescents from the better neighborhoods.

4. The reason or reasons for the overprediction of delinquency are not clear. An obvious possibility is that a considerable amount of delinquency goes unrecorded.[13] If this "hidden delinquency" could somehow be put into the record, the predictions might well seem more accurate. Another possibility is that delinquent tendencies were somehow "nipped in the bud." Troublesome preadolescents were salvaged. The difficulty with this interpretation is that the planned program of intervention did not result in a lower delinquency rate in the treatment group as compared with the control group. As a matter of fact, Table 3 suggests more strongly than the overall treatment group-control group comparison that a boomerang effect might have occurred.[14] The difference between the treatment group and the control group in the "good" neighborhoods was greater than the difference in the "worst" neighborhoods. This difference can be explained by sampling peculiarities. On the other hand, it is clear that the program of intervention was not *more* successful in the better residential neighborhoods. Since delinquent peer group influences are relatively weak in better residential neighborhoods, one would expect a program of delinquency prevention to have a *better* chance in such neighborhoods. The planned treatment program of the Cambridge-Somerville Youth Study staff may have been ineffectual; yet there is still the possibility that unplanned circumstances intervened to arrest delinquent tendencies. For example, parents may have moved to more wholesome communities to escape the delinquent influences of the slum.

TABLE 3. Delinquency Among Treatment Boys and Control Boys in the Cambridge-Somerville Youth Study, by Type of Neighborhood

Type of Neighborhood	*% of Convictions in Treatment Group (N=233)*	*% of Convictions in Control Group (N=250)*
Good	38	26
Fair	37	33
Poor	40	44
Worst	46	49

[12] Walter C. Reckless, Simon Dinitz, and Ellen Murray, "Self-Concept as an Insulator Against Delinquency," *American Sociological Review*, 21 (December, 1956), pp. 744–747; Simon Dinitz, Frank R. Scarpitti, and Walter C. Reckless, "Delinquency Vulnerability: A Cross Group and Longitudinal Analysis," *American Sociological Review*, 27 (August, 1962), pp. 515–517.

[13] Fred J. Murphy, Mary M. Shirley, and Helen L. Witmer, "The Incidence of Hidden Delinquency," *American Journal of Orthopsychiatry*, 16 (October, 1964), pp. 286–296.

[14] William and Joan McCord, *Origins of Crime*, pp. 71, 204.

(The neighborhood ratings in the Cambridge-Somerville files date from the start of the study; they do not take into account subsequent moves.) The possible benefits of movement into low-delinquency neighborhoods is, unfortunately, pure speculation.

New York City Youth Board Prediction Study

The New York City Youth Board Prediction Study differed from the Cambridge-Somerville Youth Study in important respects. In the first place, all the boys for whom delinquency predictions were made came from two high-delinquency neighborhoods. Second, the predictions were based on home visits by social workers when the youngsters entered the first grade. They gave negligible weight to a factor particularly stressed in the Cambridge-Somerville Youth Study, the boy's own behavior. The critical question, of course, is: By what mechanism do "bad" family situations lead to delinquency in high-delinquency neighborhoods? Consider two quite different mechanisms by which a bad family situation might lead to delinquency:

1. Parental rejection and neglect damage the personality of the developing child. Lack of impulse control results from pathological socialization.[15] The psychopathic or neurotic boy reacts with violence to trivial provocations, sets fires, and steals purposelessly.

2. Parental inadequacy and neglect, by reducing family control, thereby orient the boy toward his agemates in the neighborhood.[16] (The family and the peer group are in a sense competing for the allegiance of boys in high-delinquency neighborhoods.) If the peer group is delinquent, a boy's desire for acceptance by his peers tempts him to participate in delinquent activities.

The Youth Board researchers do not make clear which of these mechanisms they suspect has greater influence. Although both are probably at work, mutually reinforcing one another to produce delinquency, a delinquency control program cannot do all things at once; hence it would seem desirable to be explicit about suspected etiological mechanisms. In point of fact, the intensive treatment program undertaken by the Youth Board addressed psychiatric problems; a clinic was set up in one of the two schools, and treatment was offered by a team consisting of psychologists, psychiatrists, and social workers to all of the boys predicted delinquent by the original Glueck scale.[17] The boys who were likewise predicted delinquent in the other school were to serve as a control group. Although the experimental program lasted four years, it failed in its objective. As in the Cambridge-Somerville Youth Study, members of the treatment group were no less likely to become delinquent

[15] Kate Friedlander, *The Psychoanalytic Approach to Juvenile Delinquency,* New York: International Universities Press, 1944.

[16] Thrasher, *op. cit.*

[17] New York City Youth Board, Research Department, *A Study in Variance from Predicted Delinquency: A Study of 20 Negro Boys Who Were Overpredicted,* mimeographed, 1962, ch. 4.

than members of the control group.[18] A possible explanation for the failure is that the treatment program was predicted on the first mechanism whereas the second mechanism may have been more relevant to the delinquency of these underprivileged boys. Let us examine the relationship between predictions and outcomes in the light of this hypothesis.

Table 4 reports the relationship between 1952 predictions and 1959 outcomes utilizing three different prediction techniques:

(1) the five-factor scale designated by the Youth Board at the beginning of the research as the official prediction device;[19]

TABLE 4. A Comparison Among the Youth Board Two- or Three-Factor Table, The Glueck Five-Factor Table, and a Single Factor (Public Assistance) in Predicting Delinquency

1952 Predictions	*Outcomes, 7 Years Later* Delinquent	Nondelinquent	*Total*
Based on Five Factors			
Probably delinquent	17	50*	67
Probably nondelinquent	4*	152	156
Total	21	202	223
Based on Two or Three Factors			
Probably delinquent	13	24*	37
Probably nondelinquent	8*	178	186
Total	21	202	223
Based on Single Factor (Economic Status of Family When Boy Entered School in 1952)			
Public assistance	13	39*	52
No public assistance	8*	163	171
Total	21	202	223

*Errors of prediction.

[18] Based on a personal conversation with Mrs. Maude Craig, research director of the Youth Board. To the best of my knowledge the New York City Youth Board has not published a full account of this experiment, apparently on the assumption that something went wrong in the execution of the experiment that did not reflect on its underlying assumptions. This attitude strikes me as dubious, particularly in view of the Youth Board's awareness of the similar results of a project in Washington, D.C., which also used the Glueck scale to identify predelinquents and which also attempted clinical treatment. *Ibid.*, p. 58.

[19] Sheldon and Eleanor Glueck, *Unraveling Juvenile Delinquency*, New York: Commonwealth Fund, 1950.

(2) a two-and three-factor scale developed late in the research to adapt the Glueck scale to the ethnic groups represented in the Youth Board population (especially Negroes);[20]

(3) a single-item predictive device (based on whether or not the family was receiving welfare assistance in 1952), the purpose of which is to provide a basis for comparing the predictive power of the Youth Board scales with predictions based on a readily available socioeconomic datum.

Note that the original five-factor prediction table made 54 errors, more than the 47 errors made by the table based on the public assistance criterion alone. The two-and three-factor table did considerably better: only 32 errors. But *why* did the two-and three-factor table do better than the five? What factors were eliminated? The revised scale used "mother's supervision" and "cohesiveness of the family" supplemented by "father's discipline" in those cases "where a father or father substitute has been in the home a sufficient length of time to have had an influence in the boy's life."[21] From this improvement of prediction resulting from the elimination of "affection of mother for the boy" and of "affection of the father for the boy," it might be inferred that these factors are not important to the etiology of delinquency in this population. (Bear in mind that the universe consists of boys from *high-delinquency* neighborhoods.) Eleanor Glueck assures skeptics that "this is not the case."[22] She explains the greater accuracy of the two-and three-factor table as compared with the original five-factor table as due to inconsistency of ratings of parental affection by social workers of different intellectual persuasions and to the difficulty of making ratings for families where the father has long been out of the home. To me this argument is not convincing. Only 28 of 224 boys lacked fathers (or father substitutes) in the home for a major portion of their lives, and presumably the absence of mothers or mother substitutes was rarer.[23] Why was "affection of the *Mother*" not a useful predictive item? Mrs. Glueck's argument is essentially that parental affection is etiologically important but that the Youth Board researchers were unable to measure parental affection reliably. An alternative interpretation is that parental *affection* is less closely correlated with delinquency in high-delinquency neighborhoods than is parental *control.*

[20] Further modifications of the Glueck scales occurred after eight years. Instead of getting rater agreement on total scores, the Youth Board researchers insisted now on rater agreement on each factor going into the score. Second, aware of the fact that the scales were overpredicting delinquency, the Youth Board researchers reviewed some cases and reclassified them from probably delinquent to probably nondelinquent. These changes were seemingly made for cogent research considerations. Unfortunately, though, they were made long after the research began and could no longer be regarded as uncontaminated "prospective predictions." For a history of these changes, see New York City Youth Board, *An Experiment in the Use of the Glueck Social Prediction Table as a Prognosticator of Potential Delinquency,* mimeographed, October, 1961.

[21] *Ibid.,* p. 10.

[22] Eleanor T. Glueck, *op. cit.,* pp. 55–56.

[23] New York City Youth Board, *op. cit.,* 1961, p. 13. Note that the total of 224 boys includes one Puerto Rican youngster not included in earlier reports I have examined and therefore not included in Tables 4 or 5.

The explanation of the greater accuracy of the shorter scale as compared with the five-factor scale may simply be that mother's supervision, family cohesiveness, and father's discipline are more closely related to parental control than are affection of the mother and affection of the father.

Is there any other evidence in favor of the hypothesis that parental control is the crucial variable affecting the accuracy of the Youth Board predictions? The Youth Board itself provided such evidence in a study of 20 Negro boys who were predicted delinquent by the five-factor Glueck prediction table and failed to become so in the subsequent eight years.[24] In a chapter entitled, "Mother's Supervision Counteracting Peer Group Environment," the author of the Youth Board monograph (Dr. Philip W. Furst) emphasizes the role of the mother or mother-substitute in preventing gang membership or defining it as undesirable (dangerous). "She uses various means: exhortation, reason, rewards, example, tongue-lashing, threats, discipline, manipulation of the environment, coaxing, cajoling. And this process goes on with ever broadening content into the middle teens and beyond."[25] *Seven* of these 20 boys had been rated in 1952 as effectively supervised by the mother—as contrasted with *two* of 14 Negro boys predicted delinquent who confirmed the prediction.[26] Four additional boys "were saved in the school years by mothers' supervision even though the mothers' original supervision ratings were poor...."[27] In another four cases, recognition of the *grandmother's* part in supervision and in the cohesiveness of the family might have led to a more hopeful prediction. For instance, one of the two boys out of the 20 considered to have the *highest* probability of becoming delinquent had little contact with his parents. "What the interviewer did not grasp in 1952...was the fact that the person who really counted in those children's lives was the marvelous grandmother in whose home the family was living."[28] Thus, 15 of the 20 incorrect predictions of delinquency might have been avoided by emphasizing parental control more strongly.

Those mothers and mother-substitutes who were concerned about supervising the activities of their sons may have been distressed at the growing crime problems of their neighborhoods. Although the schools were selected by the Youth Board in 1952 because they lay in high-delinquency neighborhoods, the delinquency rates in the two neighborhoods increased over the ten-year period of the study. Three families moved from the Bronx to rural areas, at least one for the express purpose of providing better child supervision.[29] Bear in mind that choice of neighborhoods was limited for these 20 Negro families. Furthermore, half of them were receiving public assistance at some time during the study, reflecting economic disabilities that must have also reduced their opportunities to relocate. Nevertheless,

[24] New York City Youth Board, op. cit., 1962.
[25] *Ibid.*, pp. 28–29.
[26] *Ibid.*, p. S6.
[27] *Ibid.*, p. S15.
[28] *Ibid.*, p. 36. See also pp. 63–68.
[29] *Ibid.*, pp. S7–8.

eight of the twenty families had moved by 1961 to better neighborhoods. Perhaps it is only a coincidence, but four of the seven families where the mother's supervision was rated effective in 1965 had relocated into neighborhoods with lower delinquency rates—as compared with four of the 13 families where the mother's supervision was poor.

Residential mobility was not confined to Negro families; 29 of the 53 white boys in the Youth Board study were Jewish, and other studies have shown that Jewish families move readily to better neighborhoods when their old communities deteriorate.[30] Mobility is not motivated exclusively by a concern for the upbringing of children, important though this is; population flow is to be expected in a large city. The Youth Board researchers have complained about the difficulty of keeping track of 61 boys scattered by 1961 in out-of-town schools in 12 states, Puerto Rico, and Malta.[31] And of course moves occured within New York City. Regardless of the motivation for residential moves, however, an important consequence is to provide a new environment for children. Of 14 boys predicted *nondelinquent* in 1952 whose families moved to a *better* neighborhood, none became delinquent; of 31 boys with exactly the same prediction score whose families moved to neighborhoods with the *same* or *worse* levels of delinquency, 7 became delinquent.[32] The Youth Board has not yet analyzed the moves of all the families in the study in relation to prediction scores and outcomes. Hence, it is not known whether boys predicted *delinquent* in 1952 were less likely to become so if their families moved to better neighborhoods. It sounds plausible.

If indeed weak family control predisposes a boy living in a high-delinquency neighborhood to become delinquent, it would be helpful to know the ethnic and socioeconomic circumstances that reinforce this tendency. The question is not *whether* the various prediction tables predict delinquency but *how* both successful and unsuccessful predictions provide clues to underlying causes and ultimately to programs of intervention. As an illustration of this approach Table 5 breaks down the relationship between the two-and three-factor prediction table and delinquent outcomes (shown in Table 4) for three ethnic groups and two socioeconomic statuses.[33] What does Table 5 reveal about the reinforcing effect of the social milieu?

Facts

1. Predictions of delinquency were more likely to be made for Negro boys than for Puerto Rican or white boys. Twenty-one per cent of the 131 Negro boys were

[30] *Ibid.*, p. 4; Nathan Glazer and Daniel Patrick Moynihan, *Beyond the Melting Pot: The Negroes, Puerto Ricans, Jews, Italians, and Irish of New York City*, Cambridge, Massachusetts, M.I.T. Press, 1963, pp. 53–67, 160–163.

[31] New York City Youth Board, *op. cit.*, 1961, p. 15.

[32] New York City Youth Board, Research Department, *A Study of Mobility and Delinquency in a Sample of Boys in Glueck Project*, mimeographed, February, 1963, p. 6.

[33] Mrs. Maude Craig, research director of the Youth Board, graciously provided unpublished data on the economic status and the ethnic background of the 223 boys in the study.

TABLE 5. Differential Impact of a "Bad" Family Situation on Economically Dependent and on Self-sufficient White, Negro, and Puerto Rican Families

Ethnic Background	1952 Predictions Two- and Three-Factor Table	*1959 Outcomes*					
		For 1952 Public Assistance Families			*For 1952 Self-sufficient Families*		
		Delinquent	*Nondelinquent*	*Total*	*Delinquent*	*Nondelinquent*	*Total*
White	Probably delinquent	1	2*	3	0	1*	1
	Probably nondelinquent	0*	0	0	0*	49	49
	□ Total	1	2	3	0	50	50
Negro	Probably delinquent	4	9*	13	4	11*	15
	Probably nondelinquent	4*	19	23	3*	77	80
	□ Total	8	28	36	7	88	95
Puerto Rican	Probably delinquent	3	1*	4	1	0*	1
	Probably nondelinquent	1*	8	9	0*	25	25
	□ Total	4	9	13	1	25	26
All	Probably delinquent	8	12*	20	5	12*	17
	Probably nondelinquent	5*	27	32	3*	151	154
	□ Total	13	39	52	8	163	171

*Errors of prediction.

given better than a 50–50 chance of becoming delinquent—as contrasted with 13 per cent of the 39 Puerto Rican boys and 8 per cent of the 53 white boys. To look at the data in another way, of the 37 boys predicted delinquent, 33 were Negro or Puerto Rican.

2. Although the number of cases in some categories were very small, e.g., only four *white* boys and five *Puerto Ricans* predicted delinquent, predictions of delinquency were more likely to be correct and predictions of nondelinquency to be wrong for Negroes and Puerto Ricans than for whites. Whereas one out of four of the white boys predicted delinquent became so, 36 per cent of the Negroes and Puerto Ricans predicted delinquent fulfulled the prediction. None of the 49 white boys predicted nondelinquent became delinquent but 8 per cent of the Negro and Puerto Rican boys did within seven years.

3. Predictions of delinquency were more likely to be made for boys from public assistance families than for boys from self-sufficient families. Thirty-eight per cent of the 52 public assistance boys were given better than a 50–50 chance of becoming delinquent—as contrasted with 10 per cent of the 171 boys from self-sufficient families.

4. Predictions of delinquency were more likely to be correct and predictions of nondelinquency more likely to be wrong for public assistance families than for self-sufficient families. This tendency was characteristic of white, Negro, and Puerto Rican families looked at separately; the fact of public assistance had an adverse effect on outcomes regardless of ethnicity.

Interpretation

1. Since the predictions of delinquency were based on pathological family situations, the greater tendency for predictions of delinquency to be made in Negro and Puerto Rican families must be due mainly to the greater incidence of family disorganization in these ethnic groups. This disorganization is highly correlated with dependency and, very likely, with employment opportunities. Note, for example, that only 16 per cent of the boys from self-sufficient Negro families were predicted delinquent—as constrasted with 36 per cent from dependent Negro families.

2. Recall that in the Cambridge-Somerville Youth Study the greater tendency for predictions of delinquency to come true and predictions of nondelinquency to be wrong in slum neighborhoods was interpreted as due to differing neighborhood traditions of delinquency. In the Youth Board study we see again a greater tendency for predictions of delinquency to come true and predictions of nondelinquency to be incorrect in disadvantaged segments of the population, this time among Negroes and Puerto Ricans and among the children of welfare recipients rather than among boys from poorer neighborhoods. Part of the explanation here may be that ethnic traditions of delinquency are analogous to neighborhood traditions of delinquency. Obviously, however, differing ethnic traditions of delinquency cannot explain the fact that boys from public assistance families were more likely to become delinquent within the same ethnic group and the same Glueck prediction category. It is unlikely that public assistance families constitute a community within a community

and that the children of such families have a distinct tradition of delinquency. Possibly boys from economically dependent families are more likely to be *recorded* as delinquents than boys from self-sufficient families who are behaving similarly; this assumes that the police know the welfare status of the family and discriminate against the most deprived. This seems to me far-fetched. More likely, economic disadvantage has adverse effects on the school adjustment and (ultimately) on the occupational opportunities of public assistance children.[34] Their greater proneness to delinquency may stem from their lesser hopes for and commitments to legitimate enterprises.[35]

3. Bear in mind that all of the preadolescent boys followed up in the Youth Board Prediction Study came from two high delinquency neighborhoods characterized by considerable gang activity. Yet those members of the Study population *predicted nondelinquent,* i.e., closely supervised by their parents, usually avoided delinquent associates and bore out the prediction. Exceptions to this generalization are Negro boys from public assistance families predicted nondelinquent; 17 per cent of them became delinquent within seven years. Perhaps the double disadvantage of race prejudice and poor economic prospects reduced their stake in conformity.[36]

4. One reason for the overprediction of delinquency is that Table 5 does not include *all* delinquencies committed by the boys in the study from 1952 to 1959; some delinquent acts were undetected or unrecorded. Another reason for the overprediction of delinquency in Table 5 is that some boys became delinquent for the first time *after* 1959. But there remains the possibility that many of the prophecies of delinquency were defeated because deliberate as well as unintentional interventions occurred in the lives of these boys. Families moved to neighborhoods with fewer delinquent gangs; boys joined boys' clubs or the Boy Scouts; social agencies helped the families to solve their problems and thereby improved parental supervision; the schools offered remedial education to slow learners.

Conclusion

The problem of delinquency control has long been the subject of jurisdictional disputes among sociologists, psychologists, social workers and psychiatrists—not to mention lawyers and the police. Recently, "early identification and intensive treatment of predelinquents" has attracted much interest, and it seemed at first that this approach offered a relatively uncontroversial technique of delinquency control.

Careful analysis of two notable experiments in early identification and intensive

[34] Richard A. Cloward and Lloyd E. Ohlin, *Delinquency and Opportunity,* Glencoe, Ill,: The Free Press, 1960.

[35] Larry Karacki and Jackson Toby, "The Uncommitted Adolescent: Candidate for Gang Socialization," *Sociological Inquiry,* 32 (Spring, 1962), pp. 203–215.

[36] Jackson Toby, "Social Disorganization and Stake in Conformity: Complementary Factors in the Predatory Behavior of Young Hoodlums," *Journal of Criminal Law, Criminology and Police Science,* 48 (May–June, 1957), pp. 12–17. Arthur L. Stinchcombe, *Rebellion in a High School,* Chicago: Quadrangle Books, 1964, Chs. 3 and 4.

treatment of predelinquents shows that intellectual confusion lurks beneath the surface plausibility of early identification and intensive treatment. The following issues have not been resolved:

1. Does early identification depend on extrapolating antisocial tendencies already observable in the preadolescent boy or girl into adolescence? Or does early identification consist of locating youngsters who have been exposed to family or community experiences known to cause delinquency?
2. Can *early* identification be accurate? The issue of accuracy is essentially a theoretical problem. Accurate early identification is possible only (a) if no crucial etiological factors make their appearance *after* the predictions are made or (b) if early experiences establish a differential vulnerability for all subsequent experiences.
3. What *kind* of intensive treatment should be given? Does the type of treatment have to be individualized according to the problem of the youngster? Or are all types of treatment equally effective with all types of delinquents providing treatment is "intensive"?
4. How intensive must "intensive treatment" be and how early must it start in order to satisfy the early identification and intensive treatment formula? (The McCords have dismissed the negative results of the Cambridge-Somerville Youth Study as irrelevant to the validity of the early identification and intensive treatment approach because the treatment program was not sufficiently intensive.)
5. How can early identification and intensive treatment programs avoid "self-fulfilling prophecies"? If the treatment program concentrates its efforts on youngsters who are especially vulnerable to delinquency, how can it justify its discriminatory policy except by stigmatizing predelinquents? And may not the delinquency-producing effects of the stigmatization equal or exceed the delinquency-preventing benefits of the treatment?
6. Finally, is it likely that an effective approach to delinquency control can emerge without clarification of the underlying intellectual issues in the etiology of delinquency? Although they approached early identification of predelinquents in theoretically distinct ways, both the Cambridge-Somerville Youth Study and the New York City Youth Board Prediction Study show that attention to the social context can improve the accuracy of predictions. The neighborhood of residence in the Cambridge-Somerville Youth Study and the dependency status of the family and its ethnicity in the New York City Youth Board Prediction Study were relevant to later outcomes. However, in neither study is it clear *why* predictions of delinquency were more likely to be correct and predictions of nondelinquency wrong for youngsters of disadvantaged social origins. The relationship among social origin, family functioning, individual self-conception, and peer group influence was ignored. Can a theoretically blind prediction technique provide the basis for effective intervention?

51. Experimental Treatment: Community Programs

The President's Commission on Law Enforcement and Administration of Justice

In recent years a number of experimental community programs have been set up in various parts of the country, differing substantially in content and structure but all offering greater supervision and guidance than the traditional probation and parole programs. The new programs take many forms, ranging from the more familiar foster homes and group homes to halfway houses, "guided group interaction" programs, and intensive community treatment. As such, they offer a set of alternatives between regular probation supervision and incarceration, providing more guidance than probation services commonly offer without the various disruptive effects of total confinement. They also greatly enrich the alternatives available in parole supervision. The advent of these programs in the postwar decades and their recent growth in numbers and prominence are perhaps the most promising developments in corrections today.

These programs are by and large less costly, often far less costly, than incarceration in an institution. Evaluation has indicated that they are usually at least as effective in reducing recidivism and in some cases significantly more so. They therefore represent an important means for coping with the mounting volume of offenders that will be pouring into corrections in the next decade. Although population forecasts indicate that the number of adult criminals who will be incarcerated in the next 10 years will increase only slightly, the projections for juveniles on the basis of present trends are alarming....It is estimated that by 1975 the number of juveniles who would be confined would increase by 70 percent; whereas in 1965, there were about 44,000 juveniles in State and Federal correctional institutions, by 1975 this number would reach about 74,000. Such an increase would place a burden on the correctional system that increased community programing could go far to alleviate.

Among the special community programs at least five types are important enough to warrant special discussion: guided group interaction programs; foster homes and group homes; prerelease guidance centers; intensive treatment programs; and recep-

Reprinted from "Special Community Programs: Alternatives to Institutionalization," *Task Force Report: Corrections,* a Report by The President's Commission on Law Enforcement and Administration of Justice (Washington: Government Printing Office, 1967), ch. 4, pp. 38–44.

tion center parole. These programs are reviewed here as examples of approaches that are capable of, and deserve, widespread application in a variety of modifications.

Guided Group Interaction Programs

Underlying one of the newer programs for treating the young delinquent in the community is the premise that juvenile delinquency is commonly a group experience and that therefore efforts to change delinquent behavior should focus primarily on a group like that within which the individual operates. A number of group counseling methods have been employed but the method called guided group interaction has been used most extensively in those programs which involved a research component.

The general strategy of guided group interaction calls for involving the offenders in frequent, prolonged, and intensive discussions of the behavior of individuals in the group and the motivations underlying it. Concentrating on participants' current experiences and problems, the approach attempts to develop a group "culture" that encourages those involved to assume responsibility for helping and controlling each other. The theory is that the offender-participants will be more responsive to the influence of their fellow offenders, their peers, than to the admonitions of staff, and less likely to succeed to hoodwinking and manipulating each other.

As the culture develops and the group begins to act responsibly, the group leader, a staff member, seeks to encourage a broader sharing of power between the offenders and the staff. At first, group decisions will be limited to routine matters, such as the schedule of the day, but over time they may extend to disciplinary measures against a group member or even to decisions concerning readiness for release from the program.

Highfields. The Highfields project in New Jersey was the pioneer effort in guided group interaction.[1] Initiated in 1950, it has been duplicated in communities and also in institutions and used with both juveniles and adults. Highfields limits its population to 20 boys aged 16 and 17, who are assigned directly to it from the juvenile court. Boys with former commitments to correctional schools are not accepted, nor are deeply disturbed or mentally retarded youths. The goal is to effect rehabilitation within 3 to 4 months, about half the average period of incarceration in the State training school.

The youths are housed in the old Lindbergh mansion. They work during the day at a mental institution immediately adjacent to their residence. In the evening they participate in the group counseling sessions. On Saturdays, they clean up the residence. Saturday afternoon is free, and Sunday is reserved for receiving visitors and going to religious services. Formal rules are few.

[1] See Lloyd W. McCorkle, Albert Elias, and F. Lovell Bixby, "The Highfields Story: An Experimental Treatment Project for Youthful Offenders" (New York: Henry Holt & Co., 1958). See also Paul Keve, "Imaginative Programming in Probation and Parole" (Minneapolis: University of Minnesota Press, 1967), pp. 137–173, and J. Robert Weber, "A Report of the Juvenile Institutions Project" (unpublished report to the Osborne Association and the National Council on Crime and Delinquency, Sept. 1966), pp. 123–126, 223–230.

Early efforts to evaluate the effects of the project on recidivism, as compared with those of the State reformatory, are still the subject of academic dispute. However, it is clear than Highfields was at least as effective as the reformatory, perhaps more effective, and that it accomplished its results in a much shorter period of time at greatly reduced monthly costs.

Pinehills and Other Developments. Important variations on the Highfields project developed at Essexfields, also in New Jersey, and at Pinehills in Provo, Utah. As at Highfields, program content at Essexfields and Pinehills centered around gainful employment in the community, school, and daily group meetings. The most significant difference was that, in the Essexfields and Pinehills experiments, the offenders continued to live at home.

The regimen at both Essexfields and Pinehills was rigorous. At Pinehills, for example, all boys were employed by the city. They put in a full day's work on the city streets, on the golf course, in the cemetery, wherever they were needed. They were paid 50 cents an hour. During the late afternoon, after the day's work was finished, all boys returned to the program headquarters where they met in daily group sessions. About 7 p.m. they were free to return home. They were also free on Sundays.[2]

In the daily group sessions all group members, not just adult staff, were responsible for defining problems and finding solutions to them. By making the program operations to some extent the work of all involved, both offenders and staff, it was possible to make a better estimate of just how much responsibility for his own life a given offender could take.

The fact that these guided group interaction programs are located in the community means that the problems with which the group struggles are those that confront them daily in contacts with their families, friends, teachers, and employers. This is one great strength of a community program over an institutional program. The artificiality of institutional life is avoided, and concentration can be placed upon the issues with which every offender eventually has to deal.

The Pinehills experiment was one of the first to set up an experimental design by which to assess the effectiveness of the project. Offenders assigned to the program were compared with two control groups: One group which was placed on probation, and another which was committed to a training school. The initial design was such that all three groups could be drawn randomly from a common population of persistent offenders living in the same county. Although there was some difficulty in exactly maintaining the research design, the data appear significant. The results, as measured in terms of recidivism, are shown in table 1.

•••

Contributions of Guided Group Programs. These projects, like Highfields, represent an authentic departure from traditional community programs for delinquents. The Highfields type of program is unique in that the group process itself shapes the

[2] For further discussion of Pinehills and Essexfields, see LaMar T. Empey, "Alternatives to Incarceration," Office of Juvenile Delinquency and Youth Development Studies in Delinquency (Washington: U.S. Government Printing Office, 1967), pp. 37–40.

TABLE 1. Effectiveness of Three Programs for Juvenile Delinquents, Utah, 1964, as Measured by Percentages of Releases Not Arrested Within 6 Months of Release

Program	*Percentage of Releases Not Arrested Within 6 Months*	
	All Boys Assigned to Program	*All Boys Completing Program*
Pinehills (experimental)	73	84
Probation (controls)	73	77
State school (controls)	42	42

SOURCE: Adapted from LaMar T. Empey, "Alternatives to Incarceration," Office of Juvenile Delinquency and Youth Development Studies in Delinquency (Washington: U.S. Government Printing Office, 1967), pp. 38–39.

culture and social system of the total program. The key element seems to be the amount of decision-making authority permitted the group, which has considerably more authority to decide than in traditional group therapy programs. J. Robert Weber, who made a study of promising programs for delinquents, said of the Highfields type of program:

> If one asks a youth in most conventional institutions, "How do you get out?" one invariably hears some version of, "Be good. Do what you are told. Behave yourself." If one asks a youth in a group treatment program, "How do you get out?" one hears, "I have to help myself with my problems," or "When my group thinks I have been helped." This implies a basic difference in the social system of the organization, including staff roles and functions.[3]

In the large institution, Weber concluded, the youth perceives getting out in terms of the problem of meeting the institutional need for conformity. In the group treatment program the youth sees getting out in terms of his solution to his own problems, or how that is perceived by other youths in the group.

Foster Homes and Group Homes

Foster-home placement has long been one of the most commonly used alternatives to institutionalization for juvenile probationers. The National Survey of Corrections reported that 42 percent of the 233 probation departments surveyed utilized this resource. A sizable proportion of juvenile aftercare programs also make foster placements a routine part of their work.

The utilization of foster homes or group homes in lieu of institutional confinement has several obvious advantages, provided the offender does not require the

[3] Weber, *op. cit.,* pp. 225–226

controls of an institution. Such placements keep the offender in the community where he must eventually work out his future. They carry less stigma and less sense of criminal identity, and they are far less expensive than incarceration.

Weber reported in 1966:

> Discussions with State administrators would seem to indicate that foster care is in an eclipse. Reception center staffs report disillusionment with foster care for delinquents. Yet a look at actual placement practices of the State agencies and local courts indicates an unabated use of foster care.[4]

The opinions encountered by Weber may be a reflection of the long and controversial history of foster-home placement for delinquents. The decision to sever family ties, even temporarily, is a hard one to make for the youth who might otherwise be placed on probation at home. And more difficult juveniles who might be sent to institutions are often beyond the capacity of the usual foster home to manage. It is obvious, however, that many delinquent youngsters come from badly deteriorated family situations and that such conditions are significant, perhaps critical, factors in generating delinquent behavior. When the delinquency-inducing impact of a slum neighborhood is added to a destructive family setting, placement of the delinquent away from home becomes increasingly necessary.

•••

Halfway Programs: The Prerelease Guidance Center*

In corrections as in related fields, the "halfway house" is an increasingly familiar program. Initially, such programs were conceived for offenders "halfway out" of institutions, as a means of easing the stresses involved in transition from rigid control to freedom in the community. The prerelease guidance centers of the Federal Bureau of Prisons are the best-known halfway-out programs in the United States. Recently the halfway house has come to be viewed as a potential alternative to institutionalization, and thus a program for those "halfway in" between probation and institutional control.

Federal Prerelease Guidance Centers. The first prerelease guidance centers of the Federal Bureau of Prisons were opened in 1961 in New York, Chicago, and Los Angeles, and others were established subsequently in Detroit, Washington, and Kansas City. Each center accommodates about 20 Federal prisoners who are transferred to it several months before their expected parole date. Thus they complete their terms in the community but under careful control.

Some of the centers are located in what were large, single-family houses; some occupy a small section or scattered rooms in a YMCA hotel; and one is located in a building once operated as a small home for needy boys. All are in neighborhoods with mixed land usage, racial integration, and nearby transportation.

[4] Weber, *op. cit.*, p. 173.

*Editor's Note: Also referred to as Community Treatment Center.

Offenders transferred to these centers wear civilian clothes. They generally move from prison to the centers by public transportation without escort. For a day or two they are restricted to the building, although they may receive visitors there. In the YMCA's they are in a public cafeteria in the building and use the public recreation areas, taking out YMCA memberships. Following a day or two of orientation and counseling, they go out to look for jobs. After they are on a job, they are gradually given more extensive leaves for recreational purposes and for visits with their families. As their parole date approaches, some may even be permitted to move out of the center, although they are still required to return to the center for conferences several times a week.

These centers are staffed in large part by persons rotated from regular institution staff who are highly oriented to counseling. One full-time employee is an employment counseling specialist. Several others, such as college students in the behavioral sciences, are employed on a part-time basis and provide the only staff coverage during the late night hours and part of the weekend. In addition to individual counseling, there are several group sessions a week. Federal probation officers, who will supervise the offenders when they go on parole, participate in the center's counseling activities. By the time a resident is ready to begin his parole, almost all of his individual counseling has been assembled by his parole supervisor officer.

A major function of these temporary release programs has been to augment the information available to correctional staff. This information includes both diagnostic data on the individuals temporarily released and information on the assets and deficiencies of correctional programs and personnel. In addition, they provide optimum circumstances for counseling, since the counseling can deal with immediate realities as they are encountered, rather than with the abstract and hypothetical visions of the past and the future or the purely institutional problems to which counseling in institutions is largely restricted.

Inmate misbehavior while on work release or in prerelease guidance centers is not a rare thing, particularly for youthful offenders. Although a majority adjust quite satisfactorily, some get drunk, some get involved in fights and auto accidents when out with old or new friends, and some are late in returning to the center. An appreciable number of the youth have difficulty in holding jobs, some fail to go to work or to school when they are supposed to be there, a few abscond, and a few get involved in further crime. The important point is that they would be doing these things in any case, and probably more extensively, if they had been released more completely on their own through parole or discharge. Under the latter circumstances, however, correctional staff would know of the releasee's difficulties, if at all, not nearly so promptly as is possible with temporary release measures.

When an individual returns from a temporary release to home, work, or school, his experience can be discussed with him by staff, to try to assess his probable adjustment and to note incipient problems. Many difficulties can be anticipated in this way. The inmate's anxieties can be relieved by discussion, and discussion may also help him develop realistic plans for coping with prospective problems. When persistent or serious misbehavior occurs, sanctions are available to staff, ranging from restriction of further leaves or temporary incarceration to renewed institutionalization, with a recommendation to the parole board that the date of parole be deferred.

A number of offenders on work release...live in prerelease guidance centers. Some of them attend school part- or full-time, in addition to or instead of working; this sometimes is called "study release." It is particularly appropriate for juvenile and youthful offenders and is highly developed at several State establishments resembling the Federal prerelease guidance centers.

...

Intensive Community Treatment

Perhaps the best known of the country's efforts at controlled experimentation in the correctional field is the California Youth Authority's Community Treatment Project, now in its sixth year. Operating within a rigorous evaluative design, it offers an excellent illustration of the profitable partnership which can develop when carefully devised program innovations are combined with sound research.

The subjects of the project consist of boys and girls committed to the Youth Authority from two adjacent counties, Sacramento and San Joaquin. While under study in a reception center, each new group is subjected to a screening process which excludes some 25 percent of the boys and 5 to 10 percent of the girls because of the serious nature of their offenses, the presence of mental abnormality, or strenuous community objections to their direct release. The remaining youngsters are then either assigned randomly to the community project–in which case they form part of the experimental group–or are channeled routinely into an institution and eventually paroled.

An interview by a member of the research staff provides the basis for classification of the offender subgroups. This categorization is made in terms of the maturity of the youth, as reflected in his relationships with others, in the manner in which he perceives the world, and in the way he goes about gaining satisfaction of his needs. A variety of standardized tests seeks to measure the extent of his identification with delinquent values as well as his general personality characteristics.

The program provided for the experimental group offers singly or in combination most of the techniques of treatment and control which are in use in corrections today: individual counseling, group counseling, group therapy, family therapy, involvement in various other group activities, and school tutoring services by a certificated teacher with long experience in working with delinquents. The goal is to develop a treatment plan which is tailored to the needs of each type of offender. The resulting plan is then implemented at a level of high intensity, made possible by the availability of carefully selected and experienced staff on a ratio of 1 staff member for each 12 youths.

A program center serves as the hub of activity; it houses the staff and provides a recreation area, classrooms, and a musicroom. A limited outdoor sports activities area also is available. In the late afternoon and some evenings, the center resembles a small settlement house operation as the wards come in after school for counseling, tutoring, and recreational activity.

An unusual and controversial feature of the experiment is the frequent use of short-term detention at the agency's reception center to assure compliance with program requirements and to "set limits" on the behavior of the participants. The detention may vary from a few hours to a few days.

Results have been measured in several ways. A repetition of the psychological test battery seeks to determine what movement has occurred in the socialization of the individual offender. The responses of the various categories of youth have revealed greater success with some than with others, and may eventually provide a more reliable indicator of who should be institutionalized. Finally, the "failure rate," as measured by the proportion who are later institutionalized because they have committed additional offenses, is carefully compared with similar information on members of the control group who have been institutionalized and then returned to the community under regular parole supervision.

The latest report of the project activity available to the Commission revealed that checks of parolees, at the end of 15 months of parole exposure, showed that 28 percent of the experimental group had been subject to revocation of parole, as compared to 52 percent of the control group which was afforded regular institution and parole handling.[5]

After several years of pilot work, the California Youth Authority decided in 1964 to extend the community treatment format to the Watts area of Los Angeles and to a neighborhood in West Oakland. Both are high-delinquency areas; both are heavily Negro in population. Essentially duplications of the original experiments, the two new program units do not have a research component. Instead of random assignment of the subject, the youths committed from a given area are screened by project staff for direct release from the reception center.

In the absence of a control group, the success of the program has been measured by comparing the failure rate of the youth assigned to it with equivalent statewide rates for youths of the same middle to older adolescent age range. At the end of 15 months of parole exposure, 39 percent of project wards had been subject to parole revocation as compared to a statewide revocation rate of 48 percent for youths of the same age bracket.

The Los Angeles and Oakland adaptations of the original demonstration were initiated, in part, to alleviate acute population pressures in the institutions. With caseloads of 15 youths per officer, the $150 per month cost per boy is three to four times as much as that of regular parole. But it is less than half the average monthly cost of institutionalizing an offender. These experiments are now handling a group that is larger than the capacity of one of the new institutions that the Youth Authority is building. Thus they obviate the investment of $6 to $8 million.[6]

[5] Communication from Keith Griffiths, chief, Division of Research, California Youth Authority, December 1966.

[6] The development of the Community Treatment Project is reported in "Community Treatment Reports" issued by the Division of Research, California Youth Authority, Sacramento, Nos. 1–7, 1962–66.

Reception Center Parole and Short-term Treatment Programs

Diagnostic parole is a program whereby all commitments from the juvenile court are referred to a reception center where they can be screened for eligibility for parole, either immediately or after a short period of treatment. This program has reached significant proportions in an increasing number of States.

While most State systems have long had some informal arrangements for returning a few cases to the community at an early date, more organized procedures developed almost simultaneously in New York, Washington, Kentucky, and California in the early 1960's. These programs were conceived in part as a response to acute population pressures in overcrowded institutions. The seemingly successful results have led to a substantial increase in the volume of cases diverted from the training school to short, intensive treatment programs followed by parole in the community.

In New York the screening is undertaken by special aftercare staff while the youngsters are in New York City's Youth House awaiting delivery to the State school system. The youths selected to return to the community are those who are thought to be amenable to conventional casework procedures. Those selected are placed in an intensive casework program. The apparent success of the original unit in New York City has led to an expansion of the program and to the practice of returning still other youngsters to the community after the intake studies carried on in the State schools.

Washington, another State with a central reception center for juvenile offenders, is also screening those committed. A significant percentage of cases are assigned to immediate placement in foster homes or other community-based programs, including four halfway houses.

The California Youth Authority apparently is making the greatest use of the reception center release procedure. Currently some 20 percent of the boys and 35 percent of the girls processed are being released to regular parole or to foster home placement at the termination of reception period. This is typically a month long, but in some instances release may be postponed for another 30 to 90 days.[7]

The California Youth Authority's Marshall Program represents an interesting variation in the practices discussed above. The program was initiated 3 years ago as a device for easing population pressures in the institutions. It provides for the selection of cases by the clinical staff and the project director for a 3-month intensive treatment program at the reception center at Norwalk.

Based on "therapeutic community" concepts, the project involves the youths in a half-day work program in institution operation and maintenance, some specialized education classes, and daily group counseling. Active participation is rewarded by progressively longer and more frequent home furloughs. Parents provide the transportation, and furloughs are scheduled so that parents can participate in group counseling activities as they return their sons to the center. Parental involvement is seen as a significant program component.

[7] Data provided by the California Youth Authority.

While the performance of the project graduates has not been subjected to comparison with a control group, agency research staff have sought to match the subjects with youths possessed of the same characteristics who have been processed through the regular institution programs. With 15 months of parole exposure time, 44 percent of the Marshall youths, as against 47 percent of the matched group, were subject to parole revocation. Moreover, the relatively short program period of 3 months, as compared against the average stay of 8 to 9 months in the State schools, means a significant saving of public funds.[8]

The success of reception center parole has been encouraging. Other States will undoubtedly develop reception centers that feature sophisticated screening techniques and intensive treatment for those offenders who are deemed most susceptible. To date, parole from reception centers has been confined to the juvenile field. However, there is no inherent reason why this approach should not be taken with adults, and hopefully it will be so used in the near future.

•••

Problems to Be Confronted

Extensive development of alternatives to institutions requires that several problems be solved, and solved simultaneously. First is the need to make administrators and legislators aware of these programs and thus create conditions favorable for developing them. Demonstration projects which duplicate successful alternatives to institutionalization will have to be set up in various parts of the country. Such a process would require changes in the funding policies of many Federal and private agencies, which usually will support only a new type of program and not a duplication of one already proved successful. Such duplication is essential if correctional personnel and citizens are to become aware of the potentials of alternatives to institutions.

A second major problem is the familiar one of manpower. Most of these programs require skills which many correctional personnel do not have. Several centers should be established at sites of successful programs of all kinds, to train workers in the skills involved. This proposal would have particular application to training personnel for the special community programs described here.

The variety among correctional administrative structures in the country makes it difficult to determine how the new community programs could best be administered. The limited history of the prototypes indicates that the State itself will have to play a major and continuing role in order to coordinate services.

In some jurisdictions, the State may well operate virtually all of the alternative programs; in others, only part of them. For example, it is anticipated that the State will usually operate community programs for parolees. For probationers the situation is different, since a number of counties will continue to operate probation services. Where the State does not operate all community programs, it should at least supply leadership and subsidies in order to promote their development.

[8] *Ibid.*

Whatever the administrative arrangement, it is essential that all elements of corrections should be involved. Special community programs must be perceived by all parts of the correctional apparatus as legitimate and integral parts of the system. There is a great tendency for each part of the system to push forward with its own existing programs. For example, institutional managers are apt to urge new institutions rather than looking at the possibility of alternative programs. Failure to involve important elements of the correctional community can jeopardize not only the creation of new community programs but the survival of those which prove successful. The Pinehills project in Provo, Utah, described earlier in this chapter as exciting both in its operation and in its research design, does not exist today. This project and other successful ones were not picked up by a correctional agency once the initial grant moneys were exhausted. It is clear that new community programs must be integrated into the main line of corrections if they are to succeed and survive.

It is also essential that representatives of allied service agencies, such as welfare and mental health, be involved in planning for community programs. Correctional foster-home placements, for example, are closely involved with such placements by welfare agencies, and consideration must be given to the needs of both systems. Many of the specialized community programs in corrections will lay demands on the same resources as mental health agencies. It is essential that corrections and the mental health field work out accommodations, so that there is a functional relationship.

Finally, one of the most critical problems in developing new community programs is to secure the involvement and participation of the community itself. Too often, promising programs such as halfway houses have failed simply because the community was not prepared to tolerate them. Thus it is essential that the public be brought into planning early and that correctional managers make intense efforts to insure citizen understanding and support.

Appendix

Recommendations from the Report by the President's Commission on Law Enforcement and Administration of Justice

1. Preventing Crime

The prevention of crime covers a wide range of activities: Eliminating social conditions closely associated with crime; improving the ability of the criminal justice system to detect, apprehend, judge, and reintegrate into their communities those who commit crimes; and reducing the situations in which crimes are most likely to be committed.

Every effort must be made to strengthen the family, now often shattered by the grinding pressures of urban slums.

Slum schools must be given enough resources to make them as good as schools elsewhere and to enable them to compensate for the various handicaps suffered by the slum child—to rescue him from his environment.

Present efforts to combat school segregation, and the housing segregation that underlies it, must be continued and expanded.

Employment opportunities must be enlarged and young people provided with more effective vocational training and individual job counseling. Programs to create new kinds of jobs—such as probation aides, medical assistants, and teacher helpers—seem particularly promising and should be expanded.

The problem of increasing the ability of the police to detect and apprehend criminals is complicated. In one effort to find out how this objective could be achieved, the Commission conducted an analysis of 1,905 crimes reported to the Los Angeles Police Department during a recent month. The study showed the importance of identifying the perpetrator at the scene of the crime. Eighty-six percent of the crimes with named suspects were solved, but only 12 percent of the unnamed suspect crimes were solved. Another finding of the study was that there is a relationship between the speed of response and certainty of apprehension. On the average, response to emergency calls resulting in arrests was 50 percent faster than response to emergency calls not resulting in arrest. On the basis of this finding, and a cost effectiveness study to discover the best means to reduce response time, the Com-

From *The Challenge of Crime in a Free Society* (Washington: Government Printing Office, 1967), pp. v-xi.

mission recommends an experimental program to develop computer-aided command-and-control systems for large police departments.

To insure the maximum use of such a system, headquarters must have a direct link with every on-duty police officer. Because large scale production would result in a substantial reduction of the cost of miniature two-way radios, the Commission recommends that the Federal Government assume leadership in initiating a development program for such equipment and that it consider guaranteeing the sale of the first production lot of perhaps 20,000 units.

Two other steps to reduce police response time are recommended:

- ☐ Police callboxes, which are locked and inconspicuous in most cities, should be left open, brightly marked, and designated "public emergency callboxes."
- ☐ The telephone company should develop a single police number for each metropolitan area, and eventually for the entire United States.

Improving the effectiveness of law enforcement, however, is much more than just improving police response time. For example, a study in Washington, D.C. found that courtroom time for a felony defendant who pleads guilty probably totals less than 1 hour, while the median time from his initial appearance to his disposition is 4 months.

In an effort to discover how courts can best speed the process of criminal justice, the known facts about felony cases in Washington were placed in a computer and the operation of the system was simulated. After a number of possible solutions to the problem of delay were tested, it appeared that the addition of a second grand jury—which, with supporting personnel, would cost less than $50,000 a year—would result in a 25-percent reduction in the time required for the typical felony case to move from initial appearance to trial.

The application of such analysis—when combined with the Commission's recommended timetable laying out timespans for each step in the criminal process—should help court systems to ascertain their procedural bottlenecks and develop ways to eliminate them.

Another way to prevent crime is to reduce the opportunity to commit it. Many crimes would not be committed, indeed many criminal careers would not begin, if there were fewer opportunities for crime.

Auto theft is a good example. According to FBI statistics, the key had been left in the ignition or the ignition had been left unlocked in 42 percent of all stolen cars. Even in those cars taken when the ignition was locked, at least 20 percent were stolen simply by shorting the ignition with such simple devices as paper clips or tinfoil. In one city, the elimination of the unlocked "off" position on the 1965 Chevrolet resulted in 50 percent fewer of those models being stolen in 1965 than were stolen in 1964.

On the basis of these findings, it appears that an important reduction in auto theft could be achieved simply by installing an ignition system that automatically ejects the key when the engine is turned off.

A major reason that it is important to reduce auto theft is that stealing a car is very often the criminal act that starts a boy on a course of lawbreaking.

Stricter gun controls also would reduce some kinds of crime. Here, the Commission recommends a strengthening of the Federal law governing the interstate shipment of firearms and enactment of State laws requiring the registration of all handguns, rifles, and shotguns, and prohibiting the sale or ownership of firearms by certain categories of persons—dangerous criminals, habitual drunkards, and drug addicts. After 5 years, the Commission recommends that Congress pass a Federal registration law applying to those States that have not passed their own registration laws.

2. New Ways of Dealing with Offenders

The Commission's second objective—the development of a far broader range of alternatives for dealing with offenders—is based on the belief that, while there are some who must be completely segregated from society, there are many instances in which segreation does more harm than good. Furthermore, by concentrating the resources of the police, the courts, and correctional agencies on the smaller number of offenders who really need them, it should be possible to give all offenders more effective treatment.

A specific and important example of this principle is the Commission's recommendation that every community consider establishing a Youth Services Bureau, a community-based center to which juveniles could be referred by the police, the courts, parents, schools, and social agencies for counseling, education, work, or recreation programs and job placement.

The Youth Services Bureau—an agency to handle many troubled and troublesome young people outside the criminal system—is needed in part because society has failed to give the juvenile court the resources that would allow it to function as its founders hoped it would. In a recent survey of juvenile court judges, for example, 83 percent said no psychologist or psychiatrist was available to their courts on a regular basis and one-third said they did not have probation officers or social workers. Even where there are probation officers, the Commission found, the average officer supervises 76 probationers, more than double the recommended caseload.

The California Youth Authority for the last 5 years has been conducting a controlled experiment to determine the effectiveness of another kind of alternative treatment program for juveniles. There, after initial screening, convicted juvenile delinquents are assigned on a random basis to either an experimental group or a control group. Those in the experimental group are returned to the community and receive intensive individual counseling, group counseling, group therapy, and family counseling. Those in the control group are assigned to California's regular institutional treatment program. The findings so far: 28 percent of the experimental group have had their paroles revoked, compared with 52 percent in the control group. Furthermore, the community treatment program is less expensive than institutional treatment.

To make community-based treatment possible for both adults and juveniles, the Commission recommends the development of an entirely new kind of correctional institution: located close to population centers; maintaining close relations with schools, employers, and universities; housing as few as 50 inmates; serving as a classification center, as the center for various kinds of community programs and as a port of reentry to the community for those difficult and dangerous offenders who have required treatment in facilities with tighter custody.

Such institutions would be useful in the operation of programs–strongly recommended by the Commission–that permit selected inmates to work or study in the community during the day and return to control at night, and programs that permit long-term inmates to become adjusted to society gradually rather than being discharged directly from maximum security institutions to the streets.

Another aspect of the Commission's conviction that different offenders with different problems should be treated in different ways, is its recommendation about the handling of public drunkenness, which, in 1965, accounted for one out of every three arrests in America. The great number of these arrests–some 2 million–burdens the police, clogs the lower courts and crowds the penal institutions. The Commission therefore recommends that communities develop civil detoxification units and comprehensive aftercare programs, and that with the development of such programs, drunkenness, not accompanied by other unlawful conduct, should not be a criminal offense.

Similarly, the Commission recommends the expanded use of civil commitment for drug addicts.

3. Eliminating Unfairness

The third objective is to eliminate injustices so that the system of criminal justice can win the respect and cooperation of all citizens. Our society must give the police, the courts, and correctional agencies the resources and the mandate to provide fair and dignified treatment for all.

The Commission found overwhelming evidence of institutional shortcomings in almost every part of the United States.

A survey of the lower court operations in a number of large American cities found cramped and noisy courtrooms, undignified and perfunctory procedures, badly trained personnel overwhelmed by enormous caseloads. In short, the Commission found assembly line justice.

The Commission found that in at least three States, justices of the peace are paid only if they convict and collect a fee from the defendant, a practice held unconstitutional by the Supreme Court 40 years ago.

The Commission found that approximately one-fourth of the 400,000 children detained in 1965–for a variety of causes but including truancy, smoking, and running away from home–were held in adult jails and lockups, often with hardened criminals.

In addition to the creation of new kinds of institutions–such as the Youth Services

Bureau and the small, community-based correctional centers—the Commission recommends several important procedural changes. It recommends counsel at various points in the criminal process.

For juveniles, the Commission recommends providing counsel whenever coercive action is a possibility.

For adults, the Commission recommends providing counsel to any criminal defendant who faces a significant penalty—excluding traffic and similar petty charges—if he cannot afford to provide counsel for himself.

In connection with this recommendation, the Commission asks each State to finance regular, statewide assigned counsel and defender systems for the indigent.

Counsel also should be provided in parole and probation revocation hearings.

Another kind of broad procedural change that the Commission recommends is that every State, county, and local jurisdiction provide judicial officers with sufficient information about individual defendants to permit the release without money bail of those who can be safely released.

In addition to eliminating the injustice of holding persons charged with a crime merely because they cannot afford bail, this recommendation also would save a good deal of money. New York City alone, for example, spends approximately $10 million a year holding persons who have not yet been found guilty of any crime.

Besides institutional injustices, the Commission found that while the great majority of criminal justice and law enforcement personnel perform their duties with fairness and understanding, even under the most trying circumstances, some take advantage of their official positions and act in a callous, corrupt, or brutal manner.

Injustice will not yield to simple solutions. Overcoming it requires a wide variety of remedies including improved methods of selecting personnel, the massive infusion of additional funds, the revamping of existing procedures and the adoption of more effective internal and external controls.

The relations between the police and urban poor deserve special mention. Here the Commission recommends that every large department—especially in communities with substantial minority populations—should have community-relations machinery consisting of a headquarters planning and supervising unit and precinct units to carry out recommended programs. Effective citizen advisory committees should be established in minority group neighborhoods. All departments with substantial minority populations should make special efforts to recruit minority group officers and to deploy and promote them fairly. They should have rigorous internal investigation units to examine complaints of misconduct. The Commission believes it is of the utmost importance to insure that complaints of unfair treatment are fairly dealt with.

Fair treatment of every individual—fair in fact and also perceived to be fair by those affected—is an essential element of justice and a principal objective of the American criminal justice system.

4. Personnel

The fourth objective is that higher levels of knowledge, expertise, initiative, and integrity be achieved by police, judges, prosecutors, defense attorneys, and correctional authorities so that the system of criminal justice can improve its ability to control crime.

The Commission found one obstacle to recruiting better police officers was the standard requirement that all candidates–regardless of qualifications–begin their careers at the lowest level and normally remain at this level from 2 to 5 years before being eligible for promotion. Thus, a college graduate must enter a department at the same rank and pay and perform the same tasks as a person who enters with only a high school diploma or less.

The Commission recommends that police departments give up single entry and establish three levels at which candidates may begin their police careers. The Commission calls these three levels the "community service officer," the "police officer," and the "police agent."

This division, in addition to providing an entry place for the better educated, also would permit police departments to tap the special knowledge, skills, and understanding of those brought up in the slums.

The community service officer would be a uniformed but unarmed member of the police department. Two of his major responsibilities would be to maintain close relations with juveniles in the area where he works and to be especially alert to crime-breeding conditions that other city agencies had not dealt with. Typically, the CSO might be under 21, might not be required to meet conventional education requirements, and might work out of a store-front office. Serving as an apprentice policeman–a substitute for the police cadet–the CSO would work as a member of a team with the police officer and police agent.

The police officer would respond to calls for service, perform routine patrol, render emergency services, make preliminary investigations, and enforce traffic regulations. In order to qualify as a police officer at the present time, a candidate should possess a high school diploma and should demonstrate a capacity for college work.

The police agent would do whatever police jobs were most complicated, most sensitive, and most demanding. He might be a specialist in police-community relations or juvenile delinquency. He might be in uniform patrolling a high-crime neighborhood. He might have staff duties. To become a police agent would require at least 2 years of college work and preferably a baccalaureate degree in the liberal arts or social sciences.

As an ultimate goal, the Commission recommends that all police personnel with general enforcement powers have baccalaureate degrees.

While candidates could enter the police service at any one of the three levels, they also could work their way up through the different categories as they met the basic education and other requirements.

In many jurisdictions there is a critical need for additional police personnel. Studies by the Commission indicate a recruiting need of 50,000 policemen in 1967 just to fill positions already authorized. In order to increase police effectiveness, additional staff specialists will be required, and when the community service officers are added manpower needs will be even greater.

The Commission also recommends that every State establish a commission on police standards to set minimum recruiting and training standards and to provide financial and technical assistance for local police departments.

In order to improve the quality of judges, prosecutors, and defense attorneys, the Commission recommends a variety of steps: Taking the selection of judges out of partisan politics; the more regular use of seminars, conferences, and institutes to train sitting judges; the establishment of judicial commissions to excuse physically or mentally incapacitated judges from their duties without public humiliation; the general abolition of part-time district attorneys and assistant district attorneys; and a broad range of measures to develop a greatly enlarged and better trained pool of defense attorneys.

In the correctional system there is a critical shortage of probation and parole officers, teachers, caseworkers, vocational instructors, and group workers. The need for major manpower increases in this area was made clear by the findings from the Commissions national corrections survey:

- ☐ Less than 3 percent of all personnel working in local jails and institutions devote their time to treatment and training.
- ☐ Eleven States do not offer any kind of probation services for adult misdemeanants, six offer only the barest fragments of such services, and most States offer them on a spotty basis.
- ☐ Two-thirds of all State adult felony probationers are in caseloads of over 100 persons.

To meet the requirements of both the correctional agencies and the courts, the Commission has found an immediate need to double the Nation's pool of juvenile probation officers, triple the number of probation officers working with adult felons, and increase sevenfold the number of officers working with misdemeanants.

Another area with a critical need for large numbers of expert criminal justice officers is the complex one of controlling organized crime. Here, the Commission recommends that prosecutors and police in every State and city where organized crime is known to, or may, exist develop special organized crime units.

5. Research

The fifth objective is that every segment of the system of criminal justice devote a significant part of its resources for research to insure the development of new and effective methods of controlling crime.

The Commission found that little research is being conducted into such matters as the economic impact of crime; the effects on crime of increasing or decreasing criminal sanctions; possible methods for improving the effectiveness of various procedures of the police, courts, and correctional agencies.

Organized crime is another area in which almost no research has been conducted. The Commission found that the only group with any significant knowledge about this problem was law enforcement officials. Those in other disciplines–social scientists, economists and lawyers, for example–have not until recently considered the possibility of research projects on organized crime.

A small fraction of 1 percent of the criminal justice system's total budget is spent on research. This figure could be multiplied many times without approaching the 3 percent industry spends on research, much less the 15 percent the Defense Department spends. The Commission believes it should be multiplied many times.

That research is a powerful force for change in the field of criminal justice perhaps can best be documented by the history of the Vera Institute in New York City. Here the research of a small, nongovernment agency has in a very short time led to major changes in the bail procedures of approximately 100 cities, several States, and the Federal Government.

Because of the importance of research, the Commission recommends that major criminal justice agencies–such as State court and correctional systems and big-city police departments–organize operational research units as integral parts of their structures.

In addition, the criminal justice agencies should welcome the efforts of scholars and other independent experts to understand their problems and operations. These agencies cannot undertake needed research on their own; they urgently need the help of outsiders.

The Commission also recommends the establishment of several regional research institutes designed to concentrate a number of different disciplines on the problem of crime. It further recommends the establishment of an independent National Criminal Research Foundation to stimulate and coordinate research and disseminate its results.

One essential requirement for research is more complete information about the operation of the criminal process. To meet this requirement, the Commission recommends the creation of a National Criminal Justice Statistics Center. The Center's first responsibility would be to work with the FBI, the Children's Bureau, the Federal Bureau of Prisons, and other agencies to develop an integrated picture of the number of crimes reported to police, the number of persons arrested, the number of accused persons prosecuted, the number of offenders placed on probation, in prison, and subsequently on parole.

Another major responsibility of the Center would be to continue the Commission's initial effort to develop a new yardstick to measure the extent of crime in our society as a supplement to the FBI's Uniform Crime Reports. The Commission believes that the Government should be able to plot the levels of different kinds of crime in a city or a State as precisely as the Labor Department and the Census Bureau now plot the rate of unemployment. Just as unemployment information is essential to sound economic planning, so some day may criminal information help official planning in the system of criminal justice.

6. Money

Sixth, the police, the courts, and correctional agencies will require substantially more money if they are to control crime better.

Almost all of the specific recommendations made by the Commission will involve increased budgets. Substantially higher salaries must be offered to attract topflight candidates to the system of criminal justice. For example, the median annual salary for a patrolman in a large city today is $5,300. Typically, the maximum salary is something less than $1,000 above the starting salary. The Commission believes the most important change that can be made in police salary scales is to increase maximums sharply. An FBI agent, for example, starts at $8,421 a year and if he serves long and well enough can reach $16,905 a year without being promoted to a supervisory position. The Commission is aware that reaching such figures immediately is not possible in many cities, but it believes that there should be a large range from minimum to maximum everywhere.

The Commission also recommends new kinds of programs that will require additional funds: Youth Services Bureaus, greatly enlarged misdemeanant probation services and increased levels of research, for example.

The Commission believes some of the additional resources—especially those devoted to innovative programs and to training, education, and research—should be contributed by the Federal Government.

The Federal Government already is conducting a broad range of programs—aid to elementary and secondary schools, the Neighborhood Youth Corps, Project Head-Start, and others—designed to attack directly the social problems often associated with crime.

Through such agencies as the Federal Bureau of Investigation, the Office of Law Enforcement Assistance, the Bureau of Prisons, and the Office of Manpower Development and Training, the Federal Government also offers comparatively limited financial and technical assistance to the police, and courts, and corrections authorities.

While the Commission is convinced State and local governments must continue to carry the major burden of criminal administration, it recommends a vastly enlarged program of Federal assistance to strengthen law enforcement, crime prevention, and the administration of justice.

The program of Federal support recommended by the Commission would be directed to eight major needs:

(1) State and local planning.

(2) Education and training of criminal justice personnel.

(3) Surveys and advisory services concerning the organization and operation of police departments, courts, prosecuting offices, and corrections agencies.

(4) Development of a coordinated national information system for operational and research purposes.

(5) Funding of limited numbers of demonstration programs in agencies of justice.

(6) Scientific and technological research and development.

(7) Development of national and regional research centers.

(8) Grants-in-aid for operational innovations.

The Commission is not in a position to recommend the exact amount of money that will be needed to carry out its proposed program. It believes, however, that a Federal program totaling hundreds of millions of dollars a year during the next decade could be effectively utilized. The Commission also believes the major responsibility for administering this program should lie within the Department of Justice.

The States, the cities, and the counties also will have to make substantial increases in their contributions to the system of criminal justice.

7. Responsibility for Change

Seventh, individual citizens, social-service agencies, universities, religious institutions, civic and business groups, and all kinds of governmental agencies at all levels must become involved in planning and executing changes in the criminal justice system.

The Commission is convinced that the financial and technical assistance program it proposes can and should be only a small part of the national effort to develop a more effective and fair response to crime.

In March of 1966, President Johnson asked the Attorney General to invite each Governor to form a State committee on criminal administration. The response to this request has been encouraging; more than two-thirds of the States already have such committees or have indicated they intend to form them.

The Commission recommends that in every State and city there should be an agency, or one or more officials, with specific responsibility for planning improvements in criminal administration and encouraging their implementation.

Planning agencies, among other functions, play a key role in helping State legislatures and city councils decide where additional funds and manpower are most needed, what new programs should be adopted, and where and how existing agencies might pool their resources on either a metropolitan or regional basis.

The planning agencies should include both officials from the system of criminal justice and citizens from other professions. Plans to improve criminal administration will be impossible to put into effect unless those responsible for criminal administration help make them. On the other hand, crime prevention must be the task of the community as a whole.

While this report has concentrated on recommendations for action by governments, the Commission is convinced that governmental actions will not be enough. Crime is a social problem that is interwoven with almost every aspect of American life. Controlling it involves improving the quality of family life, the way schools are run, the way cities are planned, the way workers are hired. Controlling crime is the business of every American institution. Controlling crime is the business of every American.

Universities should increase their research on the problems of crime; private social welfare organizations and religious institutions should continue to experiment with advanced techniques of helping slum children overcome their environment; labor unions and businesses can enlarge their programs to provide prisoners with vocational training; professional and community organizations can help probation and parole workers with their work.

The responsibility of the individual citizen runs far deeper than cooperating with the police or accepting jury duty or insuring the safety of his family by installing adequate locks–important as they are. He must respect the law, refuse to cut corners, reject the cynical argument that "anything goes as long as you don't get caught."

Most important of all, he must, on his own and through the organizations he belongs to, interest himself in the problems of crime and criminal justice, seek information, express his views, use his vote wisely, get involved.

In sum, the Commission is sure that the Nation can control crime if it will.

Index